ACTS OF BRAVERY
Deeds of Extraordinary American Heroism

*From the Personal Records
and Reminiscences
of the Courageous Americans
Who Risked Everything
for Their Comrades and Country*

Edited by
W.F. Beyer and O.F. Keydel

Illustrated

1993

A Platinum Press Book

This special reprint edition originally published
in 1907 is now republished by:

Longmeadow Press
201 High Ridge Road
Stamford, CT 06904

in association with

Platinum Press Inc.
311 Crossways Park Drive
Woodbury, NY 11797

ISBN 0-681-45504-7

0987654321

Printed in the USA

Library of Congress Cataloging-in-Publication Data

(Revised for vol. 2)

Deeds of valor.

    Originally published: Detroit, Mich.: Perrien-Keydel Co., 1903.
    Vol. 1 has subtitle: How America's Civil War Heroes won the
Medal of Honor.
    Vol. 2 has special title: Acts of Bravery.
    "A Platinum Press book."
    Includes index.
    Personal reminiscences and records of officers and enlisted
men who were rewarded by Congress with the Medal of Honor for
conspicuous acts of bravery during wartime, on the high seas, and in
Arctic explorations, prior to World War I.
    1. Medal of Honor. 2. Military Decorations — United States. 3.
United States — History, Military — To 1900 — Anecdotes. 4. United
States — History, Naval — To 1900 — Anecdotes. 5. United States —
Armed Forces — Biography. [1. Medal of Honor. 2. United States —
History, Military — To 1900 — Sources.] I. Beyer, Walter F. II. Keydel,
Oscar F. (Oscar Frederick), b. 1871.
    E181.D385 1992 355.1'342'092273 [B] 91-47984
    ISBN 0-681-41567-3 (v. 1)
    ISBN 0-681-45504-7 (v. 2)

THE CONGRESSIONAL
MEDAL OF HONOR

THE ARMY

EXTRACT FROM REGULATIONS RELATIVE TO THE MEDAL OF HONOR.

B Y DIRECTION of the President, the following regulations are promulgated respecting the award of Medals of Honor:

Medals of Honor authorized by the Act of Congress approved March 3, 1863, are awarded to officers and enlisted men, in the name of the Congress, for particular deeds of most distinguished gallantry in action.

In order that the Congressional Medal of Honor may be deserved, service must have been performed in action of such a conspicuous character as to clearly distinguish the man for gallantry and intrepidity above his comrades — service that involved extreme jeopardy of life or the performance of extraordinarily hazardous duty. Recommendations for the decoration will be judged by this standard of extraordinary merit, and incontestible proof of performance of the service will be exacted.

Soldiers of the Union have ever displayed bravery in battle, else victories could not have been gained; but as courage and self-sacrifice are the characteristics of every true soldier, such a badge of distinction as the Congressional Medal is not to be expected as the reward of conduct that does not clearly distinguish the soldier above other men, whose bravery and gallantry have been proved in battle. * * *

THE NAVY

Recommendations for medals on account of service rendered subsequent to January 1, 1890, will be made by the commanding officer at the time of the action or by an officer or soldier having personal cognizance of the act for which the badge of honor is claimed, and the recommendation will embrace a detailed recital of all the facts and circumstances. Certificates of officers or the affidavits of enlisted men who were eyewitnesses of the act will also be submitted if practicable.

In cases that may arise for service performed hereafter, recommendations for award of medals must be forwarded within one year after the performance of the act for which the award is claimed. Commanding officers will thoroughly investigate all cases of recommendations for Congressional Medals arising in their commands, and indorse their opinion upon the papers, which will be forwarded to the Adjutant-General of the Army through regular channels.

AT THE commencement of the great struggle now known to history as the War of the Rebellion, the United States Navy consisted of only twenty-six steamers, as follows:

Six screw-frigates—The Niagara, Merrimac, Wabash, Minnesota, Roanoke and Colorado.

Six first-class sloops (in later naval parlance termed corvettes)—The Richmond, Brooklyn, San Jacinto, Lancaster, Pensacola and Hartford.

Five second-class screw-sloops—The Pawnee, Mohican, Wyoming, Iroquois and Dakota.

Two third-class screw-sloops—The Narragansett and Seminole.

Four first-class side-wheel sloops—The Powhattan, Susquehanna, Mississippi and Saranac; besides the three small side-wheel steamers Michigan, Water-Witch and Saginaw.

The greater number of these vessels were either abroad, in foreign waters, or in southern ports, and therefore not immediately available for the grave emergency. The personnel of the navy numbered at that time 7,600 men, of all ranks. While the crews held on faithfully to the cause of the Union, not less than 259 naval officers of the line either resigned or were dismissed, amounting to forty-three per cent. of the corps.

Under such conditions the task of the Navy Department seemed a desperate and hopeless one; sailors and especially their officers could not be readily recruited, for, under all conditions, they must necessarily have a thorough technical training. Outside of this there was the lack of ships to cover a sea-coast of 3,600 miles against a foe who had at the time the moral and material support of the two most efficient naval powers in the world, England and France.

"If we had had a hundred gunboats the rebellion could have been smothered at its start." This utterance of Admiral Porter, U. S. N., pictures the situation concisely.

But little did the foreign naval powers, who watched the development of this national cyclone with such discriminating interest, imagine that the pigmy sea force of the apparently outclassed Northern States would teach the world a lesson, from which it learns to this very day, namely: the matchless co-operation of the military bodies on land and on sea for attaining the ultimate result. It was the aid the northern men of the sea gave along in this portentous struggle to their hard-fighting comrades on land which forms forever one of the most precious gems in the crown of glory of the United States Navy. In short, the efforts of the men entrusted with this branch of the defense of the Union are unparalleled in history.

Creating a fleet was naturally slower and more difficult work than the improvisation of land forces, as will be seen from the following statistics: All the ships, steam and sail, in commission, in March, 1861, were 42; on July 4, 1861, 82; December, 1861, 264; December 1, 1862, 467; December 7, 1863, 588; December, 1864, 671.

At the beginning of the war, therefore, it was impossible for the navy either to aid the operations of the Union Army by bombarding any southern sea-ports or to establish an effective blockade to cut off the most important source of subsistence of the seceded states. Finally, after four years of hard struggle, colossal effort and great sacrifices, the navy, with a personnel of 50,000 men and 671 ships of war, was ready to perform her share in the so-called Anaconda plan; that is, to encircle the enemy by land and by sea, and then press forward concentrically with superior force and so finally crush them as in the vise-like grip of a giant snake.

The first great success of the war belongs to the navy; it was the capture of Forts Walker and Beauregard, in the Port Royal Sound, by Admiral Du Pont, on the 9th of November, 1861. He won the first laurels with seventeen men-of-war.

From Port Royal Sound, the largest bay on the whole coast, south of Chesapeake Bay, and situated between Charleston and Savannah, it was possible by the further aid of the fleet to extend the operations of the land forces to the important islands along the coast, and thereby effectively menace the coast lying behind this line of operations.

The second great success was the co-operation of the Mississippi flotilla, under Commodore Foote, with General Grant's army, in the spring of 1862.

This flotilla forced its way 110 miles up the Tennessee River, destroyed Fort Henry and a great amount of war supplies, passed then into Cumberland River and captured, together with the army, the powerful Fort Donelson, where 14,000 prisoners fell into the hands of the Union forces. Now the line of defense of the Southern States on the northwestern theatre of the war was broken, Kentucky won back for the North, and Tennessee laid open to the farther advance of the Union army.

The next strategical success won by the navy was the reconquering of the mighty waterway of the lower Mississippi, in stubborn and daring fights, and thus creating an operating base of decisive importance.

Then, on April 24, 1862, followed Admiral Farragut's glorious action before New Orleans. In a night fight in which both sides had fifty-five ships as active units, Farragut forced the entrance to the Mississippi in spite of obstructions, and after silencing the forts, which formed the main defense, he pushed on to New Orleans. This city, the greatest and most important commercial emporium of the South, lay defenseless under the guns of the Union fleet and surrendered to the northern forces without further attempt at resistance.

The splendid co-operation of the navy and army, especially in the three last years of the war, was the real cause of the final debacle of the rebellion; the "Anaconda ring" contracted more and more, and against its merciless force the most heroic bravery and self-sacrifice on the part of the Southerners proved of no avail. But in some instances, as is well known, their tenacity was indeed splendid. There was Vicksburg, the strongly fortified center of a desperate resistance, which held out more than a year against the most strenuous efforts on the part of the besieging Union Army, and the final capture of this stronghold was only rendered possible by the co-operation of the navy and her transports.

The brilliant conclusion of the magnificent and successful activity of the United States Navy in supporting the army operations was Admiral Farragut's victory at Mobile, on the 5th of August, 1864. This action stands out forever as one of the most glorious deeds on the sea, and the heroic admiral's curt order: " Damn the torpedoes; full speed ahead!" will well be remembered as the fighting motto of the American Navy for all time to come.

After a most sanguinary combat of three hours, the Confederate flagship Tennessee struck; the other vessels of the enemy were all destroyed with the exception of a single one, which made good her escape.

The power of resistance of Mobile, which had always been rated as impregnable, was broken; on the 23d of August the largest and strongest fort surrendered. Again the navy had here stood the brunt of the battle and the main share of the work.

Not only as a whole, but also in its individual units, in the actions between ships—Kearsarge and Alabama, Monitor and Merrimac, the sinking of the Albemarle by Lieutenant Cushing—the United States Navy played in the great and bloody drama a part which secured for it, as to quality if not to number, the very first place among the navies of the world; likewise for the men of this service, who earned, by their splendid behavior and qualities, the acknowledged gratitude of the whole nation.

Subsequent events, in the Spanish-American war, have shown that this service can boast of plenty of able pupils of Farragut, Porter, Cushing and all the others, who represented the best. There is no apprehension that it might be otherwise in the future.

The following is a chronological list of the important naval actions fought from May 26, 1861, to June 3, 1865:

May 26, 1861—Attack on Aquia Batteries, Potomac River, by Commander Ward.

June 27, 1861—Attack on Mathias Point, Potomac River; Commander Ward killed.

August 28 and 29, 1861—Capture of Forts Clark and Hatteras.

September 13, 1861—Destroying of Confederate privateer schooner Juda, by Lieutenant Russell of the United States frigate Colorado, at Pensacola Navy Yard.

October 13, 1861—Action in Mississippi River, near Southwest Pass.

November 7, 1861—Destroying of the Confederate steamer Rusk, and capture of privateer Royal Yacht, by Lieutenant Jouett and cutting-out party from United States frigate Santee, in Galveston Harbor.

November 9, 1861—Capture of Port Royal (Forts Walker and Beauregard), by Flag Officer Du Pont.

February 6, 1862—Capture of Fort Henry, on the Tennessee River, by Mississippi Squadron, Flag Officer Foote.

February 8, 1862—Capture of Roanoke Island, Albemarle Sound, by Commander S. C. Rowan.

February 10, 1862—Capture of Cobb's Point Fort and Confederate gunboats, by Commander Rowan.

February 13, 1862—Capture (in co-operation with General Grant's army) of Fort Donelson on the Cumberland, by Flag Officer Foote and the Mississippi Squadron.

March 9, 1862—The fight between the Monitor and the Merrimac, Lieutenant Worden, U. S. N., and Commodore Buchanan, C. S. N.

March 16-April 7, 1862—Bombardment and Capture of Island No. 10 by Flag Officer Foote and the Mississippi-Squadron.

April 16-28, 1862—Capture of New Orleans and the entrance to the Mississippi, by Flag Officer Farragut and the West Gulf Blockading Squadron.

April 25, 1862—Capture of Fort Macon, Beaufort Harbor, N. C., combined action of army and navy, under Major-General Burnside and Commodore Lockwood.

May 10-June 4, 1862—Bombardment and capture of Fort Pillow, by Captain C. H. Davis, successor to Flag Officer Foote, as commander of the Mississippi Squadron.

May 18, 1862—Engagement on James River; gunboats of Commander Rodgers, U. S. N., and Confederate battery on Drury's Bluff.

June 6, 1862—Capture of Memphis and opening of the Mississippi to Vicksburg.

June 28, 1862—Farragut's first action before Vicksburg.

August 6, 1862—Rebel ram Arkansas destroyed by Porter before Vicksburg.

October 3, 1862—Engagement on Blackwater River, near Franklin, N. C., by Lieutenant Flusser, with the United States gunboats Commodore Perry, Hunchback and Whitehead.

November 16, 1862—Engagement of Confederate batteries at Columbus by gunboats Taylor and Lexington, under Commander Walke from Foote's Mississippi Squadron.

November 20, 1862—Lieutenant Cushing's adventure in New River Inlet, N.C.; the loss of the gunboat Ellis.

December 12, 1862—Blowing up by torpedo of the U. S. ironclad gunboat Cairo, Lieutenant Commander Selfridge, in Yazoo River.

January 1, 1863—Recapture of Galveston by the Confederates; capture of the Harriet Lane by the Confederates; death of her captain, Commander Wainwright. Destruction of the Westfield.

January 11, 1863—Confederate privateer Alabama sinks the U. S. gunboat Hatteras in Galveston Bay.

January 31, 1863—Naval Engagement in Charleston Harbor.

February 14, 1863—Queen of the West captured by rebels in the Red River.

February 27, 1863—Montauk destroys the Nashville in Ogeechee River, Ga.

March 14, 1863—Admiral Farragut passes the Port Hudson batteries on the Hartford.

March 19, 1863—Admiral Farragut passes the Grand Gulf, Miss., batteries, and anchors below Vicksburg on the 21st.

March 23, 1863—Rebel ram Vicksburg captured by Admiral Porter. Pensacola burned by Federals.

March 25, 1863—Federal ram Lancaster sinks while passing Vicksburg batteries.

March 31, 1863—Admiral Farragut silences Grand Gulf batteries.

April 7, 1863—Admiral Du Pont attacks Fort Sumter; the Federal monitor Keokuk sunk; Admiral Farragut destroys Bayou Saraha.

April 16, 1863—Five gunboats and three transports run the Vicksburg batteries; the Queen of the West recaptured at Grand Lake, La.

April 22, 1863—Six gunboats and twelve transports, carrying advance of Grant's army, pass batteries at Vicksburg.

April 30, 1863—Admiral Porter passes the batteries at Grand Gulf, Miss.

May 4, 1863—Engagement and capture of Fort De Russy, Ark., by Admiral Porter.

May 6, 1863—Admiral Porter's fleet captures Alexandria, La.

May 8, 1863—Admiral Farragut commences bombardment of Port Hudson.

May 20, 1863—Admiral Porter destroys navy yard at Yazoo City, Miss.

May 24, 1863—Eight rebel steamers destroyed on Yazoo River by detachment of Porter's fleet.

June 12, 1863—Tacony captured by the rebel privateer Clarence and converted into a privateer; Clarence burned.

June 17, 1863—Rebel ram Atlanta captured.

June 19, 1863—Rebel ram Chattahoochee blown up.

June 25, 1863—Tacony, converted rebel privateer, captures the Archer, converts her into a privateer and is burned.

June 26, 1863—Converted rebel privateer Archer captured in attempted raid on Portland, Me.

July 8, 1863—Port Hudson, La., surrenders to Banks, Mississippi thereby opened.

September 8, 1863—Naval engagement in Charleston Harbor; attack on Fort Sumter repulsed.

October 5, 1863—Rebels attempt to blow up Federal warship Ironsides.

October 31, 1863—Furious bombardment of Fort Sumter.

December 6, 1863—Monitor Weehawken sunk in a gale. Steamer Chesapeake captured by rebel passengers.

January 12, 1864—Gunboats and transports of Porter and Sherman, on expedition up Yazoo River, attacked by 3,000 rebels.

February 2, 1864—Rebel attack on Newberne, N.C., repulsed; Federal gunboat Underwriter captured and destroyed by the rebels.

February 28, 1864—Bombardment of Fort Powell, Mobile Harbor, by Admiral Farragut.

March 30, 1864—United States steamer Maple Leaf blown up in St. John's River, Fla., by a rebel torpedo.

April 9, 1864—Engagement between Federal gunboats and rebels at Falls City, La.; rebels defeated, with a loss of 600 killed and wounded. Failure of a rebel attempt to blow up Federal frigate Minnesota at Kingston Roads.

April 12, 1864—Steamer Golden Gate, with U. S. Government stores, captured by rebels near Memphis. Fort Pillow recaptured by Confederates under General Forest.

April 18, 1864—Federal gunboats Bombshell and Southfield sunk at Plymouth, N. C., by a rebel ram.

May 1, 1864—Federal gunboat Eastport and three transports blown up by Union forces near Alexandria, La., to prevent their falling into the enemy's hands.

May 9, 1864—Expedition of Admiral Porter and General Banks up Red River returns and passes the Falls near Alexandria by aid of the Bailey dams.

June 19, 1864—Sinking of the Alabama by the Kearsarge, off Cherbourg, France.

August 5, 1864—Admiral Farragut with his fleet passes Forts Morgan, Gaines and Powell in Mobile Bay; captures Confederate Admiral Buchanan and ram Tennessee, as well as gunboat Selma; Union monitor Tecumseh sunk by torpedo.

August 7, 1864—Failed attempt of rebels to recapture Admiral Buchanan at Pensacola.

August 8, 1864—Fort Gaines surrendered to United States forces, with 874 officers and men and 26 guns.

August 23, 1864—Fort Morgan, Mobile Harbor, surrendered with all stores to United States.

October 7, 1864—Rebel privateer Florida captured by Federal steamer Wachusetts at Bahia, Brazil.

November 29, 1864—General Butler's dispatch steamer Greyhound destroyed by fire.

December 6, 1864—Admiral Dahlgren and General Foster land at Pocotaligo and cut the Charleston Road.

December 7, 1864—Gunboat Narcissus blown up by torpedo in Mobile Bay.

December 24, 1864—First attack on Fort Fisher by Admiral Porter and General Butler; explosion of the powder boat.

January 13, 1865—Second attack on Fort Fisher by Admiral Farragut and General Terry.

January 14, 1865—Capture of Pocotaligo, S. C.

January 15, 1865—Capture of Fort Fisher.

January 17, 1865—Loss of monitor Patapsco in Charleston Harbor.

January 18, 1865—The Harriet Lane destroyed at Havana.

January 25, 1865—The rebel ironclad Virginia blown up at the descent of the James River; other rebel vessels driven back.

March 4, 1865—Federal transport Thorne blown up by torpedo in Cape Fear River.

March 19, 1865—Rebel schooner Anna Dale, in Matagorda Bay, cut loose from under two rebel batteries and burned.

April 23, 1865—Rebel ram Webb escapes past Union fleet on Red River; is run ashore, deserted and blown up.

April 28, 1865—Foundering of transport Sultana, laden with soldiers, near Memphis; 1,500 lives lost.

June 3, 1865—Rebel ironclad Missouri, in Red River, surrenders to Commander W. E. Fitzhugh, U.S.N.

AT MATHIAS POINT

THE reader cannot be too often reminded of the deplorable state in which the Union Navy found itself when the declaration of war came upon the country in 1861, like a mighty thunderbolt. While the capital at Washington was in immediate danger at the hands of the fast advancing enemys, all possible stress was brought to bear upon the Navy Department for the protection of the Potomac River. Deserted by nearly half its officers, deprived through Southern machinations of the greater part of its stores and the control of some of the few ships then seaworthy, the navy saw itself indeed *vis-a-vis de rien*. So much more honor and credit to the faithful officers of this service for their energy, their effort, their resourcefulness and the fearless devotion with which they met the almost hopeless emergency, and in May had ready for service a flotilla, a small and frail one, indeed, but one with which its gallant commanding officer, Commander James H. Ward, managed to wrench success from defeat, and laid down his own life as the price, he being shot through the body while aiming one of the guns.

On the 26th of May, Commander Ward attacked fiercely the strong confederates batteries at Aquia Creek with three little craft, the Freeborn, the Anacostia and the Resolute, of respectively 200, 200 and 92 tons. It was the first naval engagement of the war, and the enemy's batteries were silenced within two hours. Of course, it could only be temporary. After the little squadron had been re-enforced by the Pawnee, Commander Rowan, the gallant Ward renewed his attack on June 27th, for a fourth time, this time against the batteries of Mathias Point. The Union squadron tried even to land a party from the vessels in order to try an assault. The attempt was unsuccessful, but Lieutenant Chapman of the Pawnee, commanding the landing party, took advantage of the inexperience and the astonishment of the enemy, and managed by his coolness to avert a serious disaster. It was a desperate struggle, even while retreating. The enemy kept up a constant fire, wounding many of the Union men. John Williams, captain of the maintop on board the Pawnee, while in charge of one of the landing boats, was wounded by a musket ball in the thigh, but he still retained command of his boat, and when the flag-staff was shot away he held the stump in his hand, waving the flag and encouraging the men until the boat reached the side of the Pawnee.

THE FIRST TO HOIST THE FLAG

WHEN we consider under what gloomy aspect and little chance of success or even appreciation the personnel of the then scanty naval force of the Union labored, the narrative of Benjamin Swearer, gun-captain, who was probably one of the first of the naval force at the taking of Fort Clark, shows their indomitable confidence in their cause and their willingness to sacrifice themselves for something they valued higher than life:

BENJAMIN SWEARER.
Captain of Foretop, U. S. S. Pawnee.
Born May 18, 1825. ,

"When the war began I was an enlisted man on the Pawnee, United States sloop; I was gun-captain of No. 1 gun on my ship, which was lying in the Potomac, near Alexandria. One morning we got the order to land in this town. I went on shore, in charge of a crew; we were under command of Lieutenant Lowry. My men and I went into the city; I hoisted the American colors on the Beal and Everett post, at the corner of King and Quinn Streets. Just while we were at this work we heard of the murder of Colonel Ellsworth, who, while pulling down a Confederate standard at the Marshall House, had been shot dead by Mr. Jackson, the proprietor. We then proceeded to Michael's Point, down the river, and, in spite of the overwhelming fire from the rebel batteries, we set fire to and burned the wharf. There was a tremendous cannonade from Mathias Point, and Captain Ward was killed by a shell.

"Our little vessels had to withdraw before the overwhelming fire. We were ordered to Norfolk, Va., from there back to Washington, and soon after to proceed to Fairmount Point, Va. From here we went, under command of Flag Officer S. H. Stringham, to restore Federal authority over Hatteras Inlet and the adjacent waters of Chesapeake Bay, which was said to have become the resort of Confederate privateers. The squadron consisted of the frigates Minnesota and Wabash, the sloops Cumberland and Susquehanna, the steamers Pawnee, Harriet Lane and Fanny. The Fanny was a transport with 860 soldiers on board, under command of General Butler; we were to co-operate with them at Hatteras Inlet. There were two forts there, Fort Clark, near the outer bar, and Fort Hatteras, further on the inside. The day after leaving Norfolk, that is on the 27th of August, 1861, we anchored off Hatteras Inlet. The works were about half a mile off to the southwest, separated from us by a shallow bay, and they mounted together twenty-five guns, which we at that time, of course, did not know.

"In the evening the land troops were put ashore on the island, under cover of the guns of the squadron. Next morning, on the 28th, the fighting began. The first day we passed up and down before the forts, bombarding all the time, with the larger ships, while the smaller ones accompanied the transport to a point further north on the island to land the troops. I was one of the landing party from the Pawnee, and shortly after noon of the first day we got into Fort Clark. I happened to be the first to hoist the Union flag in this fort, for which deed I was granted the Naval Medal of Honor. Towards noon the second day, the 29th, Fort Hatteras showed the white flag. We took 615 Confederate prisoners, with 25 guns, 1,000 muskets and a large supply of ordnance stores."

"CUTTING OUT OF THE ROYAL YACHT"

At the beginning of November, 1861, the Federal Navy Department had a small squadron of vessels, under command of Captain Henry Eagle, blockading the coast of Texas. Eagle's flagship was the sailing frigate Santee. Information reached the captain that the Confederates were fitting out a privateer, the Royal Yacht, in the harbor of Galveston. It was also known that the Confederate war-steamer General Rusk was at anchor under Pelican Island Fort in the harbor.

Captain Eagle wishing to destroy the privateer before she could get out to sea and also, if possible, to capture the General Rusk, decided to send a cutting-out party from his ship into the harbor for this purpose.

Consequently, early in the morning of November 7, 1861, an expedition left the Santee in two launches, each armed with a howitzer and carrying a selected crew of men, under command of Lieutenant James E. Jouett. Jouett had with him a pilot who was to take the Royal Yacht out to sea.

The entrance to the harbor and the Point and Bolivar Forts was guarded by an armed schooner. The two launches managed to pass this schooner unnoticed, also the two forts named, but when they neared Pelican Island Fort, where the General Rusk lay, they ran aground and sentinels from the fort gave the alarm.

Lieutenant Jouett at once made up his mind that any further attempt to reach the Rusk would, under the circumstances, lead inevitably to disaster. He therefore directed his boats towards the Royal Yacht. Her crew had in the meantime been aroused, too, and everybody on board was ready to receive the bold Santee men in proper fashion, with cutlass, pike and revolver. But the Yankees never hesitated. Trusting in the protection of darkness, they boarded the schooner. The struggle was short but sharp. The Confederates, thirteen in number, were made prisoners. Lieutenant Jouett had received a bad wound from a boarding pike in the hands of an enemy, one of the boat crew was killed, another one mortally wounded, and Gunner

THE DESTRUCTION OF THE ROYAL YACHT.

Carter and Seaman George Bell were severely wounded. As the forts had in the meantime opened with full force on the Royal Yacht, and Jouett's pilot, who was to take the schooner out, had been shot, the Lieutenant gave up bringing her out, but spiked her only gun and set her on fire, totally destroying her. Lieutenant Jouett and his daring party reached the Santee safely, where they were warmly received by their ship-mates, and well did they deserve the praise which Captain McKean bestowed upon them. Among the men who especially distinguished themselves on this day was George Bell, captain of the afterguard on the Santee, who steered one of the boats. While the party was boarding the Royal Yacht he was severely wounded in the encounter, but notwithstanding his suffering from the wound he kept in the fight and otherwise displayed extraordinary courage under the most painful and trying circumstances.

NAVAL HEROES AT FORTS HENRY AND DONELSON

THROUGH the abandoning of the Norfolk Navy Yard by the Federal Navy about 1,400 serviceable guns of all calibres fell into the hands of the Confederates. Up to the end of winter 211 of these guns had been recaptured, the greater part of the rest were used by the enemys to strengthen the works of Fort Henry on the Tennessee and Fort Donelson on the Cumberland into first-class fortifications. These two forts commanded completely the navigation on the two rivers named, thus blocking all access to Kentucky and Tennessee from the north. General Grant, fully recognizing the great importance of these two strongholds, had his plans ready to destroy and capture them at the beginning of February, 1862. He started down the Tennessee from Cairo with 17,000 men on the 2d of February and landed his army at Bailey's Ferry, just outside of the range of Fort Henry. Grant and Admiral Foote had agreed that while the land forces were to attack the main fortifications, on the east bank, from the rear, the navy should attack from the front. Fort Heiman, on the east bank, was abandoned by the Confederates, who concentrated all their strength in Fort Henry as soon as they became aware of the intended move of the Federals. Grant, not knowing this, detailed a brigade under General Charles F. Smith against Fort Heiman. The rest of the forces, under McClernand, he directed against Fort Henry simultaneously with the gunboats of Foote. The latter's squadron, consisting of the Essex, 9 guns, Commander William D. Porter; the Cincinnati, flagship, 13 guns, Commander Stembel; the Carondelet, 13 guns, Commander Walker, and the St. Louis, 13 guns, Lieutenant Paulding, besides the wooden gunboats Conestoga, Taylor and Lexington, all in all mounting 76 guns, got under way at two o'clock on the 6th of February. Soon the gunboats reached the forts and began their fire, shortening the distance by-and-by to about a third of a mile. The cannonade soon became a very hot one; after the gunboats had reached their proper station and obtained their range their fire became very destructive; almost every shot told.

The army, on account of the bad weather and consequently terrible condition of the roads, was unable to reach its destination in time. So the navy had to fight it out alone. For a little over an hour did the forts bravely resist—then the white flag appeared; the navy had won.

Only about twenty minutes before the surrender a shot hit the gunboat Essex, piercing and exploding the boiler and disabling the ship. Twenty-nine officers and men of the crew were killed or put out of action by this disastrous shot. The second master of the Essex, James Laning, described the scene on board at the time of the accident as follows:

"As we could only see the bow batteries, the four ironclads could bring only 11 guns to bear. The fort, although mounting 17 guns, could also bring only 11 to bear; so it was a fair and square fight, and the problem was about to be solved whether ironclad gunboats could compete with earthworks. Under the old-system warfare, I believe, it was conceded that one gun on land was about equal to three on the water.

"Upon arriving at the head of the island, the flagship Cincinnati opened fire, which was the signal to begin the general engagement. I had, however, received orders from Captain Porter not to fire until he had particularly noted the effect of the Cincinnati's shots, so as to profit by their mistakes, if they made any, in elevation. The first three shots from the flagship fell short, so there was twenty-four dollars' worth of ammunition expended. A lesson had, however, been learned on board the Essex, and orders were at once given to increase elevation. At that moment the captain's aide appeared on the gun-deck with orders to fire high, and blaze away; and before I could repeat the order the No. 2 port gun belched forth her fiery flame and sent a nine-inch shell plump into the breastworks. which, exploding handsomely, caused a considerable scattering of earth and called forth a cheer from the fleet, whilst it produced great consternation in the fort. The Essex had therefore won the honor of putting the first shot into the enemy's breastworks.

"And here I must record the fact, in justice to the memory of a brave man who lost his life in that engagement, that the honor of that shot belonged to Jack Matthews, captain of No. 2 gun. Jack was an old tar who had seen much service on men-of-war in both the English and American navies, and was always restive under the command of a volunteer officer. Jack, ever on the alert to put in the first licks, and feeling, no doubt, jealous and insubordinate, had increased the elevation of his gun, and just as I was in the act of repeating the captain's order, pulled his lockstring and blazed away. Our fleet kept slowly approaching the fort, and the elevation was decreased from seven degrees to six, five, four and then three, and every shot went straight home, none of the Essex's falling short.

"Captain Porter, coming below, complimented the lieutenant of the first division for their splendid execution. By orders, I turned over the command of the battery to the third master, and ordered the first division to give way to the second. Captain Porter then ordered the first division to the stern battery. A few of my men, however, reluctant to quit the scene of action, among them Jack Matthews, lingered by their guns on the forward gun-deck. In the twinkling of an eye the scene was changed from a blaze of glory into a carnival of death and destruction. A shot from the enemy pierced the casemate just above the port-hole on the port side, then through the middle boiler, opening a chasm for the escape of scalding steam and water. I, who had gone aft in obedience to orders only a few moments before, was met by Fourth Master Walker and a crowd of men rushing aft. Walker called to me that a shot from the enemy had carried away the steam pipe. I ran to the stern of the vessel and, looking out of the stern port, saw a number of our brave fellows struggling in the water. The steam and hot water had driven all who could get out of the ports into the water. A few were fortunate enough to cling to the casemate outside. I ordered Walker to take the boats and pick up the men.

"When the explosion took place Captain Porter was standing with his aide, Brittan, directly in front of the boilers. He at once rushed to the starboard port-hole and threw himself out, expecting to go into the river. A seaman caught him round the waist, and, supporting him with one hand, clung with the other to the vessel, until with the assistance of another man he succeeded in getting the captain on a narrow projection which ran around the vessel, and so enabled him to make his way to the after port, where I met him. As soon as the steam would admit, the forward gun-deck was explored. The pilots, who were both in the pilot-house, were scalded to death. Marshall Ford, who was steering when the explosion took place, was found at his post at the wheel, standing erect, his left hand holding the spoke, his right hand holding the signal bell rope. Pilot McBride had fallen through the hatchway to the deck below; he was still living, but died soon after. The captain's aide, Brittan, had fallen by a shot as it passed through the gun-deck before entering the boiler. A seaman named James Coffey, who was shot-man to the No. 2 gun, was on his knees in the act of taking a shell from the box to be passed to the loaders. The escaping steam had struck him square in the face, and he met death in that position. Jack Matthews had gone overboard badly scalded. Third Master Terry was badly scalded and died in a few days.

"Our loss in killed, wounded and missing amounted to thirty-two; about one-half of the wounded recovered. The flagship continued approaching nearer and nearer to the fort, until the enemy showed the white flag."

The surrender of Fort Henry was followed by the same action on the part of Fort Donelson, on the Cumberland. But this latter victory belonged, as Admiral Porter expresses it, exclusively to General Grant and the army under his command, the navy taking a secondary part in it.

The result of the overwhelming of these two forts was important: Kentucky was won back to the Union, Tennessee laid open to the advance of the Federal armies.

Matthew Arthur, signal quartermaster on the Carondelet, became the cynosure of all hands during both these engagements by reason of the effective way in which he handled the rifled bow gun, of which he took voluntary charge, and the valiant manner in which he encouraged his shipmates to stand by their posts in the time of need. For this devotion to his voluntary duty, and the general good effect his actions had on the men, he was awarded the Medal of Honor.

A DESPERATE SITUATION

IMMEDIATELY after the capture of the forts on Roanoke Island, in the Pamlico Sound, by Commander S. C. Rowan and his squadron of gunboats, Admiral Goldborough, the commander-in-chief in those waters, ordered Rowan to follow up the escaped Confederate vessels which had entered Albemarle Sound and destroy them. Rowan had no knowledge of the state of affairs farther up the sound, but he did know that if there were any fortifications the fleeing enemy would make for them for protection. The ships put at his disposal were the Louisiana, Hetzel, Underwriter, Delaware, Perry, Valley City, Morse, Lockwood, Ceres, Shawsheen, Brinker and Putnam, all of them more or less frail vessels. But this fact did not at all affect Commander Rowan's determination to seek the enemy and attack them wherever he might find them. He did find them under cover of Cobb's Point Fort, which mounted four heavy 32-pounders. Opposite it was moored the schooner Black Warrior, mounting two heavy 32-pounders; between these two points of support the enemy's squadron was seen drawn up in line of battle diagonally across the channel. Rowan depended on swiftness for success, and had thoroughly explained to his officers that he meant to dash right into the enemy and fight them at as close quarters as possible. The Confederates opened fire on the Union vessels as soon as these came within range of the heavy guns. While shot and shell crashed hail-like into their midst the Federal boats did not answer the fire, but at the signal of the leader, "Dash at the enemy!" they went at them with all the speed that was in them. Before the astonished Confederates knew what was happening to them their attackers were on board. After a struggle of about fifteen minutes the victory was won; all the enemy's vessels had either been run ashore or fired or captured, with the exception of one, which managed to escape. The crew of the Black Warrior set fire to their vessel and fled; the men in the fort, seeing the destruction of their vessels, also fled in confusion.

But Commander Rowan was not yet satisfied with his brilliant exploit. He sent some of his vessels as far as Elizabeth City and Edenton. The garrison of the former city, when they saw the enemy's gunboats approaching, set fire to the place and fled Rowan, who was quite aware that this setting fire to the city would afterwards be charged to the Federals, hurriedly sent a detachment on shore, which succeeded in extinguishing the flames, colored people helping them willingly.

Among naval men this action, although seemingly of not first-class importance, was admitted to have been one of the most cleverly conceived and most energetically executed in the war.

"HE DID NOT FLINCH."

John Davis, quarter gunner on board the Valley City, won here his Medal of Honor. In the attack upon the hostile gunboats the Valley City, together with the Whitehead, formed the squadron's reserve. A shell of the enemy caused fire to break out on the first-named vessel, close to the powder magazine. Davis, who was one of the men in charge, saw an open barrel full of powder, and sparks and flames shooting towards it. Quick as lightning, and without gauging his chances he jumped to the barrel and sat upon it, thus preventing the fire from reaching the powder. He got there just in the nick of time, the sparks and cinders flying all about him, setting fire to his clothes and burning him severely. But he did not flinch, and stuck to his rather undesirable place of rest until comrades had put out the flames. Thus did the brave man prevent the explosion of the magazine and the destruction of the ship. The report of his commanding officer gave him full credit for his heroic act, and secured for him the well-deserved medal.

THE FAMOUS SEA DUEL

Ericsson's Monitor was launched on the 30th of January, 1862, in Thomas R. Rowland's shipyard at Greenpoint, Brooklyn. The difficulties the inventor had in convincing naval officers and naval constructors of the soundness of the principles underlying his plan are too well known to need more than mention here.

On the 25th of February she was turned over to the government and put in commission; Lieutenant J. L. Worden was appointed her captain and Lieutenant S. D. Greene her executive: the crew was selected from volunteers of the North Carolina and the Sabine, then lying in New York Harbor. The vessel was manned by twelve officers and forty-six men of various ranks, fifty-eight in all.

She left New York for Hampton Roads on the 6th of March. There are narrations of this trip by several of the crew; all agree as to the poor sea-going qualities this vessel showed. During the first night the wheel-ropes became jammed and the ship's safety depended entirely on the hawser that connected her with her tug, the Seth Low.

On the afternoon of Saturday, March 8th, while rounding Cape Henry, the men could distinctly hear the distant roaring of guns. It was the fight of the Merrimac with the Cumberland, Congress and Minnesota, some miles away. The Monitor stripped and cleared for action. After darkness had set in and the vessel approached Hampton Roads the burning Congress gave the crew the first intimation of what had happened. At 9 o'clock the Roanoke was reached. Worden reported to the commander, Captain Marston, who sent him to the aid of the grounded Minnesota. The ship was reached near midnight.

Officers and men of the Monitor were well-nigh exhausted by their first trip of three days; there had hardly been any sleep during the voyage for anyone; cooking had been impossible, and the fare consisted of wet hardtack and an occasional potato baked before the fires. The news received could not be gloomier than they were. Evil forebodings on the part of the worn-out men might have been excusable on this occasion; but there were none whatever. The men on the Monitor had confidence in their commander, their ship and themselves. The men were lookers-on when the Congress finally blew up between 1 and 2 o'clock, and many were the earnest pledges to get even with the Merrimac in the morning.

At 7 o'clock on this memorable morning of the 9th of March the Monitor was ready and waiting for her enemy. Half an hour later the latter came in sight, steaming straight for the Minnesota. As yet the enemys knew nothing of the presence of the Monitor. Suddenly the crew of the Merrimac espied the nondescript vessel emerging from behind the frigate. "What's that thing?" "What have the Yanks put up there?" the Merrimac officers and men asked each other in wonderment. The Merrimac was then commanded by Lieutenant Catesby Jones, a former officer of the U. S. Navy, Captain Buchanan having been wounded the day before. The rebel ironclad fired the first shot of the battle at the Monitor from her bow pivot-gun, a 7-inch rifle. After that she meant to ignore the Monitor entirely, and made for the Minnesota. This was at about 9 o'clock.

Lieutenant Worden manœuvred as if he had expected this. He kept persistently between the Minnesota and her dreaded foe, heading straight for the latter. When at close range the Merrimac fired her starboard broadside, one 6-inch rifle and three 8-inch smooth-bore guns. The two 11-inchers of the Monitor bellowed back their answer and the battle had begun.

According to Confederate statements the Ericsson vessel did not fire very fast. Captain Ericsson ascribed the slow firing to the fact that Lieutenant Greene, commanding the turret, instead of turning the turret off for loading the guns, had the gun-crews handle the pendulum port-stoppers after each firing, a ponderous and comparatively slow manipulation, which was only provided for emergencies. The entire gun-crews were required for it, while turning the turret off could be accomplished by one man.

As it was, the Monitor delivered about forty shots, the fight lasting somewhat over two hours.

When the Confederate captain saw that his invulnerable and plucky little adversary would not let him get at the Minnesota he tried to board the Monitor and "have the crew smothered below," presumably by stuffing the blower pipes. The two vessels lay several times nearly alongside. Taking advantage of such a chance, boarders were sent away from the Merrimac; but they had to crawl back on board immediately, as there was no time for them to act on account of the fire from the Minnesota. The sharpshooters of this ship kept a good lookout. A man on the Merrimac who crawled out of a port-hole to look around was immediately shot down and rolled overboard dying.

No shot had up to this time penetrated either ship. The Merrimac had her smokestack knocked over, and the Monitor had one officer, Acting-Master Stodder, disabled. Stodder was working the turning engine of the turret and leaned incautiously against the side, when a shot struck in the vicinity and the powerful shock knocked the man down and contused him to such a degree that he had to leave his station.

Lieutenant Greene complained later about the difficulty of obtaining and holding the aim with the turret and locating the bearings; also the difficulty of communicating with the captain forward in the pilot-house. In order to make sure of avoiding firing the guns too far forward and thus endangering the pilot-house, Greene, according to his statement, fired every shot himself.

Towards noon the supply of ammunition ran short in the turret and Lieutenant Worden hauled the ship off for about fifteen minutes, as during the replenishing of the supply the turret had to be kept stationary so that the two scuttles, one in the turret-floor and the other in the deck, should be in line. During this lull Worden passed through a port-hole out upon the deck to get a good look all around.

Although the Merrimac had received some heavy shocks, no shots had so far penetrated to the inside. At the same time officers and men realized their inability to reach the inside of their adversary. When, during the lull, Lieutenant Jones made a quick tour of inspection of his ship he met a whole gun-division in the battery standing "at ease," saying that it was no use to waste powder on the Monitor, it being just as effective to snap one's fingers at her.

Jones determined to run the Monitor down. His ship was here at a double disadvantage; she was much slower and more-unwieldy then the Monitor and also had

THE MONITOR'S HEROES AT WORK IN THE TURRET.

to confine herself to a small area in her manœuvring on account of her twenty-two feet of draught, the Monitor only drawing twelve feet.

When the battle began afresh Jones rammed the Monitor; the effect was almost nothing. The Monitor glanced off and one of her guns managed to plant a 180-pound shot at a distance of fifteen yards against the forward casemate.

The Confederates now concentrated their aim on the Monitor's pilot-house. A hostile shell, fired at a distance of no more than ten yards, struck against one of the slits in the pilot-house and exploded. While the top of the latter was torn and lifted the gases and flames from the exploding powder struck Worden, who stood close behind the slit, full in the face, burning him and blinding him completely.

He had to leave his station while his brave wheelman, Peter Williams, who stood right beside him, escaped unhurt and stuck to his now exposed post, assuring his commander that he would take care of the movements of the vessel until Lieutenant Greene should come up. Williams steered the Monitor away from the Merrimac, and Worden, summoning all his strength and holding himself up against the ladder of the pilot-house, sent for Greene.

In about twenty minutes the Monitor attacked again, Chief Engineer Stimers being left in charge of the turret. But when her bow was turned toward the Merrimac it was seen that she was retreating. A few shots were fired at her and then the Monitor went back under the side of the Minnesota, which had been saved by the little ironclad.

Worden was transferred to a steamer and sent to New York; he had engaged and come out victorious in the first battle of ironclads ever fought, a combat which rendered his name and that of his vessel famous all over the world and sealed the fate of the old wooden sailing fleets.

The Merrimac claimed the fight a draw; all the rest of the world called it a glorious victory for the North.

Peter Williams, the cool-headed wheelman, received for his circumspection, presence of mind and courage the Medal of Honor, the only man awarded one in this historical engagement.

The Merrimac never came out again and was destroyed by her crew on June 11, 1862.

FORCING THE ENTRANCE TO THE MISSISSIPPI

WILLIAM McKNIGHT.
Coxswain U. S. S. Varuna.
Born in Ulster Co., N. Y., 1841.

A S EARLY as November 12, 1861, an order was issued by President Lincoln for the fitting out of an expedition to capture New Orleans. Captain D. G. Farragut, with the title of flag officer, was appointed commander-in-chief. By the middle of March, 1862, the first division of Farragut's squadron, the steam vessels, had assembled at Key West. Later on this force was re-enforced by the division of mortar schooners in command of Commander David D. Porter.

The defenses of New Orleans consisted of two powerful works, Forts Jackson and St. Philip, which included obstructions on the river itself; besides a quite formidable naval force. The two forts were situated in a commanding position at a turn of the river, Jackson on the east and St. Philip on the west bank, mounting together 128 guns. The Confederate fleet counted fourteen vessels with thirty-nine guns.

Farragut's forces—not including the mortar boats—counted 177 guns. While his vessels were all wooden, some of the enemy's were armored. The squadron of steamers was divided into three divisions, as follows: First division, Captain Bailey; Cayuga, Pensacola, Mississippi, Oneida, Varuna, Katahdin, Kineo, Wissahickon. Second, center division, Flag Officer Farragut; Hartford, Brooklyn, Richmond. Third division, Captain Bell; Scioto, Iroquois, Kennebec, Pinola, Itasca, Winona.

At the signal given these divisions were to force an entrance and subdue the forts and hostile naval forces, in the order named.

The mortar flotilla was moored on the west bank of the river, at a point screened from the forts by a thick growth of woods. The mortars were to assist the fleet by their fire, and they did indeed capital service, as Captain Farragut acknowledged himself.

Everything being in readiness, the bombardment was opened on the morning of April 16th and continued until the night of the 23d of April.

On the morning of April 24th the signal set the fleet moving. The odds were decidedly against the Federal forces.

The first division, of course, had naturally to stand the brunt of the enemy's fire, before the other divisions could close in. The Pensacola and Mississippi, advancing through a hail of shot and shell as close as the depth of the channel allowed on to Fort St. Philip, succeeded in driving the gunners of this fort into shelter. The difficulty of manœuvering such a number of ships, under such a heavy fire, in a narrow channel, against a current of about three-and-a-half miles an hour, was obvious. The Varuna was fiercely attacked by two of the enemy's vessels; one of them, the Stonewall Jackson, ramming her twice. The Federal ship was doomed; she filled rapidly through the fatal wound received under the water line in her starboard side. To save the lives of those on board her commander had to beach her, when the Pensacola and Oneida rescued what was left of her crew.

Farragut's own flagship, the Hartford, was set on fire by a fire-raft which the enemy managed to shove against her side. During the efforts to avoid contact with this dangerous foe she grounded on a shoal. Only the captain's coolness and circumspection saved her from destruction. She was successful in backing off the shoal, freeing herself from the fire-raft, and the crew extinguished the fire. All the other ships experienced similar precarious situations. But the skill and coolness of the Federal officers forced success. An hour and ten minutes after getting under way the three divisions were past the forts, with the exception of the Kennebec, Winona and Itasca, which on account of their slow speed had to suffer too long under the fire of the forts and were compelled to fall back. After the other ships had passed the mortar steamers withdrew from their position before the water battery, back behind the shelter of the bank, where the mortar schooners were anchored.

After silencing the Chalmette batteries, farther up the river, Farragut anchored off New Orleans at noon of April 25th. His object was attained, as the Confederate

"THE MANASSES STRUCK US A DIAGONAL BLOW."

land forces had abandoned the city and left her defenseless at the mercy of the Federal fleet.

Captain Porter, in the meantime, with his mortar vessels shelled Fort Jackson, whose resistance was broken on the 28th of April, on which day the Confederate commander communicated his willingness to capitulate. The capitulation was signed on the following day. On the 28th of April New Orleans surrendered.

The Union fleet lost in this famous engagement one ship, the gunboat Varuna, 35 men killed and 128 men wounded. The ships which suffered most were the Pensacola, 27; Brooklyn, 35, and Iroquois 28.

As to individual experience in this memorable action we have a graphic account by an eye-witness and combatant, Gunner Cornelius Cronin, then one of the crew of the Brooklyn. He says: "The first bombardment continued, with intermissions, until the morning of April 24th, when, at 2 o'clock, after the display of a preconcerted signal from the flagship, which consisted of two vertical red lights at her mizzen peak, the signal for battle, all the ships got under way, beat to quarters, and steamed towards the forts.

"My station during the action was on the poop-deck, with several others, when, as we rounded the point behind which we had enjoyed up to this time a comparative immunity from the direct fire of the forts, a shot struck close to our stern, almost drenching us with water. A minute or so thereafter, being now under a raking fire from both forts, I had been speaking to our signal quartermaster, Barney Sands, and had just turned away from him, when a cannon shot struck him and Midshipman John Anderson, killing both instantly. The latter was knocked overboard and we saw no more of him, while the former, with the assistance of another man, I carried below, returning at once to my station.

"By this time the action had become general, and from the density of the smoke it was almost impossible to see anything. The gunboat Kineo, at this juncture, ran foul of us; while we, in turn, collided with one of the hulks used by the enemy in obstructing the channel. One of our kedge anchors placed on each quarter, having a hawser attached to each, to be used in springing the ship should she become disabled, fouled the hulk, carrying away the stopper of the anchor, so that we actually had the hulk in tow. I reported this to the captain, and was ordered to cut the hawser, which with an ax was shortly done, freeing us from the encumbrance.

"And now the shot and shell were flying and bursting around us in all directions, crashing through our ship, scattering splinters and bolts on all sides, killing and wounding our men in a terrible manner. Nevertheless, our brave captain stood on the forward part of the poop-deck during the battle, and did not seem at all disconcerted, while shot and shell were flying around him from every point of the compass, giving his orders as coolly as if taking his ship into an open roadstead in broad daylight.

"1 must confess for my part, though, that I cordially disliked the business, as these big 100-pound shells, moving with a fiendish velocity within a few feet of a man, make the most hellish and disagreeable noise imaginable. I thought every shot was within a few inches of my head, or aimed directly at me, and, as a matter of course, I felt, as it were, compelled to dodge frequently to avoid them.

"We were now actively engaged, not only with both forts, but also with the rebel gunboats. One of them appearing upon our port beam, about fifty yards distant, was effectually silenced by the contents of our entire port battery. She was crowded with men, and it was evidently their intention to board us. Fortunately for themselves, they were not destined to succeed.

"As day dawned, we found ourselves abreast of the enemy steamer McRae, but as our captain mistook her for one of our ships he did not, of course, fire into her. Had this not been the case, however, we might have made short work of her. I was very sure myself that she was the McRae, but as I was a subordinate I deemed it prudent to hold my tongue, which I did. Soon afterwards the ram Manassas was discovered on our starboard bow. Nearly everyone saw her and cried out, 'The ram!' 'The ram!' Our captain having seen her from his point of vantage, the poop, ordered the helm hard-aport, and to the engineer in charge, 'Full speed ahead.' The ram, then heading for our starboard gangway, struck us a diagonal blow, causing the ship to career several strakes, discharging her bow gun simultaneously at us. As we could not depress our guns sufficiently to strike her, she drifted astern, and by the combined action of the swift current of the river and the opposing speed of both ships, was quick as a flash out of reach. She was subsequently attended to, however, by the frigate Mississippi, who rammed her ashore, compelling her crew to leave her as best they could in all directions, they having first laid a train to her magazine, which caused her destruction by a terrific explosion shortly afterwards.

"The battle of the forts and gunboats being now virtually at an end, cheer after cheer by us made the welkin ring, our heroic old captain participating with us in this gleeful demonstration. Following this, the flagship made signal that all the ships come to anchor and bury their dead.

"The casualties on the Brooklyn were nine dead and twenty-seven wounded. In a rude cemetery, devoid of all embellishments of art or other evidences of material grandeur, on the west bank of the Father of Waters, rest in silent repose the honored dead of all of our ships.

"After we had had our breakfast the ships all got under way and steamed up the river, the negroes exhibiting great signs of joy at seeing us above the forts by cheering us on our way, while the whites were much less enthusiastic.

"Next day Chalmette Point batteries on both sides of the river were discovered, which opened fire on us as soon as we got within range. We now formed in close order, the flagship leading, and under the raking fire from the batteries their shots flew around us pretty lively. We regretted that we were unable for some little time to use other than our bow and forecastle guns in replying to theirs. Rapidly advancing up stream, however, and as soon as we could bring our other guns to bear, the Hartford delivered a full broadside to the battery on the right bank, and, sheering off to starboard, left the field open to us. Our captain then cried out: 'Boys, hold your fire, and I will lay you alongside that battery!' while to the engineer in charge he signaled, 'Go ahead full speed.' We then gave a cheer and opened on them with grape and cannister at a distance of fifty yards, completely silencing their fire. Manning our starboard battery, we moved toward the left bank, whither the Hartford had preceded us, getting in her work, and let them have it there with 9-inch shell. It was really comical after this to notice the stampede and general demoralization which prevailed among the Confederates as they ran away from their guns in all directions to escape the murderous fire of the fleet. By this time all the ships were up and the battle was shortly afterwards terminated.

"The ships now ascended the river a distance of three miles from the batteries, and came to anchor in front of the city of New Orleans, where, the river being high, they presented a formidable and commanding position and appearance. But the anarchy and confusion which prevailed in and around the city — steamships, coal and other inflammable and combustible material adding to the general conflagration — presented a scene of desolation and wanton destruction of property such as beggars all my powers of description to portray.

"Immediately upon the anchoring of the fleet before the city Captain Theodorus Bailey, second in command, was dispatched by the flag officer on shore to demand of the mayor or other constituted authorities the surrender of the city, coupled with the order that the flag of the United States be hoisted upon all public buildings. The correspondence between the mayor and the flag officer was quite spirited towards this end, but of course as they had no alternative but to surrender, possession of the city was taken in the name of the United States by the victorious squadron and the flag of the Union raised upon the Postoffice, the Customs House and the Mint.

"On the 26th we visited Carrollton, seven miles above the city, and found the batteries there abandoned and the guns spiked, while the welcome news soon followed by the arrival of the Cayuga that Forts Jackson and St. Philip had capitulated on the 26th, and the flag of the United States was again waving over those strongholds."

Twenty sailors of the squadron were granted the Medal of Honor for their valiant behavior in this memorable engagement. There were eight from the lost Varuna, three from the Pensacola, one from the Wissahickon, one from the Brooklyn, one from the Mississippi, one from the Owasco, one from the Pinola, three from the Cayuga and one from the Colorado, as follows:

John McGowan, quartermaster, and Amos Bradley, landsman of the Varuna, stood at the wheel during the entire fight, although the guns were raking the deck from behind them, their position being one of the most responsible on the ship.

When it was seen that the Colorado could not participate in the battle, owing to her too deep draught, Christopher Brennen, seaman, volunteered and received permission to join the crew of the Mississippi. The energy and zeal with which he worked made him the life and soul of the gun's crew, and drew forth unstinted praise from both officers and crew.

In the heat of the action fire broke out on the berth-deck of the Pinola, in close proximity to the powder magazine, the flames threatening to make their way to the powder. I. B. Frisbee, gunner's mate, saw the danger, and leaving his gun ran swiftly around the fire and into the magazine, closing the heavy iron door behind him. Here he stayed in momentary danger of being blown up with the magazine, until the crew had subdued the fire.

During the attack Thomas Lyons, seaman, was lashed on the port sheet chain, outside of the Pensacola, with lead in hand, to guide the ship past the forts, and never flinched in spite of the terrific cannonade the Pensacola was exposed to from the enemy's forts and gunboats.

James Buck, quartermaster of the Brooklyn, stationed at the wheel, was painfully wounded by a heavy splinter early in the fight, but for seven hours stood bravely at his post, refusing to go below until positively ordered to do so, and next morning in his wounded condition he stole to his station and steered the ship for more than eight hours.

Thomas Flood, boy, of the Pensacola, assisted very materially in the action by taking up the duties of the signal quartermaster, who was shot down.

Louis Richards, quartermaster of the Pensacola, steered the ship through the barricade amid the din and roar of battle with the utmost coolness, and his watchful devotion to orders contributed greatly to successful passage.

The others rewarded for exceptional bravery are:

Thomas Bourne, seaman and gun-captain of the Varuna.

John Green, captain of the forecastle and gun-captain of the Varuna.

George Hollat, third-class boy of the Varuna.

William McKnight, cockswain gun-captain of the Varuna.

William Martin, seaman, gun-captain of the Varuna.

Oscar E. Peck, second-class boy of the Varuna.

Henry Shutes, captain of the forecastle of the Wissahickon.

Edward Farrell, quartermaster of the Owasco.

William Parker, captain of the afterguard of the Cayuga.

Edward Wright, quartermaster of the Cayuga.

William Young, boatswain's mate of the Cayuga.

James McLeod, captain of foretop, of the Colorado.

AMIDST DEATH AND DESTRUCTION

THE hardest fight that occurred on the James River was the engagement of Commander John Rodgers's gunboats, especially his ship, the Galena, with the fort on Drury's Bluff, Fort Darling, about eight miles below Richmond. Rodgers had at his disposal the so-called "ironclad" Galena, ten 100-pounder guns, the Monitor, two 9-inch guns, and three unarmored gunboats. The Galena had been pronounced as "not sufficiently protected" by Lieutenant D. D. Porter, who had inspected the ship while she was being fitted out. Besides, it was by that time generally admitted in the navy that ships alone had not good chances in a fight against strong forts, unless they were supported by land forces. Drury's Bluff rises on the river bank to an elevation of about

JOHN F. MACKIE,
Corporal on U. S. S. Galena. Born in New York City in 1835.

200 feet. Commander Rodgers, burning with ambition and the desire for activity—notwithstanding the obstructions of sunken vessels and barriers of driven piles in the James River—considered his chance had come when the Army of the Potomac was moved south to Yorktown and operations were begun to recapture Norfolk. On the 15th of May, Commander Rodgers decided to make a demonstration and, perhaps, also to show the enemy that a Federal naval force might be expected to undertake and dare almost anything. The struggle was entirely one-sided, and its results were merely of a moral nature, in favor of the attacking force; but the heroism of the Galena's crew and the professional skill displayed by the leader of the attacking force stand unequaled.

Corporal John F. Mackie, of the Galena, who won his Medal of Honor on this day, gives the following graphic description of this sanguinary action:

"On the morning of the 8th of May Captain Rodgers was ordered to advance up the James River as far as Richmond, if possible, and to capture, burn and destroy all Confederate works wherever found, reporting as frequently as possible. The gunboats Port Royal, 6 guns, Captain George N. Morris; Aroostook, 6 guns, Captain John Beaumont; and the revenue steamer Naugatuck, 3 guns, Captain Stevens, were to assist him in this work.

"As we started up the river it was reported that Yorktown had been evacuated and 10,000 troops had been landed at Sewell's Point, opposite Norfolk, by General Wool; all of which was glorious news. The passage up the river was resisted at every available point, during which three severe battles had been fought, resulting in the capture and destruction of the places offering resistance. As the fleet arrived at City Point the Confederates set fire to the place and abandoned it.

"On the 13th of May Captain Rodgers's fleet was joined by the ironclad Monitor, Captain William N. Jeffers, when all hands got under way again and started up the river for Richmond. The river, which was quite wide up to this point, now became very narrow, only about 200 yards wide, crooked as a ram's horn, with very high banks, heavily wooded on both sides, from which the fleet was constantly being fired on by Confederate sharpshooters hidden in the underbrush.

"About 6 o'clock on the morning of the 15th the fleet arrived off Fort Darling, a heavily casemated battery of ten guns on a high point called Drury's Bluff, about eight miles below Richmond. Here the river was found to be completely obstructed by sunken vessels. The Galena advanced so close to the obstructions that we could step on board of them, but Captain Rodgers found them impassable.

"The line of battle was formed in the following order: Galena on the right, distant from the fort about 100 yards; Monitor, Port Royal, Aroostook, Naugatuck, in single line. But Captain Rodgers found a few minutes later, after opening fire, that we were too close. We could not get sufficient elevation to our guns. He got under way with the whole fleet, dropped down about 200 yards, and came to anchor again in the same order. This was all done under a heavy fire from the fort on the hill, during which several men were killed and wounded. Captain Rodgers, being badly cut in the face by a splinter, refused to have it dressed by the surgeon until after the close of the fight.

"About 7 o'clock the action began in earnest and raged with great fury on both sides for the next three hours, during which the fleet and fort suffered severely. The Naugatuck burst her 100-pound rifle and was obliged to withdraw to a lower position. Captain Jeffers reported that the Monitor was too close, and if allowed to drop a little lower down the river could be of more service, which was permitted.

"A severe fire was kept up by the sharpshooters on the banks of the river, which killed and wounded several men. The fire of the fleet had silenced the fort for nearly half an hour, when the Aroostook, Captain Beaumont, and Port Royal, Captain Morris, dropped down the river about 1,000 yards on account of the sharpshooters, besides being very much exposed to a plunging fire from the fort, endangering the steam boilers.

"This left the Galena alone in front of the fort. About 11 o'clock Fort Darling was re-enforced by the Merrimac's crew, which had been sent down from Richmond. They sprang upon the parapets and gave three cheers. We were so close to them that we could see the stripes on their uniforms.

"They then sprang to their guns and reopened fire on the fleet, particularly on the Galena, smashing every one of our six small boats, cutting so many holes in the smokestack that it reminded one of a nutmeg grater, tearing great gaps in our spardeck and smashing all the spare spars. One shot struck the quarter deck wheel and binnacle, knocking them overboard. The ship began to fly all to pieces, and in a short time we were a complete wreck. But no officer or man flinched from his duty, and our work went bravely on.

THE GALENA BEFORE FORT DARLING.

"A few minutes later Gunner Boreum came up out of the magazine and reported to Captain Rodgers, who was forward at the time, that we had fired all but five rounds to each gun of our fixed ammunition. 'Send it up as long as it will last, and then we will use solid shot,' replied Captain Rodgers.

"As the gunner turned to go below an 8-inch solid shot pierced the port side, killing him and four other men instantly and wounding several. This was followed almost within a moment by another 8-inch solid shot hitting a little farther forward, killing and wounding six men. After this shell came one which exploded on our deck, killing and wounding several men. Among these was a powder boy in the act of passing a cartridge, which exploded.

"While this dreadful work was going on forward the after division fared still worse. A 10-inch solid shot, followed immediately by two other 8-inch solid shot, struck this part of the ship, killing and wounding the entire after division of twenty-five men and disabling all the guns.

"Death and destruction reigned supreme here for about ten minutes; everybody believed the ship was on fire.

"Twelve men of the marine guard under my command and I were at our ports, taking care of the sharpshooters on the opposite river bank, and I barely escaped being struck by the 10-inch shot. As soon as the smoke cleared away a terrible sight was revealed to my eyes: the entire after division down and the deck covered with dead and dying men. Without losing a moment, however, I called out to the men that here was a chance for them, ordering them to clear away the dead and wounded and get the guns in shape. Splinters were swept from the guns, sand thrown on the deck, which was slippery with human blood, and in an instant the heavy 100-pounder Parrott rifle and two 9-inch Dahlgren guns were ready and at work upon the fort. Our first shots blew up one of the casemates and dismounted one of the guns that had been destroying the ship.

"Order in the meantime had been restored forward by Captain Rodgers and the guns set at work once more, returning a very destructive fire on the fort.

"The coolness of the officers and men in this dreadful crisis was extraordinary; everybody behaved handsomely, to say the least.

"A captain of a gun was thumbing the vent of a 9-inch Dahlgren as the men rammed home a 10-pound cartridge of powder, when he was knocked down by a splinter uncovering the vent. George Smith, a seaman, placed his bare thumb on the hot gun and kept the vent closed until the men finished loading; he was burned severely, but never left his station.

"A part of a shell entered the boiler-room, cutting the steam escape pipe and unseating the safety valve, filling the fire-room with steam and driving everybody out. The boilers were losing steam at a terrible rate, when a young fireman, Charles Kenyon, rushed in at great risk of his life and seated the valve, a most heroic act.

"At this time Captain Rodgers was signaling to the fleet below when a shot cut the signal halyards, throwing them down on deck, and leaving a white signal flying at the fore. The signal quartermaster, Jeremiah Regan, saw the situation at a glance and sprang into the forerigging, climbing aloft under a heavy fire from the sharpshooters on the bank. He cleared the halyards, threw the white signal overboard, and then slid down the back-stays and returned to his station unhurt. When asked by Captain Rodgers why he threw the white signal overboard, he replied: 'I wanted to show those damned enemys that we had no use for white flags.' This was the spirit that animated all of the crew of the Galena.

"At 11:30 o'clock Captain Rodgers gave orders to cease firing, as there was no prospect of our being able to capture the fort, and the river was so seriously obstructed that until those obstructions were removed it was absolutely impassable. So slipping our cables we turned and headed down the stream, followed by the other vessels. The enemy kept up a heavy fire as long as we remained within reach of their guns.

"Thus ended the first attempt to take Fort Darling. The Galena, as she steamed away from the fort, was a complete wreck. She had been hit by 132 shots in different places, pierced on the gun-deck in twenty different places, breaking in about four feet of woodwork at each place. The port side was shattered so badly that the guns had to be shored up underneath to keep them from falling into the coal bunkers. And, worst of all, we had lost two officers and eighteen men killed and thirty-eight men and two officers wounded, a loss of sixty men out of a ship's company of 150 officers and men, forty per cent. of the entire crew.

"No man flinched from his station. If his mate fell dead by his side he took his place without orders or any question of rank or duty. Where necessary, the men discharged their duty in positions where they were practically sure of being killed. The first man who paid for his heroism with his life was the leadsman, Thomas Ready, taking soundings outside of the ship, under the guns of Fort Darling, exposed to a heavy fire from the sharpshooters. Every man was ready to sacrifice his life in the discharge of his duty.

"The Galena remained in the James River all summer and fought in every battle on the peninsula within the reach of her guns and practically saved the Army of the Potomac from capture by the Army of Virginia, under the command of General R. E. Lee, at Malvern Hill, July 15, 1862. Captain John Rodgers's courage and bold seamanship kept the river open so that General G. B. McClellan's supplies and re-enforcements reached him in time and opened the way for his escape."

President Lincoln visited the Army of the Potomac at Harrison's Landing, opposite City Point, in July, and also Admiral Goldsborough on the Wachusetts, the Monitor and the Galena, where he and his escort were received with appropriate honors.

After exchanging the usual courtesies the President, Secretary of the Navy Welles, Admiral Goldsborough and Captain Rodgers inspected the ship. Seeing her condition, the President remarked: "I cannot understand how any of you escaped alive." On his return to the spar-deck all of the distinguished party had assembled on the quarter-deck, facing the crew on the port side, and the President made a short speech, thanking the officers and men for their magnificent services.

Captain Rogers then called Lieutenant Newman and ordered him to have the following men report at the main-mast;

Corporal John F. Mackie, Quartermaster Jeremiah Regan, and First-class Fireman Charles Kenyon. They stood there for a few minutes, when presently Captain Rodgers, followed by President Lincoln, Secretary Welles, and nearly all of the distinguished company, came up and halted before them. Captain Rodgers said: "Mr. President, these are young heroes of Fort Darling battle," and he related briefly how Regan had cleared away the halyards, throwing the white flag overboard; how Kenyon had rushed into the steam-filled fire-room and saved the ship by fixing the safety-valve; how in the terrible crisis Mackie had rallied the marines and taken charge of the after division when all the men had been killed or wounded.

The President then took them all by the hand, personally thanked them for their gallant conduct, and ordered them rewarded with the Medal of Honor and promotion.

CARONDELET AND ARKANSAS CONFLICT

THE Confederate ram Arkansas was made ready for her short though destructive career about July 12, 1862. She was armored with half-inch iron plates and railway iron, with a battery of ten guns. She started on her career July 14, running down the Yazoo to Old River, where she overhauled the ironclad Carondelet, the wooden gunboat Tyler, and the ram Queen of the West. Their meeting was the signal for trouble.

The Carondelet fired broadside against the ironclad sides of the ram in vain; the shots glanced off harmlessly and dropped into the water. The ram then ran into the Carondelet with a fearful crash and the gunboat suffered severe punishment from the enemy's fire. Five shots went through the captain's cabin, exhaust pipes were shot in two and the steam escaped. All the starboard boats were carried away, and ten men killed and fifteen wounded. The Federal captain tried to board the ram; but the enemy, noticing the intention, drew away. It was at this juncture that Cockswain John G. Morrison, of the Carondelet, gave evidence of his courage and fearlessness. He at the first call acted as leader of the boarders, and was the first on deck to lead the hand-to-hand fight. The men, however, had to retire, as the enemy's could not be reached. With keen presence of mind in all this turmoil Morrison, taking advantage of a good opportunity, ran down into the battery and caused a broadside to be fired into the ram while she passed. As he had shown conspicuous presence of mind and courage on many other occasions, this last distinguished act of bravery caused the commanding officer to recommend Morrison for the Medal of Honor.

The Arkansas now moved down the river to its confluence with the Mississippi. Here the entire Union fleet was lying, the combined flotilla of Davis and Farragut. The Arkansas ran the gauntlet of the whole fleet, and safely anchored under the batteries of Vicksburg.

Commodores Farragut and Davis then resolved to make a general attack on Vicksburg, and, if possible, sink or capture the Arkansas. In the evening the vessels

"THE ARKANSAS RAN THE GAUNTLET OF THE WHOLE FLEET."

of both fleets moved down the river and opened fire upon the Confederate batteries.

For over two hours the bombardment was heavy. Davis engaged the upper batteries while Farragut's ships passed on below. The air was lighted up with bursting shells, and the heavy broadsides of the Richmond and Hartford were perceptible above the general din. The upper batteries were silenced and the town set on fire in several places. During all this fight, however, the Arkansas lay off the water batteries and did not fire a single shot. The ram Sumter attempted to sink her during this engagement, but did not succeed.

On the 20th Commander Ellet took the Queen of the West and went down to see if he could destroy the monster. Under a terrific fire from the batteries and broadsides from the ram, he ran the Queen, under a full head of steam, at the Arkansas. The blow, although slightly glancing, shook both vessels terribly; some of the Confederate crew jumped overboard, thinking that the vessel was sinking. Commander Ellet then drew off for another blow, and on moving toward her again the Queen missed her and ran into the bank. The engines were reversed, the Queen backed off and ran past the batteries up the river to join the fleet, where she arrived terribly riddled by shot and shell.

Early in August General Breckenridge planned an expedition to recapture Baton Rouge, which was held by a small force under General Williams. On the 5th Breckenridge moved upon the city from the rear, while the Arkansas, which had been strengthened at Vicksburg, was to co-operate with him from the river, assisted by two gunboats, the Webb and the Music.

The Confederate vessels stopped at the bend above the town, as Commodore Porter was at Baton Rouge with a force of gunboats. The land forces of the enemy attacked General Williams at 4 o'clock in the morning, and were repulsed as soon as Porter's gunboats could shell them from the river.

While leading his men General Williams was shot through the heart. The gunboats, in order to reach the enemy, had to fire over the town, their shots being directed by a signal officer stationed on top of the State House.

As soon as the enemy were driven off, Commander Porter, with the Essex, Cayuga and Sumter, started up the river to look after the Arkansas, which had not made her appearance below in consequence of an injury to one of her engines.

As soon as Porter got sight of her he opened fire with incendiary shells, and in twenty minutes she was discovered to be in flames. The crew backed her ashore and got a line out, which soon burnt off, and she swung into the river, where she continued to burn until she blew up with a tremendous explosion.

A DARING RECONNOISSANCE

THE operations of the North Atlantic Squadron during the summer of 1862 were limited to small expeditions up the sounds and rivers around Pamlico and Albemarle Sounds. Some of these exploits, although not productive of important strategical results, were severe tests of the endurance, the skill and courage of those who participated in them, officers and men sharing the hardships alike. One of the most ambitious, daring and energetic of the younger officers in the squadron was Lieutenant C. W. Flusser, the captain of the steamer Commodore Perry. He simply enjoyed hazardous enterprises which, mostly without a prospect for reward or even recognition, offered pretty good chances for losing one's life or getting wounded. Of this kind was the reconnoissance which he undertook on the 9th of July, 1862, from Plymouth, N. C. On this vessel, the Commodore Perry, he had a captain of the Ninth New York Volunteers, Hammell, and twenty of his men. The small steamers Shawsheen and Ceres completed his little flotilla. The Ceres had on board Lieutenant Green and ten men of the regiment named above.

Flusser's aim was the capture of the unimportant little town of Hamilton. He had not gone far up the Roanoke before running into the fire of thick lines of enemy sharpshooters who occupied the south bank of the river, seemingly in large numbers. This was shortly after noon. The three vessels returned the fire, of course, and pushed on. Their speed was slow, for they had to be on the lookout for some hidden fortification. For two hours they ran the gauntlet, losing twelve men, two killed and ten wounded. Then Hamilton hove in sight, where Flusser expected armed resistance. He got his "forces" ready to attack the town, when on closer observation he found that the enemy had decamped. It seemed that Flusser's reputation sufficed in this case to have his opponents decide for the "better part of valor." So he "captured" Hamilton and a small schooner into the bargain, his success being also his only reward.

But the risk of life and vessels had been considerable, and the work of his little force of a hundred sailors and soldiers so praiseworthy that two of the crew of the Ceres, Quartermaster Alexander Hand and Second-class Fireman John Kelly, whose behavior bordered closely on recklessness, were awarded the Medal of Honor for their good conduct and bravery.

FOUNDERING OF THE MONITOR

THE famous Monitor foundered at sea in a gale off Cape Hatteras in the night between December 30 and 31, 1862; glory and drama were the ushers in and out in this memorable vessel's short but momentous career of only a little over nine months' duration.

As to whether her tragical end was inevitable or avoidable was never settled; for either view sound and competent minds have held their own.

But as the deplorable catastrophe did take place it brought out again in a most beautiful and touching manner the unselfish, unconscious and hardy heroism of the men who manned the Union ships.

The Merrimac, the Monitor's dangerous adversary, was destroyed by her own crew when the Confederates evacuated Norfolk, and the Monitor joined the squadron in the James River under Commodore Rodgers. After an unsuccessful engagement with Fort Darling, which lasted four hours, the vessel returned to Hampton Roads, and finally, in the fall, went up to Washington for the repair of her destroyed pilot-house. In November she went back to Hampton Roads, with her old executive officer, Lieutenant S. D. Greene, and Commander J. P. Bankhead as captain.

On the 29th of December, 1862, she started for Beaufort, N. C., under escort of the sidewheel steamer Rhode Island, which had her in tow with two 12-inch hawsers. On the second day out the weather became severe, and towards noon had increased to a gale. The ships were then about fifteen miles directly off Cape Hatteras. While the Rhode Island steamed slowly but steadily ahead, the heavy sea pitched and rolled over the little ironclad so that those on board the Rhode Island had the impression more than once that the Monitor was gone. Imagine the situation of the crew of sixty-five officers and men on board this vessel. According to Lieutenant Greene's own statement, referring to ordinary weather, "probably no ship was ever devised which was so uncomfortable for her crew, and certainly no sailor ever led a more disagreeable life than we did on the James River, suffocated with heat and bad air if we remained below, and a target for sharpshooters if we came on deck." If, in the present situation, we substitute for sharpshooters the huge and many times more dangerous waves of the roused Atlantic we might gain some faint idea of the conditions on board. Francis B. Butts, one of the survivors of this memorable and last trip, describes his remarkable experience, as follows:

"The wheel had been rigged temporarily on top of the turret, where all the officers, except those on duty in the engine-room, now were. I had taken my turn at the wheel, and, being a good hand, I was kept there. I heard the remarks of the officers and watched closely the movements of the vessel, so that I exactly understood our condition. The vessel was making very heavy weather, riding one huge wave, plunging through the next as if shooting straight for the bottom of the ocean, and splashing down upon another with such force that her hull would tremble, and with a shock that would sometimes take us off our feet, while a fourth would leap upon us and break far above the turret, so that if we had not been protected by a rifle-armor that was securely fastened and rose to the height of a man's chest we should have been washed away.

"About 8 o'clock, while I was taking a message from the captain to the engineer, I saw the water pour in through the coal-bunkers in sudden volumes as it swept over the deck. About that time the engineer reported that the coal was too wet to keep up steam, which had run down from its usual pressure of eighty pounds to twenty. The water in the vessel was gaining rapidly over the small pumps, and I heard the captain order the chief engineer to start the main pump, a very powerful one of new invention. This was done.

"About 8:30 o'clock the first signals of distress to the Rhode Island were burned. She lay to, and we rode the sea more comfortably than when we were being towed. The Rhode Island was obliged to turn slowly ahead to keep from drifting upon us and to prevent the tow-lines from being caught in her wheels. At one time, when she drifted close alongside, our captain shouted through his trumpet that we were sinking, and asked the steamer to send us her boats. The Monitor steamed ahead again with renewed difficulties, and I was ordered to leave the wheel and was kept employed as messenger by the captain. On account of the wet condition of the coal the captain ordered the chief engineer to slow down and put all steam that could be spared upon the pumps. As there was danger of being towed under by our consort, the tow-lines were ordered to be cut, and James Fenwick, quarter-gunner, was swept from the deck and carried by a heavy sea leeward out of sight in attempting to obey the order. Our daring boatswain's mate, John Stocking, then succeeded in reaching the bows of the vessel, and he also was swept by a heavy sea far away into the darkness.

"About 10:30 o'clock our anchor was let go with all the cable, and struck bottom in about sixty fathoms of water. This brought us out of the trough of the sea, and we rode it more comfortably. The fires could no longer be kept up with the wet coal. The small pumps were choked up with water, or, as the engineer reported, were drowned, and the main pump had almost stopped working from lack of power. Upon learning this, the captain ordered me to see if there was any water in the ward-room. I went forward, and saw the water running in through the hawse-pipe, an 8-inch hole, in full force, as in dropping the anchor the cable had torn away the packing that had kept this place tight. I reported my observations, and at the same time the chief engineer reported that the water had reached the ash-pits and was gaining very rapidly. The captain ordered him to stop the main engine and turn all steam on the pumps, which were soon working again.

"The clouds now began to separate, a moon of about half size beamed out upon the sea, and the Rhode Island, now a mile away, became visible. Signals were being exchanged. The method of communication from the Monitor in daylight was by writing in chalk on a blackboard, which was held up to view, the Monitor having no mast on which to hoist the regular code used by the Rhode Island. As night approached, the captain of the Monitor wrote, while they could yet see, that if we were forced to abandon our ship we would burn a red light as a signal. About 10 o'clock the signal was given. I again went to the ward-room and found the water just above the soles of my shoes, which indicated that there must be more than a foot in the vessel. I reported this to the captain, and all hands were set to bailing — bailing out the ocean as it seemed — but the object was to employ the men, as there now seemed to be danger of excitement among them."

Many questions have been raised as to the nature of the leak or leaks which caused the rapid filling of the vessel and finally her foundering. Her captain, Commander Bankhead, was of the opinion that the shocks from the heavy tossing in the seas had caused her upper and lower hulls to separate. But the builder, Captain Ericsson, did not share at all in this belief. He ascribed the leaking to the bad preparation of the vessel for sea. Ericsson learned from one of the Monitor's engineers that oakum was packed under the base of the turret to make sure of a water-tight joint. Now, the base of the turret, being accurately faced underneath, rested on a flat ring of bronze let into the deck and faced very smooth in order to form a water-tight joint without the employment of any elastic packing. The plaited hemp rope, rough and uneven, which had been inserted at the turret's base, did not form a perfect joint at all; "the water came down under the turret like a waterfall," as the executive officer, Lieutenant Greene, had it in his report. Captain Ericsson scorned the statement or even suggestion that the upper and lower hulls separated, which, he said, could only be imagined by persons who possessed no knowledge of the method of the builders in joining the upper and lower hulls.

Captain Rodgers rode through a fearful gale off Chincoteague Shoals with the monitor Weehawken on January 22, 1863, standing upon the turret the whole time He reached the conclusion that "the monitor form had great sea-going qualities; if leaks were prevented no hurricane could injure such vessels." So there remains a good reason for believing that if the water had been kept out of Ericsson's famous craft she would have reached her place of destination in safety.

Butts continues as follows: "The weather was clear, but the sea did not cease rolling in the least, and the Rhode Island, with the two tow-lines wound up in her wheel, was tossing at the mercy of the sea and came drifting against us. The first boat was then lowered by the Rhode Island, under command of Acting Ensign Taylor. Although the sea smashed against the side of the Rhode Island and stove in the starboard gunwale the boat was kept afloat and managed to bring away sixteen men from the Monitor. At that time this vessel lay with her stern close under the Rhode Island's quarter.

"For the third time I went to examine the water in the ward-room, which I found to be more than two feet above the deck. The water had gained so as to choke up the main pump. There were three or four cabin-boys pale and prostrate

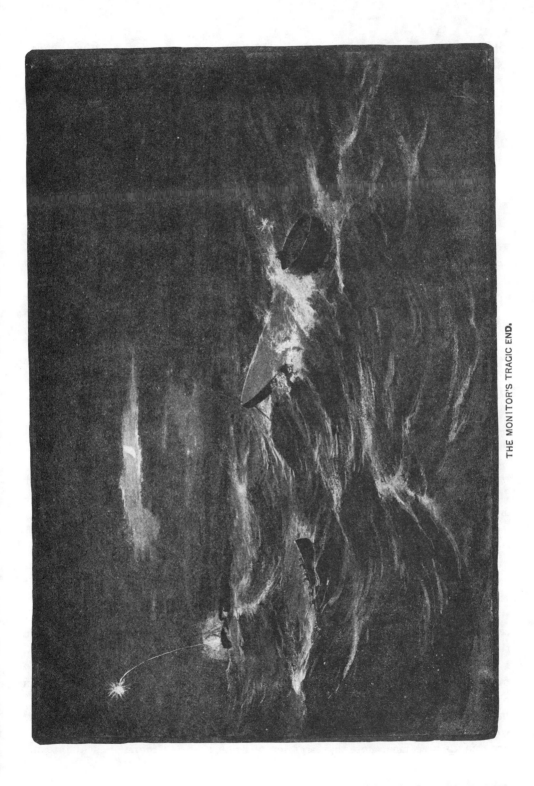

THE MONITOR'S TRAGIC END.

with seasickness, and the cabin-cook, an old African negro, under great excitement was scolding them most profanely.

JOHN JONES,
Ordinary Seaman, U. S. S. Rhode Island.
Born in Bridgeport, Conn.

"As I ascended the turret-ladder the sea broke over the ship and came pouring down the hatchway with so much force that it took me off my feet; and at the same time the steam broke from the boiler-room, as the water had reached the fires, and for an instant it seemed to me that we had gone down. Our fires were out, and I heard the water blowing out of the boilers. I reported these facts to the captain, and at the same time I saw a boat alongside. The captain again gave orders for the men to leave the ship, and fifteen of them crowded into the first boat. I was disgusted at witnessing the scramble, and resolved to stick to the ship as long as my officers. I saw three of these men swept from the deck and carried leeward into the swift current. Bailing was now resumed. I occupied the turret all alone, and passed buckets from the lower hatchway to the man on top of the turret, feeling that our noble ship was not yet lost. As I raised my last bucket to the upper hatchway I noticed that there was no one there to receive it. I scrambled up the ladder and found that we below had been deserted. I shouted to those on the berth-deck, 'Come up; the officers have left the ship, and a boat is alongside.'

"As I reached the top of the turret I saw a boat made fast to the weather quarter filled with men. Three others were standing on deck trying to get on board. One man was floating leeward, shouting in vain for help; another, who hurriedly passed me and jumped down from the turret, was swept off by a breaking wave and never rose. I was excited, feeling that it was the only chance to be saved. I made a loose line fast to one of the stanchions, and let myself down from the turret, the ladder having been washed away. The moment I struck the deck the sea broke over it and swept me as I had seen it sweep my shipmates. I grasped one of the smoke-stack braces and, hand-over-hand, ascended, to keep my head above water. It required all my strength to keep the sea from tearing me away. As it swept from the vessel I found myself dangling in the air nearly at the top of the smoke-stack. I let myself fall, and succeeded in reaching a life-line that encircled the deck by means of short stanchions, and to which the boat was attached. The sea again broke over us, lifting my feet upward as I still clung to the life-line. I thought I had nearly measured the depth of the ocean, when I felt the turn, and as my head rose above the water I was somewhat dazed from being so nearly drowned, and spouted up, it seemed, more than a gallon of water that had found its way into my lungs. I was then about twenty feet from the other men, whom I found to be the captain and one seaman; the third man had been washed overboard and was now struggling in the water. The men in the boat were pushing back on their oars to keep the boat from being washed on to the Monitor's deck, so that the boat had to be hauled in by the painter about ten or twelve feet. Lieutenant Greene and other officers in the boat were excitedly shouting, 'Is the captain on board?' and with severe struggles to have our voices heard above the roar of the wind and sea, we were shouting 'No,' and trying to haul in the boat, which we at last succeeded in doing. The captain, ever caring for his men, requested us to get in, but we both, in the same voice, told him to get in first. The moment he was over the bows of the boat Lieutenant Greene cried, 'Cut the painter! Cut the painter!' I thought 'Now or lost,' and in less time than I can explain it, exerting my strength beyond imagin- ation, I hauled in the boat, sprang, caught on the gunwale, was pulled into the boat with a boathook in the hands of one of the men, and took my seat with one of the oarsmen. As we were cut loose I saw several men standing on top of the turret, apparently afraid to venture down upon deck, and it may have been that they were deterred by seeing others washed overboard while I was getting into the boat.

"After a fearful and dangerous passage over the frantic seas, we reached the Rhode Island, which still had the tow-line caught in her wheel and had drifted about two miles to leeward. We came alongside under the lee bows, where the first boat, that had left the Monitor nearly an hour before, had just discharged its men; but we found that getting on board the Rhode Island was a harder task than getting from the Monitor. We were carried by the sea from stem to stern, for to have made fast would have been fatal. The boat was bounding against the ship's sides; sometimes it was below the wheel, and then, on the summit of a huge wave, far above the decks; then the two boats would crash together. Lines were thrown to us from the deck of the Rhode Island, which were of no assistance, for not one of us could climb a small rope; and besides, the men who threw them would immediately let go their holds, in their excitement, to throw another, which I found to be the case when I kept hauling in rope instead of climbing.

"It must be understood that two vessels lying side by side, when there is any motion to the sea, move alternately; or, in other words, one is constantly passing the other up or down. At one time, when our boat was near the bows of the steamer, we would rise upon the sea until we could touch her rail; then in an instant, by a very rapid descent, we could touch her keel. While we were thus rising and falling upon the sea I caught a rope, and, rising with the boat, managed to reach within a foot or two of the rail, when a man, if there had been one, could easily have hauled me on board. But they had all followed after the boat, which at that instant was washed astern, and I hung dangling in the air over the bow of the Rhode Island, with Ensign Norman Atwater hanging to the cat-head, three or four feet from me, like myself, with both hands clinching a rope and shouting for some- one to save him. Our hands gave us great pain and all the time grew weaker, until

I saw his strength give way. He slipped a foot, caught again, and with his last prayer, 'O, God!' I saw him fall and sink to rise no more. I still clung to the rope with aching hands, calling in vain for help. But I could not be heard, for the wind shrieked far above my voice. My heart here, for the only time in my life, gave up hope. While I was in this state, within a few seconds of giving up, the sea rolled forward, bringing with it the boat, and when I would have fallen into the sea it was there. I can only recollect hearing an old sailor say, as I fell into the bottom of the boat, 'Where in hell did he come from?'

"When I became aware of what was going on no one had succeeded in getting out of the boat, which then lay just forward of the wheel-house. Our captain ordered them to throw bow-lines, which was immediately done. The second one I caught, and, placing myself within the loop, was hauled on board. I assisted in helping the others out of the boat, when it again went back to the Monitor. It did not reach it, however, and after drifting about on the ocean for several days it was picked up by a passing vessel and carried to Philadelphia.

"It was 12:30 on the morning of December 31, 1862, when I stood on the fore-castle of the Rhode Island, watching the red and white lights that hung from the pennant-staff above the turret. Now and then they could be seen as we would per-haps both rise on the sea together, until at last, just as the moon had passed below the horizon, they were lost, and the Monitor, whose history is familiar to us all, was seen no more.

"The Rhode Island cruised about the scene of disaster the remainder of the night and the next forenoon in hope of finding the boat that had been lost; then she returned direct to Fort Monroe, where we arrived the next day."

Three boats were employed by the Rhode Island in the attempt to get the men off the doomed Monitor, a launch, a whaleboat and the first cutter. It was the latter boat which saved Butts and Captain Bankhead. Ensign Brown of the Rhode Island commanded her. Twice the brave cutter crew had accomplished their extremely toilsome and perilous trip to the Monitor and back. They started a third time, as there were still four officers and twelve men on board the helpless and water-logged ironclad. But when the brave men thought they had reached the spot where a few minutes ago still shone the red light from above the turret nothing was to be seen but the huge waves which threatened to swamp and swallow them. The famous Monitor had found her last berth at the bottom, ten miles east of Cape Hatteras.

The Rhode Island very likely considered the cutter and her crew lost, for when day broke the lookouts could find no trace of her. But Fate, the skill of Ensign Brown and the endurance of the cutter kept the boat afloat until picked up.

The members of this brave crew, Luke M. Griswold, seaman; Lewis A. Horton, seaman; John Jones, landsman; Hugh Logan, seaman; George Moore, seaman; Charles H. Smith, cockswain, and Maurice Wagg, cockswain, were awarded the Medal of Honor.

AT STONO RIVER

IN JANUARY, 1863, the gunboats McDonough and Isaac Smith were stationed in Stono Inlet, below Charleston, S. C., on patrol duty.

The Isaac Smith was a 450-ton steamer, armed with one 30-pounder Parrott and eight 8 inch Columbiads. On the 30th of January, 1863, she was ordered to reconnoiter in the Stono River, beyond Legareville. Arriving in this locality late in the afternoon, the vessel was suddenly and unexpectedly attacked by several batteries of siege and field guns hidden in the woods bordering the river banks. The Isaac Smith had just anchored opposite Grimball's plantation, when the rebels opened fire. Although she had a lookout in the masthead, nothing had been discovered in the presence of these hidden batteries. Lieutenant Conover slipped his cable and engaged the enemy at once. As the Federal vessel's battery was inadequate to silence the hostile batteries, she tried to escape down the river, being exposed to the guns of two batteries for the distance of a mile and a half. When abreast of one of the batteries, some 200 yards off, a shot disabled her engine, and the vessel grounded. Eight men had been killed and seventeen wounded, some of them mortally. Among the killed was Acting Second Assistant Engineer Turner, and the wounded included the commander, Lieutenant Conover, Paymaster Hills and Third Assistant Engineer Barry.

The gunboat McDonough hastened to her relief as soon as the cannonade was heard, but she arrived too late. When the Isaac Smith came in sight, the white flag was seen just being hoisted. Three heavy field batteries were firing upon the McDonough, and she had to retire.

So the Isaac Smith fell into the enemy's hand, and all her survivors became prisoners of war.

Richard Stout, landsman, one of the unfortunate vessel's crew, received the Medal of Honor for his bravery and devotion in this action. His right arm was torn off by a rebel shot, but heedless of the pain and the orders to retire below, he managed with the assistance of a comrade to stop the rapid discharge of blood from his wound, and with the crippled arm stayed at his post and fought until the Smith surrendered.

HAULED THE FIRES AND SAVED THE SHIP

THE strengthening of the blockade of Southern ports compelled the Confederates to seek out new channels through which to obtain necessary supplies from abroad. The most important of these channels was the Mexican country, from where the contraband found its way to the Confederate country east of the Mississippi and the Red River. The Red River joins the Mississippi between Vicksburg and Port Hudson, which two places had been strongly fortified by the rebels. Admiral Farragut recognized the imperativeness of preventing Confederates obtaining ammunition from abroad through the Red River just after his victory at New Orleans. But the inability of obtaining the necessary support by an army force held back the execution of his plan until spring, 1863. Having, after many vain endeavors, secured the promise of assistance by a land-force under General Banks, the admiral proceeded to action towards the middle of March. On the 12th of this month Farragut and his squadron arrived at Baton Rouge, and on the 14th he anchored not far above Profit Island, seven miles below Port Hudson. Below this port seven fortified works stretched along the eastern bank, the northernmost fort being nearly abreast the town.

Farragut had with him seven ships from his own fleet, besides the Essex and the Sachem and a flotilla of mortar schooners, under protection of the two last named vessels. The works counted an armament of nineteen heavy cannon and some thirty-five field pieces.

For the passing up stream Farragut employed here for the first time his own plan of coupling vessels in pairs. The small ones were to make fast alongside the stronger ones on the off side, so as to guarantee some motive-power for the latter in case these should be disabled by the enemy's fire. The order in which they were to pass was: Hartford and Albatross, Richmond and Genesee, Monongahela and Kineo, and last in the line the old Mississippi. She was a side-wheeler, and it seemed best, on account of her paddle-boxes, to leave her single.

At 10 o'clock in the evening the squadron got under way. It was about 11 o'clock, and the Hartford, leading, had already passed some of the lower batteries, when the enemy fired rockets and opened upon the ships.

On account of the damp, heavy air the smoke from the cannonade rolled low upon the water, and the darkness increasing the difficulty, the ships could not see where they were going. The Hartford, although under a heavy fire and having once slightly grounded with her bow, passed the forts and the bend all right. But the Richmond, the second in the line, received, when almost past the batteries, a 6-inch shot through her steam-pipe, tearing away her safety valves. Thus disabled, she was compelled to drop down the river out of the fire.

As soon as the shot tore away the steam-pipe, and the engine-room and fire-hold began to fill with steam, Joseph E. Vantine, fireman, took off his woolen shirt, tore it into four parts and ran up on deck and soaked them with water. Then after giving Mathew McClelland, John Rush and John Hickman each a piece of the shirt, Vantine and these three plucky men covered their faces with the soaked woolen and made their way again to the hold. There in the face of the scalding steam they laboriously hauled the fires and thus saved the ship, the combined effects of fire and steam compelling them to relieve one another at intervals until the work was accomplished. Their heroism was rewarded by the gratitude of the whole crew and the award of the Medal of Honor.

The Monongahela, next in line, ran aground directly in front of the principal battery, lying there for half an hour as a motionless target for the enemy, losing six killed and twenty-one wounded, among the latter her captain, McKinstry. Her final escape was due to the splendid exertions of her engine's crew. Chief Engineer Kutz risked the doubling of the steam pressure in the boilers, and with the additional power thus created managed to back the ship off. But by the extraordinary effort the forward crank pin became heated, and the engine, after the ship was free, had to stop. With the assistance of her consort, the Kineo, the Monongahela made her way back down the river into safety.

The Mississippi ran aground just below the inner corner of the bend. The enemy raked her with shot and shell for thirty-five minutes, and after every effort was made to release her without success, in which Andrew Brinn, seaman, Peter Howard, boatswain's mate, and P. H. Vaughn, sergeant of marines, not only worked heroically to get her off, but also exposed themselves to the raking fire of the enemy, Captain Melanchthon Smith considered further sacrifice useless and proceeded to abandon the ship, setting her on fire. Sixty-four of her crew were afterwards reported killed or missing, 233 saving themselves in the boats.

Harris Webster, then assistant engineer of the Genesee, and consequently an eye-witness of the occurrence, gives the following stirring narrative:

"As the smoke slowly drifted to leeward we caught sight of the old frigate Mississippi, hard and fast aground, apparently abandoned and on fire.

"When we first discovered her, the fire was already crawling up the rigging. From every hatch the flames were surging heavenward, and it seemed but a question of minutes when the good old ship must blow up.

"Every mast, spar and rope was outlined against the dark background of forest and sky, and it was a sad and at the same time a beautiful spectacle.

"While all hands were speculating on the causes of the disaster, the stanch old craft, which had braved the gales of every clime, slowly floated free from the bank, and, turned by an eddy in the current, swept out into the river and headed for the fleet as though under her helmsman's control. This was at about 3 o'clock in the morning.

"As the burning ship neared those at anchor in her path, her guns, heated by the flames, opened fire, one after another, in orderly sequence, and as their breechings had been burned away the recoil carried them amidships, where, crashing through the weakened deck, they fell into the fiery depths, showers of sparks and fresh flames following the plunge.

"Fortunately for us, her guns had been trained upon the bluffs, so her shots flew wide of the fleet and spent themselves in the forest below the batteries of Port Hudson.

"Majestically, as though inspired with victory, the ship, which by this time was a mass of fire from stem to stern, from truck to water-line, floated past the fleet, down past Profit Island, into the darkness of the night.

"Suddenly, as if by magic, her masts shot into the air all ablaze. A tremendous tongue of flame pierced the sky for an instant, and amid the muffled thunder of her exploded magazine the Mississippi disappeared in the stream whose name she had borne so bravely and so long."

The Hartford and her consort, the Albatross, were the only ships, therefore, which succeeded in the task set them by Farragut, and it is safe to say that they were successful only because under his immediate supervision.

THE ATTACK ON VICKSBURG

THE attack on Vicksburg on the 22d of May, 1862, by the Union forces, by the navy from the front and the army under Grant from the rear, had not been successful. The 42,000 Confederate troops under Pemberton kept their ramparts.

On the 27th of May a request from the army reached Admiral Porter to send some gunboats down the river to clear out a battery of two guns which was said to hamper the extension of General Sherman's right flank. The Cincinnati, thirteen guns, under command of Lieutenant George N. Bache, was detailed for the work. She started the next morning down the river to seek out the small battery mentioned in General Sherman's request and destroy it. The Confederates had on a bluff a strong battery

THOMAS E. CORCORAN,
Landsman, U. S. S. Cincinnati. Born at Dublin, Ireland, 1839.

consisting of eleven heavy guns commanding this whole stretch of the river down to the "small battery." The commander of this work, Colonel Higgins, formerly a

THEY SWAM TO AND FROM SHORE, SAVING THEIR COMRADES.

lieutenant in the U. S. Navy, had lowered these guns a short time before this from their carriages, partly to avoid the fire from the ships, but partly also as a ruse to deceive the enemy. And the ruse succeeded completely and sealed the fate of the Cincinnati.

The army, when the guns were no longer to be seen, got the impression that they had been removed somewhere else and informed the navy accordingly. But Higgins, who had managed to get hold of the Federal signal-code, and had therefore learned in time of the preparation and destination of the Cincinnati, remounted these guns unnoticed during the night and blended them with brushes so that they could not be seen in the daylight.

The Cincinnati, on getting within range of the "small battery," had just fired her first broadside at it when the heavy battery on the bluff opened on her stern. The very first shot struck the Cincinnati's magazine and then crashed through her bottom. Another shot disabled the steering-gear, shot after shot, each following the other in rapid succession, raking the doomed ship, which could not elevate her guns sufficiently to return the fire. Lieutenant Bache tried the only thing he could under the circumstances. Under all the steam that could be had he put in along the shore and headed up the river looking for a convenient place to beach the vessel. Against the heavy current the headway was very slow, about three miles an hour, but Bache succeeded in running her into the bank in such a position that a plank could be thrown ashore as a means of saving the crew. A hawser was made fast to a tree, but before the men could start to get out the hawser gave way and the ship slipped back into deeper water and sank in about three fathoms. Many of the crew, and Lieutenant Bache himself, were unable to swim. The fire of the hostile battery was withering. The small boats had all been destroyed by it. The order to abandon ship was given. Brave Lieutenant Bache took up the flag which had been shot down with the staff, and with the assistance of Frank Bois, quartermaster, nailed it to the stump under a most galling fire. The two men were in full view of the enemy in a most exposed part of the ship, a hail of shot and shell falling all around them, and when the flag was again floating to the breeze Bache left the ship with the assistance of two sailors. Fifteen of the crew were drowned and twenty-six were killed and wounded. Those who could swim sufficiently rendered material assistance in helping to save the lives of some of their less fortunate shipmates. Among these were Henry Dow, boatswain's mate; Thomas Jenkins and Martin McHugh, seamen, and Thomas E. Corcoran, landsman. Corcoran worked valiantly at the guns, but when the boat went down and most of the survivors saved themselves by swiming ashore, he, and his three above named companions devoted themselves to rescuing those who were unable to leave. While under a constant and accurate fire from the rebel batteries these four men, led by Corcoran, swam to and from the shore, helping those who could be landed in that way. Then they pulled half a dozen or more of the wounded to the upper deck, found a small boat, which had partly been stove in, fixed it up, and towed the wounded, with Lieutenant Bache, who could not swim, to the rest of the Union flotilla, where they were safe. Quartermaster Thomas W. Hamilton, although severely wounded at the wheel, refused to leave his post, and kept on working to get the disabled gear into shape again.

The lowering of the water in the river enabled the Federals a few days later to save the guns of the Cincinnati, which did good service to Sherman's right flank as a naval battery on shore under command of Lieutenant-Commander Selfridge.

REFUSED TO LEAVE HIS FALLEN COMRADES

AFTER the occupation of New Orleans the little steamer Commodore, of Commander H. H. Bell's squadron, was employed for patrol duty in the neighborhood of the coast, but on November 20, 1863, she was ordered to Ship Island Sound with a force of colored infantry on board who were to destroy some salt works on shore.

On the next day the steamer reached her destination and made fast to the river's bank, which rose some ten feet above her decks.

The army officer in charge landed his troops and, throwing out skirmishers in order to guard against a surprise, proceeded with the rest of his men to the destruction of the property.

Not far from the bank stood a lone, apparently deserted building, and an officer and twenty men advanced towards it with the intention of setting fire to the house. When close under its walls a volley suddenly rang out from within the building and two Federals fell, one dead and the other helplessly wounded. The rest of the party fled precipitately on board the steamer and the skirmishers were hastily recalled from the flanks and proceeded towards the vessel under cover of the high bank.

Paymaster's Steward Richard E. Seward of the Commodore, a seasoned salt, became indignant on account of leaving those two men behind. Before anybody could prevent it he rushed up the bank towards the house, heedless of the galling rifle fire poured at him from the rebels within. Quickly he placed the groaning, wounded man upon his shoulders and hurried back with him, reaching the vessel in safety.

The body of the dead soldier still lay close to the house, and in spite of the remonstrances of his comrades Seward made a second trip toward it to secure the body before it should fall into the hands of the enemy. With a dash he reached the side of his fallen comrade, bullets whistling close to his ears, and some passing through his clothing. Throwing the prostrate form over his shoulder he started back for the ship, which he again reached in safety. His action was so deliberate in the face of the heavy fire from the enemy that the officers and men were nonplused at his behavior, and when he had both the wounded and the dead man in a place of safety his comrades sent up a cheer that made him forget momentarily the danger he had just passed through.

SURPRISED BY THE REBELS

JAMES MILLER,
Quartermaster U. S. S. Marblehead.
Born in Denmark, September, 1836.

A REMARKABLE engagement took place on the Stono River, near Charleston, S. C., on Christmas day, 1863. While the army, under General Gillmore, was completing its preparations for the attack on the forts, Admiral Dahlgren had a small squadron, comprising the Pawnee, Commander Balch, the Marblehead, Lieutenant-Commander Meade, and the mortar schooner Williams, stationed in the Stono River on picket duty. These three vessels kept in communication with an outpost of about 100 men of General Schimmelpfennig's Brigade, thus forming, so to speak, the left wing of the besieging land forces.

On the 24th of December, the Marblehead was at anchor at her station, a little above Legareville. She was a small side-wheel gunboat of about 600 tons displacement, mounting one 11-inch Dahlgren pivot-gun, one 20-pounder Parrott rifle on the top-gallant forecastle and four brass 20-pounder Dahlgrens in broadside. Although her full complement was 100 men, at the time she had only seventy.

Theenemys underthat active artillery general, Del Kemper, knew of her presence, but as she was out of reach of the next fort and the wooded banks of the river lacked fortifications, the situation appeared secure, the ship being anchored in midstream.

However, the resourcefulness and ingenuity of General Del Kemper had apparently been underrated. Employing large gangs of slaves, he built silently behind the dense fringe of the woods on the bank a powerful fort and mounted it with 8-inch guns. On the 25th of December, shortly after midnight, all was ready for the surprise. The slaves now cleared the fringe of bushes and woods away down to tbe bank, and towards 5 o'clock in the morning the rebels opened fire.

Imagine the effect of these first shots upon the astonished crew of the Federal gunboat. Captain Meade was asleep in his cabin; the watch had just started to wash down the deck, according to the usual daily routine, and had pivoted the big 11-inch gun amidship for more room, when the first shells came tearing through the air and the rigging. The officer of the deck, Ensign Harriman, rushed into the captain's cabin, shouting: "Captain, quick; the enemys!" Captain Meade jumped hurriedly out of bed. He thought it meant a boarding party. Buckling his sword and revolver over his night-shirt, he rushed on deck. This was rather light clothing for a fresh December morning, but the action of theenemysfurnished all the necessary temperature. While he rushed on the bridge, started the engines and had the cable slipped and sails unfurled, Boatswain's Mate William Farley, captain of the big pivot-gun, hastened to get it ready, and soon the little Marblehead thundered back her reply. No sooner was the gun in working order than a shot crashed into the first sponger, tearing the unfortunate man into shreds. The second sponger paled for a moment before picking up the sponge, and was ready to bolt, but Farley whipped out his revolver instantly and pointing it at the man said: "Pick up that sponge, and damned quick." A second command was not necessary, for the determined action of Farley sobered him into complete coolness, and he bent to his work with energy. Farley now set to work with a will, firing the heavy gun with great rapidity, setting a noble example of true devotion to duty to all the men.

During this time great damage had been done on board. The upper parts of the hull were all torn up and three men killed and six wounded. The enemy evidently

THE CREW RUSHED TO THE GUN.

had the range. Commander Meade moved his ship closer in and as near as possible under the bank of the river. This manœuvre improved matters considerably. The enemy had lost the range and fired mostly too high. But the gunners on the Marblehead did not. Grape, shell and shrapnel went flying like hail into the hostile works.

When the ship was being manœuvred, Quartermaster James Miller was in the starboard fore-chains casting the lead and calling out his soundings, and when the starboard guns were brought into action he was exposed to a terrific fire from the enemy. Commander Meade, full of consideration for the intrepid man, called him in, but, pretending not to hear the order, he continued to cast his lead and call out his soundings as if the ship were just going into her berth in a peaceful harbor instead of being in the midst of a fury of shot and shell. The fire becoming too hot, the commander peremptorily ordered him in, whereupon he took his place at the wheel cool and stolid, handling it most admirably under trying circumstances.

In the after part of the ship the guns were doing their duty in the hands of a noble crew that stood manfully by them amid the heavy cannonade from shore. Shots plunged into her sides, sweeping her decks, covering them with blood, one ricochetting from the rail, tearing off a gun-captain's head, which flew against Charles Moore, landsman, knocking him down. A splinter also struck him, tearing off half his scalp, but notwithstanding his injuries, he jumped up and attempted to resume his duties. He fell over and was carried below, where his wounds were dressed, and as soon as the surgeon's back was turned he again slipped up on deck and took his position; but he could not long hold out in his wounded condition, and when he fell in a faint from loss of blood he was again carried below and restrained from further attempts to reach his gun.

During the hottest of the fight Robert Blake, contraband, could be seen in the apparent confusion running back and forth from the powder magazine to the various guns with ammunition. He was a fugitive slave who had enlisted in the Federal Navy, and, though listed under the term "contraband," he acted as Commander Meade's servant, and when that officer started on his night-robe rush on the battle morning "Blackie" Blake rushed faithfully after him, waving the commander's clothes and imploring him to put them on. Being of no service to his master on the bridge he went below and voluntarily acted as powder-boy, in which capacity he worked with such fearlessness and good nature that the gun-crews, no matter how hard pressed the strain of the fight, were compelled to laugh and cheer whenever he appeared with his cartridge, a broad grin on his black face and uttering some happy remark, as he passed the ammunition to the cannoneers with the grace of a man offering a Christmas cake. The alacrity and extraordinary courage displayed by him merited the admiration of all and secured for him the Medal of Honor.

After two hours of hot fighting, the Confederates abandoned the fort and fled, leaving two 8-inch guns behind them, together with equipments and entrenching tools. The Pawnee, which came up the Kiowah River and enfiladed the enemy, completed the victory. Commander Meade went on shore with his gig and planted a Federal flag from the Marblehead upon the captured works, and three days after he landed with 100 men and brought away the two abandoned guns.

A CONSPICUOUS MARK FOR BULLETS

O N the 29th of February, 1864, a fleet of five gunboats and a monitor—the Osage—started up
the Red River, the Black River, and the Washita
River successively, to break up some enemys camps
that were being fortified around and near Harrisonburgh, La. Arriving at the town of Trinity, the
junction of the Little and the Washita Rivers, on
March 1st, they were attacked by a battery of
12-pounder guns and some sharpshooters under
General Polignac. The ships immediately opened
fire and in a few minutes drove the enemys from the
town.

HUGH MOLLOY,
Ordinary Seaman, U. S. S. Fort Hindman.
Born in Comerford, Ireland, Sept. 25, 1841.

The next morning the fleet started up the Washita in the following order: The Osage, Fort Hindman,
Conestaga, Cricket, Washita, and Lexington, and
when within about two miles of Harrisonburgh Polignac again attacked it, directing his 12-pounder rifled guns chiefly at the Fort Hindman, she being the flagship.
Shot and shell crashed into her with frightful rapidity, and whenever they struck
her squarely the missiles plowed their way through the thin iron plating and two-
inch planking, which proved to be of little or no protection to the men. Twenty-
seven missiles from the 12-pounders had pierced the Hindman within half an hour,
one of them, a solid shot, disabling her starboard engine. With only the port engine
working, she was unable to maintain proper steerage-way, and consequently swung
to and fro in the current, giving the enemys a good opportunity to fire into her. A
well-directed shell pierced the bow casement a little to the right of No. 1 gun, killing
the first sponger. As he fell he dropped his sponge out of the port into the forecastle. Hugh Molloy, seaman, who was one of the gun's crew, saw the sponge fall
out on the port and instantly jumped through the opening down on the forecastle,
where, exposed to the severe fire of the enemy, he recovered the sponge and sponged
and loaded the gun from the outside, while shell and musket-bullets from the sharpshooters struck the ship all around him. To all on board it looked as if Molloy
would never regain the protection of the ship, but, strange as it may seem, he was
not struck by the enemys, and as soon as he had the gun loaded he crawled through
the port into the ship again.

Just after Molloy had regained the deck a enemy shell burst at the muzzle of one
of the Hindman's guns, setting fire to the tarred yarn of a cartridge, which had been
put into the gun preparatory to being rammed home. James K. L. Duncan, seaman,
saw the tie burning and before the fire could eat its way through the covering of the

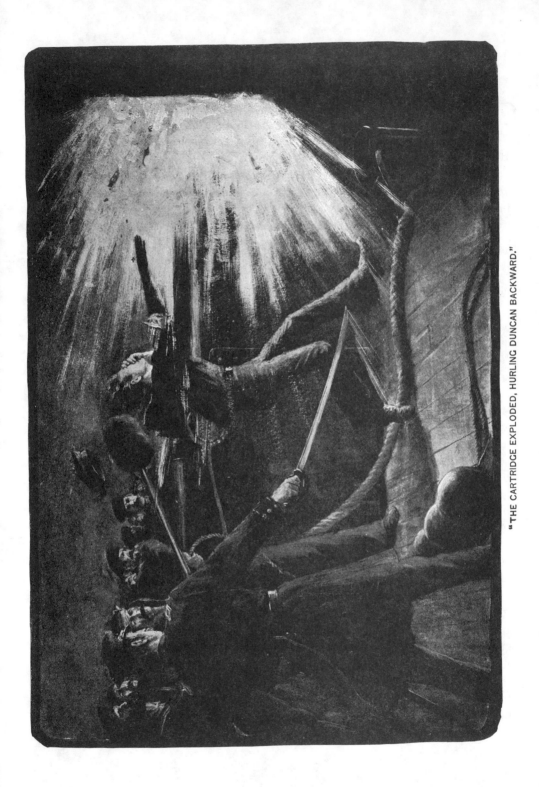

cartridge and explode in the gun he sprang forward, seized the cartridge with his bare hand, by its blazing end, and exerting all his strength he wrenched it from the muzzle. Rushing to the port with the burning cartridge, he threw it out. Hardly had he loosed his hold when the cartridge, still in the air, exploded, hurling Duncan backward across the deck. His shipmates, however, caught him and prevented him from falling, but when he regained consciousness it seemed to him as if all the sounds of conflict had ceased. In describing the situation Duncan says:

"When I regained consciousness after the explosion of the cartridge I looked about me in surprise, for there were the men rushing about, loading and firing the guns, but all was inaudible to me. Upon recovering from my amazement I became convinced that I was deaf. This belief was confirmed by the surgeon, who pronounced the drum of my right ear completely destroyed, and the other temporarily impaired."

All parts of the ship were receiving their quota of the enemy's missiles. The whistling balls and screeching shells, the cries of the wounded, the groans of the dying, could be heard on every side, while the good ship reeled and shook from stem to stern as she was being pounded here and there by the deadly hail. One by one the ship's crew fell, inch by inch the white planks were becoming crimsoned with the life-blood of the Hindman's willing crew, but no one flinched.

Even when wounded, the men would stick to their guns until they were overcome.

William P. Johnson, landsman, was wounded early in the engagement, the bones of his left hand having been shattered by the fragments of a shell. He deliberately bound up the quivering, bleeding flesh as best he could with a strip of cloth torn from the sleeve of his shirt. A few moments later a shot crashed through the sides of the ship, disabling a sponger of one of the guns. Johnson immediately took the wounded man's place and sponged and loaded the gun throughout the entire engagement.

At the close of the action Seamen Molloy and Duncan and Landsman Johnson were highly commended by their officers and later received the Medal of Honor.

LOSS OF THE SIGNAL AND COVINGTON

ON May 5, 1864, the two light gunboats Signal, Acting Lieutenant Morgan, and Covington, Lieutenant Lord, were lost to the Federal Navy in a spirited skirmish with crushing superior forces of the enemy below Alexandria, on the Red River, this engagement closing the ill-starred Red River Expedition.

While Admiral Porter was piloting his gunboats through the famous dam constructed by Lieutenant-Colonel Bailey, corps of engineers, the Signal and Covington convoyed the little transport Warner, which was filled with soldiers, down the river. The Warner was ahead, the gunboats covering the rear. At Dunn's Bayou the Warner was suddenly greeted by an intense artillery and infantry fire from the banks. In a few minutes the Warner was disabled by the shooting away of the rudder. She drifted helplessly down the current and grounded soon at the next bend, blocking the channel for the two gunboats. The fire grew in intensity; the gunboats answering with all the energy that was in them, for three full hours. Then the Warner showed the white flag. Lord, from the Covington, while keeping up his fire, sent a boat to burn her. But upon Colonel Bailey's statement that there were fully 125 killed and wounded on board, this plan was abandoned to save some lives.

At this time the Signal also became disabled, whereupon the Covington tried to save her by towing her up stream, under the heavy fire of the enemy. Shot and shell crashed into the sides of both ships, doing fearful destruction, one of the shots carrying away the Covington's rudder and another cutting the tow-line, thus causing the Signal to again rely upon her own resources, drifting helplessly down stream until she could let go her anchor. All this time the crews exerted every energy to handle the guns and the disabled ships. Perry Wilkes, pilot on the Signal, was in a most trying position at the wheel. While the shot and shell were falling thickly around him, crashing into the pilot-house, he remained at the wheel until one of the bursting shells disabled it, he escaping death with but slight injuries.

In an attempt to get out of range of the field batteries and sharpshooters the officers of the Signal ordered the cable slipped. While the officers and men who were disengaging the end of the cable were under slight shelter, John Hyland, seaman, who was assisting them, was exposed to the full view and range of several hundred sharpshooters. When he first took this exposed position a sharpshooter's bullet struck him, but as the work of slipping the cable would not take long he proposed to stick to his duty. It was but a few moments, however, before a second bullet struck him, this time completely disabling him.

All this time the two boats, in spite of their desperate situation, fired bravely back at the enemy. Finally the ammunition gave out. Lord managed to escape with the remnant of his crew, after setting his vessel on fire. When they assembled under the shelter of the woods lining the bank it was found there were thirty-two left out of a total of seventy-six. The Signal had so many wounded on board that her commander, Lieutenant Morgan, surrendered, instead of destroying her.

Besides Wilkes and Hyland, the following received the Medal of Honor for working the guns and performing their duties after they had been wounded early in the action: Charles Austin, quarter-gunner; George Butts, gunner's mate: Michael McCormick, boatswain's mate, and Timothy O'Donoghue.

AN ATTEMPT TO DESTROY THE ALBEMARLE

WHEN in April, 1863, Captain Melanchthon Smith was assigned to the command of a squadron of gunboats in Albemarle Sound, one of the objects pointed out to him was, if possible, to destroy the ram Albemarle. This Confederate iron-clad, commanded by a former officer of the Old Navy, Lieutenant A. F. Warley, had made her name feared by destroying the Southfield and disabling the Miami, causing the death of her brave captain, Commander C. W. Flusser, on the 18th of April. On the 5th of May she came out again from Plymouth and attacked the whole squadron, and, after beeing rammed by the Sassacus, came near disabling and sinking this vessel. Although the gunboats fought bravely and well, the heavy battering which the ram withstood, apparently with little damage, created an uncomfortable feeling in the North about her strength and dangerousness, and it was highly desirable to put her out of the way.

From the crew of the Wyalusing, Lieutenant-Commander Queen, emanated a plan to destroy her with torpedoes. Five daring men of this ship were willing to risk their lives in the undertaking. After having secretly reconnoitered the river and its banks they started on the 20th of May. They were: Cockswain John W. Lloyd, leader; Firemen Alex. Crawford and John Laverty, and Coalheavers Charles Baldwin and Benjamin Lloyd. They had all their apparatus, two torpedoes containing 100 pounds of powder each, and a contrivance of guiding lines, in a dinghy. When near Plymouth and the Albemarle's berth, which place they reached after darkness hat set in, they carried the torpedoes on stretchers to a hidden place by the north bank. Laverty had been left in charge of the boat secreted in the bushes, while Cockswain Lloyd and Coalheaver Baldwin swam across the river to the Plymouth side with lines which they fastened securely not far from the town. They were then, by means of another guide-rope, to haul the torpedoes across the bow of the ram, where Baldwin intended to fasten them, and Crawford was to explode them from the opposite bank. All went well until Baldwin neared the

THE SASSACUS RAMMING THE ALBEMARLE.

Albemarle. A sentry saw him, an alarm was given and the men had to cut the lines and swim for their lives. Cockswain Lloyd and Laverty reached their ship in their boat, the others being picked up later in a swamp, nearly exhausted and starved.

Although these five men were not successful, their behavior and bravery won for them their Medals of Honor.

THE SINKING OF THE ALABAMA

ALL the history of privateering shows nothing comparable to the record of the Confederate steamer Alabama. Under her unscrupulous but clever and resourceful commander, Raphael Semmes, she captured, ransomed or destroyed within the short space of twenty-two months a Federal war vessel and some sixty ships of the then prosperous merchant navy of the United States, until fate finally overtook her on the 19th of June, 1864. The damage this vessel inflicted upon the merchant marine of this Republic can hardly be computed. In money value it was estimated at over $10,000,000.

Semmes was a commander in the Old Navy and had some thirty years' service behind him when he resigned his commission with the Federal Government in February, 1861. It was he who suggested first a system of privateer service to the Confederate Government. His suggestions found ready ears, and in April he was commissioned as captain of the Sumter, a slow 500-ton steamer, the first enemy privateer. Although this vessel had been declared unfit for sea by a board of naval men at New Orleans, Semmes ran her through the blockade of the Mississippi, in June, 1861, barely escaping capture by the Brooklyn. After taking fifteen prizes, most of which he destroyed, he escaped over the Atlantic, running into Gibraltar. Lacking funds and being closely watched by two Federal gunboats, he was forced to sell the Sumter and proceeded to Southampton. In order to facilitate the bargaining of a Confederate naval commission in England for some fast ships he determined to get out of the way and sailed to Nassau, Jamaica. This was in June, 1862.

In August news reached him that the "No. 290," afterwards known as the Alabama, was awaiting him in England as her captain. Semmes joined his vessel at Terceira, a small island belonging to the Azores group. Here English supply vessels had waited together with the "290" for Semmes's arrival. He took the "290" and the supply-boats out to sea, to avoid complications of international character, fitted his vessel out and put her in commission as the Confederate cruiser Alabama. She was well designed and built for her purpose, barkentine rigged, of beautiful symmetry in her lines, and capable of making easily eleven miles under steam, and fifteen miles under steam and sail combined. Her tonnage was a little over a thousand, her draught fifteen feet.

On Sunday, the 24th of August, 1864, Semmes set out, under sail, on his destructive career. He chose the North Atlantic, which was then being traversed by the home-bound North American whalers, for his first hunting grounds. Within a hundred days he captured and destroyed sixteen prizes, most of them valuable ships with full cargo. From the beginning he made it his custom to send the captured crews and occasional passengers on shore at the first opportunity.

In November the Álabama, to replenish her bunkers, shaped her course for one of the islands in the Carribean Sea, where a coal steamer had arranged to lie in wait for her about that time. As Semmes was thoroughly informed of the goings-on in the Northern States by the mail almost regularly obtained through the prizes, he learned of the prospective expedition of General Banks to attack Galveston and invade Texas. He decided at once to try a coup against this expedition. Regulating his course so as to arrive at just the time when the transport must anchor off the harbor, he made for it. But when nearing the harbor he sighted five men-of-war—Commander Bell's squadron—instead of harmless transports. The squadron had seen the smoke of the Alabama and sent out the gunboat Hatteras to identify the stranger· It was towards evening, January 11, 1863, when the Hatteras approached to hailing distance. According to some reports the Alabama had hoisted the British war-flag; according to others it was too dark to distinguish colors. On Captain Blake's hail: "What ship is that?" the Alabama replied: "Her British Majesty's ship Vixen." Captain Blake then said he would send a boat, to which the dark unknown agreeably assented. The boat had hardly left the Hatteras when the latter received a full broadside from the Alabama, and a voice—that of Semmes—cried: "This is the Confederate cruiser Alabama!"

The Hatteras, a former river passenger steamer, was in no sense a match for her reckless adversary, besides being entirely unprepared for an attack. The first broadside had shattered her overhead walking beam and otherwise disabled the engine, the second settled her fate. Pierced in several places on the water-line, the unfortunate vessel was sinking rapidly. The bold privateer condescended to save the crew. The latter were afterwards landed on the beach near Kingston and left there, utterly destitute, to themselves.

The small boat from the Hatteras escaped the destructive fire and carried the news of her fate to Galveston.

The Alabama then pursued her evil course in the South Atlantic, creating havoc among the homeward-bound East Indiamen. Towards the end of April she crossed the Atlantic, to the Cape of Good Hope, where she nearly ran foul of the United States steamer Vanderbilt, which vessel would have put a swift end to her career— but Semmes was not to be caught as yet. In Simon's Town the Vanderbilt had the privateer cornered. "I am not going to fire a shot at the fellow: I shall run him down and sink him," Commander Baldwin is said to have remarked to the British admiral in command of the station. But there arose one evening a heavy southeast gale with thick weather, and when the Federal vessel went scouting for the Alabama in the morning she was gone. Semmes took the usual route for sailing vessels bound east in the South Indian Ocean, going south until he could use the "brave west winds" for a speedy trip to the other side. Near the Australian coast he changed to a northerly course and appeared next in the Sunda Islands, where his usual good luck brought several American East Indiamen across his way. These were promptly destroyed. There was a Federal cruiser in those waters, which tried to find him, but in vain. Semmes coaled in Singapore and then crossed over to East Africa, passed through the Strait of Mozambique to Cape Town, and after a short stay made again for the coast of Brazil, his track being lighted all along by burning vessels of the American merchant marine. Semmes hardly exaggerated when in a speech to his crew he said that the Alabama had by this time "swept the American commerce from the seas." But even this indefatigable rover had now reached a state where rest and repair could no longer be put off. So he started for Europe. On the 11th of June, 1864, the Alabama entered Cherbourg, on the northeast coast of France. Semmes wanted to dock her, but permission had to be asked from the French Emperor, who happened to be then absent from Paris. Ere his decision could be obtained, precious days were lost in delay—and this was fatal. The end was at hand.

The United States ship Kearsarge, Captain John A. Winslow, was lying at anchor in the Schelde, Holland, when, on June 12th, her commander received information of the Alabama's arrival at Cherbourg. Without losing an hour, Winslow put to sea and announced the stirring news to his crew. On the 14th the Kearsarge reached the breakwater before Cherbourg, and there the jubilant crew beheld, lying within the breakwater, the coveted prey, the white Confederate war-flag, with the stars and bars in the upper corner, waving defiantly from the privateer's peak.

The Alabama was a splendid sea-goer and a swift vessel, but not built for a fight. Her battery mounted six 32-pounders broadside and two pivot-guns, a Blakely 100-pounder rifle forward and an 8-inch solid-shot abaft the mainmast. The Kearsarge had two 11-inch smooth pivots, one 30-pounder rifle and four light 32-pounders, the 11-inchers rendering her armament considerably the heavier. The Kearsarge's company was 163, the Alabama's 150. In all other respects the ships were almost entirely equal, although the engines of the latter were then badly in need of overhauling. But Captain Winslow had covered the side of his ship abreast of the engines with the sheet anchor chain as an improvised armor, and subsequent events showed that by this he had rendered his vessel decidedly superior to her antagonist. Oftentimes the question has been asked in wonderment how such a resourceful and intelligent commander as Semmes could have neglected similar precaution.

Winslow, in order to keep strictly to the neutrality limitations, decided not to enter the port, but to watch the entrance rigidly.

As the case was, this proved hardly necessary, for Semmes had decided to fight and sent to the Federal vessel a challenge, stating "that he would come out as soon as necessary arrangements could be completed."

Winslow was willing; he got the Kearsarge ready for action and waited.

A beautiful day broke on Sunday, June 19, 1864; the sun rose brightly, and the sea was breathing in a light heave. The Kearsarge's people meant to observe the Sabbath according to the usual routine. The crew had been inspected in their Sunday's dress at quarters and were assembling aft for divine service. Captain Winslow had opened his book and looked a last time over the sermon he was going to read. The ship's bell tolling solemnly announced the commencement of the service.

It was about 10:15. The quartermaster on duty lowered his long ship's glass upon an outcoming steamer. Suddenly the deep silence was broken by his stirring shout: "There comes the Alabama!" And instead of a prayer the stern command rang out from the captain's lips: "Beat to quarters!"

On she came, the dreaded "No. 290," the beautiful, merciless Alabama, an object of admiration even to her foe.

In order to draw the Confederate vessel as far away as possible from the line of the maritime league, three miles off shore, Winslow put his ship about and headed seaward. The French frigate Couronne, which escorted the privateer out of the harbor, turned back at the end of the maritime league.

About six miles out the Kearsarge wheeled and went for the enemy's starboard bows, presenting her starboard battery. When nearly a mile distant, the Alabama opened with her starboard broadside. Winslow answered immediately in the same manner. It was 11 o'clock. Winslow ordered full speed and tried to close in on the Alabama or rake her, but Semmes would not have it and sheered off. So the two ships began soon to circle around each other, each one presenting the starboard side, both about 800 yards apart. Seven such circles, under a port helm, were completed, ranging, under the influence of a strong westerly current, in a line in the direction west by north. The distance of the ships was decreasing gradually down to 400 yards. While Semmes, standing on the horseblock abreast the mizzenmast, observed that his shells and even his solid shot did not do much damage to his opponent, it was evident from the first on board the Kearsarge that their own fire surpassed that of the enemy's by far in both accuracy and effect. The zeal and confident enthusiasm of the Kearsarge's crew can better be imagined than described. Shell after shell the men saw crashing into the enemy's hull, while her angry shots struck against the heavy chain armor at the sides and dropped harmlessly into the sea. Cheer followed cheer, and hats flew into the air on the Kearsarge after each broadside.

All at once, the seventh circle just being completed, there was an ominous stir on board the Alabama; steam was seen rolling out from every opening, it seemed, and the fore-sails and fore-trysails were set. The Alabama drew off with a starboard helm and tried to make for the harbor. One more broadside from the Kearsarge, while the ship hastened to cut off the evidently mortally wounded privateer from the shore.

A few more well-directed shots and the enemy colors were seen to sink slowly down on board the Alabama. A white flag appeared over her railing. Winslow ceased firing.

A volley of cheers from the Kearsarge; the battle was over. A boat from the privateer came alongside to ask for assistance, as the ship was rapidly sinking. Captain Winslow lowered the only two boats which were not disabled, and sent them to save the enemy crew. Just then the British yacht Deerhound, belonging to a Mr. Lancaster, passed by, and the Federal captain, realizing that his means of aid were inadequate, and wishing that as many lives as possible be saved, asked how to assist in getting off the men from the doomed ship.

The Alabama's stern was then just awash. Presently her bow rose high above the waters—the ship stood straight up on her end for a second, and then disappeared beneath the sea, which took thus to her bosom the most famous privateer that ever sailed the ocean.

The duel had lasted a little over an hour and a quarter. The losses were: Kearsarge—Three wounded, one of them, Seaman William Gouin, mortally. Alabama—nine killed, ten drowned, twenty-one wounded. All of the wounded were safely taken out before the ship foundered. Among the drowned was Assistant Surgeon D. H. Llewellyn, an Englishman. Captain Semmes, thirteen of his officers and twenty-six men were saved by the Deerhound and landed in Southampton. The rest were saved by the Kearsarge and two French pilot-boats.

The far superior marksmanship of the Kearsarge's gunners is evident from a comparison of the number of shots fired and their effect. The Alabama fired 370 times; the Kearsarge was struck twenty-six times without receiving serious injury. The Kearsarge fired only 173 times, and according to an estimate of some of her own officers the Alabama is said to have been struck between fifty and sixty times.

Special praise was due to the engineers of the Kearsarge and their men in the engine-room. The ship went into action under artificial draft, with safety-valves lashed down, and thus she fought under her utmost speed throughout the engagement. It was her speed which enabled Captain Winslow to force the circling tactics upon Semmes and to prevent him thus from escaping eventually within the neutral zone. Seventeen of the Kearsarge's crew earned the Medal of Honor for marked coolness and good conduct during this duel. They were: William Bond, Thomas Perry, boatswain's mates; John A. Bickford, Robert Strahan, captains of top; Michael Aheam, paymaster's steward; James Haley, captain of forecastle; Mark G. Ham, carpenter's mate; George H. Harrison, James H. Lee, Joachim Pease (colored), George E. Reed, Charles Moore, seamen; John Hayes, Charles A. Reed, cockswains; William B. Poole, James Saunders, William Smith, quartermasters.

HEROIC DEEDS AT MOBILE BAY

ADMIRAL FARRAGUT's victory at Mobile Bay is the most glorious achievement ever recorded of an American naval commander; as to daring and skill of execution it has no peer in the naval history of the world.

It seems that people both in this country and abroad have never fully realized and appreciated the grandeur of the battle of Mobile Bay and the greatness of the venerable old sea-hero who planned and won it. Nelson's wondrous skill, judgment and daring at Copenhagen have rendered the latter name the brightest gem in this standard naval idol's wreath of glory. Nelson was at that time in the prime of his manhood. The difficulties, risks and dangers at Mobile Bay outclassed

CORNELIUS CRONIN,
Chief Quartermaster, U. S. S. Richmond.

those at Copenhagen, and he who overcame them was in his 64th year at the time.

As in several other instances in this war, there would never have occurred the occasion for such a momentous feat if it had not been for the negligence, incompetency, helplessness, or whatever one might call it, of the powers governing the Northern forces by land and sea.

Farragut anticipated the importance which Mobile gained during the last half of the war at the very beginning; right after his victory before New Orleans he urged the occupation of the bay by a combined naval and army force, which at that time could have been effected with comparative ease. Again and again he pointed out the latent danger to the Navy Department, but nothing was done. Finally, towards the end of 1863, after the enemys had fortified the entrance to the bay so as to impress upon them the term "impregnable," and after they had built and launched the ram Tennessee there, the strongest ironclad the Confederates ever possessed, the Federal authorities deemed it timely to determine upon the reduction of the place, in consequence whereof they ordered Farragut to do it. After many vain endeavors the admiral succeeded in obtaining the addition of four monitors, the Tecumseh, Manhattan, Winnebago and Chickasaw, to his wooden fleet. On the morning of August 5, 1864, subsequent to a reconnaissance undertaken with the little steamer Cowslip, Farragut went ahead.

Chief Quartermaster Cornelius Cronin, of the ship which earned the largest number of medals in this fray, tells the story of the fight:

"In September, 1863, I joined the U. S. S. Richmond, Commanded by Captain Thornton A. Jenkins. We left New York in the month of October, making a quick passage to New Orleans, thence taking up blockading duty off Mobile, which, as the

RESCUING THE CREW OF THE MONITOR TECUMSEH.

sequel has proven, was to last for the following ten months. In January, 1864, Admiral Farragut arrived with the flagship, the Hartford, and at once began to make preparations for the capture of Forts Morgan, Gaines and Powell, as soon as the army was ready to co-operate. Several weary months passed, until late the following July, when, the army having perfected all its arrangements, and assurance being given and received that conjointly in action an attack was to be made upon the enemy defenses,the ships were sent to Pensacola, there to dismantle send spare spars on shore and otherwise to prepare for the conflict which was now to follow.

"In preparing for battle, Captain Jenkins ordered his ship stripped to her lower masts, splinter-nettings to be placed fore and aft the bulwarks, engines and boilers protected by anchor-chains outside, sand-bags inside in the bows. Having thus made every preparation that human skill and ingenuity could suggest for the safety of his ship and men, the Richmond left Pensacola on the morning of August 4, arriving off Mobile the same afternoon, with the monitor Tecumseh. During the evening a large percentage of our crew, being perhaps cognizant of the ordeal through which

BARTHOLOMEW DIGGINS,
Captain of the Watch, U. S. S. Hartford.

they must pass very soon, preferred to remain up until a late hour singing, talking and exchanging notes concerning the battle of the morrow.

"At 12, midnight, a heavy rain-squall set in, lasting until 4 o'clock A. M., when all hands were called to 'weigh anchor and prepare for action.' The Port Royal, selected as our consort, now came on our port side and made securely fast to us. Each other ship had a gunboat also as consort on her port side to pull her through in the event of becoming disabled during the action.

"Having now formed in line of battle, the Brooklyn leading, the Hartford next, our ship, the Richmond, being third in line, we steamed slowly until the vessels got in close order. The four monitors, Tecumseh, Manhattan, Winnebago and Chickasaw, were stationed between the wooden ships and Fort Morgan. While moving up towards the forts the enemy gunboats together with the ram Tennessee were closely observed by us, also on the move. The weather now cleared up, with a light breeze from the westward, and, lessening our distance from the fort, we opened fire with our bow and forecastle guns, these being all we could bring to bear, while in the interim, and until we could use our broadside guns, the enemy were replying and kept us under a scorching, raking fire. As soon, however, as we got abreast of Fort Morgan we let them have it with our broadside batteries, which had the quite observable effect of silencing their fire to a very great extent. At this juncture the monitor Tecumseh was blown up by a

enemy torpedo, which sank her in three minutes. A boat was dispatched at once from the Metacomet, which succeeded in rescuing her pilot and nine of her crew.

"Torpedoes being now reported ahead, the Brooklyn, still leading, stopped and backed down on the Hartford, delaying the advance of the entire fleet, which caused their bows to fall off, heading toward the fort and nearly athwart the channel. Fortunately at this juncture the flagship took the lead, passing the Brooklyn, and we, by backing our consort and going ahead with our own ship, soon brought our

broadside guns to bear, when we poured into the fort and water batteries, at a range of 150 to 300 yards, a continuous and rapid fire of shell and grape, driving the enemy from their guns. By this time the action became general. The fleet presented a fine appearance in double column, with the American flag flying at their peaks and each masthead. I noticed that the topmasts of the Hartford and Brooklyn were plainly visible above the smoke of the battle, while nothing could be seen above the smoke to indicate the presence of the Richmond, her topmasts being down. She was completely hidden, otherwise we should have fared badly while under the raking fire of the fort. Probably no ship ever engaged in battle better prepared for her own safety and that of her crew than the Richmond, owing to the wise precautions of Captain Jenkins.

"Having now passed the forts, we opened fire on the Tennessee with solid shot, without making any impression on her. This was done, however, to keep their men from loading their guns. Shortly after this, and while continuing up the bay, dealing out death and destruction to the enemy gunboats, a heavy rain-squall came up, accompanied by fog, which lasted some little time. When the weather cleared we found that the Selma, one of the enemy gunboats, had been captured by the Metacomet, and the Gaines, another of the enemy, having sprung a leak through the heavy fire of the fleet, had been burned by her own men. The others were steaming in under the shelter of the fort. Being up the bay now a distance of four miles from Fort Morgan, we came to anchor and piped to breakfast.

"Only a few minutes afterwards, and before we had time to swallow a mouthful of breakfast, it was reported that the Tennessee was moving up towards the fleet, then at anchor.

"All mess-gear was hurried aside, and, slipping our cables, we at once beat to quarters. Signal was made to the monitors to destroy the ram, and to the Monongahela, Lackawanna and Ossipee to ram her and open fire on her with solid shot.

As soon as she arrived within 400 yards of the fleet the Monongahela went at her, striking her squarely amidships. All the other ships and monitors now dashed at her. After manœuvring for a little more than an hour, during which time her smokestack and stearing-gear were shot away, causing her to drift aimlessly and uncontrolled with her head down stream, she, together with her master-spirit, Admiral Buchanan, who was himself disabled by a broken leg, was placed hors de combat, and, showing a white flag at 10 A. M., surrendered to the fleet. A boat crew was now sent on board of her and the Union flag hoisted. She was afterwards taken in tow by the Chickasaw and anchored near the flagship. Admiral Farragut subsequently pronounced this 'the fiercest naval combat on record.'

"The Hartford lost more men in this battle, in proportion to the complement of both ships, than the Victory lost at the battle of Trafalgar. The loss of the Hartford was twenty-five killed and twenty-eight wounded.

"This finished the fight for the day, the battle commencing at 7:07 A. M. and ending at 10 A. M., a little less than three hours."

In the afternoon of the same day the Chickasaw stood down the bay to Fort Powell, engaging it for an hour at a distance of 300 yards. That night the fort was evacuated and blown up. The following day the same monitor went down and shelled Fort Gaines, which also surrendered next day. Fort Morgan now being the only fort holding out, we transported a portion of the army, under General Granger, by siege train from Dauphin Island to Mobile Point, and made preparations for bombarding the fort, having landed a number of heavy guns with crews from the several ships. On the 22d of August, at daylight, the bombardment opened from the batteries, ships and monitors, continuing for twenty-four hours, when the white flag was hoisted at 7 A. M. on the morning of the 23d and the fort surrendered. The city, however, was not captured until the succeeding spring, its reduction being virtually of no special importance until later on, as the fleet now held the bay.

JOHN LAWSON,
Landsman U. S. S. Hartford.

Thus after the short period of eighteen days from the firing of the first gun all the defenses, stationary and afloat, guarding the approaches of the city of Mobile had been reduced, and the Union flag was again triumphantly waving over the places where for a time the emblem of the Rebellion had held its vaunting sway.

Among the more conspicuous individual acts of exceptional bravery performed on this occasion for which the Medal of Honor was awarded are the following:

Landsman Wilson Brown of the Hartford was stationed at the shell-whip on the berth-deck when a man was killed on the ladder above him and thrown with such violence against Brown as to knock him into the hold, where he lay for a short time unconscious; but on recovering he immediately returned to his station. Besides him, only one of the original six on duty there, John H. Lawson, had escaped death.

Cockswain Thomas Fitzpatrick's gun was almost disabled by the bursting of a shell which killed seven men and wounded several others, among the latter himself.

He had the dead and wounded removed, replaced the breeching, truck and tackles, got a crew, and in a little while was firing the gun as usual.

Martin Freeman, pilot of the Hartford, found himself handicapped by the dense smoke of the action. in guiding the ship, whereupon he immediately went aloft and stood in the maintop, directly above Admiral Farragut's position in the futtock-shrouds, where he was exposed to the heavy fire of the enemy's sharpshooters. In this position he could look over the smoke, which thus enabled him to pilot his ship with accuracy.

John McFarland, captain of the forecastle, was at the wheel on the Hartford during the whole battle, and when in the heat of the action the Lackawanna ran into her the excitement was intense. For a moment McFarland was in great danger of being crushed

WILLIAM D. NEWLAND,
Ordinary Seaman, U. S. S. Oneida.

to death, but fearlessly he stood at his post unmindful of his peril and attended strictly to his duties, thus keeping the ship under control and preventing further damage and perhaps loss of life.

Bartholomew Diggins, seaman, received his medal not only for his brave behavior in this engagement alone; he had distinguished himself on several previous occasions. He was on board of Admiral Farragut's flagship from beginning to end, and had been four times wounded. At Vicksburg he volunteered to serve as powderman in the first attack, although being on the sick list on account of a shattered arm. On the 5th of July, 1864, he went with Flag-Lieutenant Watson inside the bay and boarded and destroyed the blockade-runner Ivanhoe, which was then discharging cargo at Fort Morgan. The feat was accomplished under a most terrible fire from the batteries. Besides, he had been a participant in a night expedition under the same officer below Natchez, on March 17, 1863, when they cut all wires and communications between Vicksburg and Port Hudson.

George Taylor, armorer, was wounded early in the fight, but after having his wounds dressed returned to his duties. While in the performance of these a shell exploded over the shell-room of the Lackawanna, setting fire to the room. Taylor ran into it, and there, among the high explosives stored within it, he put out the fire with his hands and saved the ship from possible destruction.

John Preston, landsman, although severely wounded, remained at his gun until obliged to go to the surgeon, to whom he reported himself as slightly hurt. He assisted in taking care of the wounded below and wanted to return to his station, but

on examining him it was found that he was wounded severely in both eyes, whereupon the surgeon refused to grant him permission to return to duty.

A boat's crew from the Metacomet, in charge of Acting Ensign H. C. Neilds, went to the rescue of the officers and men of the monitor Tecumseh, when this vessel was blown up by a torpedo. This boat's crew, under their gallant leader, went within 200 yards of one of the forts under a fire which Admiral Farragut expressed as "one of the most galling" he ever saw, and succeeded in rescuing from death ten of the crew of the Tecumseh. Their conduct elicited the admiration of both friend and foe and won for them the Medal of Honor.

WILLIAM R. PELHAM,
Landsman, U.S.S. Hardford.
Born in New York City,
December 24, 1845.

The members of the brave crew were: Henry Baker, quarter-gunner; John Harris, captain of forecastle; Patrick Murphy, boatswain's mate; John Noble, landsman; John Donnelly and Henry Johnson, seamen.

Others in this memorable action whose heroic conduct was rewarded with the Medal of Honor were:

FROM THE RICHMOND:

THOMAS ATKINSON, Yeoman.
JOHN BRAZELL, Quartermaster.
ROBERT BROWN, Captain of Top.
WILLIAM M. CARR, Master-at-Arms.
JAMES B. CHANDLER, Cockswain.
THOMAS CRIPPS, Quartermaster.
CORNELIUS CRONIN, Chief Quartermaster.
CHARLES DEAKIN, Boatswain's Mate.
WILLIAM DENSMORE, Chief Boatswain's Mate.
WILLIAM DOOLIN, Coalheaver.
ADAM DUNCAN, Boatswain's Mate.
HUGH HAMILTON, Cockswain.
THOMAS HAYES, Cockswain.
JOHN H. JAMES, Captain of Top.
WILLIAM JONES, Captain of Top.
JAMES MARTIN, Sergeant of Marines.
JAMES McINTOSH, Captain of Top.
ANDREW MILLER, Sergeant of Marines.
JAMES H. MORGAN, Captain of Top.
GEORGE PARKS, Captain of Forecastle.
HENDRICK SHARP, Seaman.
LEBBEUS SIMKINS, Cockswain.
JAMES SMITH, Captain of Forecastle.
JOHN SMITH, Cockswain.
WALTER B. SMITH, Seaman.
DAVID SPROWLE, Orderly Sergeant.
ALEXANDER H. TRUETT, Cockswain.
WILLIAM WELLS, Quartermaster.

FROM THE BROOKLYN:

WILLIAM BLAGEEN, Ship's Cook.
JOHN BROWN, Captain of Forecastle.
WILLIAM H. BROWN, Landsman.
JOHN COOPER, Cockswain.
SAMUEL W. DAVIS, Seaman.
J. HENRY DENIG, Sergeant of Marines.
RICHARD DENNIS, Boatswain's Mate.
WILLIAM HALSTEAD, Cockswain.
MICHAEL HUDSON, Sergeant of Marines.
JOSEPH IRLAM, Seaman.
JOHN IRVING, Cockswain.
NICHOLAS IRWIN, Seaman.
BARNETT KENNA, Quartermaster.
JAMES MACHON, Boy.
ALEXANDER MACK, Captain of Top.
WILLIAM MADDEN, Coalheaver.
JAMES MIFFLIN, Landsman.
WILLIAM NICHOLS, Quartermaster.
MILES M. OVIATT, Corporal of Marines.
EDWARD PRICE, Cockswain.
WILLIAM SMITH, Corporal of Marines.
JAMES E. STERLING, Coalheaver.
SAMUEL TODD, Quartermaster.

FROM THE GALENA:

THOMAS JORDAN, Quartermaster.
EDWARD B. YOUNG, Cockswain.
EDWARD MARTIN, Quartermaster.

FROM THE LACKAWANNA:
  JOHN M. BURNS, Seaman.
  MICHAEL CASSIDY, Landsman.
  LOUIS G. CHAPUT, Landsman.
  PATRICK DOUGHERTY, Landsman.
  JOHN EDWARDS, Captain of Top.
  SAMUEL W. KINNAIRD, Landsman.
  ADAM McCULLOCK, Seaman.
  WILLIAM PHINNEY, Boatswain's Mate.
  JOHN SMITH, Captain of Forecastle.
  JAMES WARD, Quarter-Gunner.
  DANIEL WHITFIELD, Quartermaster.

FROM THE CHICKASAW:
  ANDREW JONES, Chief Boatswain's Mate.
  JAMES SEANOR, Master-at-Arms.

FROM THE METACOMET:
  THOMAS TAYLOR, Cockswain.

FROM THE HARTFORD:
  RICHARD DUNPHY, Coalheaver.
  JAMES R. GARRISON, Coalheaver.
  JOHN LAWSON, Landsman.
  CHARLES MELVILLE, Seaman.
  THOMAS O'CONNELL, Coalheaver.
  WILLIAM R. PELHAM, Landsman.
  WILLIAM A. STANLEY, Seaman.

FROM THE ONEIDA:
  WILLIAM GARDNER, Seaman.
  JOHN E. JONES, Quartermaster.
  THOMAS KENDRICK, Coalheaver.
  DAVID NAYLOR, Landsman.
  WILLIAM NEWLAND, Seaman.
  JAMES S. ROANTREE, Sergeant of Marines.
  JAMES SHERIDAN, Quartermaster.
  CHARLES W. WORAM, Seaman.

Farragut's fleet counted eighteen ships, and the Federal army force under General Granger, operating against Fort Morgan, consisted of 5,500 men.

The losses in the Federal fleet were 146 killed and drowned, 169 wounded and 4 captured; in the army detachment, 7 wounded. The Confederate fleet lost 12 killed and 20 wounded.

THE BLOWING UP OF THE ALBEMARLE

WHILE Admiral Porter was fitting out the fleet which he was to command in the intended attack on Fort Fisher, in the fall of 1864, the Navy Department was greatly troubled on account of the Confederate ram Albemarle, repairing at Plymouth, N. C. The reputation the Albemarle had gained in the North by her sinking the Southfield, disabling the Miami, and her engagement with the "double-ender" squadron of Captain Melanchthon Smith in Albemarle Sound in the spring of this same year was the cause of this alarm.

Admiral Porter, having been apprised of the views of the department in this matter, suggested a plan to blow up the Albemarle with steam launches and by means of torpedoes. The plan was approved, and details arranged forthwith for the building of three steam launches by Naval Engineers Wood and Lay.

Lieutenant Porter selected the young and indefatigable lieutenant, William D. Cushing, for the command of this hazardous expedition. Cushing accepted rejoicingly and started with the three launches about the middle of October from the New York Navy Yard for Hampton Roads. Here he arrived on the 24th with one badly battered launch, he and his crew utterly exhausted from the week's trip. Of the other two launches one had foundered shortly after leaving New York, the second had run ashore on account of a terrible storm in Chesapeake Bay and surrendered to the Confederates. Cushing alone, storm or no storm, pushed ahead and reached

CUSHINGS DARING AND SUCCESSFUL EXPLOIT.

his destination. Admiral Porter ordered Cushing and his men to rest while the battered launch was put in ship-shape again.

Just at that time the admiral was ordered to prefer charges against Cushing for the supposed violation of some neutral rights while in command of a vessel in those waters. Cushing felt greatly distressed about this, but the admiral, after a brief investigation, reported the young officer free from blame, and at the designated time Cushing in his launch started on his forlorn-hope trip, jubilant at having so fortunately slipped off from a possible court-martial. Passing through the Dismal Swamp Canal, Cushing, on the 27th of October, reached the Roanoke River in Albemarle Sound and reported to Captain Macomb on the flagship Shamrock.

This same night he completed his arrangements and started up the Roanoke to find his prey. It was said that at the wreck of the Southfield, about seven miles up the river, there was a guard of armed schooners. So Cushing took with him against them, in case they should discover him, an armed boat from the Shamrock. His own launch carried fourteen volunteers, officers and enlisted men from Captain Macomb's squadron, mainly from Picket Boat No. 1. The Albemarle was made fast to a wharf about a mile above where the Southfield lay. The attackers knew that her crew and all the pickets along the banks of the Roanoke kept a sharp lookout against any surprises, for an unsuccessful torpedo attack had been made against the ram on the 25th of May by a party of daring men from the Wyalusing.

The weapon Cushing intended to use was a boom torpedo. When the daring party shoved off from the Shamrock all of its members, as well as those in the squadron, were convinced that the Albemarle would be destroyed or they would never return, such was the reputation of young Cushing's unbending and daring nature.

The launch with the Shamrock's boat in tow proceeded up the river unmolested, although the infantry pickets had a good many fires burning on the banks, which were hardly 200 yards apart. The Southfield was reached and passed without disturbing or rousing anybody.

Soon a dark object loomed up before the anxious men, who kept the keenest lookout. It was the Albemarle. Cushing cast loose the armed boat, with instructions to take care of armed hostile boats which might come to interfere with him, and then made for the ram. When within twenty yards of her he saw that she was protected against a torpedo attack by a boom of logs extending about ten yards from her sides. At this moment a sentry from aboard hailed them.

Cushing, standing ready at the torpedo boom, which was raised, started his launch at full speed against the obstruction. The sentry gave the alarm. In a moment the deck of the ram swarmed with men. Two field guns discharged a hail of grape at the launch. Sharpshooters also opened a hot fire. But while the launch was pushing the logs under and Cushing was lowering the torpedo boom he had his 12-pound howitzer in the bow of his boat fire canister into the human mass on board, which drove them for a moment under shelter. In the next second there was a tremendous roar and a huge column of water rose high in the air, lifting the Albemarle several feet. Then the ram settled in a sinking condition, from a fatal wound in her side. The little launch was swamped by the falling water, and drifted down the river with some of her crew still on board, while others, among them Cushing, were struggling in the water trying to get beyond the light of the fires and the reach of the rifles of the infantrymen.

The following men composed Cushing's crew: From picket boat No. 1—William Howarth, master's mate; William Stotesbury, assistant engineer; Bernard Harley, Edward Houghton, William Smith, seamen; R. H. King, Lorenzo Demming, Henry Wilkes, landsmen; Samuel Higgins, fireman; R. Hamilton, coalheaver. From Otsego—T. S. Gay, master's mate; C. S. Steever, assistant engineer; F. Swan, assistant paymaster. From Commondore Hull—John Woodman, master's mate.

Cushing, Woodman and Higgins left the launch or were hurled out of her. The rest of the crew, with the exception of Houghton, some of them wounded, were picked up by the Confederates and taken prisoners. Cushing himself had been wounded in the wrist. He drifted in the icy cold water until his strength nearly gave out. He came across Master's Mate Woodman, who was crying for help. Cushing's strength, although he tried to save the man, failed and Woodman was drowned. Fireman Higgins, too, lost his life in the river. The bodies were afterwards found washed on shore and buried by the Confederates.

Finally managing to reach the bank, Cushing hid in a dense swamp half a mile below Plymouth. Here, his hiding place being near a path leading alongside the river bank, he heard two passing rebel officers talking about the sinking of the Albemarle, whose smokestack only remained visible above the water. The exhausted man remained in the swamp until the next evening, when, having obtained some reliable information from a faithful old negro, he continued his toilsome wandering down the river, coming finally to a small creek, where he found an empty boat. He took it, and, pulling, exhausted as he was, all the following day until late into the night, he came towards 11 o'clock within hailing distance of a Federal gunboat. It proved to be the Valley City. He called for help and collapsed unconscious in the boat. It took some time ere the suspicious crew of the Valley City overcame their distrust and sent a boat down to the drifting object. Somebody recognized Cushing, and he was saved. Soon afterwards he was able to make his way back to his admiral's flagship at Hampton Roads and report the details of his daring achievement. Cushing and Houghton were the only two members of the expedition who escaped imprisonment or death.

Cushing was promoted a lieutenant-commander for this most heroic act. From his men the following, all of picket boat No. 1, were awarded the Medal of Honor: Bernard Harley, William Smith, Edward J. Houghton, seamen; Lorenzo Demming, Henry Wilkes, R. H. King, landsmen; R. Hamilton, coalheaver. These formed the original crew which had brought the boat from New York.

THE CAPTURE OF PLYMOUTH

IMMEDIATELY after the destruction of the Confederate ram Albemarle in Roanoke River on the 27th of October, 1864, Captain Macomb set out to capture the town of Plymouth, situated a little over eight miles up the river, and on the 29th, toward noon, he was under way with the whole squadron. Near the wreck of the Southfield, the Federal gunboat sunk by the Albemarle, the expedition found the river so thoroughly obstructed by sunken schooners that farther advance was rendered impossible.

Macomb turned back, sending one of his ships on a reconnoissance of the Middle River entrance. This latter being reported free, he started again with his squadron. During the passage of the Middle River, Macomb dropped shells into Plymouth across the intervening woods. Towards night he reached the river proper, where he lay till daybreak.

MICHAEL C. HORGAN.
Landsman, U. S. S. Tacony.

The next morning the engagement began. The Whitehead was lashed to the off-side of the Tacony, the Bazley and Belle to the Shamrock and Otsego respectively, and the Commodore Hull led the line to the attack. A hot cannonade ensued, lasting about an hour. Then a lucky shot from the Shamrock exploded a magazine in the opposing fort, which caused the Confederates to abandon the works and withdraw.

Captain Macomb occupied Plymouth then without further resistance. His force had suffered a loss of six men killed and nine wounded. The Commodore Hull and Tacony had especially distinguished themselves by their clever manœuvring and firing. Six men earned the Medal of Honor. They were:

From the Tacony—James Tallantine, quarter-gunner; Michael C. Horgan, Henry Brutsche, Robert Graham, and Martin Howard, landsmen.

These men were sent out in a boat to land at the water-battery and spike a gun, while other guns were still firing, a task which they accomplished with much skill and daring, under a heavy fire from the enemy.

From the Commodore Hull—Patrick Colbert, cockswain. He was captain of the forward pivot-gun. Although painfully wounded by a shell, which killed a comrade at his side, he remained at his post until the close of the action, and appeared as cool during the engagement as if at target practice.

ADMIRAL PORTER AT FORT FISHER

DANIEL DICKINSON STEVENS,
Chief Quatermaster, U. S. S.
"Canonicus".
Born at La Grange, Tenn.

THE splendid energy of the Union Navy in blockading a sea-coast of nearly 3,500 miles had such effect that a year after the commencement of the war there were practically only two ports open along the whole hostile coast—Charleston, S.C., and Wilmington, N. C. They were the channels through which the Confederate States, by means of daring and fast blockade-runners, communicated with the outer world and obtained all the supplies and provisions they wanted in exchange for their cotton. It was impossible for the navy to close those two places at the time being with the sea-forces available and without the co-operation of the army; but the army had its hands full just then in other parts of the theatre of war.

After the Federal Navy finally succeeded in blockading Charleston closely, Wilmington became the base of operations and the headquarters of the Southern blockade-runners. There are two entrances from the sea to Cape Fear River, both passable for ships of light draught, the southern inlet protected by Fort Caswell, the northern by a number of earthworks which in time developed into the most powerful cluster of works afterwards known as Fort Fisher.

The blockade-running trade from Wilmington brought at the time enormous profits to those engaged in it. They were paid for their ventures in Confederate cotton at the rate of eight cents a pound, then worth one dollar in the North and eighty cents in England. The later blockade-runners, much perfected and built for the purpose in England, were long, narrow, shallow steel vessels with a speed of fifteen miles. They could cross the bar at any time of day or night.

The Federal gunboats constituting the blockading squadron were generally of too deep draught to follow them over the bar, and at night the war vessels had to be extremely careful in making signals or firing guns lest in the darkness they should hit each other. So it came about that even at the time when the Federal blockade was closer than any ever maintained on any coast before eight out of ten of the runners would succeed in breaking through. But at the rate of profit prevailing their owners were paid handsomely for their risks if only one out of three vessels escaped. There was a time when blockade-runners could even be insured in England against capture, and when in Wilmington people awaited the regular arrival of the runner as confidently as if she were a liner in time of peace.

Such was the state of affairs, when on the 22d of September, 1864, Rear-Admiral Porter was assigned to the command of the North Atlantic Squadron. The Navy Department had obtained assurances of aid by the army, and Admiral Porter went to City Point, Va., to confer with General Grant.

FOR THE THIRD TIME THE FLAG WAS REPLACED.

Admiral Porter's request was for about 8,000 troops and enough vessels to fire 150 guns in broadside. As most of the ships would be wooden vessels and Fort Fisher had seventy-five guns mounted behind heavy earthworks, the granting of this request still left the odds against the navy.

The fleet under Porter assembled at Hampton Roads by October 15, 1865, to the number of 121 vessels. It was divided into three divisions, each under command of a commodore, and by the end of October the navy was ready. On November 1st General Butler came on board Admiral Porter's flagship and unfolded to him a novel plan, that of bringing a boat containing 150 tons of powder as close as possible under the fort and blowing up the vessel; the tremendous shock, it was supposed, would level the fort or at least dismount the guns.

LOUIS C. SHEPHERD.
Seaman, U. S. S. Wabash.
Born Sept. 2, 1841, at Ashtabula, Ohio.

After thorough investigation by competent men the plan was viewed as perfectly feasible and as prospective of complete success, provided the whole cargo of 150 tons could be detonated simultaneously. This some army engineers said could be done easily enough, and Admiral Porter telegraphed the Navy Ordnance Department for the powder. In his haste, according to his own statement, he wrote two zeros too many in the telegram, and Captain Wise of the Ordnance Department shook his head in amazement when he received the request to furnish the squadron with 15,000 tons of powder. He telegraphed back: "Why do you not ask us to send you Niagara and Vesuvius down there; that would satisfy you." There was considerable merriment about this otherwise harmless mistake.

The steamer Louisiana, an old vessel, was selected to serve as the "powder-boat" and was taken down from Newberne to Hampton Roads, where she received her dangerous cargo, brought together from both army and navy magazines and stowed away on board in bags.

In Beaufort, N. C., the "powder-boat" was fitted out for her perilous trip, fuses being carefully laid to assure the simultaneous explosion, which was to be started by candles and some system of clock-work. The fleet had in the meanwhile left Hampton Roads and anchored off Fort Fisher, twenty-five miles from the shore, on the 16th of December, in twenty fathoms of water. The army transports and General Butler with his flagship were at anchor off Masonboro' Inlet, out of sight of the naval squadrons. The admiral intended to send the "powder-boat" in on the 18th and informed General Butler accordingly.

General Butler objected to the date as being premature, and nothing was done on the 18th, although the weather was comparatively calm, with only a light swell on

the sea. The next day a heavy gale set in from the southeast, and the way in which the large number of vessels rode out this hurricane, each with two anchors out, in twenty fathoms of water, and 120 fathoms of chain out on each anchor, was a glorious sight to see, and a feature which reflected the greatest credit on the seamanship of our navy.

The powder-boat started at last on the night of the 23d of December, and finally anchored as near the beach as possible. She was in command of Commander Rhind and the following officers and men, who volunteered for this dangerous mission: Lieutenant Preston, flag-lieutenant of the admiral, Second-Assistant Engineer Mullan, Master's Mate Boyden, Gunner's Mate Charles J. Bibber, Quarter-Gunner John Neil, Seamen James Roberts, William Garvin, Robert Montgomery, Charles Hawkins, Dennis Conlan and James Sullivan, Firemen William Hinnegan and Charles Rice. The men were all from Commander Rhind's vessel, the Agawam.

RICHARD BINDER,
Sergant of marines, U. S. S. Ticonderoga.
Born in Germany July 26, 1841.

Admiral Porter, who seems to have regarded the clock-work and candle arrangement with some skepticism, suggested that it would be wise to light some pine-knots in the cabin before leaving the boat, so as to make sure of the explosion anyway. His advice was followed. Commander Rhind and Lieutenant Preston lighted the candles and Engineer Mullan the pile of pine-knots in the cabin, after which the members of the crew made their escape hurriedly in small boats. The candles and the clock-work were to explode the ship in an hour and a half. After nearly two hours there was an explosion, but only the after-part of the powder boat went up. It is reasonable to believe that the clock-work "missed fire" and Porter's pine-knots did the work. Of course, they did not cause a simultaneous explosion, and consequently the enterprise failed. Although the shock of the explosion was considerable, not the least damage was done to the fort. The next day a boat with four deserters came on board the Malvern, and Admiral Porter asked one of them about it. "Oh, it was terrible, Admiral; we all woke up from it," said he.

On the morning of the 24th, Admiral Porter, according to agreement with Butler, proceeded with his fleet to the attack. Shortly before noon the bombardment began, the ironclads Canonicus, Ironsides, Monadnock and Mahopac leading. Then followed the Minnesota, Colorado and Montana; the Ticonderoga, Shenandoah, Tacony, Mackinac and Vanderbilt; the Osceola, Santiago de Cuba, Fort Jackson, Sassacus, Chippewa, Monticello, Rhode Island, Quaker City and Josco, in the order named. They all reached their prescribed position with splendid, seaman-like quickness and accuracy, and by noon the pandemonium of battle had broken loose with its utmost fury. The shot and shell crashed into the fort at the rate of 115 per

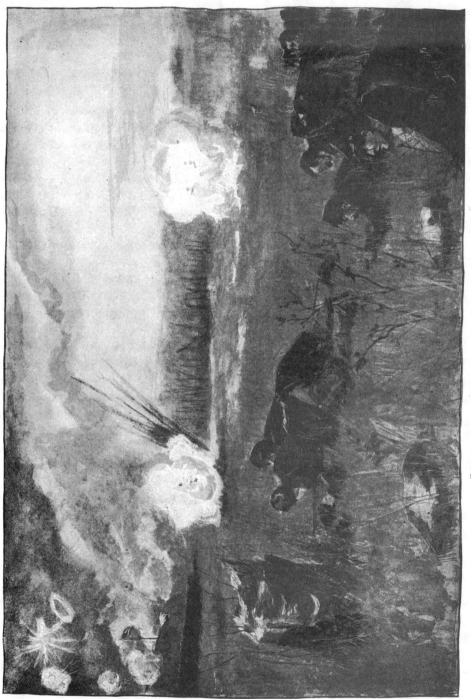

"WE CRAWLED THE ENTIRE DISTANCE TO OUR POSTS."

minute; it was impossible to stand such infernal fire. Two magazines blew up, the woodwork of the works was in flames, and an hour and a quarter after the first shot had been fired into it the fort was silenced. As this was all the navy could do, the admiral reduced the activity of his ships to moderate firing and waited for the army. At sunset General Butler arrived with a few transports.

The tremendous fire of the fleet had so quickly chased the gunners in the fort under shelter that not a single man on board had been injured by the enemy. But the 100-pounder Parrott guns proved treacherous weapons for those who worked them. On not less than five ships of the fleet there were casualties from the bursting of these guns. One burst on the Yantic, killing an officer and two men; one on the Juanita, killing two officers and wounding ten men; one on the Ticonderoga, killing ten men and wounding fifteen; one on the Mackinac, killing one officer and wounding five men; one on the Quaker City, injuring three men, making forty-nine casualties in the fleet caused by the inferiority of the material of its own guns. The men thereafter handled the 100-pounder Parrotts with suspicion and evil forebodings.

On the 25th the rest of the transports arrived. The squadron detached seventeen gunboats to protect the army forces and aid them in landing. The fleet formed in line of battle, and the attack was renewed. As the firing from the forts was slow, the ships confined themselves to the same practice, their purpose being to distract the enemy's attention from the army without wasting ammunition.

While the admiral was watching the soldiers reconnoitering and skirmishing near the forts, some men even reaching the parapets, the startling communication reached him that the army was re-embarking. In spite of this news, and although ammunition began to run short, the fleet kept up a moderate cannonade until sunset.

Next morning the admiral received the astonishing information that the generals found the assault impracticable, and General Butler stated in a letter that it was his intention to return with his command to Hampton Roads, which he did.

General Grant, at Admiral Porter's request "to send other troops and another general," ordered General A. H. Terry to take command of the army end of the expedition, and on the 12th of January the fleet and transports started again for Cape Fear.

Early the next morning, the 13th of January, 1865, the landing of the troops began; by 2 o'clock 8,000 men, with cannon and provisions, were on shore. One hundred and twenty boats had been employed in the landing, and seventeen gunboats, anchored inside the line of transports about a hundred yards from shore, swept the ground during the whole operation with a terrific fire way down to Cape Fear River, a distance of about 1,000 yards. This was to protect the landing forces from a sudden land attack by the Confederates.

The Confederate garrison had been increased to 2,500 men, and General Bragg had been put in command of the defenses, General Hoke having the immediate command of the troops.

While the Federal forces were being landed under the protection of the gunboats the rest of the fleet proceeded to the attack, in three columns, together with the four ironclads on an inner line. The Saugus, Ironsides, Canonicus, Monadnock and Mahopac, anchored within 800 yards from the fort to draw the fire from the batteries and unmask the guns for the fleet. The three lines took their respective positions handsomely, and the ships kept firing until some time after dark. Then the wooden ships were withdrawn.

As the admiral noticed that some of the heavy guns in the fort were still standing, and as he wished that there should be no guns to bear upon the assaulting forces, he renewed his attack on the 14th at noon, the small gunboats being particularly directed to go in and fire their heavy 11-inch guns at the pieces in the fort.

At a conference after this day's work between the admiral and General Terry the hour for the assault was set for 3 o'clock P. M. next day, and the fleet was to furnish 1,600 sailors and 400 marines to assault the fort from the sea-side.

Thus on the 15th the fleet renewed its attack, beginning the bombardment at about 11 o'clock, preparatory to the assault. The naval brigade, which had been landed, had intrenched itself some 600 yards in front of the fort and was awaiting the signal to storm. The plan was to let the sailors rush the parapets while the marines were to act as sharpshooters and keep the defenders in check. Unfortunately most of the sailors were only armed with cutlasses and revolvers, the marines alone carrying the Sharpe rifle.

At 3 o'clock the signal was given for the general assault, but as the army was a trifle late in reaching its place, the sailors were the first to rush on. The Confederates, taking the naval men for the main assaulting forces, massed upon the parapets and opened a withering fire upon them. The failure of the marines to support the latter by their fire, together with the steady and accurate fire of the enemy, caused the sailors to become demoralized, and although some naval officers, among them Cushing, Breeze, Parker, Preston, and B. H. Porter, dashed ahead with great daring and intrepidity, still the sailors could not be induced to charge; they retired precipitately, only the following men remaining at the front near the fort, until night set in, for which bravery and good conduct they were awarded the Medal of Honor: Gurdon H. Barter, landsman; David L. Bass, seaman; John Rannahan, corporal of marines; John Shivers, marine; Henry Thompson, marine; Othniel Tripp, chief boatswain's mate; Franklin L. Wilcox, seaman; Henry S. Webster, landsman; Philip Bazaar, seaman; Thomas Connor, seaman; John Griffiths, captain of forecastle; Thomas Harcourt, seaman; Thomas Cane, captain of the hold; Charles Mills, seaman; George Province, seaman; Auzella Savage, seaman; Lewis C. Shepard, seaman; John Swanson, seaman; Edward Swatton, seaman; A. J. Tomlin, corporal of marines; Albert Burton, seaman; Isaac N. Fry, sergeant of marines, and Richard Binder, sergeant of marines.

Sergeant Binder says of this assault: "After the storming parties had formed in line volunteers were called for to go to the front and act as sharpshooters. The advanced position that was to be occupied was extremely dangerous owing to the nearness of the enemy and the continuous rain of shot and shell that swept over it, also to the unpleasant fact that the whole ground immediately in front of the fort was mined. Volunteers were not plentiful; indeed for a time not a single one offered his services for the undertaking. Then Lieutenant Williams volunteered the whole guard of which I was sergeant as sharpshooters. We fixed our accoutrements and started for our position, Lieutenant Williams, Sergeant Isaac N. Fry and I in the lead. We crawled the entire distance to our posts, and when we got there we were compelled to stay from 1 o'clock until dark amid the bursting of shells and the whizzing hail of bullets. During that time no one would venture to go to the rear, nor did anyone from behind come out to us; to show your hat above cover meant almost instantly to have it knocked off by a bullet.

"As it began to get dark we left our posts and returned to the rear. Lieutenant Williams and I were the last to leave our position in the front."

Eight of the above men—John Griffiths, captain of forecastle, and John Swanson, Edward Swatton, George Province, Auzella Savage, Philip Bazaar, Lewis C. Shepard, and Albert Burton—further distinguished themselves at the time of the panic among the sailors by entering the fort, they being the only ones who did so.

The naval attack, although repulsed, had by no means been in vain, for the enemy, taking these storming parties as the main column, concentrated their forces against them. The surprise of the Confederates when they suddenly received the deadly fire of the assaulting army forces from the rear was complete.

A furious hand-to-hand fight began and lasted for nearly five hours in the fort. From traverse to traverse the rebels defended every inch with stubbornness and reckless bravery. Upon the admiral's orders the Ironsides trained her guns by the aid of the calcium lights from the ships—for it was dark by this time—upon the struggling mass of Confederates on the traverses and mowed them down by the score.

At last the gallant soldiers of General Terry forced the fighting foe out of the central fort towards the Mound, or Battery Lamb, and from there to Federal Point. Here the enemy finally surrendered at 10 o'clock that night. Fort Fisher and the inlets were won to the Union. When the shouts of the victorious army rang out from Federal Point as the Confederates laid down their arms the ships' crews answered with ringing cheers and the blowing of whistles.

While the forces on shore were so desperately engaged the men aboard the various ships were performing heroic work in the bombardment, and among the more prominent individual deeds which were rewarded by the Medal of Honor were the following:

Daniel D. Stevens was quartermaster on board the ironclad Canonicus, and in order to attend to the signals during the attack he had to remain outside the turret exposed to the enemy's fire; he had also to take and call the soundings under a terrific fire, a most important duty, as the Canonicus went so near the fort on that day that time and again there was not more than a foot and a half of water under her keel. The flag of the ship was shot away three times, and three times Stevens replaced it; the first two times he climbed the staff in accomplishing the work, but the third time, the staff being broken by a shot, Acting Master Decker aided Stevens in fixing the flag in its place.

As has been narrated above, during the first attack on Fort Fisher, December 24, 1864, five 100-pounder Parrott guns burst on different ships, one of them on the Ticonderoga, killing ten and wounding fifteen men. William Shipman was captain of a gun next to the one that burst. When the catastrophe happened and his men saw so close before them the fearful havoc that had come like a flash upon the ship, the mangled bodies of the dead, the mutilated wounded writhing and groaning in indescribable agony, courageous hearts stood still for a moment, and horror shook the crew of Shipman's gun and made them weak. Shipman alone did not lose his composure for a second. Coolly turning towards his men he said aloud: "Go ahead, boys; that's the fortune of war." These words reassured the men, and in another second Shipman's gun let fly at the enemy again as if nothing had happened.

In addition to those already mentioned the following men were awarded the Medal of Honor for highly meritorious conduct during the several engagements with Fort Fisher, in December, 1864, and January 1865: James Barnum, boatswain's mate; John Dempster, cockswain; William Dunn, quartermaster; Thomas English, signal quartermaster; Charles H. Foy, signal quartermaster; Joseph B. Hayden, quartermaster; Edmund Haffee, quarter-gunner; Thomas Jones, cockswain; Nicholas Lear, quartermaster; Daniel S. Milliken, quartergunner; George Prance, captain of the maintop; William G. Taylor, captain of forecastle; Joseph White, cockswain; Augustus Williams, seaman; Richard Willis, cockswain; Edward R. Bowman, quartermaster; William Campbell, boatswain's mate; Robert Summers, chief quartermaster.

The navy lost 21 officers and 309 men killed and wounded, the casualties having been almost entirely due to the fire of the rebel sharpshooters during the assault.

TWO THOUSAND MILES IN A GIG

WILLIAM HALFORD.
Cockswain U. S. S. Saginaw.
Born August 18, 1841, in Gloucester-
shire, Eng. Highest rank attained:
Chief Guner, U. S. N.

EVEN in times of profound national peace the sailor, when on his chosen element, is forever at war. In a moment's notice an emergency, unexpected, incalculable, may arise to put his courage, self-reliance, endurance and sound judgment to a far severer test than the most distressing circumstances in the midst of the fiercest battle on land could possibly exact. It is for this reason that the history of seafaring life records instances of individual heroism and devotion unequaled elsewhere.

The following narration of William Halford, then a cockswain on board the ill-fated U. S. S. Saginaw, will be found to offer a good illustration.

During the year 1870 he was serving on board the Saginaw, as a cockswain of the gig. The ship had been engaged in surveying and deepening the entrance to the lagoon at the Midway Islands in the Pacific Ocean. The appropriation being about all expended and the season getting late, work was discontinued, and on the evening of October 28th, the ship started on her way to San Francisco. Commander M. Sicard, in command of the ship, decided to run down to Ocean Island to see if there were any shipwrecked men on the island, it being out of the track of shipping. She ran down under easy sail, expecting to make the island about daylight, but overran her reckoning, on account of the strong unknown currents, and at about 3 A. M. was in the breakers outside the reef surrounding the island. Before sail could be got off the ship, or the engines backed—the ship being under banked fires—she struck heavily and stove in her bottom, throwing the boilers out of position. The heavy breakers lifted the ship and threw her higher on the reef with every sea. She began breaking up almost immediately, throwing her foundered parts around at right angles, making a shelter for the crew to work in. The weather boats having been washed away, they succeeded, after considerable trouble, in getting their lee boats over the reef into the lagoon, thus saving only three small boats—a gig, an old cutter and a dinghy—very much battered up. The crew were taken off, without the loss of a man, and landed on a low sand island inside the lagoon, a barren, desolate spot. There was nothing alive on the island but sea birds and a few seals on the beach; no trees or shelter of any kind. A small amount of provisions that washed out of the ship and over the reef into shoal water in the lagoon was saved. The water was so clear that everything could be seen on the bottom and fished up with a hook; in this way considerable was saved, but not enough to last over two or three months on quarter rations. In order to make the provisions last longer, members of the crew were detailed to kill birds and seals, which were made into soup, and, along with some fish that were caught, the crew of ninety-six men managed to exist. The day after the wreck Commander Sicard, seeing no prospect of any relief in this out-of-the-way place, decided to put out an expedition to go to Honolulu for assistance, as it was only a matter of a short time before they would all starve to death.

The expedition would have to pull and sail over 2,000 miles. Lieutenant Talbot, the executive officer, took command of it, and Peter Francis, James Muir, John Andrews and William Halford formed the crew. The gig was gotten out of the water and repaired as well as could be done with the material on hand—just a little wreckage from the ship. The makeshift and her crew left the island on November 18, 1870, on her trip to Honolulu. The men reckoned that they had provisions for twenty-five days on quarter rations, unfortunately about three-quarters of it being composed of beans, rice, wheat and peas, all mixed together, which had been fished from the water when the ship went to pieces, dried in the sun, then cooked and put in tins. When the little craft got out to sea this mixture was all fermented and rotten. It caused dysentery, and in two or three days the men were weakened so that they were almost powerless to help themselves. This stuff was then thrown overboard.

"We had a small amount of dessicated potatoes left," says Cockswain Halford, "and these were dealt out twice a day, one spoonful morning and evening, and with what fresh water we had in the boat we would soak our potatoes to a sauce to soften them as well. We had five gallons of sperm oil in the boat for our light, but we lost the lamp the third day out and had no way of getting another light, everything being wet; no matches, nor flint and steel. The oil was therefore useless to us. I suggested to the men that they use it on their food, but they were so weakened that they could not retain it. I therefore had the whole five gallons to myself.

"After about twenty-five days the potatoes gave out. Then things began to look pretty blue, but the next day God furnished us with rations. The weather being fine for the first time during the voyage, I was sitting steering, while the rest slept, when a large sea bird (booby) came along and alighted on the boat close to me. I grasped it, wrung its neck, stripped off the feathers, cut it in five pieces and served it out warm and bloody. That was our ration for that day. The next we went hungry. The following morning just before daylight I was alone steering the boat when something struck me in the face and dropped alongside of me. It was a small flying fish, about four inches long. I ate it just as it was. Shortly after a school of them came skimming along and six dropped into the boat. I secured them and served them out. That was our last meal.

"As the morning broke land was in sight, but a long way off and to windward; it was the Island of Hawaii. We tried our best to make it that day and the next, but it was slow work—with nothing to eat. As night came on the weather began to change for the worse. Lightning, thunder, rain and heavy squalls came down on

"I GRASPED THE BIRD AND WRUNG ITS NECK."

us, but we were making such fair progress that by the next night we were close up with the land. In attempting to debark we got caught in the breakers on the reef, about a mile from the beach. The boat was capsized and all hands were lost except myself, the little craft turning over and over several times before she got through the breakers and into comparatively smooth water. The masts of the boat had been carried away when she turned over the first time. I got hold of some of the rigging and held on. It was hard work, but I kept my head, and felt ten times my natural strength all the time. I should think it was between 2 and 3 A. M. at the time. I remained with the boat until she got in towards the beach. Then I got the dispatch box, containing the report of the wreck of the ship to the admiral of. the station, and to the Secretary of the Navy, secured it to my shoulder and left the boat for the beach. I remember striking the shore; that was the last.

"When I awoke, or regained consciousness, my feet were in the water and my head up clear. I tried to rise, but found that one of my legs refused duty; I had a bad wound in the knee-joint. I found a piece of driftwood and used it for a crutch. Then in looking around I found that if I had gone twenty-five feet more to leeward I should have dashed to pieces against the perpendicular rocks. Where I landed was a sandy beach. Well, I found some natives, but none spoke English. They treated me kindly and one went off and got a half white native who spoke English, He got some clothing to cover me, as I was stark naked, and then took me over the mountain to a plantation kept by a gentleman named Mr. Bent. He took me in charge and doctored me up, giving me food, very little at a time, and dressing my wounds. I stayed with him two days.

"I was anxious to get to Honolulu, so engaged a small native schooner to take me there, ninety miles distant. On my arrival at Honolulu I went directly to the United States Consul, also to the resident United States Minister. That night they had a 200-ton schooner sail for the wreck of the Saginaw, with provisions and medical stores. Two days after the sailing of the schooner a steamer was started. The steamer arrived first and was taking the last load of men off when the schooner arrived, so all she could do was to turn around and go back.

"Two days after my arrival at Honolulu the steamer from San Francisco came in and left again the day following. I returned to San Francisco with the dispatches, which I delivered to Admiral Winslow, commanding the Pacific fleet, then went to the Naval Hospital, Mare Island, was promoted to gunner and granted the Medal of Honor.

"We had sailed over 2,000 miles in a small boat, suffered untold hardships from cold and hunger, and had not someone been left to tell the story in all probability the ninety-six men left behind would have starved to death before any assistance would have reached them.

UNDAUNTED HEROISM OF SAILORS

IN August, 1866, the American schooner General Sherman, a merchant vessel, was at anchor in the Ping-Yang River, Corea, when, for some reason never sufficiently ascertained, the treacherous natives unexpectedly sent fire-rafts against the vessel on a dark night, boarded her in the ensuing confusion and murdered the crew to the last man.

To retaliate for this act of barbarism a squadron under the gallant Commodore John Rodgers, consisting of six warships — the Colorado, Alaska, Monocacy, Ashuelot, Benicia and Palos — appeared on May 30, 1871, before the Han River, on which Seoul, the capital of the Kingdom of Corea, is situated. A reconnoissance being necessary, the Palos and Monocacy, the only ships of sufficiently light draught, were sent in, accompanied by four steam launches, to survey. The Americans were just rounding a bend of the river when they were suddenly greeted by a volley of some hundred gingals and several 32-pounders mounted on one of three heights on the river bank. One sailor was wounded, but in a few minutes the guns of the expedition cleared the fort of the impudent rabble of slit-eyes.

WILLIAM F. LUKES,
Captain of the top, U. S. S. Colorado,
Born in Berlin, Germany, February 19, 1847.

On receiving the report of this treacherous act Commodore Rodgers demanded forthwith a satisfactory explanation or apology from the government, or those who pretended to represent one. As after ten days' waiting nothing had come forth, another expedition was fitted out to punish the evil-doers. The two gunboats mentioned, with four launches and twenty boats, having on board 550 sailors, 100 marines and seven pieces of artillery, under command of Captain Homer C. Blake, set out on the 10th of June. Soon the fort, or forts, for there were five works in all, was reached. The Monocacy, which was in the lead and had her artillery strengthened by two 9-inch guns from the Colorado, cleared the first fort of its garrison and shot the surrounding stone wall to pieces at the river front. It was growing dark. The landing force disembarked and went into camp some 800 yards below the forts.

The next morning the attack began on the middle fort. With the Monocacy shelling from the river, the enemy were chased pell-mell out of it to take refuge in the last line of works located on a high and extremely steep bluff. There were 153 guns and gingals in this fort.

While the Monocacy was throwing her shells against the walls of the fortification and in it, and the landing artillery frustrated a sudden dash of thousands of the enemy on the American flank, the attacking column went forward to the storm. The men had to climb the steep incline in front of the fort under a hail of shell and gingal shots, and under the rays of a broiling sun finally engaged in a hand-to-hand fight with the enemy within the walls. The slaughter was complete, although the real struggle did not last over half an hour. Three hundred and fifty Coreans were slain in the fort, only twenty being captured alive. Five fortified works, fifty flags, twenty-seven heavy guns and some 450 gingals fell into the hands of the dauntless attackers. The Americans had lost three killed, among them Lieutenant McKee from the Alaska, and ten wounded.

During the attack on the forts the gallant Lieutenant McKee from the Alaska fell mortally wounded while leading his men, whereupon Frederick Franklin assumed command. As the brave Lieutenant fell Alexander McKenzie, Samuel F. Rogers and William Troy fought at his side to protect him from the enemy, and were also wounded. Then John Coleman tried to rescue them, but succeeded only in rescuing the wounded McKenzie from the hands of the Coreans.

In connection with the death of Lieutenant McKee, a most gallant act of loyalty and sacrifice was performed by William F. Lukes, landsman, and Seth Allen and Thomas Murphy, seamen, of the Colorado.

When McKee fell, Lukes was near by and quickly noticed what had occurred. As for the time being the overwhelming numbers of the enemy made it imperative that none of the men should leave the fighting line, Lukes rushed forward with the others until they had put the enemy to flight. Without resting a moment he then started out to find his wounded officer, and discovering a band of fleeing natives, dragging with them what proved afterward to be the body of Lieutenant McKee. Lukes's call for volunteers brought to his aid Seamen Seth Allen and Thomas Murphy, and these three then sprang at the natives. A desperate hand-to-hand fight ensued. The struggle had been observed from the fort and a detachment of marines hurried to the rescue. When they arrived they found both Allen and Murphy dead, and Lukes, with eighteen sword and spear wounds, lying unconscious on the body of his lieutenant. The man lay for thirty-nine days unconscious in the Colorado's sick-bay, and as a result of the terrible hacking he had gone through became an invalid for life. The Medal of Honor was the reward for his unswerving devotion.

The following men also received the Medal in this engagement: Frederick Franklin, quartermaster; Alexander McKenzie, boatswain's mate; Cyrus Hayden, carpenter; Charles Brown, corporal of marines; Samuel F. Rogers, quartermaster; William Troy, seaman; Michael Owens, marine; JohnColeman, marine, of the Colorado. H. P. Grace, chief quartermaster; John Andrews, seaman; James Dougherty, marine, and Michael McNamara, marine, of the Benicia.

"A DESPERATE HAND-TO-HAND FIGHT TOOK PLACE.

IN AN ARCTIC STORM

IN 1873, the United States steamer Tigress was sent to the far North in search of the exploring ship Polaris, and to rescue those of her officers and men who were still alive. She was driven about by the wind and current in the great fields of ice and thousands of icebergs in Baffin's Bay until finally, in September she was able to force her way through Cumberland Gulf, where she remained for two weeks in order to repair the damage done while being buffeted about in the ice.

When these repairs had been made, Commander Greer brought her out, but before she had fairly fought her way out to the pack ice of the stream, a fresh northeaster blew up. Every effort was made to get her out of the pack before the gale increased in fury, for to be caught in the pack in a heavy gale meant rough usage, with much damage to the ship. Her bluff nose plowed its way into the ice until she was fast. Then she would back off a sufficient distance, when under full speed she was again sent ahead into the pack. During this operation the wind was steadily increasing until it was blowing a gale, causing a short, choppy sea, which ground the ice into the sides of the Tigress and twisted her so that her timbers creaked and groaned under the strain. But she kept on, seeking, against terrible odds, to make her way out of the ice into the open sea, which she finally succeeded in doing, only to meet new dangers in the way of enormous icebergs. All hands, from captain to cook, kept a sharp lookout for these dangerous bergs which menace the passage of ships at night as they drift silently and unseen in the darkness. Now that she was out in the open water, she was tossed about like a cork on the huge waves, which were gaining in force and size every hour. For four days she was kept on her course, now riding on the top of a huge wave only to plow head first into the next one, sending the water over her decks in torrents, and carrying everything with it that was not secured.

One day when the gale was at its height the spanker was half way brailed, with only a reefed staysail forward. The ship was lying as close up to the wind as possible and the engines were kept going to hold her. All hands except Chief Engineer Melville's engine room crew were on deck that day, clinging to the life-line or to the weather-rail to escape the heavy seas that washed over her, and anxiously watching the fore-topgallant sail, which was adrift and flapping with great violence. As the seas came on board, all hands clung tighter to the life-line and ducked below the rail, thus missing the full force of them. Anxious faces were turned up to that topgallant sail as it flapped defiantly in the wind, everyone expecting it would cause the mast to go by the board. At length a petty officer, Geo. Willis, apprehending the great danger the ship was in, hauled himself aft, hand over hand, along the lifeline to the mainmast, where Lieutenant-Commander Henry C. White, the executive officer, was holding fast.

"Commander White," he said, "that topgallant sail must be furled, or the mast will go," and he held fast to the life-line with one hand as he touched his cap in saluting.

"It must," replied the officer, "but no man will be ordered aloft in this gale to do the work. We must hope for good luck to carry us through. It may hold."

"Someone must do it; it will never hold out. Send me."

"God bless you, Willis, for the offer, but I shall never order you aloft in this gale."

"But, good God! forty-four souls are at stake. If you won't order me to do it. I'll go without your orders," insisted Willis.

Without further parley he hauled himself forward to the weather-shrouds, and watching his opportunity he sprang up on the rail, but was twice thrown back by the wind and sea before he succeeded in reaching the ratlines.

All eyes were turned on him and not a man thought other than that Willis was going to certain death; for, even should he succeed in passing the foretop, and reaching the topgallant yard, it was almost certain that he would be carried away by the wind and the rolling of the ship and hurled into the seething, boiling sea, where no boat could live to rescue him.

With the agility of a cat he went up the ratlines and gained the foretop; then slowly he got up the shrouds of the topgallant mast, reaching the yard in safety. But now the perilous work began. Inch by inch he worked his way out to the weather-yard end on the foot-ropes and began furling the flapping sail. Those below expected momentarily to see the sail carried away and Willis with it. But he bravely stood out on those foot-ropes, tugging and hauling and lashing up the flapping spread of wet, frozen canvas, almost tearing off his finger nails as the wind would blow it out. He never faltered in his task, doing what in less severe weather would require the services of several men.

Willing hands on deck brailed up the canvas, when Willis signaled to them, and little by little he furled the sail until he reached the mast. Out on the leeward foot-ropes the intrepid man now clambered, holding on with a firm hand. The greatest caution was imperative, for in brailing up the canvas on the windward side of the yard that on the leeward side flapped and bellied out to the wind in a dangerous way, making it doubly perilous to step on the foot-ropes. But, nothing daunted, Willis began furling the sail from the mast outboard, stepping little by little along the swaying foot-rope all the time, clinging close to the yard to keep the flapping sail from throwing him overboard. Having successfully reached the end of the yard-arm and furled the sail, he started back along the foot-ropes to the mast. Upon reaching it, he hung on for a time to rest himself. He remained in that position so long that one of the officers, fearing he was exhausted and that he could not reach the deck again, offered $50 to anyone who would go aloft and rig Willis in a boatswain's chair to send him below to the deck. No one accepted the proffered money. No one ventured to the aid of the man who risked his life in an endeavor to save the ship's crew.

Willis, after regaining his strength, cautiously worked his way out to the wind-ward side and slowly made his way down to the shrouds safely to the deck, which it was believed he would never again reach after he started up the shrouds on his self-imposed mission of heroism.

WILLIS VOLUNTARILY FURLING THE SAIL ALONE.

IN the preceding narratives no naval officers are mentioned as possessors of the Medal of Honor. Unlike the act of Congress relative to the Army Medal of Honor, which states that the Medal is to be awarded to such officers and enlisted men as especially distinguished themselves in action, the act conferring this decoration upon naval men specifically states that the Medal of Honor is to be awarded to enlisted men and marines. Thus the officers are excluded.

There are other cases of naval men having been awarded the Medal of Honor which are not mentioned in "Deeds of Valor." This is due to the fact that the personnel of the navy became scattered so far and wide over the world after the War of the Rebellion that all effort to reach some of the rewarded men proved futile. Among the instances of great heroism on board ship must be included those of saving life at sea. These instances, though most heroic in themselves, do not properly come within the scope of Deeds of Valor, as they did not occur in battle, but, inasmuch as they were rewarded with the Medal of Honor, they are recorded on the following four pages.

Under varying conditions men found themselves struggling in the water in a desperate attempt to save themselves from drowning, and they would have perished but for the undaunted courage of shipmates, who jumped overboard and at the great risk of their own lives rescued the unfortunate men from watery graves.

HEROIC INSTANCES OF LIFE-SAVING

JAMES CAREY,
Seaman, U. S. S. Huron. Born in
Ireland in 1847,

THERE were actions of bravery performed in time of peace by men of the navy which secured for them the well-deserved Medal of Honor.

On April 12, 1872, Commodore A. F. Crossman and a number of men of the U. S. S. Kansas were drowned near Graytown, Nicaragua, on which occasion three men, Boatswain's Mate John O'Neil, Seamen Austin Denham and Richard Pile, displayed such extraordinary coolness and bravery that the Medal of Honor was deservedly bestowed on them.

There are many cases where men of the United States ships endangered their lives in saving those of others. In every instance known to the department these men were awarded the Medal of Honor. The following list gives instances from all over the globe where American seamen thus displayed undaunted courage:

Cockswain William Anderson, for rescuing an apprentice boy from drowning on the 28th of June, 1878.

Seaman J. F. Auer, of the Lancaster, saving a Frenchman from drowning at Marseilles, France, November 20, 1883.

Seamen Richard Bates, John Brown and Thomas Burke, of the De Soto, rescuing two men of the Winooski off Eastport, Me., May 10, 1860.

Seaman W. H. Belpitt, of the Monocacy, jumping overboard and saving a Chinaman from a capsized sampan at Foo Chow, China, October 7, 1884.

Seaman James Benson, of the Ossipee, trying to save a comrade who had fallen overboard, on June 20, 1872.

Landsman Alexander Bradley, of the Wachusett, saving a man off Cowes, England, August 7, 1872.

Apprentice David M. Buchanan, of the Saratoga, saving a comrade off the Battery, New York, on July 15, 1879.

Seaman James Carey, of the Huron, saving three shipmates from drowning on three different occasions. He received the Medal of Honor three times, the third instance being at Rio de Janeiro, Brazil.

Apprentice August Chandron and Boatswain's Mate Hugh Miller, of the Quinnebaug, for saving a man at Alexandria, Egypt, on November 21, 1885.

Seaman Michael Connolly, of the Plymouth, saving a citizen from drowning at Halifax, N. S., August 7, 1876.

Landsman William Corey, of the Plymouth, saving a man at the navy yard, New York, July 26, 1876.

Seaman John Costello, of the Hartford, saving a man at Philadelphia on July 16, 1876.

Boatswain's Mate T. Cramen and Seaman H. C. Courtney, of the Plymouth, for saving a laborer at the Washington Navy Yard.

Landsman George W. Cutter, of the Powhatan, at Norfolk, Va., May 27, 1872.

Landsman Joseph H. Davis, of the Dale, at Norfolk, Va., January 22, 1886.

Seaman John Davis, of the Trenton, at Toulon, France, February, 1881.

Seaman John Dempsey, of the Kearsarge, at Shanghai, China, January 23, 1875.

Seaman Michael Deneef, of the Swatara, at Para, Brazil, on December 1, 1875.

Apprentice Frank Du Moulin, of the Sabine, at New London Harbor, on September 5, 1867.

Landsman Walter Elmore, of the Gettysburg, at sea, latitude 36 deg. 58 min. N., long. 3 deg. 44 min. E., on October 1, 1878.

Landsman John Enright, of the Ranger, at Ensenada, Mexico, January 18, 1886.

Seaman Isaac L. Fasser, of the Lackawanna, at Callao, Peru, on June 13, 1884.

Boatswain's Mate John Flannagan, of the Supply, at Havre, France, on October 16, 1878.

Quartermaster Christopher Fowler, of the Fortune, saving part of a drowning boat's crew at Zapotitlan, Mexico, May 11, 1874.

Seaman Charles Giddings, of the Plymouth, at New York, July 26, 1876.

Boatswain's Mate Matthew Gillick, of the Lancaster, at Marseilles, France, November 26, 1883.

Quartermaster John Handran, of the Franklin, at Lisbon, Portugal, January 9, 1876.

Apprentice John Hayden, of the Saratoga, at New York, near the Battery, July 5, 1879.

Seaman William Hill, of the Minnesota, at Newport, R. I., June 22, 1881.

Quarter-Gunner George Holt and Landsman Paul Tobin, of the Plymouth, at Hamburg, July 3, 1871.

Cooper William Johnson, of the Adams, at Mare Island, Cal., November 14, 1879.

Seaman Thomas Kersey, of the Plymouth, at New York, July 26,1876.

Seaman Hugh King, of the Iroquois, at Delaware River, September 7, 1871.

Landsman P. J. Kyle, of the Quinnebaug, at Port Mahon, Minorca, Balearic Islands, March 13, 1879.

Seaman Thomas Larkin, of the Narragansett, at Mare Island Navy Yard, Cal., November 24, 1874.

Seaman Emile Lejune, of the Plymouth, at Port Royal S. C., June 6, 1876.

Seaman George Low, of the Tennessee, at New Orleans, La., February 13, 1881.

Apprentice Boy John Lucy, of the training ship Minnesota, at Castle Garden, New York, July 9, 1876.

Seaman Edward Maddin, of the Franklin, at Lisbon, Portugal, January 9, 1876.

Quartermaster Henry J. Manning, of the training ship New Hampshire, at Newport, R. I., January 4, 1882.

Ship's Printer John McCarton, of the training ship New Hampshire, off Coasters' Harbor Island, near Newport, R. I., January 4, 1882.

Boatswain's Mate Hugh Miller, of the Quinnebaug, at Alexandria, Egypt, on November 21, 1885.

Seaman John Millmore, of the Essex, at Monrovia, Liberia, October 31, 1877.

Landsman Thomas Mitchell, of the Richmond, at Shanghai, China, November 17, 1879.

Boatswain's Mate Francis Moore, of the training ship Portsmouth, at the Washington Navy Yard, January 23, 1882.

Seaman Philip Moore, of the Trenton, at Genoa, Italy, September 21, 1881.

Corporal John Morris, of the marines, on board of the Lancaster, at Villefranche, France, December 25, 1881.

Seaman William Morse, of the Shenandoah, at Rio de Janeiro, Brazil, September 19, 1880.

Seaman Joseph B. Noil, colored, of the Powhatan, at Norfolk, December 26, 1873.

Landsman J. A. Norris, of the Jamestown, at the New York Navy Yard, December 20, 1883.

Landsman James O'Conner, of engineers' force of the Jean Sands, at Norfolk, June 15, 1880.

Seaman John Osborne, of the Juniata, at Philadelphia, June 21, 1876.

Seaman Christian Osepins, of the tug Fortune, at Hampton Roads, Va., March 7, 1882.

Boatswain's Mate Alexander Parker, at Mare Island, Cal., on July 25, 1876.

Seaman Thomas Robinson, of the Tallapoosa, off New Orleans, La., July 15, 1866.

Seaman Johannes Rouning, of the Fortune, at Hampton Roads, Va., May 7, 1882.

Seaman John Russell, of the Trenton, Genoa, Italy, September 21, 1881.

P. J. KYLE,
Landsman, U. S. S. Quinnebaug.

Seaman Richard Ryan, of the Hartford, at Norfolk, Va., March 4, 1876.

Seaman William Sadler, of the Saratoga, at Coasters' Harbor Island, R. I., June 25, 1881.

Seaman Isaac Sapp, of the Shenandoah, assisting Midshipman Miller in saving Seaman Charles Price; date not given.

First-class Fireman Henry Simpson, of the Essex, at Monrovia, Liberia, October 1877.

Seaman John Smith, of the Shenandoah, at Rio de Janeiro, Brazil, on September 19, 1880.

Seaman Thomas Smith, of the Enterprise, at Para, Brazil, October 1, 1878.

Seaman William B. Stacy, of the Rhode Island, Cape Haytien; no date given.

Corporal of Marines James Stewart, of the Plymouth, at Villefranche, France February 1, 1872.

Boatswain's Mate James F. Sullivan, of the training ship New Hampshire, at Newport, R. I., April 21, 1882.

Landsman William Sweeney, of the engineers' force of the Jean Sands, at Norfolk Navy Yard, night of June 15, 1880.

Seaman Robert Sweeney, of the Jamestown, at New York Navy Yard, December 20, 1883.

Ship's Corporal James Thayer, of the Constitution, at Norfolk Navy Yard, Va. November 16, 1879.

Seaman Henry Thompson, at Mare Island Navy Yard, Cal., on June 27, 1878.

Seaman Michael Thornton, of the Leyden, near Boston, Mass., August 25, 1881.

Landsman Paul Tobin, of the Plymouth, at Hamburg, July 3, 1871.

Fireman J. M. Trout, of the Frolic, at Montevideo, April 20, 1877.

Chief Boatswain's Mate Jeremiah Trout, of the training ship New Hampshire, at Newport, R. I., April 21, 1882.

Seaman Alexander Turvelin, of the Trenton, at Toulon, France, February, 1881.

Seaman Albert Weisvogel, of the Plymouth, at sea, April 27, 1876; also for saving life on board the Benicia, on January 11, 1874.

Ship's Cook Adam Weissel, of the training ship Minnesota, at Newport, R. I., August 26, 1884.

Seaman Louis Williams, of the Lackawanna, for saving life on two occasions, at Honolulu, March 16, 1883, and at Callao, Peru, June 13, 1884.

T HE Indian, now practically civilized, has always figured prominently in our country's history. The
pioneer as he gradually spread out and settled on
new land, thus advancing civilization, was in continual
conflict with him. The stories of many of these encounters are thrilling and fascinating, revealing deeds
of self-sacrifice and fortitude which cause the blood to
run warmer. Ever since the first white men settled in
North America there had been a constant clash between
them and the red men, until now what remains of a
once numerous and hardy race is huddled together upon
small reservations in various sections of the United States. A retrospective view of
the early struggles with King Philip's tribes, the Seminoles, the Black Hawks, etc.,
makes these events seem less bloody than they actually were; but the Indian outrages
and massacres of later years, still fresh in our minds, abound with treachery and cunning and a fiendishness that in some instances is positively indescribable. It is
these later wars, from 1860 down to a recent date, that bring out more prominently
the true character of the wily red men, showing them to be a most picturesque,
interesting and withal an intelligent race. Their character was so diverse from
their white aggressors that it was difficult to understand them, and therefore they
seldom got the benefit of just criticism from their foes.

So long as the red man could roam in freedom over the vast hunting grounds
from the shores of the Atlantic to the shores of the Pacific, he was happy and contented; but when the exterminating process was begun he was gradually driven
toward the setting sun, and as his confines were narrowed down to smaller and
smaller areas he resisted the action of the white men, put on his war paint and
proceeded through the settled portions killing, burning and laying waste. This pillaging, together with the fights between tribes which are hereditary mutual enemies,
necessitated the continual presence of troops to quell these outbreaks.

If we judge the Indian by his morals we find that originally he stood fairly high. He is acknowledged at first to have been trustworthy and hospitable; in the prominent tribes like the Sioux the women enjoyed an excellent reputation for virtue. Their institutions were all thoroughly democratic, not only in theory but also in practice, and fitting the wants and views of a people who appreciated liberty and freedom.

The evil change in the red man's character came with the advent of the white desperadoes on the frontier. These white men, reckless and unconcerned, belonged with very few exceptions, to the very scum of their race, and their behavior towards the redskins was that of brutal, inconsiderate bullies. Many wars on the frontier were brought on by the actions of these white men; and when the provoked Indians finally took the warpath, in the instincts of their savage nature, they committed unspeakable outrages, and were denounced as treacherous wild beasts who should be hunted down as such.

In later times, after the establishment of Indian reservations, it was often the dishonesty of the government agent which deprived the reservation tribes of their subsistence and caused their suffering, want and starvation. All these evils were seldom counted in favor of the Indians by the men on the frontier. The red man's best friends in these remote regions were the United States troops, the men who had to fight him hardest after he had taken the warpath.

Not often was the sensible advice heeded which went to Washington from the military commanders at the frontier posts; when the agent had stirred up the redskins and could no longer control them he would try in time to save his own hide and pack up, while the soldiers had to round up the raiding Indians in most fatiguing and relentless warfare.

The campaigns and scouts against the Indians from 1860 to 1898 in the following pages are arranged in chronological order, with particular attention given to those fights in which some of the brave regulars won the Medal of Honor.

THRILLING INCIDENTS FROM ARIZONA

COL. BERNARD J. D. IRWIN,
Asst. Surgeon U. S. A.
Highest rank attained: Colonel U. S. A.
and Assistant Surgeon-General.
Born in Ireland.

A RIZONA, the sunniest part of the Union and the home of numerous tribes of Apaches, had been "opened to civilization" up to 1861 by but few frontiersmen. The desperate resistance of the Indians had allowed these daring settlers to gain but little foothold, and even the almost continuous warfare with Union troops could not intimidate the treacherous redskins, who aimed to drive the hated whites out of their domain.

At that time the territory was unexplored, and, excepting the military road passing east to west, through the southern part from Fort Thorn, New Mexico, via Tucson to Fort Yuma, California, and a short one from Tucson to Sonora, there were no public highways. The region embraced between the Rio Grande on the east and the Colorado River on the west, and from the international line on the south to the country of the Navajoes on the north, was then but little known—a veritable *terra incognita*, inhabited by nomadic tribes of hostile Apaches, embraced under the various tribal designations of Mescalero, Mogollon, Cayatero, Tonto, Pinaleno, Yuma, Mojave, Hualapi and last—but the most savage of all—the Chiricahua. The Pueblo or Montezuma Indians—Pimas, Maricopas, Papagoes and Moquis—lived from time immemorial and still live in the villages or fixed habitations, and have always maintained friendly relations with their white neighbors, but were obliged to defend themselves against the constant raids of the predatory Apaches. The usual home or rendezvous of the Chiricahuas, when not roving over the border in the Sierra Madre, Mexico, was in the mountain range situated in the southern part of Arizona and named after that tribe. This range had been their stronghold for many years and they always felt secure when, being chased by troopers, they had managed to reach it. From there they made forays in quest of plunder, or they laid in wait ready to pounce upon small parties of incautious travelers en route to Mexico or California. Such parties were usually ambushed, the men slaughtered, and the women and children subjected to bondage and ill-treatment much worse than the most cruel death.

The Medal of Honor which was awarded to Colonel Bernard J. D. Irwin ranks in cronological order as the first one on record, he having earned it by his voluntary, hazardous trip to rescue besieged soldiers in Apache Pass, Arizona, February 13 and 14, 1861. The act of Congress creating and awarding the medal, approved March 3, 1863, included all exceptional deeds of valor performed during the years 1861 and 1862.

The chief of the Chiricahuas at that time was Cochise, after whom one of the counties of Arizona has been named. He was then in the prime of life, tall and well-formed in face and figure, about thirty years old, and at least six feet in height. His presence was bold and warlike, presenting the attributes of a superb specimen of robust, physical manhood. Conscious of the evil reputation of his tribe, and fearing that retribution for their many wicked deeds might overtake him, he declined all overtures and offers made to induce him to visit the military posts. The highway leading to and from Apache Pass was dotted with the graves or stone tumuli that covered the remains of the victims of his treachery, slaughtered by his bloodthirsty followers, who were ever on the lookout from their mountain fastnesses for the approach of the careless wayfarers, constrained to enter the dreaded pass in quest of water and transit through its range of heights.

Early in 1861, while Captain Ewell was encamped at the pass, endeavoring to conciliate the Chiricahuas with presents, two young Mexican girls—part of the spoils of a recent foray over the border—were discovered in their possession, and were rescued by purchase from their cruel fate and restored to their parents. While detained there, awaiting the pleasure of the independent and haughty chief of the tribe, he was aroused one night by a courier seeking his aid to succor a party consisting of three discharged soldiers and their families who had left the post of the Seventh Infantry shortly after his departure, and desiring to get through the dreaded pass, on their way to the States, while he was encamped there, had been attacked. Two of the men, who had served as sergeants in the army during many years, were killed while defending their wives and children. Their horses and mules had been carried off by a party of savages who had joined and camped with them during the night and partaken of breakfast, after which they withdrew to the screen afforded by a neighboring ravine, from where they attempted the destruction of the party whose hospitality they had enjoyed only a few moments before. Such was the character of the Apache Indians of Arizona in 1861. One and all were then alike treacherous, bloodthirsty and cruel, and ever on the alert to ambush small parties or incautious travelers, without risk to themselves, the chances being always in favor of their success. Men had been waylaid and shot down within 300 yards of the only post guard-house in the territory in 1860, and the government herds had been stampeded repeatedly by Indians who lurked in the ravines and bushes in the vicinity of the military post, watching for a favorable opportunity to make a dash upon the coveted animals. All of that, and much more of a similar character, occurred before the arrival of the Seventh Infantry in the territory. A raid upon a beef contractor's cattle, which were trailed to the mountain home of Cochise, brought the Seventh Infantry in contact with these murderous Indians, in February, 1861, and gave an excuse to punish them as they deserved.

The owner of the stock, Mr. Wadsworth, had followed the trail of the stolen cattle until he became satisfied that they had been taken by the Chiricahuas. He came to the post and reported the robbery, and his convictions that the marauders were of that tribe. The commanding officer of the station, Colonel Pitcairn Morrison, directed Lieutenant George N. Bascom to take sixty men of that regiment and follow up the trail until the cattle were found and recovered. If the trail were found to enter the camp of Cochise, Bascom was ordered to demand the immediate restoration of the stolen property, and in the event of refusal to use the force under his command in recovering it.

Lieutenant Bascom having followed the trail of stolen cattle to the stronghold of the Chiricahuas, marched his command to the mail station situated within the pass and in the vicinity of the only water in that neighborhood. A station employe named Wallace, who was acquainted with Cochise, volunteered to go to his village to apprise him of the nature of the duty which had caused the troops to visit that place. That having been done, the chief, accompanied by several of his people, visited Lieutenant Bascom's camp, but when demand was made upon him for the restoration of the stolen property he scoffed at the idea of force having been brought there to compel obedience on his part.

Argument having failed to produce any effect upon the disposition of the chief, Lieutenant Bascom then determined to detain him and some others of his party as hostages, until the tribe should deliver up a captive boy, carried off with the herd, and surrender the stolen animals. That determination was only reached as a dernier resort and after every effort at peaceful persuasion had proved futile. When Cochise was informed that he would not be allowed to depart until after the demand made by the representative of the government had been complied with, he arose from where the party was seated and, yelling to his companions to follow him, boldly dashed through the bystanders, and with some of the warriors escaped into the adjacent ravines, from where they, with others who had been waiting to learn the outcome of the visit, opened fire upon the occupants of the mail-corral.

Next day a squaw was dispatched with a message informing the chief that the hostages detained would be taken to Fort Buchanan, and confined there until the captive and the cattle were restored.

The overland mail coach from California could not be apprised of the situation by the garrison in time and on entering the pass that night was attacked by a well-prepared ambuscade, but, after a wounded horse had been cut adrift, miraculously escaped. The driver, with a shattered leg, and with one of his passengers shot through the chest, finally succeeded, with the remaining horses, in bringing the coach into the corral.

There being several wounded soldiers at the station, one of them volunteered to lead a mule over the steep and untraveled hillside and endeavor to escape during the night towards Fort Buchanan in quest of aid. The brave man having succeeded in creeping through without detection, reached the mail station at Dragoon Spring early next day, and, after receiving a remount, arrived at the post the second night of his weary and dangerous journey. On the same day, in response to the message sent him, Cochise approached the mail station with a white flag and called for a talk with the "Soldier Captain," which was accorded, Lieutenant Bascom, two soldiers, Wallace and two other mail employes meeting the chief with an equal number of his followers at a point about 150 yards from the corral. The parley had hardly commenced when a sentinel posted on the roof of the station house discovered a large number of Indian warriors crouching from view in a ravine close behind Cochise. The soldier called an alarm, and had scarcely concluded his warning when a dash to surround Bascom's party and cut off his retreat was made, the warriors in the ravine opening fire on him as he fell back. He escaped without injury, although several rifle bullets passed through his clothing and one through his hat. Wallace and his companions, presuming upon their intimacy with the Indians, incautiously advanced too far and were seized and dragged into the ravine, after which they were not again seen alive. At that critical moment the hostages attempted to escape from guard. One of them was shot and killed, and another knocked down and transfixed by the bayonet of a sentinel, the weapon passing through his abdomen without wounding the viscera, as evinced by his speedy recovery and his ability to walk with other prisoners a mile and a half to the place of execution, where he and five other warriors were hanged seven days later.

At that time there had been quite a heavy fall of snow at the pass, which was used until it became impracticable to melt a sufficient quantity of it to supply water for the men and animals at the place. It then became necessary to resort to the spring, situated about 8,000 yards from the corral.

On the third day after this outbreak part of the herd was driven from the station to the spring, but ere the mules had reached the water the Indians pounced from all directions and succeeded in stampeding the animals. During this affair several of the guard and quite a number of warriors were shot down. As the attack had been expected, half the mules were to be detained to be sent forward after those sent to be watered should have returned, but through an error all got out at once.

The daring soldier who during the darkness of the night had stealthily scaled the steep and pathless mountain side and groped his way out to the plain where his command was surrounded by several hundred blood-thirsty savages, had meanwhile reached the post and related the events which had just taken place.

There being no mounted troops at Buchanan, an order was at once sent to Fort Breckenridge to dispatch two troops of cavalry to the assistance of Bascom's force. Assistant Surgeon B. J. D. Irwin, who was to accompany them at once, volunteered to take a small but picked number of men through the Apache Pass direct to Fort Breckenridge, about 100 miles north of Buchanan. Fourteen reliable infantrymen were selected for the hazardous service. James Graydon, a discharged soldier, who was ever ready for an adventure, joined the party, which, mounted on mules, set out in the face of a heavy snow-storm on February 13.

"THEY WERE TIED TO THE WHEELS AND BURNED TO DEATH."

As 100 miles had to be traversed to reach the pass, two days were required to accomplish the weary and fatiguing journey, sixty-five miles of which—to Dragoon Spring—were made during the first day's march. On the Second day, February 14, while crossing the plain west of the Chiricahua range, a party of Indians, evidently returning from a raid, were discovered driving a herd of cattle and horses. They were pursued, and after a long and exciting chase, including a running fight of several miles, abandoned the stock, consisting of some thirty ponies and forty cattle, all of which, with three Indian warriors, were captured. Knowing that Bascom's party was short of provisions, it was determined to drive the animals along, as well as for the further reason that, in the event of being attacked within the pass, escape would be facilitated through the desire of the enemy to stampede and recapture the large drove. The prisoners were secured and every precaution taken for defense while passing through the long and tortuous canyon leading to where Bascom's party was beleaguered.

On arriving at the entrance of the canyon a train of five wagons was found plundered and burned in the road. To the partially consumed wagon wheels the naked remains of eight human bodies were lashed—the unfortunate and unsuspecting victims having been captured, stripped, tied to the vehicles and then slowly tortured to death by the burning of the outfit.

By a fortunate incident the little party under Irwin escaped destruction, which would have been inevitable had the Indians guarded the western entrance to the pass. After the success the Indians had in driving off the stock from the spring they drove the animals out on the west side of the mountain range, and, while running them to the northwest they discovered a company of infantry on the march changing station from Fort Breckenridge to Fort Bliss, on the Rio Grande. Suspecting that that force was marching to the east side of the pass for the purpose of attacking them in the rear, they followed that command and thereby left the western entrance unguarded.

The arrival of the relief party at the mail station was hailed with shouts of joy, as it was feared that they had been intercepted and wiped out. The wounded were attended, and two days later, on the arrival of two troops of cavalry, a scout through the southern part of the mountain range was made, but on seeing the concentration of troops for their punishment the Indians had vanished in various directions. Two more days were spent in seeking the camp or village of Cochise, which was found and destroyed. While on the march in quest of his home a flock of buzzards was observed some distance to the right of the trail leading to the chief's favorite camping ground, and on riding over to the place from where the birds had flown the ghastly remains of six human bodies, upon which the vultures had been banqueting, were discovered. The evidence was indubitable that the skeletons were those of the unfortunate Wallace and his companions and three other prisoners who had fallen into the power of the savages.

It was then and there determined to execute an equal number of Indian warriors confined at the mail station in retaliation.

The punishment was an extreme mode of reprisal, but was demanded and justified by the persistent acts of treachery and the atrocious cruelties perpetrated by the most treacherous and intractable tribe of savages infesting the territory.

When some six months after the events related the same troops again traversed the pass the bodies of the Indians executed still dangled in the oaks over the graves of the murdered men, and the debris of the train burned at the entrance to the canyon gave sad evidence of the devilish work perpetrated at that point before the execution of the Indian warriors.

By the untiring energy and perseverance of such officers as Generals Crook, Crawford, Lawton, Gatewood, David, Maus, Wood and others, the Chiricahuas were finally brought to bay, and through the efforts of General Miles were transported from the scenes made memorable by the perpetration of their diabolical cruelties.

THE MINNESOTA MASSACRE

THE Minnesota Massacre, perpetrated by Winnebago and Blackfeet Sioux in August, 1862, on the Upper Minnesota, ranks among the darkest and bloodiest episodes in the life-destroying struggle between Indian and white man on the Northwestern frontier. The saddest feature of it was that this wholesale butchering of some 700 whites of all ages and sexes was undoubtedly the result of the shameful unscrupulousness and dishonesty of some of the representatives of our Government in the latter's immediate dealings with the savages of those regions.

The treaty which existed between the Indians and the United States as to lands abandoned by the former in Minnesota, stipulated that the sum granted by our Government was to be paid annually in gold, per head of their members, to the tribes concerned. Those Indians, like most of the red men of those days, knew the value of money, and, furthermore, being superstitious, would not touch or accept paper money. In accordance with their wishes, it was promised that they should receive their annuties in gold.

When pay-day arrived, in 1862, the Indians were assembled in the two agencies, the Upper and Lower Agency of the Upper Minnesota Valley. The paymaster was present and began with the paying of that part of the annuity that consisted of "naturalia" and "materialia," ammunition, blankets, and so forth. When this was finished, the official produced paper money to settle the cash account. The Indians promptly refused to accept it. In vain were they told that the paper had the same practical value as gold. They were not to be convinced. Finally they were quieted with the promise that the paymaster would go back to fetch gold and would return in a short time.

Weeks passed and no paymaster returned. The Indians grew restless. Not only their belief in having been cheated, but their actual want, rendered them unusually excited. Add to this that the traders in the agencies denied them credit, that the buffalo was not to be found in that region at this time of the year, and the need in the villages of the Indians grew daily, until finally the bucks had to go begging at the settlements. The farmers, mostly Germans, gave them willingly what they had to spare, hoping thus to keep on good terms with the starving and despairing red men.

Soon after there came warnings that serious trouble was to be expected from the Indians. A fair-minded Indian by the name of Other Day brought word to some settlements that his kinsmen were holding secret gatherings in which the protests against the faithlessness of the white men grew louder and more menacing every day, and that an outbreak was immediately pending. Other Day ran the risk of being declared a traitor to his kin; from the last and decisive meeting of his red brethren he had to flee, leaving his hat and coat behind. He arrived at the Upper Agency, which was farthest away from the nearest point of possible refuge, and saved sixty white people, men, women and children, by leading them over out-of-the-way tracks to a point of safety.

The Civil War, which was then raging in its most fearful intensity, had necessarily deprived this Northwestern country of almost all military protection. The whole effective force of the defense on the entire frontier from Pembina to the Iowa line did not exceed 200 men, and most of them militia.

There were thirty soldiers at Fort Ridgley, thirty at Fort Ripley, and a company of some fifty men at Fort Abercrombie, the rest scattered in similarly small details along the line.

On August 17, 1862, the Chiefs Little Crow, Little Priest and the ill-reputed Inkpaduta, a Winnebago marauder, met in council and decided to cut loose.

Now it was learned that an uprising had taken place at the agency, and most all whites there killed and their properties destroyed. The savages had immediately branched out and were on their way to capture and destroy New Ulm. They were coming in large bands on all roads and murdered and pillaged whatever came into their way.

The little town of New Ulm, founded by Germans, was the main settlement, and distant about eighteen miles from Fort Ridgley. The inhabitants of this place and the surrounding settlers, mostly Germans and Scandinavians, had not the slightest fear of an outbreak, as they had all aided the distressed and starving Reds to their best ability and felt sure of their friendship.

On the 17th of August the citizens of this peaceful town were startled by the appearance of a company of volunteers, mostly half-breed Indians, which had been mustered in by Uncle Sam's officials for the protection of the agencies. This troop was escorting one of the foremost government officials, who declared that urgent business called him to Fort Snelling, 100 miles away. It was hardly credible that

NEW ULMER CITIZENS BEHIND BARRICADES.

this man was not informed of the coming storm; anyway he took the greater part of the protecting force, which was insignificant enough as a whole, away with him.

On the 18th of August a fleeing white man aroused the people of New Ulm, with the terrifying cry that the Indians were on the warpath and were coming. At his heels came fugitives, men, women, children, pouring into the little town, helpless, half dead from fright and exhaustion.

On the forenoon of this day a recruiting party for the United States Army had left New Ulm in wagons, with a band, to go to Milford, a small town some eight miles away. This party was just crossing a bridge over a gully near Milford, when a volley was fired into them from the surrounding bushes, and three of the people in the first wagon fell dead to the ground; they were the first victims of the Indians from New Ulm. Several others were wounded; the remnant of the party, taking their wounded with them, fled back to the town, where one of the neighboring settlers, who had watched the dastardly murder from a distance, had preceded them with the alarming news.

The New Ulmers now felt that time was precious and hurried to the utmost in establishing a defense. The sheriff appointed a courageous citizen, Jacob Nix, as commandant of the town, and all the available men were organized. They formed three companies, one of rifles, under Louis Theobold, another one of men with double-barreled shot guns, under E. F. Brunk, and a third one, under J. Chaikowitz, armed with all sorts of guns, mostly old-fashioned. Besides there were some twenty men with guns, who wished to act independently. As a reserve they had a number of men with hay-forks and similar weapons.

Barricades were erected in haste at the extremities of the main streets. New Ulm, with its 1,000 inhabitants, was not to be easily defended, the 200 houses being rather widely scattered. Within a day some 600 women and children had arrived as fugitives.

On the afternoon of the 19th the alarming news was spread that a party of farmers from near Cottonwood had been cut off on their way to New Ulm and was now being surrounded by the Indians about a mile from the town. Theobold's sharpshooters were despatched to the scene, and later on Brunk's company too, to bring the endangered party in.

This news of the Cottonwooders, however, had been a "canard," which came near settling the fate of the New Ulmers. The dispatched men had hardly been away half an hour, when the Indians were sighted by Engineer Brockmann, stationed with a telescope on top of a brick building. The savages, with infernal yells, immediately rushed upon the town. They made for one of the barricades behind which the greater part of the tiny force of defenders was lying. The ensuing fusillade proved serious enough; the citizens lost two dead and several wounded.

The situation became most desperate. The few men already contemplated plans to kill their women and children and themselves before allowing the red devils to take them prisoners, when a dispatched detail, on its return, brought help, just in the nick of time. Deployed as skirmishers, the undaunted men, mostly former citizens from Cincinnati and experienced sharpshooters, attacked the savages from the rear and scattered them, for the time being, in all directions. Soon the detached men united with those within the town, and fresh hope was instilled in the brave little band.

The renewed attacks of the Indians grew more reckless and daring, and the ammunition of the citizens began to run short. The women gathered casks of shot from the different stores and melted the lead into lumps from which they casted bullets for the rifles. The loss of the whites had now reached a serious proportion, and it took all the courage and steadfastness of the leaders to keep up the spirits of their men.

It was at 4:30 in the afternoon, when an unforeseen ally in the shape of a thunderstorm broke loose with all the force peculiar to the electric storms of this region. It grew dark, and the superstitious Indians, taking this explosion of the forces of nature as a bad omen, lost heart and withdrew. At 5 o'clock the firing had ceased. During the fight the Indians had managed to set fire to six houses.

The citizens, and especially their leaders, Roos and Nix, who had served against Indians as leaders of militia companies before, knew that the red men would leave them alone during the night, so these hours were devoted to the wounded and the women and children, who during the day had been gathered and taken care of by Dr. C. Weschke. The defenses were also strengthened.

It was estimated that over 900 Indians had been in the attack of the 19th. It proved afterwards that their repulse by the brave little band of settlers decided the fate of the Upper Minnesota Valley. Had New Ulm fallen, the next important town, Mankato, twenty-eight miles below New Ulm, and situated in grounds entirely unfavorable for any defense, would have undoubtedly shared the same fate; the red men would have been masters of the valley.

In the morning it was found that the Indians had left and were on their way to capture Fort Ridgley. The joy of the inhabitants may better be imagined than described. A feeling of safety came over the harassed population, strengthened through the arrival of twenty-five mounted citizens from St. Peter and the neighboring country, under Captain Bordman. This detail came in on the evening of the 19th, just after the firing had ceased and was enthusiastically received.

But the country surrounding New Ulm did not escape as luckily as the little town. All the farms and settlements were heaps of ruins, the inhabitants were massacred, the women having suffered outrages too horrible to describe.

Fort Ridgley, garrisoned by Captain Marsh and one company of the Fifth Minnesota Volunteers, received the first news of the Indians being on the warpath, from the Upper Agency, some forty miles above the fort, which asked for help. Brave Captain Marsh took fifty men and started forthwith, Before the command reached the Lower Agency, which was situated about twelve miles above the fort, they had gathered in a great number of fugitives, mostly women and children, who had taken temporary refuge in the cornfields. At the ferry, running between the two banks of the Minnesota, the little band of soldiers ran into an ambush; thirty-seven men, among them Captain Marsh, were killed; the remaining thirteen men reached the fort. The command here then fell to a sergeant of the regular army, by the name of Jones. He had about twenty men left, including the survivors from Captain Marsh's detachment.

But re-enforcements arrived; armed farmers, some of them ex-soldiers, flocked into the fort for protection, and a company, under Lieutenant Sheenah, ordered back from Fort Ripley, reached Ridgley at about the same time. Besides there were some field-pieces left by the former garrison, which formed the most important part of the defense.

On the 20th the redskins were discovered in front of the fort and proceeded to the attack. They had no chance of success here. Although the garrison suffered a loss of several killed and many wounded, the sound of the cannon soon took all the heart out of the Indians. They retreated in the afternoon, taking, according to their fashion, their dead and wounded with them. Their loss could, therefore, not be ascertained, but was estimated at from fifty to seventy.

Meanwhile the menaced New Ulm had received more re-enforcements; armed detachments from St. Peter and Mankato arrived at midnight of the 19th, under the command of the worthy Judge Flandreau, who was one of the most esteemed settlers in the district. The command of New Ulm was transferred to him. During the night and the following day more aid arrived.

The Indians, however, did not appear again until the 23d of August, when, undaunted by their second repulse before Ridgley, they renewed the attack upon New Ulm. At 10 o'clock in the forenoon they began to advance under cover of the smoke of fired fields and outlying buildings. In their first effort they succeeded in taking possession of the Turner Hall, a building on a rise of ground overlooking the town. It was a commanding position. Not far from this building and on the same elevation was a large wind-mill, occupied by the commands from Mankato and Le Sueur. These held the enemy in check and were supported by citizens holding the postoffice, a brick structure, which afforded good covering against the deadly fire of the savages, who were splendidly armed and seemed to be amply supplied with ammunition.

The south and southeast sides of the town were the weakest points in the defense, and cunning Little Crow, the chief who directed the hostiles again on this occasion, was not slow in noticing it. The southeast side was formed by the German Park, a piece of ground then covered with high grass, just the place where the red men could display the cleverest side of their warfare. They were soon thick in this park and managed to push forward towards Minnesota Street until they reached abandoned houses in the latter street, from which they opened a deadly fire into the center of the town.

Towards noon two men, Captain Dodd from St. Peter and a former German soldier by the name of Krieger, of Milford, attempted a daring reconnoissance in that direction. They had hardly galloped 200 yards before they were both shot. Krieger managed to ride back to town, but Dodd had to be rescued by a party of daring citizens, of whom one paid with his life for his devotion. Dodd died after a few hours, Krieger succumbed to his wounds after several months of suffering.

The Indians were gaining ground step by step. Towards 4 o'clock they occupied a large blockhouse at the southwest corner of Minnesota and Center Streets. This was the strongest position in that part of the town. The conviction forced itself upon the defenders that they must drive the enemy from it or perish. Judge Flandreau and Captain Nix gathered some seventy men and made a most desperate attack on the redskins, some 200, who were in this blockhouse. The savages were driven out, but the attackers lost five killed and eighteen wounded.

It was now necessary to sacrifice all the outlying buildings by firing them, in order to deprive the enemy of the chance of again gaining strong positions. The great glow of the burning town was a magnificent sight that night.

Later on in the morning the Indians in the Turner Hall, anticipating correctly a determined attack by the settlers, fired the building and fled.

Then firing on their side ceased entirely, and the besieged commenced to fight the flames. The greater part of the town was in ruins. Only the center, where the women, children and wounded were sheltered, remained—not more than thirty houses.

On the 24th of August the Indians were held at bay and withdrew. But the besieged found their stay in the ruined city unsafe, and, although some of them bravely objected, an organized exodus of the whole population took place on the 26th of August. The column reached Mankato the next morning, without further hardship.

The Indians, after being twice repulsed, did not show up again before New Ulm, which was reached and occupied by Captain Dean and a company of United States volunteers on the 27th.

On the 29th of August the inhabitants began to return; the first ones finding troops and not Indians in possession of the destroyed town.

Details of affairs at Fort Ridgley were then learned, which disclosed the fact that the Indians had again retreated to that place and had made a most determined assault, which had forced the besieged garrison to seek shelter within the buildings and every spot where concealment against the shower of bullets was possible.

Probably five hundred Indians were engaged in the assault. There had been no time to construct any defensive works, or to remove or destroy the wooden structures or haystacks behind which the enemy could take position and shelter. And to render the situation of the beleaguered garrison still more critical, the magazine was situated some twenty rods outside the main works on the open prairie. Men were at once detailed to take the ammunition into the fort. This perilous duty was performed while Indian bullets rained across the open space over which they had to pass, until the last ounce was safely within the barracks.

Many deeds of bravery were exhibited during this fight and the men, although wounded, would not leave their places even when ordered to do so by their commander.

The fight continued until dark, the artillery all the while shelling the ravine at close range, and the rifles and muskets of the men dropping the yelling demons like

"ALTHOUGH WOUNDED, THE MEN WOULD NOT LEAVE THEIR PLACES."

autumn leaves. Meantime the Indians had gotten into some of the old outbuildings and had crawled up behind the haystacks, from which they poured heavy volleys into the fort. A few well-directed shells from the howitzers set fire to their places of shelter, and when night closed over the scene the bright light of the burning buildings shot up with a fitful glare, revealing to the watchful eye of the sentinel the head of each one of the foe as soon as it appeared. The Indians retired with the closing day, and were seen in large numbers on their ponies, making toward the agency.

All the vast region over which the savage up to this time had carried desolation and death was abandoned by the inhabitants who survived. During that entire week, over all that wide region, the midnight sky was red with the flames of burning buildings and stacks. In two days a population of 30,000, scattered over some eighteen counties on the western border of the state, on foot and horseback, with teams of oxen and horses, under the momentum of panic, had fled to places of safety.

After the described attacks the red devils retreated towards the northwest, their path being marked by death and destruction. Several small villages were burned to the ground, sharing the fate of New Ulm.

United States troops were now on their way to put an end to such atrocities. Fourteen hundred soldiers, under command of Colonel H. H. Sibley, were hurried from Fort Snelling in pursuit of Little Crow and his followers. A succession of desperate fights on both sides followed, which always ended in favor of the troops. Such defeats as were inflicted upon the Indians at the battle of Birch Coolie, which was the most bloody of any in which the forces were engaged, and also that at Wood Lake, where 300 Indians were terribly cut up by the troops, put an end to all hopes which Little Crow had entertained.

A large number of his warriors, and especially those of the Wapeton tribe, surrendered, but the notorious chief and his outlaws managed to escape and continued the war until the following year. Deprived of all comfort and deserted by his followers, he roamed through the woods and prairies, accompanied only by his son, until fate brought him before the gun of a white hunter, whose bullet finished his bloody career.

Had Little Crow been caught alive, his fate would have been the same as that of the ringleaders of the outbreak, thirty-eight of whom, after having received a regular trial, were hanged on one gallows. The hanging of these thirty-eight murderers at the same time was most gruesome, yet picturesque, and the punishment administered to the tribes thereby bore the best of results, as it taught them that every crime would be punished as it deserved

THE CHIVINGTON BUTCHERY

THE Minnesota massacre had matured an intense feeling for revenge in the white man against the Indian. The question as to where was the real right or wrong found seldom a place for consideration in these strifes; it was simply a matter of to be or not to be between the frontier settlers and the red man beyond.

Consequently a force set out into the Platte country as soon as the slackened strain of the ebbing of civil war granted a chance.

This force, amounting to 750 cavalry and artillery, started one night late in November, 1864, from Bison Basin towards the northwest. The weather was so bitterly cold that old trapper Jim Beckwith, the guide, gave out and a half-breed had to take his place.

After a march of some 200 miles the head of the column came upon the village of 120 Cheyennes and eight Arapahoe lodges, stretching along the bank of a little river, the Sand Creek.

The command bore down upon this hapless camp just before sunrise; only a few of the redskins had risen from their night's rest when the clattering of the cavalry became noticeable in the distance.

The camp was practically surprised, and the enraged soldiery proceeded to one of the most merciless butcheries ever committed by white men in recent times. Not only were the women and children ruthlessly destroyed, but, if reports of eye-witnesses may be trusted, there were numerous cases of scalping of murdered women and even children, and many of those who tried to surrender were shot down like animals and mutilated in a manner rivalling the brutality of the red man himself.

Two squaws and five children were the only prisoners taken. About 300 Indians were slaughtered, half of whom were women and children.

The loss of the whites was seven killed and forty-seven wounded, seven of the latter mortally.

The ferocious acts on the part of the white soldiery at this bloody affair had naturally much to do with the subsequent relentless fierceness which the red tribes of the Northwest showed during the intense struggle lasting all through the latter sixties, the seventies and eighties, and ending with the battle at the Wounded Knee in 1891.

The man who planned and superintended this ill-renowned and atrocious deed on the Sand River was Colonel I. M. Chivington of the First Colorado Cavalry, under whose name it is generally known.

SAVED FROM STARVATION

CHARLES L. THOMAS,
Sergeant Co. E, Eleventh Ohio Cavalry.
Born in Philadelphia, Pa., February 12, 1843.

THE Powder River expedition, lasting from June 20 to October 7, 1865, was planned to punish the various Indian tribes, notably the Sioux, Comanches, South and North Cheyennes, the Arapahoes, Kiowas and Apaches, who were continually harassing and obstructing the newly opened Platte and Arkansas overland routes. Only a month before the expedition started the Indians had attacked a train on the Arkansas River, killed five men and robbed and destroyed the train. A station on the Smoky Hill route was attacked, stages were burned and cattle and stock carried off. Every day brought news of some act of hostility and treachery on the part of the Indians, and summary action became imperative.

The situation in reference to Indian matters about this time was a peculiar one. The Indians complained of great wrongs inflicted upon them by their agents. Some of the tribes claimed that they had received the government annuity but once within the past ten years, and they knew that it had been sent them regularly.

Other tribes asserted, with much apparent truthfulness, that they had received only a moiety of what was intended for them. It was, as General G. M. Dodge expressed it, dishonestly frittered and speculated away by agents. This, of course, bred hatred and incited the Indians to many of their outrages.

Previously treaties were made which neither party would carry out, and were therefore easily broken. A spirit of independence and rebellion had grown up among the tribes, which manifested itself in ever-increasing atrocities. Life and property of the white man were nowhere safe in sections where any of the above-mentioned tribes were located.

Such was the situation at the time of the Powder River expedition, which was conducted by Major-General Dodge. The plan of the expedition was this:

General P. E. Connor was to move against the northern Indians in three columns; General J. B. Sanborn in three columns against the southern Indians, and two separate columns were to move to the country between the Platte and Arkansas Rivers to protect the great overland routes.

One of General Connor's three columns, under Colonel Nelson Cole, consisted of eight companies of the Second Missouri Light Artillery, equipped as cavalry, eight companies of the Twelfth Missouri Cavalry and a train of 140 six-mule wagons. The total number of men was about 1,400. The artillery comprised one section of three-inch rifled guns, manned by men of the Second Missouri Light Artillery.

On July 1 this command took up the line of march towards Columbus, on the Loup Fork of the Platte, following the line of the Pacific telegraph. From Columbus the route left the Platte and followed up the north bank of the Loup, leaving the last vestige of civilization at the Pawnee Mission, 110 miles from Omaha.

After passing the Mission a lieutenant's escort brought dispatches from General Connor containing full instructions as to the destination and route of the columns, which up to then were not known.

It was unquestionably an act of prudence on the part of either General Dodge or General Connor to have kept the leader and men in ignorance as to the nature of the expedition. For, had they known in advance through what desolate country they were to march, what obstacles they were to overcome, what deprivations they were to suffer, many of them who now started on the march with cheerful heart and expectant mood might have hesitated to participate in the hardships, and Colonel Cole's difficulty would have been increased a hundred-fold.

After much hardship they reached the Loup River, where wood, water and grass were found in plenty, and with few exceptions scarcely any serious obstacles to the march were encountered. Anticipating the frequent use of tools in the construction of bridges and cutting of embankments, a company of the Second Missouri Light Artillery was organized as a pioneer company. By keeping this company some distance in advance with the guides the road was prepared with sufficient dispatch to occasion but little delay in the movement of the column. After the first 150 miles had been traversed few creeks or rivulets emptied into the river. Near the head of the Loup the wood gave out entirely and the command was forced to resort to buffalo chips, of which a very limited quantity could be found.

Serious misgivings as to the practicability of moving the command across the country, which according to the best information obtainable was a barren, sandy desert, without fresh water, wood or grass, were harbored by the commander, and two parties were sent out, one on Lieutenant Warren's trail and another to the north or most direct line to the Niobrara River, to reconnoitre. The former reported an impassable route, the latter a practicable one with grass and water in abundance.

The latter course was adopted. This part of the country consisted of ridges from 200 to 500 feet in height, of deep, loose sand, which made the draught heavy on the mules, necessitating the frequent dismounting of the men, and the pulling of the guns and the army wagons with drag ropes. Continuous marches brought the command to the head of Antelope Creek, and thence it proceeded to the White Earth River; from there through Les Mauvais Terres to the South Fork of the Cheyenne River. Recent rains rendered the crossing of this stream very difficult. The banks were submerged and made almost impassably miry, compelling the construction of corduroy roads before the trains could be gotten over. Here, not far from camp, was discovered the first trail of a small party of Indians, indicating the recent passage of some roving band. On the march through the Bad Lands they had found no water fit for· use until reaching the South Fork of the Cheyenne, but here again there was a scarcity of grass.

Many trails, evidently five or six days old, of parties of from five to fifteen Indians were seen; older and heavier trails, tending down the valley, were observed, denoting it to be one of their highways.

Scurvy had now become prevalent in the command, and the absence of the usual scorbutic remedies resulted in many fatal cases.

From here to the westward the troops moved over a gently undulating country, without water, save that in a couple of holes, which, with its brackish taste and thick consistency, was almost unfit for use. It was nearly night when the head of the column arrived at the edge of a cliff in sight of the Powder River. This cliff was hundreds of feet in height and no place of descent could be found. It seemed utterly impossible to traverse the rough and broken country, and it was decided to move into the valley of O'Fallon's Creek, where, happily, a small pool containing possibly half a dozen barrels of brackish water, which the buffalo had been within a short time wallowing in, was discovered. The intense heat of the day, along with the dust-laden air, had created too strong a thirst among the men to cause them to hesitate at drinking the water discovered, although it was impregnated with the excrement of these animals. Of forage there was none to be had, and the stock had to be tied up the entire night without water or grass.

At 3 o'clock the next morning they moved to the edge of the cliffs again, where the guides discovered an Indian trail leading down to the lower plain. By cutting along this path, across divides and through canyons the trains were advanced about three miles that day. It was necessary, however, to station men on the sides of the hills with ropes to steady the wagons, which were frequently on the point of upsetting upon the mules or sliding sideways down the numerous precipices along the brinks of which they were compelled to pass.

The following day was intensely hot, and the great labor of working through canyons and over masses of rock, ofttimes necessitating the men to dismount and pull the fieldpieces and wagon by drag-ropes, together with the excessive dust, intensified the weariness and exhaustion of the entire command. The valley was reached at a point about fifty miles from the Yellowstone River.

The instructions given by General Connor were to proceed to Panther Mountains, at the base of which, on the Tongue River, there was to be found a depot of supplies. Rations by this time were nearly exhausted, and it was necessary to communicate with the general as soon as possible to procure a fresh supply. To expedite this Lieutenant Hoagland, Second Missouri Light Artillery, with Raymond, a most reliable guide, and a detachment of twenty men, was sent to scout across the Tongue River, to ascertain the best route by which to move the column; also, if possible, at what point General Connor was lying with his command.

The scouting party returned September 1st. They had traveled fifty miles and reported no depot of supplies in sight, nor any indication of any having been around there at any time before. Panther Mountains were simple masses of red volcanic rock without the slightest sign of vegetation.

Upon the receipt of this report the rations were ordered to less than one-half. No Indians, nor any traces of any, had lately been seen.

Presently a report was brought that the Indians had attacked the men herding stock a mile distant from the camp and had driven off some of the animals. Immediately the entire command was ordered out, save sufficient to guard the camp.

HAULING THE FIELD PIECES BY DRAG ROPES.

The advance engaged the Indians and succeeded in recovering most of the captured stock. Captain Rowland, Second Missouri Light Artillery, with a party of seven men, reached the ground first and pressed the Indians closely, killing a number of them. He was pursuing one of the small detached bands when another party of about forty-five suddenly dashed upon him and his men from a ravine to their right and killed or mortally wounded all of the small detachment, with the exception of Captain Rowland himself.

When the main body of the command reached the scene of action, the Indians fell back out of sight rapidly, and the troopers, with their broken down horses, could not pursue. The result was a loss of four men killed and two mortally wounded.

The greatest bodies of Indians were seen in the direction of the Little Missouri River and the most of them retreated along the trail through the "Bad Lands." During the afternoon a column of smoke was seen distinctly rising toward the mouth of the Powder River. Knowing that there were hostile Indians in the neighborhood, the commander felt satisfied that there was a large body of warriors or a village on the Yellowstone River. It was concluded that the smoke was evidently a signal made by the Indians, or else General Connor, unable to get down the Tongue River Valley on account of its barrenness, had availed himself of the fertile valley of the Big Horn to reach the Yellowstone and was endeavoring to attract attention by signal fires. Either case being true, it was the proper course to pursue to move in that direction, especially since it was expected to find there game in plenty and with sufficient buffalo to feed the command.

On the morning of September 2d they crossed to the west bank of the river and followed the trail of Colonel Walker, Sixteenth Kansas, who marched about three miles ahead of the main force, through a country that offered nothing but cottonwood bark for forage.

After marching for about twenty-five miles, scouts were sent out to examine the territory. The waters of the stream sank into the sand about eight miles away and the bed was comparatively dry. The Indian trails scattered and were lost in the quicksands of the river, where the horses could not for an instant control themselves. During the night a terrible storm set in, a kind of storm that is liable to sweep over this country in any season and during which the temperature of the atmosphere suddenly changes from intense heat to extreme cold. The want of nourishing forage, the exhaustion from the intense heat of the day's march, together with the effects of the storm, proved fatal to a large number of horses. Very reluctantly the command turned back on the next morning, September 3d, to the point where they started and where they could at least find some grass for the dying stock. During this march down the river and back to grass 225 horses and mules died, and in consequence a number of wagons had to be destroyed, as also a considerable amount of now superfluous quarermaster's stores.

On the following morning Indians were discovered in large numbers in the hills to the west.

Larger detached parties showed themselves on the adjacent hills and many hundreds were discovered in the ravines beyond, who thus far had not shown themselves. Large bodies also moved up the valley toward the south and a considerable force manœuvred on the east bank of the river.

The Indians made efforts to attract small parties of men from camp and frequent attempts to get at the horses of the men who were on foot on the skirmish line, but the gallantry of the men and the excellence of the Spencer arm invariably frustrated these designs.

On one hill a large number of them had collected; a red flag and the constant use of their signal glass — a piece of looking glass flashed in the sun — denoted it to be their headquarters. Guns were trained on that particular spot, which drove the Indians out of sight. Continuing up the river on September 8th, Colonel Walker, who was still three miles in advance of the main body, sent information that he was being attacked by between 3,000 and 4,000 Indians, who were driving him back. The command was rapidly pushed forward, and by quick action drove the Indians in all directions, then the river was crossed and a camp was formed of both commands.

After getting into camp a storm blew up, which grew worse as night came on and finally became terrific in its fury. From rain it turned to hail, then in succession it snowed and sleeted, yet freezing all night long. Picket officers were forced to march their men in circles at the reserve posts to prevent them from being frozen to death, as fires were not admissible. Nothing could be done to protect the stock from the peltings of this terrible storm, and whole numbers of them died during the night. When daylight dawned it had not abated in the least, and owing to the unsheltered position of the camp was especially severe on the men as well as the stock, so much so that it was determined to move to some point within a few miles where shelter could be secured in heavy timber to save the remnant of the rapidly failing animals. Two miles and a half of march route were marked with dead and dying horses and mules. During the thirty-six hours of the storm 414 animals perished at the picket ropes or along the roads between the camps.

On September 10th the command was compelled to cross the river under cover of artillery fire, for the Indians had, vulture-like, hovered around the exhausted and starving command and made a detour around to a position on the bluff in the rear, prepared to dash down and finish up. However, a generous amount of shells thrown among them kept them at a respectful distance.

Fatigue and starvation had now done their work on both men and stock so that they were unfit to pursue the savage foe that circled around their starving way through this desert. The rations by this time had been reduced to less than quarter rations, and the horse and mule flesh was used to sustain life.

At this critical juncture there appeared like a messenger from heaven a stranger —a mere youth—in Colonel Cole's camp, and by his timely arrival and valuable information, of which he was the bearer, an entire command was saved from an almost inevitable fate of death and destruction.

This man was Sergeant Charles L. Thomas of Company E, Eleventh Ohio Cavalry. He came, a courier from General Connor, to apprise Colonel Cole of the proximity of the general's camp and point out a way of safety amidst the dangers that beset the colonel and his helpless troops and lead him along an avenue of escape.

How the wonderful feat of the brave soldier, whose presence seemed like a miracle to the downcast command, was accomplished, and for which a Medal of Honor was awarded him, is told in the hero's own narrative, as follows:

"We had marched 400 miles northeast to the Powder River, established a stockade fort called Fort Connor, at a base of supplies, proceeded in the same direction to Clear Creek, where another fort—Fort Carney—was constructed, and marched to the junction of the Tongue with the Yellowstone River, where on August 22d our scouts reported the location of a large Indian village. A detachment was sent after daybreak to attack the habitation, which was pillaged, burned and destroyed, many Indians being killed and about 700 horses and mules captured.

"Our chief guide was a Major Bridge, and a better guide or better posted pilot through this territory could not have been found, for he had spent forty-two years of his life in this section and among the Indians. In fact, he had a wife in every tribe and children galore.

"On September 7th we reached the Yellowstone River, where we were to meet Colonel Cole's command.

"Not finding the division at this place, General Connor was greatly concerned and worried as to its whereabouts, because he knew that by this time Colonel Cole would have exhausted his rations and feared that he was in a serious plight. Scouting parties were at once sent out, but they all returned and reported the surrounding country full of swarming Indians, to such an extent, even, that it was impossible for a small command to get to the Powder River. Reports also came in to the effect that artillery firing, the roar of cannons, could be heard distinctly somewhere along the river. All agreed that no human help could reach Colonel Cole, as he was surrounded and completely hemmed in by thousands of Indians.

"General Connor knew that Colonel Cole must be apprised of the location of his own camp and base of supplies or perish with his entire force, even should he escape the clutches of the 6,000 or 7,000 Indians.

"He asked for volunteers to go to the colonel's relief.

"On the morning of September 12th I went to the general and offered my services. General Connor was pleased.

"'Go get your breakfast, fill your canteen with coffee, take some buffalo-jerk and all the ammunition you can carry, and prepare yourself for your journey. I expect there will be others to join you,' he said.

"I did as he bade me and waited, but not another man came forward to undertake the mission.

"General Connor ordered me to appear before him, and, emphasizing the dangers of the task I had volunteered to accomplish, asked me if I still was willing to carry out an undertaking so hazardous, yet, if successful, so eminently important.

"I said I was. And why shouldn't I? I was young—22 years old—vigorous, considered a good horseman, and admittedly the best shot in the regiment. I was recklessly fearless and could stand almost any amount of hardship. I rather liked an errand like that.

"My captain gave me two of his most reliable Pawnee Indians to take along, as he did not want to see me go alone to my almost certain death.

"We rode out of camp on September 12th, at 8 o'clock in the morning, and for an hour and a half saw no Indians, and then observed only a few who were too far away to shoot at. We rode as fast as the condition of our horses would permit.

"By 3 o'clock we had reached the top of the divide between the rivers and met two Indians with a travis, upon which they carried a wounded warrior. We made them drop their comrade, and one of my Pawnees jumped from his pony, gave his tribe's warwhoop, struck the helpless Indian in the face with the handle of his whip, placed his foot on the brave's neck and in an instant was holding his scalp high in the air. A shot through the head put the finishing touch on the mutilated foe. My proud Pawnee companion then remounted and we rode on, exchanging frequent shots with numerous Indians whom we met on our dashing ride. When darkness fell we could observe the small Indian camp-fires and had no trouble in avoiding them. Yet, I dreaded to encounter a party of these Indians in the dark, and therefore entered the first draw I found leading into the river. How I missed the elbow touch of a white comrade that night. Here I was almost deserted in a wild, unknown country, surrounded by hordes of bloodthirsty Indians riding on madly through the dark, pursued by the hideous howls of the hungry wolf and hostile Indians.

"I reached Powder River just at daybreak. At the mouth of the canyon, along which I and the Pawnees were riding, a horse appeared and immediately afterward an Indian came out from under the shelving rocks where he had been sleeping. He was less than ten feet from me as he raised up, threw his blanket off his shoulder and held his rifle in his left hand. I shot him dead. The incident was sudden and made me and my Pawnees somewhat excited. It was too bad, for had I kept my head a second Indian, who likewise appeared from behind the rocks, would have shared his fate. But this Indian got away by jumping over the embankment, a distance of fifteen feet, and escaping into the dense bushes. We rode for about six miles along the banks of the Powder River. Then in a comparatively cool spot we let our horses drink and rest up a little. Now we could hear distinctly the signal calls of the Indians from six or seven different directions. It was apparent that our presence was known to the Indians, so I decided to push on as fast as I possibly could, realizing that lingering would mean almost certain death with no show for a defense. So riding out into the valley we discovered Colonel Cole's trail leading in a southerly direction, or up the river, and followed this trail, hurrying on our horses to the greatest possible speed. We pushed on unmolested by Indians until about 9 o'clock, when we struck a small stream. The valley below was strewn with carcasses of horses and mules. The sight brought the cold sweat to my brows. I thought Colonel Cole's entire command had been massacred down there, but soon reassured myself when I rode down into the valley and found that there was not a single human corpse among these bodies, and also discovered that the animals had all been shot in the head. Shortly after leaving this ghastly valley I noticed an Indian riding into a chaparral alongside of the trail. There was no way of avoiding an encounter. Neither could we tell whether that Indian was alone. We drew revolvers and charged right past the chaparral. We were immediately followed and fired on by seventeen Indians. Answer was given with shots

"WHAT IN GOD'S NAME ARE YOU DOING HERE?"

from our rifles, which killed one Indian on a horse and drove the others across the river. As we continued on our course, these Indians recrossed and followed in our rear, increasing in number as we proceeded until there were too many of these red-skins on our heels to count. For mile after mile, hour after hour, a hot chase and running fight was kept up. The longer this chase continued the more excited it grew. At every crook and turn in the trail I expected to find Colonel Cole.

"This fighting, running, shooting, chasing at break-neck speed lasted from 10 o'clock in the morning until 3 o'clock in the afternoon. Then, away in the distance where the valley was narrow, I saw a body of men drawn across the trail. I was sure they were men of Colonel Cole's command, and my heart beat faster as I urged my horse on to still greater speed. But what a disappointment when, on coming closer, we found them to be Indians—a large body of Sioux!—and no alternative but to break through that file or fall in the attempt. I realized that some scalping would be done, and rather anticipated that my own head would have to furnish such a trophy. Nevertheless I was determined to sell my life as dearly as possible, and, instructing my faithful Pawnees, rode up to within fifty yards of this line of Indians. Then we fired our rifles at them. One Indian dropped to the ground dead; the others ran hither and thither, opening the way for us to make a swift dash. We dismounted two more warriors, when the rest fled as if Satan himself were on their heels. Still another Indian was struck by our bullets, and he fell off his horse in the trail. He was tied to his pony by a hair lariat and was dragged along for some distance. I separated him from his horse and took the animal to have a remount should my own horse give out or get shot, which I expected every moment.

"I discovered that the Indian's horse I had taken belonged to a member of the Sixth Missouri Cavalry. I still found his letters and pictures in the saddle-pockets. There was also in one of the pockets a tintype picture of the Indian himself and $95 in United States notes. How I longed to scalp this fellow! But my time was too precious to indulge in acts of vengeance. After riding for a short distance I saw a white man lying behind a stone and small sage-bush. I rode up to him.

"'What in God's name are you doing here?' I asked him.

"He stammered, hardly audibly, that he was one of Colonel Cole's command. 'I'm played out. My feet are full of thorns and thistles. Would that the Indians only come and end my misery!'

"I got him on my reserve horse and carried him along. We still had a distance of four miles to cover until we reached camp, and had to fight every inch of our way. It was sundown when we finally arrived at the picket-line. I at once reported to Colonel Cole and was able to direct him to Fort Connor, about 150 miles distant.

"I found the men of the command in a most deplorable condition—they were a starved, disconsented body of men.

"I left Camp Connor with over 350 rounds of ammunition and had 17 shots left when I arrived at Colonel Cole's camp. My horse, which had carried me throughout the expedition, came down with lockjaw the next day, and I was compelled to shoot the faithful animal."

THE FETTERMAN MASSACRE

The rush of settlers to the Northwest, following the disbandment of the large armies of the civil war, made it necessary to build roads in that remote region, the undisputed home of the most warlike tribes of American Indians. To protect these roads forts had to be constructed. Fort Phil Kearney, built by General Carrington in the year 1866, was one of the line of forts intended to protect the Montana Road from the attacks of the Dakotas, or Sioux. At that time the most dreaded savage in the Powder River region was Red Cloud, the leader of the Ogalallas.

Fort Kearney was one of the largest posts ever erected in the wilderness, and was surrounded by an extensive stockade. While the building was in progress the soldiers at work were continually harassed by the roaming savages. The commander of the troops in the fort, which consisted of two small detachments of cavalry and infantry, was Colonel Fetterman. An important part of the military life around the new post was the cutting of the timber for the new buildings and pallisades, and the soldiers had to do this work, so that the protection of these wood-cutting details from the surprises of the hostiles became one of the trying tasks of the garrison.

On December 6, 1866, the wood-cutters were attacked in the timber, two miles from the fort. Colonel Fetterman, who hastened to their aid with a detail of cavalry, was lured into an ambush and escaped from disaster only through the timely arrival of support under General Carrington himself. Lieutenant Bingham and several soldiers were on this occasion killed by the Indians.

On December 21st it became necessary to obtain a large quantity of timber, and a force of some ninety men was detailed to cut it. Colonel Fetterman secured the assent from the general to look after their protection. The wood-cutters had hardly left the stockade when Indians were appearing in the surrounding woods, first in clusters of three and four, but soon in considerable numbers. Only a short time after the wood-cutters had left the lookouts from the signal station reported that the detail was surrounded by savages and had gone into corral to defend itself. Colonel Fetterman started immediately for the relief with a combined force of cavalry and infantry, counting, including himself, three officers and eighty-two soldiers.

The command soon disappeared in the woods and its effect upon the Indians was apparent, when the lookouts from the signal bluff reported that the wood-cutting detail had broken corral and was on its way back.

Nothing was observed of Fetterman's command until, towards noon, heavy firing was heard in the distance. As it kept increasing in intensity, General Carrington sent all the rest of the garrison available towards the sound of the firing. This party reached a ridge from behind which the firing seemed to come. But when the troops were crossing it the firing had ceased.

From the crest of the ridge the soldiers could see dense swarms of Indians in the woods in front, the redskins challenging the troops with provoking boldness to come down and fight. From Fetterman's party nothing could be detected.

The officer in command of the supporting troops went determinedly down and attacked the savages, who retreated after a short and not very vigorous resistance.

After a short advance the soldiers came to a large boulder, and on the ground around this boulder, within a space of perhaps fifty feet square, they found the butchered remains of forty-eight of Fetterman's detachment and the body of the officer himself. Nearly overcome by the ghastly sight, the relief party had had hardly time to count the dead when the Indians came on again in a furious attack. Their numerical superiority was such that the little force was compelled to withdraw back to the fort, which was reached at nightfall.

After this longest of winter nights had passed in depressing dreariness and sorrow for the people in the fort General Carrington went out, as soon as the sun came up, with a detachment of eighty men, determined, if possible, to obtain the full details of the tragedy. This time the Indians were not inclined to resist. The troops reached the fatal spot unmolested. In vain did they send out searching parties for possible survivors; all the searchers found were the bodies of Lieutenant Grummond, two civilian volunteers and thirty-two soldiers lying towards the further end of the divide. Lieutenant Grummond had been in command of the cavalry detachment, the civilians had volunteered in their eagerness to test a couple of Henry rifles, which were at that time a much admired novelty in the Northwest.

Colonel Fetterman and the third officer, Lieutenant Brown, lay close together at the foot of the boulder, each one with a shot through the left temple. This led to the conjecture that in the last moment both took each other's life in order to escape capture and torture. But one cannot help thinking it strange that in the midst of bloody slaughter the swarm of undisciplined savages should have spared the two officers to the last just to give them a chance to escape being taken by blowing each other's brains out.

The bodies were horribly mutilated; such butchery had never been known before, on even Indian murder-fields. The rocks around the fatal spot were strewn with torn-out eyes, knocked-out teeth, hacked-off heads, limbs, ears, noses; the lifeless trunks were filled with arrows; in one of the bodies were counted no less than thirty-seven. This was the devilish work of the Indian boys after their elders had done the killing.

The eighty-five bodies, or rather what remained of them, were buried around the spot where the men had fallen.

Shocking as this horrible massacre was, the climax of the evil-doings of its perpetrators was yet to come. Red Cloud, who instigated this murder and led his bands into committing it, found his own deviltry outstripped by his tribesman, Sitting Bull, when the latter, nearly ten years later, slaughtered brave Custer and his men at Little Big Horn.

THIRTY-TWO AGAINST THREE THOUSAND

WHEN the government in 1866 decided upon the necessity of constructing a road through some of the Indian reservations in Dakota to Montana, consent was obtained from the Sioux, through whose territory the proposed highway was to run. The concession was granted and a treaty signed by all the Sioux chiefs, except one— Red Cloud. He regarded the demand of the "Great Father in Washington" as an invasion and succeeded in gathering about himself a formidable force of Sioux and Cheyennes, upon whom his fierce eloquence, firm attitude and warlike spirit had made a great impression, and who like Red Cloud himself were determined to resist the proposed "invasion" to the bitter end.

In the meantime the government had built in July, 1866, a fort right in the heart of the Sioux domain and called it Fort Phil Kearney. Red Cloud and his hordes placed every obstacle possible in the way of the construction of the fort, attacking small detachments sent out to cut wood, lying in ambush for small details and ready at all times for a coup to annihilate an inferior force. The Fetterman massacre was the sad result of this treacherous conduct.

In February, 1867, Sergeant George Grant, of Company E, Eighteenth United States Infantry, came near falling into the hands of these savages and losing his life, when he voluntarily undertook to deliver a dispatch from the newly constructed fort to Fort C. F. Smith in Dakota. His sufferings from the hardships of very severe weather, lack of food and the dangers of an invisible, yet powerful, merciless enemy made his trip one of the most heroic and the success of his mission a grand achievement.

About the latter part of July of the same year Captain James Powell, of the Twenty-seventh United States Infantry, left the fort with fifty-one men and one officer, Lieutenant J. Jenness, to protect a "wood party," which, under the eye of a contractor, was cutting fuel for the garrison.

The contractor had two encampments of lumbermen, one in the center of a small plain well situated for effective defense, another on the other side of Little Piney Creek, near the foot of the mountains. Both encampments were about a mile apart. The captain detailed part of his soldiers to protect the working parties and to escort the wood trains on their trips to and from the fort.

With wise precaution Captain Powell, who had a force of one lieutenant, twenty-six men and four civilians left at his disposal, made his position on the plain as strong a defense as he could.

He had fourteen empty wagon-beds, top parts of large wagons, the running gears of which were being used to haul wood, which he placed on the ground in such a manner as to form an oval-shaped fort. At the point on each side a wagon on wheels established the connection between the beds. These wagons contained the necessary supplies for the troops.

Red Cloud's warriors were swerving ominously about the vicinity of the corral, but for three days everything was quiet. Then came the clash—the final and last clash, which forever crushed the Indian chief's ambitious hopes.

On August 2, 1867, 200 Indians attacked and drove off the men in charge of the herd attached to the camp; 500 attacked the train on the foot of the mountain, compelling the men to flee, and burning the wagons. A number of soldiers were killed and wounded, few arriving at the fort.

Then followed a concerted attack on Captain Powell's corral. The Indians, numbering some 3,000, were certain of their prey. Indeed, they had brought their squaws along to assist in the torturing of their victims and add zest to their enterprise. As they lined up, garbed in their war costumes of many colors, parading hither and thither, they were a picturesque and repulsive set.

Now the attack began. Captain Powell was fully prepared—each man had his instructions, each his designated post. "Fight for your lives now," was the commander's last admonition before the charge.

Eight hundred Indian horsemen came dashing on with the force of a whirlwind. When they were within 100 yards of the corral, Powell commanded "Fire!" and a sheet of flame from behind the wagon-beds was the answer. Another volley and still another, and of the charging savages nothing could be seen but a mass of dead bodies, and a number of wounded on the ground and a few fleeing in confusion toward the hills. That was the end of the first charge. Red Cloud was watching awe-stricken the destruction wrought to his braves from a mysterious arm so cleverly handled by the soldiers. It was his first acquaintance with the breech-loading gun, which had just been introduced in the army.

He now began to encircle the corral, sending out first his sharpshooters, who, creeping forward, dodging behind stump and boulder, hiding in the hollows, slowly came nearer and nearer to the wagon-beds, and by constant firing occupied the attention of the few defenders. Charge after charge was made, five times in succession, every time with the same result—death and defeat before the murderous gun of the accurately firing soldier. For three long hours did Red Cloud lead his horde of followers before the fatal muzzles of the mysterious gun, but when hundreds of his braves had been slain on the field, hundreds wounded and he had lost nearly half his force either by death or wounds, he desisted from further attack and gave up the hopeless task. He retired to the hills, just as re-enforcements arrived for Captain Powell and his band of heroes, who had lost one officer—Lieutenant Jenness—and five men killed and two wounded.

ON THE ARICKAREE

WHEN after the War of the Rebellion disbanded soldiers and others flocked in great numbers into the northwest and the railroads began to build their lines, the warlike Indian tribes who considered that vast region their own and indisputable territory became greatly aroused. From mere excitement and turbulence to actual aggressiveness it was only a small step with these fierce aborigines. Towards the end of 1866 the situation on the border was ripe for the crisis, and from many signs and sources the military garrisons took their warning and prepared the best they could for the gathering outbreak. The storm center was felt developing within the haughty and powerful Sioux nation, and particularly among the Cheyennes.

At Fort Ellsworth, in Kansas, the commander of the post, General Palmer, had an important conference, a "big talk," with the Cheyenne chieftains, Black Kettle, the superb Roman Nose and some others. The demeanor of the Indians was defiant in the extreme; they declared unanimously that if the building of the railway through their country was not stopped immediately and for good it would be war. "This is the first time," said the towering giant, Roman Nose, "that I shook the white man's hand in friendship; if the railway is continued I shall again be his enemy for evermore." General Palmer was unable to promise anything, but assured the indignant warriors that he would faithfully submit their complaint to the Great White Father in Washington.

The next move on the part of the government was to send General Hancock with a mixed force of some 1,500 troops into the endangered region, with strict orders to avoid bloodshed if possible, but to announce to the Indians in unmistakable terms that they must henceforward refrain from any acts of molestation or depredation, and keep away from the lines of travel.

The Indians' answer was a number of raids and murders committed among the white frontier settlers. All the Cheyennes and Sioux between the Arkansas and Platte went upon the warpath.

In the summer of 1867 General Hancock was relieved by General Phil Sheridan; the latter had on his staff Brevet-Colonel George A. Forsyth, a trusted aide during the civil war, a man of iron will, iron constitution and absolute fearlessness. The emergency required quick action, and General Sheridan directed Forsyth to hire fifty civilians, if possible expert frontiersmen, at the rate of thirty-five dollars per month, each to bring his own horse and equipment, receiving forty-five cents per day for its use, but to be supplied with arms, ammunition and rations by the government. Forsyth did not lose any time and soon had his force in readiness. It was sent out at once to the aid of white settlers between Harbinger Lake and Bison Basin, who were in immediate danger from large Indian war parties. On the march the command, or rather posse, discovered traces of criminal acts of some of these Indians near the head waters of Beaver Creek. Forsyth took up the pursuit of this band, and on the 14th of September his men struck a fresh trail of a large force of hostiles. From all signs their proximity was evident, and the command marched with all necessary precaution. On the afternoon of the 16th the whites had no more provisions left except biscuit for one day, and their leader was extremely anxious to close in with the enemy. Forsyth's good judgment led him into camp on this day at about 5 o'clock, instead of marching on till nightfall. He wanted to give the horses rest and good fodder so that they should be fresh the next day on which he hoped to catch up with the hostiles. It was afterwards found out that only three miles from where he halted the Indians were lying in ambush for him in such a position that had Forsyth run into it his force would undoubtedly have been annihilated.

Forsyth's camp was close to the bank of the Arickaree, a tributary of the Republican. In the middle of the stream, which had a depth of only a few inches, was a sandy island fringed with willows and with a few stunted trees distributed over its surface. The surrounding country was an undulating plain, with the nearest divides about one mile away. The place offered good grazing, and the horses, carefully picketed and under guard, were soon enjoying it. When night came the men lay down near their horses, with arms in hand.

The commander was up and reconnoitering long before daylight. While peering through the gloom of early morning twilight he saw some indistinct figures stealthily creeping over the plain towards his camp. His men were quietly notified that the enemy were coming; everybody secured his horse and prepared for the attack.

Presently the Indians rushed in, howling and shaking blankets and buffalo robes with the intention of stampeding the horses, their usual introductory act at battle. They were not successful; a few well-aimed volleys drove them off. When day broke it was at once seen that the enemy were overwhelmingly superior in numbers, and Colonel Forsyth began forthwith to transfer his camp to the sand island. This was about 200 by 40 feet in extension. The horses were tied to the scanty shrubbery, the men distributed in a circle, and set at once to the digging of rifle pits, which was soon accomplished in the sandy ground. In the meantime a few good marksmen on the main bank of the river kept advancing crowds of hostiles at bay.

Forsyth stood unprotected among his men, and only after several Indian bullets had barely missed him he consented to protect himself in a pit which one of his men had dug.

Shortly after 9 o'clock the Indians proceeded to the first great assault. In the distance the men on the island could distinguish the magnificent Roman Nose by the crimson sash which General Palmer had presented to him on the occasion of his visit at Fort Ellsworth. Roman Nose organized his mounted braves, who were to deal the decisive blow in the attack. Swarms of dismounted Indians, with breech-loading guns of latest pattern, and even boys armed with bows and arrows, preceded the onrush of the mounted force, covering the island with a perfect fusillade of missiles. The men on the island were directed by their leader not to answer this galling fire, and they obeyed to the letter.

Presently the Indian women and children who as spectators fringed the slopes of the flanking elevation, started a terrific, ear-tearing yelling and whooping, and the mass of mounted warriors, with Roman Nose far in the van, came thundering on in all their savage splendor. At about 200 yards from the river they all let loose their unearthly war-whoops and urged their ponies to the utmost speed. Forsyth had warned his men earnestly to wait with their fire until they should hear his command. When the roaring wave of redskins was not farther away than fifty yards the Colonel's command rang out: "Now!" The sharpshooters' bullets crashed into the dense column of horses and men with unerring directness; volley after volley swept with lightning-like rapidity into the fast-moving ranks. The horses went down in rows and the riders fell in heaps. Some bodies of men and horses lay right in the stream, only a few yards from the rifle pits. But the great mass, wavering a moment, split in two under the fearfully telling fire, and, describing wide, flanking curves to the right and left, swept back into safety.

Right in front of the rifle pits, the shallow waters of the Arickaree rippling about the lifeless bodies of rider and horse, lay Roman Nose, the wicked and merciless hater of the pale-face, superb and defiant even in death.

The Indians, discouraged though they were by the collapse of their daring attack, resorted to their boldest tricks to recover the body of this renowned warrior, but the guns on the island held them in check.

Roman Nose's death meant a fatal blow for the hostiles. Twice in the course of the day they repeated the attack, but their energy did not nearly come up to their first effort; both attempts were easily frustrated by the steady hands and the cool heads behind the guns in the sand island's rifle pits.

The brave white men had suffered severely. Lieutenant Beecher, of the Third U. S. Infantry, second in command, having been shot through the abdomen, died in great agony; the doctor of the outfit was killed early in the day; Colonel Forsyth was dangerously wounded in three places. Before 10 o'clock a bullet pierced his right thigh; later another shattered his left leg at the knee, and in the afternoon a third one grazed his skull, scooping the bone. Two other men were dead, two mortally and sixteen more or less severely wounded. Every horse and mule had been killed.

Towards evening a drizzling rain began to fall, adding to the discomfort, dreariness and hopelessness of the situation. Fort Wallace, the nearest place from which help might be obtained, was almost 100 miles away.

But the little band, encouraged by the marvelous example of their leader, did not despair, They dug a well through the sand, stripped meat off the dead horses and mules and strengthened their line of defense with saddles and the bodies of the dead animals. Towards midnight two men, Pierre Trudeau and John Stillwell, left the camp to reach Fort Wallace, if possible, and summon relief. By unusual

"THE INDIANS PROCEEDED TO THE FIRST GREAT ASSAULT."

care, combined with good luck, they accomplished their task. Wearing moccasins they had made from boot-tops and with blankets wrapped around them Indian fashion, they managed to crawl through the lines of the hostiles in the first night, making three miles. The next day they spent lying hidden in a washout between the Arickaree and the South Republican. During the second night they continued their dangerous trip, meeting and avoiding several parties of Indians, and towards daybreak they reached the South Republican. The next day they spent like the first, lying concealed under the river bank; the Indians swarmed all around them, and it was a wonder to themselves that the wily savages failed to discover them. During the third day they were lying in a bison swallow when some scouting Indians came within thirty yards of their cover and Stillwell had to quiet an alarming rattlesnake by spitting tobacco juice on its head. The following night Trudeau, who was an elderly man, came near breaking down. But they kept on, and on the fourth day, towards noon, they met two mounted couriers going to Colonel Carpenter at Lake Station, which was about sixty miles from Forsyth's camp. Colonel Carpenter, as soon as these two men informed him, started with his whole command and relieved Forsyth on the ninth day.

The Indians had given up the siege on the fifth day, but Forsyth's command was by that time in such a state of exhaustion that nobody could move. The relief party found the men helpless and near death, lying among the dead animals in an atmosphere rendered pestilent from the decaying bodies.

The day after Carpenter reached this veritable island of desolation a second relief force arrived from Fort Wallace. The sufferers were transported to the latter place, but some of them never recovered. Scout Trudeau died in the following spring; Forsyth had to have his shattered leg amputated and was put on the retired list.

The Indians said afterwards that their whole force against the fifty men had amounted to 900 warriors, of whom 75 were killed.

EXCITING SCOUT FOR A TRAIL

A PRETTY little Indian story tells of the dangers which beset the explorer who in days not far remote dared to follow an Indian trail.

The scene of action was in picturesque Arizona. The time was in the early spring of 1868 — a few months before the great Indian uprising.

The Apaches had become unruly. They harassed and annoyed the settlers and stole and plundered. An expedition was expected to restore peace and safety and punish the offending savages.

Two cavalry troops, B and L, of the Eighth United States Cavalry, and two companies of the Fourteenth United States Infantry, left Camp Verde, Arizona, some time during the latter part of May, 1868, on their mission. A large pack train, conveying a sufficient supply of rations, ammunition and other accessories to an expedition, greatly impeded the progress of the command, especially since the route itself offered an abundance of obstacles. The destination was the Tonto Basin, where the rebellious Indians were supposed to be in hiding. The march to the edge of the Basin consumed five days. The first stop was made at San Carlos River not far distant from the edge of the basin; just near enough to remind the troops that they were almost within sight of their field of operations, and to make some of the soldiers, who knew the Indians only by reputation, tremble with fear. Seven men of Troop B stole away from camp and deserted.

EDGAR L. ASTON,
Private, Co. L,
8th U. S. Cavalry.

WILLIAM G. CUBBERLY,
Private, Co. L,
8th U. S. Cavalry.

Trouble began at the edge of the basin, which was a mass of gigantic walls of solid rock, with no path or passageway leading to the bottom. Yet the descent had to be made, though it would take nearly all day, and was the occasion of many a thrilling escape from death. The descent began early in the morning; in the evening camp was pitched 4,000 feet down the valley near a running stream.

The presence of the Apaches was soon made known to the troopers, for they announced themselves early in the evening by shooting innumerable arrows into the camp, but without inflicting any damage except to kill a horse.

A detachment of forty cavalrymen was sent after them, but the wily Indians got away and kept out of sight.

On May 27th Troops B and L left the camp at San Carlos River and started on a two days' scouting tour, leaving the infantry and the pack train behind them in camp.

Four cavalrymen were ordered to remain with the pack train: Sergeant Richard Fisher, Corporal William Thomas and Privates Edgar L. Aston and William G. Cubberly.

There was also attached to the train an old trooper, a most original and quaint character called "Cap" Shere, who acted as a guide. He, Aston and Cubberly started out to find a passable trail.

"On the morning of May 28th," says Private Aston, "'Cap' Shere saddled up his mule. Without saying a word the old fellow got ready to leave camp.

"'Say, Cap, what are you going to do?' I asked him.

"'H'm,' he replied, without looking up. 'Going to hunt up a trail. There must be some way to git out o' this here valley, I reckon.'

"The idea struck me as an excellent one, but neither I nor my friend Cubberly wanted to see the old man go alone, so we obtained permission to go along with him,

"We had left the camp and journeyed about a mile, when at the foot of the hills we struck Indian signs, and, of course, continued on the trail a mile or two farther, till we could see that there was quite a large party of redskins—at least nineteen—ahead of us.

"We followed the trail down a very steep decline in a canyon and then turned abruptly to the left. The tracks of the Indians were now fresh and plain.

"Every moment I expected a big Indian to jump out and swing his tomahawk. I needn't say that I did not feel quite comfortable.

"Cap Shere halted. 'Look here,' you fellows,' he said to us; 'do yer want to go on or do yer want to go back?'

"'You're running this trip. Whatever you say goes,' I replied, and Cubberly nodded assentingly.

"'Well, then,' Cap remarked, 'I ain't satisfied yet about this here trail. What I want to find out is, what becomes of the trail at the top of the hill.' That settled it. We continued our lead, Cap going at the head, Cubberly and I bringing up the rear.

"Before we reached the top of the hill the old man discovered that the Indians had left the trail, and once more he halted to ask us whether we still wished to go ahead. Our reply was the same as before. Then Cap declared himself:

"'Now,' said he, 'it's just about like this: if we turn back the Indians 'll surely think we're afraid, and jump on us, and if we go ahead, they'll git ready and lay fer us. You kin bet your lives they'll try to git us, if they kin. If you fellers are a mind to stick by me, we kin give 'em all the fight they want. I'm fer goin' ahead.'

"Having delivered himself of this speech, he faced about and on we went for another six miles till the top of the hill was gained and the best kind of trail leading out of the valley found. We now concluded to retrace our steps.

"We fully knew, of course, that our troubles would now commence and we prepared to find the Indians lying in wait for us.

"But we had to go back' no matter how great the danger.

"The thought that our discovery of a passable trail was of great importance inspired us with courage and hastened our return.

"The six miles back from the top of the hill was about the most uncomfortable six miles I ever made in my life, and when we arrived within about a hundred yards of the place where we first stopped old Cap halted and gave us the following orders:

"He was to take the lead and Cubberly and I were to follow. But we were first to turn our animals loose and drive them down to him, so that he could lead them off as they reached the bottom of the hill.

"Cap started, but the Indians did not molest him.

"Cubberly and I, however, had not proceeded more than 150 yards, when the redskins suddenly appeared and with a whoop and yell opened up on us. We continued on our retreat, but also made our Spencer carbines talk.

"How we did fire! The Apaches, too, were furious and sent arrows and bullets after us, till we were in a shower of missiles.

"WE MADE OUR SPENCER CARBINES TALK."

"We managed to reach the bottom of the hill without injury, and after crossing the canyon to the other side knew that we were safe from further attacks. We halted to make an inventory. Cubberly's mule was shot through the nostrils, my horse was wounded along the tail, the bullet passing clean through the intestines. Cap had a lock of hair cut off his forehead as nicely as though it had been done with a pair of scissors. His forearm was also slightly injured.

"There is no doubt but what we would have been killed had we taken to our heels and simply ran, and that only by keeping up a hot fire we held the Indians at bay."

Privates Aston and Cubberly were both rewarded with the Medal of Honor for the valuable information which enabled the troops to follow the Indians with their wagon train after the encounter.

From this time on to the end of October troops B and L were constantly engaged in encounters with the Indians, but the principal work was done and the greatest hardships endured during the months of August, September and October.

The Apaches kept all Arizona in a state of terror by their depredations, and it was only by the most persistent hammering that the troops, particularly B and L, kept the territory open to the settlers. During these three months the Indians were murdering men, women and children mercilessly and stealing live stock and other property, and all real progress in the territory was prevented. The Apaches did not give battle to the troops except when cornered by them; their idea being primarily to steal, and then to kill without being killed. Many times were these two troops, amounting to not more than fifty or sixty men, attacked from ambush, and before the startled troopers could respond the redskins fled to their mountain strongholds, where if by chance they succeeded in carrying a prisoner they would inhumanly torture him. But this method of warfare did not deter the troopers, who, although they spent the greater portion of every twenty-four hours in the saddle, and were exposed to the treacherous fire of the Indians, nevertheless persistently kept at them until they finally drove them into subjugation.

For their gallantry in these actions against the Apaches and their successful efforts in keeping the territory open to the settlers the following men of the Eight U. S. Cavalry were awarded the Medal of Honor:

THOMAS CARROLL, Private, Company L.
GEORGE CARTER, Private, Company B.
CHARLES CRUNDLE, Private, Company B.
CHARLES DAILY, Private, Company B.
WILLIAM DOUGHERTY, Blacksmith, Company B.
JAMES DOWLING, Corporal, Company B.
HENRY FALCOTT, Sergeant, Company L.
THOMAS P. HIGGINS, Private, Company D.
JOHN KEENAN, Private, Company B.
AKBERT KNAAK, Private, Company B.
JAMES LAWRENCE, Private, Company B.
THOMAS LITTLE, Bugler, Company B.
BERNARD McBRIDE, Private, Company B.
JAMES McDONALD, Corporal, Company B.
WILLIAM SHAFFER, Private, Company B.
ANDREW J. WEAHER, Private, Company B.
GEORGE G. WORTMAN, Sergeant, Company B.

DANIEL FARREN, Private, Company B.
WILLIAM H. FOLLY, Private, Company B.
NICHOLAS FORAN, Private, Company L.
CHARLES GARDNER, Private, Company B.
THOMAS H. GAY, Private, Company B.
PATRICK GOLDEN, Sergeant, Company B.
JOHN HALL, Private, Company B.
CLAMOR HEISE, Private, Company B.
DANIEL McKINLEY, Private, Company B.
CHARLES H. McVEAGH, Private, Company B.
GEORGE W. MILLER, Private, Company B.
JOHN O'CALLAGHAN, Sergeant, Company B.
MICHAEL O'REGAN, Private, Company B.
LEWIS PHIFE, Sergeant, Company B.
JOHN A. SUTHERLAND, Corporal, Company L.
BENONI STRIVSON, Private, Company B.
JOHN KAY, Private, Company L.

COOLNESS PREVENTED A DISASTER

JOHN B. BABCOCK,
First Lieutenant Fifth U. S. Cavalry. High-
est rank attained: Brigadier-General
U. S. Volunteers.

THE patience of the government with the Indians had reached its limit; forbearance with them had ceased to be a virtue. The boldness and audacity of some of the largest tribes had reached a point that demanded prompt and immediate attention; they had committed atrocities and acts of barbarism which aroused public indignation throughout the country, and from all quarters came the cry for retaliation. Within a few years no less than 800 white men had been butchered by these savages, scores of women had fallen into their hands to be mutilated, outraged or dragged into captivity, where their sufferings were too horrible and revolting to relate. The Indians had torn away the infants from their mothers and tortured them before their parents' eyes; older children they simply carried along and brought them up amidst the dismal surroundings of their miserable villages. They devastated farms, pillaged small, unprotected settlements and looted and destroyed many thousands of dollars' worth of white men's property. These deeds were always perpetrated during the summer. In the winter these marauding bands retired to the snow-covered deserts and prairies, where they felt fairly safe from attack and prosecution, as military operations in the severe climate of these regions were deemed impracticable. Here they would pass the winter months in celebrating and glorifying their robberies and butcheries and in practicing and inventing new cruelties to torment the captive white women. Winter over, they would again start out and renew their deviltries. This had been going on for years, the Indians growing bolder, more daring, more audacious, more bloodthirsty with every succeeding year.

Finally, in 1868, the government called a halt to further depredations, slaughter of human life and outrages of women. It was decided to punish the Indians, and punish them hard. They were to be taught a lesson which they would not soon forget. At that time Lieutenant-General Phil H. Sheridan was commander of the military division of the Missouri, and as such had charge of all military operations within this large district, which, at the time, included all the territory extending from the British boundary on the north to the Mexican frontier of the Rio Grande on the south, and from Chicago on the east to the western boundary of New Mexico, Utah and Montana on the west.

In this territory there were living some ninety odd Indian tribes, the principal ones being the Sioux, Northern and Southern Cheyennes, Crows, Chippewas, Poncas, Assinaboines, Flatheads, Piegans, Gros Ventres, Bannocks, Shoshones, Utes, Arapahoes, Pawnees, Winnebagoes, Pattawatomies, Omahas, Kickapoos, Miamis, Otoes, Kiowas, Comanches, Apaches, Navajoes, Pueblos and others. Of these the Sioux, Cheyennes (both tribes), Kiowas, Comanches, Arapahoes, Utes and Apaches had shown themselves most hostile toward the whites; others had only occasionally trangressed into the white man's domain, while still other tribes remained peaceful and lived up to the treaties.

General Sheridan was entrusted with the execution of the government's resolution to punish the offending tribes, and formulated a plan which was calculated to make order of lasting effect. He organized a campaign for the winter of 1868, fitting out three expeditions which, starting out in November, trailed and met the Indian at his own home village at a time when he least expected an attack and was least prepared for one.

This campaign was highly successful; about 12,000 Indians were surrendered at the various military posts, while over 300 of them were killed, 89 wounded and 53 captured.

The next year, 1869, the campaign was continued with equal vigor and lasted all summer and the following winter. It was during this campaign that an occurrence took place which forms the subject of the following narrative:

One of the expeditions organized by General Sheridan was commanded by General E. A. Carr. In the spring of 1869 General Carr was directed to proceed with a column of seven troops of the Fifth United States Cavalry across the country from the Arkansas to the Platte and carefully patrol the valleys of the intermediate streams and round up all the roving bands of Indians he found lurking there.

The expedition started on its long march from Fort Wallace, Kansas, May 10th, and three days later struck the first Indian trails at Beaver Creek.

The advance guard under Lieutenant Ward made a reconnoissance and observed a large Indian village some eight miles from Elephant Rock. Their presence, however, was discovered by a party of Indians who had been hunting, and within an incredibly short time they found themselves surrounded by an overwhelming force of warriors. The detachment had to charge through the ranks of Indians to avoid capture, which every soldier knew would mean torture, scalping, death.

Another incident, still more thrilling, occurred three days later, on May 16th. The command, learning of Lieutenant Ward's experience, proceeded to attack the Indians, and found them massed to cover the retreat of their families. A charge was ordered and the redskins were completely routed. Their camp was destroyed, twenty-five Indians being killed and fifty wounded. The loss to the command was three soldiers killed and four wounded. General Carr followed up his brilliant victory with energy, following the trail of the fleeing Indians, until he arrived at Spring Creek, Nebraska. Here the command was rested to water the animals and forage.

Before breaking up General Carr decided to feel his way cautiously and carefully, and ordered Lieutenant J. B. Babcock to scout the country with his troop "M."

Realizing that the expedition was over a country comparatively unknown and full of hostile bands of Indians, he detailed that expert of all scouts, William F. Cody, to accompany the lieutenant. Babcock pushed on about two miles, when he detailed Lieutenant Volkmar with four men to go in advance a short distance to survey the topography of that section of the country. The latter was carrying out his order when suddenly and without the slightest warning he found himself confronted with a large force of Indians. From all directions they came; they seemed to be literally growing on the ground. Volkmar and his companions lost no time in rejoining Lieutenant Babcock's detachment. The Indians followed in still increasing numbers and were preparing for an onslaught on the whole command. The sudden appearance of so many yelling and howling Indians created no little consternation among the few men of Babcock's command. Some of the soldiers were badly rattled and began to retreat, others were frightened, and but a few kept their nerve in the face of the wild-eyed, yelling, devilish looking foe.

Lieutenant Babcock realized that his command could be saved only by the most determined and prompt action. To retreat would lead to a rout and bring disaster. The only salvation was to meet the attack and face the Indians, even though they outnumbered his men about one to ten.

His command: "Forward!" brought the wavering men to their senses.

"Trot!" he commanded next—and all further confusion within the ranks ceased.

He led his troop to the top of the slope, thus selecting the most favorable ground to repulse an attack. Here he quickly ordered the men to dismount, form into a circle and shield themselves behind the prostrate bodies of their horses, which served them for breastworks, each man holding the bridle-rein over his right arm. "Now let the red devils come!" Lieutenant Babcock exclaimed. "In the position you are now, boys, you can whip any number of Indians."

This talk, together with the coolness displayed by the lieutenant, who alone remained in the saddle, occupying the most conspicuous position in the middle of the circle and directing the fire of the men, had a most reassuring and encouraging effect upon the latter.

Then the Indians came. First singly, then in groups they swarmed around the human circle. A well-directed fire kept them at a respectful distance. Every man was aiming as accurately as he could; every shot told in the ranks of the savages.

Scout Cody, known as a crack shot, coolly picked off the Indians one by one as they came within the range of his rifle. Some of the braves, more daring than the others, threw themselves over the necks of their horses, thus shielding themselves behind the bodies of the animals, and ventured closer to the circle. A well-directed bullet paid them for their daring. This manner of fighting was continued for some time, the Indians being held at bay in spite of their superiority of numbers.

Lieutenant Babcock remained steadfastly on horseback in his dangerously conspicuous position and refused to yield to the urgent pleas of his men not to expose himself in such manner. Calmly he directed the fire of his men, now cautioning

"THE INDIANS COMMENCED CIRCLING."

this one of the approach of the Indian, now commanding that one to fire into a group of advancing warriors. It was almost miraculous that he himself escaped the deadly missiles of the foe, whose easy target he seemed to be. His horse was shot and fell just as a large body of cavalrymen sent in all haste by General Carr, who had heard the firing, came to his rescue.

Upon arrival of the re-enforcements the Indians desisted from their attack and reluctantly left the small detachment, the members of which they had counted on as their prey. They retired before the new arrivals and disappeared behind the many small hills of the prairie.

Lieutenant Babcock's coolness and presence of mind had saved the day and averted what would unquestionably have turned out to be a disaster. A Medal of Honor was the reward for his conduct on this occasion.

DEATH OF CHIEF BLACK KETTLE

A TREMENDOUS punishment administered to the hostiles in the memorable winter campaign of 1868-9 was carried out by General George W. Custer against the notorious Chief Black Kettle and his numerous followers while they were encamped for the winter. The hostilities carried on by the Indians, described in the foregoing story, had reached their climax, and these atrocities they expected to continue until the approach of winter, when the inclemency of the weather would give them ample security, and they could live on their plunder, glory in the scalps taken and the debasement of the poor unfortunate women whom they held as prisoners.

Depredations of this character for many years, with comparative security to themselves, had made the Indians very confident and bold. To disabuse their minds of their fancied safety, and to strike them at a period when they were helpless, became a necessity, and a winter campaign was authorized, which was commenced October 9, 1868.

At this time the operations of the Indians had been mostly transferred to the line of the Arkansas River and Santa Fe Road, owing to the presence of troops under Colonel Forsyth, General Bradley and General Carr, north of the Smoky Hill River and on the Republican, as well as to the near approach of winter, which caused them to work in the direction of their families, then supposed to be on the headwaters of the Red River.

To make this campaign General Getty was directed to quickly organize a small column at Fort Bascom, New Mexico, General Eugene Carr to organize a column on the Arkansas River, while a third column composed of eleven companies of the Seventh cavalry, twelve companies Nineteenth Kansas Cavalry, and three companies of the Third and one company of the Thirty-eighth Infantry, were directed to concentrate at the junction of Beaver Creek with the North Canadian, 112 miles south of Fort Dodge.

On November 5th the Nineteenth Kansas was in readiness and moved from Topeka via the mouth of the Little Arkansas to Camp Supply — the point before alluded to at the junction of the North Canadian and Beaver Creek; and on the 11th of November the Seventh Cavalry and Third Infantry moved from Dodge to the same destination. The column from Bascom had already moved, and Carr's column from Lyon was ordered to move on November 12th. The main column from Camp Supply was expected to strike the Indians either on the headwaters of the Washita, or still further south, on the Sweetwater and other branches of the Red River. A furious snow-storm commenced on the evening of November 21st, which continued during the night and next day, making the situation very gloomy, especially on account of the non-arrival of the Nineteenth Kansas, expected to reach Camp Supply about this time.

Indians were seen by General Sheridan, who was then on his way to Camp Supply, and two days after he arrived he directed General Custer to move his regiment, storm or no storm, on the morning of November 23d. This order was responded to with alacrity by the officers and men of the Seventh Cavalry, and on the morning of the 23d the regiment moved at daylight, although the snow continued to fall with unabated fury.

General Custer, on the evening of the 26th, struck the trail of the war-party, which had passed north. This party was composed, as was afterwards learned, of Black Kettle's band of Cheyennes and some Arapahoes. They had been north, killed the mail carriers between Dodge and Larned, an old hunter and two expressmen. As soon as Custer struck the trail he corralled his wagons, left a small escort with them and followed the Indian trail, which was very fresh and well marked in the deep snow, until it led into Black Kettle's village. The next morning, before daylight, the Osage Indian trailers discovered the village and stock of the Indians and notified Custer, who at once made a most admirable disposition of his command for the attack and capture of the village. At dawn the attack was made, the village captured and burned, 103 warriors killed and 53 women and children captured, the horses and ponies being killed in accordance with orders.

While this work was going on, all the Indians for a distance of fifteen miles down the Washita — Cheyennes, Comanches, Kiowas and Apaches — collected and attacked Custer, but were driven down the stream for a distance of four or five miles, when, as night was approaching, Custer withdrew. The loss at the attack on the village was Captain Louis M. Hamilton and three men killed, and three officers and eleven men wounded. Unfortunately, Major Elliott, of the regiment, seeing some of the young bucks escape, followed with the sergeant-major and fifteen men, to capture and bring them in; after capturing them, and while on their way back to the regiment they were surrounded and killed.

No one, so far as could be learned, of those with the regiment knew of their having followed the Indian bucks; no one heard the report of their guns, and no one knew of their exact fate until they were discovered, some two weeks afterward.

The first news of the whereabouts of the Nineteenth Kansas was brought to Camp Supply on November 25th by Captain Pliley and about thirty men. The regiment had lost its way, and becoming tangled up in the deep snow of the canyons of the Cimarron, and running out of provisions, could not make its way out, and was in a bad fix. Provisions were immediately sent, along with guides, to bring it in. It had been subsisting on buffalo meat for eight or nine days, and as buffalo were plenty no great suffering was occasioned for want of food. November 30th, Colonel Crawford, commanding the regiment, came into Camp Supply with four companies, and a few days after the remainder of the regiment arrived in a crippled condition.

Although Custer had struck a hard blow and had wiped out Black Kettle and his murderous band, the work was not yet finished. The Indians were to see fully how helpless they were, even at this season, when the government was in earnest. So on the 7th of December, after getting the Kansas regiment as well up as possible, a movement towards the head waters of the Washita was commenced.

Snow was on the ground and the weather very cold, but the officers and men were cheerful, notwithstanding the men were supplied with shelter tents only. They moved south until they struck the Washita, near Custer's fight of November 27th, the thermometer registering about eighteen degrees below zero.

The next day the troops started down the Washita, following the trail of the Indians, and crossed numerous ravines by digging and bridging with pioneer parties. This was continued until the evening of the 16th, when they came to the vicinity of the redskins—principally Kiowas. They did not dream that soldiers could operate in such cold and inclement weather, and the troops marched down on them before they knew of their presence in the country. After night they saw their fires, and by means of relays communicated with General Hazen, and obtained a letter from him saying that the Kiowas were friendly. This was a pretty good joke, as Sheridan's troops had just followed their trail from Custer's battlefield, and a section of this band had just come from Texas, where they had murdered and plundered in the most barbarous manner.

Sheridan did not strike these Indians on account of General Hazen's letter, and because he did not at the time know the extent of their guilt. As soon as they found he was not going to attack them, the old system of lying and deception was revived, by their proposing that all the warriors should join his column and march with it to Fort Cobb, while their villages moved to the same point on the opposite bank of the Washita. But this was a decoy, as toward night all the warriors slipped off, as they said, to help the women along with the villages, leaving only about twenty chiefs and principal men, and early the next morning these escaped, except Santanta and Lone Wolf, the head chiefs, whom Sheridan ordered Custer to arrest. On reaching Fort Cobb that evening, he found that the villagers, instead of moving to Fort Cobb, as they proposed, were going down toward the main Red River, west of the Wichita Mountains, in an opposite direction, as fast as possible, and that some of them were nearly 100 miles distant; and that the proposition of Lone Wolf and Santanta was a decoy to get their villages out of the way. Sheridan immediately issued orders for the execution of Lone Wolf and Santanta, unless the villages came back in two days and delivered themselves up at Fort Cobb. They all came back eventually under this pressure, and at a gait as fast as that of their flight, and Santanta and Lone Wolf were saved.

At Fort Cobb Sheridan found most of the Comanches and Apaches; they had hastened into the reservation after the fight with General Custer. While these operations were going on, Lieutenant-Colonel A. W. Evans moved, as heretofore mentioned, from Bascom up the main Canadian to Monument Creek, there established his depot, and with the most commendable energy struck off to the south, on the headwaters of the Red River, where he discovered a trail of hostile Comanches, who had refused to come in, following it up with perseverance. On the 25th of December he attacked the party, killed, as near as could be ascertained, twenty-five, wounded a large number, captured and burnt their village, destroyed a large amount of property, and then moved in to a point about twelve miles west of Fort Cobb, where Sheridan communicated with him.

Meanwhile, General Carr was scouting along the main Canadian, west of the Antelope Hills, and the country was becoming so unhealthy for Indians that the Arapahoes and the remainder of the Cheyennes concluded to surrender and go to the reservation designated for them. The operations of the troops had forced these bands over into the eastern edge of the Staked Plains, where they surrendered and agreed to deliver their people at Fort Cobb as speedily as possible.

The Arapahoes were faithful to their promise, and delivered themselves up under their head chief, Little Raven. The Cheyennes broke their promise and did not come in, so Sheridan ordered Custer to move against them. He found them in a very forlorn condition, and could have destroyed most of the tribe, certainly their villages, but contented himself with taking their renewed promise to come into Camp Supply, and obtained from them two white women whom they held as captives. The most of the tribe fulfilled this latter promise as to coming into the vicinity of Camp Supply, and communicating with the commanding officer; but Tall Bull's band again violated the promise made, and went north to the Republican, where he joined a party of Sioux, who, on the 13th of May, 1869, were attacked and defeated with heavy loss, whereupon the remainder of the tribe moved into Camp Supply.

Meantime, while the Arapahoes and Cheyennes were negotiating with Sheridan to surrender, the Oua-ha-da, or Staked Plains Comanches, sent a delegation over to Bascom. General Getty arrested the delegation, who were ordered to Fort Leavenworth, and finally returned to their people on condition that they would deliver themselves up on the reservation at Medicine Bluff or Fort Sill. This was complied with, thus ending a successful campaign.

A WELL-PLANNED SURPRISE.

WILLIAM F. CODY,
Chief of Scouts, Fifth United States Cavalry.
Highest rank attained: Colonel.
Born in Scott County, Iowa.

A QUIET June evening in 1870 found the troops stationed at Fort McPherson, Neb., enjoying a well-earned rest after many a hard chase and expedition. Of the stirring incidents that brought their brief recreation to a sudden termination, Colonel William F. Cody has this to say:

"I was chief of scouts under General Phil H. Sheridan, and knowing the boys well, having led them on many a dangerous journey, joined them to enjoy the refreshing breezes of the evening. A detail had left the fort to water the government herd of horses and mules in the near-by Platte River, when presently shots were heard. Everybody was on his feet the next moment and we learned that a war-party of Sioux Indians had dashed from among the cottonwood trees on the little islands in the river, shooting, shouting and waving blankets, which stampeded the herd of about 400 animals. The Indians also killed two of the herders and wounded another. Some of the herd ran for the corral, where they were accustomed to going for the night, but the Indians got away with about 200 and started for the bluffs south of the fort. In less time than it takes to tell it, all was excitement at the fort. All knew it was an Indian attack. As was my custom, I had my war horse, old 'Buckskin Joe,' near at hand and was mounted in time to note the ravine or canyon in which the Indians disappeared with the government stock. General William H. Emory, who was in command, immediately ordered his bugler to sound boots and saddles, and by the time I returned for instructions, five troops of cavalry were busy saddling up, getting their arms, ammunition belts, etc. Company I, Fifth United States Cavalry, was the first troop saddled and ready for the chase. Their officer, a young lieutenant by the name of Earl D. Thomas, just from West Point, was delighted when he received the order from General Emory to take his troop and follow me. The general stated that he would be supported by the other troops as soon as they were ready, but ordered him to follow the Indians and recapture the animals. By this time the Indians with such of the herd as did not get away from them were at least five miles away in the hills. Thomas at once counted fours, 'fours right, trot, gallop, march!' and we were off. Striking the trail, it was followed in a gallop till dark, but it did not bring us in sight of the Indians, and the tracks of their horses showed that they were still on the run. The lieutenant called a halt to rest the puffing horses and to consult me as to what he should do. His orders were to follow the Indians and recapture the animals, but his men had had no supper and had neither rations nor water and the way the Indians were headed it was still thirty miles to water. I told Thomas that it was possible to follow the trail all night and awaited his answer. He said he was told to follow me, and where I went he proposed to go.

"'Mount and forward!' was at once the order, and the chase was continued. During the night the Indians repeatedly doubled on their trail, with all the horses. They would drive them in a circle, and use every means known to a crafty Indian to throw anyone who might be following off the trail, and several times during the night it took some time to get the trail straightened out. While this was being accomplished, the troops would get some sleep. Such delays, however, increased the distance between us and the Indians, and we did not reach the head of Medicine Creek, where we got water for men and horses, until 11 o'clock next day. Here we consulted again while the horses were drinking and nibbling a few mouthfuls of grass, and some of the men, with empty stomachs, caught a few minutes' sleep. The trail of the Indians showed that they were several hours ahead of us and headed southwest in the direction of Red Willow Springs, about thirty miles distant.

"There is no water between Medicine Creek and Red Willow Springs, and this made me feel sure that the Indians would make a stop at the latter place, for it was many miles from there to the next water. This was well considered by the lieutenant as we talked over the situation. No one in the little party had had anything to eat since dinner the day before, and there was no possible way of getting any before the next morning, and then only by overtaking the Indians, surprising them, whipping them and capturing what dried meat they had. These were long chances, but we decided to take them. Again the order: Bridle up, mount, forward! was given. Nearly all the Fifth Cavalry soldiers knew the country, as they had followed me through those dry, hot sand hills on many a scout. Thirty miles to water and no canteen in which to carry any, nor anything to eat in twenty-three hours, and nothing in sight, was a hard proposition for our little troop, yet no one demurred at the thought that every mile took us farther into those hot sand hills. Most of the men were in their shirt sleeves and had not even a blouse to protect them from the night air. When we left the green grass that bordered the creek and entered the dry sand hills I listened to hear if there should be any complaints.

"Not a word. Grim, silent, like sleuthhounds they came. They were on a hot trail for Indians. Indians who had killed their friends. They were ready to starve, to thirst, if only the prospects of a fight were good. They were American soldiers of the Indian-fighter type, Sheridan's cavalrymen. Soon after leaving the creek the Indians began their old tricks of trying to hide the trail, but no attention was paid to this, for we now knew the next stopping place and were as familiar with that part of the country as they were. We kept straight on for the springs, with the exception that occasionally we went out of the direct line to keep in low places between the sand hills, so as not to be seen. At 9 o'clock that night we halted about four miles from the springs. I advised Thomas to allow the men to unsaddle and unbridle, letting each second man hold two horses by their halters and so let them

"BOTH INDIANS FELL TO THE GROUND—DEAD."

feed on grass. By changing the men every two hours they could get some sleep. Meanwhile I was to disguise myself as an Indian, locate the hostiles and be back in time so that we could attack them at daylight. No fires were to be lighted. All must be silent until my return.

"Tired men go to sleep quickly, and before I left half of my little band were slumbering. I took the saddle and bridle off from old Joe and left him to graze, knowing he would not leave. One hour later I found the Indians just where they were expected to be. The tired horses, some grazing, some sleeping, were corralled. Four Indians were guarding them and one sentinel or scout was lying down on a little sand hill back from camp on the trail peering into the night to signal our coming. I knew every inch of ground around the spring, and knew where to bring the troop for an attack. Going back I found the boys as I had left them. Quietly they were called to saddle up, and told what they were to do, those who were to capture the herd and the ones who were to attack the camp being instructed in their duties. I had estimated the Indians to number thirty, and there were forty-two of us. Ten of these were to creep up to the sleeping Indians on foot, while twenty, besides the lieutenant and myself, were to charge on horseback, and the other ten were to bring up the remaining horses, take care of the mounted Indian herders, and round up the animals. We were to attack them just at the break of day, which we did, and a more surprised lot of Indians never awoke to face the woes of this world. The very next moment nine of them went to sleep again forever. Indians on the warpath always keep their war horses near them and some of these redskins got to their horses and thus escaped. I saw two Indians mount one horse, and they were on none other than my favorite war horse, 'Powder Face,' which was with the government herd when captured by the Indians. I gave chase as soon as I saw that we had won the fight, which took less time than it takes to tell it, but by this time the two Indians on 'Powder Face' were half a mile away heading for the hills. I knew my old friend to be nearly as swift a horse as 'Buckskin Joe,' but he had double weight to carry and Joe soon began to gain, so that within a few minutes I was getting near enough for a shot. The Indian who was riding behind kept shooting back with a revolver, but I feared to chance too long a shot for fear of killing or wounding 'Powder Face.' By this time we were in the rough sand hills, and as they were about to go out of sight over a mound I fired, with the result that both Indians fell to the ground, the bullet having passed through both of them. I soon caught 'Powder Face' and returned to our little battlefield, where the boys were then in high glee. They had found a lot of dried buffalo and deer meat, which they ate hungrily, between copious draughts of spring water. A detail was sent to bury the dead Indians and gather up all the stock.

"Certainly the results of our chase raised the spirits of our brave troopers to a point of enthusiasm hardly to be described. I felt great sympathy with these courageous fellows, and knew that on our trail would soon be following the support that General Emory said would be sent, presumably in command of at least a major. If this supporting command reached us, Lieutenant Thomas and his brave boys would have to share their glory with others. It was my intention to prevent this by getting away as soon as possible, and by not taking our trail back to the fort. We kept a few miles away from our former route so that the supporting troops could not see us, and thereby succeeded in avoiding a meeting. The supporting troops had the unenvied pleasures of following our entire trail, on the second half of which they certainly noticed the scheme. When our boys "tumbled" to what was being done they gave me a hearty cheer. We reached the fort the next evening much fatigued but joyful.

The Lieutenant and his men were complimented by special order, and shortly afterwards I had the distinction of receiving a Medal of Honor.

THE SIXTH CAVALRY AND THE INDIANS

WITH the coming of spring in 1870 the Indians in Northwestern Texas became extremely dangerous and daring. White outlaws in great numbers kept the small detachments of troops then stationed in the vast region amply occupied, and the Indians saw the time was opportune for an assault upon the mail stage. Their attack upon the stage began in early July, and the troops were sent from all sides to chastise the bold marauders.

Captain C. B. McLellan, of Troop L, Sixth United States Cavalry, commanding a mixed detachment of three officers and fifty-three men of Troops A, C, D, H, K and L of said regiment, was the first to come across the Indians and force them to fight.

He left Fort Richardson, Tex., on the 6th of July in pursuit of a party of Indians who had captured the mail at Rock Station, sixteen miles west from the post. Marching generally in a northwesterly direction, passing Rock Station and picking up information and evidence of the doings of the marauders while he went along, McLellan reached the Middle Fork of the Little Wichita on the 9th of July.

The weather was bad; heavy rain-storms visited the detachment several times. A severe one kept the command in camp at the last-named place until the 12th of July, when camp was broken. The troops moved in a westerly direction, with the heavy rain pouring down, and came upon the Indians towards noon. The latter were recognized as superior in numbers, but the captain deployed into line and intended to charge them, when hostiles were discovered on both flanks threatening the pack train left in the rear. The troops halted, dismounted and opened fire, which was promptly answered by the enemy. Within half an hour the Indians nearly surrounded the detachment, and the necessity of retreating to some stronger point of defense caused McLellan to move his force slowly back to some crests where he thought he could meet the redskins on equal terms.

This retreat was far more difficult than was anticipated.

The country was a rolling prairie interspersed by marshy places which threatened to cut off outlying details of the command. For four hours and a half the small band of soldiers moved slowly back from one crest to the next under a heavy fire, without finding a spot where they might hope to cope successfully with the ever-increasing swarms of Indians.

According to Captain McLellan's opinion there were some 250 of them against his fifty odd soldiers.

The retreat, always under a hot fire and over unknown ground, was stopped between 3 and four o'clock in the afternoon, when the Indians gave up hope and withdrew.

Two American soldiers were killed, the surgeon and ten other men wounded. All the wounded were saved, but the killed fell into the savage enemy's hands.

The Indians lost fifteen killed; the number of their wounded could not be ascertained.

The order, discipline and devotion shown throughout this remarkable action are indicated by the fact that the swift and clever Indians were unable to get hold of any of the property of the command except some baggage belonging to the officers, which they themselves decided to abandon to avoid unnecessary exposure of their men.

Twelve non-commissioned officers and soldiers earned the Medal of Honor for exceptional gallantry. They were recommended by Captain McLellan in his official report as having "made themselves conspicuous in acts of bravery in the engagement." They were:

First Sergeant A. Stokes, Sergeant Thomas Kerrigan, Corporal John Connor, Corporal Charles Smith, all of Company H; Farrier Samuel Porter, Bugler Clarion Windus, Corporal James Watson, Private Solon Neal, Sergeant John May, of Company L; Sergeant William Winterbottom, of Company A; Sergeant Geo. Eldridge, of Company C, and Corporal John Given, of Company K, Sixth Cavalry.

At noon of July 14th the detachment reached Fort Richardson, after having marched 200 miles.

The department commander complimented this expedition in a general order, concluding with the words that "this engagement doubtless saved the frontier counties in Northwestern Texas from a most destructive raid from a band of 250 Indians."

But the Indians, in ignorance of the fact that more troops were to be encountered, pushed their boldness further. They were all from the Fort Sill Reservation and infested the entire northwestern part of Texas, where outrages increased in number and atrocity.

Another expedition against the red fiends started from Fort Richardson on September 26th under Captain Rafferty and twenty-two men. They were all of

Company M, Sixth Cavalry. They marched towards the headwaters of the Trinity River, passing over part of the ground of Captain McLellan's exploit. A few Indians were seen and pursued, but they escaped into the trackless fastnesses of the rocky desert. On October 4th a new trail, discovered by Scout Dozier, was followed, and on the 5th of October the command came up with the Indians near the Little Wichita, early in the morning. The soldiers attacked without delay and surprised the redskins. It was a war-party of about fifteen. Two were killed and one wounded, but the latter crawled in the underbrush and made his escape with the rest of the band. Eighteen horses were captured by the detachment, together with a considerable quantity of clothing and property belonging to white settlers, showing that the red devils were just returning from a raid.

For this exploit, the success of which was due in great measure to the efficiency of Scout Dozier, the latter received the Medal of Honor, together with five enlisted men: Sergeant Michael Welch, Corporals Samuel Bowden and Daniel Keating, and Privates James Anderson and Benjamin Wilson.

SIX MEN AGAINST 400 COMANCHES

R. G. CARTER,
Second Lieutenant Fourth U. S. Cavalry.
Highest rank attained: Captain, U. S. A.

FOR ten years or more immediately following the close of the War of the Rebellion the entire borders of Texas, Kansas, Montana, Nebraska, Wyoming, Arizona, Utah and neighboring territories were ablaze with Indian wars. One raid followed another, and many depredations and massacres were committed by the Sioux, Cheyennes, Arapahoes and other affiliated bands of Kiowas and Comanches, followed by fire, rapine, pillage and plunder.

In September, 1871, the Fourth U. S. Cavalry had returned from a long and arduous expedition against Kicking Bird's and Lone Wolf's bands of hostile Kiowas, when Colonel Ronald S. Mackenzie, commanding the regiment, learned that a band of hostile Oua-ha-da Comanche Indians, under Mowwi, the "Hard-Shaker," and Para-o-coom, the "He Bear," were in the Pan Handle of Texas, outside the reservation. It was said that they held several white captives, among them two boys and one little girl, stolen some time before near San Antonio, Texas, besides many horses and herds of cattle driven off during the almost constant raids. Colonel Mackenzie reorganized the command at Old Camp Cooper, the former reservation of the Comanches, on Tecumseh Creek, near Fort Griffin, Texas, and on the morning of October 3d the column moved out with wagon and pack trains for the purpose of beating up this nest of freebooters, recovering the captive children, and either destroying the village with its accumulated plunder or driving the Indians back into the reservation, from which they had been absent for years in utter defiance of the government. Lieutenant Henry W. Lawton, regimental quartermaster of the Fourth Cavalry, was in charge of the wagon train. On October 7 Duck Creek was reached, where a permanent supply camp was established. It was determined to surprise the village by moving at night and attacking at daybreak. About 7 o'clock on the morning of the 8th Troops A, B, F, G, H, I, K and L left the supply camp with a pack train of about eighty mules for this purpose. The village was supposed to be somewhere on the Freshwater Fork of the Brazos River, or up on the numerous canyons of the Staked Plains. The Ton-Ka-Way scouts had been sent out on the night of the 7th for the purpose of locating it.

About midnight, after a hard march over a very rough country, further progress of the command was blocked by a precipitous bluff, which in the impenetrable darkness it was found impossible to scale, and the command bivouacked on the trail. At daybreak the march was resumed by passing around the obstacle. The Freshwater Fork was reached about 9:30 A. M. of the 9th, too late for any decisive action. The locality was recognized as being near the spot where Lieutenant P. M. Boehm of the Fourth Cavalry had a skirmish with this same band two years before. The command unsaddled and got breakfast. In the afternoon Captain E. M. Heyl, with a squadron, was sent out on a reconnoissance. The Ton-Ka-Way scouts sent out from Duck Creek came in, but while hastening along some ravines on high ground unexpectedly ran upon a group of Comanches busily intent upon watching the reconnoitering column. The scouts reported the village to be up Catfish or Canyon Blanco (White Canyon), near by. At 3 P. M. the command saddled up, moved across and down the Freshwater Fork, Captain Clarence Manck with one squadron being left behind on guard with instructions to join the advance later. After proceeding two miles or more a shot was heard. Colonel Mackenzie immediately rode to the rear, sending word to Captain Wirt Davis to countermarch the column, but after proceeding some distance, on discovering that it was an accidental shot by a careless soldier, the march was resumed. Much valuable time had been lost. The country was rough with foothills and small ravines or arroyos, making frequent halts necessary, so that it was nearly dark before the command was fairly straightened out and ready to go into bivouac. The absent squadron was sent for, and under the shadow of a line of abrupt hills, scarcely 100 yards from the stream, the command camped. The horses were staked out and the men were allowed to make small fires. The missing squadron came in after dark, and, not finding much room, crowded up pretty close to the rear company, the horses being huddled upon their grazing ground. It was a long picket, with the line of small bluffs or hills close to camp on one side and the treacherous quicksand stream on the other; an excellent camp—provided there were no Indians about.

"THE INDIANS IMMEDIATELY CLOSED IN UPON THE DETACHMENT."

Shortly after midnight the camp was attacked by a large body of Indians who rode along the line of hills referred to, and by firing, yelling, shaking dried buffalo robes and ringing bells, succeeded in stampeding the horses. As the fire was immediately returned the flashes of carbines and pistols showed, at intervals, that the ridge which skirted the entire camp was alive with Indians, riding and yelling like so many demons. The cry rang out above the tumult: "Every man to his lariat! Stand by your horses!" Pandemonium reigned for a few moments. At every flash the horses and mules, about 600 in number, could be seen rearing, jumping, snorting and running, with a strength that terror and brute frenzy alone could inspire, while ropes could be heard snap like the cracking reports of pistols. Iron picket pins were whistling through the air, more dangerous than bullets; men, crouching as they ran, vainly endeavored to seize the pins as they whirled and swished, only to be dragged and thrown among the heels of the animals, with hands lacerated and burnt by the ropes running so rapidly through their fingers. The herd thundered off in the distance; the yells of the retreating Indians came back on the midnight air with a peculiarly taunting ring, telling all too plainly that the Oua-ha-das, Mow-wi's wild band, had been found at last.

As soon as the confusion had somewhat subsided, orders were given for a portion of the command to saddle up, and Captain Heyl and Lieutenant W. C. Hemphill were ordered with detachments from their respective troops, K and G, to scout about the camp for the trail of the stampeded horses, of which some sixty-five or seventy had been driven or "circled out" by the Indians. At daybreak Lieutenant R. G. Carter, then second lieutenant, Fourth Cavalry, while engaged, by order of Colonel Mackenzie in inspecting the picket posts, and endeavoring to find the trail of the outgoing horses, heard a shot, then a loud shout. Riding in that direction, he met Captain Heyl and Lieutenant Hemphill galloping from different directions, both riding towards the sound of the shot. Upon looking down a long and narrow valley from the ridge they were on, a small party of Indians was seen running off some eight or ten horses. All gave chase. About two miles from camp the detachments came to a break or abrupt shelf in the prairie. Here the Indians suddenly released the captured horses, being then under pistol fire from their pursuers, and turned toward quite a prominent bluff or butte. Lieutenant Hemphill, with most of the men of both detachments, stopped here, as it was a difficult place to cross. Captain Heyl, however, with some six or seven men of his own troop, jumped, and scrambled through this abrupt break, closely followed by Lieutenant Carter and Sergeants Jenkins and Foley and Privates Gregg, Downey and Melville of Troop G. It was not yet light enough to see far, and the ground for 300 yards or so gradually ascended. As the pursuers passed over this slight rise, terminating in an open, smooth prairie ridge or knoll, they suddenly came upon the main body of Indians, variously estimated at from 400 to 600, and but five to six hundred yards distant. The Indians gave one shrill yell of intense satisfaction and moved out rapidly to cut off the retreat of the detachment. All drew rein on the ridge as one man, and without a word each looked at the other, and then raised a simultaneous shout of surprise. It was like an electric shock. For a moment the blood fairly congealed and the heart of every man in that little party stood still. All realized what the ruse of the Oua-Ha-Has had meant, knew that they had been drawn into an ambuscade, and the almost hope lessness of their situation. Capt. Heyl, who was riding near Lieutenant Carter, ex claimed: "Heavens, look at the Indians, we are in a bad nest!" Lieutenant Carter, while fully realizing the danger of all, quickly suggested that the men dismount immediately and open fire, to gain time until Colonel Mackenzie could hear the firing and come to their relief. Captain Heyl gave orders to this effect. There was no shelter whatever, it was nearly three miles from camp, and the horses were almost exhausted from the long run over rough ground. It was certain death to one and all should they turn and seek shelter in the ravine they had just left, now some 500 or 600 yards to the rear, for the Indians had already commenced circling and were endeavoring to get around the flanks of the little party. Captain Heyl, who was more than 100 yards to Lieutenant Carter's right, with his men in line, dismounted, deployed and firing, upon observing this movement of the Indians, without giving Lieutenant Carter any other instructions, or without notifying him of his intentions. suddenly mounted, and with his men started on a run for the ravine. The Indians, seeing this, charged down upon Lieutenant Carter, who, seeing that it would be certain death to all should he join the retreating party, mounted his five men, gave them instructions to keep well deployed, maintain a rapid fire and to commence falling back, but on no account to turn and run. The leading Indians, led by Para-o coom himself, in black war paint—stripped to his breech-clout—wearing a full war bonnet of feathers reaching to his horse's tail, and mounted on a coal black pony, immediately closed in upon the detachment. Private Gregg of Troop G was killed by the chief, and Private Downey of the same troop was slightly wounded. All would undoubtedly have been killed in a few moments, although all were determined to sell their lives dearly, had not Lieutenant P. M. Boehm, with the Ton-Ka-Way Indians, of whom he had charge, gallantly come to their rescue. He had met Captain Heyl at the ravine, and with the men who had halted there when the pursuit first commenced— together with two citizens, Messrs. Stockton and James, who had accompanied the expedition to identify their stock if found—in all about twenty-five or thirty, he had reached the scene of action at just the right moment. The dust of the column could now be seen coming out of an adjacent valley, and the Indians, fearing they might be attacked from the rear in open ground, and by a superior force in front, commenced falling back into the hills. A running skirmish was kept up for nearly half an hour until the arrival of Colonel Mackenzie with the column. It is believed that this decisive action of Lieutenant Carter, in temporarily checking the pursuit by the Indians of Captain Heyl and his fleeing men until Lieutenant Boehm's arrival, saved the lives of the entire party, excepting the unfortunate man who was killed, and it was because of such prompt, brave action, that Second Lieutenant R. G. Carter was brevetted first lieutenant, who was also, for "most distinguished gallantry in this action," granted the Medal of Honor.

DARING SINGLE-HANDED COMBAT

JOHN NIHILL,
Private, Co. F, Fifth U. S. Cavalry.
Born in Tipperary, Ireland, 1850.

IT was nothing new when, on the morning of July 13, 1872, a Mexican ranchman rode into the military post at Camp Crittenden, in the extreme southern part of Arizona, and reported that a band of Apaches with large herds of stolen cattle had passed his ranch, for all summer the Indians had been committing all kinds of depredations and terrorizing the inhabitants. The military protection was somewhat inadequate, only a small force—one company, Troop F, Fifth U. S. Cavalry—being stationed at the post, and three-fourths of these few men were usually disabled and laid up by fever, chills and other physical ailments due to the climate. Thus the military post exerted little deterring influence and furnished slight protection.

However, when this Mexican came in with his complaint, Lieutenant W. B. Hall immediately started in pursuit of the thieving Apaches. His detail consisted of First Sergeant Henry Newman and seven privates. The chase is described by Private John Nihill, who was one of the participants.

"The trail," he says, "was found within 600 yards from the post, and, as it had been raining the day before, the ground was soft, so that there was little difficulty in following it while in the open country.

"It headed towards the Whetstone Mountains, which were distant about fifteen miles, southeast of the post. We traveled as rapidly as the nature of the ground would permit, hoping to overhaul them before they reached the mountains. As we approached the mountains our progress was necessarily slow. The Indians had in several places split up their band, so as to throw us off the trail, which invariably came together again at some given point.

"Late in the afternoon we passed some cattle that the Indians abandoned in a deep ravine, as they were thoroughly exhausted and unable to travel any farther. This caused us to make as much haste as possible, for we knew that they would strike into some of the deep canyons in the mountains, where it would be almost impossible to follow them.

"About two miles from where we passed the cattle the trail led into a deep canyon, where we had the greatest difficulty in following it, and then could only do so by dismounting and leading our horses.

"We had advanced in this manner about a mile when we were suddenly attacked by some forty Indians, who were concealed behind rocks 800 feet above us. The side of the ravine where the Indians had taken up their position was nearly vertical, so that it was almost impossible to get a shot at them. At the time the Indians made the attack I was following the trail of some who had gone up the opposite side of the canyon, and had taken a position behind a small tree, which had a fork about five feet from the ground; in this fork I rested my carbine to steady it. I watched for every opportunity to fire at an Indian, but they were so well concealed behind rocks that it was almost impossible to catch more than a fleeting glance of them. During this time some of our party were wounded, and to make matters worse the Indians commenced to roll rocks down from the top of the cliffs with such force and noise that the horses became unmanageable.

"It was then that Lieutenant Hall made up his mind to retreat and gave the men orders to do so, he and First Sergeant Newman taking the post of danger, in the rear, assisted by Private Michael Glynn, who displayed great courage and bravery throughout the fight, thus giving the wounded men a chance to get out first. Glynn alone drove off eight of the hostiles, killing and wounding five. I was watching a chance to get a shot at an Indian who was dodging behind the rocks on the opposite side of the canyon, and did not notice that I was being left behind until our detail had got a considerable distance ahead of me. However, I started to catch up. I was dismounted, with the bridle-rein over my arm, and my carbine in readiness for whatever might turn up. After I had gone about 300 yards I was fired at by an Indian, but the gun missed fire, and before he could make a second attempt I fired and dropped him. In the meantime, three others rushed down the side of the canyon, with the intention of cutting me off from the remainder of the detail. One of them stopped long enough to shoot at me, but missed. I returned his fire, and was fortunate enough to bring him down also. The other two concealed themselves behind rocks, directly in front of me. I turned my horse loose and drove it ahead to draw the fire of the Indians. Then I moved about thirty or forty yards to the right of my horse, making as little noise as possible. When within about thirty yards of the redskins they came crawling around the rocks to the side where they were exposed to me, and just as soon as they discovered me I fired, killing one; the other jumped into a ravine and I saw him no more. I kept on and rejoined the detail, which was waiting at the mouth of the canyon."

Sergeant Newman and Privates Nihill and Glynn were awarded the Medal of Honor for the active part they took in this action.

WHERE THE COMANCHES WERE PUT TO FLIGHT

DAVID LARKIN,
Farrier, Co. F, 4th U. S. Cavalry.

ALTHOUGH no general Indian war took place in 1872, there were several expeditions and crusades against bands of savages. The number of murders, outrages and depredations by small parties of redskins was greater than the preceding year, especially in Kansas, Nebraska, Minnesota and Dakota, and those states where the building of railroads marked the advent of a new era of civilization. About this time the Northern Pacific Railroad had reached the Missouri River, and the surveyors were at work as far west as the Powder River, 200 miles beyond the Missouri. The Santa Fe and the Southern Pacific Railroads were both in course of construction, and small groups of surveyors, engineers, contractors, etc., were scattered all over this large territory, challenging the attention of certain tribes of Indians who were always on the lookout for plunder and murder, and ready to go on the warpath at the slightest provocation. The dawn of a new civilization, which the building of these roads signified, furnished a sufficient pretext for many a chief to gather his braves and look for trouble.

An expedition commanded by Colonel Mackenzie was consequently ordered to scout over the Staked Plains of Texas to locate some of the turbulent hostiles' camps, and started out, marching as far as Fort Bascom, N. M., without detecting the presence of Indians in any considerable number. Owing to the exhausted condition of the horses and the prevalence of disease among the men, the command returned to the supply camp, arriving there September 27, 1872.

The day following Colonel Mackenzie left his camp again, having provided himself with new operating material in men and horses, taking with him Companies A, D, F, I and L of the Fourth United States Cavalry.

After riding one day at a good steady gallop, the command reached the North Fork of the Red River, where a camp of Comanches of considerable size was sighted. A charge was ordered and the command swooped down upon the lodges, numbering 280, with vigor and dash. The Indian pony herd stampeded and made a mad rush for the village, giving the first alarm of the approach of the troopers to the unsuspecting redskins, who at once prepared to resist the sudden attack.

Lieutenant Hudson with Troop I led the advance, and in jumping from the bank to the bed of the river the lieutenant's horse and the horses of some of the men got stuck in the quicksands and could neither advance nor retreat. Colonel Mackenzie ordered Sergeant William Wilson of Troop I to take command of the troop, continue the charge and hold the right of the village.

This order Wilson executed with skill and bravery and complete success, holding his position until recalled at sunset. In the meantime the remainder of the command attacked the left of the village, and after a fierce and bloody fight of three hours defeated and routed the Comanches, who had to flee to avoid annihilation. The entire camp outfit, 300 squaws and over 3,000 ponies, fell into the hands of the troopers, whose loss consisted of one man killed, three wounded and a number of horses shot. The bodies of twenty-three Indians were gathered up and buried.

This stinging defeat so discouraged the Mow-wi tribe of Comanches that they subsequently gladly surrendered at Fort Sill, after having been on the warpath for seventeen years.

Besides Sergeant Wilson the following men distinguished themselves in this encounter: First Sergeant William McNamara, Sergeant William Foster, Privates Edward Branagan and William Rankin, Farrier David Larkin, of Troop F; Corporal Harry A. McMaster, of Troop A; Corporal William O'Neill and Blacksmith James Pratt, of Troop I.

Sergeant Wilson, a few months previous, on March 28, 1872, had a fight with Indians which furnished him an opportunity to distinguish himself, and for which he likewise received a Medal of Honor.

This fight occurred on the Colorado River near Fort Concho, Texas, when he and twenty privates of Troop I attacked a band of Indians and Mexican cattle thieves. After a short engagement the hostiles were driven off with a loss of four killed, several wounded and one prisoner in the hands of the sergeant himself. In addition, the marauders lost their entire camp equipage. Sergeant Wilson's capture proved to be important, as much valuable information in reference to the location of hostile camps was obtained from his prisoner.

THE BATTLE IN THE LAVA BEDS

T HE southwestern part of Oregon was formerly the home
of the powerful Indian nation of the Klamath. A
large, narrow stretch of lakes, the Upper and Lower Klamath, run nearly parallel to the mountains which reach
over the frontier down to California. East of the lower
Klamath, divided by the frontier, lies a third lake, the
Tule, into which the Lost River empties its waters.

In 1873 the Upper Klamath touched towards the northeast, the southwest corner of the Indian Reservation of the
Klamaths, who counted among one of their offshoots the
warlike tribe of the Modocs.

JOHN GREEN,
Major, 1st U. S. Cavalry,
Born in Germany, Nov. 20th, 1825.
Highest rank attained: Lieut.-Col,
and Brevet Brig.-Gen. U.S.A.

The Modocs, then under the leadership of Captain Jack,
did not live on the reservation, but occupied a stretch of
land about the Lost River.

This region was the original home of the Modocs. But after the government
road had been laid through the heart of their country and the immigrants began to
come, trouble naturally arose. There was a massacre of seventy-five whites in 1852,
and a treacherous murdering of forty-one Modocs, who had been invited to a peace
council, as retaliation for the former act.

In 1864 the Klamaths, Modocs, Yakooskins and Snakes gave up their territory, as
agreed to in a treaty, for the exchange of the above named reservation farther
north. The Modocs, it seems, were the ones who meant to keep most strictly and
faithfully to their agreement; they began to cultivate the land assigned them with
skill and diligence. But the Klamaths, now their immediate neighbors, annoyed
them so that they simply left, after only a few months' stay, and returned to their
old home.

In 1869, after having been given all sorts of promises and assurances of protection
against the Klamaths, they let themselves be coaxed into coming back to the reservation and started anew, with earnest effort, to create for themselves new homes.
But the promises of the government's representatives proved to have been wind, and
the provocations and annoyances by the Klamaths grew more unbearable than ever,
they going so far as to claim tribute for fish, grass, timber and water. The Modocs
were helpless themselves, as the Klamaths far outnumbered them. So they appealed
to the White Father, through his Indian Agent. This man, instead of following the
appeal with protection and help, simply removed the guiltless Modocs again to
another place; they went there, insulted and taunted by their overbearing enemies,
and losing all the work and time spent upon their former grounds.

The Klamaths did not leave them alone in their new country, and again the
Modocs appealed to the government agent. The latter, instead of checking their
aggressors, tried to move the Modocs again, to still another place. But their
patience was exhausted, especially as the new region appeared to them altogether

unsuitable. They left the reservation for their old hunting grounds. Here in the meantime the whites had settled more or less thickly, and there was no longer room for the homeless red man. Soon difficulties arose, and complaints against the Indians were frequent. Then—this was in 1871—the Superintendent of Indian Affairs tried, by sending a special commission, to induce them to return to the reservation. They refused and declared their wish, to settle with the superintendent in person and permanently. They wanted to be separated from the Klamaths and claimed a small reservation on Lost River for their home.

Demonstrations against them were of no avail; the white settlers grew more and more urgent in their demands to have the Indians removed, as they, Indian fashion, could not resist from committing all sorts of minor offenses and misdemeanors, which rendered them dangerous and highly undesirable neighbors.

It happened that the command of the Department of the Columbia was then in the hands of Brigadier-General E. R. S. Canby, a soldier of great professional experience, natural tact and thorough comprehension of the situation, and consequently eminently qualified to deal with it.

When a joint petition of the white settlers of the Lost River district and the Indian Agent asking for the removal of the Indians reached the superintendent he took the side of the settlers and communicated to General Canby the desirability of removing the Modocs by force.

General Canby investigated. In a short letter, which proved afterwards his remarkably good judgment and true conception of the state of affairs, he recommended moderation. He was not heeded. In the fall of 1872 the agent demanded directly and peremptorily from the Modocs that they should comply with his wishes and return forthwith to the part of the reservation assigned to them. They defied him. The next step was an appeal by the agent, in the name of the Central Office in Washington, to the commanding officer at Fort Klamath to furnish a force sufficient to compel the Modocs to return to Camp Yainak. The commanding officer, Major John Green of the First U. S. Cavalry, had to comply, and detailed Captain Jackson with about thirty men for the purpose Jackson left Fort Klamath on November 28, 1872, and thus started the Modoc War.

On the 29th the troop reached Captain Jack's camp before daylight; the Indians were still asleep. The clattering of the hoofs of the United States cavalry horses among their tents brought them quickly to their feet.

A short "talk" ensued, during which Captain Jackson endeavored to point out to Captain Jack the imprudence of resisting the United States Government, and urged him to accept the request of the Indian Agent and to return to the Klamath Reservation. The officer promised that the Modocs would this time be protected against any transgressions whatever from the Klamaths. But Captain Jack, having apparently become too distrusting by preceding events, would not listen. Jackson finally ordered the Indians present to lay down their arms. Some of them complied, but a warrior by the name of Scar Faced Charlie refused to obey, and when an officer approached him with a cocked pistol in hand two shots were fired; the Indians claimed the officer had fired first, and the military claimed that the Indians had been the aggressors. A fight was the result, in which a party of citizens joined as opponents of the red men. Nine warriors lost their lives, the rest were driven into the hills; one soldier was killed and seven wounded.

The Indians selected as their stronghold a stretch of country known as the Lava Beds, south of Tule Lake, a most inaccessible region. The Lava Beds comprise an intricate net of gorges, crests and crevices, amply supplied with water from Tule Lake, and covering a surface of four by seven miles.

The next expedition was started against the hostiles towards the middle of January. It numbered some 400 men, officers included; 225 were regulars, the rest volunteers. After the commanding officer had obtained a true insight of the almost absolute inaccessibility of the country and the character of his foe, things which he could not have known beforehand, he reported that 1,000 men might have been equal to the task.

During the whole fight hardly half a dozen Indians were seen by the soldiers, although the attacking force lost between forty and fifty killed and wounded.

While on this occasion many deeds of valor on the part of the troops came to light, the most conspicuous personage during the whole fight was Major John Green, the commander at Fort Klamath, whose conduct won the admiration of all who observed him.

Major Green commanded a line of skirmishers. As the battle ground was of such peculiar formation that an unbroken line of skirmishers would a few minutes later find itself split up in small detachments cut off from one another by impassable crevices and exposed to sudden flanking fire from an unseen enemy, extreme precaution was required to avoid disaster. The rank and file, who felt their prey continuously slipping away from them, between their fingers, so to speak, while the hostile shots told only the more severely, were likely to lose heart and confidence in themselves. So it happened that, when the command came to advance, the men in some part of Major Green's line appeared none too eager to execute the orders; they had sustained severe losses without any visible counter effect upon the Indians, and the position then held was a sheltered one. Major Green, seeing this, at once stepped forward and commenced walking coolly up and down, fully exposed to the enemy's fire, showing his men by his own example that the hostile bullets were not worthy of notice. During the whole engagement he exposed himself with a recklessness that could not fail to impress his men. Under fire it is the example of the superior which inspires the soldier to disdain death and danger and to devote his whole energy to the fulfillment of duty.

As the United States forces were not at all adequate to cope with the foe under the heavy odds against them they were finally "withdrawn to their camps."

This second effort to force the Modocs back to the Klamath Reservation had thus failed.

Re-enforcements were asked for. At this stage the Central Office in Washington considered it wise to resort again to a peace commission. Then it was deemed timely to take General Canby into the confidence of the Indian Affairs Department. Canby advised that now, after the first clash had taken place, there was only one way to assure success, and that was to crush the Indians by a superior force, bring them to terms, and then, after their forced surrender, treat them fairly.

But in spite of his proposition the peace commission, consisting of Mr. A. B. Meacham, Rev. Dr. Thomas and the Indian Agent, L. S. Dyar, arrived and conferred with the general. The latter, from his experience, foresaw the futility of an attempt to pacify the fully aroused savages now by any other means but force. On the 5th of March a telegram arrived from the Secretary of the Interior to the commission, saying: "I do not believe that the Modocs mean treachery. Continue negotiations." A subsequent meeting with the representative Indians on April 2d showed their suspicion, fully awakened now to a degree far beyond the possible influence of "negotiation." Besides, there were the warnings of an experienced scout and interpreter by the name of Frank Riddle, and his wife, a full-blood Modoc woman, who had always been loyal to her husband and his friends, and proved to be so to the last.

But all these signs and warnings availed not with the majority of the commissioners.

General Canby had by this time assembled all his troops, surrounding the enemy's fastnesses.

After several fruitless meetings the Indians sent several of their tribe and the two famous warriors, Bogus Charley and Boston Charley, to propose a meeting the next day at a certain place, both negotiating parties to be unarmed.

They were so urgent and apparently so sincere that even the sharp Canby was deceived. It was agreed to meet on the next day; Meacham, Dyar, Dr. Thomas and General Canby were to go as the representatives of the White Father. The two Indian rogues, Bogus Charley and Boston Charley, were kept in camp over night and treated with friendly consideration and kindness. Commissioners Meacham and Dyar had their suspicions, but were overruled. Tobe, the wife of Scout Riddle, implored the commissioners not to go, as her tribesmen planned treachery and murder; but her entreaties were in vain.

Next morning the party started for the council-tent. They were General Canby, Dr. Thomas, Meacham, Dyar, Riddle and his Modoc wife, and the two warriors, Bogus Charley and Boston Charley; they carried no arms whatever; General Canby took a box of cigars with him.

At the council-tent they met six chieftains, armed; Captain Jack, Schonchin, Shacknasty Jim, Ellen's Man, Hooker Jim and Black Jim. Their pistols could be seen sticking out of their blankets. The two Charleys, who had been treated so

"MAJOR JOHN GREEN RESCUED THE WOUNDED."

friendly in the white camp, forthwith joined their comrades, disappeared for a while and came back armed. Canby and his companions now saw plainly that they had been entrapped. But Canby stepped forward coolly and invited everyone to sit down for the meeting. The whites sat on one side of a small sage-brush fire, the redskins on the other; Riddle and Tobe were near General Canby. The latter handed around his box of cigars, and the council farce began.

Suddenly Hooker Jim arose and, taking an overcoat from Dyar's horse, said sneeringly while putting it on, "Here is Mr. Meacham." The commissioners thought to ignore the incident, although it was of bad enough significance; only Meacham said: "Well, take my hat, if you want to," to which the savage replied in his own language, "Just wait a bit and I will, too." The crisis was in sight.

General Canby, in a dignified little speech, explained to the Indians, through Riddle, that wherever he had dealings with them he had always looked out fairly for their interests, so that Indians of several tribes with whom he had negotiated had acknowledged to him their gratitude in various ways. He expressed the hope that some time he would also be successful in winning the friendship of the Modocs.

The chieftains received this speech with impudent sneers and contemptuous laughter.

Schonchin arose and began a harangue which was characteristic of his fierce and murderous inclinations. With loud shouts he insisted that all the soldiers should be sent home immediately and the Hot Creek region given to the Modocs as their reservation.

While he was talking, evidently only to kill time, two Modoc warriors came in, each one carrying three rifles.

Dr. Thomas, kneeling down, said: "I believe the Great Spirit sent us here to make peace. I know my heart and those of my friends, and I know they are good; we want no more war. The Great Spirit made all men, the red man and the white man. We are all brothers and will live in peace together."

Captain Jack had quickly gotten up and, springing behind Dyar's horse, cocked his pistol. Two more armed Indians rushed upon the scene. General Canby rose and demanded sternly: "Captain Jack, what does this mean?" The answer was a shot from Jack's pistol, the bullet striking the General in the face, right under his left eye. He jumped forward, but Ellen's Man shot him through the head from behind, and Canby fell dead. Boston Charley then sent a bullet through the lungs of poor Dr. Thomas, whose guest he had been during the preceding night. Dr. Thomas fell, raised himself again on his arm and said to the treacherous savage: "Boston, stop shooting; I am dying now." The Indian sneered: "Damn ye! Maybe you will believe next time what squaw (Riddle's wife) tell ye," and he shattered the doctor's brain with a second bullet.

Dyar, when the shooting began, succeeded in running away, out of harm's reach.

Meacham was attacked by the bloodthirsty Schonchin, who sent several bullets into him. Meacham fell and would have been scalped had not brave Tobe, Riddle's wife, suddenly raised the cry: "The soldiers are coming!" It was a ruse, but a clever one and saved Meacham's life.

The Indians fled into the lava beds. When the soldiers finally did come they were all gone.

Now, that the long-foreseen outrage had been committed and two precious lives sacrificed for nothing, the eyes of the central authorities opened sufficiently to size up the gravity of the situation, and prompt action was taken at last to make an end of the dangers and atrocities in this region forever. The Modocs must be exterminated.

The wily and desperate redskins, who must have been aware of what was awaiting them, kept still, hidden in their lava crevices.

Colonel Gillem of the First United States Cavalry, who only escaped the chance of sharing Canby's and Thomas's fate by being too ill to accompany the hapless peace-party, was ordered to attack without delay with all his available forces.

The troops, flanking the lava beds, joined at the lake front and cut off the water supply of the Indians. The latter had to come out, and desperate fighting followed, lasting three days. The troops proved too weak to prevent their foe from finding another strong position, where they again defiantly awaited further developments.

A reconnoissance was ordered, and Captain Thomas of the Fourth United States Artillery went forward, his command consisting of five officers, a surgeon, sixty-five enlisted men and fourteen friendly Warm Spring Indians. The detachment left early in the morning. The objective point was reached at noon, and as no hostile Indians had been observed, the command halted for a rest. Unfortunate men! Before they had finished an impromptu meal a volley came suddenly pouring in, well aimed, and instantly creating a panic. The men ran to escape the bullets; the officers and non-commissioned officers, with a few fearless men of the rank-and-file, rallied, made a gallant stand, and after a desperate and heroic struggle met their fate.

Some Warm Spring Indian scouts who attempted to bring succor to the ambushed party, but were by mistake fired at by the whites, rushed back to camp and reported the latter's desperate plight. Major Green, ever ready, gathered in the utmost hurry all the available forces and hastened to the spot. But of the five line officers four were found killed, Captain Thomas and Lieutenants Cranston, Wright and Howe, and Lieutenant Harris mortally wounded. Besides there were eighteen men killed and seventeen wounded of this gallant band, which when it assembled for the last stand had hardly numbered fifty men. Major Green rescued the wounded, among whom was also the surgeon of the party, Dr. Semig, who escaped death in a miraculous way. He had been twice severely wounded and lay helpless between the rocks, hearing, while still conscious, how the hostiles endeavored to reach him and lift his scalp. Finally consciousness fled, and when he came to he was in the hands of friends, he having lain there fully twenty hours. Major Green had come in time. The rapidly advancing soldiers kept the savages from crawling towards their intended victim, as they would have been compelled to expose themselves had they done so.

This new disaster increased the energy of the military, and on the 2d of May General Davis reached the scene with a goodly force of fresh troops.

"THEY TURNED AND OPENED THE ATTACK THEMSELVES."

Two friendly Modoc squaws were sent into the lava beds as spies; after some days' absence they returned with the information that the enemy had gone.

Instantly a vigorous pursuit was ordered.

The exhausted savages had not been able to make much headway in their flight, and when they became aware that the soldiers were after them they turned and opened the attack themselves. This time they were badly beaten and scattered, and finally fell back again to the lava beds, defending every inch of the ground against the vigorously pushing troops. The latter took the enemy between two lines, and the situation of the sandwiched redskins became hopeless. They began to quarrel among themselves and split soon into two parties, both of which succeeded in sneaking out of the lava beds unseen. But soon the troops were after them. On the 22d of May one band surrendered, and almost immediately after this a Modoc captive, who had enjoyed Captain Jack's full confidence, betrayed the whereabouts of the latter. On the 1st of June the famous chief and his band were surprised and scattered; many of them were killed, some captured, but Jack escaped. On the 3d of June he and three loyal followers were surrounded and gave themselves up. Jack explained stoically that he would not have been caught had not fatigue overcome him.

During these last days of desperate fighting and pursuing it was again Major John Green who, in courage, zeal, instruction and intelligence, proved a model soldier, and impressed his men more than any other officer with the idea of absolute fearlessness. Self-protection and shelter were ever secondary in his mind to the accomplishment of what he had in view, and he richly deserved his Medal of Honor.

The subdued Modocs were all brought to the Tule Lake, which place they reached on the 5th of June. Captain Jack, Schonchin, Black Jim, Boston Charley, Barncho and Sloluck, the six leaders, were afterwards tried by a military commission at Fort Klamath on the 1st of July, found guilty and sentenced to death. The sentences of Barncho and Sloluck were commuted to imprisonment for life, while the other four were hanged at Fort Klamath on October 3, 1873.

This was practically the end of the Modocs; the remnants of the band were conveyed to a small stretch of land near Baxter Springs, Kansas, where they now offer an illustration of the slowly-dying-out process, and Barncho and Sloluck withered away to their graves in the prison at Alcatraz.

RESCUING THE GERMAINE GIRLS

MANY of the Indian uprisings were like the convulsive struggles of a dying race, the last efforts of a people doomed to final extinction against the irresistible and relentless march and progress of civilization. The white man's civilization was as ruthless in the removal of all obstacles and the extermination of every race or nation that proved a hindrance as the cruelty and barbarism of the savage himself, differing only in the methods. The Indian exerted his brute force, the white man his intellectual superiority; the result could be but fatal to the former.

A characteristic uprising of this kind was planned and inaugurated by the Southern

FRANK D. BALDWIN,
First Lieutenant, Fifth U. S. Infantry. Highest rank attained: Colonel 27th U. S. Inf. Born in Washtenaw County, Mich., June 26, 1842.

Cheyennes, Kiowas, Arapahoes and other bands in the Indian Territory in 1874, and the first serious occurrences took place in June of that year, with Texas as the main scene of action. The events which led up to and culminated in the outbreak were accumulative rather than of one single and definite character.

Civilization was making rapid progress; the white man was penetrating the forests, colonizing at streams and waters and covering the plains and prairies. The establishment of military posts, trading stations and settlements, the building of railroads, gradually changed the character of whole sections of the country. Nor was this accomplished with consideration or regard for the Indian's feeling of piety and respect. Places of ancient worship were demolished, to be replaced, perhaps, by a prosaic railway station; old burying grounds, regarded by the Indian with justifiable veneration, were made to disappear by the hand of the white man, who claimed ownership of the sacred spot. The Indian's anger grew as he observed these changes in conditions, which in his eyes were but evidences of rude vandalism.

Again, the white man was depleting the Indian's hunting ground by his wholesale slaughter of buffalo. From this animal the savage derived his clothing, food and shelter; yet the white man killed them by thousands. The greed of the frontiersman, who found in the skin of the buffalo a ready article of trade, knew no bounds. Statistics show that within a few years over 4,000,000 buffaloes were killed by white hunters.

Some time early in June the aforementioned Indian tribes met at Medicine Lodge, Indian Territory, and at a general council aired their various grievances. The chiefs were bitter in their denunciation of the invaders' vandalism and reckless brutality, and war was decided upon to stop further acts of this kind. Subsequently bands of these tribes began to leave their reservations, cross the boundary lines and harass and disturb the settlers along the Texas frontier. War opened in earnest when a body of several hundred Indians advanced to attack some buffalo hunters. Fortunately for the latter, the attack was planned on a Sunday, when the hunters were assembled together for mutual rest and recreation, and thus were able to present a united front to the attacking warriors. They were crack riflemen, too, these hunters, and easily repulsed the savage foe, killing nearly one-fourth of the entire Indian force.

This sudden attack, however, induced the government to order an expedition against the rebellious tribes, and thus the Indian War of 1874 followed, during which one of the most pathetic incidents of any of the Indian wars occurred.

The Cheyennes had crossed from their reservation to the territory of Western Kansas. Their path was marked by plunder and devastation. Among the first victims were the members of a family by the name of Germaine, consisting of man and wife, a grown-up son and daughter and four smaller children, girls, aged fifteen, thirteen, nine and seven years respectively. The Germaines originally lived in Georgia, but had later moved to Western Missouri, and now were on their way to Colorado. Although their journey was slow, they were well provided with food, carried along a fairly large stock, including several horses and an outfit of several wagons. Thus far their travels had been uneventful and free from adventure, and they were already congratulating themselves on having been spared the many dangers which in those days usually lurked in the path of the pioneer. But their joy was premature, and disaster struck them when they least expected it. A cruel fate came between them and their hopes and ended the journey of the little family.

The Cheyennes surprised them, killed Germaine and his wife, also the son, and carried off the four girls as captives, together with all their property.

For some reason or other they did not want to keep the oldest of the Germaine girls, but killed her in the presence of her trembling little sisters. These they dragged along with them on the retreat to their camp, and later kept them prisoners in their village. It is almost impossible to describe the fate to which these children were doomed among the uncouth savages. The life they had to endure, the tortures to which they were subjected, are too revolting to recite. Their innocence and tender age offered no protection from the outrages of their captors; their prayers and tears failed to move the hearts of their fiendish tormentors. They were looked upon by the males as common property and by the squaws as objects of pleasure and pastime for their consorts.

The expedition organized by the government and directed in these sections by General Nelson A. Miles began operations in June and continued all through the summer and autumn, the Indians being driven back into their reservations, wherever they showed themselves. Hostilities did not cease when winter came, but the pursuit was vigorously kept up during the cold season, and over territory where the Indians had heretofore felt themselves free and undisturbed. Wherever their trail was discovered, it was followed as long as it could be traced.

During one of these winter expeditions the command of First Lieutenant Frank D. Baldwin, Fifth United States Infantry, consisting of a force of friendly Delaware Indians, twenty-five frontiersmen, expert riflemen, scouts and men accustomed to the Indian's way of fighting, Troop D, of the Sixth United States Cavalry, commanded by Lieutenant Overton, and Company D, Fifth United States Infantry, Lieutenant Bailey commanding, at daylight, November 8, 1874, was moving through a rough country, bordering the east of the Staked Plains of the Pan Handle of Texas, when scouts, coming back suddenly at breakneck speed, reported the presence of a large Indian camp only a short distance in front in the breaks. Lieutenant Baldwin, without waiting for re-enforcements, at once closed up his command, preparatory to an attack, and sent Scout Schmalsle to General Miles to notify him that an Indian camp had been located and an attack would be made upon it immediately, regardless of the numerically vastly superior Indian forces.

After dispatching the scout, Baldwin ordered his command to advance as rapidly as possible, until it was within range of the camp.

Then Company D fired a volley into the camp and drove the surprised and unprepared Indians to the brow of the hills overlooking the plain. Here the warriors rallied, and turning suddenly made a most desperate effort to repulse the soldiers and retake their camp and abandoned property.

Lieutenant Baldwin now brought the cavalry into action and once more forced the braves to flee, chasing them hotly for a distance of over twelve miles. The

"THEY DROVE THE SURPRISED INDIANS TO THE BROW OF THE HILL."

victory was complete and resulted in the capture of the entire Indian camp and the rescue of the two younger Germaine girls, Adelaide and Julia.

It was Chief Gray Beard's own camp of Cheyenne Indians, the very same savages who had perpetrated the outrage upon the wayfaring Germaine family, that had been captured by Baldwin.

The rescue of these two little girls was the reward of his quick and decisive action. For had he delayed the attack only for a short time, the Indians would undoubtedly have murdered their white captives and managed their escape.

Freed from the clutches of their tormentors the little girls were boundless in their joy. They cried and laughed, their eyes beamed with delight; they kissed and hugged their deliverers and knew not how to express their childish gratitude.

Those who were present when the children were led away from the camp where they had suffered so much will never forget the scene. Soldiers surrounded them; now one, now the other, would take one of the little ones in his arms and carry her along for a distance, and many a grim warrior cried as he heard the child tell her revolting experience. They clenched their fists and vowed vengeance upon the savages. "By all that is holy, there won't be a rest till we get the other two girls!" they exclaimed, and they kept their word. The two children were, under proper care, sent to Fort Leavenworth, Kansas, while the pursuit of the Indians was continued with unrelenting vigor. For two months this warfare was kept up, when at last the Indians began to weary of further hostilities and showed evidences of submission.

A trusted and friendly Indian was sent to the camp of the warriors with a message from General Miles demanding their surrender, and coupled with the further condition that they bring in alive the prisoners they had in their hands. The message made it plain that there would be no peace granted until these prisoners were restored. The Indian messenger had still another mission. He was told to find the Germaine girls and hand them a photograph of their sisters who had been liberated. On the back of the photograph the general had written: "Your little sisters are well and in the hands of friends. Do not be discouraged. Every effort is being made for your welfare." This picture and message the faithful Indian slipped into the hands of the captive Germaine girls after his arrival in the hostile camp, and thus brought a ray of hope and sunshine to the two unfortunate girls. They had almost despaired of ever hearing of their sisters, and with sullen resignation prepared themselves to die among the savages, far away from their friends and white people.

The Indians were only too glad to have a chance to secure peace. In spite of snow and ice and the hardships of winter travel, they journeyed over 200 miles to their agency, where they surrendered. At the beginning of the march the chief ordered special care to be taken of the Germaine girls, who now were treated with the greatest kindness and consideration.

At the agency the Indians were lined up and the girls told to point out the perpetrators of the murder of their parents, brother and sister and their own worst tormentors. The girls passed along the line and pointed out seventy-five Indians. These were placed under guard and taken to St. Augustine, Florida.

The sisters subsequently were united at Fort Leavenworth, where they were educated, General Miles becoming their guardian. They each received $2,500 from the government.

That a sad story thus had a happy conclusion was due primarily to the brilliant and decisive victory of Lieutenant Baldwin, the hero of the Indian war of 1874, a man whom nature had designated to be a soldier, who was endowed with those qualities which alone prepare a man for a soldier's life — gallantry and bravery. For this voluntary attack and its successful issue he was awarded the Medal of Honor.

His conduct during the War of the Rebellion furnishes additional proof of this and brought him suitable reward and recognition from the government. An achievement at Peach Tree Creek, Georgia, July 20, 1864, earned for him his first Medal of Honor.

He was captain of Company D, Nineteenth Michigan Infantry, at the time, and, under a galling fire, led his company against the enemy, entering the Confederate lines ahead of his own men where, single-handed, he took two commissioned officers prisoners and carried off the guidon of a Georgia regiment.

WITH GENERAL MILES THROUGH TEXAS

THE pursuit of the Indians in the uprising of 1874 carried General Miles's command to the Staked Plains of Western Texas, as has been related in the previous story. It now becomes necessary to describe his march briefly, leading up as it does to occurrences of more than passing importance and which form the subject of the present narration.

General Miles left Fort Dodge, Indian Territory, on August 14th, in a southerly direction, and for the remainder of the month covered a distance of many hundred miles through a country that had been devastated by a peculiar scourge—the plague of locusts—and, in addition, offered many other natural disadvantages. The almost unbearable heat of the hottest season of the year, when the mercury seldom, if ever, drops below 110 degrees in the shade, together with the large bands of ever-alert and hostile Indians, contributed to make this expedition one of the most memorable in the history of the Indian wars.

The beds of the many small rivers and creeks were completely dry. For days the troops marched without a drop of water. Sometimes the ground over which they had to pass was a mere desert, and this added to the misery of men and beasts. Sometimes, after many hours of weary marching, the soldiers, with rapturous delight, would hail the sight of a rivulet which promised the much-needed refreshment, only to find upon arriving at its inviting banks that the water was so impregnated with minerals as to be absolutely unfit for drinking purposes. Hardships and disappointments all along the route put the military spirit, the endurance and tenaciousness of the command to the highest test, but the American soldier proved here, as always, that he was, under all circumstances, equal to the occasion, and General Miles bestowed the highest praise upon the excellent conduct of his men during this trying march. They not only braved the fatigues of weather and territory, but met the constant attacks and harassing manœuvres of the hostile Indians with unabated courage, defeating and routing them wherever the savage hordes showed themselves.

In this fashion the march was continued towards the Canadian River in Texas, when, on August 27th, the main trail of the Indians was finally struck at the Sweetwater River. It was followed with eagerness and was of such character the day following as to lead the command to believe that they were in the immediate proximity of the long-looked-for main body of the enemy. This infused new life into the weary troops, who, incredible as it may seem, marched sixty-five miles during the next two days in their ardor to meet the redskins.

On the morning of August 30th, Lieutenant Frank D. Baldwin, the hero of the foregoing story, and his detachment of scouts, two miles ahead of the main column, were attacked by a large band of hostiles, who with the usual hideous ado sprang from their places of concealment lining the bluff which bordered the level plains, and with reckless daring charged right into the small detachment.

Baldwin's men at once took position, dropped to the ground and used their rifles with unerring and unfailing effect. With the detachment were a number of friendly Delawares under their aged chief, Fall Leaf. This veteran warrior summoned about him his faithful braves, and with glittering eyes and streaming gray hair he swung his rifle and dashed, the very picture of an Indian hero, at the head of his men against the hated enemy. The hostiles were held at bay till the main column arrived upon the scene of action, but they came none too soon, for the Indians, too, had received re-enforcements, and thus what was at first but a mere short and sharp fight now turned into a real battle, lasting for some hours and ending in a complete route of the Indians, who were driven across the Red River into the Staked Plains and pursued for more than twenty miles.

After the victory, the troops, now thoroughly fagged out, halted at the bed of the Red River, about half a mile wide at that point. A small, stagnant pool, saturated with gypsum and alkalai, was the only water in sight, and that nobody could drink. How the men suffered! General Miles states that he saw some of them open the veins of their arms to moisten their parched lips with their own blood.

The next day the command moved into the Staked Plains, and there, in a locality where water was abundant, rested to await the arrival of a new supply train from Camp Supply, Indian Territory.

The arrangement by which these supplies were to be transported was this: Captain Wyllys Lyman, Fifth United States Infantry, with his company, and Lieutenant Frank West, Sixth United States Cavalry, with twenty men, were sent to meet the supply train, which General Miles knew had left Camp Supply some days previously. The two detachments met September 7th, and the stores were transferred, a violent storm rendering the work rather difficult and of slow progress. The return march was eventful. At the outset the Indians made their presence felt in a most annoying manner. A teamster, for example, who had imprudently wandered away a short distance, fell into their hands, was scalped, killed, and his body left on the trail. The farther the train proceeded, the bolder these savages grew, increasing, too, in numbers all along the route.

On September 9th, just as the train emerged from a deep ravine, the Indians, who, it now appeared, were Kiowas and Comanches, who had left their reservations, attacked the rear of the train. They numbered fully 300, and, relying upon their strength, displayed unusual boldness and audacity. They came within 100 yards of the train, shot Lieutenant G. Lewis, Fifth United States Infantry, a sergeant and several soldiers. It was by almost superhuman efforts that the brave men composing the small detachment foiled the impetuous attack of the Indians.

The train continued to wend its way slowly and cautiously across the Washita River into Texas territory, and finally came to a halt one mile north of the river· Then all further progress ceased. · The Indians had increased to such a strength that they were able to completely surround the entire detachment.

In spite of the most vigorous and gallant resistance, in which First Sergeant John Mitchell, Sergeants Fred S. Hay, William Koelpin, Corporal John James, John J. H. Kelly, John W. Knox and Private Thomas Kelly, of the Fifth United States Infantry, and Sergeants George H. Kitchen, Fred S. Neilon, Josiah Pennsyl and Corporals William W. Morris and Edward C. Sharpless, of the Sixth United States Cavalry, distinguished themselves, the savages would have succeeded but for the personal bravery of that daring young scout, Schmalsle.

On the second night, when darkness had fallen, Schmalsle mounted his horse and dashed through the lines of the warriors with such reckless speed as to completely surprise the braves. A number of them attempted to pursue the daring rider, but Schmalsle had the better mount and was the better rider, and proved too speedy for his pursuers.

He was chased into a herd of buffaloes and escaped in the tumult and under the cover of darkness.

Schmalsle continued his wild ride till his horse became completely exhausted and dropped dead on the road. The young scout then traveled on foot, and after two nights of continuous marching—he was compelled to hide during the day— finally reached Camp Supply, where he furnished information of the critical situation of the supply train.

SERGEANT NEILON CARRYING AMMUNITION TO THE BESIEGED TROOPERS.

Colonel Lewis at once sent Major Price with a battalion of the Eighth United States Cavalry to the relief. The appearance of this large force caused the Indians to raise the siege and disperse in all directions.

"The Indians," First Sergeant George K. Kitchen, of Troop I, Sixth United States Cavalry, relates, "concentrated their entire force, and made a vigorous and united charge on the train. This charge was repulsed after a hard fight, the Indians coming to within fifty yards of the train, and repeatedly attempting, after being beaten off, to overwhelm the troops by dint of superior numbers.

"The wagons were then, as it was impossible to advance, put 'into park' as rapidly as possible, forming in an egg shape. The infantry was thrown out on a skirmish line round the hastily formed corral, some 25 yards from the wagons. When this movement was completed, the little band of cavalry found themselves, at the end of some hard fighting, about 500 yards away from the skirmish line, and surrounded by the enemy. To regain their comrades of the Fifth Infantry they had to charge through a mass of Indians, who concentrated themselves between them and the wagons. This was successfully done.

"On reaching the 'park' we secured our horses inside the enclosure, and were then ordered out on the skirmish line.

"The hostiles now divided, and about 400 of them at this time made two unsuccessful charges on the right rear of the corral, defended by about one-half of the command. These charges were made in column of platoons, and the alignment was as precise and well maintained as regular troops could do it. Each time they came up to within forty yards of the line in admirable order, and only the perfect steadiness and continuous, well-directed fire of our troops prevented this well-conceived and daringly executed movement from being successful.

"By our heavy fire, however, we at last succeeded in repelling them in confusion from the very muzzles of our guns.

"The enemy then, unsuccessful in storming us, took up position on the numerous sand hills around, some as far away as 400 yards, others at about only 200 yards, surrounding us by a complete circle. As we lay beneath them we were exposed to a severe and vexatious fire from all points, and our return fire was comparatively harmless. When darkness arrived we were divided up into squads, and orders were given to dig rifle pits, from twenty to thirty yards distant, around the corral. The enemy followed our example and were occupied in entrenching themselves on the sand hills they held during the day. Their object now appeared to be to starve us out, as they knew we had no means of quenching our thirst. The Washita was one mile away, and the one water-hole near us had been inaccessible during the day, and our repeated attempts to get at it at night proved futile. Several details tried to reach the water, but the Indians placed a strong guard around it, and their fire was too well-directed to allow of our men getting near. They would permit us to get within fifty yards of the hole, in fancied security, before opening on us, and then poured in their fire, which balked every effort to reach the desired spot. In the meantime a desultory fire was kept up by them on all sides of us.

"Next day this fire became regular and continuous, and was returned by us from the rifle pits. We killed many a brave, but his place was taken at once by a comrade, after the dead body had been carried off. This was done always by two Indians, riding at full gallop, one on each side of the dead man, who was picked up by them without their making the slightest halt, and dragged into shelter.

"When we first went into corral the command had but very little water in the canteens, and this was saved for the use of the wounded. From the 9th to the morning of the 14th of September no one, except our wounded, had one drop of water. On the third day, when driven almost to despair by the torments of thirst, some men opened a barrel of vinegar, and undertook to drink it when sweetened somewhat by sugar. It was with difficulty that they were prevented from swallowing too much of the mixture. One of the ten men whom I had in my rifle pit drank, in spite of my efforts to prevent any excess, so much of the vinegar that he became delirious and very violent. We had to tie him hand and foot to keep him inside the pit; he frothed at the mouth, bit and fought, and exhibited every token of insanity. It was two days before he recovered from the effects.

"The fighting, until the night of the 13th of September, was continued in the same way, we staying in our rifle pits, exhausted by heat and thirst, and returning as best we could the fire of the Indians, who remained in possession of their sand hills.

"On the morning of the 14th we saw, with relief, the whole band of Indians pull out and move south. If we had had water, we could have lasted a long time. Without it, we could not have stood the siege for many more days."

A few days prior—on September 12th—another no less thrilling incident occurred at about the same place, the Washita River.

General Miles had sent a detachment of six men, Sergeant Z. T. Woodall, Company I; Privates Peter Roth, Company A, John Harrington, Company H, and George W. Smith, Company M, Sixth U. S. Cavalry, and Scouts Amos Chapman and William Dixon, to carry a dispatch to Camp Supply.

On the way this party was attacked by a force of warriors numbering about 125. Four of the six men were wounded at the beginning of the fight, Private Smith mortally, and the other three severely. Surrounded by a foe outnumbering them twenty-five to one, the men were facing almost certain death; yet they were determined to sell their lives as dearly as possible.

Private Harrington describes the fight as follows:

"Between us and the Indians was a good-sized ravine, to which we advanced and rode into. We had scarcely time to dismount and leave the horses in charge of Smith, before the Indians were on us from all sides. We hurriedly sought shelter on the sides of the ravine. Smith was shot through the arm and compelled to abandon the horses and join us. About twenty-five Indians then charged down the ravine and stampeded our horses, taking all but one. Concluding that things were getting too warm for us, and that we would have to find some better position, we formed a skirmish line and fell back, the one horse left by the Indians following us. An Indian attempted to capture it, when Sergeant Woodall turned and fired, and the Indian fell.

"We again retreated in skirmish line, receiving their fire from all directions. Whenever we attempted to secure a knoll or other vantage ground, the Indians would be ahead of us in such numbers as to make us change our direction. None of us expected to get out of the fray alive, with such fearful odds against us, but all determined to die hard and make the best fight possible. We continued our skirmishing, and whenever a shelter was secured, took what little rest we could until driven out by renewed attacks.

"At every halt the Indians, dismounted, would surround us, closing in from all sides. The 'medicine man,' decorated with buffalo horns and an immense head-dress of eagle feathers reaching to his horse's tail, looking like the devil himself, tried to force them to charge over us; each time, as they circled into within about twenty-five yards, we would jump up, yell, and run towards those in our rear. The Indians could not fire for fear of hitting their own party, but would open out and allow us to pass through their line, firing at us as we went through.

"It seems almost incredible that we should have received their fire as long as we did without serious injury; but it could not go on so forever. We kept up these tactics until about 4 o'clock in the afternoon. The 'medicine man,' now the only mounted one of their party, kept riding around us all the time, getting bolder and firing his pistol when he came in range. Chapman, the scout, said, 'not to mind him, for he couldn't hit anything,' but at last he came within about twenty yards, when Scout Dixon fired at him, after which we saw no more of the bold 'medicine man.'

"By this time we were about done out, and our ammunition, of which we had 200 rounds per man in the morning, was nearly exhausted. Determining to make one last stand, we broke for a small knoll, on the top of which was a buffalo wallow. While attempting to gain this position, Smith was again shot and fell, mortally wounded. Woodall was shot in the groin, and I in the hip. All gained the knoll but Smith."

Sergeant Woodall adds the following: "At this stage of the fight we were eye-witnesses to some magnificent feats of horsemanship, that could not be equaled by any like number of men in the world—men rising readily from the stirrups while their horses were in rapid motion, and standing erect on the backs of their animals while they delivered their fire, and then instantly dropping, as if shot, into the stirrups; swinging themselves rapidly under their horses' bellies, in which position they could easily aim and fire. These tactics were continued by them for some time. There was one spot on the prairie where the grass stood over five feet high. Toward this place the Indians would ride as fast as their ponies could go, and I noticed every time any of the men fired at an Indian near this place the latter would drop as if hit, while his pony would continue on until finally caught by some of the squaws. Fully twenty of them dropped in this manner, leading us to believe that they were all hit. Nothing more was seen of them for about an hour, during which our attention was engaged in an opposite direction by another party of Indians, who repeatedly charged us, eventually forcing us from our position. In moving to higher ground we approached the bunch of tall grass before referred to, near which we had seen so many Indians drop. We got within fifty yards when a line of Indians sprang up, presenting as good a skirmish line as any body of soldiers could form, and poured a murderous fire into our party, droppingSmith and severely wound-ing Amos Chapman, Harrington and myself."

Smith, who had fallen outside, was thought to be dead. In a little while, how-ever, he was seen to move, and Chapman heroically volunteered to attempt to rescue him. Chapman tells the story of his noble act in the following words:

"'Now, boys,' said I to my comrades as I started out, 'keep those infernal redskins off me and I will run down and pick up Smith and bring him back before they can get at me.'

"I ran full speed to Smith and attempted to shoulder him. Smith was not a large man, but I declare that he seemed to weigh a ton. Finally I laid down and got his chest across my back, and his arms around my neck, and then got up with him. It was as much as I could do to stagger under him, for he couldn't help himself a bit. By the time I had got twenty or thirty yards, about fifteen Indians came for me at full speed on their ponies. They all knew me, and yelled, 'Amos! Amos! we have got you now!' I pulled my pistol, but I couldn't hold Smith on my back with one hand, so I let him drop. The boys in the buffalo wallow opened on the Indians just at the right time, and I opened on them with my pistol. There was a tumbling of ponies and a scattering of Indians, and in a minute they were gone. I got Smith up again and made the best possible time, but before I could reach the wallow another gang came for me. I had only one or two shots in my pistol, so I didn't stop to fight, but ran for it. When I was within about twenty yards of the wallow a little old scoundrel that I had fed fifty times rode almost on to me and fired. I fell, with Smith on top of me, but as I didn't feel any pain I thought I had stepped into a hole. The Indians couldn't stay around there a minute—the boys kept it red hot —so I jumped up, picked up Smith, and got safe into the wallow. 'Amos,' said Dixon, 'you are badly hurt.' 'No, I am not,' said I. 'Why, look at your leg,' he said, and, sure enough, the leg was so badly shattered just above the ankle joint'that I had been walking on the bone, dragging the foot behind me, and in the excitement I never knew it."

Night came, and with its merciful darkness an end was put to the unequal strug-gle. The bodies of more than twenty Indians lay stretched upon the ground.

The savages had no further desire to engage in a combat with that small but heroic band of soldiers and scouts and left the scene before the break of day.

Private Smith died early in the morning of September 13; Sergeant Woodall, Private Harrington and Scout Chapman were so severely wounded that they were unable to move, and Private Roth and Scout Dixon, though injured themselves, had to remain in the same small ditch to watch over the corpse of their dead comrade and comfort their wounded friends. The entire day passed before relief came. They were without food, and to quench their thirst were compelled to drink the filthy water that had collected in the trench and been mixed with their own blood.

At night Major Price, with a strong command, came and took them to Camp Supply.

In speaking of this affair General Miles says: "The simple recital of their deeds and the mention of the odds against which they fought; how the wounded defended the dying, and the dying aided the wounded by exposure to fresh wounds after the power of action was gone; these alone present a scene of cool courage, heroism and self-sacrifice which duty, as well as inclination, prompts us to recognize, but which we cannot fitly honor."

AMOS CHAPMAN BRINGING IN SMITH

HAND-TO-HAND FIGHTS WITH INDIANS

SIMULTANEOUSLY with the operations of General Miles in Indian Territory were those conducted by Colonel R. S. Mackenzie, who was moving with his command, Troops A, D, E, F, H, I, K, Fourth Cavalry, towards the Red River, Texas, from the south.

The torrents which follow the dry season made the roadbeds almost impassable for wagons, and impeded the progress of this column seriously. In spite of the difficulties of the march and the many privations which resulted therefrom, the troops preserved a most excellent spirit, and easily repulsed two determined attacks made by the Indians. After crossing the head of the Tule Canyon Colonel Mackenzie located five camps of Southern Cheyennes and their allies at Canyon Blanco, a tributary of the Red River, and immediately proceeded to attack them.

In the subsequent fight, which lasted two days, September 26 and 27, 1874, the Indians were put to utter rout, leaving their entire camp outfits and their herds of ponies, some 1,400 animals, in the possession of the victors. The Indians lost four killed and several wounded, while of the troops but one was wounded, and he only slightly. Corporal Edwin Phoenix and Privates Gregory Mahoney and William McCabe, of Company E, were especially conspicuous for their gallantry in this conflict and received the Medal of Honor in consequence. A like honor was conferred upon Private Adam Paine, who as an Indian scout rendered invaluable services to Colonel Mackenzie.

After this victory the column continued its march and had many other engagements with the redskins. In the fight on November 3d Farrier Ernest Veuve, of Company A, had an interesting encounter with a hostile Indian who faced him at a most unexpected time and when he was completely separated from his comrades. The intrepid farrier, however, proved equal to the emergency, and after a brief hand-to-hand fight put the Indian to flight.

Private John W. Comfort, of the same company, two days later had a similar experience, but with a more fatal result, as far as the attacking savage was concerned. Comfort killed his adversary outright during the struggle.

The chase after the Indians continued all winter and lasted till the spring of the following year. The hostiles, wherever found, were attacked and driven back to their reservations.

At one time First Lieutenant Lewis Warrington, of the Fourth Cavalry, had been pursuing a small band of savages, when, on December 8th, at Muchague Valley, he found himself suddenly attacked by five Indians. In his ardor to get close to the warriors he had become separated from his detachment, and thus found himself face to face with five savages, who, with taunts and sneers in true Indian style, demanded his surrender. The lieutenant, however, was loath to part with his scalp, and he replied to their sneers by firing a shot, which disabled one of them; another shot and a second Indian was placed where he could do no harm. The Indians were no longer inclined to keep up an acquaintance with a soldier who could aim so accurately and shoot so rapidly, and rode away, taking their wounded with them.

Private Frederick Bergendahl, a member of the band, and John O'Sullivan, of Company I, also had an encounter, on the same day, with a body of Indian braves whom they were pursuing, and desperately fought with them until the Indians retreated, leaving several of their dead and wounded to show the gallant work done by these two soldiers.

A successful chase under the direction of First Sergeant Dennis Ryan, of Company I, Sixth United States Cavalry, also belongs to this campaign. The sergeant, accompanied by a detachment of twenty men, discovered a large band of Indians on Gageby Creek, Indian Territory, December 2d. Fully realizing the danger of attacking so large a force of savages, the sergeant, nevertheless, charged and chased them for ten miles, capturing some fifty ponies and destroying a large amount of property belonging to the hostiles.

SNATCHED FROM A HORRIBLE FATE

IF the stories of the encounters civil engineers and surveying parties had with the Indians in the wild, unsettled regions could be written they would be found replete with stirring incidents of adventure, of splendid courage and heroism. The trackless wastes, the rugged mountain fastnesses, the impressive stillness of nature, furnish each a scene for hostile action, and it was rare, indeed, that the white man did not encounter his natural foe, the Indian, before he was many days on the ground. At a time perhaps when least expected, a savage horde would appear on the brow of a mountain or its ambushed presence would be made known by the whizz of an arrow. There was no time for parleying or preparation; but, instantly put upon the defensive, the white man would take up his cause with his handy arms and a gallant fight was the result.

In the year 1874, when Lieutenant King, of the Fifth Cavalry, was detailed to make surveys of a military reservation in Arizona, he had an experience which, in thrilling adventure, might be taken as the original of a story one reads in a book for boys. There is much in the beauty and grandeur of the territory to attract the student of nature and the artist, and one may be allowed the liberty of believing that Lieutenant King and his party looked forward to enjoying themselves in a country where little is tame or common in its scenic character.

If the hope was indulged at all, it was dashed to pieces at the very outset. Their advent was marked by an unexpected uprising of the Apaches, who had resisted every effort to civilize them. They were not the only Indians in the territory, but none of the others could surpass them in relentless cruelty and savagery toward the white man. During the winter months, preceding the arrival of the surveyors, near Sunset Pass, Arizona, they accepted the bounty of the government, with the poorest grace, and with the coming of spring they threw off the clothes the government had provided them with, and, armed with the rifles the government had given them for purposes of hunting, went forth to kill the white invader. It was of small consequence that the troops pursued the savages. The latter knew the mountains and had a deadly mode of warfare in which they were masters. Gifted also with a cunning which seemed to anticipate every move of the military, the soldiers were obliged to meet the Apaches on their own terms.

The Indian fighter cheerfully accepts the fortunes of his lot, and seldom counts the cost; but a sturdy heart was needed to face the Apaches on their own stamping ground. This was what Lieutenant King did when he went forth to try conclusions with the savages, and had it not been for the remarkable coolness and courage of a sergeant at the first encounter, the day would doubtless have ended disastrously for the lieutenant. On the first of November, after days of hard riding, in the hope of administering a decisive blow to the Indians, Lieutenant King advanced some distance ahead of his command. Suddenly he came upon a band of the enemy, ambushed and waiting for him. He turned into the underbrush, in order to flank his position, when an arrow whizzed past, almost striking him in the head. Then followed another, which cut the muscles at the corner of his eye, making an ugly wound, and in another moment a rifle ball pierced his arm. Lieutenant King's men, who were witnesses of how their officer was faring, hastened with all speed to his aid. King was exhausted from his wounds and only half conscious, and after a few steps his foot caught in the root of a tree and he fell to the ground. An experienced Indian fighter, he knew what fate awaited him should he fall into the hands of the Apaches. There seemed no hope of rescue, and only a matter of choice as to the manner of death. Like the soldier he was, King drew his revolver, and but for the timely arrival of Sergeant Bernard Taylor would have taken his own life. Taylor, who had dashed out of the woods, was a big, strapping, powerful fellow, and taking his superior officer in his arms forged ahead of the Indians, stopping every few paces to send a bullet among them. Lieutenant King was no light burden, and under favorable conditions to carry him would have been less of a feat for a man like Taylor, but the Apaches, thoroughly roused, trained their arms upon the sergeant. Arrows and bullets flew thick and fast, singing ominously as they passed him. But Taylor kept on, determined to save his lieutenant if he could, and to die hard if he must. King feared the worst for both, and told Taylor to leave him and save himself. Taylor believed that the circumstances justified him in disobeying orders, and one can almost hear his emphatic "No!" as he passed on resolutely with his burden. King implored, then ordered his subordinate to return to the troops; but Taylor refused, for well did he know that should the Indians once capture either of them death by means of torture too horrible even to contemplate would be the result.

Sergeant Taylor carried his wounded officer for nearly half a mile, under the constant fire of the savages, over rocks and ravines, until safe within the picket line, and for his heroic conduct he was awarded the Medal of Honor.

CHASING INDIANS BY RAILROAD

MARCUS M. ROBBINS,
Sergt. of Troop H, 6th U. S. Cavalry.

THE military operations against the hostile bands in the Indian Territory, were continued during the winter, and well into the spring of 1875, and at length, early in March, the Southern Cheyennes, completely broken down, gave up the contest, and under principal chief, Stone Calf. the whole body of that tribe, with a few trifling exceptions, surrendered themselves as prisoners of war, restoring at the same time the two elder Germaine girls, who had been captives among them for nearly eight months. Although the conditions of surrender required the Indians to deliver up their arms, only a few guns and a large quantity of bows and arrows were turned in, the greater part of their more valuable firearms being hidden away where no search by the troops would be likely to find them.

Orders were received, when the Indians began to surrender, to select from among them the principal ringleaders who had incited or led bands of hostiles in the recent outrages, to be sent to the sea coast, there to be kept in confinement, for a time at least. Seventy-five men were accordingly picked out from the several tribes. On April 6th, whilst shackling Black Horse, one of the Cheyennes who were thus to be disposed of, he broke from the guard and ran directly towards the camp of his people. He was pursued by Captain Bennett, Fifth Infantry, with the guard, who fired upon and killed Black Horse. The shots being in the direction of the Indian camp, several passed beyond the escaping pris·oner and wounded some persons there. After a volley of bullets and arrows upon the guard, about one-half of the tribe fled to the sand hills on the south side of the Canadian, opposite the agency. The troops under command of Lieutenant-Colonel T. H. Neill, Sixth Cavalry, followed, but the Indians, well supplied with firearms they had hidden in that vicinity, occupied a difficult hill and defended themselves against the troops for several hours until nightfall. By night the troops had forced their way nearly to the crest of the hill occupied by the Indians, but at daylight it was found the enemy had fled during the night. Eleven Indians were found dead, and nineteen soldiers were wounded. Troops from other posts in the vicinity were ordered to assist in the pursuit, and eventually most of the Cheyennes gave themselves up.

A party of about sixty or seventy, consisting of the worst criminals of the tribe, who had murdered the Germaine family and others, and being afraid on that account to surrender with the rest. crossed the Arkansas River west of Fort Dodge and attempted to make their way to the Sioux country, north of the Platte.

"WE SPRANG UP THE BANK AND DIRECTLY INTO THE PIT."

The commanders of the troops, however, were on the alert, and with quick wit they utilized the then partly completed railways running through Kansas. Lieutenant A. Henley was dispatched with forty men of the Sixth Cavalry to chase them by rail and then head them off. On the 23d of April this was accomplished, on the North Fork of Sappa Creek, southeast of Fort Wallace, Kansas. It was during the severe action that followed, and, by conceiving and executing a dangerous move ment with a small detail of men, turning the trend of the fight, that Private Marcus M. Robbins and several others of Company H, Sixth Cavalry, won their Medal of Honor. A description of the affair is given by Robbins as follows:

"In the evening of April 21st a telegram was received by our commanding officer at Fort Lyon, Colorado, stating that the band of hostile Cheyennes, who had made good their escape, had been fording the Arkansas at the crossing of the Cimmaron, headed to the north, and directing him to send a detachment of cavalry in pursuit.

"A party of forty men was detailed under Lieutenant Henley, first lieutenant of Company H, with orders to take a special train from Las Animas, a small town five miles from the fort, to Fort Wallace, Kansas, there leaving the train and march in an attempt to head off the hostiles and punish them.

"In order that the plan may be understood, it is well to state that at this time there were two parallel lines of railroad crossing Kansas und Colorado, from east to west, the Atchison, Topeka and Santa Fe Railroad, following the Arkansas Valley, and the Kansas Pacific Railroad along the Smoky Hill River. There was also a branch line running diagonally from Las Animas on the Santa Fe to Kit Carson on the Kansas Pacific. And it was by means of this branch that we were expected to head off our foes.

"We were on board, horses and men, by 9 o'clock that evening, and, after a back-breaking ride over a new road for nearly 100 miles, we reached Fort Wallace early the next morning. Unloading our horses from the train, we stopped only long enough to feed them and then we started for the hunt.

"At about 10 o'clock the trail was discovered, leading across the railroad, almost due north, the hostiles having made over 100 miles on their ponies in 24 hours. We pushed along on this trail until dark, running across some buffalo hunters who were fleeing to the railroad, and learning that we were near the Indians' camp, we accordingly laid down under arms. No noise or fires were allowed, and each man retained his horse's halter. At 3 o'clock in the morning we were silently aroused and ordered to creep cautiously forward to the valley where the camp was supposed to be. Crawling to the edge of the bluffs we were rewarded by a full view of their camp, with the entire herd of nearly 400 animals a half mile away and no one guarding. Ten men were at once sent forward to capture the herd, and the rest charged down the slope-through the creek and into the camp of the half-wakened and wholly bewildered Indians.

"It was a complete surprise, and all who were not killed at the first charge, or made their escape, took refuge in the natural rifle pits along the bank of the stream, made by the washouts at high water. In these pits the hostiles gave us a hot reception, the man who had the temerity to poke his head over the bank getting it —literally—'in the neck.' We lost two men in this manner in as many minutes.

"At this time I saw what I believed to be a fine chance to rout the rascals out of their holes, and communicated the plan to Lieutenant Henley, who approved it. Taking four or five men with me, we made a detour down the creek until out of sight of the hostiles; then getting into the creek, we waded in the mud and water back up the stream until directly behind the rifle pits, doing this without attracting the attention of the Indians. Then, making the signal agreed upon, we sprang up the bank and directly into the pit, while the rest charged from above at the same time.

"I had run my head into many a 'hornet's nest' in my time, but they did not compare with that which buzzed around us for a while. I still have a hazy recollection of emptying my revolver into an Indian who sprang up in front of me, and of my 'bunkie' saying I had saved his life, but how I did it is impossible for me to tell, so frenzied in 'battle fever' was I at the time. The contest was all over, for there were no more foes to fight. We lost two men killed and one horse wounded. Nineteen Indians were killed in the fight, all bucks. We captured the entire camp, which was rich in buffalo robes, beaded moccasins, war bonnets and the different adornments of savage life, and also captured 367 horses, ponies and mules.

"On our return trip a dreadful blizzard—although it was the latter part of April —caught us on the prairie and we suffered terribly, nearly all of us going on the sick report when we arrived at Fort Wallace. After a sojourn of only two weeks here we were able to return to our proper station, where we were given a royal welcome, the band and all the garrison turning out to receive us."

Lieutenant Henley recommended not only Private Robbins for the Medal of Honor, but also Sergeants Richard L. Tea and Frederick Platten, as well as Privates James Lowthers, Simpson Hornaday, Peter W. Gardiner of the same company and regiment, these being the men who were with Robbins during his desperate fight. Trumpeter Michael Dawson and Private James F. Ayers, also of Company H, received the Medal of Honor for their display of heroic courage in the same affair. Of both it is reported that their conduct was so exceptionally brave and inspiring that it challenged the admiration of all who participated in the dash upon the hostiles.

ADVENTURES WITH INDIANS IN 1875

B Y the treaty of 1869 the Indians were granted various reservations west of the Missouri River, and in addition to these they were allowed a large range of country as hunting grounds over which they were permitted to rove without molestation in the pursuit of game. But this treaty was not rigidly adhered to by either the Indians or the government, and as a result constant trouble was had with the various bands, especially the Sioux, during the year 1875.

While the great chiefs, Spotted Tail, Red Cloud and others, made strenuous efforts to keep their people on the reservations and carry out the terms of the treaty the younger element, emulating the spirit of Chief Crazy Horse, who was one of the younger chiefs, would organize raiding parties and go on long expeditions against other Indian nations, or, as was most frequently the case, against the white settlers. In many of these raids terrible atrocities were committed; surveyors, settlers and travelers were killed without warning, while women and children were carried into captivity to suffer untold horrors.

Again, some of the bands had never accepted the reservation system, would not recognize the authority of the government, and insisted upon remaining wild and perfectly free from control. Among these were the bands who followed Sitting Bull and Crazy Horse, who were, properly speaking, not chiefs, but head-men, and whose immediate following did not exceed 40 and 120 lodges, respectively. These unruly redskins roamed about the country striking terror to the hearts of all settlers with whom they came in contact for purposes of trading. They would go into a trading post, obtain their necessary supplies, chat in a cordial manner with the whites, and upon leaving the post in apparently the friendliest spirit they would suddenly turn about and fire volley after volley into the startled traders. Then before the whites could regain their composure the devils would stampede and run off their herds of stock.

During the summer of this year General Custer conducted an expedition into the Black Hills, and later an expedition under General Crook went out against this hostile element of the Sioux, in an endeavor to subjugate them. The expedition started out from Fort Laramie late in the fall and followed the Indians over the roughest kind of country, with great persistence, finally encountering the hostiles under Crazy Horse near the headwaters of the Tongue River, where a most spirited fight took place. When Crazy Horse saw that he could not cope with the well-armed and skillful white soldiers he turned heel and with his band escaped into the fastnesses of the mountains. A portion of Crook's command under General Reynolds later surprised Crazy Horse and captured a herd of horses, thus depriving the wily chief of some valuable animals. Reynolds then started back to the main body of this command with his captured horses, followed by the Indians, who were awaiting an opportunity to recapture the beasts. This opportunity presented itself to the redskins a few days later when Reynolds was overtaken by a terrific snow-storm. The men plodded along through the snow unconscious of Crazy Horse's intention, and when they went into camp the Indians stealthily approached the troops, under cover of the blinding snow, and succeeded in stampeding the herd, thus recapturing them. Winter had by this time set in with all its hardships and further attempts to corral the hostiles were given up.

During the early part of the year campaigns were being prosecuted against the Indians in various parts of the western country also for the purpose of rounding up those who would not remain on their reservations.

The expedition against the Kiowas and Comanches, in the Department of Texas, under Colonels Mackenzie, Davidson and Buell, in co-operation with the column under Miles, was prosecuted with such energy that these two tribes gave up the unequal contest and went into Fort Sill, first in small parties and then in larger numbers, surrendering there, and by June the last of the bands absent from their agencies, the Quehada Comanches, also came into the fort and surrendered themselves, with large numbers of ponies and mules, to Colonel Mackenzie, commanding at that post. Colonel Davidson had in the meantime made an important capture on the Salt Fork of the Red River. He met a band of Kiowas at that place, and in a sharp fight with them he captured 65 warriors and 175 women and children, with 375 ponies and mules. The prisoners, including Lone Wolf, Red Otter and Lean Bull, three most dangerous characters, all surrendered unconditionally with their arms and ponies.

Many small engagements and skirmishes marked these expeditions, among the more important of which was the following:

Lieutenant Bullis with a detachment of three men of the Twenty-fourth Infantry was out scouting on the 26th of April and came upon a band of about twenty-five Indians, on the Pecos River, Texas. The lieutenant and his three men approached the Indians unseen, and when within close range they attacked the redskins, killing three and wounding one. This little quartet of soldiers fought bravely during the short time the engagement lasted and then retreated safely to their command. Sergeant John Ward, Trumpeter Isaac Payne and Private Pompey Factor, all Indian scouts of the Twenty-fourth Infantry, constituted Lieutenant Bullis's detachment, and they were rewarded with the Medal of Honor for their exceptional bravery in standing by their officer against those twenty-five Indians.

On May 5th, Sergeant Marshall, with a detachment of Troop A, Tenth Cavalry, attacked a band of Indians at Battle Point, Texas, and on June 3d Lieutenant J. A. McKinney, with a detachment of the Fourth Cavalry, in pursuit of thieving Indians, overtook a band of Osages robbing a cattle herd on Hackberry Creek, Indian Territory. A corporal and two men in advance attempted to arrest the Indians, but the latter opened fire and a fight ensued in which one Osage was killed and several wounded.

The Sioux Indians in Dakota, however, were causing the most trouble, and on July 6th a band of about 200 of them attacked the Ponca Agency in that territory. As soon as the attack was made Sergeant Danvers was immediately r- '-1 -t a point of vantage with a detachment of eleven men of Company G, First Infantry. This little band of eleven withstood the brunt of the attacking forces of Indians, and with an old cannon which they pressed into service fought them valiantly. Lacking regular shot and shell, the men loaded this piece with old scraps of iron, and with their improvised ammunition successfully drove off the attacking party in three assaults, whereupon the hostiles withdrew. The latter part of October Captain J. M. Hamilton, with Troop H, Fifth Cavalry, left Fort Wallace in quest of the Indians, and met a band of them near the Smoky Hill River, Kansas, where in the subsequent fight he routed them, killing two of their number and wounding many others.

In November the closing actions of this year took place in Texas, near the Pecos River, where Lieutenant A. Geddes, of the Twenty-fifth Infantry, with two troops of the Tenth Cavalry, attacked a large band of renegades, killing one and capturing five; and in Nebraska, near Antelope Station, where a detachment of Troop G, Third Cavalry, under Lieutenant E. Crawford, had a fight in which they drove the Indians before them for many miles.

During the entire campaign of 1875 the troops were kept busy pursuing the Indians, driving them into their respective agencies, and protecting the settlers and emigrants from frequent raiding, and although there were no large battles in accomplishing the tasks set before them they nevertheless acquitted themselves bravely in the many small encounters and suffered many privations during the excessively hot and cold seasons of this year.

THE LITTLE·BIG HORN

OF all the Indians contesting the advance of the white man in the
Northwest, the Dakotas, more commonly
called Sioux, were by far the most warlike
and powerful. They formed a federation
of many related tribes, as for instance the
Ogalallas, Uncpapas, Brules, Minneconjoux, Assiniboines, Santees, Yanctonnais,
Cheyennes (partly), Tetons and Sans Arcs.

By treaty in 1868 the United States Government assigned to these Indians the vast
tracts of land they claimed in what was
then the Territory of Dakota. But when
the discovery of gold in the Black Hills
attracted white adventurers by the hundreds and thousands, the integrity of the
treaty could no longer be strictly main-

JEREMIAH J. MURPHY,
Private, Co. M, Third U. S. Cavalry. Born in Ireland,
February 2, 1858.

tained. Crime followed crime on this frontier, and although the whites were by no
means blameless, the savages finally showed such a ferocity, boldness and lawless-
ness that their subjugation became imperative.

As late as 1876 the United States Government had no control over these savages,
who roamed free and independent over an area more than 100,000 square miles in
extent; the horrors and atrocities committed by their raiding parties along the
frontier, and which culminated in the Little Big Horn massacre of June 25, 1876,
actually beggar description.

The leading spirits among these savages were Sitting Bull, the powerful "head-
man" of the Uncpapas, the foremost figure in later Indian history, a man equally
strong and unbending in character, resources and crime; Crazy Horse, Gall and Red
Cloud, all three Ogalallas, and Rain-in-the-Face, an Uncpapa.

The task which confronted the troops was a most difficult one, as very little
knowledge had been obtained about that particular stretch of the country and the
number of the hostiles was problematical. A guess in that respect by the highest
and best authorities in Washington fell far from the actual figures, so far indeed
that to it was due in a measure the shocking catastrophe of the Little Big Horn.

After an exploring expedition by General Custer in the summer of 1875 and a
fruitless expedition against Crazy Horse and his followers by General Reynolds in
the spring of 1876, the main expedition was ordered out by General Sheridan in
May of the latter year, with Generals Terry and Crook in charge.

General Sheridan was under the impression that the winter season was the most opportune time to "catch" the Indians, and three columns were consequently fitted out in all haste.

One was organized by General Gibbon, to start from Fort Ellis, on the Yellowstone, Montana; one at Fort Russell, under General Crook, and a third at Fort Lincoln, Dakota, by General Custer; but the latter having incurred the displeasure of President Grant, General Terry was ordered to accompany this column.

There was no reliable information at that time as to the whereabouts of the Sioux. Terry was under the impression that they had camped near the mouth of the Little Missouri; later he learned that they were some 200 miles farther west, near the Dry Fork of the Missouri.

The extremely cold weather in the early spring prevented the three main columns from starting. But the impatient General Crook sent out a reconnoitering party under Colonel I. I. Reynolds, which left Fort Fetterman early in March, working slowly towards the head waters of the Powder, the Tongue and the Rosebud Rivers. Old Chief Crazy Horse was reported camping in the vicinity of these streams with a numerous band of Sioux and Cheyennes.

The columns consisted of troops A, B, E, I and K of the Second and troops A, E, F and M of the Third Cavalry. These troops suffered terrible hardships on the march, the thermometer registering forty degrees below zero on March 17th. Notwithstanding, Reynolds succeeded in completely surprising the enemy, who was found in camp on the Powder River, at the mouth of Otter Creek. The squadrons rushed the village, the enemy fled and the troopers destroyed all the lodges, 105 in number, and captured 800 of the hostiles' ponies.

But the success of the troops was only temporary. The Indians, soon perceiving their own great superiority in numbers, rallied, made a vigorous and desperate counter-attack and forced the command back. Although the troops kept perfect order in their retreat to Fort Fetterman, the rear-guard could not prevent the Indians from stampeding the captured ponies, which thus again fell into the hands of their former owners.

While the attack upon the village was in full swing an Indian band managed to sneak between the main forces of the troops and an outlying picket, consisting of a corporal and five men of Company M, Third Cavalry. The little squad fought with the courage of desperation to break through the lines of the redskins and reach their retreating comrades, but one after another they were shot down.

Finally, Private J. J. Murphy was the only one left not disabled. When one of the wounded called to him in a heartrending voice: "O, Murphy; for mercy's sake, do not leave me in their hands," Murphy fearlessly turned back, lifted the groaning man on his shoulders and tried to make his way through the advancing savages, who poured a rain of bullets at him. The wounded man was again hit, and Murphy's carbine-stock smashed by a rifle-ball. He managed to draw his pistol and fired until the last cartridge was spent; then, being without ammunition and seeing absolutely no chance of saving his comrade, he was compelled to abandon him and succeeded, to the surprise of his officers, who watched his movements, in reaching his comrades. His uniform was pierced by several bullets, but the brave man escaped unscathed. For his heroism, so gallantly displayed, he was awarded the Medal of Honor.

Among those men who covered the retreat and fought the attacking Indians with the utmost intrepidity, showing a seemingly reckless courage, was Blacksmith A. Glavinsky, of Company M, Third Cavalry, who had to be recalled several times by his officers from self-selected, exposed positions. He also earned the Medal of Honor.

The weather continued inclement during March and April, and the main body of the troops made preparations for the final start, as soon as the weather would permit.

At last, on May 29th, General Crook moved out from Fort Fetterman, with his column, consisting of five troops, A, B, D, E and I, of the Second Cavalry, ten troops, A, B, C, D, E, F, H, I, L and M, of the Third Cavalry, and five companies of infantry, C, G, H, of the Ninth, and D and F, of the Fourth. They started for Goose Creek, where they established a supply camp on June 8th.

A peculiar incident happened here, which, though insignificant, in all likelihood saved Crook's command from the fate reserved for the unfortunate Custer.

General Crook had been expecting a large war-party of friendly Crow Indians, deadly enemies of the Sioux, which had promised to join his command. On one of the last days of May the general decided to send his best three scouts, Gruard, Pourrier and Richard, to the Crow Agency, some 300 miles away, in Montana, to bring the tardy Crow warriors in.

At 11 o'clock, on the night of June 8th, at the Goose Creek Camp, the sentries were stirred up by most extraordinary outcries like the howling of coyotes, but supposed to emanate from Indians. The general sent Scout Arnold down to the Tongue River to ascertain the cause of the shouting in that direction. Arnold hailed the mysterious shouter and thought he recognized the Crow dialect. "Any Crows in your camp?" asked the unknown cautiously. Arnold, who suspected Sioux, replied in that language, and there was no further reply.

Afterwards it was learned that an advance party of the expected Crow scouts had hailed the command, but hearing the dreaded Sioux dialect, immediately withdrew.

General Crook, who had guessed the truth, was very angry that evening; the prolonged absence of the Crow re-enforcement caused delay. Yet Crook was thereby prevented from getting to the Rosebud River and into a trap which two weeks later sealed Custer's fate on the Little Big Horn.

Towards evening, on the 9th of June, a party of Sioux made the first attack on Crook's camp. They were easily repulsed, Colonel Mills attacking them with four dismounted troops and driving them from the bluffs whence they had been firing into the camp.

An Indian bullet pierced the pipe of the stove in Colonel Mills's tent, and a report sent to a newspaper stated that someone had sent a ball through the colonel's stove-pipe; whereupon the editor could not refrain from criticising, in a scathing editorial, the recklessness of a colonel wearing a stove-pipe during battle.

On the evening of June 14th, to the joyful surprise of all, and not the least to the general commanding, the faithful scouts rode into camp with a following of some 200 Crow Indians, in war paint and full of eagerness to meet their deadly foe.

General Crook learned from the Crow chiefs that the main force of the Sioux was encamped on the Rosebud, near the Yellowstone.

Early on the morning of the 16th the whole command started in that direction, leaving the wagon train, tents, etc., behind.

The following morning the column halted in a valley on the Rosebud, to give the tired mounts a rest, while the scouts were sent out to reconnoiter. They did not have to reconnoiter far. Shortly before 9 o'clock they rushed in with their reports that the Indians were at hand, and immediately after the latter came on furiously to the attack. "Heap Sioux!" yelled the panic-stricken Crows and Snake warriors, whom the appearance of their hated and dreaded enemy seemed to have completely upset.

In a few moments the battle raged all along the line. The troops drove the enemy from one line of bluffs to the next, and then to one still farther back. The Indian allies aided by noisy and boisterous demonstrations rather than by active participation.

General Crook realized soon after the beginning of the fight that his opponents were not stray bands, but organized forces of unusual and unexpected numerical strength. But even his calculations did not approach the actual numbers. Afterwards it was ascertained that Crazy Horse's followers, many times multiplied by a constant stream of bucks from Sitting Bull's village and malcontents from the different agencies, had been the general's adversaries. There were between 2,000 and 2,500 of them, while the actual fighting force of Crook's command did not reach 1,000 men.

In the attack upon the third bluff the troops suffered severely, especially Company L, of the Third Cavalry, under Captain Vroom, who had ventured too far forward. It was only the skill of Captain G. V. Henry of Company D, Third Cavalry, and Colonel Royal, who brought up re-enforcements, which prevented the cutting off and, of course, consequent cutting up of this troop. In the melee Captain Henry was shot through the face. The gallant officer, with blood rushing from his mouth, kept on his horse, although for the time being completely blinded; finally he fell from the saddle fainting and exhausted. So close together were the contestants that a party of howling Sioux actually charged over the captain's prostrate body. But they were quickly repelled, as was the whole hostile line.

It was during this melee that First Sergeant J. H. Shingle, of Troop I, Third Cavalry, won his Medal of Honor. Shingle had been placed in command of the

"PRIVATE MURPHY WAS THE ONLY ONE LEFT NOT DISABLED."

horses of a battalion of four dismounted troops, by Captain Henry. When the Indians swarmed around them, and Shingle saw some of the men waver, he left the horses in command of a sergeant, mounted his horse, rushed into the thickest of the fight and did exceedingly valuable service in rallying the breaking ranks, which finally enabled the hard-pressed battalion to keep the Indians at bay until the oncoming supports under Colonel Royal put the redskins to flight.

JOSEPH ROBINSON,
First Sergant, Co. D, 3d U. S. Cavalry.

Among the troopers engaged in this fight, whose bravery was rewarded by the Medal of Honor, were: First Sergeants John Henry, of Company I, Michael A. McGann, of Company F, Sergeant Joseph Robinson, of Company D, and Trumpeter Elmer A. Snow, of Company M, Third Cavalry; the last-named receiving wounds through both arms.

It was now late in the day, and the Indians retreated. The troops had forced them back in battle for about five miles, but the result of the encounter was far from satisfactory to General Crook's command. The Indians left behind thirteen Crow and Shoshone scalps, 150 dead horses and a few blankets. Eleven dead bodies of the enemy were counted on the field.

The command lost ten whites killed and twenty-three, including Captain Henry, wounded; and of the Crows and Shoshones two warriors were killed and eleven wounded.

As the rations were almost completely used up and 25,000 rounds of ammunition expended, the general considered it proper to fall back upon his base of supplies on Goose Creek, eighty miles to the rear. Again the Indians had, morally at least, been victorious.

While General Crook's column was supposed to act independently, General Terry was the assigned commander of the other two. That fitting out and starting from Fort Ellis was in command of Colonel Gibbon; he had four companies of cavalry and six companies of infantry, some 450 men in all, and marched out in April to unite finally with Terry, which junction was effected in the latter part of June, on the Yellowstone, at the mouth of the Rosebud River.

Custer had his troops ready at Fort Lincoln, Dakota, towards the middle of May. The command included the entire Seventh Cavalry, 12 companies with 28 officers and about 700 men; two companies of the Seventh and one of the Sixth Infantry, 8 officers and 135 men, one battery of Gatling guns, manned by 2 officers and 32 men of the Twentieth Infantry, and forty Indian scouts.

On the 17th of May this expedition left Fort Lincoln for the Yellowstone, and on the 27th of May the troops crossed into the Bad Lands. The 30th found Custer on a reconnoissance with four troops, returning on the same day without having seen anything of hostile Indians. On the 1st and 2d of June the command was unable to proceed on account of a severe snow-storm.

By this time pack mules, eleven to each troop, were allotted to the Seventh Cavalry, and soon the rumor spread of a prospective scout of the regiment up the Powder River. All was bustle in the camp of the cavalry.

On the 10th of June, Major Reno, of Custer's regiment, was sent to reconnoiter up the Powder River, his detachment comprising six troops, with twelve days' rations.

The rest of the column marched to the mouth of the Powder River, and, after a short delay, farther up to the mouth of the Tongue River, where it halted until the 19th in expectation of news from Reno's party. On this date rumors began to circulate that Reno had found a three-weeks-old Indian trail, indicating a party of not less than 350 lodges, which he had followed up the Rosebud for forty miles.

It was on the 17th, just while Crook was fighting his battle not forty miles away, that Reno decided to turn back. Both commands, of course, were unaware of each other's proximity, and in all probability the Indians had no knowledge of Reno's advance.

On the 21st Custer's column reached the mouth of the Rosebud. Here he found Terry, who had left the command to meet Gibbon, whose column had traveled from Montana. The three leaders had a conference, with the result that the Seventh Cavalry, in command of Custer, was ordered to proceed up the Rosebud in pursuit of the Indians whose trail was discovered by Major Reno a few days prior. The rest of the order of Terry to Custer, the regimental commander, left all further dispositions to the judgment of this experienced Indian fighter. The bugle sounded officers' call as soon as the conference — which Custer had left seemingly excited — had ended. The regiment was to take fifteen days' rations of hardtack, coffee and sugar, twelve days' rations of bacon, and fifty rounds of ammunition per man on the mule pack train; besides each man in the command was to carry 100 rounds carbine and 24 rounds pistol ammunition on his person or in the saddle-bags, and forage of twelve pounds of oats to be carried on the horse.

This meant a heavy pack for each charger—some eighty pounds, besides the rider's average weight of 150 pounds and the saddle equipment.

At 12 o'clock noon, on the 22d of June, the Seventh Cavalry marched out from the mouth of the Rosebud in column of fours, the band playing the commander's favorite battle tune, "Garry Owen."

Every man, every officer, knew and felt that serious times were ahead.

After a twelve miles' march the regiment went into camp at four o'clock in the afternoon, and immediately the officers' call wafted its well-known tune over the stirring rabble of men, horses and mules.

After they who were called had assembled in the cheerless tent of their leader, the latter announced that no more trumpet calls would be sounded except in case of emergency; that according to the reports of the Indian Office in Washington they might have to meet from 1,000 to 1,500 hostile Sioux; that the march would thenceforward begin at 5 o'clock in the morning; that only two things from now on would be regulated from headquarters: viz., when to move out of and when to go into camp, and that for all the rest he would hold the company commanders responsible.

He also mentioned an offer by General Terry of a battalion of the Second Cavalry and of the Gatling detachment, but that he had declined, as he thought that if the Seventh could not meet emergencies successfully, the aid of a battalion would hardly turn the scales, and that the Gatlings might hamper quick movement in the difficult and unknown country to be traversed.

Officers who knew Custer well and were present at this conference were very much impressed with his manner, and one of them remarked to a comrade who was leaving the conference with him: "I believe Custer is going to be killed; I never heard him talk so seriously about a coming fight."

The 23d and 24th of June were spent in marching, and brought the first fresh signs of Indians. On the latter date the command made a short halt near a large "sun-dance" lodge, in which was found the scalp of a white man, supposed to be one of Gibbon's force murdered a short time before.

Late in the evening on the 24th the general assembled his officers once more, telling them that the march would be continued at 11:30 that night; that the enemy were located by scouts over the divide, in the Little Big Horn Valley, and that he was anxious to get the troops as near this divide as possible before daylight, so that they could bear down upon the hostiles at sunrise, as he had done in his famous battle of the Washita.

After a march of ten miles, from 11:30 P. M. to 2:00 A. M., the column halted for six hours, most of the troops unsaddling their mounts to give them relief, for the animals were sorely used up. Towards 8 o'clock on the morning of the 25th the scouts came in and reported the Indians camping twelve or fourteen miles beyond the divide in the Little Big Horn Valley.

Promptly at 8 the march was again resumed and continued until half-past 10, when the whole command was brought to a halt in a ravine, evidently for the purpose of escaping detection by the enemy, if such were possible.

The Little Big Horn and the valley mentioned were now to the front and left of the force; towards the northwest was the river—which is a rapid mountain stream twenty to forty yards wide, with steep, soft banks. The country north and east of the valley is a plateau, rough, broken ground with many steep hills and narrow, deep gulches. The "divide" mentioned above is formed by the Little Chetish mountains. In front of the command, where it now was, flowed a little creek, in a northwesterly direction, towards the bend of the Little Big Horn. At that time the creek was nearly dry, and the trail of the Indians followed its bed down into the valley.

Custer had gone forward to where the scouts were to scan the valley and obtain, if possible, a view of the enemy. On account of a bluff cutting into the valley from the north it was impossible to see all parts from his place of observation, but what he saw strengthened his belief in the correctness of his calculation as to the enemy's number. But even had he then had a true conception of the real magnitude of his task he could not have withdrawn. With the hostiles before him, and the War Department behind him, there was only one way: forward.

JOHN H. SHINGLE,
First Sergeant, Troop I, 3d
U. S. Cavalry,
Born in Philadelphia, 1842.

There were then encamped in the valley some 15,000 redskins, counting between 2,000 and 3,000 warriors, with a pony herd of some 30,000 head, the order of the tribal villages being from south to north—the Uncpapas, Sans Arcs, Minneconjoux Ogalallas, Brules, Cheyennes and Arapahoes.

When the general had finished his scout he made up his mind to make the attack the next morning at day break. But on his return to camp he found from the observations of some of his officers that the Indians were well aware of his whereabouts; he thought they might possibly escape, and therefore ordered the attack to be made immediately.

The divide was crossed by the command a little before noon. The regiment, which had so far advanced as one body, was now divided into three battalions, as follows:

The advance battalion, under Major Reno, containing troops M, Captain French; A, Captain Moylan and Lieutenant De Rudio; G, Lieutenants McIntosh and Wallace; the Indian scouts and Interpreter Girard, under Lieutenants Varnum and Hare; Surgeons DeWolf and Porter, and Lieutenant Hodgson as acting-adjutant.

The battalion of Captain Benteen, containing troops H, Captain Benteen and Lieutenant Gibson; D, Captain Weir and Lieutenant Edgerly; and K, Lieutenant Godfrey.

The battalion under Custer himself, containing troops I, Captain Keogh and Lieutenant Porter; F, Captain Yates and Lieutenant Reily; C, Captain Tom Custer and Lieutenant Harrington; E, Lieutenants Smith and Sturgis; L, Lieutenants Calhoun and Crittenden; Dr. Lord as surgeon, and Lieutenant Cook, the regimental adjutant.

The pack train, under Lieutenant Mathey, was escorted by Troop B, Captain McDougall.

Reno's detachment advanced into the valley along the bed of the little creek, followed by Custer and the pack train; Benteen advanced farther to the left, towards a high bluff, from where he was to scan the front, and, in case he saw the enemy, to report immediately.

At the place where the regiment was divided nobody could anticipate the extremely difficult nature of the ground. After struggling over several lines of bluffs

"THE END OF CUSTER'S COMMAND."

without seeing a sign of the enemy Benteen was forced to join the trail just in front of the pack train and follow the main body.

Reno's advance guard had in the meantime reached a burning tepee, chasing some Indians who had fired it. In the tepee was the body of a trooper killed in General Crook's battle at the Rosebud. Custer sent an order to Reno to hurry forward and charge the village, and the whole force would support him. Reno trotted ahead until he reached the river. Crossing it he sent word to Custer that the Indians were in front of him in large numbers. After moving forward about two miles Reno dismounted his men, advancing them as a line of skirmishers, with his Ree scouts to the left. Two horses ran away with their hapless riders, carrying them right into the hostiles' lines, whence a demoniacal howl arose, leaving no doubt as to their fate.

Custer had in the meantime swerved to the right, thus putting the river and a line of high bluffs between his own and the other two battalions.

This was without doubt the fatal move which decided the day. "Custer's mistake of his life," as one of the veteran company commanders of Reno's battalion put it.

Reno was by this time hotly engaged with the hostiles; he occupied a position across the valley about one mile south of the river bend. A mounted Indian force rushed against his line; the Ree scouts fled, and Reno, seeing no force coming up as a support, retreated to the river. His position was a strong one, as both his flanks were covered by the bends of the river, and the dry river bank, fringed with timber, protected his front. But for some unknown reason he concluded to retreat up the river to some high bluffs towards the southeast, on the other side of the stream. The order to mount created confusion; fifteen soldiers, the interpreter, Girard, two scouts, and also Lieutenant De Rudio, whom the order had not reached, were abandoned among the bushes.

Reno's retreat made the Indians bold, and they pressed the column hard. The major, who rode at the head of the retreating command, was aware that he could not reach the ford by which he had crossed when entering the valley; so he kept close to the river and was lucky to strike a pony trail that led him to a fordable place at the steep bank, just opposite a ravine in the bluffs. No evidence of an organized resistance on the part of the troops during this retreat was displayed, which, by the time they reached the river, apparently had degenerated into flight. Casualties became numerous as soon as the command got out of the timber. Reno lost during this retreat, beside those abandoned in the timber, three officers and twenty-nine men and scouts killed, and seven men wounded. Lieutenant McIntosh was shot dead soon after leaving the second position at the river bank. Lieutenant Hodgson's horse received a bullet in the body; in its agony it jumped into the river, unseating its rider, whose right leg had been pierced by the same bullet. Hodgson shouted loudly for someone to help him. A comrade grabbed the wounded man, who, clinging to his rescuer's stirrup, was thus dragged through the stream to the opposite bank; but on reaching it a bullet crashed into his head, killing him instantly.

Dr. DeWolf fell dead while seeking a way up the ravine to the bluffs.

Charley Reynolds, the famous scout, was killed while crossing the river.

When the battalion had finally reached and occupied its new position the Ree scouts were nowhere to be seen. In fact the cowards, when put to flight in the first clash with the enemy, never stopped until they reached the supply camp at the mouth of the Powder. The Crow scouts remained faithfully with the troops.

During the crisis of this retreating movement a deed of most gallant daring and loyalty came under the observation of many of the officers and men.

Benjamin Criswell, sergeant in Company B, was the man who had helped Lieutenant Hodgson out of the stream and to the other side. When Hodgson was killed the sergeant was so occupied with rallying the men that he could not take care of the body. But as soon as order was somewhat restored he turned his horse and rode fearlessly back, down the river bank, picked up the body, took the ammunition from the saddle-bags of several fallen horses and returned thus laden to his comrades under a most galling fire of the savages, who yelled fiendishly and seemed frantic that the sergeant's deed should deprive them of such a valued trophy.

Criswell was rewarded for his extraordinary exploit with the Medal of Honor.

Up to this time the Sioux were firmly convinced that they had fought and routed the whole body of troops under "Long Hair" Custer, they not having noticed the departure of the latter's battalion.

Custer had entered the valley about two miles east of the creek, from where he had started and rode in a northwesterly direction, slightly diverging from the general course of the river until he reached a high bluff, about three miles distant. While his column pushed down near the river the Indians discovered their new and unexpected foe, and from what they afterwards related the sight of this body of troops spread terror into their lines.

This happened just when Reno decided to abandon his second position and was retreating to the bluffs. Cunning Chief Gall, who anticipated Reno's intention, was already on the way with his numerous band to cut off Reno's line of retreat and trap him, when suddenly one of the Uncpapa lookouts came running after him, shouting with all his might, "More pony-soldiers; look!" and pointed to the bluff, where part of Custer's squadrons could be seen rapidly filing past.

Gall abandoned his plan immediately, rallied his band and rushed back to the river, crossing it at the mouth of what was afterwards called Reno's Creek.

By this time all the Indians were aware of the coming of Custer's troops and concentrated against him, abandoning gradually their position in front of Reno.

Custer had Calhoun and Keogh occupy the knoll mentioned by their two dismounted troops. Gall, who pressed with his Indians up the bed of a dried-up creek, observed their horses being led away. Immediately the redskins set out to stampede the excited animals, and were successful.

Meanwhile Custer had deployed his whole line along the ridge. Smith's company joining with its left wing Keogh's right, and with its right wing the troops of Yates and Tom Custer, who extended down to within half a mile of the river from another knoll, now known as Custer's Hill. Here the general, too, took his stand.

By this time a sergeant from Custer met Benteen and brought orders to hurry the pack train up. Shortly after another messenger, a trumpeter, met Benteen with the following message signed by Adjutant Crook: "Benteen, come on; big village; be quick; bring packs." Evidently the Custer battalion was in need of the reserve ammunition.

Benteen rushed forward, to comply with the order; his command was drawn out in line, with pistols in hand. Finally, the valley came into full sight; thick clouds of smoke rolled over the ground, cutting off the view. A great number of horsemen could be seen galloping to and fro through the clouds of smoke and dust. Away off, on a bluff to the right, a body of fighting troopers could be distinguished, and some Crow scouts hurried by, and, pointing to the troops on the bluffs, shouted that they were soldiers. Benteen followed their beckoning and turned to the right towards the bluffs, where he found Reno's command, which was still slightly engaged.

The Indians now commenced to withdraw from the attack. They were all massing against Custer, leaving just enough braves in front of Reno to keep him in check.

On the other side of the battlefield Keogh's and Calhoun's companies lost their saddle-bag ammunition with their stampeded horses. Gall and his band kept the skirmishers firing until they calculated their ammunition well-nigh exhausted, when the Indians made a rush, on foot and on horseback, in overwhelming numbers. There was no standing up against this demoniacal wave, which swept over the brave little cluster of heroes, killing every one of them.

Crazy Horse, Crow King and several other Sioux chieftains had in the meanwhile gathered all their available forces in a ravine leading up to a ridge opposite Custer's Hill. They rushed up to this ravine and, spreading along the crest of the ridge, fell on Yates's, Tom Custer's and Smith's rear and right flank. While they were pouring an overwhelming fire into the rapidly thinning lines, Gall's victorious hordes, bloodthirsty and intoxicated with their recent success over Keogh and Calhoun, rushed up from the front and left flank.

In this onslaught the scanty remnants of the three troops were annihilated; while defending their honor and lives until the last drop of blood, the last cartridge was spent.

Thus died Custer and his 223 men, including 13 commissioned officers of the Seventh Cavalry.

In the meantime, the soldiers under Reno heard the distant firing. It was towards 3:30, when two heavy volleys were distinctly heard on the bluffs. Instinctively a sensation came over many that this was Custer's signal for help, and so it was, alas, the last signal which came from yonder side.

Captain Weir and Lieutenant Edgerly could no longer endure the suspense of uncertainty, so they started with the troop down the ravine in the direction of the firing. Weir, who was ahead, reconnoitering, perceived in time the approach of a large band of Indians and warned Edgerly, who regained a safe position.

Captain McDougall joined Reno now with the pack train. Of those who had been left in the timber at the river bank thirteen men and a scout rejoined their commands at about this time; they had lain hidden in the brush until the departure of the Indians towards Custer's stand gave them an opportunity to escape.

Reno now made an attempt to push down the river and ascertain the whereabouts of Custer's command. The advanced troops reached the high bluff which rose in the direction of the junction of the Little Big Horn and a small creek where some of Reno's men said they had seen Custer waving his hat while he was fighting the oncoming Indians in the valley.

A haze of dust and smoke hanging over the valley rendered distinct observation impossible, but the groups of stationary or moving horsemen could be recognized as Indians. On the western slope the immense pony herd of the savages could be seen, but not a trace of Custer or any part of his command. The impression prevailed that the general had been repulsed and had very likely marched off to join the column under Terry and Gibbon; no anxiety whatever was felt.

Soon swarms of mounted Indians moved swiftly from all sides upon the position which Reno now held, and opened a heavy fire. Major Reno withdrew all the squadrons to the bluffs formerly occupied and installed himself there, as well as he could for the defense, where within a short time the soldiers were encircled by savages.

RICHARD P. HANLEY,
Sergeant, Troop C, 7th U. S. Cavalry.

During the retreat to the bluffs Sergeant Richard P. Hanley, of Troop C, exhibited fearlessness and coolness of an unparalleled nature, which gained him the Medal of Honor. A pack mule, loaded with precious ammunition, had become frightened by the incessant whizzing of the bullets and broke away, making straight for the hostiles' lines.

Hanley, seeing the runaway mule, mounted his horse and ran out to head him off. Instantly the Indians concentrated their fire upon the daring man. The mule had a good start, and its pursuer didn't overtake it until within dangerous proximity to the Indians. The latter immediately directed their fire toward the fearless trooper. Bullets fell like hailstones. Hanley seemed not to notice the bullets which by dozens splashed up the sand and dust around his horse's hoofs. The mule tried to evade its pursuer, who had succeeded in heading it off, and ran up and down the firing line; his comrades and the officers yelled and shouted to Hanley to let up and come in, but in vain. He was determined to capture this mule, and capture it he did, at last. During this twenty minutes' chase Hanley had run the gauntlet of a perfect hail of bullets, but he escaped uninjured and brought his mule in with the ammunition. Loud cheers greeted him when he passed within the circle of his comrades.

When darkness began to set in the Indians dropped back from the firing line, and soon all shooting ceased. But silence was to be banished in the valley during this terrible fight. Down in the hostiles' camp sheol broke loose and lasted without intermission until daybreak. Evidently the red fiends were enjoying a scalp dance. The terrific yelling and howling, together with the incessant sound of the tam-tams and gun-firing, sent chills down the backs of that thirsty, wearied, hungry and discouraged handful of troopers upon the bluffs. All night the men worked with knives and

HE WAS DETERMINED TO CAPTURE THE MULE.

whatever came handy, to dig pits for better shelter, as the crisis was to be expected with the break of day.

Some of the Indian scouts of the command went out to establish communication with Custer, but they soon returned with the news that the whole surroundings were thickly covered with Sioux.

The attack was renewed early in the morning, before 3 o'clock. At sunrise the firing was general all around the position. The Indians did little damage, but still they succeeded in drawing the fire and thus forced the soldiers to spend their scant ammunition. Captain Benteen's troop suffered severely; his men occupied the south front, which was open to the long range fire of the Indians from the north bluffs. Many of his troopers had but three cartridges left. Benteen finally went to seek Reno, leaving to Lieutenant Gibson strict orders not to retreat from the position. On this side of the position, the Indians showed incredible daring and recklessness, partly, in all probability, on account of the scantiness of ammunition, which necessitated a slackening fire. A man in Benteen's line was shot and killed. The copper-colored slayer dashed up into the line, touched the body with his "coup-stick" and tried then to run back into shelter. But he was felled by a dozen bullets ere he could run as many steps.

Benteen at last obtained Major Reno's consent to get Captain French's company, M, into the thinned line on the south front as a support. With the sharpened instinct of an old Indian campaigner, Benteen felt that the enemy knew the weakness of this part of the position and would ere long rush it with overwhelming forces. To discourage such a plan Benteen rallied all the available men in the lines and made a rush, out of the pits and down the slopes, at the astonished redskins. They had, in fact, already been gathering in a ravine for the final assault, which the gallant Benteen anticipated and frustrated so timely.

Many deeds of daring happened on the bluff during this memorable day. Sergeant Thomas Murray, of Company B, brought the rations up to the command, passing to and fro several times through the terrific fire of the exasperated savages. He had already distinguished himself on the first day of the siege, bringing the pack train within the reach of the command and into a comparatively sheltered position.

Corporal Charles Cunningham, of Company B, had been shot through the neck during the fight of the 25th, and was ordered to retire, but he refused positively to leave the line, and held out bravely during the whole day of the 26th, saying that he could do better lying on his belly with gun in hand than on his back among the helpless in the rear.

Private Henry Holden, of Company D, repeatedly went for ammunition for his comrades, being exposed to the heaviest of fire. Again and again he sought his way through the storm of Indian bullets to keep his company's line supplied with food for the guns.

The worst thing was the lack of water, especially for the wounded. If the burning thirst was maddening to the uninjured, its quenching became a question of life and death with the injured. The situation was terrible and became more so the higher the sun rose. Towards noon something had to be done at all hazards, to obtain water.

Nineteen brave men volunteered to take their lives in their hands and try for it. Four of them, Sergeant George Geiger, Blacksmith Henry W. B. Mechling, Private Charles Windolph, and Saddler Otto Voit, of Troop H, were instructed by their captain to take an exposed position outside of the line and protect those soldiers who would go for water from the fire of the Indians. These four brave men kept in their dangerous position for nearly four hours, and it was due to their vigilance and reckless exposure that none of the water carriers were killed by the enemy.

OTTO VOIT,
Saddler, Troop H, 7th U. S. Cavalry.

Sergeant Stanislaus Roy, Privates D. W. Harris and Neil Bancroft, of Troop A; Sergeants R. D. Hutchinson and C. H. Welch, and Privates Thomas Callan and James Pym, of Troop B; Privates Abram B. Brant, William M. Harris, Frederick Deetline, George Scott, T. W. Stevens, Frank Tolan, of Troop D; Private Peter Thompson, of Troop C, and T. W. Golden, of Troop G, reported themselves ready to fetch the water. They carried camp-kettles and singly they slipped out from the right wing of Benteen's line, making a dash for the river. A space of about eighty yards, which they rushed over, brought them into a deep ravine, which afforded shelter and led down to within fifteen yards of the river. The men would, upon reaching the ravine, rush over the remaining distance, dip their camp-kettles into the river and then return with them.

HENRY W. B. MECHLING,
Blacksmith, Troop H, 7th U. S. Cavalry.
Born at Mount Pleasant, Pa.,
October 14, 1851.

While they were dashing over the exposed spaces, Geiger, Voit, Mechling and Windolph kept their rifles cracking to check the enemy's fire. A group of Indians had concealed themselves in some bushes, from which their rifles had good command of the exposed stretches of the water carriers' path, and they would, undoubtedly, have killed some of the carriers but for the vigilance and skill of the four sharpshooters. The result was that only one of the carriers, Peter Thompson, was wounded. He was shot through the head, but, notwithstanding, he made two more successful trips for the water, even though his sergeant ordered him to go to the rear. Although the hostiles wounded only one man, there were nevertheless many narrow escapes, for several camp-kettles were smashed by bullets. The courageous and self-sacrificing men who had thus exposed themselves and risked their lives for their comrades were all awarded the Medal of Honor.

About 2 P. M. of the 26th the fire of the Indian line began to slacken. The fire against the water carriers, however, was kept up until 3 o'clock. Shortly thereafter the savages abandoned their position. They fired the grass, and under the screen of the smoke the village was abandoned. The besieged troops could see through the smoke the whole cavalcade moving briskly away, in almost military order, towards the Big Horn range.

It was now near 7 o'clock and sighs of relief went up from the exhausted and sorely-tried white warriors on the bluff. There was not the slightest doubt in

"FOUR BRAVE MEN KEPT IN THEIR DANGEROUS POSITION."

their minds that Custer had by this time united with Terry and that aid was near. But the moving of the Indian village excited suspicion, and it was decided to move into a new position down the slope, in order to escape the stench of the decaying bodies of men and horses. The losses of the command during this day had been eighteen killed and forty-two wounded.

The evening of this never-to-be-forgotten day had a joyful surprise in store for the men; towards 9 o'clock Lieutenant De Rudio, Private O'Neal, Scout Jackson and Interpreter Girard, who had been left in the timber during the retreat from the second position in the valley, joined their comrades, hale and hearty, and the stories of their thrilling adventures were listened to in wonderment. De Rudio and O'Neal's escape was remarkable. On the 25th they concealed themselves in the bushes at the river-bank; they saw the squaws come out after the fight and multilate the bodies of the fallen. De Rudio was once so overcome by the horrid sight that he cocked his revolver to shoot down some of these human hyenas. But O'Neal pointed out the inevitable result, and the officer prudently desisted.

Towards evening they saw what they in hopeful expectation took for Lieutenant Smith's gray horse squadron come trotting along. There could be no mistake, thought De Rudio; there were the campaign hats and the blue tunics; the horsemen, then, must be American cavalry. De Rudio stepped out of shelter and shouted: "Ho, there, here we are, take us away from here." A fiendish yell from the personage supposed to be the lieutenant showed De Rudio his mistake, and a volley from the mounted band chased him and his companion back into the brush. Those men were Indians clad in soldiers' uniforms, and riding soldiers' horses. De Rudio and his companions outwitted the redskins and remained hidden in the brush until darkness set in, when they slipped away and joined their command.

When De Rudio told the command of the Indians wearing soldiers' uniforms, some soldiers ventured the statement that they had seen Custer's cavalry guidons in the ranks of some of the beleaguering Indians, and gloom spread over the men on the bluff.

The night passed without further incident. The next morning, towards 10 o'clock, while preparing to resist any attack which might be attempted, the dust of a moving column was seen approaching in the distance. Soon it was discovered to be troops who were coming, and in a little while a scout arrived with a note from General Terry to Custer, saying that some Crow scouts had come to camp stating that Custer had been whipped, but that their story was not believed. About half-past 10 o'clock in the morning General Terry rode into Reno's lines and the fate of Custer was ascertained.

Precisely what was done by Custer's immediate command, subsequent to the moment when the rest of the regiment last saw them alive, has remained partly a matter of conjecture, no officer or soldier who rode with him into the valley of the Little Big Horn having lived to tell the tale.

The only person who came away with his life from Custer's command after firing began was the Crow scout, Curley. He managed to sneak through the Sioux lines by arranging his blanket in their fashion. His version throws no light upon the point mentioned. There is no good reason, however, why Custer should have been spared to the last; it was certainly not in his nature to go out of death's way, and the Indians said afterwards that they did not see him nor even know where his stand was.

The only real evidence of how the men of Custer's command came to meet their fate was the testimony of the field where it overtook them.

Custer's trail, from the point where Reno crossed the stream, passed along and in rear of the crest of the bluffs on the right bank, for nearly or quite three miles. Then it came down to the bank of the river, but at once diverged from it again, as though Custer had unsuccessfully attempted to cross; then turning upon itself and almost completing a circle, the trail ceased. It was marked by the remains of officers and men horribly mutilated, and the bodies of horses, some of them dotted along the path, others heaped in ravines and upon knolls where halts appeared to have been made. There was abundant evidence that a gallant resistance had been offered by Custer's troops, but that they were beset on all sides by overpowering numbers.

The officers known to be killed were General Custer, Captains Keogh, Yates and Custer, Lieutenants Cooke, Smith, McIntosh, Calhoun, Porter, Hodgson, Sturgis and Reily of the Seventh Cavalry, Lieutenant Crittenden of the Twentieth Infantry, and Acting Assistant Surgeon DeWolf; Lieutenant Harrington of the cavalry, and Assistant Surgeon Lord were missing. Mr. Boston Custer, a brother, and Mr. Reed, a nephew of General Custer, were with him and were killed.

THOMAS J. CALLAN,
Private, Co. B, 7th U. S. Cavalry.
Born in Ireland, on July 13, 1853.

Twenty-three bodies, among them those of Lieutenants Harrington and Porter, were never found; the fate of those who once animated them has remained a mystery; were they tortured, or did they sink and disappear in the quicksand of the Little Big Horn? It will never be known. The Indians claimed afterwards that they had no prisoners, and could consequently not have tortured any — but who is to believe an Indian? On the other hand, according to all signs, Custer never came nearer than half a mile to the river. His men can therefore not have fallen into the quicksand.

What the outcome of the battle might have been if Reno's command had firmly held on to its first position, or if it had come over the plateau later on from the bluffs and attacked the enemy in the rear, is not within our province to discuss here. Sioux who had fought in the battle said afterwards, when asked, that in both cases they would have fled.

When Reno was pressed back in his second position towards the river bank, Gall and his band, as has been mentioned, hastened to cut off his retreat to the bluffs and set a trap for him.

Had Custer appeared later so that Gall's band could have fallen upon the retreating Reno, bringing him thus between two fires, Reno's command would certainly have been annihilated. The Indians would then still have had time to deal with Custer alone, and, after they got through with him, to finish the small command of Benteen and the pack train.

The news of the disaster shook the country from end to end, but Sitting Bull's evil-bearing influence among the tribes on the warpath grew stronger than ever.

Agency Indians sneaked away by the hundreds to join the rebellious bands, and the War Department set all the necessary power in motion to stamp out the scandalous menace.

THREE DARING COURIERS

AFTER the battle of the Little Big Horn the relief column of General Terry and Colonel Gibbon's force took back the wounded and remnants of the Seventh Cavalry to the Rosebud Landing on the Yellowstone, where they remained for the time being, awaiting re-enforcements, just as General Crook did, farther down south, in his supply camp at Cloud Peak.

All kinds of rumors and reports reached both commanders as to the whereabouts of the hostile Indians. On July 9th General Terry found it desirable to impart certain weighty information to Crook, which had to be done by couriers. The task was an extremely dangerous, if not a hopeless one, as nobody exactly knew where the hostiles might have their scouting parties roaming. Two attempts to deliver the dispatches had been made and both failed, but a third succeeded. Three brave men volunteered to undertake this trip: Privates James Bell, Benjamin F. Stewart and William Evans, all three of Company E, Seventh Infantry. They reached General Crook's camp safely on July 14th and returned with dispatches from this officer. The Medal of Honor was their reward for this brave deed. On this trip they lay hidden during the daytime and traveled at night. Singular as it may seem, they did not come upon any Indian war-party or across any trail, which, of course, did not render the act less conspicuous as a heroic deed.

General Crook was to be joined by General Merritt's column, with the Fifth Cavalry, which force was delayed by Merritt's brilliant exploit against the Cheyennes under Yellow Hand. As is well known, the Cheyennes were surprised and defeated at the War Bonnet Crossing, where their chief, Yellow Hand, was slain by Buffalo Bill in a single-handed duel. The two columns effected a junction on the 3d of August at the Goose Creek. The combined column mustered now 2,000 fighting men, all tents and baggage having been sent back by order of General Crook, with the exception of the mule pack train carrying the reserve ammunition and rations for fifteen days.

Terry's column joined Crook's near the Yellowstone, bringing the expedition up to 4,000. As there was no chance that the Indians would stand up against such a force, Terry separated from Crook on the 24th of August to cross to the left bank of the Yellowstone.

Crook's command then started on an expedition which as to hardships and physical suffering, as well as determination and boldness of conception, has no equal in warfare against the Indians.

On the afternoon of September 4th the column—in the truest sense of the word a "flying column," for no man, from the general down to the packer, had more clothing or package with him than what he could carry on his own or his animal's body —crossed the Little Missouri. The command was then about 200 miles from the northern edge of the Black Hills and about 150 miles from Fort Lincoln, with rations sufficient for but two and a half days.

Here, in a wretched, rain-soaked camp, Crook decided on the 5th of September to push on to the Black Hills. "It's hard, I know it," said this indefatigable hunter of Indians, "but we'll live on our horses and half rations." Under continuous rain and hail-storms the column pushed on.

On the evening of the 7th a column of 150 men from several companies of the Third Cavalry was sent ahead under Captain Anson Mills to try and get some supplies from the Black Hills settlements.

After they started the men of the main force began to kill horses for food. They had had no shelter for several days from the ever-pouring rain, and no wood to build fires through nearly ninety miles of marching.

Early in the morning of September 9th a packer rode into camp with the announcement that Mills had met and surprised a party of Sioux at Slim Buttes that he had attacked, but was opposed by a superior force and needed re-enforcements without delay. General Crook started immediately himself with 100 men of the Third, 50 men from the Second, and the whole of the Fifth Cavalry.

Captain Mills had taken only fifty rounds for each man, in order to march light and swift. He came upon the Indian village of American Horse at Slim Buttes, Dakota, unexpectedly, and attacked without hesitation, capturing the entire village of about thirty-seven lodges, with quantities of supplies, arms and ammunition, and about 175 ponies. Among the articles taken from this village were a guidon of the Seventh Cavalry, a pair of gloves marked with the name of Colonel Keogh, Seventh Cavalry, who was killed with Custer, and many other things which were recognized as belonging to that command. The battalion of Captain Mills suffered a loss of one enlisted man killed, six wounded, and Lieutenant A. H. von Luettwitz, Third Cavalry, so seriously wounded in the leg as to require amputation. The loss of the Indians was American Horse, mortally wounded, four Indians killed and about a dozen captured. The village of Crazy Horse was only a short distance away, and after the first flight from camp the Indians returned in increased numbers and attacked Mills's command, but, the main column of General Crook having arrived, the Indians were worsted in several encounters which took place.

The Indians would hover around the command, taking positions in ravines from which they had to be dislodged, and which they defended with desperate determination. In order to get a glimpse of their foe the soldiers had to expose themselves, and many acts of bravery were performed here. Scout Charley White was shot through the heart, Private John Wenzel, one of the best horsemen of Troop A, Third Cavalry, died from a bullet which passed through his head, Sergeant Edward Gloss of Troop E, same regiment, was wounded. Sergeant John A. Kirkwood and Private Robert Smith of Troop M, of this regiment, showed exceptional fearlessness, and gained for this fight the Medal of Honor.

The Indians under the mortally wounded chief, American Horse, finally surrendered. Several squaws and even a baby pappoose had lost their lives in this most desperate fight, which abounded in revolting scenes characteristic of the border warfare of those times.

BATTLE OF WOLF MOUNTAIN AND CEDAR CREEK

JAMES S. CASEY,
Captain, 5th U. S. Infantry.
Highest rank attained: Colonel, U.S.A.
Born in Philadelphia, Pa.,
January 28, 1833.

PREPARATORY to the winter campaign of 1876-77 against the Sioux and Northern Cheyennes, under Sitting Bull and Crazy Horse, in Montana, Colonel Nelson A. Miles equipped his command, the Fifth United States Infantry, as if he were organizing an expedition for the Arctic regions. His foresight was commendable, for frequently the thermometer registered as low as fifty degrees below zero. They were abundantly supplied with food and clothing, and every precaution was taken to protect both men and horses against the severity of this intense cold. The command, numbering about 400 men and one piece of artillery, when dressed in their blankets and furs, looked more like a large body of Esquimaux than like white men and United States troops, and when they wore their woolen masks over their heads it was impossible to distinguish one from the other. Thus equipped the men were well prepared to battle with both the elements and the Indians during this trying campaign, which opened early in October, 1876.

A cantonment had been established at the mouth of the Tongue River by Colonel Miles, and on the 10th of October a train of ninety-four wagons started for it from Glendive Creek with supplies, but was attacked and driven back. With a new escort of 185 men of the Twenty-second Infantry, under Colonel E. S. Otis, the train again started out, but was a second time attacked by 700 Indians on Spring Creek. The train, however, formed in compact lines, pressed on, the infantry escort charging the Indians repeatedly and driving them back, while the wagons slowly advanced. Three or four scouts from Colonel Miles's command were met here, having been attacked by Indians, and one of their party killed. The train proceeded, with the escort skirmishing, until Clear Creek was reached. Here the Indians made a most determined attack, firing the prairie, and the wagons were obliged to advance through the flames. Compactly arranged in four lines, the wagons proceeded, the entire escort being engaged in alternately charging the Indians, driving them back and then regaining the moving teams.

"COLONEL MILES MET SITTING BULL BETWEEN THE LINES."

While the train was thus advancing, an Indian runner approached and left upon a hill the following communication :

YELLOWSTONE:

I want to know what you are doing traveling on this road. You scare all the buffalo away. I want to hunt in this place. I want you to turn back from here. If you don't, I will fight you again. I want you to leave what you have got here and turn back from here.

I am your friend,

SITTING BULL.

I mean all the rations you have got and some powder. Wish you would write as soon as you can.

Colonel Otis sent out a scout, with a reply to Sitting Bull's note, stating that he intended to take the train through the Tongue River and would be pleased to accommodate the Indians with a fight at any time.

The train again proceeded, the Indians surrounding it and keeping up firing at long range, but after a short time two Indians appeared with a flag of truce and communication was again opened with the hostiles, who stated they were hungry, tired of the war and wanted to make peace. Sitting Bull wanted to meet Colonel Otis outside of the lines of the escort, which invitation, however, Colonel Otis declined, though professing a willingness to meet Sitting Bull inside the lines of the troops. This the wary savage was afraid to do, but sent three chiefs to represent him. Colonel Otis made them a present of 150 pounds of hard bread and two sides of bacon, said that he had no authority to treat with them, but that the Indians could go to the Tongue River and there make known their wishes regarding surrender. The train moved on and the Indians fell to its rear, finally disappearing altogether.

On the night of the 18th of October Colonel Otis met Colonel Miles with his entire regiment, who, alarmed for the safety of the train, had advanced to meet it. The supplies were then taken to the cantonment at the Tongue, and the wagons returned in safety to Glendive.

Shortly after meeting Colonel Otis and learning from him the immediate situation, Colonel Miles, with the Fifth Infantry, started after Sitting Bull, overtaking him near Cedar Creek, Montana, north of the Yellowstone. Colonel Miles met Sitting Bull between the lines of the troops and of the Indians, the latter having sent a flag of truce to Miles, desiring to communicate.

After some conversation Sitting Bull desired to know what the troops were remaining in that country for, and why they did not go back to their posts or into winter quarters. He was informed by Miles that they were out to bring him and his Indians in, and that they did not wish to continue the war against them, but that if they forced the war it would end disastrously for the Indians. He was told that he could not be allowed to roam over the country, sending out war-parties to devastate the settlements. Sitting Bull claimed that the country belonged to the Indians and not to the white men, and declared that he had nothing to do with the white men and wanted them to leave that country entirely to the Indians. He said that the white man never lived who loved an Indian, and that no true Indian ever lived that did not hate the white man. He declared that God Almighty made him an Indian and did not make him an agency Indian either, and he did not intend to be one. After much talk the interview closed unsatisfactorily and Colonel Miles's column, numbering 398 rifles, moved and camped on Cedar Creek, so as to intercept the movement of the Indians, Sitting Bull being told to come again the next day.

While the command was moving north between the Indian camp and the Big Dry River, the Indians again appeared and desired to talk. Another council followed between the lines, October 21st, Sitting Bull and a number of principal men being present. Sitting Bull wanted peace, if he could have it upon his own terms. He was told the conditions of the government. He then said he would come in to trade for ammunition, but wanted no rations or annuities and desired to live free, as an Indian. He gave no assurance of good faith, and as the council broke up he was told that a non-acceptance of the terms of the government would be considered an act of hostility.

Sitting Bull and the men who accompanied him then returned with all speed toward their lines, calling out to the Indians to prepare for battle, and the scene was, for the next few minutes, one of the wildest excitement. The prairies were covered with savage warriors, dashing hither and thither, making ready for battle. At the end of the time mentioned, Miles ordered an advance of the entire body of troops, and immediately the Indians commenced setting fire to the dry prairie grass around the command, together with other acts of hostility. An engagement immediately followed, in which the Indians were driven out of their camp for several miles, and on the two following days were hotly pursued.

The Indians lost a few of their warriors and a large amount of property, both in their camp and on their retreat, including their horses, mules and ponies.

At one time the command was entirely surrounded by Indians, and the troops, although outnumbered three to one, were formed in a large hollow square in open order and deployed at five paces, with all the reserves brought into action; yet not a single man left his place or failed to do his full duty.

The energy and persistence with which the attack was made created such consternation in the Indian camp that after a pursuit of forty-two miles they sent out another flag of truce and again requested an interview. During this interview 2,000 of them agreed to go to their agencies and surrender, five chiefs giving themselves up as hostages for the delivery of men, women, children, ponies, arms and ammunition at the agencies. Sitting Bull himself escaped northward with his own small band, and was joined later by Gall and other chiefs with their followers. Having returned to Tongue River Cantonment, Colonel Miles organized a force numbering 434 rifles and moved north in pursuit of Sitting Bull, but the trail was obliterated by the snow in the vicinity of the Big Dry River. A band of 119 lodges, under Iron Dog, crossed the Missouri in advance of the command and dissolved itself in the

Yanktonnais camp, Sitting Bull continuing to hover about the neighborhood of the Missouri River and its branches for some time afterwards.

On December 7th, First Lieutenant F. D. Baldwin, with Companies G, H and I, Fifth Infantry, numbering 100 officers and men, overtook Sitting Bull's camp of 190 lodges, followed and drove it south of the Missouri, near the mouth of Bark Creek. The Indians resisted Baldwin's crossing of the river for a short time and then retreated into the Bad Lands. Ten days later this same force, under Lieutenant Baldwin, surprised Sitting Bull's band of 122 lodges near the head of the Red Water, capturing the entire camp and its contents, together with about sixty horses, ponies and mules. The Indians escaped with little besides what they had upon their persons and scattered southward across the Yellowstone.

The large cantonment at the mouth of the Tongue River having been established, from this point as a base the pursuit of the remnants of the Sioux and Northern Cheyennes, with Sitting Bull and Crazy Horse, was energetically pressed by the troops under Colonel Miles. The low state of water in the river now gave the troops on the Yellowstone a three-fold task of great difficulty, to shelter themselves by building huts, to bring up their supplies by tedious hauling from the head of navigation, and to prosecute, simultaneously, in the midst of winter, vigorous field operations against the hostiles.

On the 29th of December, Colonel Miles, with Companies A, C, D, E and K, Fifth Infantry, and Companies E and F, Twenty-second Infantry, numbering 436 officers and men, with two pieces of artillery, moved out against the Sioux and Cheyennes under Crazy Horse, whose camp had been reported south of the Yellowstone, in the valley of Tongue River. As the column moved up the Tongue, the Indians abandoned their winter camps, consisting of about 600 lodges, and the column had two sharp skirmishes on the 1st and 3d of January, driving the Indians up the valley of the Tongue, until the night of the 7th, when the advance captured a young warrior and seven Cheyenne women and children, who proved to be relatives of the head-men of the tribe. A determined attempt was made by the Indians to rescue the prisoners, and preparations were made for the severe fight to be expected next day. The next morning about 600 warriors appeared in front of the troops and an engagement followed, lasting about five hours. The fight took place in a canyon, the Indians occupying a spur of the Wolf Mountain range.

As the fight opened the two Napoleon guns exploded shells within the Indians' lines, creating great consternation among the savages At one time they had completely surrounded the command, but the key of the position was a high bluff to the left of the line of troops, and the sharpest fighting was for the possession of this ground. The Indians who held it were led by Big Crow, a Medicine Man. He rushed out in front of the warriors, attired in a most gorgeous Indian battle costume of the brightest colors, and with a head-dress made of the waving plumes of the eagle falling down his back, jumped up and down, ran in a circle and whooped and yelled like a madman.

Then a charge was made by troops under Captains James S. Casey, Fifth Infantry, and Edmund Butler, Fourteenth Infantry, and Lieutenants Robert McDonald and Frank D. Baldwin, Fifth Infantry. It was done with splendid courage, vim and determination, although the men were so encumbered with their heavy winter clothing, and the snow was so deep, that it was impossible to move faster than a slow walk. They were conspicuous in this charge for their boldness and excellent judgment. In the very midst of their daring acts of bravado, Big Crow fell, pierced by a rifle shot, and his loss, together with the success of the charge that had been made and the important ground gained, seemed to cause a panic among the Indians. and they immediately fled in utter rout up the valley down which they had come a few hours before. The ground was covered with ice and snow to a depth of from one to three feet, and the latter portion of the engagement was fought in a blinding snow-storm, the troops stumbling and falling in scaling the ice and snow-covered cliffs from which the Indians were driven, with serious loss in killed and wounded, through the Wolf Mountains and in the direction of the Big Horn range. For this gallant charge Captains Casey and Butler and Lieutenant McDonald received the Medal of Honor.

DAVID ROCHE,
First Sergeant, Co. A, 5th U. S. Infantry.
Born at Kerry, Ireland, July, 1853

If the troops had met with disaster it would have been many weeks before any relieving command could have reached the ground from the nearest possible source of aid. Every officer and soldier knew this, and that a mistake meant disaster, and that disaster or defeat meant annihilation, and were therefore inspired to deeds of heroism and fortitude and a corresponding confidence. The fighting that occurred on the left of the line, as already described, was for a time very close and desperate, in which the troops lost three men killed and eight wounded. The column then returned to the cantonment at the mouth of the Tongue River.

The prisoners which Colonel Miles's command captured from Crazy Horse's village proved a valuable acquisition in communicating with the hostiles and in arranging for their surrender. On Febuary 1st Miles sent out a scout with two of the captives, offering terms on which a surrender would be accepted, informing the hostiles that a non-compliance would result in a movement of the troops against them. Following up the trail from the scene of the engagement, near the Wolf Mountains, the Indians were found camped on a tributary of the Little Big Horn. The mission was successfully executed by the scout, and on February 19th he returned with nineteen Indians, mainly chiefs and leading warriors, who desired to learn the exact conditions upon which they could surrender. The terms were repeated, viz: unconditional surrender and compliance with such orders as might be received from higher authority. The delegation returned to their village, the camps moved near the forks of the Powder River for a general council, and after another interview with Colonel Miles, Crazy Horse's uncle, named Little Hawk, with others, guaranteed to bring the Indian camp to the cantonment at Tongue River, or to take it to the lower agencies, leaving in Colonel Miles's hands, as a pledge of good faith, nine hostages, prominent men and head-warriors of both tribes. Three hundred Indians, led by Two Moons, Hump, and other chiefs, surrendered to Colonel Miles on April 22d. The largest part of the bands, numbering more than 2,000, led by Crazy Horse, Little Hawk, and others, moved southward and surrendered at the Red Cloud and Spotted Tail Agencies in May.

Crazy Horse and his people were placed on the reservation near Camp Robinson, where, for a time, they appeared quiet and peaceable, but in a few months the restraints of this new position became so irksome to Crazy Horse that he began to concoct schemes again involving his people in war. It was determined, therefore, to arrest and confine him. While on his way to the guard-house he broke from those around him and attempted to escape by cutting his way, with a knife, through the circle of sentinels and bystanders. In the melee he was fatally wounded and died on the night of September 7th.

In the meantime Sitting Bull's camp had gathered near the Yellowstone, and when Crazy Horse and his confederates decided to place themselves under subjection to the government, Sitting Bull's band, in order to avoid surrendering and to escape further pursuit, retreated beyond the northern boundary and took refuge on Canadian soil, the party being in a very destitute condition, almost out of ammunition and having lost nearly everything excepting their guns and horses.

The campaign against these Indians, which brought abought the preceding results, was carried on by the troops under the most unfavorable conditions and against greatly superior forces of Indians. The men not only withstood the rigors of the cold weather with great fortitude, but also fought the savages in the several engagements from Cedar Creek to Wolf Mountains with a vigor that challenged admiration.

Among these brave and hardy troopers were men who displayed exceptional acts of heroism and gallantry in these actions that won for them the coveted Medal of Honor.

They are as follows:

John Baker, Musician, Co. D, 5th U. S. Inf.
Richard Burke, Private, Co. G, 5th U. S. Inf.
Denis Byrne, Sergeant, Co. G, 5th U. S. Inf.
Joseph Cable, Private, Co. I, 5th U. S. Inf.
James S. Calvert, Private, Co. C, 5th U. S. Inf.
Aquilla Coonrod, Sergeant, Co. C, 5th U. S. Inf.
John S. Donelly, Private, Co. G, 5th U. S. Inf.
Christopher Freemeyer, Priv., Co. D, 5th U. S. Inf.
John Haddoo, Corporal, Co. B. 5th U. S. Inf.
Henry Hogan, 1st Sergeant, Co. G. 5th U. S. Inf.
David Holland, Corp., Co. A, U. S. Inf.
Fred O. Hunt, Private, Co. A, 5th U. S. Inf.
Edward Johnston, Corporal, Co. C, 5th U. S. Inf.
Philip Kennedy, Private, Co C, 5th U. S. Inf.
Wendelin Kreher, 1st Sergeant, Co. C, 5th U.S. Inf.
Bernard McCann, Private, Co. F, 22d U S. Inf.

Michael McCormick, Private, Co. G, 5th U. S. Inf
Owen McGar, Private, Co. C, 5th U. S. Inf.
John McHugh, Private, Co. A, 5th U. S. Inf.
Michael McLoughlin, Sergeant, Co.A, 5th U.S. Inf.
Robert McPhelan, Sergeant, Co. E, 5th U. S. Inf.
George Miller, Corporal, Co. H, 5th U. S. Inf.
Charles H. Montrose,, Private, Co. H, 5th U.S. Inf.
David Roche, 1st Sergeant, Co. A, 5th U S. Inf.
Henry Rodenburg, Private, Co. A, 5th U. S. Inf.
Edward Roonty, Private, Co. D, 5th U. S. Inf.
David Ryan, Private, Co. G, 5th U. S. Inf.
Charles Sheppard, Private, Co. A, 5th U. S. Inf.
William Wallace, Sergeant, Co. C, 5th U. S. Inf.
Patton G. Whitehead, Private, Co. C, 5th U.S. Inf.
Charles Wilson, Corporal, Co. H, 5th U. S. Inf.

CAPTURE OF LAME DEER'S VILLAGE

A FTER the surrender of the greater part of the Cheyennes under Crazy Horse and the escape of Sitting Bull's band into Canada, there still remained a band of renegades, chiefly Minneconjous, under Lame Deer, who had determined not to yield to Colonel Miles.

It was learned that these renegades had moved westward, and as soon as the necessary forage could be obtained Colonel Miles with a force consisting of four troops of the Second Cavalry, two companies of the Fifth and four of the Twenty-second Infantry, on the 5th of May started up the Tongue River in pursuit of them.

After a march of about sixty miles from the Yellowstone they crossed the trail of Lame Deer's camp, and after leaving the wagon-train with an escort of three infantry companies the rest of the command moved up the Rosebud River, they having scarcely halted at any time for rest until they reached a high divide between the Rosebud and the Big Horn Rivers, from the top of which could be discerned an Indian village some fifteen miles away as the crow flies, near the mouth of Muddy Creek, Montana. Having assured himself that it was Lame Deer's village, Miles moved his troops under cover of darkness within close proximity of the Indians, and at dawn of day on the 7th charged upon the village, the mounted infantry and scouts stampeding the Indian horses while the battalion of cavalry attacked the camp. The ponies, horses and mules were handsomely rounded up and brought to the rear of the fighting battalion. The Indians, after a short but sharp engagement, fled from their camp to the high hills in the vicinity.

Before the attack was made Colonel Miles called on the Indians to surrender; Lame Deer and Iron Star, his head warrior, appeared desirous of doing so, but after shaking hands with some of the officers the Indians, either meditating treachery or fearing it, again began firing. This ended peace-making and the fight was resumed, the hostiles being driven, in a running fight, eight miles, across the broken country, to the Rosebud. Fourteen Indians were killed, including Lame Deer and Iron Star, 450 horses, mules and ponies, and the entire Indian camp outfit were captured, including fifty-one lodges well stored with supplies. Lieutenant A. M. Fuller, Second Cavalry, was slightly wounded; four enlisted men were killed and six were wounded. The Indians who escaped subsequently moved eastward to the Little Missouri and the command returned to the cantonment.

Five men were awarded the Medal of Honor for distinguished gallantry in this action, they being: First Sergeant Henry Wilkens, Corporal H. Garland, Farrier William H. Jones, and Private William Leonard, of Troop L, and Private Samuel D. Phillips Troop H, of the Second U. S. Cavalry.

The following interesting episode relative to this action is told by General Miles in his "Personal Recollections":

"When the Indians were attacked they fled from their camp, taking only what they carried in their hands, up among the high bluffs and rugged hills in that vicinity.

"In the surprise and excitement of the wild onset of the charge, a group of warriors was forced away from the others and became separated from the rest of the tribe. Before making the attack I had ordered our Sioux and Cheyenne Indians to call out to the Lame Deer Indians that if they threw down their arms and surrendered we would spare their lives. I was anxious to capture some of them alive, as we hoped thereby to secure the surrender of all the Indians in the camp. As we galloped up to this group of warriors they apparently recognized the purport of the demand and dropped their arms upon the ground. In order to assure them of our good will, I called out 'How-how-kola' (meaning friend) and extended my hand to the chief, Lame Deer, which he grasped, and in a few seconds more I would have secured him and the others, as, although he was wild and trembling with excitement, my adjutant, George W. Baird, was doing the same with the head warrior, Iron Star. Unfortunately, just at that time one of our white scouts rode up and and joined the group of officers and soldiers with me. He had more enthusiasm than discretion, and I presume desired to insure my safety, as he drew up his rifle and covered the Indian with it. Lame Deer saw this and evidently thought the young scout was going to shoot him. I know of no other motive for his subsequent act than the belief that he was to be killed whether he surrendered or not. As quick as thought, with one desperate, powerful effort, he wrenched his hand from mine, although I tried to hold it, and grasped his rifle from the ground, ran backward a few steps, raised his rifle to his eye and fired. Seeing his determined face, his set jaw, wild eye, and the open muzzle of his rifle, I realized my danger and instantly whirled my horse from him, and in this quick movement the horse slightly settled back upon his haunches; at that moment the rifle flashed within ten feet of me, the bullet whizzed past my breast leaving me unharmed, but unfortunately killing a brave soldier by my side. Iron Star broke away from Adjutant Baird at the same time. This instantly ended all efforts to secure their peaceful surrender and opened a hot fight that lasted but a few seconds. A dozen rifles and revolvers were opened on the scattered warriors who were fighting us, and all went down quickly beneath the accurate, close and deadly fire. The whole incident was over in a much less time than it takes to describe it.

"The main object of our expedition being now accomplished, and not desiring to risk more lives in an encounter than the circumstances absolutely demanded, we turned back and bivouacked at Lame Deer's camp, which was one of the richest I had ever seen. It was composed of fifty-one beautiful lodges, richly stored with robes, horse-equipments and every other species of Indian property. Whatever was desired by the troops was taken possession of and the remainder burned. The herd of horses were round, fat, sleek and in excellent condition.

"On the morning following commenced the greatest circus I have ever witnessed. Two hundred of the war and buffalo ponies were selected with which to mount our foot-troops. The Fifth Infantry was afterward completely equipped in this way, and on the frontier was sometimes known as the Eleventh Cavalry, there being then ten cavalry regiments in the army organization.

"Selecting the gentle and trained ponies from the vicious brutes was a difficult problem. The soldiers who were fortunate enough to select well-trained buffalo or war ponies congratulated themselves in being able to put Indian bridles and saddles upon them, but even then they were not safe in mounting. Frequently it required the aid of two men to get one into the saddle. The ponies seemed as suspicious of the white man as the American horse is of the wild Indian.

"Still, many of the men succeeded in mounting, and in place of spurs used the Indian 'quirt,' a stick about a foot long with a rawhide lash. These men were highly elated, and their derisive remarks to their more unfortunate comrades were equal to the best witticisms I have ever heard on the stump or under canvas. Some of the ponies would not allow a white man to go near them; others as fast as the scouts or Indians could rope them would submit to being bridled and saddled; in fact would look meek and calm, waiting for a good opportunity. With the help of one or two men the infantryman would mount, or at least reach his place above the saddle and beast for the time being, whereupon the pony would double up like a ball, make a bound into the air, coming down stiff-legged, jump about over the prairie, and repeating this exercise with lightning rapidity in almost every direction at the same time: then the soldier's hat would fall, and before many minutes he would follow suit, and frequently the pony would not stop until he had freed himself from the saddle; or, sometimes he would gallop around over the prairie and come back to the herd with the saddle underneath.

"Two hundred soldiers on the same field endeavoring to subdue the same number of wild horses created a scene of excitement which was not only humorous but also somewhat dangerous. Fortunately they did not have far to fall, and the ground was covered with a heavy crop of green grass. This scene continued until the command was completely mounted and the ponies and infantry had become better acquainted, and by that time we were ready to take up our return march to the cantonment."

CAMPAIGN AGAINST THE NEZ PERCES

WILLIAM R. PARNELL,
First Lieutenant, 1st U. S. Cavalry.
Highest rank attained: Major, U. S. A.
Born in Dublin, Ireland,
August 13, 1836.

THE trouble with the Nez Perce Indians broke out early in the summer of 1877 and terminated in the fall of the same year. This tribe had lived in Idaho, and up to this time had always been at peace with the white population of the surrounding country. As a matter of fact the thrifty Nez Perce was regarded as one of the friendliest Indians of that section of the country, who had always treated the white traveler and explorer with hospitality and generosity. The same treatment was not accorded them by the white settlers, who from fear or general prejudice had always been more or less hostile. Nevertheless, these Indians remained quiet and peaceable, attending strictly to their own affairs and pleasures.

The direct cause of the trouble was a controversy for the possession of the Wallowa Valley. A band of white settlers claimed ownership of the land; the Indians pointed out that since the land had been given them by treaty as part of their reservation they were the rightful owners.

The result of the dispute was the Nez Perces were compelled to yield. The settlers succeeded in impressing the government at Washington with the importance of their claim for the possession of the valley, and to their intense satisfaction saw a military force moving to enforce their demands. This placed the Indians before the alternative of fighting for rights or abandoning their cherished land. The general sentiment seemed to favor the latter. Rather than begin hostilities they would emigrate. Looking Glass and Chief Joseph, the leading chiefs, prepared for the removal. Then an occurrence happened which changed the whole plan by which hostilities were forced upon the tribe. Some of the hot-headed settlers had become impatient, and, tired of waiting for the retirement of the Indians, began to annoy them. One white man, more imprudent than the others, shot and killed a Nez Perce. With this one shot the discontent of the savages that had been smoldering for some time was now fanned into open rebellion. The quiet, undisturbing, harmless Nez Perce at once became as violent and valiant a foe as was ever encountered by the American soldier. And although the subsequent campaign was not of long duration, it was exciting while it lasted, full of thrilling episodes, included a number of sharp encounters, entailed a severe loss of life to the military forces and, when it finally ended, did not tend to decrease the respect which the civil and military authorities had always entertained for this savage tribe.

The first act of hostilities on the part of the Indians was the murder of a white settler. A brother of the Nez Perce who had been shot retaliated by taking the life of his brother's slayer. A hue and cry was raised among the white settlers, who feared a general massacre, and the military was urged to step in and prevent further outrages. On the other hand, the Indians were fully cognizant of what the result of the act of one of their tribesmen would be, and hastened to get away. They left their reservation and moved in a northeasterly direction toward Montana. They were pursued alternately by General Howard, Colonel Gibbon and Colonel Sturgis.

At the first sign of a disturbance General Howard sent an expedition under Captain David Perry and J. G. Trimble, consisting of Troops F and H, First United States Cavalry, to the scene of the disorder.

The impression prevailed in military circles that the uprising was not of a general character, especially since this Indian tribe was known to be very peacable and friendly.

The expedition then was intended by General Howard more in the nature of a demonstration rather than active hostilities. The sight of the troops was thought to be sufficient to restore peace and tranquillity. To this failure to comprehend the grievances of the Nez Perces and appreciate the seriousness of the situation was added another mistake. White settlers of the district of Idaho, threatened by the pillaging Indians, had grossly exaggerated the conduct of Chief Joseph and his tribesmen. "The Nez Perces are so loaded up with plunder and booty that they are hampered in their own progress and are able to proceed very slowly only," they said. General Howard gave these stories more credence than the facts warranted and acted accordingly. His orders to Captain Perry were: "Get to the scene quickly, take away from the Indians their loot and chase them back to their reservation." The result was, that when the command moved on its mission—believed to be so simple and easy—it left Fort Lapwai poorly equipped and not even sufficiently provided with ammunition, Troop F having but forty rounds for carbine and twelve for pistol, Troop H not being much better off. The strength of the force did not exceed 90 men.

General Howard's first information about the trouble reached him June 15, 1877, and the next day found Captain Perry's expedition on the march. Prompt action had almost assumed the character of undue haste.

It was known that the Nez Perces were in camp in the White Bird Canyon, Idaho, and thither the command moved quickly, rapidly reaching its destination after an exacting and exhausting ride—wearing out the men and horses—of twenty-four hours. A surprise awaited the troops on their very appearance on the scene.

The Indians were occupying a strong position and had prepared themselves for a fray. Their attitude indicated plainly that they would not yield to a "demonstration," and that, if the soldiers wanted to recapture the plunder, they would have to fight for it. They then realized that they would have to fight anyway, since a retreat was impossible. And thus the battle of White Bird Canyon, which resulted in a very serious disaster for the cavalrymen, occurred on June 17, 1877.

Captain Trimble, who commanded Troop H, at the outset realized that as far as the command was concerned the fighting could be defensive only, the Indians outnumbering the soldiers eight to one and being in an unassailable position.

To his right there was an elevation on rocky ground, which offered all the advantages of a strong defense. Accordingly, he at once placed there his first sergeant, Michael McCarthy, with a detail of six men, with orders to hold that point at all hazards.

Now the fight began. The Indians broke forth, yelling, screaming, filling the air with hideous howls and showers of bullets.

As soon as this rush was made—it looked as if hades itself had been turned loose—eight citizens, settlers who had been most loud in their denunciation of the Nez Perces and demands for vengence, took to their heels and ran away as fast as they could. The soldiers, too, were not prepared to meet this furious and awe-inspiring onslaught and wavered. Soon most of the men of Troop F were hurrying to the rear. Captain Perry, doubting the advisability of a defense, ordered a general retreat.

MICHAEL McCARTHY,
First Sergeant, Troop H, 1st U. S. Cavalry.
Born April 19, 1847, at St. John's, N. F.
Highest rank attained: Captain
Washington Nat'l Guard.

Captain Trimble did not lose his head in the general confusion. He galloped to the commanding officer and beseeched him to recall the order.

"What is to become of McCarthy and his men?" he said; "they are in a strong position. If we re-enforce him and hold the ground there, we shall check the attack."

Captain Perry saw that the proposition was plausible and consented to the plan.

Quickly Captain Trimble ordered the men to turn about and again face the savage foe, taking the lead himself, and thus by his personal example inspired the fear-stricken men to renewed confidence.

In the meantime the Indians had not been slow in taking advantage of the confusion within the ranks of the cavalry. They dashed forward with increased vigor and mingled shouts of triumph with their ugly warcries.

From his elevated position Sergeant McCarthy with his small command was able to hold the advancing savages by sending into their ranks a hot and accurate fire.

He, too, observed the change of tactics, when the troops suddenly turned and formed for an attack, and hurriedly rode from his position to assist his captain in steadying the men. As soon as the attack was organized he joined his faithful six men at the former post.

However, Captain Trimble's well-conceived plan failed of success. It was simply impossible to withstand the onslaught of such an overwhelming force. Men fell wounded from their horses on all sides, and to maintain the fight much longer would have been like reckless slaughter. Once more the troops retreated before the

"HELD HIS POSITION AGAINST THE STORMING FOE."

exultant Nez Perces, galloping to some hills which promised protection about a mile away. Their retreat was much faster than the Indians were able to follow. This second retreat left McCarthy and his detail in a serious plight. Completely surrounded by savages, he nobly and heroically held his position against the storming foe.

The struggle was observed by his comrades on the hills, who followed every phase of it with anticipations of awe and terror. Closer and closer the Indians drew their circle around the gallant little band. One could now see them shoot, strike or club the foremost of the redskins. Now it was a hand-to-hand fight. Now they could no longer be seen They ooomed to have been swallowed up by the hundreds of the triumphant Nes Perces. Many of the soldiers turned away from the distant, sickening sight. But lo! Again the figure of McCarthy, still surrounded by his comrades, loomed up.

The gallant little band was cutting its way through the ranks of the hostiles.

A detachment under First Lieuteuant W. R. Parnell, Troop H, hastened to their help.

McCarthy was successful in escaping from the savages' grip and reaching the lieutenant's detail. But two of his six comrades fell into the hands of the foe during that brief but terrific ride.

Re-enforced by Lieutenant Parnell's detail, another stand was made against the Indians,—but in vain. Finally the Lieutenant, who handled this small force of heroes with phenomenal galantry, ordered the retreat.

McCarthy was truly omnipresent, now fighting, now helping a poor dismounting comrade from falling in the hands of the savage foe, now encouraging and steadying his men. He seemed to know of no danger and fought like a lion. One horse was shot from under him. He mounted another. Slowly he and his men retreated. Again his horse was killed and in the general melee that ensued the brave sergeant was separated from his comrades.

With great presence of mind and unabated energy he made a dash through the shouting and yelling Indians and made for a nearby clump of bushes in the bed of the creek, where he crawled as far as he possibly could and kept in hiding. He heard the shooting, saw the victorious savages ride by, observed the soldiers fleeing for their lives. He gnashed his teeth at the helpnessness of his position, to be the eye-witness of sad defeat and not to be able to turn the tide and help his comrades. But his own situation was extremely perilous and common prudence dictated to him the necessity of remaining quietly in his place of concealment.

Near by him lay a dead comrade—a dear comrade. Presently a number of squaws came up to rob and mutilate the dead hero. His own big cavalry boots stuck out of the bush. One of the women saw them and, concluding that they betrayed the presence of another soldier, called the attention of the other women to the boots. McCarthy, however, followed every move of the squaws and promptly anticipated their action. He slipped his feet out of the tell-tale boots and crawled still farther into the undergrowth. The squaws got the boots, but they failed to get their owner. Some soldier dropped them here in his hasty flight, they thought, and desisted from further investigation.

After many hours of patient waiting McCarthy, bootless and with empty gun, made his escape by crawling down the bed of the creek and finally gaining the timbered mountains some miles away. From here he wandered over rough territory, hiding by day, marching by night, living on the scant rations he had with him, until after untold hardships he at last reached his camp at Mount Idaho, thoroughly exhausted, where his safe return caused great rejoicing, since every one of his comrades and superior officers had believed that he had suffered the horrible fate of a captive in the hands of the torturing redskins.

In this engagement the troops lost one commissioned officer and thirty-three men—over one-third of the entire command. The Nez Perces, however, continued their march toward Montana.

Besides Parnell's heroic attempt to rescue McCarthy, he returned with a few men in the face of a heavy fire from the pursuing Indians, and at imminent peril rescued a soldier, whose horse had been killed, leaving his rider behind in the retreat.

Lieutenant Parnell and Sergeant McCarthy were awarded the **Medal of Honor** for the part they played in this action.

BATTLE OF THE BIG HOLE

THE Nez Perces Indians were so elated over their success after repulsing Captain Perry's forces at the White Bird Canyon, Idaho, that they committed numerous crimes and outraged white women in a most brutal and fiendish manner.

These crimes were brought to the attention of General Howard, who at once took the field in person, determined to punish the savages who had committed them Detachments were sent out to scout the country and attack the Indians wherever they found them. These crimes must be stopped and drastic measures were a necessity.

One of the detachments encountered them at the Clear Water River, Idaho, and in this fight both the whites' and the Indians' losses were quite heavy. The Indians had succeeded in driving the soldiers away from a howitzer and two field guns, thus allowing them to fall into the Indians' hands. First Lieutenant Charles F. Humphrey, Fourth Artillery, upon seeing his men driven back and the guns abandoned at once called a few of his men together and voluntarily led them, in the face of a withering fire, to the abandoned guns, which were lying within a few yards of the hostiles. A most desperate fight ensued between him and the Indians for the possession of the guns, and in a short time he had them safely within the lines, hauling them by hand, as the horses had been shot down. Lieutenant Humphrey was warmly commended for this brave act and was awarded the Medal of Honor.

The troops were continually on the move in order to harass the Indians and intercept them whenever they attempted to leave Idaho, but notwithstanding their vigilance the hostiles broke up into several small bands and made for the "buffalo country" in Montana by way of the Lo-Lo trail.

General Howard at once notified General Gibbon, commanding the district of Montana, of the Nez Perces' escape and the probable route they would pursue, whereupon General Gibbon dispatched Captain C. C. Rawn, commanding Fort Missoula, to look for the hostiles and head them off. Captain Rawn promptly threw a small force consisting of his company, Captain William Logan's and a few citizen volunteers, into the Lo Lo Pass, where they intrenched themselves in the canyon and awaited the arrival of Chief Joseph and his Nez Perces into Montana. Small scouting parties were sent out to ascertain whether Joseph was coming on that trail, but they returned without seeing any signs of the approaching Indians. A few hours after their arrival, however, two of Joseph's Indian runners came through with messages stating that Joseph and his band wished to pass through the Bitter Root Valley on their way to the buffalo country, and that they would not molest the settlers if they were allowed to do so. Joseph's past record was such that the request could not be complied with and the two messengers were forthwith arrested. Captain Rawn then sought a conference with the Nez Perces, with the hope of detaining them until General Howard's troops, or expected assistance from Fort Shaw, under Gibbon, should arrive. At this conference Joseph was informed that if his band would surrender their arms he would allow them to pass. This Joseph positively refused to do, and cunningly leaving a few Indians to make a feint, he at once climbed the hills and passed around Rawn's flank into the Bitter Root Valley. Rawn left a small force behind to guard the post and immediately gave chase, but when he overtook them it was found that most of the citizen volunteers had deserted him and that his remaining force of less than 100 was wholly inadequate to stand a fight with Joseph's braves, who outnumbered his men four to one. He therefore withdrew his command and returned to his post near Missoula.

General Gibbon in the meantime had collected from the several posts in Montana all the available troops and started out from Fort Shaw for Missoula, 150 miles away, and by making forced marches over a rough country accomplished the trip in seven days. Upon his arrival at Missoula, Gibbon's command was re-enforced by Rawn's company, thus bringing up his force to a total of 146 men, 17 officers, and some citizen volunteers. With this small force he set out in pursuit of Chief Joseph, who had on the 28th of July started up the Bitter Root. Joseph having a start of several days, moved slowly, believing that it would be some time before his pursuit would be resumed, but after five days of terrible climbing over the rugged and broken country the Nez Perce village was sighted by the troops on the evening of August 8th in the Big Hole Basin, Montana.

About 10 o'clock that night General Gibbon moved his command stealthily down to within a few hundred yards of the sleeping Nez Perce warriors, and as day began to break, the troops in perfect silence, moved to their positions for attack, being compelled to cross a slough with water waist deep before reaching the Indian camp. Captains Logan, Williams and Rawn were sent with their companies to the extreme right to cross and attack the camp near a small creek, while Lieutenant Bradley with a small force went farther down the stream to attack.

After proceeding some distance Bradley's men encountered a mounted Indian who was on his way to the pony herd. He was immediately shot down. This shot was quickly followed by others, and the line of men sprang forward to the charge. A heavy fire was at once opened along the entire length of the Indian tepees, the startled Nez Perces rushing from their lodges in every direction, many taking refuge in the brush behind the bank of the creek, along which the village lay. For a few minutes no effective fire was returned, but soon the hostiles recovered somewhat from their surprise, and, getting under cover of the brush, they opened a destructive fire on the troops as the latter came into the open ground. The fire was particularly destructive on the right end of the line where Logan was sweeping forward. He and his men—Company A, Seventh Infantry—were in the rear of the hidden Indians who turned, as the soldiers came along, and fired into them with terrible effect. The greatest slaughter of the day took place here, Logan and others of the brave men laying down their lives.

In less than twenty minutes from the time the charge was begun the soldiers were in full possession of the camp and orders were given for its destruction. While part of the men were engaged in burning the lodges, the Indians kept up a fire from their sheltered positions, officers and men falling rapidly under these well-directed shots, until General Gibbon reluctantly withdrew his men from the village and took shelter in the timber. Although the Indians were driven from their camp, they were, however, not beaten, and as the troops sought shelter in the timber the Indians became more confident of themselves and came out from their shelter into the camp again. Another charge was ordered and the troops dashed back into the camp, engaging in a hand-to-hand fight. This deadly encounter lasted but a few minutes, when the Indians again retired to their shelter, all the while firing into the brave little band of soldiers.

General Gibbon now ordered a charge in opposite directions for the purpose of driving out the Indians who were in the woods, but as the soldiers advanced the Indians retreated still farther into the dense underbrush. When it became evident to General Gibbon that it would be unwise to hold his position in the valley, he ordered the men to retire up the hill and again take shelter in the timber. This movement was successfully accomplished, the troops carrying off with them such of their wounded as could be found, the Nez Perces following closely and keeping up a constant fire. Fighting continued all day, the Indians several times attempt_ing to burn out the troops by setting fire to the grass and woods, and during the night

"A HEAVY FIRE WAS AT ONCE OPENED."

shots were occasionally discharged into the position of the troops and in the evening of the 10th the Indians gave them a parting volley and disappeared.

The losses on both sides were very heavy, those of the troops being sixty-nine killed and wounded out of a strength of 191.   The number of wounded among the Indians could not be ascertained, but their killed number eighty-nine.

Among this band of soldiers, every one of whom fought heroically, were five whose actions were of such a conspicuous nature that they were awarded the Medal of Honor.

These men were: First Sergeant; Wm. D. Edwards, Sergeant Patrick Rogan, Private Lorenzo D. Brown, Musician John McLennan, all of Co. A, 7th Infantry and Private Wilfred Clark, Troop L, Second Cavalry,

CHIEF JOSEPH'S CAMP SURPRISED

AFTER the battle of the Big Hole, the famous pursuit of Chief Joseph and the Nez Perces was begun.   They proceeded south, murdering settlers and stealing stock as they went.   They crossed the Rocky Mountains into Idaho and back again, moving rapidly to the Geyser Basin, and through that to the Yellowstone, which they crossed, and thence on to the junction of Clark's Fork and the Yellowstone, hotly pursued by General Howard's wearied troops and a detachment of Colonel Gibbon's command.

On the morning of August 20th the Nez Perces succeeded in capturing about 100 mules from General Howard's troops.   Major Sanford, with two troops of the First Cavalry, one of them in command of Captain James Jackson, hotly pursued the Indians, overtaking them at Camas Meadows, Idaho, when after a sharp fight the troops recaptured about fifty of the animals.   In this action several troopers had been wounded, among them a trumpeter.   Captain Jackson saw him fall from his horse, and immediately he dismounted and went to his side.   In the face of a desperate fire from the yelling Indians he called upon one or two men, who quickly responded, and together they carried to a place of safety, out of the reach of the savages, the body of the trumpeter who had been shot and killed.   For his heroic action while thus exposed to the Indians' severe fire, Captain Jackson was warmly commended, and he was rewarded by the Medal of Honor.

Hither and thither the escaping hostile Nez Perces proceeded through Northern Idaho and Montana, in the vicinity of the Yellowstone, leading the troops in a hot chase, in which the latter lost their trail.   This, however, was again picked up early in September by the Seventh Cavalry, under Colonel Sturgis, and by forced marches of fifty and sixty miles a day the Indians were pursued until the 14th, their rear frequently attacking the troops.   For days at a time the latter were wholly without rations, and the limit of endurance having been reached by both men and animals Colonel Sturgis gave up the chase and awaited the arrival of General Howard's forces.

On the evening of September 17th Colonel Miles was informed that the Nez Perces were beyond the reach of their pursuers and was requested to join in the chase, especially since the colonel, who with his forces was stationed at the junction of the Yellowstone and Tongue Rivers, was believed to be in a position to intercept the Indians by a much more direct and consequently shorter route.

HENRY ROMEYN,
First Lieutenant, 5th U. S. Infantry.
Born June 1, 1833, at Galen, N. Y.
Highest rank attained: Brevet
Major, U. S. A.

The request was acted on immediately. That same night the troops were taken across the Yellowstone and early the following morning Colonel Miles started in pursuit of the warriors. His command consisted of a detachment of guides and scouts and thirty friendly Cheyenne Indians under the command of Lieutenant P. M. Maus, First United States Infantry, Troops F, G and H, Second United States Cavalry, Troops A, D and K, Seventh United States Cavalry, Companies B, F, G, I and K, Fifth United States Infantry, one Hotchkiss breech-loading and one twelve-pounder Napoleon gun.

The command took a northwesterly direction toward the Missouri River, which was reached early on the morning of September 24th.

Colonel Miles pressed a passing Missouri steamer into service and ferried his force, except one small detachment, across the stream. This was fairly accomplished when he was informed that the Nez Perces were on the other side of the river and the boat, which had already steamed away, had to be recalled at once to take the force back. According to the information, the Indians were in the vicinity of the Bear Paw Mountains, a range of mountains connected by a low divide with the Little Rocky Mountains.

On September 30th, after a forced march through a difficult country, the trail of the long-looked-for savages was discovered at last and followed with much caution and great secrecy, the whole command marching stealthily along the base of hills and mountains.

Colonel Miles had given strict orders that not a shot be fired, and that the numerous buffalo, deer and elk be left unmolested and undisturbed—an order which led many a hunter among the soldiery into dire temptation.

The colonel himself recounts a unique incident.

Lieutenant Maus, who commanded the scouts, came across a grizzly or silver-tip bear. The animal raised upon its hind legs and was ready for a "scrap." Lieutenant Maus's sporting blood was aroused in a second, and he ached for the possession of such costly trophy. He brought his rifle to the shoulder, aimed—and one second more and a shot would have, in all probability, put a quietus on Mr. Bear's pugilistic ambitions. But there was the order not to fire a shot! Slowly the rifle sank from its raised position; the captain remembered the order, and his sense of duty conquered over his desires as a hunter.

The Nez Perces were located within the curve of a crescent-shaped cut bank in the valley of Snake Creek and also in the ravines leading into that valley.

The Indians seemed perfectly unconscious of the approaching danger. Their scouts failed to detect the troops, the buffalo grazed quietly, the elk, the deer moved about without show of fear or fright. What, then, was there to alarm the camping braves?

The last eight miles along the trail were covered in almost spectacular style, the whole command riding and marching to the impending fray as on pleasure bent. The soldiers laughed, joked, hummed the popular tunes of the day—in fact the finest of military spirit prevailed.

Captain Tyler was ordered to take the Second United States Cavalry on a slight detour, attack in the rear and capture the herd, so as to render an escape of the Indians impossible.

This order was executed with great zest and dash and proved a complete success, Captain Tyler capturing about 800 ponies.

The Seventh United States Cavalry and Fifth United States Infantry then charged directly upon the village. The surprise of the Indians, however profound, was not complete, nevertheless. The tramp of the horses had given them warning. and when the troops came upon the village they were met with a hot and deadly accurate fire. This was a somewhat unexpected reception, and for a minute checked the advance. But for a minute only. Again the troops charged ahead, and soon had a portion of the Indians driven from the camp into the ravines. The combat raged fiercely, the Indians putting up and maintaining a stout resistance. Colonel Miles, however, arranged his force in such a manner as to completely encircle the camp, first in a wide and large circle, but gradually tightening his grip and slowly driving the Indian force into the ravines.

OSCAR F. LONG,
Second Lieutenant, 5th U. S. Infantry.
Highest rank attained: Major and Quarter-master, U. S. V.

This was not easily accomplished, and resulted in a great loss of life to the troopers. The Nez Perce proved to be a perfect marksman. Moreover, he knew how to select his victims and used his rifle with telling discrimination. He seemed to pick out the officers.

A few minutes stopped the advance of the Seventh. In the meantime White Bird and several other warriors rushed out from their camp, mounted their horses and made for the hills. The Second Cavalry had become widely scattered over the valley. Captain Tyler had captured more than 300 Indian ponies; Lieutenant Jerome had also secured a large number. Lieutenant E. J. McClernand, with but a few men, had moved far down the valley, where he had captured several hundred

"HE WAS CARRIED OFF THE FIELD BY FOUR OF HIS MEN."

ponies. While he was driving them back he encountered the Indians who made their escape from the camp and they made a vicious effort to regain possession of the horses. In the sharp fight that followed Lieutenant McClernand successfully beat off the enemy and got his men and horses back to an opening in the hills in safety.

By this time the troops had completely encircled the Indian camp, but it had been done at awful cost. Captain Hale and Lieutenant Biddle of the Seventh Cavalry were lifeless upon the ground; Captain E. S. Godfrey and Captain Myles Moylan, who had led their troops at full gallop against the Indians, were severely wounded; Assistant Adjutant-General George W. Baird was shot through the arm and had one ear carried away while bringing orders to different parts of the battle-field.

Four of the five officers of the Seventh Cavalry battalion had been killed or wounded in the first charge, and Lieutenant Henry Romeyn, of Company G, Fifth Infantry, mounted on a captured Indian horse, was put in command also of troops A and H. With his own company and the cavalry Romeyn charged down the steep bank to cut the enemy off from water. He had scarcely got the men moving when he was struck by a bullet in the right breast, breaking a rib where it entered, and another where it passed out near the spine. Another bullet pierced his belt, the handle of his hunting knife was shot away, his field-glass case was shattered and a ball had gone through his ear after grazing his shoulder. He was carried off the field by four of his men, who risked their lives in the act, but his wounds were considered mortal and he was left to die, something being given him to ease his pain. Lieutenant Mason Carter, of the Fifth Infantry, had continued the charge after Romeyn's injury, and succeeded in dislodging the Indians, inflicting heavy loss upon them.

Lieutenant Oscar F. Long had been directed by Colonel Miles to order one of the cavalry troops to advance. Finding both of its officers wounded, Lieutenant Long voluntarily assumed command and took the troop forward under a heavy fire. While the men were falling rapidly, Major and Surgeon Henry R. Tilton seemed everywhere among them giving them his best aid, notwithstanding the rain of bullets about him. He rescued by admirable courage quite a number of fallen soldiers who would have received finishing bullets by the Indians had they not been taken care of by him. Two officers and twenty-two soldiers had been killed; half a dozen officers and thirty-eight soldiers had been wounded. Colonel Miles had now to fear that the Indians who had escaped would bring the hostile Sioux to the assistance of the Nez Perces. The wounded were too many to be properly cared for, and he dared not risk another assault upon the Indian camp, knowing that a siege would be the safer though slower method of bringing the enemy to time. To make matters worse snow began to fall, and the suffering of the soldiers was intense. The next day, however, a flag of truce was sent out from the Indian camp and a parley followed, which resulted three days later in the complete surrender of the Indians.

Strange to say, Lieutenant Romeyn survived his wounds, although he had been prepared for burial. The next morning it was found that life was not extinct, and shortly after he regained consciousness. Seven days later he was placed in an army wagon filled with brush and grass, and after seven days of this sort of travel arrived at the Missouri River, where with the rest of the wounded he was put on board a steamer and taken down the river.

For gallantry in this engagement Medals of Honor were given to Captains Edward S. Godfrey and Myles Moylan; Lieutenants Henry Romeyn, Mason Carter, George W. Baird, Oscar F. Long, Edward J. McClernand and Major Henry R. Tilton.

THE BATTLE OF MILK RIVER

EDWARD P. GRIMES,
Sergeant, Troop F, 5th U. S. Cavalry.

DURING the latter part of August and the early part of September, 1879, frequent reports came in to General Pope, commanding the Department of Missouri, that the White River Utes had started several extensive fires in the mountains west of Hot Sulphur Springs, Colorado, that they had fired on an agency employe, attacked his house, driving him out and injuring him, and that the lives of the people at the agency were in great danger.

Satisfying himself that the reports were true, General Pope informed the War Department of the state of affairs, and orders were at once received for the nearest military commander to send a force to the White River Agency to protect the agent and arrest the ringleaders in the outrages reported.

Accordingly General Crook, commanding the Department of the Platte, sent Troops D and F, Fifth Cavalry; E, Third Cavalry, and Company E, Fourth Infantry, under command of Major Thornburgh, to the scene of the trouble.

This force, numbering about 200 officers and men, left Fort Steele, in Southern Wyoming, on the 21st of September, and by rapid marches through rugged mountain passes and over barren plains, reached Fortification Creek, in Upper Colorado, where the infantry company was left to establish a supply camp, while the cavalry pushed on to Bear Creek. On the afternoon of the 26th, while the command was at Bear Creek, several prominent Ute Indians came into the camp and talked with Major Thornburgh about the troops coming to the agency, and being assured of the mission of the troops the Indians left in apparent good humor. This conference, however, did not satisfy the Indians at the agency, and the next day several other prominent Indians carried a letter to Major Thornburgh from the Indian agent, to the effect that the Indians at the agency were greatly excited and begging that the troops advance no farther, but that the major and five soldiers should come to the agency for consultation.

Major Thornburgh replied that he would meet the agent and five chiefs on the road some distance from the agency, after he had marched his command to a suitable camping place.

Two days later, on the 29th, a courier brought a letter from the agent saying he would leave the agency with several chiefs on the morning of the 30th, to meet Major Thornburgh.

It looked now as if the difficulties could be amicably settled and Major Thornburgh, who had by this time reached Milk River, left Troop D to continue the march along the road with the wagons, while he with the rest of the troops turned off from the road and took up a trail leading to his left.

The troops with Major Thornburgh had gone scarcely a mile when, in crossing a high bridge, they came suddenly upon the Indians in large force.

This was less of a surprise to the troops than their hostile attitude, in view of the proposed meeting between the major and the Indian agent on the morrow. Major Thornburgh immediately dismounted and deployed his men, at the same time endeavoring to open communication with the Indians. His efforts were in vain and drew forth a volley from the redskins, whereupon a hot engagement began, in which the Indians had the advantage in both position and numbers. Slowly did they drive the troopers back toward the wagon train, which had "parked" near the Milk River, the soldiers leading their horses and firing back into the Indians with deadly aim. Again and again the Indians attempted to break the skirmish line, but each time they were driven to cover, and only when they realized that the troops were not in precipitate rout did they attempt to get between them and the wagon train. They succeeded in gaining a strong position on a knoll commanding Thornburgh's line of retreat, but a desperate charge by about twenty men under Captain Payne routed the Indians and opened the way to the wagon train.

Sergeant Edward P. Grimes, of Troop F, Fifth Cavalry, had covered the left flank of the troops with a party consisting of two non-commissioned officers, one trumpeter and seven men. Grimes's company commander ordered his troop to mount and charge. While the men ran to their horses Major Thornburgh came riding along, countermanding the order and directing Grimes to keep his position of defense on the bluffs. Grimes could only get the trumpeter and two men, as the others had already mounted and followed the rest of the troop. These few men defended their position with the greatest bravery until ordered by their company commander to mount and withdraw to the wagon train.

About the same time Lieutenant Cherry, Fifth Cavalry, called for volunteers to cover the retreat of the command to the wagon train. Grimes was again the first one to follow the summons of the lieutenant. With him Corporal Edward F. Murphy and Blacksmith Wilhelm O. Philipsen, of Troop D, Fifth Cavalry, jumped off their horses, and other men of both the Third and Fifth Cavalry followed their gallant example. The heroic band fought with unflinching devotion; their ammunition was running short, the Indians had them nearly surrounded, and some of these brave volunteers were already wounded—Lieutenant Cherry immediately saw that their position was becoming desperate, and that their chances of escaping were growing less, with all the wounded to care for and protect. The officer called for a volunteer to make his way to the wagon-train for ammunition and support. Grimes realized that the effort was well-nigh hopeless, but fearlessly informed the lieutenant that he would attempt it. He mounted his horse, for what he fully believed to be the last time, and started on his mission. The Indians seemed to divine his purpose, and at once started in pursuit. His horse being stronger and speedier than the ponies of his pursuers, carried him safely to the wagon-train, where the desired ammunition and support were obtained.

The daring ride was made in full view of all the Indians and soldiers, and the encouraging shouts of the latter cheered the intrepid rider on his daring and dangerous mission.

In the meantime Major Thornburgh, trying to supervise the arrangements for

HENRY JOHNSON,
Sergeant, Troop D, 9th U. S. Cavalry.
Born June 11, 1850, in Virginia.

protecting the wagon train, had himself started for it, but was shot and instantly killed when within 500 yards of it. The wagons were formed into an elliptical corral, about 200 yards from the river, the side towards the stream being exposed to a furious fire from the Indians, who were now making determined efforts to capture or destroy the train. The horses were rapidly falling under the unerring fire of the hostiles. The wounded were quickly laid in sheltered places within the corral, while the wounded horses were led to the exposed side of the huddled group of men, wagons and horses and shot there, to form a defense for some of the men who were acting as sharpshooters.

The contents of the wagons were then quickly piled on top of the horses and behind this meager shelter the troopers kept up their fire; but against one more deadly from the screeching, half-frantic redskins. Not content with the advantage they had over the small corral, the wily Indians set fire to the tall grass and sage-brush down the valley. The flames, fanned by the high wind, spread rapidly towards the troops, igniting bundles, grain-sacks, wagon-covers and other combustible material, adding the horrors of fire to the rain of lead and arrows. The entire train was threatened with destruction. The troopers, besides being compelled to with-

"HIS HORSE CARRIED HIM SAFELY TO THE WAGON TRAIN."

stand a fusillade of bullets from the hostiles, were obliged to cease firing and exert their energies to extinguish the flames and care for their wounded, whose cries and moanings added to the weirdness of the scene. The sun was rapidly sinking behind the mountains and as twilight set in the Indians redoubled their efforts to dislodge the men, but the troopers took courage in the thought of approaching darkness and fought with renewed vigor, picking off a redskin every time he silhouetted his head and shoulders against the deepening gloam. Thus the fight was kept up from 3 o'clock in the afternoon until darkness put an end to the desperate struggle. In a final effort a large party of the reds had charged down upon the corral, firing volley after volley into the huddled-up mass of men, horses, wagons and debris.

With the cessation of hostilities a new difficulty presented itself. Water and ammunition were needed. The command was surrounded by the enemy on three sides, making it almost suicidal to attempt to leave the entrenchment. The command was not to be left in this predicament, however, without an attempt, at least, to obtain water and ammunition, and Sergeant E. P. Grimes and Corporal H. M. Roach volunteered to make the effort. They stealthily crept out of the intrenchments toward the river, and at almost point blank range secured water, going back and forth until a sufficient supply had been obtained. Grimes then crept to a supply wagon some distance away from the corral and secured enough ammunition to last another day. Roach bravely repeated his mission on the two succeeding nights, and luckily escaped the vigilance of the wary hostile guards.

During the first night of their camp, while Grimes and Roach were obtaining water and ammunition, those of the troopers who were not wounded dug better intrenchments, cared for the wounded, dragged away the dead animals and ate lightly of their rations, and at midnight couriers, among them Sergeant John S. Lawton and First Sergeant Jacob Widmer, of Company D, slipped away toward the railroad with dispatches reporting what had occurred and asking for aid.

On the following day, September 30th, the Indians kept up an incessant fire, killing all of the remaining animals excepting fourteen mules. The troopers, being comparatively well protected now by their intrenchments, held their fire except when a good opportunity presented itself to pick off an unwary Indian. At nightfall the Indians again gave the weary troopers a rest, but after that they worried them unceasingly with all the tricks known to them, all the time firing with a seemingly inexhaustible supply of ammunition.

The couriers who had slipped away traveled through a region infested with hostiles until they met Captain Dodge and Lieutenant Hughes with Troop D, Ninth Cavalry, late in the afternoon of the 1st of October, who were scouting in that section of the country. Captain Dodge immediately went into camp for the purpose of deceiving any Indians who might be in the vicinity, issued 225 rounds of ammunition and three days' rations. Then, under cover of darkness, he broke camp and pushed to the relief of the men at Milk River, with his two officers, thirty-five men and four citizens.

The beleaguered troopers in the trench, waking from their restless slumbers on the morning of the 2d, were greeted with the sight of advancing cavalrymen, who with some difficulty made their way between the Indians and joined the almost encircled men. It was Captain Dodge's command; and immédiately after they entered the trenches the Indians opened fire. With these re-enforcements the troops kept up a vigorous attack, and the battle waged for the next three days. The troopers never lagged or flinched under the terrific fire of the Indians, who were now infuriated by the renewed vigor with which the troops fought. Many a brave fellow seemingly exposed himself needlessly in his ardor to get a better shot at the red man, many helped the wounded to places of safety, but among those whose daring, almost sheer recklessness, was most conspicuous in the narrow confines of the corral were Sergeant John Merrill, who, though severely wounded, remained on duty and rendered gallant and valuable service; Corporal George Moquin, Corporal Edward Murphy, and Sergeant John A. Poppe. Sergeant Henry Johnson, on the night of the 2d, voluntarily left a sheltered position and under heavy fire at close range made the rounds of the pits to instruct the guards; and also, on the next night fought his way to the river and back to bring water to the wounded.

The couriers who went out on the night of the 29th, after meeting and informing Captain Dodge of the trouble at Milk River, pushed on and succeeded after many hairbreadth escapes in reaching headquarters with their requests for aid. Colonel Wesley Merritt with Troops A, B, D and M, Fifth Cavalry, was immediately dispatched from Fort D. A. Russell to the relief and in a short time was on a special train for Rawlins, a few miles west of Fort Steele, Major Thornburgh's starting point when he went to the relief of the White River Agency. From Rawlins the remainder of the distance had to be made over the mountains, and by a march of almost unparalled rapidity, in something over forty-eight hours Colonel Merritt's column, consisting of 350 men, one half of whom were infantry following in wagons, marched 170 miles over an almost impassable road and reached the command at Milk River at 6 o'clock on the morning of the 5th of October.

Upon the arrival of Colonel Merritt's column at Milk River the crippled and exhausted command gave as hearty a cheer as they could muster in their pitiful condition, after which they were tenderly cared for, given rations and then sent back to the railroad at Rawlins. The Indians retired from their concealed places when the relief column came within sight, but were followed by Colonel Merritt's command, which had been re-enforced by other troops. Merritt pushed on to the White River Agency, the Indians having all disappeared before him, and upon his arrival there he found that they had burned and utterly destroyed the agency, had killed the employes and agent, and had carried off all the females. The bodies were buried and preparations made for the continuance of the pursuit when orders were received to suspend operations at the request of the Indian Department, which was negotiating with the Utes for the release of the captive females and the surrender of the ringleaders in these outrages.

During the cessation of hostilities various reconnoitering parties were sent out from Colonel Merritt's command, and one of these on the 20th, consisting of five men under Lieutenant Wm. P. Hall, Fifth Cavalry, was attacked by thirty-five Indians about twenty miles from the White River. They defended themselves behind some sheltering rocks, Lieutenant Hall several times exposing himself to draw the fire of the enemy, thereby giving his small party an opportunity to respond with telling effect. They kept up the unequal fight until night, when they succeeded in returning to camp with the loss of Lieutenant W. B. Weir, of the ordnance department, and Chief Scout Humme, both of whom were killed.

The loss sustained by the command at the Milk River fight from September 29th to October 5th, when it was relieved by Colonel Merritt, was Major Thornburgh, Fourth Infantry, and nine enlisted men, Wagonmaster McKinstry, Guide Lowry and one teamster, killed; Captain Payne and Second Lieutenant Paddock, Fifth Cavalry, Sergeant Grimes, forty enlisted men and two teamsters wounded.

The Indians who numbered 350 and were well supplied with ammunition, admitted a loss of thirty-seven killed. The number of wounded, which must have been large, was never known.

All the non-commissioned officers and enlisted men, herein mentioned for conspicuous acts of courage and gallantry were awarded the Medal of Honor.

HUNTING INDIANS IN THE SNOW-DRIFTS OF MONTANA

T. B. GLOVER,
Sergeant, Troop B, 2d U. S. Cav.
Born January 2, 1852, at New York City.

SMOKE from the tepees of the "friendlies" curled lazily up, then floated into straight lines, as the sun went down on a day shut in and blasted with the death of a Montana winter, but far out and beyond the sheltering hills of Fort Keogh there was murder in the chill air. That afternoon, February 3, 1880, word had come to the headquarters of the Second United States Cavalry that the treacherous Sioux were again riding with death; that a man had been murdered on Mizpah Creek, and his multilated body with that of another, fatally wounded, had been found. "Spotted-Tail's work," commented the scouts, from experience.

The bearer of the ghastly news and his horse were exhausted from fatigue and exposure to the biting cold in their race across the white wastes. There were fifteen of the murdering reds, the rider stated.

The sun had gone down bleak and cheerless, and over the endless waste of snow the midwinter night fell quickly, on the porch of the mess the thermometer read fifty-six degrees below zero. The prospect was not inviting, but every man knew that before sunrise troops would be in pursuit; that this roving band of renegade Sioux must be caught and punished, and the women and children in their white-roofed homes protected from the deadliest peril.

"Leave before daylight, with a detachment," was the order given to Sergeant Thaddeus B. Glover, of Troop B. "Ride to the scene of the depradations, pursue and capture the band of wandering Sioux."

Fifteen in number, the little party floundered through the deep drifts at the post gate, then out along those desolate wastes and on through the gray dawn, where finally the rising sun threw a cold, cheerless light on the crackling, snapping snow, beneath the horses' feet. The cold cut into the very bodies of man and beast, and the vapor from their breath froze upon mustache and nostril, as they rode on under the command of Sergeant Glover. All that day over the bleak, drift-covered prairie, the men and horses pushed their way, struggling against the gnawing pain produced by a temperature unknown until experienced. Dragging and hauling, now up, now down, they pushed on in the face of the rising storm. At 7 o'clock that night, hours after darkness had again come upon them, they came suddenly upon the tracks of the Indians. It was pitch dark, and the cold was intense; the country was strange and nothing could be done except wait for daylight; so there among the snow-drifts the little detachment spent the long winter night, stamping a path about the horses to keep the blood in circulation, and to fight off the deadly stupor which the cold brought, benumbing to the senses.

In the gray dawn they remounted their horses, just as a scout came creeping up to report the dead body of an Indian, covered with withered frozen leaves, at the foot of a near-by tree. From this tree led a trail, barely perceptible, but sufficient. It was quickly taken by the Indian scouts, and on again went the little band, through the drift and the maddening cold. After three hours of heart-breaking march, the men stiffened and rigid in their saddles, another halt was made.

The Indian scouts, treacherous and bold in this extremity, came back to the column and grunted that they could go no farther. Their horses, they said, were exhausted and useless from the work of breaking through the snow-drifts. They would do no more.

Sergeant Glover gave a hurried order. The troopers fell from their saddles and disarmed the Indians, taking them captive to the rear. This action of the scouts was evidence that they were hard upon the trail of the band of Spotted-Tail. Then forward again, another hour, with no word spoken, and each man suffering in silence. Sergeant Glover stopped upon the summit of a snow-covered hillock. Dismounting, he went on a little farther until the troop was brought to a sudden halt, huddled together in a valley, wind-swept and filled with whirling, stinging snow. The smell of smoke had come down on the wind to the quick sense of the sergeant. He crept on alone through the snow-banks and, peering over the icy ledge, he saw below him, on the plain, the band of murdering Sioux—the warriors of Spotted-Tail.

Orders were at once given to corral the pack train, which done, the men, benumbed and stiff, slid from their saddles. One-half of the detachment, under Corporal Edwards, was sent by a circuitous route to a deep ravine far on the left. The rest, under the sergeant, moved to the right, where in whispers they received their instructions. They were to separate, converge upon the Indians, and at a given signal fire simultaneously upon the band, still unconscious of their presence.

"We had been creeping and floundering through the drifts for some time," said Sergeant Glover, "keeping as quiet as possible and taking every precaution to screen ourselves from the watchful eyes of the Indians in the hollow below. Suddenly a shot rang out, sharp and clear in the desert stillness. A private of the troop, in the other wing, had pushed too far forward in his eagerness to get a shot, and exposed his body to view over the snow-covered ridge for an instant. A puff of smoke from the camp below, followed by the crack of a rifle, and Private Douglass pitched forward over the ridge, shot through the head. Further concealment was useless and both divisions of the little command opened fire simultaneously. I stationed my men on all the elevated points about the rude fortifications the Indians had hurriedly thrown up. We kept up a heavy fire until dark, when I saw that such methods would prove futile. The Indians were too securely intrenched; they must be either shelled or starved out. Under cover of darkness I sent a courier back to

"I STATIONED MY MEN ON ALL THE ELEVATED POINTS."

Colonel Miles, asking for a Gatling gun, then disposed my men around the hostile camp, forming a chain guard. In that way there could be no reliefs, and during the long hours of that bitter night we suffered intensely.

"When daylight again straggled slowly over the bleak hills, I examined more carefully the position taken by the hostiles. They were actually inside of a great hollow rock, the most remarkable natural fortification I had ever seen. With provisions, water and good weather, six men could have held a regiment off for a month. Shortly after I withdrew a part of my force, ordering the rest to keep up a vigorous fire.

"At that moment, however, a scout rode out to me and reported that the Indians wished to surrender. I knew that some change of conditions, which had so far escaped us, must have forced the hostiles to this decision. Glancing over the dazzling horizon I saw, far to the west, mere specks on the waste of snow, a body of horsemen approaching. I determined to postpone the surrender of the Indians until the identity of the riders should reveal itself. On they came, their horses throwing up clouds of snow as they galloped toward us.

"Could they be hostiles? No; the sharp eyes of the Indians had seen them first, and they were willing to give up a practically impregnable position. Finally, we saw them rise in their stirrups, and a cheer—a very faint one, but no less a good trooper cheer—came down on the wind. We leaped to our feet and cheered back. It was Captain Snyder, now Colonel Snyder, with re-enforcements. After acquainting himself with the situation Captain Snyder ordered me to accept the surrender of the hostiles, and with them we returned that night to the post."

In that engagement in the snow-drifts, sixty miles from Fort Keogh, with the thermometer showing fifty-six degrees below zero, Private Douglass, of Company E, Second Cavalry, lost his life, and Private Guernsey, Company B, was severely wounded. The Indian scouts rode on to the post, and from their saddle-bows dangled the scalps of two Sioux.

For this "gallantry and vigor" General Miles excused Sergeant Glover and his men from all post duty for a period of one month, and Glover was furthermore rewarded with the Medal of Honor.

This was not the only bold capture of murderous redskins in which Sergeant Glover figured prominently. In the Mizpah Creek expedition of April, 1879, a party of Indians, members of the same band that massacred Custer in that awful slaughter of the Little Big Horn, had terrorized the Creek. Sergeant Glover was ordered to pursue and capture them. They had murdered a telegraph operator at the Powder River Station.

For three days he followed, stalking them night and day. With all the wiles of their cunning they attempted to throw him from their trail, but the avenger was an old and resourceful Indian fighter.

On the morning of the third day Sergeant Glover and his men came up with the Indians. The command was at once deployed for advance.

"We were then in the Little Big Horn Mountains," said Sergeant Glover. "I advanced but a short distance, when I saw two Indians standing on a rock silhouetted against the background of sky, signaling with the white flag. I advanced and accepted their surrender. Turning, I heard the sound of furious firing in the rear. The two Indians had been joined by others and treacherously opened an attack as my men were leaning quietly on their arms. Not an Indian got away. We captured them all, and under a strong guard I took them back to the post. They were tried and convicted of murder, but cheated the executioner, for, Indian-like, they all hanged themselves in the jail at Miles City."

Thus ended the last chapter in the history of Little Wolf's band of Cheyennes.

THE SURRENDER OF RAIN-IN-THE-FACE

ELI L. HUGGINS,
Captain, 2d U. S. Cavalry.
Highest rank attained: Major U. S. A.
Born Aug. 1, 1842, Schuyler County, Ill.

A NUMBER of Indian Chiefs, among others Broad Tail, Kicking Bear, Spotted Eagle and the noted Rain-in-the-Face, surrendered to the military authorities in 1880. The subjugation of these notables and their tribesmen was accomplished by a series of successful military operations in conjunction with the telegraph and telephone. The soldier and his rifle caused fear and respect; the appliance of modern invention awakened awe and reverence, mingled with terror, in the Indian.

The use of the telephone and telegraph to bewilder the simple-minded savages was a clever piece of strategy on the part of the military authorities at Fort Keogh, Montana, and the manner in which it was accomplished forms the text of a rather amusing story.

A number of Indians had been rounded up and captured, and messengers were sent to their tribes to notify them of the capture and demand the surrender of the remainder of their people.

In reply to this summons a delegation of eighty big, burly warriors came from Sitting Bull's camp to Fort Keogh under a flag of truce to learn the conditions of the proposed surrender. At that time the military post and adjoining village were quite up-to-date in the way of modern conveniences. There was a telegraph station at the fort and a telephone plant in the village.

When the Indian delegation arrived it was treated with exquisite civility and politeness, but back of this show of deference was the determination of the military authorities to show these Indians something they had never seen before.

The Indian is always boastful when referring to his own deeds of valor. On this occasion the soldiers were equally as ostentatious with the display of their power and resources, and very soon had their unsophisticated visitors at their mercy.

Colonel Miles took the braves into the room where the telegraph clicker was in operation.

"With this here," he said, pointing to the instrument, "we can talk to the Great White Father in Washington."

The Indians examined the mysterious contrivance, listened to its incomprehensible click, click, but the significance of it all was beyond their understanding.

"How can you make this thing talk to the Great Father?" one of the old warriors asked.

"By means of electricity," was the reply.

"And what is electricity?" they questioned

Colonel Miles, in narrating this incident, confessed his discomfiture. He could not find a definition which suited the mental horizon of his guests, but with the ready wit for which he is noted he replied: "The Great Spirit has loaned the white man His lightning," and to still more clearly demonstrate his unique definition he darkened the room and set the instruments at work. The blue little electric sparks set the Indian to serious thinking.

The demonstration with the telephone had still more startling results.

The Indians were divided into two groups, and separated from each other for quite a distance. One Indian was placed at each end of the line.

The oldest of the delegation was told to place the receiver against his ear. Presently he heard his own native Dakota tongue. He recognized the voice. He knew who was speaking to him. He knew he was far away. He looked into the instrument and could not see him. His hand trembled; he shook from head to foot and dropped the receiver.

"The Whispering Spirit has spoken to me," he said with an expression of awe, and ever since that is the name by which the telephone has been known among these Indians.

Colonel Miles dismissed the delegation in the kindest possible manner. What was said and told about the white man's strange powers in the Indian villages nobody knows, but the results proved that the plan was a complete success. The Indians had no desire to oppose a foe who had borrowed the lightning from the heavens and was in league with the "Whispering Spirit," and they surrendered to the number of fully 2,000.

As has been previously stated, the military operations which preceded and led up to the incident at the fort were equally successful. They were undertaken primarily to stop the Sioux from stealing horses. As a horse thief the Indian has no superior. To him stealing a horse is a sport he has developed to the degree of a fine art. To make it more exciting the horse must belong to another tribe; to steal it from a fellow-tribesman would be a crime punishable with death. Without going into details of the Indian's manner of stealing, it may safely be asserted that upon the planning and execution of a horse-stealing raid as much care, cunning and

"THEY THREW THEMSELVES FLAT ON THE GROUND AND OPENED FIRE."

intelligence are bestowed as upon any enterprise in which the warrior interests himself. In summer the young brave who is about to pay a visit to a hostile camp garbs himself green, paints himself green, and rides a roan pony, so as to make himself less conspicuous on the grass-covered prairie. In the winter, when snow covers the ground, his face is white, his dress is white, and his mount is white. He sneaks and moves stealthily and cautiously, watches and observes, and finally at the opportune time, mostly at midnight, when sleep prevails in the hostile camp, dashes into the village, gathers the ponies and makes his escape. Then begins a mad race for home and safety, and triumph and joy reign when he reaches the tents of his tribe and boastingly exhibits his stolen animals as evidence of his prowess.

Sitting Bull and his band, after the massacre of General Custer, had taken refuge on Canadian territory just north of the boundary line.

For a time he and his followers kept quiet, though they steadfastly refused to accept the terms of the Unitad States Government and return to their reservation. By-and-by his camp was increased by new accessions from Sioux tribes, until he had gathered about himself a force of several thousand warriors. Then trouble began. The Sioux could not resist engaging in the racial sport—horse-stealing— and small bands crossed the border continually to raid. Horses were stolen from the Crows, friendly, unoffending Indians, later from farmers and settlers, and finally even from the military posts.

In 1880 these expeditions occurred with such frequency and annoyance that Colonel Miles resolved to put an end to them.

The immediate cause was the theft of a herd of fifty ponies from the Crow scouts at Fort Custer, on March 24th.

The next day at sunrise Captain E. L. Huggins, Sixth Cavalry, with 32 men, six Cheyenne scouts and twenty pack mules left Fort Keogh in pursuit of the marauding Sioux. The first day the command rode seventy-five miles through rain and mud toward the Rosebud River without finding any trace of the Indians. The troops marched up the river and finally struck the trail, which was several days old and frequently obliterated by rain and snow storms. But Captain Huggins stuck to his task with wonderful tenacity. As soon as the trail was lost he called his scouts and would not yield until it was again located. This kind of marching was wearysome in the extreme , tiring and exhausting for men and beasts, especially since the rations were not plentiful, and the food, toward the last, consisted only of coffee and hard bread.

The trail led the command by a circuitous route through the Bad Lands and across the Tongue and Pawnee Rivers.

Finally on April 1st the scouts reported the presence of a Sioux camp at the head of O'Fallon's Creek. The stolen pony-herd was grazing a few hundred yards away.

Captain Huggins decided upon immediate action, Lieutenant L. M. Brett with ten men was directed to make a dash for the ponies and capture the whole herd.

Another officer was given a sufficient number of men to make a detour and cut off the retreat of the Indians. The captain himself moved to attack the camp.

Lieutenant Brett executed his part of the program with singular success. The ponies were in his possession before the Sioux braves had time to think. When the whole band of warriors made a dash for their horses it was too late, and they were forced to run back. Five of them became separated and were taken prisoners, one was killed. The others took refuge in a slight fringe of cottonwood trees, threw themselves flat on the ground and opened a heavy fire on the troops, now advancing for an attack. A sergeant was shot through the head and one of the horses disabled. For a short time the charge was checked. The Sioux took advantage of the situation by retiring to a position in a washout, which was admirably suited for defensive purposes. They were now completely surrounded, although it was not considered feasible to attack them in their stronghold. Night was coming on. The troops were exhausted, chilled, and in much need of rest. But long before midnight it was discovered that the wily Indians had made their escape, leaving no trail with their moccasined feet on the frozen ground.

Satisfied with having recaptured the entire herd, Captain Huggins and Lieutenant Brett returned with their prisoners to the fort, having made a complete circuit and averaged about sixty miles a day since the pursuit began.

The capture of the five Indians, however, proved to be of great importance, as it let up to the surrender previously mentioned, of over 2,000, and put an end to the horsestealing along the Canadian border.

Captain Huggins as well as Lieutenant Brett were rewarded with the Medal of Honor.

PURSUIT OF CHIEF VICTORIA

IN September 1879, the notorious Chief Victoria with his murdering and thieving band of Indians held New Mexico in a state of terror by his raids and outrages on the settlers. Coming out of Old Mexico these maurauders practically swept over the whole territory of New Mexico, and so rapidly were their movements that the military had great difficulty in following them up.

The first attack made by the hostiles was upon the herd guard of Troop E, Ninth Cavalry, near Ojo Caliente and the attack was so well conducted by them that no less than eight men were killed in the short struggle. Victoria's band which had been re-enforced by Mescaleres and some Chiricahuas prior to this attack, then made for the hills, and although pursued by the troops they succeeded in carrying off with them .about fifty horses. With this attack began a series of fierce and murderous raids, which struck terror to the hearts of the people throughout the territory for it was evident that the few troops alone could not check these maurauding Indians. Citizens at once organized themselves into quasi-military companies and volunteered to aid in checking and subdoing these savages.

Near Hillsboro a party of these citizens encountered about 100 of Victoria's followers and in the ensuing engagement they displayed great courage but were unable to inflict much damage on the redskins whose spirits were buoyed up by reason of their successful escape from the troops and the fact that they were fighting with armed citizens and not trained soldiers. The Indians therefore brought into play their worst traits of savagry with the result that the whites were driven back with a loss of ten killed, a number wounded and scalped and all their stock captured. This occurred on the 17th of September and on the 18th another fierce battle took place at the head of Las Animas River, this time with the troops. Captain Dawson of the Ninth Cavalry in his pursuit of Victoria was attacked at this place by the Indians who held an impregnable position from which it was impossible to drive them, and were after being re-enforced by two troops under Captain Beyer of the same regiment the hostiles still had the advantage. The concerted efforts of the troops proved unavailing and that night, after fighting the wily redman in his stronghold all day, it was found necessary to withdraw the troops, whose losses were considerable, five soldiers, two Navajo scouts and one citizen having been killed, many wounded and thirty-two horses lost.

Victoria then proceeded north, with the troops in hot pursuit, and on the 29th was overtaken and again attacked by Major Morrow near Ojo Caliente with a force of 200 men. Two days of fierce fighting ensued in which the soldiers succeeded in stampeding the Indian herds and recapturing sixty horses and' mules, among them a number of those captured from Troop E on September 4th. On the second day of the fight the Indians killed and wounded several of Morrow's men and then retreated, successfully covering their trail. From a squaw prisoner who was captured on

October 1st, Morrow learned the position of the Indians, and by a rapid night-march Victoria's strongly fortified camp was captured and destroyed, the Indians, however, escaping in the dark.

During these three days and nights Morrow's command was without water, and as their rations and ammunition were nearly exhausted, the men and animals were utterly worn out.

Morrow's force, now reduced to less than 100 available men, continued in pursuit of the fleeing Indians, following them by very hard marches over the mountains, through swollen streams and canyons, dragging their well-nigh exhausted horses after them in a tough foot-climb up the mountain side, or down through the dark ravines, and on October 27th again overtook Victoria about twelve miles from the Corralitos River, Mexico. Taking about forty men with him, Morrow charged down upon the Indian breastworks in the moonlight, and drove the Indians from them, with a loss of but one scout killed and two wounded.

The soldiers presented a picturesque appearance as they quietly rode toward the breastworks, their felt sombreros with upturned brims, their erect forms and their carbines being sharply outlined in the bright moonlight, and in regular order the men approached the hostiles' camp. When within a short distance of the Indians the order to charge was given and away went horses and men with a dash, completely surprising the startled redskins. For a short time the fight was fast and furious, the Indians gradually backing off until they could make a dash for the dark ravines, where they secreted themselves. Work was then begun on the destruction of the camp and in a short time the sky was lighted up by the burning debris of what was a few minutes before Victoria's stronghold.

Further pursuit of the Indians was abandoned and the troops returned to Fort Bayard, New Mexico, reaching there November 3d.

TULAROSA SAVED BY TWENTY-FIVE CAVALRYMEN

O<small>N</small> the second day of January, 1880, Victoria and his band of Indians were reported raiding and murdering in Southern New Mexico, whereupon all the cavalry in that section of the country were sent out at once to round up this noted chief and his thieving band.

The Mescalero Agency at the Fort Stanton Reservation had largely served as a base of supplies and recruits for the raiding parties of Victoria, and it was determined to disarm and dismount the Indians then on the reservation and thus cut off the supplies of the raiders. Generals Pope and Ord, commanding the Departments of the Missouri and Texas, arranged that a force under Colonel E. Hatch, Ninth Cavalry, numbering 400 cavalry, 60 infantry and 75 Indian scouts, should arrive at the Mescalero Agency simultaneously with Colonel Grierson and a force of the Tenth Cavalry and Twenty-fifth Infantry. These two forces set out early in January and marched toward each other, each having, on the way, several encounters with the Indians. While Grierson was moving north and engaging the hostiles Hatch's force was driving Victoria south toward the Mescalero Agency. In this manner both forces worked ahead over a rough country until they met at the Mescalero Agency, where, on the 16th of April, Colonels Hatch and Grierson made the attempt to disarm and dismount the Indians, but they put up a brave fight and made a desperate effort to escape. This effort, however, proved futile and the hostiles, numbering about 250, were captured, only about forty escaping. The captured Indians were disarmed and dismounted and taken into the agency.

Major Morrow, with a portion of Colonel Hatch's force, then pursued the escaping Indians and overtook them in Dog Canyon, where he killed three warriors and captured twenty-five head of stock.

After disarming and dismounting the Indians at the agency Colonel Hatch began again the pursuit of Victoria, assisted by troops from the Department of Arizona, but the campaign resolved itself into a chase of the hostiles from one range of mountains to another, with frequent skirmishes but no decisive fights, until the Indians again escaped into Old Mexico. One fight took place at Tularosa on the 14th of May which is described by Sergeant George Jordan, Troop K, Ninth Cavalry, as fol lows:

"On the 11th of May I was ordered to Old Fort Tularosa with a detachment of twenty-five men of the Ninth Cavalry for the purpose of protecting the town of Tularosa, just outside the fort. Besides our own rations we had extra rations for the rest of the regiment which was pursuing Victoria's band of Apaches. On the second day out we struck the foothills of the mountains, where our advance guard met two troops of Mexican cavalry. The captain of one of them told me that it would be impossible for me to get through with the small body of men I had, and advised me to return to the regiment. I replied that my orders were to go through and that I

"THE INDIANS SURPRISED US AND FIRED ONE HUNDRED SHOTS."

intended to do so, notwithstanding the fact that large bodies of hostiles were still roaming about outside the Mescalero Agency. After leaving our Mexican friends we pushed along with our wagon-train bringing up the rear, until that evening we struck the Barlow and Sanders stage station, where we went into camp. At the station all was excitement. The people were throwing up breastworks and digging trenches in the expectation of an attack by the Indians. My command, being dismounted cavalry, was pretty well exhausted from our day's march over the mountains and we were all ready for a good night's rest; but within an hour after our arrival at the station, and just before sundown, a rider from Tularosa came in and wanted to see the commander of the soldiers. He told me that the Indians were in the town and that he wanted me to march the men the remainder of the distance to save the women and children from a horrible fate.

"My men were in bad condition for a march, but I explained to them the situation as the rider had put it before me, and that I would leave it to them whether they wanted to continue the march that night or not. They all said that they would go on as far as they could. We then had supper, after which each man bathed his feet so as to refresh himself, and at about 8 o'clock we started to the rescue. But our progress was slow. Besides the poor condition of the men we were hampered by our wagon train in that rough country. Once one of the wagons was upset as the train was coming down a steep hill and we lost valuable time righting it. About 6 o'clock in the morning we came in sight of the town, and I deployed the men and advanced quickly toward it, believing that the Indians were already there. We stealthily approached the town and had gotten to within a half mile of it before the people discovered us. When they recognized us as troops they came out of their houses waving towels and handkerchiefs for joy.

"Upon our arrival in the town we found that only a few straggling Indians had gotten there ahead of us and had killed an old man in a cornfield. The people gave us shelter, and after we had rested up a bit we began making a stockade out of an old corral, and also a temporary fort close to the timber.

"On the evening of the 14th, while I was standing outside the fort conversing with one of the citizens, the Indians came upon us unexpectedly and attacked. This citizen was telling me that the Indians had killed his brother that very morning and wanted me to go out and attack them. I could not do this, as my orders were to protect the people in the town. It was then that the Indians surprised and fired fully 100 shots into us before we could gain the shelter of the fort. As the Indians' rifles began to crack the people rushed to the fort and stockade, all reaching it in safety except our teamsters and two soldiers who were herding the mules and about 500 head of cattle. The bloodthirsty savages tried time and again to enter our works, but we repulsed them each time, and when they finally saw that we were masters of the situation they turned their attention to the stock and tried to run it off. Realizing that they would be likely to kill the herders I sent out a detail of ten men to their assistance. Keeping under cover of the timber, the men quickly made their way to the herders and drove the Indians away, thus saving the men and stock. The whole action was short but exciting while it lasted, and after it was all over the townspeople congratulated us for having repulsed a band of more than 100 redskins.

"Our little detachment was somewhat of a surprise to the Indians, for they did not expect to see any troops in the town, and when we repulsed them they made up their minds that the main body of the troops was in the vicinity and would pursua them as soon as they heard of the encounter. The remainder of the regiment did arrive the next morning, and two squadrons at once went in pursuit, but the wily redskins did not stop until they reached the mountains. There they had encounters with the troops and were finally driven into Old Mexico."

Two other important fights took place in this chase of the hostiles after the engagement at Tularosa, one of them on the 24th of May at the head of the Polomas River, New Mexico, where fifty-five Indians were killed in one of the hardest fought battles of the pursuit. The other took place on June 5th. In this action Major Morrow, with four troops of the Ninth Cavalry, struck the hostiles at Cook's Canyon killing ten and wounding three of them Among those killed was the son of the fleeing chief, Victoria.

In August of the following year Sergeant Jordan was commanding the right of a detachment of nineteen men at Carrizo Canyon, New Mexico, in an action with the Indians. He stubbornly held his ground in an extremely exposed position and gallantly forced back a much superior number of the enemy, thus preventing them from surrounding the command. His bravery in this action and his skillful handling of the detachment and also his fearlessness in the engagement at Tularosa won for Sergeant Jordan his Medal of Honor.

SAVED FROM ANNIHILATION

GEO. R. BURNETT.
Second Lieutenant, 9th U. S, Cavalry.
Born in Montgomery Co., Pa.
April 21, 1858.

A BAND of Indians under the notorious Chief Nana in the month of July, 1881, had committed a number of outrages, killed several women and children and stolen considerable property along the San Andreas Mountains in New Mexico, and Colonel E. Hatch with eight troops of the Ninth Cavalry and eight companies of infantry was sent to punish the savages and recapture the plunder.

The command started in pursuit at once and in a number of encounters drove the hostiles persistently from one point to another.

A notable engagement occurred on August 12th near Carrizo Canyon, in New Mexico. Nana's band was struck by a detachment of nineteen men under Captain Parker. In the ensuing fight the troopers were outnumbered three to one by the hostiles and lost one killed and three wounded, while one soldier was captured. The Indians, however, also lost heavily and were finally forced to withdraw. That the affair had such a successful ending and was not turned into a serious defeat was due largely to the extraordinary courage of Sergeant Thomas Shaw, of Company K, Ninth Cavalry, who with his few men stubbornly held the most advanced position and refused to yield an inch of ground. He was an excellent shot, his bravery so dismayed the Indians that they gave up the attack and retreated. A still larger engagement followed a few days later.

On August 16th, Troop I, Ninth Cavalry, First Lieutenant Gustavus Valois in command, and Second Lieutenant George R. Burnett on duty with same, was lying in Camp Canada Alamosa, New Mexico, recuperating from an arduous campaign in quest of hostile Apaches, when about 9:30 or 10 o'clock in the morning a Mexican whose ranch was a few miles down the canyon came charging into the town shrieking at the top of his voice that the Indians had murdered his wife and children, and were coming up the canyon to attack the town; in an instant all was excitement, men, women and children ran hither and thither screaming, crying, cursing and piteously calling on the "Good Father" to have mercy on them and save them.

In the cavalry camp orders were at once given to "saddle up," and in an incredible short time this was accomplished. Lieutenant Burnett requested and received permission to take the first attachment ready and proceed toward the scene of trouble. The ranch referred to was soon reached and the ranchman's story corroborated in the finding of his dead wife and a number of small children all horribly mutilated.

The trail was taken up and followed across the creek and up over the "Mesa," where the Indians were sighted about a mile off, heading toward the Cuchilla Negra Mountains, about ten miles distant. They were heavily encumbered with a large quantity of stolen stock and other plunder that they were endeavoring to get away with.

At the ranch Lieutenant Burnett had been joined by a number of mounted Mexicans, bringing his force up to about fifty men. The Indians, as nearly as could be estimated, numbered between eighty and one hundred. Immediately on sighting the Indians Lieutenant Burnett deployed his command, placing his First Sergeant, Moses Williams, in command on the right and one of the Mexicans on the left, remaining in the center himself. As soon as the advance was begun the Indians dismounted to make a stand, and commenced firing. Favored by the rolling country, the fire of the Indians soon became so warm that Lieutenant Burnett was obliged to dismount his command and to send a part of it under Sergeant Williams to flank the Indians from their position. This the sergeant succeeded in doing, and as soon as he signaled that the Indians had broken and were on the run Lieutenant Burnett mounted the balance of his command and charged them, keeping up a running fight until the Indians came to the next ridge, when they dismounted again, compelling the command to do likewise and to repeat the former tactics of flanking them ont of position and then charging.

The fight was so continued for several hours, the Indians fighting hard and contesting every foot of the ground in order to save as much of their stock and plunder as possible, but so closely were they pressed that they lost a number in killed and wounded, were obliged to abandon a large quantity of their stuff and a number of their ponies and shoot others to prevent their capture.

Finally the foothills of the Cuchilla Negra Mountains were reached, and here the Indians made a determined stand. Being unable to flank them on their right as usual, Lieutenant Burnett decided to make an effort to get around their left flank and if possible keep them out of the mountains. In working this detour he was accompanied by only about fifteen soldiers. The Indians observing his movements and apparent purpose, and his small force, offered no opposition for some time, when suddenly they found themselves in a pocket and surrounded on three sides by a heavy fire, and to make matters worse the Mexicans in the rear were firing into the bank against which the men were seeking to shelter themselves. Fortunately the pocket of basin-shaped formation was so deep that all shots passed just overhead and among the rocks and did no harm except to wound some of the horses. The Indians kept crawling nearer, their shots striking dangerously close, and the situation was growing desperate for the little detachment, unless they could get relief. Orders were given to reserve their revolver fire and fight to the last man.

It was at this juncture that Trumpeter John Rogers, at the suggestion of Lieutenant Burnett, volunteered to carry a message to Lieutenant Valois, whom he knew must be somewhere in the vicinity. Rogers endeavored to crawl out, but getting discouraged with his progress ran to where his horse was picketed and quickly mounting him rode to the rear amid a hailstorm of bullets, miraculously escaping harm, although his horse was wounded.

Rogers found Lieutenant Valois and delivered Lieutenant Burnett's message, which was to take a large hill to the right which commanded the position. Lieutenant Valois endeavored to comply with the request, but the Indians anticipated his purpose, and leaving Lieutenant Burnett's position got their first, greeting him with a volley that dismounted ten men, Valois among their number. From Lieutenant Burnett's position the Indians could be seen rallying from all points toward the hill, and divining the cause he proceeded to withdraw for the purpose of reenforcing Valois' Mounting his men and taking about thirty Mexicans who had then joined him, he started to the right and rear. On coming up over the little rise he saw Lieutenant Valois's entire command on a slight ridge about a quarter of a mile distant, dismounted and seeking shelter behind some prairie dog mounds, about the only thing in sight, and it looked as if the Indians, only a few hundred yards off, were just about to charge them. Without halting an instant, the command being deployed and at a gallop, Lieutenant Burnett ordered it to charge. This was done in a magnificent manner, the command charging splendidly up to and beyond Lieutenant Valois's line; and, dismounting, held the Indians in check until Lieutenant Valois was enabled to get his wounded and disabled men to the rear, when the whole line was ordered to fall back, as its position was untenable.

Lieutenant Valois had commenced the backward movement before the charge was made, and in doing so had left four of his men behind unobserved, in places of comparative shelter. When the general order to fall back was given, one of the men called out: "For God's sake, Lieutenant don't leave us; our lives depend on it."

At this time Lieutenant Valois and most of his command was well to the rear and apparently did not hear the cry. Lieutenant Burnett seeing the position these men were in called for volunteers to go to their rescue. Two men only, First Sergeant Moses Williams and Private Augustus Walley, responded to the call. Lieutenant Burnett directed his men to crawl to the rear while he, with Williams and Walley, behind such shelter as they could find, would try to stand off the Indians, who, emboldened by the troops falling back, were making a desperate effort to kill or capture those remaining behind. The marksmanship of the trio, all being good shots, caused the Indians to pause, and two of the soldiers were enabled to get to a place of safety, a third, who made no effort to escape was apparently wounded. This man was Walley's "bunky", so he asked for permission to go to his assistance. Going back to where his horse was picketed he mounted, rode rapidly up to where the man was lying, assisted him in the saddle, got up behind him and galloped safely to the rear.

Strange as it may appear, the Indians made no apparent effort to get Walley, but seemed to concentrate their efforts on Lieutenant Burnett whom they readily recognized as an officer among the colored troopers, and his solitary companion First

"THE INDIANS KEPT UP A CONCENTRATED FIRE ON LIEUTENANT BURNETT."

Sergeant Williams. Finally the fourth man who was left behind was seen wandering off in the direction of the enemy, or rather away from his own lines, and acting very strangely. He was apparently badly rattled. Indians could be distinctly seen making an effort to cut him off. Lieutenant Burnett, realizing that if this man was to be saved no time must be lost, ran to his horse, mounted him, and golloping toward the soldier managed to place himself between him and the Indians and finally drove him to the rear. All the while the Indians kept up a concentrated fire on Lieutenant Burnett, to which he replied with his revolver, but in their excitement they shot wildly and only succeeded in recording two hits, both on his horse,

Lieutenant Valois had in the meantime taken up a new position and assisted by some Mexicans the fight was continued until nightfall. Many horses were recaptured or prevented from falling into the hands of the Indians. The ammunition being about exhausted the command fell back to camp, and at daybreak started on the trail again and followed it until obliged to turn back at the Mexican border.

Medals of Honor were awarded to Lieutenant Burnett and his colored troopers, Williams and Walley, for their courageous conduct and rescue of life under such perilous circumstances.

Lieutenant Valois reported to the district commander that "Lieutenant Burnett's heroic charge had undoubtedly saved from annihilation his entire detachment."

Following this battle an engagement occurred August 19th about fifteen miles from McEver's ranch, New Mexico.

Lieutenant Smith with a detachment of twenty men, after a severe fight, defeated the hostiles, but the lieutenant and four of his men were killed. At the most critical moment of the combat a party of citizens joined the military forces and rendered valuable services. In this encounter Sergeant Brent Woods of Company B, Ninth Infantry, distinguished himself not alone as a brave and gallant fighter, but also the heroic manner in which he went to the succor of his wounded comrades and injured citizens saving them from falling into the hands of the savages. Nana's band was finally driven across the Mexican border, when the chase, under orders from the government, was abandoned.

THE TREACHERY AT CIBICU CREEK

During the summer of 1881 there appeared among the White Mountain Apaches in Arizona a rising star in the guise of a Medicine Man named Nockay det Klinne. This oracle gradually inflamed the minds of the Indians and became so infatuated by his success that he doubtless believed the truth of his own weird dreams. So long as he confined himself to ordinary incantations there was no special cause for anxiety. In common with more civilized charlatans, however, he had gradually mulcted the faithful believers of much of their limited wealth, and it became necessary for him to make a bold stroke to conceal the falseness of his prophecies.

Considering the length of time the White Mountain Indians had been associated with the whites and their intelligence, it is inexplicable how this fanatic imposed upon the tribe so seriously as to make large numbers of them believe

WILLIAM H. CARTER,
First Lieutenant, 6th U. S. Cavalry.
Highest ranks attained: Lieut.-Col. and
Asst.-Adjt.-Gen. U. S. A.
Born in Davidson County, Tennessee.

that if they would rise and murder the whites he would restore to life all their ancestors. He had been promising to raise the dead for some time, and he was growing rich through the bounty of his foolish patrons. When he announced that all the dead Apaches were risen, except that their feet were held down waiting for the whites to be driven from the Indian country, the time for interference had arrived.

Fort Apache is an isolated post in the midst of the White Mountain Reservation. Colonel E. A. Carr, of the Sixth Cavalry, had been ordered there for temporary duty during the early part of the summer, when there was no indication of Indian trouble. As dissatisfaction among the Indians became daily more apparent, its source was located and Colonel Carr had an interview with the Medicine Man and several chiefs, in which he explained how futile would be their efforts to rise successfully against the white race. Nockay det Klinne was repeatedly summoned to report to Agent Tiffany at San Carlos, but ignored all orders and retired to his camp on Cibicu Creek, about forty miles from Fort Apache. Agent Tiffany's police having failed, he requested Colonel Carr to arrest the Medicine Man.

Recognizing this very serious turn of affairs, Colonel Carr telegraphed the department commander recommending that additional troops be sent at once to Fort Apache to overawe the Indians and prevent an outbreak, by convincing them of the folly of an uprising. Troops were not sent, but Colonel Carr temporized with the Indians, who were growing more bold and insolent day by day, hoping to impress upon the authorities the absolute necessity of re-enforcements to prevent an Indian war, expensive alike in blood and treasure. Orders were ultimately issued for more troops to proceed to Fort Apache, but through some strange mischance, or ill advice, they were not allowed to proceed over the mountains from the Gila river, seventy miles away from the scene where soldierly diplomacy was arrayed against Indian fanaticism and wily cunning. The hours for parleying reached their limit when the agent made a formal demand that the military arm should be set in motion and the recalcitrant Medicine Man be brought before him dead or alive.

During the excitement of the dances inaugurated by the Indian Messiah, the craze became widespread and involved the Apaches in nearly all the camps in the White Mountain Reservation. The Indians brewed "tizwin," a frightful intoxicant made from corn, which added to their weird madness.

As soon as the department commander telegraphed the order for Colonel Carr to comply with the agent's request, the Indians cut the line and occupied the only practicable road and mountain trails, thus completely isolating the garrison. Warning had been received that the scouts, hitherto of unblemished character for fidelity, were strongly fascinated with the uncanny doctrines of the plausible and silver-tongued medicine man.

Upon receipt of his orders to arrest or kill Nockay det Klinne, Colonel Carr sent a runner to his camp with a message that no harm was intended toward him, but he must come in and report as desired by the agent. An evasive answer was received. It was learned he was to visit the camps adjacent to the post for another big dance and arrangements were made to secure him, but he grew suspicious and failed to put in an appearance.

On Monday, August 29th, Colonel Carr paraded his little command, consisting of two troops of his regiment, D and E, with a total strength of seventy-nine men and twenty-three Indian scouts, and marched on the trail to Cibicu Creek. There was but one officer for duty with each organization. Oné small infantry company was left for the protection of the garrison. The command moved leisurely and camped in a deep gorge at the crossing of Carizo Creek.

Some days prior to this time it had been deemed advisable to withdraw the ammunition in the hands of the scouts. Colonel Carr now thought that it was more judicious to have a plain talk with them, and assume an air of confidence. No overt act had been committed by any of them, and in past years they had accompanied the troops on innumerable scouts, exhibiting at all times courage, untiring energy and vigilence. The object of the expedition was explained and the ammunition restored to all the scouts.

Sergeant Mose was selected to precede the command and notify the Indians that no hostile action was contemplated, and that the only purpose was to have Nockay det Klinne come to the post. Mose carried out his instructions faithfully.

Next morning the command toiled slowly up the narrow trail on the top of the canyon and crossed the divide. Upon arriving in the valley of the Cibicu the scouts took the trail leading along the creek, but Colonel Carr chose the fork along the high open ground. While still several miles from the Medicine Man's camp, Sanchez, a well-known chief, rode out of the creek bottom, shook hands with the officers at the head of the column and then calmly and deliberately rode down the line counting the men. He then turned his pony and galloped back to the creek which, at this point, ran between low bluffs and hills. This was the first and only suspicious act noticed by anyone.

The column marched steadily forward and turned into the bottom, crossing the stream not far from the Medicine Man's "wicky-up." Officers and men had all been cautioned to be in readiness for treachery, but the Medicine Man surrendered so readily that the warning seemed unnecessary. Colonel Carr directed the interpreter to state plainly that Nockay det Klinne and his family would be taken to the post and no harm was intended to them, but if any attempt at rescue was made the Medicine Man would be killed.

Lieutenant Thomas Cruse, who commanded the scouts, was directed to take charge of the prisoners with the guard, and follow in the column between Troops D and E. Colonel Carr, with his staff, then led the way across the creek by a different trail from the one used in going over. This trail led through high willows and underbrush, and it was not discovered, until too late to rectify the mistake, that Lieutenant Cruse had missed the entrance to the crossing and was going down the opposite side of the lower crossing, followed by Troop E.

Colonel Carr selected an excellent camp sight and the packs were taken off, the horses of Troop D were turned out under the herd guard and the usual preparations made for camping in a country where tents were seldom used.

At this time it was observed that mounted Indians were coming up the creek from the gulches which the column had avoided, and that they were collecting around the Medicine Man's guard. When the guard crossed the creek and was about entering the limits of the camp, Colonel Carr told Captain E. C. Hentig to quietly warn the Indians away from the camp, and directed Lieutenant W. H. Carter, regimental quartermaster, to separate the scouts and put them in camp. These two officers walked only a few paces to where the Indians were. Lieutenant Carter called the scouts and directed Sergeant "Dead Shot" to put them in camp. The scouts left the other Indians, but appeared uneasy and demurred about camping because of numerous hills of large red ants, common to all parts of Arizona. The scouts arranged themselves at intervals along the crest of the "mesa," or tableland, which had been selected as a camp ground.

Captain Hentig passed a few yards beyond the scouts and called out to the Indians, to all of whom he was well known through his five years of service at Camp Apache, "Ukashe," which means "Go away." As he raised his hand to motion to them, a half-witted young buck fired and gave the war cry. The long-delayed

"THE WOUNDED MEN WERE RESCUED BY LIEUTENANT CARTER."

explosion took place at the moment when the men on foot had been warned not to show any signs of expecting a fight.

Captain Hentig and his orderly, who was between him and Lieutenant Carter, fell at the first volley, but the bodies of the wounded men were rescued by Lieutenant Carter and carried to the rear. The dismounted men of Troop D seized their arms; the small headquarters guard, engaged in putting up a tent for Colonel Carr, advanced on the scouts with brave Sergeant Alonzo Bowman in the lead, and opened fire. At this time there were more than 100 Indians besides the scouts in camp, and less than forty dismounted men engaged in a hand-to-hand conflict.

Colonel Carr walked calmly towards the position just vacated by the mutinous scouts and called firmly to the guard. "Kill the Medicine Man!" Sergeant McDonald, who was in charge of the guard, fired, wounding Nockay det Klinne through both thighs, but the sergeant was immediately shot by the scouts. The Medicine Man and his squaw endeavored to reach the scouts, the Messiah calling loudly to the Indians to fight, for if he was killed he would come to life again.

Lieutenant Carter's orderly trumpeter was going towards the guard with a saddle kit, and when Colonel Carr called he drew his revolver, thrusting the muzzle into the mouth of the yelling Medicine Man, and fired. The squaw was allowed to pass out of the camp chanting a weird death song in her flight.

The scouts and other Indians were promptly driven from the immediate vicinity. Lieutenant Stanton, whose troop had been at the rear of the column, was just forming line mounted, when the fight began, and as the scouts drew off into the underbrush the troop was dismounted and charged through the bottom, driving the Indians out at the other side of the creek.

Sanchez and a few followers shot the herder nearest the stream, and with wild yells stampeded such horses as had been turned loose. The mules still had on their aparajos and remained quietly standing in the midst of all the turmoil around them until the packers were ordered by the quartermaster to take them to the bottom for protection.

There was but a moment's respite during the retreat of the Indians to the neighboring hills. The command was immediately disposed to resist the attack, which commenced as soon as the Indians had gotten to cover in their new positions.

Colonel Carr had but three officers, Lieutenants Stanton, Carter and Cruse, and the small size of the command required everyone on the firing line. Assistant Surgeon McCreery was kept busy with the wounded, whom he attended under fire with perfect composure and courage. The loss in this fight was Captain Hentig and six men killed. That the loss was no more was due in a great measure to the coolness and courage of Colonel Carr.

A situation better calculated to try the mettle of a command could scarcely be imagined. Having effected the object of the march—the arrest of a notorious and mischief-making Medicine Man—without difficulty, and with no resistance on the part of his people, the troops had set about making camp for the night, when suddenly they were fired upon, not alone by the friends of the Medicine Man, but by their own allies, the Indian scouts, who had hitherto been loyal. The confusion and dismay which such an attack at such a time necessarily caused might well have resulted in the annihilation of the entire force, and constituted a situation from which nothing but the most consummate skill and bravery could pluck safety.

When darkness settled over the field the dead were buried in a single grave prepared inside of Colonel Carr's tent. The burial party and a few men who could be spared from the firing line stood about the grave with bared heads while Colonel Carr recited the burial service. As the last sad notes of "taps" died away the column prepared to return to the post, toward which small parties of Indians had been seen going all through the afternoon.

Before leaving the field Colonel Carr sent Lieutenant Carter to examine the body of the Medicine Man and determine if life was extinct. Strange to say, notwithstanding his wounds, he was still alive. The recovery of this Indian, if left in the hands of his friends, would have given him a commanding influence over these superstitious people, which would have resulted in endless war. Colonel Carr then repeated the order for his death, specifying that no more shots should be fired. Guide Burns was directed to carry out the order with the understanding that a knife was to be used. Burns, fearing failure, took an ax and crushed the forehead of the deluded fanatic, and from this time forward every person murdered by these Apaches was treated in a similar manner.

The column then started and marched all night, arriving at the post during the next afternoon. Many of the Indians had preceded the command, and all night they were haranguing in the vicinity. They covered the roads and trails, and killed a number of citizens, besides the mail carrier and three soldiers coming from duty at the ferry on Black River.

On the following morning, September 1st, the Indians burned some buildings in the vicinity, and in the afternoon attacked the post, but were driven off. Captain Gordon was wounded during this attack while at the corner of the main parade.

There was much in the situation to produce gloomy forebodings, not for the safety of the post, but for that of the scattered settlers. There were not enough troops in Arizona to handle a general outbreak, and it could not be determined just what tribes were implicated in the revolt. The first thing necessary was to open communication. This was accomplished by sending Lieutenant Stanton, with thirty-three men, to Fort Thomas. That part of the road which was in the mountains was covered in the night, and the balance of the seventy miles was made during the following day. Colonel Carr's command had been reported for several days as massacred, and the papers of the entire country were filled with dire forebodings as to the results of this outbreak. The news carried by Lieutenant Stanton was the first to lift the clouds from the grief-stricken relatives and friends of the Fort Apache garrison.

First Lieutenant William H. Carter, Sergeant Alonzo Bowman and Private Richard Heartery were awarded the Medal of Honor.

TREACHERY OF THE SCOUTS AVENGED

THOMAS CRUSE,
Second Lieutenant, 6th U. S. Cavalry.
Born at Owensboro, Kentucky, Dec. 29th, 1857.
Highest rank attained: Major, U. S. Vols.

THERE was great rejoicing when the report, spread by the treacherous Apaches, that they had killed the entire command of Colonel E. A. Carr was contradicted, yet the loss was severe enough to keep public indignation alive and arouse a demand from all parts of the country that the traitors and their allies be punished. This caused the expedition of 1882, of which Second Lieutenant Thomas Cruse, Sixth United States Cavalry, gives a full and graphic narration in the following:

"The spring of '82 saw us still out in the field after the hostiles. But in June they all appeared to have gone into the deep recesses of the mountains of Old Mexico, many miles below the line; so that the Fourth of July was spent at our post, Fort Apache, and was celebrated in befitting style with horse racing, wrestling, running, target matches, etc. The morning of the 9th of July, however, brought a telegram stating that a band of hostiles had dashed into San Carlos, killed the chief of scouts, several Indian policemen, friendly Indians and all the white people that could be found in that vicinity, except the agent. The telegram also stated that the hostiles had started toward Tonto Basin, and directed us to march toward Cibicu Creek and try to intercept them when they crossed the Black River. We were further notified that two companies of the Third Cavalry, from Fort Thomas, were after them, and that one troop of the Sixth, with a company of Indian scouts from Fort McDowell, under Captain Chaffee, had been ordered to watch them from the west and intercept them, if possible. The command, consisting of Troops E and I of the Third, and Troops E and K of the Sixth U. S. Cavalry, under Major Evans of the Third Cavalry, left the post that day. On the morning of the 16th, on one of the small branches of the Black River, fresh signs of the Indians were found, and that night, about 8 o'clock, while we were encamped, we were much surprised to hear that Captain Chaffee with his troop from McDowell was only about a mile away. Word was sent to him and he came and had a consultation with Major Evans. It was decided that it was highly probable that the Indians would be overtaken the next day, and would probably fight. Chaffee was ordered to break camp, at his own suggestion, very early in the morning and attempt to climb the precipitous bluffs which surround the country, called Tonto Basin, and the main command was to follow on, after he found the Indians. This program was carried out, and about 11 o'clock word was sent back that the Indians had been located and were evidently waiting for us. We were much amazed to hear this, because the Apaches never fight unless they have every advantage on their side, and then they become the most dangerous foe of any of the Indians. A year or two later this was explained to me by one of the men who was in the fight by saying that their scouts, whom they had left in the rear on the trail, had seen Chaffee's troop, which was mounted on white horses, and had determined to prepare an ambuscade for it, knowing full well the small number of men he had, but being in ignorance of the fact that re-enforcements were in the vicinity, as they had never seen Major Evans's command. Five troops now moved forward at a gallop and soon came up to the spot where the Indians were waiting. Their place was certainly well chosen, it being where the trail which led from the Apache Reservation to the Navajo Reservation crossed over a deep crack in the earth—a branch of the celebrated Canyon Diablo. This country is near the celebrated Colorado Canyon, and abounds in cracks and ravines of volcanic origin, which are absolutely impassable for men. The troops were ordered to advance as quietly as possible within about a mile of the canyon and dismount. One troop, I, Third Cavalry, commanded by Lieutenant Converse, was deployed along the bank to fire at the Indians and attract their attention, while two troops were sent around to either flank, with the idea of getting on the other side of the canyon and capturing the redskins, or at least holding them so that they could not get away. This arrangement brought Troops E and I of the Sixth Cavalry together on the right flank, and Troop D of the Third and K of the Sixth on the left.

"E was my own troop, commanded by Captain Adam Kramer, an officer of the War of the Rebellion and hero of many an Indian fight. Major Evans now turned the actual command of the forces over to Captain Chaffee, who certainly was the right man in the right place. The Indians opened fire at about 3:30 o'clock in the afternoon. Troop I lined the edge of the canyon and replied, and the other four troops moved off quietly and rapidly to get across the numerous obstacles in their way, one of which was the canyon, apparently a stone's throw across, but about 300 or 400 feet deep. I remember as we crossed it we found a nice stream of water, and someone glanced up and remarked that the stars were shining, although it was still early in the afternoon. The task that was set before us was one that taxed our energies to the utmost, but finally, about 5 o'clock, we succeeded in getting across this canyon and to the right and rear of the Indians; and then the fun began. Troop I ran into their pony herd, killed the herders and captured the entire lot. Up to this time the Indians apparently were not aware of our presence, and had started in to make a counter attack on Troop I, but our fire on their flanks soon brought to their mind the fact that there was somebody else there, and they began to fight for some way to get out and escape. Troop E was deployed near the edge of the canyon, and it was my good luck to have command of the left wing and to fall in with Al Seiber, one of the most noted scouts and guides in Arizona and New Mexico. I had been in several fights before this, but never found them very exciting affairs, as the Apache is not given to exposing himself for theatrical effect like the Sioux and the Cheyenne, but merely keeps behind a rock, well hidden, waiting a

"I TOLD HIM TO LIE QUIET."

chance to kill without taking any chance whatever himself. On this occasion, how-ever, as we advanced it became absolutely necessary for them to get out of the entrenchments they had hastily prepared and run, and for the first time I had a chance to shoot at something as well as to be shot at, Seiber, who was on my immediate left, would call out once in a while: There he goes! and would raise his rifle and shoot, and sure enough, an Indian would jump up from behind a rock, not more than 150 yards away, and, with a shriek, throw up his hands and fall. Directly they began running in bunches and things became highly exciting. I called on my men to advance, saying that some of these Indians were my scouts and now was our chance to get even with them for their treachery of the year before. With this idea in mind, I, with eight or ten men, started across a small ra-vine, beyond which we could see the main camp of the Indians.

"As I started through the forest, which was park like and with no undergrowth, I was very much amazed at hearing Seiber call out after me: "Lieutenant, don't go through there; that place is full of Indians!" But it was too late; I thought all the Indians in that part of the field had been killed, so we went—Sergeant Horan, Blacksmith Martin and six or eight privates of troop E, right after me.

"We got into their camp after firing several shots, and saw some of them run; when suddenly, about ten feet away, two Indians raised up slightly above the level of the ground and shot at me. I thought at the time I was hit, and Captain Kramer called out: "I am afraid they have got Cruse." So I judge from that, I must have dropped pretty quickly. At the same time Private McClellan, who was about two feet from me, went down in a heap also. The Indians dropped back behind a rocky ledge and were pretty well concealed. I called out to McClellan: "Are you hurt?", and he answered—"Yes, I think my arm is broken." I told him to lie quiet so that the Indians could not get another shot at him and that I would watch them. I got in a shot or two, then Blacksmith Martin came to my assistance and we succeeded in getting McClellan out of way of the Indians. In the meantime they had appar-ently sprung up on three or four sides of us, and things were very lively in that vicinity for the next five or ten minutes. During that time Sergeant Conn, of our troop, was shot through the neck and several other casualties occurred. As nearly as could be it was a hand-to-hand conflict all around, and when the melee was ended it was dark and I did not see any more Indians and began to think about getting across the Canyon to our pack-train.

"Private McClellan proved to be worse hurt than we supposed, for the bullet, in addition to breaking his arm, had gone through his chest, and he died about 11 o'clock that night.

"We squared up with those treacherous Apache scouts however. Four of them were hung at Fort Grant, Arizona; four more were sent to Alcratraz Island and five or six were killed in the fight I speak of."

During the attack First Sergeant Charles Taylor, Troop D, Third United States Cavalry, displayed the most wonderful bravery. He advanced far ahead of his comrades and in a cool and deliberate manner picked out one brave after another, killing them by his unfailing accuracy as he advanced amidst howls and shrieks.

Troop I, Sixth United States Cavalry, at one time of the fight was in a threatening position. It had crossed a deep canyon and was crawling up a steep cliff on the northern side, when bands of Indians suddenly appeared on all sides. The men were retreating toward the bottom of the canyon, when First Lieutenant Frank West rallied them and successfully outflanked the Indians.

During this movement an interesting incident occurred, which Second Lieutenant George H. Morgan, of the Third Cavalry, who volunteered to go with the detachment of Lieutenant West, tells interestingly as follows:

"By crossing the canyon it was a hard, dangerous climb both down and up, and when at the top we found that the mesa ended at the side of the canyon by a ledge of rock, probably six feet high. The top was defended by a small force of renegade Apache skirmishers.

FRANK WEST,
First Lieutenant, 6th U. S. Cavalry.
Born in Mohawk, N. Y., 1850.

"Forming our men below the ledge, they were ordered to jump over and take to the nearest tree. After seeing all the men move forward I followed and dropped down behind my tree, selected before I started. By a natural and excusable mistake six of my men had chosen the same tree. It was not the largest there, but we were all safe, as owing to the disinclination of the men to expose themselves the Indians could not hit us, their bullets hitting the tree about three feet above the ground. The men, however, were uneasy, there being so little tree and so much of a crowd, and without a word all jumped up and ran back, fortunately without loss. As it was safer, and a good place, I crawled up to my vacated tree. A chief just in front of and very close to me—thirty feet—thinking the entire party had gone, sprang out from his cover and commenced a war dance. After stopping his play in short order, I became anxious to know how far back my party had gone, and went back with much haste and little dignity. I was glad to find the men under the ledge cool enough and wondering where I was. We tried the advance again and in better form, and gained the top."

The chase after these Indians had been so energetically conducted that during the night following and the next morning there were twelve cavalry troops assembled on the scene from four posts—a remarkable concentration of scouting columns all in search of the same marauders.

The scouts crossed the canyon and found the hostiles had fled, abandoning everything and leaving six prisoners in the hands of the troops and sixteen dead bodies

"SIX OF MY MEN HAD CHOSEN THE SAME TREE".

upon the field. A severe hail-storm set in, lasting four hours, which covered the trail so completely as to prevent pursuit. The troops remained two days near the scene of the fight. Litters were made and the wounded transported by hand eight miles back to the open country, where ambulances could reach them.

Seventy horses and much camp plunder were captured. Among the dead were two of the renegade scouts who mutinied in the Cibicu fight. The troops lost one man killed, seven wounded, and two officers of the Third Cavalry, Lieutenants Converse and Morgan, wounded. The rugged nature of this part of the Mongollon Mountains prevented the hostiles from being again brought to bay, and they escaped to the various Indian camps about the reservations where they were secreted by their kindred.

CHASING GERONIMO AND NATCHEZ

THE surrender of Geronimo and Natchez, the leading chiefs of the Apaches, concluded the campaign of 1886. It marked the closing of a long and tedious war with the Apaches who had terrorized the whole southern part of Arizona and northern part of Mexico and restored peace and prosperity to the inhabitants of a vast stretch of territory of two republics. Of all Indian savages the Apache is known to be the most brutal, unruly and barbarous. His treachery is proverbial, his cruelty notorious.

The young Apache warrior could not hope to command the respect of his tribe unless he had accomplished a "heroic" deed. This consisted of an outrage upon some hostile Indian, an American or Mexican ranchman, or a lone traveler. The more cruel the act, the greater the "heroism"; the more "heroic" deeds, the greater the honor and respect among his own people. This principle inculcated in the child, actuated the youthful warrior and was practiced by the old and experienced. It made the Apaches the most dreaded and feared of all Indian races.

In 1886 General Miles was called upon to subdue these turbulent and desperate bands and restore order in the territory mentioned.

The mountainous character of the country furnished these murderous savages with innumerable places of hiding and refuge and rendered them extremely difficult to get at. Many expeditions and campaigns had been previously undertaken and failed before the seemingly insurmountable obstacles. In preparing for his campaign General Miles was determined to chase and hound these hostiles and keep chasing and hounding them and not let up on them until sheer exhaustion should force them into final subjection.

It was to be a war to the finish between the white man's perseverance and endurance and the same qualities of the redskin, the outcome of which, General Miles figured, would inevitably be in favor of the better equipped and infinitely more intelligent white man.

There was not the slightest doubt in General Miles's mind that the Apaches could be subdued, and in assuming the command of the Department of Arizona he selected such officers for the discharge of important missions and duties as agreed with him on the general proposition and were sufficiently energetic to carry out the common idea.

Then the general formulated a definite and systematic plan of campaign, reorganized the troops, restored the confidence of the men, infused new hope into the minds of the timid ranchers and brought order out of the chaos.

For the first time in the history of American military operations General Miles during this year made use of the heliostat and adopted the system of heliographic messages—signaling by mirrors—for the transmission of orders and reports of the movements of the hostile Indians.

Experiments with this system, invented by an English officer some twenty years before, had been previously made by American generals, but it was not finally adopted and practically used until General Miles conducted his Apache campaign in 1886. Stations were established on the highest peaks of the mountains all over the country. Thus the movements of the savages were kept under constant observation, and much time, money and labor were saved in unnecessary and long and tedious marches in search of the elusive enemy. One more word about the Apaches.

General Miles described them as follows:

"They were vicious and outlaws of the worst class. They were clad in such a way as to disguise themselves as much as possible. Masses of grass, bunches of weeds, twigs or small boughs were fastened under their hat bands very profusely, and also upon their shoulders and backs. Their clothing was trimmed in such a way that when lying upon the ground in a bunch of grass or at the head of a ravine, it was almost impossible to discover them. It was in this way that they were wont to commit their worst crimes. An unsuspecting ranchman or miner going along a road or trail would pass within a few feet of these concealed Apaches, and the first intimation he would have of their presence would be a bullet through his heart or brain."

The campaign began in the latter part of April. The Apaches themselves made the first move. They boldly left the mountain fastnesses in the Sierra Madres and came down upon the terror-stricken people of Northern Mexico. Among the first outrages committed was that of which the Peck family became victims. The sad story is told by Captain Leonard Wood, assistant surgeon, United States Army, in short but graphic words as follows:

"Peck's ranch was surrounded by Indians, the entire family was captured, and several of the farm-hands were killed. The husband was tied up and compelled to witness indescribable tortures inflicted upon his wife until she died. The terrible ordeal rendered him temporarily insane and as the Apaches, like most Indians, stand in great awe of an insane person, they set him free as soon as they discovered his mental condition; but otherwise he would never have been allowed to live. He was afterward found by his friends wandering about the place."

The family had two daughters, one of whom was outraged and shared the fate of her mother; the other, a little girl of ten years, was dragged upon the back of a horse and carried away into captivity. She was recaptured. On their flight through Mexican territory the Apaches met a force of seventy Mexicans. A volley was fired, killing an Indian woman, and the Indian who carried the child was wounded. This Indian's horse was shot at the same time. The little girl bravely ran away from her savage captor and was picked up by the jubilant Mexicans. The Indian retreated towards the rocks and there stood off the entire Mexican force, killing seven of them, each of whom was shot through the head. He then made his escape.

On another occasion the hordes rode through a wood choppers' camp and killed seven white men. Another time they crept stealthily into a small creek and murdered five Mexican placer miners.

Many other instances of the most reckless brutality and cruelty marked the opening of the campaign.

The command which was selected by General Miles for the expedition was placed in charge of Captain Henry W. Lawton, Fourth United States Cavalry, and composed of the best officers and men available. Troops were frequently changed and provisions made for fresh transports to replace the tired and worn-out horses and pack-mules.

The pursuit of the Indians was now taken up and continued with untiring perseverance. Over prairies, mountains, through valleys, across streams and thundering rapids, now about the peaks of giant mountains, now way down through canyons deep and narrow, wherever the trail of the Indians led the command followed. The Indians would pass straight over the highest ranges of the roughest mountains, abandon their horses and descend to the valleys below, where they would supply themselves with fresh animals by stealing them; the soldiers would send their horses around the impassable heights, climb the ascent on foot and slide down the descent. They would suffer from cold on the peaks and from an almost intolerable heat in the depths of the canyons. On one occasion the command marched twenty-six hours without a halt and was without water for eighteen hours in the intense heat of that season. The Indians were driven from one place to another, from Arizona to Mexico, with the tenacious troops clinging to their heels.

There was an agreement with the Mexican Republic and the government at Washington by virtue of which United States troops could enter Mexican territory when in pursuit of hostile Indians, so that in this campaign the boundary line between the two republics created no obstacles.

Several times the Indians were brought to bay and forced to fight, for example, in the Pinito Mountains, in Sonora, Mexico, May 3, 1886, where in the midst of the battle Lieutenant Powhatan H. Clark, Tenth United States Cavalry, dashed among the howling Apaches and at the peril of his own young life snatched from them a corporal who had been wounded and fallen into their hands.

The dash was made well in advance of his troopers, who were themselves so busily engaged in keeping the hostiles at bay that they had not noticed the absence of their comrade. Clark's intrepidity and exceptional courage displayed by dashing among the savages, firing as he advanced and killing several of the hostiles before he reached the place where the corporal was lying, prevented the massacre of the man before the eyes of his own comrades.

"LIEUTENANT CLARK DASHED AMONG THE HOWLING APACHES."

The hostiles were badly defeated. Again twelve days later at Santa Cruz, Sonora, another engagement took place in which Sergeant Samuel H. Craig, of the Fourth United States Cavalry, was severely wounded, but nevertheless fought in the front ranks of the troops and with blood-covered face led a most gallant charge. The Indians were compelled to flee for their lives and leave the entire camp in the hands of the troops.

For three long months this inexorable chase was kept up until on July 13th the last and decisive blow was struck on the Yaqui River in Sonora in a section of the country that was almost impassable for man or beast.

Geronimo and Natchez evidently considered themselves safe from all attack, but Captain Lawton, by skillful manœuvring, managed to surprise the whole camp and seize everything in sight, the Indians themselves having a very narrow escape from capture.

The savages now were tired of being the hunted game of the United States soldiers and yearned for peace. Geronimo especially was willing to submit to the inevitable and sent two of his women to open negotiations. He agreed to an unconditional surrender, begging only that he and his followers' lives be spared. This was promised. And thus Geronimo, the dreaded Apache chief, became a prisoner. He remained loyal, too, for when on the return march the command met a large Mexican force, which assumed a threatening attitude, and could have rendered the situation critical enough to make the outcome doubtful, Geronimo and his Apaches stuck to the command, and so eager were they to assist those to whom they had surrendered only a short time before that a clash between them and the Mexicans was narrowly avoided. On September 3d Geronimo surrendered to General Miles in person at Skeleton Canyon, whither the commander had journeyed to join Captain Lawton's camp.

Natchez still refused to come in, but General Miles brought about his surrender by a stroke of clever diplomacy, which had worked wonders on a former occasion.

He overawed Geronimo with the marvels of the white man's civilization. Among other things he showed him the heliostat and explained to him that by means of the instrument he could talk and receive information hundreds of miles away.

At the request of the superstitious Indian warrior the general inquired concerning the health of a brother of Geronimo, who was held a captive at a distant military post.

When the young chief had received the news he had asked for he was more terror-stricken than surprised, and sent a messenger to Natchez urging him to surrender, "as the white man was in league with powers strange and weird, and which he was not able to understand."

Natchez, perhaps glad to have a pretext to give up the hopeless and unequal struggle, followed the advice and surrendered on the same terms as Geronimo. His capture ended the Apache war.

HAZARDOUS, BUT SUCCESSFUL

MARION P. MAUS,
First Lieutenant, 1st U. S. Infantry.
Born in Maryland.
Highest rank attained: Lieut.-Colonel, U. S A.

An interesting account of the hardships and adventures which our troops had to contend with during the memorable campaign of 1886 against, the hostile Apaches under Geronimo and Natchez is vividly described by Lieutenant-Colonel Marion P. Maus, then a first lieutenant of the First United States Infantry.

His excellent soldierly qualities were instrumental in several instances during this campaign in extricating the troops to which he was attached from dangerous positions in which they, owing to the nature of the extremely mountainous country, had fallen, and the undaunted courage and heroism which he displayed won for him the Medal of Honor.

Lieutenant-Colonel Maus narrates:

"Our command, fully equipped for field service, left Apache, Arizona, on November 11, 1885, for Fort Bowie. Here it was inspected by Lieutenant-General Sheridan and Brigadier-General Crook, and with words of encouragement from these officers the command started south by way of the Dragoon Mountains, endeavoring to find the trail of a band of Indians who were returning to Mexico after a raid into the United States.

"Thoroughly scouting through these mountains without finding the trail, we went on to the border and crossed into Mexico twenty miles north of the town of Fronteras, with the object of pursuing the renegades to their haunts in southern Sonora. We believed that if we could trace this band we could find the entire hostile camp under Geronimo and Natchez. Under instructions from Captain Crawford, I preceded the command to the town of Fronteras to notify the presidente of the town of our approach, of our object in coming, and to gain information. It was a small place, composed of the usual adobe buildings, and its people lived in a constant state of alarm about the movements of the hostiles. The command arriving, we proceeded to Nocarasi, a small mining town in the Madre Mountains. On account of the roughness of these mountains we found great difficulty in crossing them with the pack-train. We found one horse which had evidently been abandoned by the hostiles, but no distinct trail.

"In marching the command it was interesting to notice the methods adopted by our Indians in scouting the country to gain information and prevent surprise. It illustrated to us very clearly what we must expect from the hostiles, who would employ the same methods. It was impossible to march these scouts as soldiers, or to control them as such, nor was it deemed advisable to attempt it. Among them were many who had bloody records; one named Dutchy had killed, in cold blood, a white man near Fort Thomas, and for this murder the civil authorities were at this time seeking to arrest him. Their system of advance guards and flankers was perfect, and as soon as the command went into camp, outposts were at once put out, guarding every approach. All this was done noiselessly and in secret, and without giving a single order. As scouts for a command in time of war they would be ideal. Small of stature, and apparently no match physically for the white man, yet when it came to climbing mountains or making long marches, they were swift and tireless. The little clothing they wore consisted of a soldier's blouse, discarded in time of action, light undergarments and a waist cloth, and on the march the blouse was often turned inside out to show only the gray lining. Nothing escaped their watchful eyes as they marched silently in their moccasined feet. By day small fires were built of dry wood to avoid smoke, and at night they were made in hidden places so as to be invisible. If a high point was in view, you could be sure that a scout had crawled to the summit and, himself unseen, with a glass or his keen eyes had searched the country around. At night only was the watch relaxed, for these savages dread the night with a superstitious fear. It was necessary to allow them their way, and we followed, preserving order as best we could by exercising tact and a careful study of their habits. Under the influence of mescal, which is a liquor made in all parts of Mexico and easily procured, they often became violent and troublesome, and we could not help realizing how perfectly we were in their power. However, no distrust of them was shown. One of my Indians, a sergeant named Rubie, followed me one day while I was hunting. I thought his actions were curious, but they were explained when he suddenly came from the front and told me to go back. He had seen the footprints of hostiles near by. In the action which followed later he came to me and warned me to cover. There was, however, very little evidence of affection or gratitude in them as a class.

"Continuing the march, we reached the town of Huasavas, in the valley of the Bavispe. Orange and lemon trees were filled with golden fruit, although it was now the 22d of December. This valley, surrounded by high mountains, was fertile, though but little cultivated. The only vehicles in use were carts, the wheels of which were sections sawed from logs. The plows were pieces of pointed wood. The people were devoid of all the comforts of life. Corn flour was obtained by pounding the grains on stones. They were a most desolate people, and completely terrorized by the Apaches, who were a constant menace to them, as they were to the inhabitants of all these towns. Here occurred the first serious trouble with the Indian scouts. One of them, who was drunk but unarmed, was shot by a Mexican policeman. At the time I was on my way to the town and met the Indian, who was running down the road towards me, followed by two policemen or guards firing rapidly. One ball passed through his head, coming out through the jaw. The other

Indian scouts were much incensed, and at once began to prepare for an attack on the town, giving us much trouble before we were able to stop them. The officers were unable to sleep that night, as many of the Indians had been drinking and continued to be so angry that they fired off their rifles in the camp. The next day I released one of them from prison, and subsequently had to pay a fine of five dollars for him. It was claimed by the Mexicans that the Indians had committed some breach of the peace.

"Here we got the first reliable news of the hostiles who were murdering people and killing cattle to the south. Crossing the mountains we passed the towns of Granadas and Bacedahuachi, the latter being the site of one of the fine old missions built by the daring priests who had sought to plant their religion among the natives many years before.

"Proceeding on our way over a mountainous country, we finally came to the town of Nacori. This place was in a continual state of alarm, a wall having been built around it as a protection against the Apaches, the very name of whom was a terror. From our camp, sixteen miles south of this town, two of our pack-trains were sent back to Lang's Ranch, New Mexico, for supplies. To our surprise a Deputy United States Marshal from Tombstone came here to arrest Dutchy. Captain Crawford declined to permit the arrest, and in a letter to the marshal asked him to 'delay the arrest till I may be near the border where protection for myself, officers and white men, with my pack-trains, may be afforded by United States troops other than Indians,' offering to return if desired. The scouts were intensely excited, and under the circumstances the marshal did not wish to attempt to arrest Dutchy, and returned without delay.

"We had now penetrated over 200 miles into the mountains of Mexico, and we were sure the hostiles were near. It was decided to move immediately in pursuit of them. In this wild and unknown land even our Indians looked more stolid and serious. One by one they gathered together for a medicine dance. The Medicine Man, Noh-wah-zhe-tah, unrolled the sacred buckskin he had worn since he left Fort Apache. There was something very solemn in all this. The dance, the marching, the kneeling before the sacred buckskin as each pressed his lips to it and the old man blessed him, impressed us too, as we looked on in silence. Afterward the Indians held a council. They said they meant to do their duty, and would prove that they would fight to those who said they would not, and they seemed very much in earnest. I am satisfied that they desired to get the hostiles to surrender, but do not believe they intended or desired to kill them—their own people. In view of their relations it was little wonder that they felt in this way.

"It was decided that all must go on foot, and that officer and scout alike must carry his own blanket, all else being left behind. Leaving a few scouts (the weakest and the sick) to guard the camp, a force of seventy-nine was equipped with twelve days' rations, carried on three or four of the toughest mules best suited for the purpose, and we started forward. We marched to the Haros River, which we forded, and then ascending the high hills beyond discovered first a small trail, then a large well-beaten one, evidently that of the entire band of hostiles. The trail was about six days old, and as we passed over it, here and there, the carcasses of cattle only partially used, were found. The hostiles had but a short time previously moved their camp from the junction of the Haros and Yaqui Rivers, a few miles to the west, and were going to the east to the fastnesses of some extremely rugged mountains, the Espinosa del Diablo, or the Devil's Backbone — a most appropriate name, as the country was broken and rough beyond description. The march was now conducted mostly by night. We suffered much from the cold, and the one blanket to each man used when we slept was scanty covering. Often it was impossible to sleep at all. At times we made our coffee and cooked our food in the daytime, choosing points where the light could not be seen, and using dry wood to avoid smoke. Our moccasins were thin and the rocks were hard on the feet. Shoes had been abandoned, as the noise made by them could be heard a long distance. The advance scouts kept far ahead. Several abandoned camps of the hostiles were found, the selection of which showed their constant care. They were placed on high points, to which the hostiles ascended in such a way that it was impossible for them to be seen; while in descending, any pursuing party would have to appear in full view of the lookout they always kept in the rear. The labor of the Indian women in bringing the water and wood to these points was no apparent objection.

"Crossing the Haros River the trail led direct to the Devil's Backbone, situated between the Haros and Satachi Rivers. The difficulties of marching over a country like this by night, where it was necessary to climb over rocks and to descend into deep and dark canyons, can hardly be imagined. When we halted, which was sometimes not until midnight, we were sore and tired. We could never move until late in the day, as it was necessary to examine the country a long distance ahead before we started. No human being seemed ever to have been here. Deer were plentiful, but we dared not shoot them. Once I saw a leopard that bounded away with a shriek. It was spotted and seemed as large as a tiger. At last, after a weary march, at sunset, on the 9th of January, 1886, Noche, our Indian sergeant-major and guide, sent word that the hostile camp was located twelve miles away.

"The command was halted, and as the hostiles were reported camped on a high point, well protected and apparently showing great caution on their part, it was decided to make a night march and attack them at daylight. A short halt of about twenty minutes was made. We did not kindle a fire, and about the only food we had was some hard bread and raw bacon. The medical officer, Dr. Davis, was worn out, and the interpreter also, unfortunately, could go no farther. We had already marched continuously for about six hours and were very much worn out and footsore, even the scouts showing the fatigue of the hard service. These night marches, when we followed a trail purposely made over the worst country possible, and crossing and re-crossing the turbulent river, which we had to ford, were very trying. But the news of the camp being so close at hand gave us new strength and hope, and we hastened on to cover the ten or twelve miles between us and the hostiles. I cannot easily forget that night's march. All night long we toiled on, feeling our way. It was a dark and moonless night. For much of the distance the way led over solid rock, over mountains, down canyons so dark they seemed bottomless. It was a wonder the scouts could find the trail. Sometimes the descent became so steep that we could not go forward, but would have to wearily climb back and find another way. I marched by poor Captain Crawford, who was badly worn out; often he stopped and leaned heavily on his rifle for support, and again he used it for a cane to assist him. He had, however, an unconquerable will, and kept slowly on. At last, when it was nearly daylight, we could see in the distance the dim outlines of the rocky position occupied by the hostiles. I had a strong feeling of relief, for I certainly was very tired. We had marched continuously eighteen hours over a country so difficult that when we reached their camp Geronimo said he felt that he had no longer a place where the white man would not pursue him.

"The command was now quickly disposed for an attack, our first object being to surround the hostile camp. I was sent around to the farther side. Noiselessly, scarcely breathing, we crept along. It was still dark. It seemed strange to be going to attack these Indians with a force of their own kindred who but a short time before had been equally as criminal. I had nearly reached the farther side, intending to cut off the retreat, when the braying of some burros was heard. These watch-dogs of an Indian camp are better than were the geese of Rome. I hurried along. The faint light of the morning was just breaking, and I held my breath for fear the alarm would be given, when all at once the flames bursting from the rifles of some of the hostiles who had gone to investigate the cause of the braying of the burros, and the echoing and re-echoing of the rifle reports through the mountains, told me that the camp was in arms. Dim forms could be seen rapidly descending the mountain sides and disappearing below. A large number came my way within easy range—less than 200 yards. We fired many shots, but I saw no one fall. One Indian attempted to ride by me on a horse; I fired twice at him, when he abandoned the horse and disappeared; the horse was shot, but I never knew what became of the Indian. We pursued for a time, but as few of our Indian scouts could have gone farther, we had to give up the pursuit. The hostiles, like so many quail, had disappeared among the rocks. One by one our scouts returned. We had captured the entire herd, all the camp effects and what little food they had, consisting of some mescal, some fresh pony meat, a small part of a deer and a little dried meat, which the scouts seized and began to devour. I had no desire for food. Every one was worn out and it was cold and damp. In a little while an Indian woman came in and said that Geronimo and Natchez desired to talk. She begged food, and left us bearing word that Captain Crawford would see the chiefs the next day. The conference was to be held about a mile away on the river below our position, and he desired me to be present. What would have been the result of this conference will never be known on account of the unfortunate attack of the Mexicans next day. It was fortunate that we occupied the strong position of the hostile camp. Our packs, as well as the doctor and interpreter, had been sent for, but unfortunately they did not arrive that night.

"We built fires and tried to obtain a little rest, but I could not sleep on account of the intense cold, and, besides, we had been without food for many hours; in fact, we had not partaken of cooked food for days. With the continual marching day and night no wonder our Indians were tired out, and now threw themselves among the rocks to sleep, failing to maintain their usual vigilance. We had no fear of an attack. At daylight next morning the camp was aroused by loud cries from some of our scouts. Lieutenant Shipp and I, with a white man named Horn, employed as chief of scouts for my companies, ran forward to ascertain the cause of alarm. We thought at first that the disturbance must have been occasioned by the scouts of Captain Wirt Davis. A heavy fog hung over the mountains, making the morning light very faint. But by ascending the rocks we could see the outlines of dusky forms moving in the distance. Then all at once there was a crash of musketry and the flames from many rifles lighted up the scene. In that discharge three of our scouts were wounded, one very badly, and we quickly sought cover. The thought that it was our own friends who were attacking us was agonizing, and we had not the heart to retaliate, but the scouts kept up a desultory fire until Captain Crawford, whom we had left lying by the camp fire, shouted to us to stop. In about fifteen minutes the firing ceased, and it now became known that the attacking party were Mexicans, a detachment of whom, about thirteen, were seen approaching, four of them coming toward the rocks where we were. As I spoke Spanish, I advanced about fifty or seventy-five yards to meet them and was followed by Captain Crawford. I told them who we were and of our fight with the hostiles, that we had just captured their camp, etc. Captain Crawford, who did not speak Spanish, now asked if I had explained all to them. I told him I had. At this time we were all standing within a few feet of each other.

"The officer commanding the Mexicans was Major Corredor, a tall, powerful man over six feet high, and he acted as spokesman. Looking to the rocks we could see the heads of many of our Indian scouts with their rifles ready, and could hear the sharp snap of the breech-blocks as the cartridges were inserted. I can well recall the expression on the faces of these Mexicans, for they thought our scouts were going to fire; indeed, I thought so myself. At the same time I noticed a party of Mexicans marching in a low ravine toward a high point which commanded and enfiladed our position, about 400 yards distant. I called Captain Crawford's attention to this as well as to the aspect of our own scouts. He said: 'For God's sake, don't let them fire!' Major Corredor also said: 'No tiras'—Don't fire. I said to him, 'No,' and told him not to let his men fire. I then turned to the scouts, saying in Spanish, 'Don't fire,' holding my hand toward them. They nearly all understood Spanish, while they did not speak it. I had taken a few steps forward to carry out the captain's instructions when one shot rang out distinct and alone; the echoes were such that I could not

tell where it came from, but it sounded like a death-knell, and was followed by volleys from both sides. As we all sought cover I looked back just in time to see the tall Mexican throw down his rifle and fall, shot through the heart. Another Mexican, Lieutenant Juan de La Cruz, fell as he ran, pierced by thirteen bullets. The other two ran behind a small oak, but it was nearly cut down by bullets and they were both killed. Nine or ten others who were in view rapidly got close to the ground or in hollows behind rocks, which alone saved them, as they were near, and formed a portion of the party that advanced. Upon reaching the rocks where I had sought shelter I found Captain Crawford lying with his head pierced by a ball. His brain was running down his face and some of it lay on the rocks. He must have been shot just as he reached and mounted the rocks. Over his face lay a red handkerchief at which his hand clutched in a spasmodic way. Dutchy stood near him. I thought him dead, and sick at heart, I gave my attention to the serious conditions existing. The fall of Captain Crawford was a sad and unfortunate event, greatly to be deplored, and cast a gloom over us which we could not shake off.

"Being next in command, I hastened to send scouts to prevent the attack attempted on our right above referred to, and after an interval of about two hours the Mexicans were entirely routed and the firing gradually ceased. They now occupied a strong line of hills, with excellent shelter, were double our strength, and were armed with 44-calibre Remington rifles, which carried a cartridge similar to our own. Our command was without rations and nearly without ammunition, the one beltful supplied to each scout having in many cases been entirely exhausted in the two fights. It was true that many of them had extra rounds, but I estimated that between 4,000 and 5,000 rounds had been fired and that some of the men had none left.

"The Mexicans now called to us saying they would like to talk, but they were too cautious to advance. When Mr. Horn and I went forward to talk to them, three or four advanced to meet us about 150 yards from our position. The brother of the lieutenant who had been killed was crying bitterly, and the whole party seemed a most forlorn company of men, and sincere in saying that they thought we were the hostiles. All their officers were killed, and I believe others besides, but how many we never knew. The fact that our command was composed almost entirely of Indians was a most unfortunate one. With regular soldiers all would have been clear. Our position at this time, confronted as we were by a hostile Mexican force, while behind us was the entire hostile band of Indians evidently enjoying the situation, is unparralleled. We had scarcely any ammunition, no food, and our supplies were with the pack-train almost unprotected—no one knew where—while we were many days' march from our own country, which could only be reached through a territory hostile to our Indians. The governor of Sonora had made serious charges against the Indians for depredations committed on the march down, and besides, there was a bitter feeling caused by this fight. If the Mexicans had attacked us in the rear, where we were entirely unprotected, our position would have been untenable. Had such an attack been made the result would probably have been the scattering of our command in the mountains, our Chiricahuas joining the hostiles.

"It looked very serious, and my future course was governed by the condition. I was bound to protect the lives of the white men of the command, the pack-train, and our Indian scouts, if it were possible. Lieutenant Shipp and I were in accord, he appreciating as I did our desperate position. The first attack had been a mistake, and the second had been brought on before the Mexicans could know what had been said to their officers who had been killed. The Mexicans deplored the affair and seemed sincere. I felt a pity for them. They asked me to go with them while they carried their dead away. A small detail took the bodies one by one to their lines, and I went with each body. They then asked me to send our doctor to care for their wounded, and to loan them enough of the captured stock to carry their wounded back. I agreed to do this, but could give them no food, which they also asked. Late in the day the doctor arrived, and after he had attended to our wounded I sent him to look after theirs, some of whom were in a dangerous way. He attended five of them.

"The next day I decided to move on, as the surgeon said that the death of Captain Crawford was a matter of but a little time, and our condition made it necessary for us to try and reach our pack-train for supplies and ammunition. I was afraid that the Mexicans might take our pack-train, as it had but a poor escort of the weak and sick. Besides, most of the packers had been armed with 50-calibre carbines (Sharps), while they had been supplied with 45-calibre ammunition. I was in hopes that when away from the Mexicans I might succeed in effecting a conference with the hostile chiefs, and possibly a surrender. This could not be done while the Mexicans were near and they would not move before we did, as they said they were afraid they might be attacked by the scouts. In order to move Captain Crawford I had to make a litter and have him carried by hand. As there was no wood in the country, I sent to the river and got canes, which we bound together to make the side rails, using a piece of canvas for the bed.

"While busy attending to the making of this I heard someone calling, and going out a short distance saw Concepcion, the interpreter, standing with some Mexicans about 200 yards away. He beckoned to me and I went forward to talk to the men, as I was the only one who could speak Spanish, Horn being wounded. I had sent Concepcion to drive back some of the captured Indian stock which had wandered off during the fight. As I advanced toward the Mexicans they saluted me very courteously, and in a friendly way said that before they left they wanted to have a talk. It was raining and they asked me to step under a sheltering rock near by; this was the very point from which they had first fired. On stepping under the rock I found myself confronted with about fifty Mexicans, all armed with Remington rifles, and a hard looking lot. I would here state that I had sent them, according to my promise, six of the captured Indian horses, which, however, they had not received,

"I CAME TO CAPTURE OR DESTROY YOU."

as they said the horses were no good, being wounded and worn out; but of this I did not know at the time. Old Concepcion was detained by them. He was a Mexican who had been stolen by the Apaches when a boy, and was employed as an interpreter, as he knew the Apache language.

"The manner of the Mexicans when they found me in their power had undergone a marked change. They became insolent, stating that we had killed their officers and that we were marauders and had no authority in their country. They demanded my papers. I explained that there was a treaty between Mexico and the United States, but that I had no papers, as Captain Crawford had left all our baggage with the pack-train. Their language was insolent and threatening. I now appreciated my position and realized that the consequence of my being away from the command with the interpreter was that there was no one with the scouts who could make himself understood by them. The Mexicans stated that I had promised them animals to take back their wounded, and had not furnished them, as those I had sent were worthless. I told them I would send them other animals on my return, and started to go, when they surrounded me, saying that I must remain until I had sent the mules.

"By this time our Indians were yelling and preparing to fight. A few shots would have precipitated matters. The Mexicans called my attention to the action of my scouts, and I told them that the Indians evidently feared treachery, and that I could not control them while away. They then said I could go if I would send them six mules, after which they would leave the country. This I promised I would do, but they would not trust my word of honor and held old Concepcion a prisoner till I sent them the mules. I demanded a receipt, which they gave, and afterward Mexico paid our government the full value of the animals.

"It was now too late in the day to move, but the next morning I proceeded on the homeward march, carrying Captain Crawford by hand. The Indians, always superstitious, did not want to help, but were persuaded, Lieutenant Shipp and I also assisting. To add to the difficulty, it was the rainy season, and the steep mountain sides were climbed most laboriously. It would be difficult to describe this march. With great effort, the first day we only made two or three miles. The wounded Indian was placed on a pony, and although badly hurt, seemed to get along very well. The two other wounded scouts and Mr. Horn were so slightly injured that they moved with no trouble.

"An Indian woman came into camp that night and said that Geronimo wanted to talk. I concluded to meet him, and the next morning, after moving about two miles, I left the command and went with the interpreter, Mr. Horn, and five scouts, to a point about a mile or so distant. We went without arms, as this was expressly stipulated by Geronimo as a condition. The chiefs did not appear, but I had a talk with two of the men, who promised that the chiefs would meet me the next day. They said I must come without arms. The next day I went to meet them and found Geronimo, Natchez, Nana and Chihuahua with fourteen men. They came fully armed with their belts full of ammunition, and as I had come unarmed, according to agreement, this was a breach of faith, and I did not think it argued well for their conduct. Apparently suspicious of treachery, every man of them sat with his rifle in an upright position, forming a circle nearly around me, with Geronimo in the center. He sat there for fully a minute looking me straight in the eyes. Finally he got up and said to me:

"'Why did you come down here?'

"'I came to capture or destroy you and your band,' I answered.

"He knew perfectly well that this was the only answer I could truthfully make. He then walked up to me and shook my hand, saying that he could trust me, and then asked me to report to the department commander what he had to say. He enumerated his grievances at the agency, all of which were purely imaginary or assumed. I advised him to surrender and told him that if he did not neither the United States troops nor the Mexicans would let him rest. He agreed to surrender to me Nana, one other man, his (Geronimo's) wife, and one of Natchez's wives, with some of their children—nine in all—and promised to meet General Crook near San Bernardino in two moons to talk about surrendering. With this understanding I returned to camp. In a short time he sent the prisoners with the request that I give him a little sugar and flour. This request I complied with, having in the meantime sent some of my scouts for the pack-train, which they had found and brought back. Here, almost at midnight, I was awakened by the scouts who had assembled saying that they had seen the Mexicans approaching to attack us, and that they must have ammunition. I had not intended to issue any more just then, as we only had about 3,000 rounds left, but they begged so hard that I finally issued 1,000 rounds, though I could hardly believe this report. No Mexicans appeared. The hostiles had plenty of money, and it was afterwards reported that our scouts had sold them ammunition at the rate of one dollar per round.

"The next day we continued our march, which was very difficult on account of our being encumbered with our wounded. On the 17th of January, while sitting with Captain Crawford, he opened his eyes and looked me straight in the face and then pressed my hand. No doubt he was conscious, and I tried to get him to speak or write, but he could not. I assured him I would do all in my power to arrange his affairs, and he put his arm around me and drew me to him, but could only shake his head in answer. This conscious interval only lasted about five minutes, and then the look of intelligence seemed to pass away forever. The next day he died while we were on the march, passing away so quietly that no one knew the exact time of his death. We wrapped the body in canvas and placed it on one of the pack mules. We now moved more rapidly, but when we reached the Satachi River we could not cross it, as it was swollen by the late rains and was deep and turbulent. We were thus forced to go into camp and lose a day. In the meantime the body of Captain Crawford began to decompose, so we hurried on, crossing the river the next day, and on the day following reached Nacori. Here we buried Captain Crawford, putting his body in charge of the presidente of the town and marking well the place of his burial. I could only get four boards (slabs) in the town, and used them in making a coffin, the body being wrapped securely in canvas.

"The disposition of the people was decidedly unfriendly, and at Baserac and Bavispe about 200 of the local troops were assembled with hostile intent. To add to the trouble, the scouts obtained mescal and were very unruly. I had to use great care to prevent a conflict at Baserac. I was obliged to pass through the town, as there was a mountain on one side and a river on the other. The officials refused at first to let me pass, but I moved some of the troops through, supported by the remainder, and avoided a conflict. At Bavispe the Indians obtained a large quantity of mescal, and the civil authorities tried to take our captured stock. I sent them out of the camp, and had they not left when they did I am sure the intoxicated Indians would have fired upon them. Here occurred a quarrel between a company of White Mountain Indian scouts and one of Chiricahuas. They loaded their rifles to fire upon each other, while the first sergeants of the two companies fought between the lines, but I finally succeeded in quelling the disturbance. The next day I hurried away, and without further difficulty reached Lang's Ranch, arriving there on February 1st. Up to that time we had marched over 1,000 miles.

"I was ordered to return, February 5th, to Mexico and look out for the hostiles who had agreed to signal their return. I camped about ten miles south of the line on the San Bernardino River, and remained there until the 15th of March, when a signal was observed on a high point about twenty miles south. I went out with four or five scouts and met some messengers from Geronimo and Natchez, near the point from which the signal had been made. They informed me that the entire band of hostiles were then about forty miles away, camped in the mountains near Fronteras. I told them to return and bring Geronimo and his band at once, as the Mexicans were in pursuit and liable to attack them at any time. On the 19th the entire band came and camped about half a mile from my command. One more warrior with his wife and two children gave themselves up, and I now had thirteen prisoners. I endeavored to persuade Geronimo and his band to go into Fort Bowie, telling them they were liable to be attacked by Mexican troops, but could only induce them to move with me to the Canyon de Los Embudos, about twelve miles below the border, where they camped in a strong position among the rocks half a mile away.

"I had notified the department commander upon the arrival of the messengers on the 15th, and on the 26th he arrived at my camp. In the interval, however, before General Crook arrived, Geronimo had almost daily come into my camp to talk to me and ask when the general would get there. On his arrival a conference was held and the hostiles promised they would surrender. General Crook then returned, directing me to bring them in. This I endeavored to do, but this surrender was only an agreement, no arms being taken from them, nor were they any more in my possession than when I had met them in the Sierra Madre Mountains. It was believed, however, that they would come in. Unfortunately they obtained liquor, and all night on the 27th I could hear firing in their camp a mile or so away. I sent my command on, and, accompanied only by the interpreter, waited for the hostiles to move, but they were in a bad humor. They moved their camp at noon that day and I then left. I met Geronimo and a number of warriors gathered together near by on Elias Creek, many of them being drunk, and Geronimo told me they would follow, but that I had better go on or he would not be responsible for my life. I then proceeded to my camp. I had ordered the battalion to camp at a point ten miles on the way back on the San Bernardino. That afternoon the hostiles came up and camped about half a mile above me in a higher position.

"I went into their camp and found trouble. Natchez had shot his wife, and they were all drinking heavily I sent Lieutenant Shipp with a detail to destroy all the mescal at a ranch near by, where they had previously obtained all their liquor. During the day all seemed quiet, but at night a few shots were heard. I sent to find out the cause and found the trouble was over some women; this trouble soon ceased, however, and quiet was restored. I felt anxious about the next day's march, as I would then cross the line and be near troops. The next morning I was awakened and told that the hostiles were gone. I caused a careful search to be made, and ascertained that Geronimo and Natchez, with twenty men, thirteen women and two children had gone during the night, and not a soul, as far as I could ascertain, knew anything of the time they had gone, or that they had intended to go. Chihuahua, Ulzahney, Nana, Catley, nine other men, and forty-seven women and children remained. The herd was brought in, and only three of their horses were missing. I directed Lieutenant Faison, with a sufficient detail, to take the remaining hostiles to Fort Bowie; then, with all the available men left, Lieutenant Shipp and I at once started in pursuit.

"About six miles from camp we struck the trail going due west over a chain of high mountains. This gave us a full view of the mountains in all directions, but the trail suddenly changed its direction to the south and went down a steep and difficult descent, across a basin so dense with chaparral and cut up with ravines as to make travel very difficult and slow, especially as every bush was full of thorns which tore ourselves and animals. Across this basin, about ten miles, the trail ascended a high mountain, very steep and rocky. The trail of the one horse with the hostiles induced us to think it might be possible to ride, but after reaching the top we found this horse stabbed and abandoned among the rocks; they were unable to take it farther. Beyond, the descent was vertical and of solid rock from 50 to 300 feet high for miles each away. Here the trail was lost, the Indians having scattered and walked entirely on the rocks.

"No doubt our pursuit had been discovered from this point when we crossed the mountain on the other side of the basin, ten miles away. These Indians were well supplied with telescopes and glasses, and a watch had doubtless been maintained here according to their usual custom. It is in this way, by selecting their line of march over these high points, that their retreat can always be watched and danger avoided. In the same way they watch the country for miles in advance. These never-failing precautions may serve to show how difficult is the chance of catching these men, who once alarmed are like wild animals, with their sense of sight and of hearing as keenly developed.

"We could not descend here, so we were obliged to retrace our steps down the mountain and make a circuit of ten miles to again strike the trail beyond. This we did, but when the stream beyond was reached it was dark, and further pursuit that night was impossible. Next morning we moved down the creek, cutting the trails which had come together about four miles below, and we followed this for about ten miles to the south. The hostiles had not stopped from the time they had left, and now had made about forty-five miles and had good ten hours the start. The trail here split and one part, the larger, crossed over the broken mountains north of Bavispe, into the Sierra Madres, while the other crossed into the mountains north of Fronteras.

"The scouts now seemed discouraged. Their moccasins were worn out by the constant hard work of the past five months, and the prospect of returning to the scenes of their last trials was not inviting. Besides, their discharge would take place in about one month. They appealed to me to go no farther, telling me that it was useless, etc. This I appreciated and decided to return. We then retraced our way and continued the homeward march. While returning, two of the escaped hostiles joined me and gave themselves up. I arrived at Fort Bowie on the 3d of April. The results of the expedition were by no means unimportant, as we had secured the larger part of the hostiles, seventy-nine in all, of whom fifteen were warriors."

THE INDIAN AT LAST SUBDUED

WITH the close of the year 1886 the Indian wars practically came to end. Not that there were no uprisings of the tribesmen after that, or that all was peace and happiness. Trouble was still brewing constantly and peace was maintained only at the price of constant vigilance on the part of the government. And that future outbreaks were not avoided is seen by the uprising in 1890, which assumed a most threatening aspect, and demanded extraordinary efforts on the part of the military authorities; but after all they were no more than the last convulsive movements of a dying race, the last delirious effort of a people doomed to extinction. The result was never in serious doubt. The epoch of real Indian armed resistance ended in 1886. It was then that he was subdued, conquered, overpowered. Brought into the reservations, the Indian was caged and kept under control. True, the reservations were vast areas of land, and furnished the savage son of the wilderness with ample space to create the illusion that he could still roam about in nature's freedom. But it was a mere illusion. He simply had a large cage, which, year after year, was made smaller, imperceptibly at first, gradually at the beginning, but with less regard for his feelings later on and always systematically and methodically. And thus one reservation after the other was taken from the Indians and opened to the wild scramble of the white settler—opened up for civilization, and the confines of the savages became narrower and narrower.

Sentimental people might deplore the fate of the Indian as something intensely tragic. As a matter of fact his fate was but the result of that inexorable rule which has been called the survival of the fittest. The Indian race's fate was sealed when the first white man set his foot upon the virgin soil of this great continent. His doom thereafter was only a question of time. The two races met, barbarism and the civilization of a new era clashed and the outcome could only be the survival of the fittest. There is no sentiment about this law of nature; it is inexorable, unchangeable. In 1886 the subjugation was complete. The Indian was no longer a menace to the safety of the country. From a foe, who spread terror and fear, he had degenerated into a "ward of the nation," the object of the government's care and solicitude; to be petted upon good conduct, spanked when refractory.

There were a few among the Indians who felt the humiliation which this condition brought upon their nation. Unable to view the situation philosophically and submit to the inevitable with resignation, imbued, too, with a true spirit of Indian patriotism they once more decided to throw off the white man's yoke and invoked the religious prejudices of their kinsmen to inflame their spirit of war. And then the great outbreak of 1890 followed.

THE MEMORABLE OUTBREAK OF 1890

CHARLES A. VARNUM,
Captain, Co. B, 7th U. S. Cavalry.
Highest rank attained: Major,
U. S. A.
Born at Troy, N. Y., June 21, 1849.

RELIGIOUS fanaticism was primarily the cause of those Indian troubles which in 1890 and 1891 commanded the attention of the entire country and placed the Indian question in the foreground of public discussion. The uprising assumed such threatening proportions that the largest and most formidable Indian war in the history of this country seemed inevitable. Happily for the people of the United States the fears were not realized, and the anticipated war was averted; happily for the white people of the United States, but happily also for the Indians themselves. The result would never have been in doubt and the extermination of whole tribes would have been the outcome. The timely death of Sitting Bull, than whom there has never been a craftier or shrewder Indian chief, averted the threatened danger and caused a complete collapse of all hostile preparations.

The religious fanaticism spoken of was created by the appearance of a Messiah among the various Indian tribes. Early in 1890 religious fervor suddenly seized the Utes. A white man appeared in their midst who by his assumed or genuine piety soon gained the respect and friendship of the Indians.

He pretended to have inspirations from above and predicted the coming of an Indian Messiah who would deliver his race from the bondage of the white man, resuscitate the spirits of the departed dear ones and restore the oppressed and enslaved tribes to the full possession of their hunting grounds and the dominion of their ancestors.

As the wish is father to the thought, so does the human mind accept for true whatever conforms to its longings and wishes.

The white man had no trouble in finding willing believers of his prophecies among the Indians, since they gratified so much their innermost and eager desires.

In order to prepare themselves for the arrival of this Messiah the Indians instituted a so-called "Messiah" or "ghost" dance, and thus lent their newly-created religious fervor a more forcible expression.

During the summer of 1890 the Sioux and Arapahoes paid the Utes their customary annual visit, and on that occasion became acquainted with the strange white preacher, the prophecy of the red Messiah and the ghost dance. They, too, readily fell victims to the new religion and carried its fascinating ceremony—the dance— to their homes in their own reservations.

Then the Messiah doctrine began to spread and extend from one tribe to another, and before it could be explained how the myth had traveled or how it could have been carried to such far-away tribes, the whole Indian race in the northwest and west became infected with the craze, for such it had now become. Every tribe expected deliverance from its own Messiah, every lodge was eager to outdo the other in preparing for the coming of this Redeemer.

Half consciously the Indian realized that his race was doomed to utter destruction. Once his nation was powerful and strong, the undisputed master of this vast country. The white man came, and with him came another civilization. Unable to either cope with the intruder or accept his civilization, he saw his race decline and decay. His powers vanished and his glory disappeared. As civilization progressed, the Indian retreated; territory after territory was taken from him by force, by fraud, by trade and barter, by promises, by any and all means, no matter how. Thus was the Indian compelled to recede, to relinquish the ancestral ground, the land where from time immemorial his tribe had lived, hunted, made merry and buried its dead.

True, the Indian sometimes revolted, resisted, went to battle the pale-faced intruder; but each war only accentuated his helplessness in a more glaring light, and sullenly he submitted to the inevitable fate, to be ruled by the white man and to await the final extinction before the relentless march of a death-bringing civilization. Left to his own resources the Indian was doomed.

Now came the new religion and a ray of hope sprung up in the heart of the despairing Indian. Heaven itself was to bring him salvation. It was to send him the Messiah. Where he was helpless the Messiah would act.

Was it strange that the new creed spread like wildfire, that it found followers? Was it so singular that the Messiah or ghost dance should be performed in every Indian camp and village?

At first the dance and the accompanying ceremonies bore a purely religious character, free from any political tinge. Soon, however, the medicine men and political schemers, ambitious chiefs and intriguing warriors seized upon the opportunity and used the dances to further their own selfish plans and ends, and ere long the movement turned into one huge political conspiracy—death and destruction to the white conqueror became the aim, America for the Indians the slogan.

The Messiah dance has been variously described, but the manner in which it is most generally indulged in is as follows:

A high priest, a leading medicine man, has entire charge of the ceremonies. He is assisted by four helpers, who have to start or stop the dance as they see fit; they are empowered to inflict punishment on any person who disobeys their orders.

Those who are to participate in the dance prepare themselves by a sweat-bath, while the high priest and his assistants engage in prayer.

The sweat-baths are taken in tents erected for this purpose. Poles are stuck in the ground and the tops are bent and securely tied. Blankets and robes are thrown over this frame-work to such thickness as to render the interior as nearly air-tight as possible. A fire is then started inside in a hole in the ground and good-sized stones

THE BATTLE OF WOUNDED KNEE CREEK.

are heated. The participants now enter the tent and proceed to force the perspiration by sitting almost naked upon these heated stones. The atmosphere is made still more disagreeable by pouring water on the stones and thus filling the interior of the tightly-closed tent with steam and vapor. Attendants keep hot stones in readiness as long as the youths are able to stand the confinement. The pipe is vigorously smoked during the sweat, and smoke, heat, vapor and steam all contribute to produce a peculiar effect upon the participants and prepare their minds for the approaching exultation at the dance.

Finally the young men emerge from the enclosure, perspiration fairly streaming from every pore.

Weather permitting, they plunge into a pool in the creek near by, but if the air be too chilly blankets are thrown about their bodies.

The high priest wears eagle feathers in his hair and a short skirt reaches from the waist nearly to the knees; the assistants are similarly dressed.

An invocation or prayer is then chanted by the high priest, while the multitude gather about the young fellows who are to execute the dance.

A sacred tree is the center of the scene, around which the terpsichorean evolutions are executed. Dancing, singing, praying, groaning and crying are kept up from beginning to end—a weird and ghost-like scene, especially at night, impressive in its earnestness, awe-inspiring in the ugliness of the participants and their peculiar motions. The dance is continued for hours, until the dancers fall to the ground exhausted and worn out.

The attitude of the authorities and those in charge of the Indians toward this new craze was such as to invite criticism. It seems to have been the general consensus of opinion that the Indian agents failed to grasp the significance of this outbreak of fanaticism, that they lacked in firmness and energy in meeting the situation, that by their own actions they themselves were responsible for the ghost dance being converted from a religious ceremony into a war dance.

Among the many Indian chiefs who from patriotic and ambitious motives were active in promoting and spreading the new movement the irreconcilable Sitting Bull was the leader.

He saw in the outburst of religious fervor a chance to arouse the warlike spirit of the noble sons of the great Wakautanka, to unite the many tribes of his great nation, the Sioux, and to be liberated from the yoke of the white oppressor.

Sitting Bull has been called an intriguer, a treacherous savage, a schemer, an Indian demagogue, a disturber, and yet, granting that he merited all these epithets, the memory of his gigantic, martial figure and commanding personality reflects him before the eyes of the world as one of the ablest and cleverest Indians that race has produced and a man whose very meanness—from the white man's standpoint—was inspired by the loftiest motives of love for the people of his race. While condemning him, nobody who has studied his remarkable career will withhold his admiration for him. True, he fomented trouble, incited his followers to rebel, inspired the war and brought misery and disaster to his people, but his aim and ideal were the liberty and independence of his race. "God Almighty made me an Indian, and he did not make me an agency Indian, and I do not intend to be one," he said on one occasion to General Miles, and now, when the Indians all over the northwest were agitated and uneasy, and he was surrounded by thousands of followers, he tried to impress this same sentiment upon the minds of the warriors.

Sitting Bull became the soul of the whole movement, the acknowledged leader of the dissatisfied tribes.

The first impetus to the general upheaval emanated from the Pine Ridge Reservation in South Dakota. The agent there, accompanied by fourteen Indian police, rode into White Bird's camp and attempted to stop the Messiah dance, which he considered to be a hostile demonstration.

But the Indians of the village met him with Winchesters and compelled him to return under penalty of death.

When the story of the boldness of these Indians and the display of weakness on the part of the agent was told it spread like wildfire. The Indians at the Rosebud and Standing Rock Reservations began to flock to the vicinity of Pine Ridge and the excitement among the whites and redskins increased.

The seat of the trouble was a tract of country embraced within the boundaries made by the Cannon Ball, Missouri and Niobrara Rivers and by a line north extending from Forts Robinson and Meade to the Cannon Ball. The number of Indians who were considered to be on the warpath was estimated at 4,000, while 6,000 others were regarded as doubtful and in need of constant observation.

At first the military force which had to cope with the situation consisted of one cavalry and two infantry regiments at Pine Ridge, one cavalry and one infantry regiment at the mouth of the Beele Fouche River, one regiment of infantry at Fort Pierre, one at Fort Yates, and one cavalry and two infantry regiments at Fort Keogh. The position of these forces was in the nature of a huge cordon that could be tightened or extended according to requirements. General Miles had charge of the military operations.

The presence of these troops was used by the Indian leaders to still further incense their warriors. "What are the soldiers here for?" they argued. "Are we to be molested even at our religious devotions?"

Large bands of Sioux had fled to the extreme north of the reservation and into the adjoining Bad Lands, where camps had been established.

The policy of the government was to mass troops, overawe the Indians and to avoid, if possible, a clash, counting upon the salutary effect which a skillful display of strength has upon a weaker foe.

General Miles was especially qualified to carry out the intentions of the government, and proved himself equal to the occasion.

The campaign which was now inaugurated had for its final object the hemming in of the hostiles, and by cutting off all avenues of escape it was intended to force them to surrender in preference to death by starvation. As winter was near and the Indians were not provided any too well with supplies, it was but a question of time till they would be forced to lay down their arms and ask for peace.

During the month of November the excitement continued with unabated strength.

Several attempts to induce the warriors by conference and persuasion to return to their reservations and villages failed.

By December 1st the government began to change its Indian agents, replacing incompetents with men of known integrity and ability. General Miles and Buffalo Bill, who had been given a commission as brigadier-general, agreed that the arrest of Sitting Bull would help to break the backbone of the rebellion and restore peace and quietness.

On December 7th General Miles reported that Lieutenant Gaston, Eighth United States Cavalry, had conferred with the Cheyennes at the Tongue River Mission, and General Brooke with a number of hostile chiefs whose warriors had gotten beyond reach in the Bad Lands. Both conferences, like all previous ones, failed of success, but the presence of so many troops and the activity of the commanders had an intimidating effect on many chiefs, and from December 12th to 15th the reports of Generals Ruger, Carr and Brooke showed that quite a number of tribes were delivering up their arms and coming in.

On December 15th it was learned that Sitting Bull was about to start out to join the hostiles in the Bad Lands, and a body of Indian police, followed by a troop of cavalry under Captain Fouchet and infantry under Colonel Drum, was sent to apprehend the Indian chief.

It was a dreary and difficult march, but the fatigues of the long and dangerous journey had been sufficiently provided against, and when the dawn of the first day appeared the expedition was within easy reach of its destination. The Indian police were the first to sight the tepees on the bank of the Grand River. The detail put the spurs to the horses and were at Sitting Bull's camp before the redoubtable chief or his warriors could realize what was about to happen. Bull Head, lieutenant, and Shaved Head, first sergeant, were in command of the police. No time was lost in parleying. The chief was hustled out of his tent and hoisted upon a waiting horse. The squad was ready to take up the return march. Sitting Bull at first raged and struggled, then, suddenly changing his mind, straightened up and began to shout commands for his own rescue. The police attempted to force him to silence by pointing their Winchesters at his head, but Sitting Bull refused to be intimidated and continued giving orders. Presently there was a shot. The policeman to the prisoner's right reeled in his saddle and fell dead to the ground. The police now became incensed and replied with a volley that had a deadly effect upon the frenzied warriors. Firing became general on both sides. In the confusion Sitting Bull's voice could be heard directing the battle, though himself a captive. He was calling upon his sons and warriors, his gaunt form far overreaching everybody else. Suddenly he dropped limp on the hard prairie, shot dead. Sitting Bull had given his last command, fought his last battle. It was some time before the police realized the great Indian's death—they thought he was shamming. His followers in the meantime began closing in from all sides, and matters assumed critical form for the brave little band of policemen. Captain Fouchet arrived just at the opportune time to assist them, and the appearance of the infantry and cavalry forced the Indians to bolt for the river.

With Sitting Bull, his two sons, Blackbird and Crowfoot, the latter a mere boy of twelve, were killed.

The death of the famous chief gave rise to considerable comment and much criticism. There was, too, another version of the occurrence, according to which Sitting Bull was shot down as he emerged from his tent in reply to a summons from a policeman and after his son, not knowing the purport of the presence of the armed force, had cried for assistance. It was also stated that one of the police lifted the old leader's scalp as a proud trophy and left his mangled body on the field, a horrible sight to behold.

It is unnecessary to state that the news of Sitting Bull's death had a depressing effect upon the hostiles in every camp. On December 17th fully 1,000 Indians surrendered. The next day skirmishes were reported at a ranch near Smithville.

On December 20th 500 friendlies left Pine Ridge to urge the hostiles in the Bad Lands to come in. A band of thirty-nine of Sitting Bull's followers also gave up their arms.

During the next week the situation became more favorable, large bands of hostiles continuing to come in.

December 27th the hostiles made two attempts to break up a camp of Cheyenne scouts on Battle Creek. Both attacks were repulsed, with several killed and wounded on both sides.

Colonel Forsyth, Seventh United States Cavalry, on December 29th located the camp of Big Foot, who, after having been captured, had made his escape and settled near Wounded Knee. Among the 150 male Indians of his camp, about one-third were refugees from Sitting Bull's dispersed band. There was likewise a large number of women and children in the tepees. In pursuance of orders from General Miles, Colonel Forsyth decided to disarm the Indians and ordered that the whole number appear before him, as he wanted to talk to them. With the sullenness characteristic of their race, the Indians obeyed and ranged themselves in a semicircle in front of the tent of Big Foot, who lay sick with pneumonia. By twenties they were ordered to give up their arms. The first batch went to their tents and returned with only two guns. This irritated Major Whiteside, who was charged with the execution of the order, and after a brief consultation with the colonel he ordered the cavalrymen, who were dismounted and formed in almost a square of about twenty-five paces, to close in. This was done and the Indians were now completely encircled. A detachment was then sent to search the tepees.

CORPORAL WEINERT WORKING HIS HOTCHKISS.

What happened next is a matter of conjecture, since it is impossible to get at the facts from the mass of conflicting statements. Two facts are, however, beyond controversy; namely, that the Indians had in their possession many arms, which they had secreted, and that the cavalrymen of the Seventh, Custr.'s regiment, had a grudge against the Indians. It is further beyond dispute that a shot was fired and fired by one of the Indians. At the same time the warriors made a rush for the troopers. And then ensued what can be termed only a carnage. Maddened by the sudden and unexpected shot and attack, without waiting for the command they reached for their rifles, and in an instant the whole front was one sheet of fire, above which the smoke rolled and obscured the scene from view. That first volley left few Indians to tell the awful story. When the atmosphere had cleared, the ground, saturated with blood, was found strewn with the bodies of wounded and dead warriors, while a few were seen to hurry away toward the bluffs to a place of safety. The wounded fought on the ground, till a blow from the butt-end of a rifle or a shot ended their miserable existence.

Big Foot lay in his tent killed, his body riddled with bullets. All about the narrow place the horribly-mangled bodies of the savages lay. Thus far the fighting was so close that the field guns could not be trained without danger to the soldiers. Now they were called into action after the fleeing Indians.

For an hour a most destructive fire was kept up, when the guns were silenced and the rifles dropped; the war of extermination had been carried out to the end. There was nothing left to shoot at.

Of the 150 male Indians only a few escaped with their lives, and these few were captured. Of the thirty-nine women captured twenty-one were wounded, while a number of them were killed on the field, together with several children.

The troops, too, lost heavily. Captain Wallace and twenty-five men were killed and two officers and thirty-four men were wounded, the probability being that owing to the close range at which the shooting was done many of the cavalrymen were struck by the bullets of their own comrades.

That during the fight many a heroic deed was performed by the troopers is certain, that more than one of the soldiers did not allow himself to be carried away by blind hatred and passion is admitted even by the unfortunate savages, and amidst the many acts of unpardonable slaughter and butchery there were, too, those of humanity and true soldierly virtues which serve to throw a ray of brighter light upon this gloomy battlefield.

Especially is this true of the following:

First Lieutenant Ernest A. Garlington, Troop A, Seventh United States Cavalry, and Second Lieutenant H. L. Hawthorne, Second United States Artillery, both of whom were severely wounded. First Sergeants Jacob Trautman, Troop I, and Frederick E. Toy, Troop G, Sergeant George Lloyd, Troop I, and Private James Ward, Troop B, the latter receiving a serious and painful wound, and Privates Mosheim Feaster, Troop E, Matthew H. Hamilton, Troop G, Marvin C. Hillock, Troop B,

George Hobday, Troop A, Herman Ziegner, Troop E, and Adam Neder, Troop A, all of the Seventh United States Cavalry, the last-named hero being severely injured.

Private John Clancey, Battery E, First United States Artillery, distinguished himself by truly heroic work in caring for his wounded comrades, and Private Joshua B. Hartzog, of the same battery, won general admiration and praise, when amidst the tumult and confusion he came to the assistance of his wounded artillery lieutenant and carried him away from the field of battle to a place of safety.

All these men received the Medal of Honor.

Corporal Paul H. Weinert, Battery E, First United States Artillery, rendered himself conspicuous by the calm and cool manner in which he served his gun, when all was excitement and confusion.

In referring to the incident, for which he was granted the Medal of Honor, Corporal Weinert says:

"After the heaviest part of the fight at Wounded Knee a lot of Indians got into a ravine, from which they were shooting with awful effect. The Seventh couldn't

PAUL H. WEINERT,
Corporal, Battery E, First U. S. Artillery.
Born in Pennsylvania, July 15, 1869.

get at them. I then took my little Hotchkiss down to the entrance of the ravine and blazed away. When I started I had three men. All of the Indians opened fire on us. One of my men went for ammunition and didn't come back. Everybody ran from the mouth of the ravine where I was to the top of and behind a hill about fifty yards away, excepting Joshua B. Hartzog and George Green. My captain called to me to come back, but I kept moving nearer the Indians, and kept on shooting. Seeing that I would not come, Lieutenant Hawthorne came toward me and was calling, when suddenly I heard him say: 'Oh, my God!' Looking around, I saw him lying on his side, and I then knew he had been hit. Hartzog ran to him and carried him back behind the hill. That left me alone with Green. I said: 'By God! I'll make 'em pay for that,' and ran the gun fairly into the opening of the ravine and tried to make every shot count. The Hotchkiss was a single-shot affair and had to be pulled off with a lanyard. They kept yelling at me to come back, and I kept yelling for a cool gun—there were three more on the hill not in use. Bullets were coming like hail from the Indians' Winchesters. The wheels of my gun were bored full of holes and our clothing was marked in several places. Once a cartridge was knocked out of my hand just as I was about to put it in the gun, and it's a wonder the cartridge didn't explode. I kept going in farther, and pretty soon everything was quiet at the other end of the line. Then the other guns came down. I expected a court-martial, but what was my surprise when gruff old Allyn Capron, my captain, came up to me and grasped me by the shoulders and said to the officers and men: 'That's the kind of men I have in my battery.'"

As has been stated before, a party of Indians, after the first few volleys, managed to break through the troops and escape to the ravine near by. They were pursued, and during the fighting that occurred here many acts of bravery were performed, notably by First Lieutenant John C. Gresham, who voluntarily led the pursuing party, and Sergeants William J. Austin, Albert H. McMillan and Private Thomas Sullivan, all of Troop E, Seventh United States Cavalry, who were also awarded the Medal.

Following this battle, reports of which had aroused the hostiles to the highest pitch of excitement, came an attack on the Catholic Mission at Clay Creek, December 30th. The Seventh Cavalry had just gone into camp after having repulsed an attack upon its supply train, when a courier brought the news of a fire at the Catholic Mission and a massacre of the teachers and pupils. Within twenty minutes the exhausted and worn-out cavalry were once more in motion on the way to the scene of action, a few miles distant. The Indians, 1,800 in number, under Little Wound and Two Strike, were found about a mile beyond the mission.

The fighting commenced at once, but on the part of the Indians peculiar tactics were followed, squads of forty warriors fighting at a time and the main body slowly retreating. Colonel Forsyth expected another ambush and refused to be drawn into dangerous ground. The Indians became cognizant of the fact that their ruse would not work and thereupon began to close in upon the regiment. They greatly outnumbered the troops and were already drawing their characteristic circle preparatory to a charge, when Colonel Henry, with the Ninth United States Cavalry, appeared on the scene and attacked the redskins in the rear. This forced the whole band of savages to flee.

In this engagement Captain Charles A. Varnum, Troop B, Seventh United States Cavalry, performed an act of great bravery, and thereby gained the Medal of Honor.

The order to retire had been given and was being carried out in the face of the steadily advancing savages. Captain Varnum realized that a further retreat would result in the cutting off of one of the troops, so disregarding orders he took the lead of his company and made a dashing charge upon the Indians, driving them back and gaining a commanding position, which he held until the Ninth Cavalry came to the assistance of the regiment.

First Sergeant Theodore Ragnar and Sergeant Bernhard Jetter, Troop K, Seventh United States Cavalry; Corporal William O. Wilson, Troop I, Ninth United States Cavalry, and Farrier Richard J. Nolan, Troop I, Seventh United States Cavalry, also displayed on this occasion, as throughout the campaign, qualities of the most conspicuous bravery and gallantry, for which they, were granted the Medal of Honor·

THE PERILS OF WINTER CAMPAIGNING

BENJAMIN H. CHEEVER, JR.,
First Lieutenant, 6th U. S. Cavalry.
Born in Washington, D. C.,
June 7, 1850.
Highest rank attained: Major, U. S. A.

TWO DAYS after the last engagement mentioned in the preceding story, on January 1, 1891, a short but sharp encounter occurred on the banks of the White River, at the mouth of the Little Grass Creek, in South Dakota.

Troop K, Sixth United States Cavalry, fifty-three men strong, was escorting a supply train to the camp of the regiment, on Wounded Knee Creek, several miles away. The day was intensely cold, the thermometer twenty degrees below zero. A sharp wind was blowing, which made the atmosphere still more icy and added to the hardships of the midwinter march. The train had covered considerable distance when presently a large band of Indians, estimated at from three to four hundred, approached.

From close observation it soon became apparent that the redskins were on the warpath and came prepared to open hostilities. Second Lieutenant Robert L. Howze, who was in command of the detachment, decided on a becoming reception for the braves, whose war-cries and howls rent the air as they came nearer and nearer. The country was slightly hilly and the lieutenant selected one of the highest knolls, which offered the best advantages for an effective defense.

This knoll was about 300 yards from the banks of the river, which was lined on both sides by a slight growth of woods.

Howze parked his horses and wagons and fortified himself as well as circumstances and time would permit. Then he calmly awaited the approach of the warriors. They made a sudden dash as if about to charge, but when within 600 yards were met with such a heavy and well-directed fire from within the barricades that they abandoned their intention and instead scattered in all directions.

Soon, however, they again collected, and now began to surround the pent-up troop. At various points they became aggressive and made determined attacks, which were repulsed through the cool bravery of the men. Sergeant Frederick Myers and Corporal Cornelius C. Smith, by chosing advanced positions, with the aid of four or five men each succeeded in frustrating several well-planned attacks of the savages.

The woods along the river offered the Indians protection from the fire of the soldiers and enabled them to maintain an annoying and threatening position.

With almost reckless bravery Lieutenant Howze with a small force made a sortie and charged the Indians concealed behind the trees, clearing the strip of woods

"WITH ALMOST RECKLESS BRAVERY THE TROOPS MADE A SORTIE."

completely. Accompanied by two brave troopers he then broke through the cordon of redskins and dispatched the two soldiers to the camp to notify the commander of the attack and apprise him of the siege. He then returned to his post and continued to hold the bloodthirsty Indians at bay until relief came.

The couriers arrived safely at the camp. They delivered their message to First Lieutenant Benjamin H. Cheever, Jr., who, after the hardships of a protracted campaign, was complacently sitting in his tent writing a letter to a friend. He was congratulating himself on a day of rest at last, and he had just penned the words: "Well, everything is quiet today, but there is no telling what moment something will pop," when he was disturbed by the couriers bringing the news of the attack on Troop K. A moment later a picket rushed by on his way to the tent of Colonel E. A. Carr. He reported heavy firing to the right of the camp, and said that it sounded like volley firing. The young lieutenant immediately reported the fact to Major T. C. Tupper, who was in command of the squadron to which he was attached, Troops F and I, and both officers ordered their horses saddled, for they knew that that squadron would be the first ordered out for detached service.

The captain of Cheever's troop was in a distant part of the camp, leaving the lieutenant in command. He ordered the men of the troop to get saddles and bridles ready, for the order was expected at once. It came a moment later, and in less than five minutes from the time the first alarm had been brought to camp the two troops were ready to go to the relief. Lieutenant Cheever sent an orderly to notify his captain of what had happened, and started out at a ringing gallop through the chilling winter air. Time was precious, and delay might jeopardize valued lives a few miles away. Waiting was not to be thought of.

A mile and a half had been quickly covered when Major Tupper, commanding the squadron, ordered the young officer to throw out an advance skirmish line of twenty men. He obeyed, taking charge of it himself, and leaving the troop in command of the second lieutenant, knowing that the captain would soon overtake his men. So quickly had the order been given, and so rapidly had it been executed, that Lieutenant Cheever had not been able to determine how many men he had with him, until the little force were deployed as skirmishers, when he found that there were but thirteen, sometimes considered an unlucky number. But he had no time just then to make inquiries and dashed ahead at a run till he and his small command were nearly two miles in advance of the main body of troops. The sound of firing in front became more and more distinct as they rushed on.

Arriving at the top of a high bluff he discovered the Indians on the opposite side of the White River. They reviled him and dared him to come up with his force. Between him and them, where the beleaguered troop was also located, flowed the river, half frozen and filled with floating ice, flanked on both sides by precipitous cliffs, which towered to a height of several hundred feet directly in front of the troopers.

There was only one descent to the valley below, and that was by a narrow trail, so that the men had to close in on the center and proceed with great care, expecting any moment to be ambushed. The Indians were in every direction. On reaching the valley the troop was deployed in order that the banks of the river might be reconnoitered and a suitable ford found. No such ford was there, and knowing that the Indians would be upon him at any moment, and that if he remained where he was till the main body of troops came up he would be at a great disadvantage, both in numbers and position—for should the Indians get possession of the opposite bank of the river he could not hold his position—Lieutenant Cheever gave the order to advance.

CORNELIUS C. SMITH,
Corporal, Troop. K, 6th U. S. Cavalry.
Highest rank attained: Captain U. S. A.

Notwithstanding the great danger of crossing the frozen river, which must be done by swimming, the plunge was made. It was something awful, the crossing of that river, men and horses swimming and scrambling in the water and battling with the ice. For a time it looked as if half the little force would be carried away, but at last, after moments that seemed hours, all stood on the farther bank, their clothes soaked and freezing to their skins. There was no time to build fires, no time to think of anything but their beleaguered comrades ahead, so they pushed on till they stood on the crest of the hill, and there the action opened at once.

It was short and vigorous. Hardly fifteen minutes elapsed before the main body of Major Tupper's command came in sight, and the Indians, knowing that they were almost equally matched in numbers, were afraid to give a fair fight. They soon commenced a rapid retreat, carrying off their dead and disabled. The troops captured three ponies from the redskins, who numbered about 300. Troop K was relieved without the loss of a man.

It was a very cold day, and as the march back to camp was about fourteen miles, it was a decidedly worn out and hungry lot of troopers that arrived there just before midnight. The clothing of many was frozen stiff.

In addition to Lieutenant Cheever, Captain John B. Kerr and Sergeant Joseph F Knight fought with such distinction and gallantry as to receive the highest praise from the general commanding, General Miles, besides being awarded the Medal of Honor. Others who won the Medal in this engagement were Lieutenant Howze, Sergeant Frederick Myers and Corporal Cornelius C. Smith.

Following this affair there were numerous other engagements and encounters, but lack of provisions, internal dissensions, the death of Sitting Bull and, above all, General Miles's masterly handling of the situation—displaying his strength rather

"MEN AND HORSES BATTLED WITH THE ICE."

than using it—soon had their effect upon the Indians and it was not long before it became clear that the backbone of the movement was broken and the reaction had set in. Tribe by tribe came in and surrendered; one chief after another submitted to the inevitable, until at the end of January the war, which had threatened to assume gigantic proportions, was completely ended and General Miles closed the campaign with a magnificent midwinter parade of the troops under his command—a military spectacle such as the assembled and completely cowed Indians had never seen before, and in all probability will never see again.

So much adverse criticism of the methods employed in treating with the Indians was directed against the authorities that steps were taken by the latter to give the Indians fair and better treatment, and consequently there were fewer uprisings, this campaign of 1890–91 being the last war against the Sioux and in fact the last against the Indians in general, for the government has them under such control as to quell any outbreak at the very start. No serious uprisings of Indians have therefore occurred between 1891 and 1898 when, during the War with Spain, the last one was promptly subdued.

In the interim occasional raids were made by hostile bands through the sparsly populated sections of the west, which were always checked by small detachments of the military and the offenders punished. These raids cannot be regarded as wars or uprisings, for they were no more warlike in character than the raids by white desperadoes which likewise had to be checked by the troops, although whenever they occurred there was hard work for the troops engaged in the pursuit, testing their endurance to the utmost.

Particularly troublesome were Mexican bandits and rebels who came across the border into the States and terrorized the inhabitants by their plundering, an incident of which is related on the following page.

FOUGHT THREE MEXICANS SINGLE-HANDED

ALLEN WALKER,
Private, Troop C, 3d U. S. Cavalry.

THE Garza rebellion in Mexico in 1891, which was a revolt against the government of President Diaz, caused considerable trouble to the United States troops stationed along the Texas border line.

The rebels and other Mexican outlaws had established their rendezvous in the country on both sides of the frontier, and whenever pressed by the troops of the Mexican government crossed on to United States territory, where they were safe from further pursuit. Here they would assemble and gather their heterogeneous forces and map out their plans for the overthrow of the established government.

To put an end to the machinations of these conspirators the United States authorities were appealed to for the rigid enforcement of the neutrality laws. This led to the display of a considerable military force in southern Texas and gave the troops ordered thither much arduous duty, coupled with hardships and adventures which furnished many good stories for the campfires.

It fell to the good fortune of Private Allen Walker, of Troop C, Third United States Cavalry, to distinguish himself during this time.

On December 30, 1891, he was sent with dispatches from one post to another, and was riding along at a good speed when he encountered three well-armed Mexicans whom he knew to be in league with the rebel cause and to have violated the laws of this country.

The young soldier appreciated that their very presence on United States territory was in open defiance of the authority of his own government, and he said to himself: "These fellows may trifle with the laws of their own country, but by God they won't do it with mine!" And with almost reckless boldness he dashed right up to the three rebels and demanded their surrender. When his demand was ignored he opened up on them, and in a sharp but short conflict had one of them wounded, the horse of another killed and the third one put to flight.

He searched his prisoners and took from them some papers which proved to be documents of extreme importance concerning the Garza rebellion, and which contained the details of a plan for an organized invasion of United States territory. So important was the seizure of these papers that Walker received the Medal of Honor as a fitting reward.

"PRIVATE WALKER SEARCHED HIS PRISONERS."

THE BEAR ISLAND UPRISING

Eᴀʀʟʏ in October, 1898, an Indian uprising occurred at the Bear Island, Reservation of the Chippewas, in Minnesota, which caused much more excitement than it deserved, and was squelched within a week. In its scope it was really nothing more serious than an armed resistance of several hundred Indians against the execution of an order from the government, but it led to a fierce fight and for a time threw the whole country into a state of anxiety, because a repetition of the Custer massacre was feared. When reliable information from the seat of the trouble reached the War Department, and not only failed to confirm the first wild rumors, but brought news of the safety of the military detachment, the minds of the people were relieved and public excitement died away.

The cause of this disturbance was a peculiar one, and dated back at least one year.

An unscrupulous white man was arrested and taken to Duluth, Minn., for selling whisky to Indians on the reservation. Among the Indians who were produced as witnesses against the defendant was one who was a real "bad Injun." Such at least was his reputation.

He is described as a man of imposing physique, tall as a pine, bony and strong. He was the typical Indian in all his ways and actions. He wore the blanket, lived in a tent or the hollow of a tree, loved to roam about, despised work and hated the pale-faces. He was the ideal Indian. The United States authorities had some difficulty in inducing him to appear as a witness at Duluth, and succeeded only after promising him plenty of money, good treatment and the means to reach his home after the trial.

The promises, which were unquestionably unauthorized and certainly illegal, were not kept, and the Indian from the Bear Island Reservation was sorely disappointed. He had to walk and beg his way home, and reached his destination in a deplorable condition. This treatment of course was not conducive to a state of good feeling on the part of the Indian. When the second trial of the same defendant came off in the fall of 1897 the United States Marshal made much less ado about securing his testimony—he simply went to the reservation and took him to Duluth, where, after the testimony had been given, the Chippewa brave was once more turned loose to shift for himself. He again returned to his home, his heart filled with hatred for the white man, and determined to get even for the insults to which he had been subjected. He vowed vengeance and kept his word. Henceforth he followed the life of an outlaw. He stole, plundered, robbed, and, the authorities say, murdered. It is said he slew an old and prominent Indian chief. This conduct had a two-fold result: first, to inspire fear and terror; second, to surround him with a number of sympathizing followers. And so he gradually became a power among the Indians of the reservation. He created discontent and fanned it by calling attention to the conduct of certain officials who were taking advantage of the inexperienced Indians in their commercial dealings. It was not long until his agitation and reckless conduct became a real menace to the white settlers in the vicinity and the military authorities, and a warrant for his arrest was finally issued and placed in the hands of the United States Marshal for execution.

Anticipating trouble, General John M. Bacon with a detachment of 100 regulars accompanied the marshal on his errand.

On the approach of the military force the Indians became uneasy. Many of them did not know the significance of the expedition; others, especially those of troubled conscience, feared for their safety. The result was that some 400 Indians deserted their places of abode and flocked together, all armed to the teeth and incited by the previously-mentioned hostile brave to offer resistance.

General Bacon reached Bear Island in the forenoon of October 5, 1898. The day was sombre and dreary and intensely cold as the force landed at Leech Lake, having crossed the small lake in rowboats.

There wasn't an Indian in sight when General Bacon and his men arrived; ominous silence prevailed as far as could be seen or heard. Scouts were sent out, but came back with the report that no traces of Indians could be found. At noon the general assembled his small force and gave the order for dinner. The men dispersed, and some of them were about to prepare their frugal meal when suddenly and without warning a shot fired from an Indian hut near the shore struck a soldier in the breast, killing him instantly. As if this fatal shot had been the signal agreed upon, a band of Indians emerged from the woods and came yelling and dashing upon the surprised troopers. However, the soldiers, although taken completely unawares, were men of the true military stamp. Most of them had faced the savage many times before and were well acquainted with the tactics of the redskin.

They at once sought shelter behind stumps of trees and opened a well-directed fire at the on-coming Indians. A few volleys and the advance was checked. The men then retreated to the shore and there took up a strong and unassailable position. Once more the Chippewas made a dash, but were forced to retreat before the fire of the plucky little squad. Then the battle was ended and no further hostilities were offered.

The loss to the troopers during this short engagement was rather severe. Major Melville Wilkinson, Sergeant William Buller and Privates Ed. Lowe, John Olmstead, John Swallenstock and Alfred Zebell were killed and sixteen men sustained injuries more or less severe, while the loss to the Indians was very much smaller. However the news of the battle brought re-enforcements to the scene almost immediately, and within less than a week quiet was restored and the ringleaders in the hands of the authorities.

General Bacon received the commendation of the whole country for the cool and energetic manner in which he faced an unexpected emergency. Hospital Steward

Oscar Burkhard was awarded the Medal of Honor in recognition of his services during the engagement and in rendering aid to the wounded.

This battle concludes the history of the Indian wars. Their end was contemporaneous with the war with Spain. No outbreak by the hostiles worthy of recording in this history has occurred since this affair, and, as civilization is spreading among even the most savage tribes of the West, it probably will be recorded as the last armed resistance in force against the United States authorities. The red man has at last approached the stage of common reason, and this tells him that he has to abandon all hope of again following the nomadic life his fathers lived, and that he and his kin must adopt the mode and morals of living of the white man if their kind is not to be exterminated.

Whether or not civilization means death and extermination to the entire Indian race cannot be prophesied as yet. The truth is that the uncivilized Indian is dying off rapidly as he is brought into proximity with the white man and no effort is made on his part to adopt civilization. However, when once successful in changing his nomadic mode of living he and his children will prosper and increase in number. The Indian race of this type is not dying out.

Our later Indian wars had constantly grown more fierce. The courageous and wily hostile, a born hunter and warrior, became accustomed to the most modern weapons and no one understood and estimated his strength better than the soldier who confronted him in battle. Fighting single-handed, oftentimes without direction of an officer and relying on his individual tactics and resources, was the lot of our soldiers in these affairs, and it can be truthfully stated that the military methods employed in our later Indian wars have been used as a basis of military tactics in modern warfare. The individual soldier is expected to depend more on his own resources in battle than formerly, and, therefore, deeds of heroism and self-sacrifice will increase rather than decrease in coming wars.

AN OFFICER'S DEVOTION TO HIS MEN

O<small>N</small> the 23d of April, 1882, a detachment consisting of six men and six Indian scouts, commanded by Lieutenant McDonald, Fourth Cavalry, was attacked by a large band of Chiricahua Apaches, about twenty miles south of Stein's Pass, near the boundary line between Arizona and New Mexico. The men put up a brave fight, holding off the Indians with rare skill and courage. By dint of rapid firing and skillful manœuvring the men held the howling fiends in check and their trusty carbines made several of them measure their lengths upon the ground. One by one the brave men of this little squad fell wounded. Escape was impossible. Annihilation was in sight unless re-enforcements were brought up. As a last resort one of the scouts slipped away from the detachment and succeeded in making his escape from the desperate situation, and notified Lieutenant-Colonel G. A. Forsyth of the plight his comrades were in. Colonel Forsyth immediately set out at a gallop with Troops C, F, G, H and M, of the Fourth Cavalry, to the relief of the rest of Lieutenant McDonald's little party.

The sixteen miles which the troops had to travel to reach McDonald's command were covered in an incredibly short time, and when they arrived at the scene of action they found McDonald's men still defending themselves against the onslaughts of the Indians, but on the approach of the column the redskins fled. Pursuit was at once taken up and the hostiles were overtaken in a strongly entrenched position in Horseshoe Canyon, New Mexico. The command dismounted and promptly attacked them among the rocky ridges, varying from 400 to 1,600 feet high. While climbing one of these narrow gorges in the mountains two soldiers, one of whom was Private Edward Leonard, asked permission to secure an Indian pony just discovered some distance up the mountain at the side of a high bowlder. The men were told that it was probably an ambuscade, but not heeding the advice they started. They had not gone very far, however, when to their surprise a volley was fired from the top of the bowlder, and then only did they realize that the officers' surmise of an ambuscade was correct, and they hurried back over the jagged rocks. Leonard slipped and fell partly behind a rock, and was immediately shot through both his exposed legs. The other man rejoined the command. First Lieutenant Wilber E. Wilder, of the Fourth Cavalry, seeing Leonard's plight, at once advanced along the gorge to his assistance. The entire distance he was subjected to a severe fire from the Indian sharpshooters, but luckily he arrived at Leonard's side in safety, and then, with the ultimate assistance of Leonard's comrade, who had followed Wilder, he carried the wounded man down over the rocks amid generous volleys from the hidden Apaches. For his intrepidity in rescuing Leonard, Lieutenant Wilder was awarded the Medal of Honor.

The Indians were driven from rock to rock among the mountains, until they dispersed in every direction and further immediate pursuit was impracticable, They left behind them in this engagement thirteen Indians killed and several wounded. A number of their animals were also captured.

W<small>ARS</small> are the stern phenomena of nations. They have their periods of gathering like the elemental disturbances in nature, and usually these are of long duration. Warfare seldom results from a single overt act. It is usually brought about by a long series of abuses, which go on until some offense which in itself might not constitute a casus belli, serves as the last straw which breaks the camel's back.

Such was the case with the Spanish-American war. The first clouds showed in the southern horizon and the low muttering of thunder was heard away back in 1826. Spain had been exhausted by wars, and her American colonies, taxed and exploited as they had been for all possible revenue, grew weary of serving as the toys of a weak nation. Mexico achieved her independence and then divided into Mexico and Central America. One by one the South American colonies broke away, and then Bolivar decided to aid the Spanish West Indies to achieve their independence and thus to prevent Spain from having any foothold in the new world which might serve as a base of supplies in case of an attempt to reconquer any of the independent territory.

These states had earned the sympathy of the United States by their successful struggle for independence, but they prejudiced their case with the slave states by emancipating all slaves. When the South Americans sought to aid Cuba to her independence, the slave interest in the United States was influential enough to prevent the undertaking. Statesmen of the slave states looked a long away ahead, and they were afraid of the influence of emancipation in Cuba. By so doing, the United States was the indirect cause of seventy-five years of misery in Cuba and much loss of life.

American diplomacy prevented the liberation of Cuba in 1825, and the result was an insurrection of the dissatisfied Cubans in the following year. From that time insurrection, or the spirit of it, was present in Cuba until her liberation was accomplished with the help of the power which had so long delayed that end. The Spanish-American war was really a part of the heritage of slavery. Slave-owners were not satisfied with preventing the independence of Cuba. Shut off from extension in the United States and determined to maintain their influence in the government, they plotted to acquire Mexican, Central American and Cuban territory by conquest. It was this spirit of conquest, egged on by the slave states, which led to the acquisition of Texas, proceeded from that to the Mexican war and the filibustering expeditions of William Walker against the Mexican and Central American states, and of Lopez and others against Cuba.

Overtures were made to Spain several times for the purchase and annexation of Cuba for the purpose of extending the area of American slave territory, but Spain rejected them with scorn. Since 1825 the Cubans had been determined to achieve their liberty, and many Americans had looked forward to the day when the island would be annexed to the United States.

In 1868 an insurrection broke out in Eastern Cuba, and the war which followed lasted for ten years. This war was by no means free from interference. Adventurous Americans who sympathized with the Cubans violated the neutrality laws in supplying arms and ammunition to the insurgents, and one of these interferences came near involving the United States in a war with Spain.

In 1895 Cuba was again a hotbed of rebellion. At first the magnitude of the revolt was not fully appreciated, but it was soon seen that every province in the island was ready for war. Funds had been accumulated. Arms had been secured and hidden away. Leaders were chosen for military operations and a republican government set up, although it never had a permanent seat and never was able to obtain recognition from any responsible power. The eastern end of the island was virtually in the hands of the insurgents, and the successful stand made by them against the Spanish troops at Bayamo gave the Cubans high hopes. The general policy of Gomez, Garcia and Maceo, the principal leaders of the revolt, was to maintain a guerrilla warfare in defiance of Spanish authority and to avoid pitched battles as much as possible.

This policy proved harassing to Spain. The insurgents were able to subsist off the country, in spite of all efforts to suppress them and starve them out. General Martinez Campos, who had secured the peace of 1878, more by diplomacy than by military skill, was censured in Spain for being too gentle and considerate. The conservative party believed that a man of the Cromwell type, who would not hesitate to use any measure that promised to crush the rebellion, was needed in Cuba. Campos was recalled and Gen. Valeriano Weyler was given complete control.

Weyler soon found that it was a costly and vexatious proceeding to undertake the running down of the rebels in their own country. His own troops suffered severely from climatic troubles and the rebels could not usually be distinguished from the non-combatant rural population known as "pacificos." The pacificos were in hearty sympathy with the rebels and gave them all possible aid and comfort. Weyler changed his plan and abandoned pursuit. He concentrated his forces at Havana, Santiago, Cienfuegos and a few other towns where they could be subsisted easily and where re-enforcement would be an easy matter, whenever the insurgents became dangerous. He established lines of defense and communication by means of trochas or barriers of barbed wire, protected by block-houses placed at intervals and guarded by squads of regulars.

Then he undertook to prevent the rebels from subsisting off the country by concentrating the rural population in the towns and thus preventing the cultivation of agricultural products. This policy soon reduced thousands of people to the verge of starvation, and it fanned the sympathy of the people of the United States into indignation. Cuba became an Andersonville prison on a mammoth scale, and the emaciated reconcentrados in every garrisoned town were a sight to move hearts of stone.

While these things were transpiring in Cuba, excitement over the war was growing to a high pitch in the United States. The people and Congress were divided into factions. Hot-headed enthusiasts were demanding the recognition of Cuban independence. Those of milder sentiments wanted a recognition of the rights of Cubans as belligerents. The more conservative element stood out for the preservation of strict neutrality. President Cleveland was of this faction, and he and his supporters sat upon the safety valve of public opionion. In spite of the vigilance of the government the owners of a number of fast tugs and steamers engaged in filibustering, and thus the insurgents were supplied with arms and food. At the same time the jingo element was so noisy and the sympathetic press was so insistent upon some form of encouragement for the rebels and some form of reproof to Spain that Spain felt that the government was less sincere in its declarations of neutrality than its chief executive.

Something had to be done to pacify the clamor of the jingoes and also to assure Spain of our good intentions, so a concurrent resolution passed both houses of Congress. It acknowledged that a state of war existed in Cuba; it pledged the United States to a policy of strict neutrality and it tendered the good offices of the United States as a mediator between Spain and the insurgents. This, of course, really meant nothing at all. Spain ignored the resolution. President Cleveland paid no attention to it, and the jingo clamor for interference went on in Congress and in the columns of the press. It became a settled fact that the United States would not intervene in behalf of the Cubans until there was some cause which would compel the conservative element to justify the interference, or at least to give passive assent.

Among the hundreds of persons arrested on suspicion or for actual participation in the rebellion were many Cubans who had at some previous time been sojourners in the United States and had either become citizens or declared their intention of so doing. These claimed the protection of the United States, and their pleas kept the jingo element in a state of excitement, which threatened to precipitate intervention.

When the republicans came into power in 1897 it was found that the Cuban situation was difficult. All previous overtures had merely served to irritate Spain. It was simply impossible for the United States to attempt a settlement in the capacity of mediator. Spain regarded the United States as a secret foe which, wearing the guise of friendship, was really encouraging the insurgents, sending them arms and money, harboring a junta representing the rebel cause and shutting their eyes to the bold operations of filibusters. Spain really believed that the United States meant to lay hands upon Cuba in a spirit of conquest whenever the slightest provocation for interference would be found.

It was evident that the republican administration would be less tolerant of Cuban abuses than its predecessor, and when President McKinley made a demand for the release of American prisoners whose pleas had formerly fallen upon deaf ears Spain released them with surprising promptness. She did not want to leave a loop-hole or a pretext for interference, and by the end of April, 1897, all American prisoners were restored to liberty and redress was promised for their wrongs.

Negotiations were begun through General Stewart L. Woodford, the American minister to Spain, and Senor Depuy de Lome, the Spanish minister at Washington. Spain agreed, at the request of the United States, to recall General Weyler, whose harsh policy had earned the condemnation of all civilized nations. She also agreed to revoke the edict of reconcentration and thus put an end to the starvation and misery which resulted. To ward off an expected suggestion to grant the Cubans their independence, Spain asked the support and mediation of the United States while she would try a system of autonomous government.

This offer from Spain was rejected by the Cuban insurgents and the United States could not, and did not, urge them to accept Spain's offer. The recall of Weyler was the only thing accomplished. The autonomous government was an irritating and unsatisfactory experiment. Affairs in Cuba went as badly without Weyler as they had under his unrestricted rule. It was evident that intervention would continue to hang fire for an indefinite period unless some overt act by one party or the other should precipitate a crisis. General Blanco, Weyler's successor, made no appreciable change in the administration. Americans in Cuba again became restless, and the sympathizers of the Cuban cause in the United States began to agitate for intervention. To assure the Americans in Havana that their government did not propose to abandon them, the government ordered the battleship Maine to that port.

THE MAINE CATASTROPHE

UP to January 24, 1898, when the Maine arrived at Havana, the United States had shown a rare delicacy by keeping their ships of war away from Cuban ports, although the two nations, being at peace, had a perfect right to send warships to each other's ports. The Vizcaya, one of the Spanish cruisers afterward destroyed at Santiago, visited New York to offset the effect of the Maine's visitation, and she was cordially received. A crisis was approaching.

February 16th was the day of fate for both Spain and the United States. As the sun sank to rest in the waters of the distant gulf, Havana's fair harbor lay serene and peaceful in its ruddy glow. The green water of the bay was tinged with gold about the dozens of ships riding at anchor or loading at the wharves. The golden tinge deepened to blood red about the glistening whiteness of the massive hull of the Maine, which had tied up at a buoy designated by the authorities. The deep thunder of the evening guns was heard as the colors on the ramparts of Morro Castle and Fort Cabanas and the Maine were hauled down.

Passengers aboard the steamers in the harbor came on deck to watch the lights of the city and to listen to band music in the distance. The harbor front was alive with people coming and going, and except for the presence of uniformed officers and men of the rank and file of the Spanish army everywhere on the streets, there was no suggestion that the atmosphere was charged with war. Astern of the Maine, not more than a stone's throw away, lay the Ward liner City of Washington. A little farther away lay the Alfonso XII and the Legazpi on the starboard bow.

The sky became overcast and the atmosphere was very close. Captain Sigsbee, of the Maine, and all of the crew of 328 men and all but four of the twenty-six officers were on board.

At 9:10 Bugler Newton sounded taps. It was the last blast of that bugle. Thirty minutes passed with outside lights out and silence aboard, the only audible sound being the soft tread of the deck watch. Presently a sharp report like an explosion under the water somewhere forward was heard. It was followed by a lifting of the vast hulk of the battleship and a deafening roar which shook every building in the city and startled the thousands of people.

Several passengers who were sitting on the deck of the City of Washington were thrown from their chairs by the shock, and then they were subjected to a rain of falling debris which had been hurled hundreds of feet in the air by the explosion. At first they thought the Maine was going to be lifted clear out of the water forward, but she settled back with a heavy plunge and began to fill and go down by the head immediately.

Captain Sigsbee and all his crew were left in inky darkness, for at the second explosion every light in the ship went out. The captain hurried on deck as soon as possible. In the passage leading to the open part of the deck he ran into a man who was coming toward the cabin entrance. It was Private William Anthony, orderly

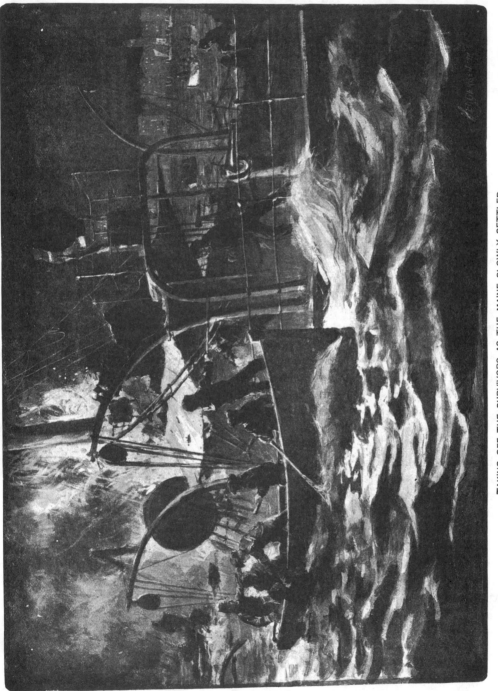

TAKING OFF THE SURVIVORS AS THE MAINE SLOWLY SETTLED.

at the cabin door. He stammered an apology and reported: "The Maine has blown up, sir, and we are sinking."

The two groped their way to the outer deck and looked about them in a dazed sort of way.

"What time is it, Anthony?" inquired Captain Sigsbee.

"The explosion took place at 9:40, sir," replied Anthony.

Lieutenant-Commander Wainright, hearing voices, made his way to the captain's side and other officers gathered about them. The most perfect discipline prevailed. The subordinates waited for orders, apparently as calmly as if the incident had been expected. The awnings were bagged with debris that had fallen after the explosion and a fire was burning forward.

"Put that fire out at once," ordered the captain, and Wainright took the matter in charge. Another officer was ordered to flood the forward magazine, but it was found to be already flooded by the sinking of the forward portion of the Maine. Lieutenant Hood and Cadets Boyd and Culverins, who made an inspection amidships to see what could be done toward subduing the fire, found the fire mains disabled, and there were no men to obey the call to fire duty. Nothing could be done, and the lieutenant so reported. It had not yet dawned upon the officers that there had been terrible loss of life.

As their eyes became more accustomed to the darkness the officers discovered one of the smokestacks hanging over the side. They also saw what appeared to be the forms of men struggling among a mass of debris in the water about the ship and faint cries for help were heard. Of the fifteen boats but three were available, the barge, the captain's gig and a whaleboat. These were immediately lowered and all possible speed was made in the work of rescue. Boats put off from the Alfonso XII, the City of Washington and other ships and gathered about the Maine, helping to rescue those who could be reached. The officers of the Alfonso XII were as zealous and courteous as men could be and some of the rescued were taken on board their ship, others on board the City of Washington, for attendance.

The Maine settled rapidly forward and then the stern began to go down. A whistling of air escaping from the bulkheads could be heard as she sank. In a short time the highest point of the quarter deck was just awash and it became necessary to abandon her. Captain Sigsbee was the last man to leave and it was with heavy hearts that he and the other officers pulled away, for they then realized that all who remained on board must be dead. They went on board the City of Washington, where Captain Sigsbee prepared the memorable dispatch to the Navy Department at Washington.

That message was like an electric shock to the people of the United States. The general impression was that the Maine had been destroyed by Spanish treachery. Upon taking second thought the more conservative newspapers came to regard the disaster as a probable accident. They felt that there could be no doubt as to the result of a war between the United States and Spain, and could not believe that the Spaniards would invite destruction by inflicting such a cowardly and dastardly wrong upon the sleeping crew of a vessel of a friendly power lying in a Spanish harbor where, if a crime was committed, it must inevitably be revealed.

On the day following the disaster it was found that only sixteen of the crew had escaped unhurt. Two officers, Jenkin and Merritt, and two hundred and fifty men had been killed. Of the one hundred and two who were saved, eight died from their injuries in the Havana hospitals. Expert divers worked about the wreck recovering the bodies and they were buried in a lot in the Havana cemetery dedicated to the use of the United States by the Spanish government. Subsequently the remains of the victims were removed to the United States.

An investigation was then conducted by American and Spanish officials, the latter holding that the explosion had been internal and therefore that no suspicion could attach to Spain. In spite of this the investigation conducted by the United States authorities showed that the Maine had been blown up by a mine placed beneath her forward section.

Proof of implicity of the Spanish officials, however, could not be obtained and therefore the Maine catastrophe was not mentioned in the declaration of war nor in the peace conference at Paris.

For forty days the people of the United States waited impatiently to learn the result of the Maine catastrophe investigation, and when it was sent in on March 28th the entire population knew what would follow. Yet, President McKinley withheld his message on the subject which was expected for fourteen days in order to give every American in Spain and in Cuba a chance to leave those countries.

The message reviewed the Cuban situation dispassionately and then announced that: "In the name of humanity, in the name of civilization and in behalf of endangered American interests which give us the right to speak and act, the war in Cuba must stop." President McKinley asked Congress to empower him to end the hostilities in Cuba, and to secure the establishment of a stable government, capable of maintaining order and observing its international obligations.

Congress empowered the president to act and an ultimatum was transmitted to Spain, whose answer to this brought a prompt declarartion of war from the United States.

THE BATTLE OF MANILA BAY

THUS, then, it was to be war! A war to free Cuba from spanish oppression.

On the following day, the 20th of April, President McKinley sent out an ultimatum to Madrid demanding Spain's withdrawal from the island of Cuba, and the Spanish minister in Washington demanded his passports. On the 21st the Spanish government notified the American minister at Madrid that diplomatic relations were suspended.

On Wednesday, the 27th of April, the Asiatic squadron of the United States Navy, commanded by Commodore George Dewey, left Mirsbay, near Hong Kong, for Manila. The ships were in the following order: Olympia (flag), Baltimore, Raleigh, Petrel, Concord and Boston, and in a separate line the revenue cutter McCulloch and the transports Zafiro and Nanshon, the latter with 3,000 tons reserve coal on board. The commodore had prepared this squadron for action with the utmost care.

The Olympia, Boston, Raleigh, Concord and Petrel had assembled in Hong Kong in the middle of March, 1898; the Baltimore, sent to increase its strength, reached there on Friday, April 22d, and was immediately docked and cleaned.

Of the American squadron the Olympia, perhaps the finest unarmored cruiser in the United States Navy, and built in 1890, measured 5,800 tons, with a speed of 20 knots; the Baltimore, laid down in 1887, measured 4,600 tons, speed 20 knots; the Boston, laid down in 1883, diplaced 3,000 tons, with 15.55 knots speed; the Raleigh displaced 3,183 tons, built in 1889, with a speed of 19 knots; Petrel, gunboat of 892 tons, with 11 knots. The revenue cutter McCulloch, with 20 knots speed, acted as dispatch-boat.

The Spanish squadron in Manila Bay, under Admiral Montojo y Pasaron, consisted of seventeen ships, but six of these were insignificant little gunboats, three were transports and one was a surveying vessel. This reduced the fighting strength of the Spaniards to seven ships, namely: The Reina Cristina (flag), an unprotected steel cruiser of 3,400 tons and 13 knots of speed; the wooden cruiser Castilla, 3,300 tons and 13 knots; the Don Juan de Austria, of 1,140 tons and 14.5 knots; the Velasco and the Don Antonio de Ulloa, of similar tonnage and speed, the latter three being steel cruisers, and the protected steel cruisers Isla de Luzon and Isla de Cuba, of 1,030 tons each and 16 knots speed. The Castilla was leaking so that she was considered unsafe in deep water. The Ulloa had her engine dismantled for repair; her armament consisted of only two guns.

In guns the Spanish ships had 14 6-inch, 22 4-inch, 34 smaller ones. The American ships had 10 8-inch, 23 6-inch and 5-inch, 20 rapid-fire 4-inch, 53 smaller rapid-fire. The American batteries were therefore superior.

On Saturday evening, April 30th, Commodore Dewey reached the entrance of Manila Bay. The ships cleared for action and towards midnight entered the bay through the southern entrance in the following order: Olympia, Baltimore, Petrel, Raleigh, Concord, Boston, McCulloch, Nanshon and Zafiro.

The southern entrance is about three and a half miles wide, with the Corregidor and Caballo Islands towards the north and El Fraile to the south. Those islands had batteries mounted, partly taken from the Spanish ships.

According to rumor the northern channel was mined, for which reason the commodore chose the southern entrance.

When the squadron was abreast Corregidor it was discovered by the enemy; a rocket went up announcing the arrival of the Americans. Some shots were exchanged with the land batteries by the Raleigh, Boston and Concord. No damage was done on either side, and the American commodore signaled to stop firing. The ships steamed now slowly towards the north, for Manila, twenty-two miles away.

At this time the McCulloch, Nanshon and Zafiro were detached from the squadron as they were not to take part in the fight.

Shortly after 5 o'clock in the morning of the 1st of May the other six ships were off the City of Manila.

The fortifications of this place consisted of the Luneta battery, immediately to the south of the town, mounting nine 4-inch Krupp guns of 22-caliber length. In the battery San Iago there were some more heavy guns behind earthworks; it is said sixteen 6-inch guns in the bastions and two smooth-bore mortars.

The Spanish squadron was lying in Canacao Bay, in Cavite, some seven miles south of Manila. At Sangley Point, the northern end of the narrow peninsula locking the Cavite Bay towards the west, was a battery of two 5.9-inch Ordonez guns and three 64-pounder Parrott muzzle loaders; a mile farther to the southwest there was one modern 4.7-inch gun behind an earthwork.

The American squadron turned southward towards Cavite when just opposite Manila. Some of the guns on shore commenced firing at long range. One or two of the American ships answered, but a signal from the commodore ordered the firing to stop.

Soon the Spanish ships came in sight, moored in an irregular line east and west, the right wing being within distant range of the southern battery, the Luneta, at Malate.

Admiral Montojo is said to have selected his position at Cavite, away from the heavier forts in Manila, in order not to endanger the city by exposing it to the American fire. He is also credited with saying that the land forts could not and did not help him as they did not get the range of the American fleet.

It seems that Admiral Montojo's plan was originally to abandon and destroy his useless ships, which could never have a chance against the far more powerful American fleet, and then use his cannons and men to strengthen the land defenses. This plan was certainly preferable to the one eventually executed; it seems that Montojo was overruled by his superior officer, the military governor of the Philippines, Augustin.

Montojo learned of the presence of the Americans near Luzon on the early evening of April 30th, when two of their ships were seen reconnoitering in Subig Bay.

An energetic commander with more initiative than he possessed might have kept this squadron ready for a dash at the enemy while the latter would pass through the entrance; in the protection of nightly darkness there might have been a chance against the vastly superior foe. But Montojo remained where he was. When the guns of Corregidor and Fraile boomed their news of the arrival of Commodore Dewey's ships, Montojo had the fires lit under the boilers of his squadron and got his ships ready for action, as ready as the meaning of the word went in a Spanish sense.

At 5:40 A. M. the foremost ship of the American squadron, the Olympia, had reached a distance of about 5,000 yards from the Punta Sangley guns when the latter opened fire. Two shells exploded at that time, well ahead of the American flagship; they were the only ones fired and did, of course, no harm.

The American squadron turned now, in stately line, slowly toward port, with a starboard helm, and at 4,000 yards the Olympia opened fire with her forward 8-inch guns, over the port bow, the other ships following immediately with their guns.

The Spaniards answered as furiously as they could, and the famous battle was on.

Commodore Dewey steamed slowly with an easterly course at about 4,000 yards along the Spanish line, firing mostly with his heaviest guns. When the shallowness of the water prohibited farther advance the ships turned by sixteen points to port and steamed the same course back until west of Sangley, when they turned again sixteen points to port and steamed as in the first round. This manoeuvre was executed five times, the American line drawing gradually nearer with each turn toward east until finally, the fifth time, they passed the Spaniards at 2,000 yards or less, and all guns were firing in the batteries of the side near the enemy.

The fire was tremendous; the decks of the Spanish ships were swept by this fearful hail of projectiles. After the fourth trip the Cristina, Castilla and Ulloa were seen burning in several places. Admiral Montojo saw that his flagship was doomed and he decided to hoist his flag on the Isla de Luzon. The transfer was executed with great boldness in the hottest American fire.

The brave commander of the Cristina, Captain Louis Cadarzo, made a last desperate effort to get at the enemy. He tried a dash at the Olympia with all available speed, but the heroic attempt was fruitless. The Olympia and Baltimore concentrated their fire on the Spanish ship, from which dense volumes of black smoke were rolling fore, amidships and aft. A shot destroyed her steering gear. The loss of life was frightful. Brave Cadarzo had to turn back in order to save the rest of the crew from useless destruction. He had previously been wounded. Now a shell from the Olympia exploded on the bridge of the Cristina, tearing her gallant commander in pieces and sweeping his remains into the sea. While the Cristina was thus beaten back two yellow launches were seen suddenly dashing out from behind Sangley and making straight for the Olympia. One was sunk by the quick-firers of the Petrel, the other one was disabled by the Olympia's quick-firers and crawled back to the shore, where she was afterwards found grounded, riddled with shot and abandoned by her crew.

It was now about 7:30; the fearful havoc their shells had done on board the Spaniards could not yet be fully seen from the American ships, and the expenditure of ammunition was reported great. Commodore Dewey, with unwilling heart, decided to withdraw out of the reach of the Spanish fire to take an accurate inventory of the ammunition left and to use the lull for giving his men a rest. The heat had been fearful and the men in the engine-room and the lower compartments of the ships suffered extremely; in some of the magazines and in the engine-room the temperature is said to have reached as high as 120 and 160 degrees Fahrenheit.

According to a report of an eye-witness, Mr. Strickney, who acted as Commodore Dewey's aide, and was standing by his side throughout the battle, the "gloom on the bridge of the Olympia" at this time "was thicker than a London fog in November." Although, as said before, three of the Spaniards were seen to be burning, it had been noticed on the American flagship that also on board the Boston fire had broken out. From the immense rain of shot and shell all over and around the ships apprehension was felt as to the loss inflicted on the other ships. The Olympia had been hit several times, though the injury inflicted was slight, and the escape from severe damage on board this ship was so extraordinary that nobody thought it might have been the same with the other vessels.

While the crews were served their breakfast and the men from below came up to get a breath of air and exchange experiences, the commodore called his captains on board in conference. Then it was ascertained that nobody had been killed, that only two officers and six men were slightly wounded on the Baltimore by splinters caused through a Spanish shell, and that the expenditure of ammunition amounted to little over fifteen per cent of the magazines' contents, instead of having only fifteen per cent left as had been calculated.

So at 11 o'clock the battle was resumed. This time the ships steamed in the following order: The Baltimore, the Olympia, Raleigh, Boston, Concord and Petrel, the Baltimore having more 8-inch shells left in proportion than the flagship.

At the return into the battle zone the Baltimore closed in at 2,800 yards and concentrated her fire on the Ulloa, which was then made out to be in a sinking condition; the Cristina and Castilla were burning brightly, before their anchors in their old positions, and it became at once evident that the fate of the Spanish squadron was sealed. The Don Juan de Austria, the Isla de Luzon and Isla de Cuba were found sunk in the shallow waters of Bakor Bay. The Raleigh, Concord, Boston and Petrel, as their lighter draught permitted it, were then sent in closer and finished the work of destruction. The Spanish ships answered for a short time feebly, then their crews abandoned them.

At 12:40 all was over and the American ships anchored abreast of the city, with the exception of the Petrel, which was sent in to destroy the remaining little

Spanish gunboats, which had hardly participated in the fight and been abandoned together with the larger disabled ships.

The man to whom credit is due for the thoroughness and good judgment shown at this work was Chief Carpenter's Mate Franz A. Itrich, of the Petrel. When Commander Wood, the captain, received his order, he gladly accepted Itrich's volunteered service and sent him ashore with seven men in the second whaleboat, which was one of the two boats left uninjured by the fire of the battle. A boy by the name of Forrester also accompanied Itrich as signal boy. It was found that the only place from where the boy could see the men in the whaleboat and the Petrel at the same time and thus signal was in the Cavite Naval Arsenal at Fort Quadeloup. When the fort was reached a landing was made, the boy hastened to the position which had been pointed out to him, and as soon as the latter reached his position Itrich stepped into the boat and ordered the men to pull for the doomed ships, which were anchored about 150 yards from the landing. Each ship was boarded by Itrich, who carefully laid his plans for ignition so that they would not miscarry by reason of the flames failing

FRANZ A. ITRICH,
Chief Carpenter's Mate, U. S. S. Petrel,
Born in Germany, 1853.

to spread over the entire ship. Thus he set fire to various portions of the ships both fore and aft, and he and his little crew left them a mass of flames. The boats so destroyed were: Don Juan, Cuba, Luzon, Duero and Velasco. Itrich showed admirable judgment in sparing the transport Manila. This ship had 350 tons of coal on board, 35 head of cattle, 45 barrels of wine and a good quantity of light artillery ammunition. The vessel was afterward transformed into an American gunboat.

Itrich, upon the recommendation of his captain, was promoted to carpenter, received the Medal of Honor and a gratuity of $100 from the Navy Department for his excellent services on that day.

So the American commodore had literally accomplished the order of his government "to find and destroy or capture the Spanish fleet," without the loss of a single man in his own squadron. The hostile ships destroyed were the Cristina, Castilla, Ulloa, all three burned and sunk; the Don Juan, Luzon, Cuba, Lezo, El Cano, Argos, Duero, Velasco and Mindanao, burned, and the Rapido, Hercule, Manila and several launches captured.

The loss in men of the Spanish squadron is given by Lieutenant Ellicott of the United States Navy as follows:

Cristina—Killed 130, wounded 90; Castilla—Killed 23, wounded 80; Cuba—Wounded, 2; Luzon—Wounded, 6; Don Juan—Wounded, 22; Ulloa—Killed 8, wounded 10; besides 6 killed and 4 wounded in the shore batteries, making a total

of 167 killed and 214 wounded, in all 381 casualties, being nineteen per cent. of the whole force, or, if the Spanish estimate of the number of their men engaged is accepted, a full one-third of the whole force, the heaviest loss ever inflicted in an action between fleets. Of officers the Cristina lost seven killed, the Ulloa three, the Castilla one; among the wounded was Admiral Montojo.

The number of hits in the Spanish ships could not be ascertained with accuracy, as their hulls were under water, and the destructive fire must have effaced the traces of many shots.

The casualties on the American side were the two officers and six men of the Baltimore slightly wounded, and one man on the Olympia injured by the recoil of an 8 inch gun, which caused a crushing of his chest. The engineer of the McCulloch fell a victim to sunstroke; Captain Gridley of the Olympia died soon afterwards from the effects of the battle on his previously weakened constitution.

The Olympia had been slightly hit three times, the Baltimore three times, the Raleigh twice, the Boston once. The fire caused on the latter ship by an exploding Spanish shell was soon extinguished without serious damage.

A few hours after the battle the American squadron was practically again ready for action.

Three hours after the surrender of Cavite the commodore demanded of the Spanish Governor-General Augustin to restrain instantly from all further attacks and molestations of the American forces and to deliver all the ammunition and military stores in his possession. Augustin complied with the first request and thus saved the City of Manila from bombardment and destruction. The occupation of Cavite Arsenal took place the next day, and on the 3d of May the Raleigh and Baltimore captured the entrance forts at El Fraile and Corregidor, which were surrendered without resistance and were provisionally garrisoned by detachments of the two ships.

On the 25th of May a brigade of infantry, 115 officers and 2,400 men strong, left San Francisco, under General Anderson, to bring re-enforcements to the American fleet before Manila. This force reached Cavite on the 30th of June, and here the independent action of the navy came to an end. The Olympia soon left with Commodore Dewey, in the meantime promoted to admiral, for home via the Mediterranean, and those of the other crews whose term of service was ended were mustered out and taken home in transports which soon arrived in numbers from the States.

ORGANIZING THE FLEET AND EXPEDITION CORPS

O^N the 25th of April President McKinley issued a call for 125,000 volunteers, of which 118,000 were mustered in by the 27th of May. Together with the regular troops these were organized into seven army corps, each containing twenty-seven regiments, in nine brigades and three divisions.

These troops were mostly concentrated in four large camps at New Orleans, Tampa, Mobile and Chickamauga Park. On the 27th of May a second call of the President summoned 75,000 volunteers more.

By the beginning of June all the forces amounted to 243,000 men, including 44,-000 regulars in the army and 25,000 men in the navy. The latter was augmented by a large number of fast merchant vessels which were adopted for auxiliary naval service, and partially manned by the naval militias of New York, Michigan, Massachusetts and Maryland.

The commander-in-chief of the maritime forces on the American east coast was Captain William T. Sampson, who had been promoted to acting rear-admiral; Major-General Shafter was put in chief command of the cuban expedition corps.

Admiral Sampson's fleet constituted the following force by the end of May:

The North Atlantic Squadron, under the immediate command of the commander-in-chief: Armored cruiser New York (flagship); battleships Indiana, Iowa and Oregon; monitors Puritan, Amphitrite, Terror, Miantonomah; cruisers Detroit, Cincinnati, Marblehead, Montgomery, Dolphin; gunboats Nashville, Wilmington, Castine, Machias, Helena, Newport, Vicksburg; armed yachts Gloucester, Mayflower, Hawk, and dynamite gunboat Vesuvius; torpedo boats Dupont, Porter, Winslow, Foote, Ericsson, Rodgers, Cushing; armed liners Harvard, Yale, St. Paul, St. Louis, and a flotilla of smaller auxiliaries.

The Flying Squadron, under Commodore Schley: Armored cruiser Brooklyn; battleships Massachusetts, Texas; Cruisers Minneapolis, Columbia, New Orleans;

The Northern Patrol Squadron, Commodore Howell: Cruiser San Francisco and armed liners Yankee, Yosemite, Prairie and Dixie.

The Spaniards had first in the West Indian waters only the old cruiser Reina Mercedes, with broken-down engines, at Santiago; the Alfonso XII, without guns and with defective boilers; the Conde de Venadito, the Infanta Isabel, the Ensenada, the latter four at Havana; and some smaller gunboats at Havana and Cienfuegos; finally an old cruiser, the Isabel II, at San Juan in Porto Rico.

On the 21st of April Admiral Sampson was ordered to blockade part of Cuba. The order of the Navy Department reached the squadron, which was filling up stores, in Key West. By 9 o'clock on the morning of the 22d all the ships had left; by 5 o'clock the same day the squadron arrived off Havana, having captured the two first prizes in the war, the Spanish merchant steamers Bonaventure and Pedro.

The three big ships New York, Indiana and Iowa remained before Havana, the other vessels scattered to their stations; the blockading order included the western coast of Cuba from Santa Clara Bay on the east to Bahia Honda on the west. These ships were all thoroughly prepared for battle, all the woodwork and wooden fittings having been cut out or taken out and left on shore, as well as nearly all the boats, the New York, for instance, retaining only three.

On the 24th the Spanish merchant steamers Catalina and Miguel Iover were captured; the same fate befell the next day the Spanish liner Panama and the Schooner Sol.

The 26th of April brought some disappointment to the American blockaders, as the Spanish liner Montserrat succeeded in running the blockade into Cienfuegos with a detachment of troops and a cargo of provisions and gold. This lucky ship ran the blockade again out of Cienfuegos on the 6th of May and got safely back to Spain.

On the 27th of April occurred the first bombardment, the New York, Cincinnati and Puritan doing a forced reconnoitering at Matanzas, on the northwest coast of Cuba. It is true the Spanish forts around Cuba had fired previously on American men-of-war, when these latter appeared before Havana on the 24th in search of the cable, but the distance was so great that the Americans did not answer to this harmless fire at all.

The fortifications in Matanzas did not amount to much; the cause for the recon-noissance was the discovery of newly-built earthworks at Rubalva in the west and Punta Maya in the east of the town. The American ships ran into the bay and drew the fire of the forts.

On the 4th of May the armed tug Leyden, escorted by the cruiser Wilmington, attempted to land a number of Cubans and supplies for the insurgents at Moriel. This was in consequence of a daring reconnoissance accomplished by Lieutenant Fremont with the torpedo boat Porter on the 25th of April. Fremont managed to land to the west of Havana and communicate with the insurgents, which meeting matured the above plan. But the American landing party at Moriel was discovered by Spaniards, who forced them to re-embark.

On the 11th of May an action took place in Cardenas, which ended seriously for the engaged American force and came very near culminating in the loss of an American torpedo boat, the Winslow.

The blockading force before Cardenas consisted of the cruiser Machias, under Commander Merry, the armed revenue cutter Hudson and the torpedo boats Winslow and Foote. They were joined on the 11th by the Wilmington, Commander Todd. It seems that the desire to distinguish themselves led the two named officers to decide on a reconnoissance into Cardenas, where they knew three small Spanish gunboats were stationed. Their object was the capture of these boats, and the Machias, whose draught was too heavy for the water inside the bay, attacked the signal station at Caya Diana, chased the guards away with an armed boat and

THE CABLE CUTTING EXPEDITION AT CIENFUEGOS.

hoisted the American flag on the station's mast. The Wilmington, which had six feet lighter draft than the other ship, went into Cardenas, accompanied by the Winslow and Hudson. On account of the shallowness of the water Commander Merry could not approach the earthworks nearer than 1,500 yards. Firing began and became lively on both sides; but the gunboats would not come out. Then the Winslow was ordered in. She went boldly close to the gunboats and engaged them with her three one-pounders, when all of a sudden masked guns from the shore opened upon her. This was shortly after 2 o'clock in the afternoon. At about 2:30 a four-inch shell from the shore crashed through the starboard side of the frail torpedo boat, destroying the forward boiler and the starboard engine and disabling the steering gear. The torpedo boat was helpless and on fire, but none of the crew of twenty-five was injured so far. The Hudson, seeing the condition of the Winslow, went bravely to her help. A hawser was thrown on board the Winslow, and her executive officer, Ensign Worth Bagley, was busy with four other men endeavoring to secure it when a Spanish shrapnel burst in their midst. All five men were killed, Bagley and Fireman Daniels instantly; the other three died within a few minutes. They were all fearfully torn by the fragments of the deadly shell. But while Lieutenant Bernadou, the commander of the torpedo boat, who was himself wounded, kept on firing the forward one-pounder as fast as he could, the Hudson managed to land another line on board, which was made fast, and thus succeeded in towing the wrecked Winslow out of reach of the Spanish guns. The five victims were the first Americans killed in the war.

CUTTING THE CABLES AT CIENFUEGOS

WILLIAM MEYER,
Carpenter's Mate U. S. S. Nashville.
Born in Germany, June 22, 1863.

Cutting the cables at Cienfuegos marked another of the events of the Spanish-American War which cannot be overlooked, if only for the conditions under which it was carried out. It occurred on May 11th, in the early stage of the war, and was one of the most perilous and exciting of the undertakings. The men were obliged to do this work in small boats, and were constantly under the fire of the Spaniards. The men were comparatively easy marks for the bullets, and but for the eventual protection given them by the Nashville and Marblehead to which the men belonged, there can be little doubt that none of them would have been spared to tell the tale.

The Marblehead and Nashville had been sent to do blockade duty on the south side of Cuba, and since the capture of the Bonaventure and the Argananta. there was nothing to occupy the time of the men on board either ship, and listless days hung heavily upon them. Consequently, when orders were received to cut the Spanish cables, there was delight on board the blockaders particularly among those who were to do the work.

Captain B. H. McCalla, of the Marblehead, the senior officer, requested the Nashville to prepare a steam and a sailing launch to guard the men while they were cutting the cables. The Marblehead also furnished launches, and marines were put on board armed with rifles, revolvers and cutlasses to act as a guard.

At five o'clock on the morning of the 11th everything was in readiness and the boats were lowered. Among those who participated in the expedition were a blacksmith and a carpenter's mate from both the Marblehead and the Nashville. Lieutenant McR. Winslow was in command of the expedition. Austin J. Durney, the blacksmith of the Nashville, who participated in this dangerous expedition and who, with all the others of the boat's crew, was awarded the Medal of Honor for this work, describes the affair entertainingly as follows:

AUSTIN J. DURNEY,
Blacksmith, U. S. S. Nashville.

"Cable cutting was something new to all of us and I did not know just how to manage it. To tell the truth, I didn't have the faintest idea of the work. To be prepared for all emergencies we equipped ourselves with every possible tool that suggested itself to us, and thus we took along chisels, hammers, axes, saws, etc. As soon as I got hold of the cable I dicovered that the only practical tool was a hack-saw, such as is used in any machine shop. We went to within about ten or fifteen yards of the shore before we could get hold of the cable. We had to search for it and pull it up with grappling irons. It was then pulled over one of the small boats and severed by the hack-saw. The task was difficult, as a rough sea was running. When the cable was cut the shore end was dropped overboard, and one of the boats of the Marblehead took the other end out to sea, where it was again cut and flung overboard, thus preventing its being picked up by the enemy and repaired. A second cable was raised close to the shore and likewise cut twice.

"The Spaniards at first did not bother us, they evidently believing that we intended going ashore. But as our object became apparent, and we began cutting the cable, the enemy commenced to rain bullets down upon us. Our marines returned the fire with a will, but the Spaniards had the advantage. They were posted on a cliff and kept out of sight of our men. Only now and then we would see one of them. This was when they were trying to get our range. Nevertheless, most of their firing went over our men. A more effective fire, however, was delivered from a lighthouse close to the shore. We did not expect that the Span-

MEMBERS OF THE CABLE-CUTTING CREW AT CIENFUEGOS.

iards would use it as a blind and a fortification, or we would have first destroyed it. But we were determined to get even, and soon after the expedition the building was leveled to the ground.

"The enemy's fire began to have a deadly effect after the cable was cut and we were returning to our ships, for the farther away we got from shore the more accurate was their fire.

"It was then that First Lieutenant Albert C. Dillingham, having taken command of the Nashville, brought her between the returning crews and the shore to save us from destruction; but he undertook no small risk, as the shore was full of rocks that projected almost out of the water. Indeed, had it not been for this the small boats would not have been used for the expedition. Thus was the perilous task completed."

BENJAMIN F. BAKER, Cockswain, U.S.S. Nashville. Born at Dennis Port, Mass., March 12, 1857.

While the cable was being cut Captain Maynard of the Nashville was wounded. The following men of the cable-cutting party received the Medal of Honor:

FROM THE NASHVILLE.

ERNEST KRAUSE, Cockswain.
AUSTIN J. DURNEY, Blacksmith.
JOHAN J JOHANSSON, Ordinary Seaman.
JOHN P. RILEY, Landsman.
DAVID D. BARROW, Ordinary Seaman.
BENJAMIN F. BAKER, Cockswain.
LAURITZ NELSON, Sailmaker's Mate.
HUDSON VAN ETTEN, Seaman.
WILLARD MILLER, Seaman.
ROBERT BLUME, Seaman.
FRANK HILL, Private, U. S. M. C.
JOSEPH H. FRANKLIN, Private, U. S. M. C.
JOSEPH F. SCOTT, Private, U. S. M. C.

THOMAS HOBAN, Cockswain.
ROBERT VOLZ, Seaman.
ALBERT BEYER, Cockswain.
GEORGE W. BRIGHT, Coal Passer.
WILLIAM MEYER, Carpenter's Mate, 3d class.
HARRY H. MILLER, Seaman.
JOHN EGLIT, Seaman.
MICHAEL GIBBON, Oiler.
PHILIP GAUGHAN, Sergeant, U. S. M. C.
POMEROY PARKER, Private, U. S. M. C.
OSCAR W. FIELD, Private, U. S. M. C.
MICHAEL L. KEARNEY, Private, U. S. M. C.

FROM THE MARBLEHEAD.

JAMES H. BENNETT, Chief B. M.
JOHN J. DORAN, B. M., 2d class.
FRANK WILLIAMS, Seaman.
HARRY HENRICKSON, Seaman.
ALBERT BADAS, Seaman.
AXEL SUNDQUIST, C. S M.
WILLIAM HART, Machinist, 1st class.
FRANZ KRAMER, Seaman.
HENRY P. RUSSELL, Landsman.
HERMAN KUCHNEISTER, Private, U. S. M. C.
WALTER S. WEST, Private, U. S. M. C.
WILLIAM OAKLEY, G. M., 2d class.

JULIUS A. R. WILKE, B. M., 1st class.
JOSEPH E. CARTER, Blacksmith.
JOHN DAVIS, G. M., 3d class.
WILLIAM LEVERY, Apprentice, 1st class.
HERBERT L. FOSS, Seaman.
NICK ERICKSON, Cockswain.
FREEMAN GILL, G. M., 1st class.
JOHN MAXWELL, Fireman, 2d class.
LEONARD CHADWICK, Apprentice, 1st class.
JAMES MEREDITH, Private, U. S. M. C.
EDWARD SULLIVAN, Private, U. S. M. C.
DANIEL CAMPBELL, Private, U. S. M. C.

About this time news was received that a strong Spanish flying squadron under Admiral Cervera had left St. Vincent, in the Cape Verdes. Commodore Schley was dispatched from Hampton Roads with his flying squadron on a scout towards the southeast, and Admiral Sampson decided on a reconnoissance to Porto Rico. With the New York, Indiana, Iowa, Amphitrite, Terror, Montgomery, Detroit, the torpedo boat Porter and the tug Wompatuck, and the necessary supply vessels, he arrived before San Juan on the morning of May 12th, where he transferred his flag to the Iowa. The town of San Juan is situated on the extreme west end of a long, narrow island, on which were three forts. The arsenal was on the southern shore facing the inside of the bay. The entrance of the harbor was obstructed by two sunken hulks, and, it is said, some mines.

Admiral Sampson closed in on the entrance and opened fire on the forts, passing them by describing an eclipse three times. After reaching the conclusion that neither Cervera's squadron nor any other ships except three little gunboats were inside Sampson gave the order to stop the fight and withdraw. So far only one shot from the enemy had taken effect on the American side, the Iowa being the sufferer, but no serious damage was done and nobody injured. Now, while the ships were withdrawing, a Spanish shell exploded on the New York, killing two men and wounding seven. The fortifications are said not to have suffered to any great extent. The Spanish lost one officer and three men killed and thirteen wounded, and among the civic population in the town thirty-one casualties were reported. The French cruiser Admiral Rigault de Genouilly, lying at anchor in the harbor, was struck in the rigging and the smokestack.

Admiral Sampson took up a westerly course, towards Key West. On the 13th of May the Solace met the squadron, bringing the news that Cervera's fleet was reported to have returned to Cadiz. The American boats then stopped off Puerto Plata until the 15th.

In the meantime the steamer Gussie, escorted by the armed revenue cutter Manning, had landed two companies of regular American infantry near Cabanas to form connection with the Cuban insurgents under Gomez. But the landed troops were soon attacked by vastly superior Spanish forces and had to re-embark.

The Spanish gunboats Conde de Venadito and Nueva Espana made a sortie from Havana on the next day, the 14th; this was probably intended to calm the minds of the people in the city by showing them that the Spanish could start an attack of their own. The boats were easily repulsed, without having attained the slightest result.

On May 15th the Porter reached Sampson with the surprising news that Cervera's squadron had been in Martinique, in the Antilles, on the 12th of May and in Curacao on the 14th; that the flying squadron under Schley was in Charleston; that cruisers had been dispatched to patrol the channels between Jamaica and Haiti and the Cairos Bank, and finally that Sampson was directed to proceed without delay to Key West.

This news was quite serious, in so far as the American ships were short of coal and in need of repairs.

The St. Louis, which met the squadron just when the latter headed westward, was directed to cut the cables at Guantanamo, Santiago and Ponce; the Yale and Harvard were ordered to coal at St. Thomas (Danish).

On the next day, when off Cape Haytien, fresh news reached the squadron, namely that the six ships of Cervera's fleet, the Teresa, Vizcaya, Oquendo, Colon, Furor and Penton, were short of coal and provisions and with foul bottoms, that Schley was under way for Key West, and that according to rumor a second Spanish squadron, consisting of five ships, had been seen off Martinique on the 14th; another dispatch brought by the Dupont on the 17th announced that Schley would be sent without delay to the blockade of Cienfuegos with the Brooklyn, Massachusetts and Texas.

The New York went at full speed to Key West, where she arrived on the afternoon of the 18th, and by the 19th the other ships of the squadron had also arrived there.

The Spanish admiral, Cervera, had left Porto Grande in the Cape Verde Islands on April 28th, with eight vessels, namely, the four armored cruisers Maria Teresa, Almirante Oquendo, Vizcaya and Cristobal Colon, the torpedo boat destroyers Furor, Terror and Pluton and the hospital ship Alicante. The most powerful vessel in this squadron was the Italian-built Colon, whose armor consisted of a complete water-line belt, tapering from 6-inch thickness amidships to 2-inch towards the ends; a central citadel 150 feet long, covered with 6-inch armor, which sheltered the bases of two barbettes, placed fore and aft and protected by 5-inch steel; besides there was a protective deck 1½-inches thick. The armament included two 10-inch Armstrong guns, one for each barbette, and ten 6-inch Armstrong rapid-fire guns of newest construction. The 10-inch guns could not be gotten ready in time, and the ship went on this cruise without them. The light battery was of the usual proportionate strength; there were four torpedo tubes above water, within the citadel, and a fifth in the bow, under water.

The other three cruisers were sister ships, and their only armor was a narrow belt 216 feet long, from ten to twelve inches thick. The upper part of the hull was not protected at all. Each ship carried two 11-inch guns in fore and aft barbettes protected by 10-inch armor; besides there were ten 5-inch rapid-fire guns established behind shields, five in each broadside; the torpedo armament consisted of eight tubes per ship, all above water, two forward, two astern and two on each broadside.

Each one of the four cruisers was rated at a speed of from eighteen to nineteen knots; of course, under proper handling and proper condition of the engines and the bottom.

The three destroyers were of the newest construction, of nearly 400 tons displacement each, built in England, and just launched before the war; they were rated at twenty-eight knots, but under Spanish handling their speed remained always below that figure.

The American strategy board had calculated that the squadron would make at least thirteen knots per hour, and after its departure from Porto Grande was known in Washington its arrival was looked for on the basis of this speed. But as nothing was heard or seen of Cervera's ships after that time some apprehension was felt that the Spaniards, intending some unforeseen trick, might make a dash at the unprotected coast cities on the North Atlantic or try to intercept or destroy the Oregon, which would then have been in the Southern Atlantic, on her long trip from the Pacific round the Horn.

On the 11th of May the auxiliary cruiser Harvard, Captain Cotton, had arrived at St. Pierre, Martinique. Here Cotton learned of a Spanish destroyer having just come into Fort de France. To verify this the captain sent an officer to the latter place and from him he learned of the presence of a second destroyer and several large steamers in the offing, outside the harbor. This news was at once telegraphed to Washington, from where it reached Admiral Sampson. Cotton learned also that the destroyer Terror would remain at Martinique, as her engines were disabled.

Thus it came about that the sudden concentration of the American sea forces at Key West took place as related above.

The United States Navy Department calculated from all recent information and the actions of the hostile squadron, that the latter would abandon the idea of reaching either San Juan, in Porto Rico, or Havana, and that it would try to sneak into Cienfuegos or Santiago. At that time it was believed that Cervera had war-stores on board for the Spanish army; therefore the conclusion was reached that he would rather try to make Cienfuegos, which was much less distant from Havana than Santiago. Events showed that the conjectures of the American Naval Strategy Board were in the main correct. Afterwards Spanish officers gave out that Cervera's intention was actually to go into Cienfuegos, but his lack of coal enabled him only to reach Santiago, which was only 600 miles away, 300 miles nearer than the other haven.

The predicament of the Spanish fleet was caused by the failure of the coal-ship Restonnel to reach or find her in time. Had Cervera been enabled to coal up his ships and then make for Cienfuegos, where he could again have replenished his stock, he might have given the American fleet many an unpleasant slip and quite a long and trying chase.

On the 19th of May Cervera reached the entrance of Santiago, and at 8 o'clock in the morning the squadron was at anchor in the harbor.

Cervera could well congratulate himself on the success of this perilous trip; but the future lay before him in hopeless gloom, filled with the most evil forebodings.

When Schley and Sampson met in Key West on the 18th, the latter gave the former orders to proceed without delay to the blockade of Cienfuegos. In compliance with this order Schley and his flying squadron started on the 19th for their destination by way of the Yucatan Channel. The general idea was that Schley should take care of the western approach to Havana and Sampson the eastern. On the next day Sampson detached the Iowa, the Castine, the torpedo boat Dupont and the collier Merrimac to join and re-enforce Schley, besides sending to the commodore a private letter in which the commander-in-chief further explained his plan in detail. This letter hinted at the probable presence of the enemy at Santiago and the consequent necessity of including this port in the circle of close observation.

On the night of the 20th of May Sampson received advice from the Navy Department that the report of Cervera's presence at Santiago was very likely correct, and that Schley should be immediately directed to proceed with all his force to this port, leaving only one smaller vessel to watch Cienfuegos. Three vessels, the Vixen, Marblehead and Eagle, accordingly left to transmit this order to the commodore. "If you are satisfied," the order read in part, "that they are not at Cienfuegos, proceed with all dispatch, but cautiously, to Santiago, and if the enemy is there blockade him in port."

Now, if the Spaniards reached Santiago on the 19th and their intended destination was Cienfuegos, there was nothing, if they left the first-named harbor without wasting time, to prevent them reaching Cienfuegos unmolested and in safety. The distance of 300 miles from Santiago to Cienfuegos was looked at as an easy day's trip for a squadron like Cervera's, even supposing their sailing speed would not exceed thirteen knots. Nobody knew or even anticipated at that time the actual run-down condition of the Spanish ships, or that Cervera might be so short of coal that even the 300 miles difference compelled his abandoning all intention of reaching Cienfuegos.

The flying squadron steamed towards its new scene of action at the rate of ten knots an hour. About midnight between the 21st and 22d of May the ships arrived off Cienfuegos, keeping in the offing, about twenty miles distant from the entrance. At daylight they steamed slowly in and cleared for action. At 8 o'clock in the morning the squadron circled before the narrow entrance at a distance of about 4,000 yards, to draw out the fire if there were any guns. But all remained silent.

At noon on the 22d the Iowa and Dupont arrived.

A second circling before the entrance brought no results, but Schley believed that he had seen the tops of a man-of-war and felt pretty sure they had located Cervera. The Dupont steamed close in to reconnoiter and reported several ships inside. Upon the mountains toward the west signal-fires were seen, evidently lighted by the insurgents to attract the attention of the ships. But Schley, who had not been informed of the signal system of the Cubans, could not understand them, and took them for signals of the enemy.

Meantime the squadron was joined by the Castine, the collier Merrimac and the armed yacht Hawk. The latter brought dispatches from the commander-in-chief directing the commodore to proceed to Santiago, where he would be expected to arrive on the morning of the 24th.

Schley, however, did not leave for Santiago before the evening of the 24th. He left the Castine before Cienfuegos, sent the Dupont back to Key West and started with the Brooklyn, Iowa, Texas, Massachusetts, Marblehead, Vixen, Hawk, Eagle and the collier Merrimac.

On the 26th the squadron arrived off Santiago. The Minneapolis, St. Paul and Yale, coming up in the evening, reported nothing seen of the Spaniards.

Meanwhile Admiral Sampson had left Key West with his flagship and arrived at his blockading station in the Bahama Channel, on the northeast coast of Cuba, on the 21st. Here he learned on the 26th, through letters from his commodore, that the flying squadron was not before Santiago on the 24th, as expected.

On the afternoon of the 27th, however, the most disquieting information, dated the 24th, reached the commander-in-chief from Schley, that the latter had ascertained the non-presence of the enemy at Cienfuegos, but would be unable to blockade Santiago on account of insufficient coal supply, that he needed two more colliers and would proceed to Mole St. Nicholas to do there the necessary coaling.

Sampson forthwith dispatched the New Orleans with additional orders to Schley and then returned to Key West in order to obtain leave to proceed to Santiago himself. In Key West he found the Oregon; this splendid ship had come in on the 26th none the worse for her long trip around the Horn and as ready as ever for sea and action

On the night of the 28th a telegram arrived from Schley saying that he would come to Key West to coal.

The commodore, not knowing at that time of the presence of Cervera in Santiago Harbor, had signaled on the evening of the 26th to proceed to Key West along the south side of Cuba and through the Yucatan Channel. The St. Paul was to remain and watch the port.

Shortly after the squadron started the machinery of the Merrimac broke down completely and she had to be taken in tow by the Yale. Four times did the hawser part, and it took twenty-four hours in the heavy sea before her chain cable was on board the auxiliary cruiser. While this was taking place the Harvard came up early in the morning of the 27th with a dispatch from Washington to the effect that the flying squadron should by all means prevent the Spaniards from leaving Santiago without a decisive engagement, and that coal was being sent to Mole St. Nicholas.

To follow orders now was impossible for Schley, so he proceeded westward.

In the evening, at about 7 o'clock, the weather improved so that coaling at sea became possible, and the Texas and Marblehead began forthwith coaling from the Merrimac. Both ships finished on the forenoon of the 28th, and at noon of the same day the squadron turned and steamed back to Santiago, where the ships were distributed for the blockade, which was thus at last established. Cervera had missed his chance, very likely without being able to use it, for want of coal and other supplies; such at least are the reasons given out from the Spanish side.

Now the gap had closed.

During the intervening time the land troops had not been idle, and preparations were made as fast as the suddenness and magnitude of the undertaking permitted for the movement of a sufficiently large expeditionary force to Cuba. A great difficulty was encountered in securing the necessary transports, as it was the intention of the government to press merchant vessels into war service, and on the other hand there was a reluctancy in some cases to withdraw vessels from their profitable carriers' occupation for the sake of the military requirements.

But towards the end of May everything was in readiness, and it became known that an army was to be landed near Santiago for an attack on that city. It was calculated that with the destruction of the enemy's naval and army forces at that place the backbone of Spain's resistance would be broken.

This view proved to be sound and correct, as subsequent events showed.

A transport fleet had at last been assembled before Tampa, Fla., which consisted of thirty-five steamers and four tenders, not including the escort of war vessels.

The intended army of invasion consisted of 15,400 men; 13,300 men were regulars, and of these 3,300 were cavalry. Only one troop of the latter was to take horses, as it had been impossible in the short time available to secure transports that would accommodate such a large number of animals. The inability to transport enough horses was unimportant, as Cuba, and especially the country around Santiago, is not favorable to cavalry action.

The organization of this army was as follows: One division of cavalry (dismounted), under General Wheeler, comprising the Third, Sixth and Tenth U. S. Cavalry, and four troops of each of the First and Ninth U. S. Cavalry under Brigadier-General Sumner and the First U. S. Volunteer Cavalry (Rough Riders), under Colonel Wood.

The First Infantry Division, under General Kent, composed of the First Brigade, General Hawkins: Sixth and Sixteenth U. S. Infantry, Seventy-first New York Volunteer Infantry; Second Brigade, General Pearson: Second, Tenth and Twenty-first U. S. Infantry; Third Brigade, General Wickoff: Ninth, Thirteenth and Twenty-fifth U. S. Infantry; three batteries light artillery, under Captains Grimes, Best and Parkhurst, and four Gatling guns, manned by infantrymen, under Lieutenant Parker.

The Second Infantry Division, under General Lawton, consisting of the First Brigade, General Ludlow: Eighth and Twenty-second U. S. Infantry, Second Massachusetts Volunteer Infantry; Second Brigade, Colonel Miles: First, Fourth and Twenty-fourth U. S. Infantry; Third Brigade, General Chaffee: Seventh, Twelfth and Seventeenth U. S. Infantry; Brigade of General Bates: Third and Twentieth Infantry; signal detachment, balloon detachment and mounted orderlies from the cavalry.

About this time, when everyone was waiting for official news as to the whereabouts of Admiral Cervera's fleet, Commodore Schley notified the War Department that he had seen the Colon and other ships of the Spanish fleet inside the harbor of Santiago.

THE SINKING OF THE MERRIMAC

IN the meantime Admiral Sampson had been at Key West, at which place he obtained the asked for permission to go personally to Santiago. On the night of the 29th he started for the latter place with the New York, Oregon, Mayflower and Porter.

Two days previous to his departure from this place he, in conference with Captains Converse and Folger and Commodore Watson, had conceived a plan to lock in the Spanish fleet, which was now known positively to be in Santiago, by sinking schooners laden with brick and stone across the entrance. Captain Converse suggested the sinking of the broken-down collier Merrimac and the admiral adopted his view. Primarily Schley was to have executed this plan, and the details of execution were to be left to him. But as now the commander-in-chief was under way to the place, he concluded to supervise the undertaking himself. During the night of the 29th he called Assistant Naval Constructor Richmond P. Hobson, who was on board the New York, into his cabin and consulted with him as to the practicability of the plan and the course to be pursued. Hobson asked permission to work out a complete plan in all its details. On the 30th he was ready; the admiral did not only fully approve of his plans, but also agreed to his request to be put in command of the expedition. Hobson's idea was to take the Merrimac in, with a small crew of volunteers, anchor her across the channel, open her sea-valves and finally blow her up with ten torpedoes, which were to be filled with guncotton. Sampson objected to guncotton, as according to his opinion the effect of the explosion would be too powerful. So ordinary black powder, eighty pounds for each torpedo, was substituted.

Early on the 1st of June Sampson and his fleet reached Santiago. Under Hobson's supervision the torpedoes and connections had all been finished on board the New York. The Merrimac was put in shape for her new and last task without delay. Her captain, Commander Miller, of the United States Navy, was very persistent in his objections to being deprived of the vessel's command; he wanted to take her in himself. But the admiral succeeded, finally, in convincing him that Hobson should have his way.

It seems that almost everybody wanted at least to participate and share the glory of this famous undertaking. Six volunteers were needed, and nearly 600 men responded to the call.

The men Hobson finally selected were: Chief Master-at-Arms Daniel Montague, Gunner's Mate George Charette and Cockswain Rudolph Clausen, all three of the ew York; Cockswain J. E. Murphy, of the Iowa; Cockswain Osborn W. Deignan, Machinist John Phillips, and Water Tender Francis Kelly, these of the Merrimac crew.

At daybreak on June 2d the Merrimac was ready; the old crew had left the ship,

THE FAMOUS MERRIMAC CREW.

LIEUTENANT RICHMOND P. HOBSON.   RANDOLPH CLAUSEN.   OSBORN W. DEIGNAN.   FRANCIS KELLY.

J. E. MURPHY.   DANIEL MONTAGUE.   GEORGE F. PHILLIPS.   GEORGE CHARETTE.

and the admiral came on board for a last inspection. But when this had been completed and before the collier was well under way the day was too far advanced, in the admiral's opinion, to allow success, and the Merrimac was ordered back. Hobson tried first not to notice the admiral's signal; but Sampson was peremptory. So the attempt had to be postponed for the next day. Before daybreak on the morning of June 3d she finally went in. The pilot remained on board, as did also the assistant engineer, who wanted to look after the engines until she reached the entrance, when both men were taken off by a steam launch in command of Cadet Powell. The latter had orders to wait outside the entrance and pick up the crew, who intended to float out on the Merrimac's catamaran, which for this purpose had been swung overboard.

Although extreme darkness prevailed, while nearing the entrance the Merrimac was discovered by a picket boat, which opened fire and caused general alarm. Shore batteries commenced firing and a shot disabled the Merrimac's rudder. This mishap prevented Hobson swinging her crosswise in the channel, as had been planned. The forts then opened fire on the ship, as did the Colon and the Oquendo, and the Reina Mercedes sent two torpedoes into her, which, according to Hobson's statement, actually rent the ship asunder. Each man of the crew fulfilled faithfully his part in the daring act. Kelly knocked the caps from the sea-valves; Murphy let go the anchor at the signal from Hobson; the latter himself was on the bridge, watch in hand; Deignan was at the helm; the others were stationed at the different quarters. All were stripped of their garments except underclothing, and while the Merrimac was sinking Hobson and his men took to the catamaran and sank with it into the water. They clung to this raft amidst a terrific fire for about an hour, all the time hoping that they would drift out into the sea, where they might be picked up by Cadet Powell, who was watching for them. Firing now ceased and a steam launch was seen approaching. Some of the latter's crew, as soon as they discovered the men in the water, raised their rifles to shoot. Hobson called out: "Is there any officer in the boat to accept our surrender as prisoners of war?" Then an elderly Spanish officer looked out from under the awning, waved his hand in assent, and directed his men to lower their weapons and help the Americans on board. This officer was the gallant Admiral Cervera himself. He treated the American sailors with friendliness, and they were taken on shore and handed over to the army. They were kept prisoners, Hobson separated from the men, for thirty-three days, when they were exchanged, arriving safely in the American camp, amidst tremendous ovations of the troops, on July 7th.

The Spanish admiral gave a handsome proof of his chivalry in connection with this famous affair.

When Cadet Powell came back with his steam launch on this memorable morning and reported that "no one had come back from the Merrimac," gloom settled over the squadron, and everybody, of course, thought that the brave men had all been killed.

But the very same day a Spanish tug boat, bearing a flag of truce, came out of the harbor and ran alongside the New York. Captain Bustamente, Cervera's chief-of-staff—afterwards mortally wounded in the trenches around Santiago—brought a message from the admiral that Hobson and his men were all safe. He took back clothing and some money for them. This news naturally changed the gloom into the greatest joy, mingled with sincere appreciation of the Spanish admiral's chivalrous thoughtfulness.

The blockade of the harbor was maintained day and night with the strictest thoroughness. From the 2d of June on all the ships of the squadron formed a semicircle around Morro as a center, first on a radius of six, later on one of four miles; the heaviest ships were in the center of the line, and during night-time a battleship went farther in and covered the entrance with her searchlight, thus rendering escape of the Spaniards practically impossible.

The situation in Santiago was a discouraging one for the defenders even at that time. There were not sufficient provisions for the garrison, and these were still further reduced by the arrival of the Spanish squadron, which brought no additional stores or provisions. The coal supply in Santiago also was insufficient, and the appliances to coal were defective, so that this process required an abnormally long time.

The blockade itself was not devoid of thrilling incidents and danger for some of the ships forming it. One dark night during the last days of May the New York, for instance, was in imminent danger of being torpedoed by the Porter. The night was extremely dark, and the Porter, which had been out on a scout, perceived suddenly on her port bow a large craft looking in the darkness extremely suspicious. The Porter closed in immediately and her captain, Lieutenant Fremont, made the night fleet signal with his electric signal apparatus. But the strange ship did not respond with a similar signal. The Porter closed in nearer, with every man on his post behind the launching tubes and the guns. Fremont hailed with thundering voice: "What ship is that?" No answer. Again he showed the night fleet signal; the stranger responded this time, but with a wrong signal. He hailed a second time; no answer came back. He then fired a shot across the stranger's bow, when one of the latter's guns fired at the torpedo boat, the shell whistling close over the heads of the crew. Imagine the mental strain of this moment upon the torpedo crew and especially the captain. Fremont, though, hailed again: "What ship is that?" "This is the New York!" rang out a strong voice from aboard, recognized at once by Lieutenant Fremont as that of Captain Chadwick, the commanding officer of the big American cruiser. An awful catastrophe was averted in the last second.

LANDING IN CUBA

A s soon as the navy had located Cervera at Santiago and the War Department had decided to land the army expedition corps there with the view of capturing the place, the commanding admiral considered it his next duty to find a place which might serve as a base of operation and where the ships might coal. He selected the harbor of Guantanamo, forty miles east of Santiago, which was the nearest one offering enough room and sufficient protection against wind and sea.

On the 6th of June Admiral Sampson went close in with his fleet to Santiago and bombarded the works in order to unmask their batteries. These batteries were in a rather dilapidated state at the beginning of the war, but the Spaniards worked hard to strengthen them, partly by mounting guns from the Reina Mercedes.

At the time of the bombardment on the 6th of June the works were mounted by but twenty-four guns of all kinds of construction and calibre, some entirely obsolete and showing the date 1769, 1718 and even 1668, their range being hardly 800 yards at the highest elevation.

The cannonade of the American fleet on the 6th did little damage to the works; the Spaniards lost but six killed and seventeen wounded on the Reina Mercedes — which had been struck by two shells — and one killed and eight wounded in the earthworks.

Mention must here be made of the daring exploit of an American naval officer, Lieutenant Victor Blue of the New York. As the admiral wanted definite and minute information about the number and names of the Spanish war vessels in Santiago, which could not directly be obtained by any action of the fleet outside, Lieutenant Blue went on shore one night in disguise and, guided by Cuban insurgents, reconnoitered the harbor and brought back satisfactory, exhaustive and unimpeachable information about the Spanish naval force inside. It was a most dangerous and praiseworthy deed.

In accordance with the admiral's orders the cruiser Marblehead and the auxiliary cruiser Yankee arrived before Guantanamo early on the 7th of June and entered the bay, chasing the Spaniards from a blockhouse on a hill. The St. Louis was already there engaged in cutting cables, and the telegraphic connection between Santiago, Guantanamo and Mole St Nicholas, on Haiti, was destroyed. The Spanish gunboat Sandoval, which attempted to come out of the bay, was driven back inside the inner harbor, which is about twelve miles in length.

On the 8th the Marblehead brought the collier Sterling into the bay and selected a site for the camp. On the 10th the transport Panther brought a battalion of some 700 marines, under Colonel Huntington. They were landed under protection of the fire of the war vessels and after a lively skirmish drove the Spaniards into the bush. The camp was at once fortified as well as possible in the short time with the meager means available, and from that time on the Americans occupied Guantanamo permanently.

On the night of the 12th the Spaniards attacked the camp with great force and in superior numbers, pushing the American marines back till nearly down to the shoreline. Here the war vessels were able to bring help by throwing their searchlights on the positions of the enemy, thus exposing them to a severe fire. Furthermore, a steamlaunch of the Marblehead rendered especially effective assistance with machine-guns. The Spaniards were now driven back into the bush with considerable loss; the Americans lost one officer — Dr. Gibbs — and three men killed and eleven wounded.

The army expedition corps at Tampa in the meantime had been embarked and was ready to proceed on the 7th of June. But a rumor that Spanish warships — it was said the ironclad Pelayo and others — had been seen on the Cuban coast retarded the departure of the fleet of transports until the 14th. The Iowa and some of the cruisers acted as an escort, and the departure of the fleet, one ship following the other closely, was a great spectacle.

Favored by beautiful weather, the fleet arrived before Cuba on the 20th and awaited the further disposition of the admiral, fifteen miles to the southwest of Santiago. Sampson dispatched his chief-of-staff, Captain Chadwick, to communicate with General Shafter, in command of the expedition. The general was on board the steamer Seguranca, and was invited by Chadwick to confer with the Cuban General Rabi, who, on the instance of the admiral, had assembled most of the other Cuban leaders at his headquarters near Aserraderos, eighteen miles west of Santiago. On the afternoon of the 20th Admiral Sampson visited General Shafter himself, and the latter declared his intention to go at once to Aserraderos. The Cubans were in possession of this part of the coast, and several hundred of them greeted the American leaders enthusiastically on their arrival on the beach. In the following conference in Rabi's tent it was decided to land the army to the east of Santiago, at Daiquiri, where use could be made of a pier, which latter, though, was in a rather dilapidated condition. General Garcia's 3,000 Cubans were to hold themselves in readiness to be transferred by transports from Aserraderos to Daiquiri on the second day; the Cuban General Castillo was stationed with 1,000 insurgents some five miles west of Daiquiri.

On the 22d of June the landing of the army began. Captain Goodrich of the St. Louis was put in command of all the available boats of the fleet and the other vessels. The lighter warships cleared the coast of Spaniards by means of their quick-firers, and everything was ready at daybreak. But the skippers of the transports, being afraid to take chances, delayed the affair by keeping too far off-shore, so that the start was not made before 9 o'clock. At Cabanas, west of Daiquiri, the light warvessels made a pretense of landing to distract the Spaniards' attention from the real landing place, in which they succeeded.

There was a rather heavy sea running in-shore that day, and the landing of the heavily-laden boats, filled with soldiers inexperienced in such a manœuvre, was by no means easy. However, before the close of the first day some 6,000 men were on shore; at the end of the 24th of June all the troops had been landed. There was no provisions for taking the animals over; they were simply made to jump into the sea and swim ashore; it is said that thereby nearly 100 mules and horses drowned, some of them in their fright turning towards the sea instead of to the shore. On the 23d landing was commenced also at Siboney, where the surf was not so heavy. On the 26th Garcia's 3,000 men were brought over to Siboney from Aserraderos, and on the 27th the Yale arrived with 1,300 infantry under General H. M. Duffield, comprising the Thirty-third and Thirty-fourth Michigan Volunteers. After they were landed the whole American force on Cuban soil amounted to 21,000 men, including 4,000 Cuban insurgents.

The Spaniards in Santiago had of course observed the arrival of the expeditonary fleet and were fully aware of what it meant. They found nothing more important to do than to close the channel between Caya Smith and the mainland by a boom and some twelve mines, thus leaving only the western channel open around the little island upon which the Caya Smith is situated. The mine-field, consisting of thirteen electro-contact mines, in two lines, between Estrella and Socapa Points, was not even examined, although it was laid in April, and therefore not in good order.

The Spanish land forces, under Generals Linares and Vara del Rey, in the immediate neighborhood, amounted to 9,000 men.

The cavalry division, forming the advance guard of our landed troops, had passed the first night on shore in camp at Siboney, from the 23d to the 24th of June.

On the morning of June 24th the Americans started from Siboney to find the enemy. There are two roads running out from Siboney; one, a cart road, runs first in an easterly direction, then north and finally west; the other one, a mere path, leads straight up over the hills, joining the former road a little north from La Quasina, about four miles in-shore from Siboney.

General Young with eight troops of the First and Tenth Cavalry, amounting to 430 men, and two Hotchkiss guns, followed the cart road; the rough riders, some 500 men, under Colonel Wood and Lieutenant-Colonel Roosevelt, took the foot path. Castillo, who was to accompany Young with 300 Cubans, did not appear, but Cubans fell in in groups with General Young's column as the latter was proceeding on its march. None of these insurgents had any knowledge about the enemy, and they soon proved utterly useless as a military force.

A short distance from the fork where the cart road and the foot path joined, the first signs of the enemy's presence appeared. The Hotchkiss guns deployed and opened fire. On their first shot volleys came back from the Spanish side. Both rough riders and regulars came in contact with the enemy simultaneously, as neither heard the other's firing. The shrubbery and grass of tropical growth were so high

GENERAL HAWKINS CHARGING EL CANEY.

and dense as to hamper progress considerably and prevent seeing farther than 100 yards. The Spanish firing line, using smokeless powder, could not be located, while the puffs of smoke from the Americans betrayed their position distinctly. So it happened that both rough riders and regulars suffered severe losses. By 8:30 the left wing of the regulars, the First Cavalry, had formed connection with the right of the rough riders. About this time the Spanish left wing began to yield before the American right, the Tenth Cavalry. The enemy concentrated their force toward the road which turns westward here toward Santiago. All the troops, rough riders and regulars, impatient with the resistance of the Spaniards, rushed the latter's position and put them to flight. They pursued them for about a mile; then the Americans halted, as they were far in advance of the rest of their army and feared they might any moment run into an ambush or against a Spanish force far superior.

This spirited engagement had a wonderfully inspiring effect upon the American troops, although they lost in the engagement one officer (Captain Capron, of the rough riders) and fifteen men killed and six officers and twenty-six men wounded.

General Joseph Wheeler, who accompanied the cavalry, was full of praise for all the troops engaged. Besides the moral effect, this fight secured for the Americans also a well-watered country farther to the front and better adapted for camping grounds.

The sufferings of the wounded were great; there were no provisions yet made for taking care of the injured. They were carried back to Siboney as well as could be done, and here they were taken on board the hospital ship Olivette the next afternoon.

The rest of the army followed the cavalry, but up to the 30th of June the whole main force had not advanced farther than about a mile beyond the ground of the engagement of the 24th. The roads were bad, the heat was oppressive, heavy rainstorms added to the discomfort of the troops, and the management of the commissariat and the sheltering of the men were abominable. It was a natural consequence of the hurried landing, which Colonel Roosevelt is reported to have characterized in these words: "We did it like everything else—in a scramble."

The brigade of General Duffield was left as a garrison in Siboney.

The Spaniards did not take advantage of the difficulties which the Americans had in establishing lines of communication with their base. General Linares concentrated his forces in a position west of Santiago, where entrenchments and wire obstructions were hastily constructed. General Parejo, who was near Guantanamo, in the rear of the Americans, with 8,000 men, did apparently nothing.

While the army was thus preparing to push on to Santiago the navy continued its close watch of the entrance. Captain-General Blanco urged Cervera to leave Santiago, notwithstanding that this seemed impossible without certain destruction. All of Admiral Cervera's representations to that effect apparently did not appeal to Blanco. As late as the 27th of June he telegraphed to Cervera: "It seems to me that you somewhat exaggerate the difficulties of leaving Santiago. There is no need to fight. All you are asked to do is to escape from the prison in which the squadron now finds itself."

Cervera considered this last message an order to leave, and reported his willingness to comply to the captain-general, which would have meant the withdrawal of 1,200 landed seamen from the firing-line in the trenches. Blanco then changed his view to that effect that Cervera should only leave "if the fall of Santiago became imminent." To hold the squadron ready for such an emergency meant keeping the fires lit, which was equivalent to a daily consumption of nearly seventy tons of coal for the whole squadron. This was about as much as the squadron could take on board during twenty-four hours. As the ships could not be coaling all the time it was evident that the contents of the bunkers were daily reduced by this measure. As a matter of fact, when Cervera finally left the bunkers of his squadron were half empty.

In America this bickering between the Spanish admiral and the captain-general became known on July 1st, when a dispatch from Madrid was printed in one of the great American dailies that "there has been a quarrel between Admiral Cervera and Captain-General Blanco, and that the admiral has been ordered to leave Santiago." This would have given timely warning to the American admiral if such had been necessary.

EL CANEY AND SAN JUAN

ON July 1st occurred the two great land battles of the war, at El Caney and San Juan.

Since the 24th of June, for six days the American army was encamped on both sides of the cart road leading from Siboney via La Quasina to Santiago; the outposts were at El Pazo, about three miles to the front. The weather was bad, extreme heat and frequent rain rendering the condition of the unsheltered and inappropriately clad troops most trying and uncomfortable. There were many other defects, too numerous to be mentioned here, and all tending to aggravate the internal difficulties of the situation. The lay of the land was unknown, as there were no maps; the only semblance of one, a rough sketch, was given to the command of the cavalry division on the evening of the 30th of June. On the same day General Shafter moved his headquarters behind the line of the outposts near El Pazo.

The distribution and strength of the Spanish troops, as far as could be ascertained afterwards, were as follows: Main line west of Santiago, 2,500 men; at El Caney, the advanced position east northwest from Santiago, 600 men; at San Juan Hill, right east from Santiago, 1,000 men; along the west shore line of the bay, 1,000 men; between San Juan and Aguadores, 1,000 men; in the forts, 1,000 men, and a naval brigade estimated between 500 and 1,200 men, distributed probably in its greater part along the main line of defense east of the city. The position of San Juan was excellent, as it commanded the defiles of the only road to Santiago from the east. The distance from the exit of the defiles to the hill had been carefully ascertained by the Spaniards. The view at the exit was extremely limited, and about there the woods ended and left an open space of several hundred yards to the foot of the hill. This ground was crossed by several lines of barbed wire fence. Behind the firing line thus fortified some navy quick-firers of light calibre had been placed.

El Caney, about three miles from San Juan, seems to have been intended as an advanced position to give a proper support to re-enforcements which might come up from the east. There were no cannon at this place, but the defense was rendered strong enough through several lines of wire fence.

The roads to the Morro could not be used by troops in considerable number for the purpose of an attack; the Spaniards need not have troubled themselves about them.

The general commanding ordered the attack upon the Spanish lines for the 1st of July. Lawton's division was to advance upon El Caney at daybreak; Kent and Wheeler were to move on the road toward Santiago as far as the San Juan River, where they should wait for Lawton, who was expected to make short work of the El Caney position. Duffield was to attack Aguadores, and Bates to act as reserve. On the 2d of July a concentration of all forces was intended to attack and carry San Juan.

Lawton started on the afternoon of June 30th; leaving El Pazo to the left he went into camp along the road leading to El Caney.

Bates left Siboney at 9 o'clock in the evening of the same day and reached a position close to the rear of Wheeler's and Kent's brigades, where he went into camp for the night.

The next morning, the 1st of July, the brigades, of Lawton, Kent and Wheeler, started with the break of day.

On Lawton's division, General Ludlow's brigade turned to the west of El Caney, Chaffee's brigade east, and Miles's brigade remained south. Captain Capron, father of Captain Capron who was killed in the fight of La Quasina, had his four guns occupy a hill to the southeast of the town, about 2,500 yards from the nearest fortified point of the enemy's line. At 6:30 o'clock Capron opened fire.

The Spaniards answered immediately from the trenches.

Chaffee's brigade advanced in extended order from the northwest, the Seventh Infantry on the right, the Twelfth on the left, the Seventeenth as reserve; Ludlow's Eighth and Twenty-second Infantry advanced in the same way from southwest, with the Twenty-second Massachusetts Volunteers in reserve. The American firing line suffered considerably, especially from Spanish sharpshooters hidden in trees, from where they had a splendid view of the advancing skirmishers, remaining unseen themselves.

In front of Chaffee's brigade, between the two firing lines, there was a sort of natural embankment which it was necessary to occupy. The Seventeenth Infantry

PRIVATE PFISTERER RESCUED HIS COMRADE.

was ordered to do this about 10 o'clock in the forenoon. Colonel Haskell led his men along the cut of the El Caney road and deployed towards the crest. The ground was simply criss-crossed by the wire fences.

The Americans could not see anything of the Spanish trenches and were suffering severely from the enemy's incessant fire.

CHARLES D. ROBERTS,
First Lieutenant, 17th U. S. Infantry,
Born at Cheyenne Agency, S. Dakota,
June 18th, 1873,
Highest rank attained: Captain 35th
U. S. Infantry.

It was here, about 400 yards from the Spanish line that the commander of the Seventeenth, Lieutenant-Colonel Haskell, fell mortally wounded in an attempt to get nearer the enemy through the tangle of the wire fences. Two officers and five men of his regiment went bravely forward to where he lay and carried him back under shelter of the embankment of a sunken road. They were afterwards rewarded with the Medal of Honor. The details of the episode were as follows: Lieutenant-Colonel Haskell and the regimental quartermaster, Lieutenant Dickinson, were passing through the bush towards the enemy in advance of the regimental line. Close behind followed Company C, under First Lieutenant B. F. Hardaway. Coming to a sunken road the advance was stopped by a barbed wire fence. Lieutenant Dickinson called for the cutters, the fence was cut and the men crossed the road, where a similar fence had to be removed. The colonel and Lieutenant Dickinson had gone ahead and the company followed in single file. There was an open field in front. Hardly had the two officers entered this when they saw the trenches before them. Instantly the Spaniards fired a volley and both were hit. Colonel Haskell sank down with a remark that he did not wish to fall into the hands of the Spaniards. Lieutenant Dickinson ran back holding his right wrist, broken and bleeding, and shouting to the men: "The colonel is shot!" Lieutenant Hardaway sprang immediately out into the open to help his commander; Second Lieutenant C. D. Roberts, Corporal U. G. Buzzard, and Privates John Brookins, T. J. Graves, George Berg and Bruno Wende followed. Berg and Brookins were shot down; they managed to crawl or roll back into shelter. The others half dragged, half carried the poor colonel behind the embankment amidst a withering fire from the trenches. As has been said, the Medal of Honor was their reward for this act of devotion and bravery.

In the Seventh United States Infantry, fighting shoulder to shoulder, so to speak, with the Seventeenth, Private Herman Pfisterer, of Company C, was so fortunate as to rescue a wounded comrade out of the Mauser fire without being injured himself. He, too, gained the Medal of Honor for this brave deed.

The cut in the road was soon filled with wounded and killed, and shortly after noon the Fourth and Twenty-fifth Regiments of Colonel Miles's Brigade received orders to deploy and advance; the First Regiment remained at Capron's battery.

The Twenty-fifth Regiment advanced in the heaviest fire up to within fifty yards of a stone house, from where the American sharpshooters were able to enfilade some of the enemy's trenches. No further advantage of ground was gained by the Americans for two hours and a half. At 1:30 Bates's Brigade, the Third and Twentieth Regiments, filed into the firing line between the Fourth and Twenty-fifth Regiments. The situation became almost critical; General Chaffee, with absolute contempt for the Mauser bullets raining about him, exposed himself recklessly and is said to have rallied in person a number of young soldiers who felt their place in the line almost too uncomfortable for keeping it.

About then an order came from General Shafter to abandon the attack on El Caney and proceed towards San Juan, where hot work was going on too. General Lawton felt that a sudden abandoning of the fight must be of serious consequences to the morale of his men. He ordered Chaffee to storm the position according to his own best judgment. Chaffee immediately ordered the Twelfth Regiment to the charge. The brave infantrymen dashed forward through wire fences and the hail of Spanish bullets, the other regiments of the brigade doing the same. The Spaniards, terror-stricken, turned and fled. Some remained in the stone house and hoisted a white flag. They were taken prisoners.

GEORGE F. BERG,
Private, Company C, 17th U. S. Infantry,
Born at Mt. Erie, Illinois, December 2, 1867.

The capture of the stone fort took all the courage out of the Spaniards; they retreated on the two existing roads to Santiago; a lot of those choosing the southern road fell into the hands of General Ludlow's men. All in all, the Americans took here 160 prisoners. The casualties on the Spanish side were apparently heavy, but could not be ascertained, as many of their wounded were taken away.

After El Caney had thus been cleared of the enemy General Lawton left a few companies there as a garrison and turned the rest of his division towards San Juan, followed by Bates's brigade. While on the road the order reached these troops to return to El Pazo. This order created an unpleasant feeling in the column, as the men, fired with enthusiasm from their recent and sanguinary success, wanted to fight. But the order was, of course, obeyed; the general led his men back to their camp near El Pazo.

Now to San Juan. This position was the key to the whole Spanish line of defense. As has been said before, the cavalry division under Wheeler and the infantry brigade of General Kent were to advance towards and up to the San Juan River, where they were expected to await the arrival of Lawton.

The cavalry division under General Sumner—General Wheeler had an attack of fever on this morning—started on the right, the division of General Kent on the left towards the San Juan River, leaving Grimes's Battery on a hill by the side of El Pazo. Grimes opened fire shortly before 6 o'clock. The Spaniards answered, at a distance of about 2,800 yards, from a battery posted behind San Juan Hill and armed with quick-firing guns from the Spanish warships. These gunners evidently knew the range to El Pazo, or rather the hill on which Grimes was posted, for their second shot, a shrapnel, fell right in the battery, killing and wounding several artillerymen, also a number from the cavalry division and some Cubans lingering there.

There was only one road, hardly five yards in width, and lined with dense brush, and the advance of both divisions on this road became very difficult. Communication with Shafter's headquarters was soon entirely impossible. The last order Sumner received was to advance in the direction of Santiago, but to await further directions at the edge of the woods. This was the first and the last order the cavalry division received on that day.

The division of Kent followed on the same road, accompanied by the balloon detachment with a captive balloon, which was sent up from the advance guard, being led along with the troops by four guide-ropes. From this balloon the observers discovered a second road to the San Juan River, forking off to the left at the confluence of the Aguadores and the Guama. The balloon was soon after disabled and sent to the ground by a shell from the above-mentioned Spanish battery; two of the three enterprising balloonists in the car were badly injured by the fall.

General Kent, with the Sixth and Sixteenth regulars, was already at the fork of the San Juan when he learned of the existence of this second road. He directed the Seventy-first New York Volunteers, the third regiment of General Hawkins's brigade, to turn into this road.

Lieutenant Parker, who with his four Gatlings had been waiting near El Pazo, received orders to go with the Seventy-first New York Volunteers. He found the regiment halted near the fork. In order to reconnoiter for a good position he passed through in a trot. This caused the men to cheer; the attention of the Spaniards was aroused and a sharp fire was opened in this regiment's direction. Instantly there was a panic, the excited men crowding back on the narrow road, thus threatening the advance of all the following troops of the Second and Third Brigades. General Kent and the officers of his staff formed a line across the road and stopped the rush of the scared New Yorkers. In this critical situation Major George S. Cartwright, the divisional quartermaster, was of great service, being the first to successfully block the flight. General Kent, seeing that these men were too excited to be of proper service at the moment, finally ordered the regiment to lie down by the roadside so that the other troops might pass. This was done. The Third Brigade, Wickoff, and two regiments of the Second, Pearson's Brigade, then passed to the front on this road; the third regiment of the Second Brigade, the Twenty-first Infantry, had followed the First Brigade on the main road.

The edge of the woods, mentioned before, reaches a little beyond the right bank of the San Juan; beyond that there is a strip of flat ground some 250 yards wide and covered with high grass, and then the ground ascended steeply, to about thirty degrees. On this slope were the trenches and block-houses; the flat strip of grass was criss-crossed with wire fences.

The Americans deployed along the edge of the woods under an almost unbearable fire by the Spaniards, who knew the exact distance of the woods and also saw how the Americans came thicker and thicker, lining this edge.

On the extreme right wing of the American position was supposed to be General Garcia, with 1,000 Cuban insurgents; but nothing was heard or seen of them. Then

CEREMONY OF PRESENTATION OF THE MEDAL OF HONOR.

Corp. G. F. Berg, Sergt. U. G. Buzzard, and Sergt. B. Wende, of the 17th U. S. Infantry, receiving their Medals of Honor at San Fernando, Philippine Islands.

came the cavalry—First, Ninth and Tenth Regiments—then the rough riders under Lieutenant-Colonel Roosevelt, as Colonel Wood had been detailed to the command of a brigade; while farther to the left were the Third and Sixth Cavalry, the whole division again under command of Wheeler, who had returned to the fighting line in spite of his illness. To the left of him followed the brigades of Hawkins, Wickoff and Pearson.

When the American line was well established it was nearly noon. The enemy's nearest position was in front of the rough riders. Shortly after 12 o'clock Lieutenant-Colonel Roosevelt led his men to the charge. Entirely ignoring the galling fire of the Spaniards, he rode at the head of his men, a conspicuous figure in the tall grass. The rough riders followed him unflinchingly, and the men of the First and Ninth Cavalry, seeing the forward move, closed in too. In a short time, but with considerable loss, the Spanish position at that point was in the hands of the Americans.

The Thirteenth U. S. Infantry was ordered to the support of this part of the line, and took up a position on the brow of the hill opposite the enemy's trenches, where the brave infantrymen lay all day exchanging a lively fire with the Spanish sharpshooters, many of whom were hidden in the dense tops of the high palm trees.

Many deeds of daring were performed during the different stages of the fight, and it is safe to say that most of them passed unobserved. In the oppressive heat and the strenuousness of the work the men seemed not to care for vainglory or reward; they simply tried to do their full duty.

Sergeant Alexander M. Quinn, of Company A, Thirteenth U. S. Infantry, distinguished himself several times during the day.

When this regiment reached the firing line in the morning a bullet struck down Lieutenant Sater, of Quinn's company. Quinn caught the wounded officer as he fell, and eased his condition as much as possible. The wound was fatal, and the lieutenant died in the sergeant's arms.

Later on, in the afternoon, when the regiment was supporting the rough riders on the right, a daring private by the name of Wiles, of Company G, had crawled forward to some shrubbery about 100 yards in front of the general line. Wiles was one of the best sharpshooters in the regiment, and as he had a splendid view of the Spaniards from his place of vantage he used his skill with great effect. The men behind were silently admiring the coolness and bravery of their comrade when suddenly he was seen to throw up his hands and roll over. He had been discovered and shot by one of the Spaniards in the palm trees.

Sergeant Quinn, who had noticed the sharpshooter's plight, ran out of cover and to his aid. There was not much more to do for him. Quinn had hardly lifted up the wounded man when the latter died. He had been shot through the left breast. Quinn took the body and also Wiles's gun and returned with his burden to the firing line, which he reached uninjured.

Quinn was lucky on this day. Some time later he was dressing the wound of Major Ellis, of the Thirteenth, when a shell burst above them; the fragments whizzed all around and between them, tearing the bandage out of Quinn's hand and wounding Ellis a second time. But the sergeant was not hurt.

For his bravery at San Juan he was afterwards awarded the Medal of Honor.

The center of the attacking line was farther away from the enemy than the cavalry, and not so fortunate. The Third Brigade of General Kent's division lost its commander, the gallant Colonel Wickoff, who was instantly killed by a bullet while exposing himself in establishing a line. The command devolved upon Lieutenant-Colonel Worth, of the Thirteenth Infantry, who soon fell also, severely

"QUINN TOOK THE BODY AND RETURNED."

wounded. Lieutenant-Colonel Liscum, of the Twenty-fourth Infantry, took the command, but within five minutes he too was wounded. Finally Lieutenant-Colonel Ewers, of the Ninth Infantry, took charge of the brigade.

GEORGE H. NEE,
Private, Co. H, 21st U. S. Infantry.

The Twenty-first Infantry, of Pearson's brigade, advancing between the Second and Tenth Infantry, got into an exposed position near a pass on top of a hill, and the enemy's cross-fire did much execution. Company H was detailed to hold the pass. In an effort to do so this company advanced still farther and got into a position which proved untenable. The company commander ordered his men back into a better place, where there was at least some shelter. After the company had been established here it was discovered that two men were lost in the previous position. Volunteers were called to bring them in. Private George H. Nee responded at once, offering to take one end of the stretcher if somebody could be found to take the other one. Thomas Kelly, another brave soldier of the same company, was willing. While they departed, Corporal Thomas M. Doherty and Corporal John F. De Swan joined them to act as escort. They had to make their way about 150 yards towards the enemy, who opened an intense fire on them. Nevertheless, the intrepid men found their comrades, but one was already dead, the other dying. They picked both up and returned to their company's position. All four were presented with the Medal of Honor.

In a similar way did Privates Alfred Poland and James J. Nash, of Company F, Tenth United States Infantry, earn their Medals. They were fighting by the side of the Twenty-first, and went back towards the Spanish line to rescue some fallen comrades. They managed to get them out without being injured themselves.

The whole American line was now under such severe fire from the hills that the situation soon became unbearable. There was no other way to get out of this inferno of bullets and shrapnel but to charge. And this was done. Suddenly there rose a cheer from a group of about fifty men in the American center, and they were seen dashing forward and up the hill with the impetuosity of a storm-cloud. Right and left the men followed, wildly cheering. Within a minute the whole line was in the charge. It was reckless and desperate work. The numberless wire fences in the wide bottom in front had to be cut and torn down in full view of the enemy, who sent volley after volley into the thin line of brave Americans. There were many casualties, but no signs of wavering. "Forward!" was the parole.

The Spaniards did their utmost to hold their own, but it could not be done. On all the four hills occupied by the defense the Americans appeared almost simultaneously and drove out the Spaniards, who ran in a wild rush for the second line of defense, about three-quarters of a mile to the rear. By 2 o'clock the Americans were occupying the position, but the situation remained critical.

The artillery had come up shortly after 2 o'clock and, posted on the second hill from the right, opened fire on the second line of the Spaniards. But the heavy puffs of smoke made the guns conspicuous and they had to withdraw behind the crest.

Parker's Gatling guns took position to the right of the cavalry and just in time to take, under fire, the retreating remnants of the Spanish forces from El Caney. The troops were first thought by the Americans to be re-enforcements for the enemy, and General Kent sent the Thirteenth and the Twenty-first Regiments to strengthen the right flank. But the Spaniards had enough; although the firing continued until sunset, it was soon felt that the enemy was beaten. The victors spent the night in the trenches, with gun in hand, among their dead and wounded.

THOMAS M. DOHERTY,
Corporal Company H, 21st U. S. Infantry,
Born in Ireland, Febuary 3, 1874,

Thus ended this awful but glorious day.

The losses of the Americans in this battle were: Eighteen officers and 117 men killed; 111 officers and 686 men wounded.

The loss of the enemy was considerable in prisoners, over 200, but the casualties were probably not as numerous as in the attacking line, because the defenders were scarcely visible throughout the fight.

The attack of General Duffield's brigade did not go beyond Aguadores. The regiment marching at the head of the column, the Thirty-third Michigan Volunteers. received the fire from the Spanish artillery while deploying at the railroad station at Aguadores. One man was killed and several were wounded.

At midnight General Bates's brigade reached the firing line and was assigned the extreme left of the position; General Lawton's division arrived at 7 o'clock in the morning of the 2d and deployed to the right of the cavalry.

The Americans were aware that the second Spanish position was possibly stronger even than the first, and the troops lost no time in fortifying themselves as best they could against a possible surprise in the night. By the break of day the whole American line was entrenched, the cannon behind emplacements. The Thirty-fourth Michigan and Ninth Massachusetts Volunteers, of General Duffield's brigade, reached the front to act as a reserve.

When daylight came on the 2d of July the battle was renewed. But this time the Americans were protected, and it was soon felt that they could easily hold their ground. When the Spaniards attempted an attack, towards 10 o'clock in the forenoon, they were easily repulsed at all points.

"THEY MANAGED TO GET THEM OUT WITHOUT BEING INJURED THEMSELVES."

It happened during this attack that in the trench of the Ninth U. S. Infantry a soldier was hit in the chest, and in his agony jumped up and rolled over the embankment toward the side of the enemy. First Lieutenant Ira C. Welborn, who was right behind his men on the line, seeing this got up and carried the wounded man back into a place of safety. The act was done without paying the slightest attention to the danger of the whizzing Mauser bullets; Welborn received for it the Medal of Honor.

At 9 o'clock in the evening there was another alarm. An American advance post was attacked by the Spaniards, and soon the lines were firing again. But this was only of short duration, yet not without casualties, among them the commander of Lawton's brigade, General Hawkins, who received a wound in the leg.

The night of the 2d to the 3d of July was passed again in the trenches. The hardships of the troops were fearful. The soldiers were lying in the ditches half-filled with water; there was absolutely no shelter from the scorching rays of the sun and the drenching flood of the tropical rain; the food, as little as was to be had, was of poor condition, and in many instances could not be eaten at all, but what the suffering soldiers regretted most of all was the lack of tobacco.

The greatest hardships fell to the lot of the wounded. The few surgeons at the front were overworked; many of the wounded were lying helplessly in the rain on the soaking ground, without blankets, without the slightest comfort, in many cases even without a bit to eat or to drink. It is doubtful whether at any time or on any occasion the endurance and patience of the soldiers were so intensely tested as immediately after the battles of El Caney and San Juan.

On the morning of the 3d the fusillade began again, but only in a desultory way. It ceased towards noon, its substitute being the tremendous roar of the heavy ships' guns in the naval battle of Santiago.

The total loss of the Americans at both El Caney and San Juan was, according to General Shafter's report, 32 officers and 208 men killed, 81 officers and 1,203 men wounded, out of a supposed strength on the firing line of 12,000 men.

The Spaniards lost two generals, Vara del Rey, killed during the attack on El Caney, and their commander-in-chief, Linares, wounded by a shot through the left shoulder; also Captain Bustamente, Cervera's chief-of-staff, mortally wounded at the attack of San Juan.

General Toral was now in command in Santiago.

Toral received during the forenoon of this day the demand by the American general to surrender unconditionally. In case of refusal Shafter announced the bombardment of Santiago, and requested the withdrawal of the foreign residents, the women and the children, by 10 A. M. of the 4th. Toral refused to capitulate; upon the request of representatives of foreign powers, who came out personally to the American commander, the latter granted a prolongation of the proposed armistice until the 5th of July.

"HE CARRIED THE WOUNDED MAN BACK INTO A PLACE OF SAFETY."

In the night of the 2d to the 3d of July the Spaniards received re-enforcements through the arrival of Colonel Escario with 3,000 men. General Garcia, who had been sent against these latter with 4,000 Cubans to drive them back, failed in his task.

On both sides the armistice was used to strengthen the lines, but after all, and especially after the destruction of the Spanish naval squadron became known, every-one felt that the Spanish cause was lost.

While thus the army had won laurels for the American nation on land, greater glory was gained by her fighting sons on the sea.

NAVAL BATTLE OF SANTIAGO

O N the 2d of July Admiral Cervera, pursuant to orders received, withdrew his sailors from the trenches on shore and prepared for his last and terrible task, the escape from Santiago. The admiral and his officers knew only too well that it was a forlorn hope. But the order of the captain-general had to be obeyed. "Ship with the greatest dispatch all your seamen and leave at once with the squadron." This was the message received.

What must have been the thoughts of these unfortunate men, who all knew that they were standing on the threshold of certain destruction; that they had now to sacrifice themselves, and a useless sacrifice at the best.

Blanco's message came in the morning. Cervera gave the order at once to have steam ready by 2 P. M. Then he summoned his captains, Moreu of the Colon, Lagaza of the Oquendo, Eulate of the Vizcaya, his flag-captain, Conchas, Villaamil, the commanders of the destroyers, and the second in command, Commodore de Paredes of the Colon.

In the ensuing conference it was decided to leave on the next morning, Sunday, the 3d, at 9:30. Captain Moreu of the Colon was in favor of going out by night; he had to yield, however, to the majority. It is also rumored that the captains, or some of them, proposed disobeying Blanco's order. Cervera would not hear of that, so the final conclusion was reached.

On the night of the 2d the cruisers got their boats aboard and shortened cables, and a little gunboat, the Alvaredo, removed some mines in the channel west of Caya Smith to open the way.

Innumerable were the criticisms coming forth afterwards against Cervera's choice of daytime for his flight. There were also weighty voices, even from some American naval officers, who sided with the Spanish admiral. But how could anyone know the true motives governing Cervera, where the chances were so manifold and un-certain, and how can full justice be done to the question without a thorough and unimpeachable knowledge of these motives?

The American fleet off the port kept as strict a vigilance as ever and never detached more than one or two of the heavy ships at the same time, thus always preserving an overwhelming superiority to the enemy.

The American commander-in-chief had his fleet divided into two squadrons: The New York, Oregon, Iowa, New Orleans, Mayflower and Porter, under his immediate command, guarded the eastern side of the entrance; the Brooklyn, Massachusetts, Texas, Marblehead and Vixen, under Schley, watched the western part.

On July 1st the New York and Iowa had been bombarding Santiago, assisting the army in its attack. On the 2d the bombardment was repeated.

On the morning of July 3d the Massachusetts left the blockading line for Guantanamo to coal, whence the Iowa had just arrived on the previous day with bunkers filled. Towards 9 o'clock the New York, accompanied by the Hist and the Ericsson, left also for Siboney, as Admiral Sampson was to attend a conference on shore there with General Shafter.

The move of these vessels was signaled from the Morro to Cervera, and this was, no doubt, another motive for his choice of hour for departure.

It was a most beautiful day, still and clear, and the crews on the American warships prepared quietly for their customary Sunday's inspection.

The ships then on guard off the harbor, ranging from west to east, were the Vixen, Brooklyn, Texas, Iowa, Oregon, Indiana and Gloucester; they were in command of the following officers: Vixen, Lieutenant A. Sharp; Brooklyn, Captain Francis A. Cook; Texas, Captain John W. Philip; Iowa, Captain Robley D. Evans; Oregon, Captain Charles E. Clarke; Indiana, Captain H. C. Taylor, and the little Gloucester, a converted yacht, Lieutenant-Commander Richard Wainwright.

The ships' bells rang out three times; it was 9:30.

On the Iowa the inspection had just been ended, and the lieutenant of the watch was ascending the bridge to relieve the navigator who had taken the watch during inspection, when the latter cried out: "What's that black thing there, coming out of the harbor? Hoist the signal!" And up went the afore-prepared signal, "The enemy is trying to escape," and the ship's gong gave the alarm to the crew.

The whole fleet was aware of what was happening yonder at the entrance. The narrow channel looked darkened by the stately black hull of the first Spanish cruiser, the Maria Teresa, with the red and yellow emblem of Spain flying from her mastheads. Thick clouds of smoke rolled over the channel, announcing the other ships of Cervera, while all the Americans rushed in concentric lines upon the entrance to the attack.

There was a flash on the Spanish cruiser, and the first shell came tearing towards the Brooklyn, striking the water in front of her. The sound of heavy cannon soon filled the air. The Spanish cruisers were now all out, nicely distanced in line ahead, with speed increasing every second, and in the order Teresa, Vizcaya, Colon, Oquendo, the two torpedo boat destroyers Pluton and Furor trying to make the entrance and gain the off-side of their ships.

On the American ships the men in the stoke-holds strained mind and muscle to their utmost to create speed, the power in which the enemy was said to excel.

When the Spaniards first emerged from the harbor they made apparently straight for the Brooklyn, which was then head-on almost in front of them. Captain Cook ported the helm of his vessel and had her circle off to starboard in order to prevent the enemy from getting between him and the rest of the American ships. The little Vixen hurried as fast as possible away from the front of the Spaniards towards the lee of her own fleet.

When the smoke-clouds began to gather around the American squadron, among the earth-rending roar of its mighty cannon, the Brooklyn seemed to be the only object the Spaniards cared for, and enveloped in a blazing, belching wreath of fire, this gallant ship seemed to be the match for all.

Minutes stood for ages in these early moments of the fearful fight.

Presently on the starboard quarter of the lonely Brooklyn loomed up the gigantic form of a battleship driving forward like a moving volcano, with glaring sheets of fire flying from her mighty sides, wrapped in waving mountains of smoke, an immense, overpowering, glorious sight. " 'Tis the Oregon," said Executive Mason to the commodore.

As the ships gained speed and the smoke would part for a second or two the flag-ship obtained glimpses of details of the cruel, although magnificent spectacle. Right behind the Oregon, somewhat on her port quarters, the sturdy Texas was plowing along putting shot and shell into the fleeing and hapless Spanish cruisers in front of her, while the powerful Iowa, her tall stacks showing above the dense smoke, with flames like glaring streamers issuing from their tops, followed. Farther to the rear the Indiana, of slower speed, strained both her artillery and engines to the extreme limit in order to do all the execution possible during the short space of time allotted to her on account of the swiftness of the chase.

The gun-fire of the American ships was probably the most terrific cannonade ever brought into play in all the history of warfare. Its tremendous power showed after a few minutes. The Teresa was seen to be on fire, and shortly before 10 o'clock she turned in-shore and ran aground at Nima-Nima cove, six and a half miles from the Morro. Only two miles farther to the west the Oquendo, also on fire, did the same. Both ships struck their flags.

The two destroyers Pluton and Furor were demolished after they had hardly come out of the entrance. Several of the big ships, the Iowa, Texas and Indiana, directed their light batteries against them, and the Gloucester, her captain, Wainwright, driving her in with conspicuous boldness, finished them. Most of their crews, among them Captain Villaamil, perished by the American shells or drowning.

The Vizcaya and Colon still held out; the latter had overhauled the Vizcaya and was fast drawing away from her pursuers. So it happened that the fire of three near vessels, the Brooklyn, Oregon and Texas, was concentrated upon the unfortunate Vizcaya. Finally, enveloped in flames, with the torpedo boat Ericsson close astern ready to torpedo her, she turned also in-shore at about 11 o'clock, near Aserraderos fifteen miles from Morro.

By this time the Colon was far enough ahead to be practically out of range. She was still gaining on her enemies. The latter consisted now of the Brooklyn, the Oregon and the Texas, with the little Vixen in the wake of the flagship. The other ships, Iowa and Indiana, were called off to return to their blockading station by the New York. This ship was about seven miles to the east from Morro when the Spaniards dashed out; she turned immediately and took up the chase, followed by the Ericsson.

The Colon had so far been most lucky. She left the harbor third in the line, being, when passing the entrance, only between 2,800 and 3,000 yards distant from the Iowa, Indiana, Texas and Oregon. All these ships fired at her, but possibly their main attention was concentrated upon the other three Spanish cruisers, and their light batteries fired at the destroyers, which were just then visible in the entrance. The Colon may also have improved her chance by shaping her course inside of the other Spanish vessels. Enough, she drew away and out of the reach of fire comparatively uninjured.

When the Vizcaya ran aground the hope entertained on the Colon for escaping must have been stronger than ever; but it did not last long. Spanish machinists and firemen were not to be classed with their American brethren in the profession. It is probable that at the time of her greatest speed she made sixteen or seventeen knots; this fell to twelve knots about noon. Soon the pursuers drew near, and the Oregon opened fire, sending two of her projectiles from the forward thirteen-inch guns after the fleeing Spaniard Within a short time both Oregon and Brooklyn were close enough to use their froward eight-inch guns. After the first shot struck her, Captain Moreu, probably utterly disheartened, turned his ship in-shore a few minutes past 1 o'clock, near Rio Tarquino, fifty-five miles from the Morro, and struck the flag.

The American ships, the Brooklyn, Oregon, Texas and Vixen, soon surrounded her, and while Commodore de Paredes and Captain Moreu surrendered to Captain Cook, sent on board by Commodore Schley, the New York, with the commander-in-chief, also came up. The struggle was over.

Within less than five hours six modern and powerful Spanish vessels were destroyed by the fire of the opposing American fleet.

It was on the same afternoon that the commander-in-chief, Admiral Sampson, announced this glorious achievement to the American people in the following dispatch which was sent from Playa, Haiti, on the following day:

"The fleet under my command offers the nation as a Fourth of July present the destruction of the whole of Cervera's fleet. No one escaped. It attempted to escape at 9:30 A. M., and at 2 P. M. the last, the Cristobal Colon, had run ashore sixty miles west of Santiago and has let down her colors. The Infanta Maria Teresa, Oquendo and Vizcaya were forced ashore, burned and blown up within twenty miles of Santiago; the Furor and Pluton were destroyed within four miles of the port. Loss, one killed and two wounded. Enemy's loss probably several hundred from gun fire, explosions and drowning. About 1,300 prisoners, including Admiral Cervera. The man killed was George H. Ellis, chief yeoman of the Brooklyn.

"SAMPSON."

President McKinley answered as follows to Admiral Sampson:

"You have the gratitude and congratulations of the whole American people. Convey to your noble officers and crews, through whose valor new honors have been added to the Americans, the grateful thanks and appreciation of the nation.

"Wm. McKinley."

Now to details.

In the first place the American officers and crews were so far superior in professional training and ability to their enemy that this fact could not fail to impress every man, from the highest to the most humble of the victors, and create an exuberance of spirit, daring and certainty of success which marks the action of the stronger in every walk of life.

The Spaniards, on the other hand, felt hopeless, from their admiral down the scale, and whatever activity or energy they showed was instigated by a mingled feeling of old-fashioned pride and desperate courage to show themselves worthy of their fancied reputation and come out alive. To deny the enemy great individual courage would be an injustice, and the personal tales of the victors bear out this view.

Finally, after the fight, during the rescue of the survivors and the surrender of the fallen foe, there were scenes so touching and dramatic that they really form the most impressive and interesting incidents of the momentous struggle.

When the Teresa rounded Socapa Point and her first guns opened fire upon the Brooklyn, Admiral Cervera dismissed his pilot, warning him to lose no time, as death and carnage were about to envelop the ship. "And do not forget to show them my certificate," concluded the considerate old warrior, "so that they pay you for to-day's service."

The Iowa was the first American ship to return the fire; the others followed suit immediately and almost simultaneously. But the first shots of the Americans fell short. This was plainly observed by Assistant Engineer Bennett, of the New York, who, while his ship was swiftly approaching, saw the sea whipped into a veritable line of moving foam by the rain of shot striking the water some distance from the fleeing targets.

The foremost Spanish ship apparently intended either to ram or cut off the Brooklyn, which the latter prevented by her loop to starboard. This manœuvre was dangerous, undoubtedly, in the dense smoke, on account of the nearness of the other battleships.

It seems that the distance over which the farthest ships, the Iowa and Indiana, opened fire on the first Spanish cruiser was in the neighborhood of 5,000 yards. All five ships, the Brooklyn, Oregon, Texas, Iowa and Indiana, directed their heavy fire naturally on the foremost enemy, the Teresa, with the result that within five minutes the smoke-cloud, enveloping her and testifying to her lively firing, had disappeared, and instead flames were shooting up from different parts of the deck. An 8-inch shell, probably from the Brooklyn, struck on one of the 5-inch gun-shields, exploded, upset two of these guns and killed every one of their crew, besides wounding many others of the second battery. Two 13-inch shells, which must have been fired by the Oregon, struck the hull right under the after barbette and exploded in the after torpedo-room. Almost every man in there was killed, the few survivors fearfully mutilated, the whole inside of the after part of the ship wrecked and a huge hole torn in the starboard side. Another big shell exploded about the same time right over her engine-room, its whizzing fragments spreading death and wreckage over this part of the ship. Besides there was the rain of smaller shells, six-pounders, one-pounders, 4-inch and 5-inch rapid-fire guns. The Spanish admiral and his flag-captain stood on the bridge amidst the infernal fire, observing the awful carnage and waiting for the fast approaching end. Captain Conchas was shot down by the admiral's side, and five of the other officers had been killed or wounded. It was difficult for the Spanish sailors to fulfill their duties under these conditions. And then it happened that cartridges did not fit the guns; that as many as seven had to be tried before one was found to fit. The fire was now blazing fiercely over the ship fore and aft; Cervera's order to flood the magazines could not be obeyed, as the men could not get to the valves on account of the overpowering smoke. The ammunition hoists became jammed, perhaps through the heat; the men no longer stood to their guns in the secondary batteries. There was no use carrying this on longer, and there was no way out. The admiral, with his heart heavy and hope vanquished, gave the command, and the Spanish cruiser, only a few minutes before so stately and strong, lay aground on the rocks of the beach a burning wreck, in whose flame-lined interior scores of wretched human beings were helplessly perishing in a most awful manner. All those who were able went overboard and tried to reach the shore by swimming. Admiral Cervera left the ship dressed in underclothes and, assisted by his son, Lieutenant Angel Cervera, reached the land in safety. Soon a cutter approached from the Gloucester under Acting Ensign Edson and the difficult work of rescuing those who still remained on the burning ship was taken up by the brave Yankee sailors with the greatest devotion and self-exposure. Cervera and the men on shore surrendered as prisoners of war and were first conveyed on board the Gloucester, where the Spanish admiral donned a light flannel suit of Captain Wainwright's. Later he was taken before the American admiral, who received and treated him with distinction. The loss of the Teresa's crew of 550 men was 46 killed and 110 wounded. The prisoners were afterwards taken on board the Harvard and brought to the United States.

The Oquendo shared the fate of the Teresa a few minutes later. This ship, the last in the Spanish line, was hit several times before she even got out of the channel. Then she had to run the gauntlet of the whole American squadron. She was struck oftener than any other Spanish ship; the American officers counted fifty-seven shell-holes on the wreck, but a good many other evidences of good marksmanship must have been obliterated by the final fire which also accompanied the destruction of this ship. An 8-inch shell from the Iowa passed through the port-, hole of the forward turret, scouring the gun and exploding inside. Every man in the turret was killed; the Americans afterwards found the dead gun-crew exactly in the positions in which they fell. In the sighting-hood the dead gun-captain was still apparently in the act of laying the gun, and another dead gunner still had his hand on the lever with which to operate the running-out machinery.

In the after-turret the air became so close that the lieutenant commanding the gun stepped to the door in the rear, opening it. At this moment a shell struck him, tearing his body to fragments. Another American shell struck in the after torpedo-room and detonated a 14-inch Schwartzkopf torpedo with terrific effect. The after part of the ship was completely wrecked thereby, and the fire-mains were broken. Fire started here with such intensity that it could not be controlled. An 8-inch shell dismounted three of the 5-inch guns in the port secondary battery, killing or disabling most of their crews. Flames sprung up on the orlop deck forward, created by an exploding 8-inch shell. The cannonade opening now against this ship made it an abode of hell. The whole American fleet directed its guns upon this unfortunate Spaniard, the Oregon at 1,500 yards, the Texas at 2,200 yards, the Iowa at 2,800 yards, the Brooklyn at 2,500 yards and the Indiana at 5,000 yards. There was no hope for this vessel; her doom was more absolute even than any of the others. Captain Lagaza turned her in-shore about two miles west from where the Teresa lay. When the Oquendo struck, both of her military masts fell and her commander, it is reported, blew out his brains in the conning-tower. The survivors of the crew were saved by boats of the Gloucester and Harvard. From a complement of 475 men 70 perished, and among the prisoners there were about 80 wounded.

When the Teresa struck the Vizcaya headed the Spanish line. This gallant ship under her brave commander, Eulate, offered by far the best resistance on the part of the Spaniards. What Eulate wanted was to disable the Brooklyn, he nourishing a hope—which would have proved vain though—that he could escape from the other American ships. But the punishment they all inflicted upon his vessel was terrible.

The Spanish gunners in the secondary battery would not stand by their guns where an incessant rain of shell and splinters swept them down and away; the officers were said to have shot several sailors who refused to keep their stations. Even in the military masts almost every one was killed by this time. The few men left perished later on when both masts fell. Horrible scenes happened on this ship. In the sick-bay the surgeons were working with superhuman effort to alleviate the cruel suffering when a shell came tearing along, exploding above and setting fire to this part of the ship. Surgeons and hospital stewards had to flee for their lives, and the wretched men in the sick-bay were left to their awful fate. A shell crashed into Captain Eulate's cabin and started a fire in the after part of the ship One 8-inch shell struck forward, exploding inside and killing or mutilating nearly sixty men. An officer on board described the terrible situation thus:

"I do not believe that a man on our ship did a cowardly act, but many of us were perfectly distracted. The exploding shells, the shriek and the roar of the missiles passing over us, and the rattle of the lighter shot on the steel deck made a fearful din. After about fifteen minutes I did not hear a single command given. The officers screamed their orders for a while, but soon they could not make themselves heard and there were few to obey,

In the engine-room the chief engineer and the greater part of his force had been killed by escaping steam from the steam-pipe, which was hit several times by shells or flying debris; the pumps were choked up and the revolving cranks blinded those who were left with flying water and oil. Captain Eulate was wounded in the head and on the side by fragments of an exploding shell. At 11 o'clock, or shortly after, he beached his ship near Aserraderos and struck the flag.

The surviving members of the crew of this vessel were in the greatest distress, for the ship was burning furiously and it was well-nigh impossible to stay on board any longer. On the shore waited the Cuban insurgents for the Spaniards, and several of the latter were shot while trying to save themselves.

It was the Iowa under Evans which brought relief to the suffering men. Evans stopped the insurgents and sent boats which rescued the survivors. Of the Vizcaya's crew of 491 men nearly 200 were killed and many wounded. When Captain Eulate was carried on to the deck of the Iowa in a chair he made an effort to rise, saluted Captain Evans gravely, unbuckled his sword, kissed the hilt affectionately and then, silent and grief-stricken, tendered the weapon to Captain Evans. The American commander refused by gesture to accept it, saying at the same time that he would not take the sword from so brave an enemy. At these chivalrous words his whole crew broke into cheers. It was a grand moment and the Spanish captain seemed greatly moved. A Spanish lieutenant, Louis Fajardo y Pinzon, impressed the Americans by his manful behavior. When reaching the deck he stood erect and saluted ceremoniously while it was seen that his left arm had been shot off above the elbow and was dangling from the stump by part of a muscle.

The officers and crew of the American ship behaved splendidly toward the stricken foe; they clothed the Spaniards, who were all naked, and provided food and other comforts for them.

It was just fifty-six minutes after the first Spanish cruiser had been discovered dashing out of the harbor that the Iowa ceased firing and lowered her boats for the rescue.

Now only the Colon was left. This ship was the best and the swiftest of the whole squadron; her extensive armor was undoubtedly an admirable protection for the men behind it, and also for the vessel itself. As she did not have her two 10-inch guns she was lighter, and the decrease in weight ought to have added to her speed. She was rated at over twenty-one knots. But after about two hours' effort, during which she may have made sixteen or seventeen knots, she fell back to twelve knots, and the Oregon and Brooklyn soon had her at their mercy.

Hardly had the first shot struck her when she was turned in-shore and the white flag hoisted. The crew threw the breech-blocks of the guns overboard, and in the stoke-holds the sea-valves were opened.

While Captain Cook rushed alongside in his steam-launch, by order of the commodore, to receive the surrender, the Brooklyn and Oregon detailed prize-crews in a hurry to save the ship. These crews were sent on board, but nothing could be done with the hull.

When Sampson had examined the situation he ordered his flagship forthwith to make an attempt to push the Spanish ship higher up on to the beach to prevent her from slipping into deep water. But it was of no avail. The Colon capsized and remained in such a position that subsequent efforts to save her proved fruitless.

The loss of the crew amounted to only one killed; the rest of the 566 men and the officers were made prisoners of war.

The greatest loss and severest punishment throughout this fight were sustained by the two destroyers, Pluton and Furor. The Pluton was commanded by Lieutenant Vasquez, the Furor by Lieutenant Carlier; on board this latter vessel was the flotilla-commander, Captain Villaamil.

As soon as these two hapless craft appeared in the entrance the Gloucester and the light batteries of the Iowa, Indiana and Texas opened on them. The unequal struggle lasted only a few minutes, although the destroyers defended themselves vigorously with their 14-pounders and 6-pounders. They made no attempt to use their 14-inch torpedoes.

The Pluton was already leaking badly and making for the shore at Punta Cabrera when a 13-inch shell from the Indiana struck her amidships. The forward boilers were exploded by the terrific shock; all the men in her stoke-hold except two were killed by the scalding steam. She sank in shallow water near the shore. Of her crew of eighty men twenty-six were saved by the Gloucester; the rest perished.

On the Furor a shell tore the boatswain to pieces and portions of his body became entangled in the steering gear. American shells exploded her ammunition and one 6-pounder shell exploded in the engine-room, killing both engineers. The ship was burning inside from stem to stern. She showed the white flag in a sinking condition. Most of the survivors jumped overboard and were rescued by the Gloucester. This happened shortly after the Oquendo had run ashore.

The New York, while passing in her chase after the cruisers, fired her only shots in the battle, three 4-inch shells, at these vessels when they were already about done up by the other ships. Captain Villaamil was hit in the abdomen by a 6-pounder shell, which tore the entrails out, and of the vessel's crew of eighty men about forty survived.

The loss of the American fleet was in all one man killed and two wounded. The killed was Chief Yeoman George H. Ellis of the Brooklyn. It happened during the engagement with the Vizcaya. Ellis was standing near Commodore Schley with his instrument to measure the distance. The commodore happened to ask: "How far?" Ellis answered: "Seventeen hundred, sir." Schley thought it a little farther, and said so. Ellis remarked: "I just took it, sir, but I will try again." He stepped off to the side and had just raised the instrument when a shell struck him in the face, taking off his head above the chin. Officers went to the body and were about to throw it overboard when Schley stopped them, directing that the body should be covered with a flag and properly buried after the battle.

The Brooklyn was hit twenty times by whole shot, besides many times by fragments of shells and machine-gun projectiles, her flag on the main and her signal halyards were destroyed, and she received other damage, none of which, however, proved serious.

The Iowa was also hit eleven times, but no serious injury was done.

The American ships fired in this engagement 9,429 shots, distributed as follows: Brooklyn 1,973; Oregon 1,903; Indiana 1,876; Iowa 1,473; Gloucester 1,369 and Texas 835.

CLOSING EVENTS OF THE SANTIAGO CAMPAIGN

THE purpose of the expedition, the destruction of Cervera's fleet, was now an accomplished fact, and as the provisions in Santiago were known to be scanty and insufficient, the surrender of the place was only a question of a short space of time.

It was probably for this reason that Shafter did not reopen hostilities on the 5th of July, although the truce ended on this day. On the next day Shafter demanded anew the surrender; Toral asked and obtained time to communicate with his goverment.

On the 9th of July re-enforcements arrived for the Americans, the First Illinois and the First District of Columbia Regiments, under General Randolph; the prisoners of the Merrimac were exchanged on this day.

The Spaniards were informed that hostilities would be definitely considered as reopened on the afternoon of the 10th at 4 o'clock.

On that day the Spaniards were the first to open fire, which was vigorously answered by both the American ships and land forces.

But the Spaniards soon ceased firing; our troops continued until darkness set in.

The next day the American bombardment was renewed, the Spaniards answering only with a desultory, weak fire.

At 2 o'clock in the afternoon the Spanish general was again asked to surrender, with the additional proviso that the Spanish troops, after disarmament, would obtain free transportation to their home country.

On the 12th Toral declared his willingness to surrender, and on the same day General Miles arrived before Santiago, not to take the supreme command, but to get a personal insight in the situation.

On the 14th of July the three generals, Shafter, Miles and Toral, met and concluded the capitulation of the part of Cuba to the southeast of the line connecting Asseraderos, Palma Soriano and Sagua de Tanamo.

On the 17th of July the Spaniards laid down their arms and the stars and stripes were hoisted over Santiago.

Affairs looked very bad in Santiago after the surrender. The population as well as the military forces were fairly starved and the aid extended immediately by the United States forces furnishing provisions averted a catastrophe which would have cost more lives than the bullets and shells in the fights of the previous days. The Spaniards cultivated the friendship of our troops and all hardships of the campaign were forgotten. Few, however, had anything but contempt for the insurgents. Their conduct had thus far been such that a hatred rather than a comradeship for them had been developed among our troops.

During and after the operations against Santiago there were smaller expeditions at several points of the coast, mainly to keep in touch with the insurgents and to reconnoiter.

In these exploits several Medals of Honor were earned by some of the participants, the details of which are given on this and the following pages.

A N act of singular bravery was performed on the 20th of July on board the Iowa by two members of her engineers' force.

Shortly before 7 o'clock in the morning it happened that a manhole gasket blew out in one of the boilers of fire-room No. 2. The fire-room immediately filled with live steam and the floor was covered with boiling water, flying from the boiler under a pressure of 120 pounds. Coppersmith P. B. Keefer and Second-class Fireman Robert Penn, who were stationed in adjoining compartments, rushed instantly to the rescue. Penn entered fire-room No. 2 just in time to save an injured coal-passer from falling into the boiling water which covered the floor. He carried the man, who had both feet scalded and a wound on his forehead, to a safe place and then ran back. Keefer, who heard the noise, had in the meantime dashed below and found his

ROBERT PENN,
Second-class Fireman, U. S. Iowa.
Born at City Point, Va.

way through the blinding steam to the two inboard furnaces and hauled the fires. In the meantime Penn had the extra feed pump turned on in the after fire-hold and built a bridge by throwing a plank across some ash buckets. Fireman Smith, who wished to assist Keefer, had both legs terribly scalded by the boiling water on the floor. Penn, while Passed Assistant Engineer Stockney held the plank in place, then hauled the two remaining fires, and thus the imminent danger of an explosion was averted by his and Keefer's fearlessness and quickness. Both men were awarded the Medal of Honor.

"AN EXPLOSION WAS AVERTED BY THEIR QUICKNESS."

SAMUEL TRIPLETT,
Seaman, U. S. S. Marblehead.
Born in Cherokee County, Kansas,
December 18, 1869.

BEFORE the American troops could be landed at Guantanamo Bay a problem presented itself to the navy the solution of which demanded tests of reckless courage and heroic intrepidity. The entrance to the bay was guarded by mines, and these had to be destroyed before the transports could attempt to enter and approach the shore. These mines were formidable affairs, French made and so constructed as to explode forty-five kilograms of guncotton at a time from a mere forty-pound blow. In other words, a ship striking them with the force equal to that blow would cause an explosion sufficient to destroy the vessel and send most of its human cargo into eternity.

To clear the harbor of these dangerous obstructions was the problem. It was accomplished by the men from the cruiser Marblehead on July 26 and 27, 1898. One of them was Seaman Samuel Triplett, who gives an interesting description of the manner in which the dangerous task was completed.

"We approached the mines in two small boats," he says. "Our boats, connected by ropes and a chain, which formed a sort of drag, moved along abreast and kept a distance of fifty yards apart.

"The Spaniards ashore eyed us keenly as we rowed toward them, and fully understanding our design waited with their fire until we would be within their reach. No sooner had we come within reach of their fire than they began to open up on us, and for a time it rained bullets and deadly missiles. Their fire did little damage, and a number of steam launches which accompanied us on the expedition protected us from a more direct and certainly more effective attack.

"As soon as the chain would strike a mine we would close in upon it, cautiously approach it and cut the contact wires. Then we would destroy the dangerous contents and render the mine harmless. In this manner we proceeded from one mine to the other until they were all disabled and the bay was cleared.

"The task was perilous in the extreme, but was accomplished expeditiously and without the loss of a single man."

RAN INTO AN AMBUSCADE

ARLY in July, 1898, and immediately after the battles around Santiago, expeditions were fitted out by the United States Government to bring supplies of ammunition to the insurgents in Cuba, of which it was known they were in great need. Such expeditions were dangerous undertakings, as great energy and daring had to be exhibited if a successful landing of the cargo of such ships was to be accomplished without drawing the attention of the enemy. The Spaniards, in a case of premature detection of such expeditions, would always have the advantage over the landing parties on account of their positions, and under such circumstances the Americans were naturally compelled to retreat.

Such an expedition was conducted by Captain J. W. Heard, Third United States Cavalry, on the wooden transport Wanderer. With a force of eleven men from his own cavalry regiment and about forty or fifty Cuban filibusters from the United States, he was to land supplies and ammunition for the Cuban forces. The landing was attempted near the mouth of the Mani-Mani River, in the Province of Pinar del Rio, and was quite a risky enterprise on account of the close proximity of the Spanish garrison of Bahia Hondo, only six miles distant.

The boat had made the voyage without a convoy, and therefore the expedition had to rely on the energy and foresight of the commander alone.

It was early in the morning of July 23d when the boat arrived in sight of the Cuban shore. When about 400 yards from the mouth of the river and shore, small boats were lowered and supplies were taken to shore under personal direction of Captain Heard.

The arrangements were that a large Cuban force should be present to receive the supplies, but this "large" force was missing. In place of it about 200 Cuban patriots were scattered along the shore, proving of very little assistance. The surroundings of the landing place were carefully reconnoitered, the sandy beach as well as the almost impenetrable jungle back of it and the beautiful and grand mountainsides in the background showing no signs of the enemy. The filibusters and soldiers landed and commenced discharging their boat-loads, when suddenly a heavy fire was opened from the woods and a force of about 1,000 Spanish cavalrymen broke forth and dashed at the landing party.

The surprise was great, and a panic would have followed had not Captain Heard kept cool-headed during the next few moments of excitement.

He ordered his men to lie down and open a rapid fire on the advancing Spaniards. Many saddles were emptied and the dash was checked. While the enemy was retiring to shelter Captain Heard hurriedly ordered his little force to re-embark and hastily return to the Wanderer.

Wheelsman William Davis and Seaman William Ross, also the Cubans, Benito Sabata, Gabriel Alvarey, Felix Lopez and Rojolu Garcia were severely wounded, and only the energy displayed by the captain saved them from falling into the hands of the Spaniards. The retreat was executed just in time, for no sooner had the boats reached the side of the Wanderer than the enemy again burst forth and opened a concentrated fire on the boat. No one on board was hit, however, and with the scars of hundreds of bullets marking her sides the Wanderer put out to sea.

As shown by later reports the Spaniards lost heavily in this engagement, and Captain Heard was awarded the Medal of Honor for heroism displayed in rescuing the wounded from the hands of the enemy.

ON the 1st of July there was an attempt to land ammunition and stores for the insurgents at Tunas near Cienfuegos. The Florida, a transport, arrived off the place and went into the horseshoe-shaped harbor, sending first a force of 200 Cubans on shore. There was a small detachment of American soldiers on board, among them a few men of the Tenth Cavalry. The landing was effected only a few hundred yards from a block-house wherein was posted a Spanish garrison. A skirmish ensued in which the small American detachment had a hard fight, but they all finally got back on board the transport towards 3 o'clock in the morning. Corporal William H. Tompkins and Private Dennis Bell, of Troops A and H, Tenth Cavalry, were conspicuous in this affair for their daring and cool behavior, and for such were rewarded with the Medal of Honor.

THE PORTO RICAN CAMPAIGN

GENERAL Miles deeming the invasion and capture of Porto Rico of the greatest importance, made a report to the War Department to that effect and was directed on the 7th of June to at once assemble such troops as were available for that purpose. These orders were subsequently changed to have the expedition operate in both Cuba and Porto Rico. When the surrender of Santiago had been accomplished by the Cuban expedition General Miles again suggested the immediate invasion of Porto Rico, and after completing his arrangements he sailed from Guantanamo on the 21st of July with 3,415 troops, under the immediate command of General Guy V. Henry, and a convoy consisting of the Massachusetts, Dixie and Gloucester.

It was Miles's intention to land at Cape San Juan on the northeast coast of Porto Rico, but when the American press dispatches disclosed his proposed destination General Miles summarily changed his plans and sailed for Guanica on the southwest coast of the island. In the meantime two other expeditions had left the United States for Porto Rico, one of 3,571 troops, under Major-General James H. Wilson, which sailed from Charleston, S. C., and another of 2,896, under Brigadier-General Theodore Schwan, which left Tampa, Fla. They were to join General Miles at Cape San Juan and therefore were not convoyed. Thus, when General Miles changed his plans and sailed for Guanica, it was thought at the War Department these two expeditions would be left to the mercy of any Spanish gunboats that might be in the vicinity of Cape San Juan, but General Miles had taken the precaution to have gunboats stationed there to notify them of his change of plans and direct them to join him at Guanica.

Arriving off Guanica on July 25th, early in the morning, the Gloucester entered the harbor first and fired a few shots, completely surprising the Spaniards. As she met with but slight resistance the transports were enabled to enter, and between daylight and 11 o'clock General Miles had his troops ashore and the American flag raised over a block-house which had been flying the Spanish flag.

On the 26th Brigadier-General Garretson's brigade had a sharp skirmish with the Spaniards, and on the following day another at Yauco, where the Spaniards were driven into the mountains and the American troops advanced on Ponce, fifteen miles east of Guanica, which place they reached on the 28th. The Dixie, Annapolis and Wasp were already in front of the town, and when the troops arrived the people surrendered without offering any resistance.

In addition to the three divisions under Generals Henry, Wilson and Schwan, a fourth expedition, under Major-General Brooke, sailed from Newport News on the 28th and arrived at Arroyo, which had already surrendered to the Gloucester. This brought the total force in Porto Rico up to 15,199 men, 106 mortars, howitzers, field and siege guns, and now preparations were made for the campaign, the purpose of which was to drive out the Spanish garrisons in the western part of the island and then proceed across the island to San Juan, the principal objective. The force was divided into four separate commands, under Generals Brooke, Wilson, Henry and Schwan, and moved eastward across the island, expelling the hostile detachments from the southern and western parts.

Meantime the Amphitrite, Puritan, Montgomery and Leyden had proceeded to San Juan to await there the arrival of General Miles, but as he had changed his plans the ships lay to in the harbor under Cape San Juan and awaited orders. On August the 6th a detachment from the Amphitrite seized the San Juan lighthouse and fortified it. Two days later the Spaniards attacked this improvised fort, but after some sharp firing in which the Amphitrite's and Cincinnati's guns covered the garrison, the Spaniards were repulsed. On the 9th this force in the lighthouse was withdrawn and preparations were made for bombarding the fortress and city of San Juan.

General Miles's forces were in the meantime rapidly advancing upon this place, carrying everything before them in the brilliantly conceived campaign, his four division commanders having taken Guayamo, Coamo, Sabana Grande, San German, Mayaguez and other less important towns, at all of which places the troops were welcomed by the natives with genuine enthusiasm, for more than four-fifths of them were in sympathy with the United States.

The Spaniards in San Juan were by this time practically cut off from retreat by General Miles's forces on shore, and had the army closed in upon the city and the intended bombardment by the warships taken place, their position would have been hopeless, but the signing of the peace protocol put an end to further operations. Thus Porto Rico was conquered by the United States with a loss of but five killed and twenty-eight wounded.

Four months later, on the 10th of December, 1898, the treaty of peace was signed at Paris upon the following basis:

Spain abandoned all rights of sovereignty over Cuba; Porto Rico and the Island of Guam in the Ladrones group were ceded to the United States; the Philippine Islands were to come into the possession of the United States upon the payment of $20,000,000 within three months after the ratification of the treaty; and Spanish merchandise was to have privileges in the Philippines equal to those of the United States for a period of ten years.

A N unfortunate misunderstanding led to the outbreak between the native Filipinos and the American troops, which developed into a serious insurrection. It is probable that this conflict could not have been avoided, for the natives had years before determined to achieve their independence and that idea had never been abandoned, even when there was apparent peace between the natives and the Spaniards. When Admiral Dewey won the battle of Manila the government of the United States regarded this blow at Spain as a war measure and nothing more. An American squadron was in Asiatic waters. A Spanish squadron was in Philippine waters. It was a very natural move for the United States to strike this squadron and destroy it, for such a feat would weaken Spain on the sea. It would deprive Spain of her Asiatic squadron, deprive her of a source of revenue, and it would place the United States in possession of the Philippines pending a settlement by treaty. The people at that time did not regard it as a permanent acquisition of territory by conquest.

When it was known that an attack was to be made upon the Spanish squadron Aguinaldo was at Singapore. Consul General Pratt, United States representative there, suggested that Aguinaldo accompany the squadron from Hong Kong to Manila, and that he should then organize land forces of natives, which would be armed by the United States, for co-operation with the American marine force. This appears to have been a very serious mistake, but it was an error of judgment quite natural under the circumstances. The squadron had no support ashore, and it needed information with regard to what was going on about Manila. Spain was offering special inducements to natives who would join her against the Americans. It was partly to prevent any such re-enforcement that Aguinaldo, a prominent rebel leader who had the confidence of the natives, was approached.

It is possible that in the excitement of the hour rash promises may have been made to the young chief of the insurrection, but he was shrewd enough to know that they were not made with authority. At first it was a matter of considerable doubt whether the United States would hold fast to the islands, and it is quite possible that unauthorized persons may have told Aguinaldo that all the United States aimed to do was to force Spain to give Cuba and the Philippines their independence. This was something that the natives had been hoping for. They were anxious to get rid of Spanish dominion and the Spanish priests and friars, to whom they attributed many of their wrongs.

Aguinaldo set off with all possible speed for Hong Kong, but did not arrive until the day after Dewey had sailed for Manila. He was received by Consul-General Wildman at Hong Kong, who conferred with him with regard to supplies of arms and ammunition for the native troops. After the battle of Manila Bay the McCulloch came over to Hong Kong and took Aguinaldo aboard. He was supplied with about 2,000 Mauser rifles and with 200,000 cartridges. The McCulloch landed the young chief all alone, at Cavite, but he proved a veritable whirlwind of energy. In six days he had thousands of natives under his banner, and Manila was practically surrounded by his bands. He was in undisputed possession of the towns of Bacoor, Imus, Benakayan, Noveleta, Santa Cruz de Malabon, Rosario and Cavite Viejo. This blocked Manila on the south, and other leaders, acting in concert with Aguinaldo, closed the Spaniards in on the north and east.

By June 9th the whole province of Cavite was under Aguinaldo's dominion. He had set up a provisional government and had taken many Spanish prisoners, besides 7,000 rifles, several cannon and much ammunition. On June 16th he declared a dictatorial government over the Philippine Islands.

The government established by him at Malolos consisted of the following cabinet officers:

President, Emilio Aguinaldo; Secretary of War, Baldomero Aguinaldo; Secretary of Foreign Affairs, Cajetano S. Arellano; Secretary of Home Affairs, Leandro Ibarra; Secretary of General Revenue, Mariano Trias; Secretary of Justice, Gregorio Araneta; Secretary of Education, Felipe Buencamino.

Senor Felipe Agoncillo was sent to Washington to represent the Filipinos at the American capital.

The army of the pseudo-republic was variously estimated at from 10,000 to 30,000 men. It was fairly well organized, although the discipline was hardly up to the standard of modern armies.

On June 20th Aguinaldo issued election notices, and on the 23d established a revolutionary government and issued notices to all the provinces. Messages were sent to several foreign powers asking for immediate recognition of his government and his authority. When Manila finally surrendered, the self-made president expected the Americans to retire and leave him in possession. He was very much hurt because the United States authorities refused to allow his men to loot the foreign quarters, to set up his presidential headquarters in the government palace and to take possession of the Spanish treasury funds and the church funds.

This was the beginning of the trouble. Repeated messages were dispatched to foreign courts asking for recognition of the native government, but no attention was paid to them or to Philippine envoys. Native troops about Manila began to show hostility toward the Americans. Those at a distance from Manila kept on attacking Spanish garrisons and making prisoners of Spanish residents, priests and laymen and collecting funds, arms and ammunition. They paid no attention to restraining orders from the United States authorities, but boldly established a camp about Manila. They sent envoys to Europe and to the United States, notably Agoncillo, Apacible and Sixto Lopez, all of whom were able men, and, looking at the case from their standpoint, they were patriots as well.

General Thomas M. Anderson, commanding the American military forces at Manila, was not slow in recognizing the purpose of the Filipino leader. He studiously avoided recognition of Aguinaldo's claims to the presidency, and acted entirely within his military function, paying no attention to the provisional republic. General Wesley Merritt, who succeeded to the command of the American troops, also avoided all official communications with Aguinaldo. When he wanted to move American troops he ordered the native troops to stand aside, but each time the wily insurgent leader would try to entangle the American commander into some recognition of his authority.

The demand for the surrender of Manila was made by Admiral Dewey and General Merritt August 7, 1898, and refused by Governor-General Augusti. A few days later, when the course of events in the Philippine capital was rapidly approaching a crisis, an order from Madrid arrived deposing Don Augusti and appointing Don Fermin Jaudenes his successor.

August 13th the city surrendered and 7,000 Spanish soldiers, officers and men, became prisoners of war of the American forces.

These are the facts.

The accompanying circumstances are not wholly beyond dispute, but granting that they, too, permit of but one interpretation, they in no wise detract from the glory of the United States.

The situation at Manila at the time of the surrender was disheartening from a Spanish point of view. Surrounded by impetuous Filipino forces of superior strength, left to defend a city the population of which was decidedly hostile, the Spanish commanders were compelled to face this unpleasant alternative: they would either have to submit to the revolutionary forces or surrender to the Americans. To attempt to lead the badly disorganized, discouraged forces against any one of the armies or both would have been the height of folly and involve only reckless butchery of human life.

It was therefore a mere matter of choice as to the lesser evil. The Spaniards detested the Filipinos and feared them; the Americans they respected even though they were their foes. And so they elected to surrender to the latter, who, it was presumed, would permit them to surrender with military honors. The plans to a certain extent miscarried, for the capture of the city was preceded by actual fighting, during which six men on the American side lost their lives and about forty were wounded.

It was early in the morning—a little after 6 o'clock—when the first operations were begun amidst a heavy thunder-storm.

On the right wing of the American forces were eight battalions of the First Brigade under General MacArthur, with three battalions in reserve, while General Greene with seven battalions and three in reserve formed the right.

The navy began operations at 8:45 A. M., and one hour later the Olympia sent the first shell into the city. Soon afterwards General Greene ordered the advance and immediately six companies of Colorado volunteers dashed toward the Spanish positions. The entrance to the suburbs was accomplished only after some severe fighting, but once the approaches of the city were in the possession of the Americans all further resistance ceased. The white flag hoisted upon the fort ended all further hostilities. By an agreement with the insurgents the American forces alone entered the city—Aguinaldo and his men remaining mere spectators, although they assisted in the fighting. The formal surrender followed the next day, August 14th. The Americans now were in possession of Manila, the stars and stripes floating from the municipal building of the Philippine capital.

Native troops deserted from the Spanish army and joined Aguinaldo. An agreement between him and General Merritt was entered into by which the natives would be restrained from sacking the city or violating the ordinary usages of war. This naturally angered the natives. Aguinaldo and General Pio Pilar wanted to make a triumphal entry into the capital. It is not at all likely that they intended to sack the city or to murder the Spanish residents and troops, for their subsequent conduct has shown a pretty strict adherence to the customs of civilized warfare. Natives who showed friendship for the Americans were ostracized by the native troops, and some of them were killed in brawls. The native newspapers were intensely bitter against the Americans.

Political clubs were formed among the natives, and these for the most part became merged into an insurrectionary society called the Katapuinan, which had for its sole purpose the expulsion of the Americans and the establishing of a republic under Aguinaldo. These clubs and branch societies became recruiting boards for the native army. They had armories established for forging bolos. They created a junta which acted as outside agent for the purchase of arms, and directed a band of smugglers who supplied them to the rebellious natives. The Filipino Congress decreed that every native above 18 years and not in the government service should be drafted into the army.

These swift operations on the part of the natives soon massed a formidable force about Manila, and they became so insolent that as a measure of safety General Merritt ordered them to withdraw outside the limits and placed a line of pickets between them and the city. Then Aguinaldo moved his temporary capital from his old home at Bacoor to the more remote town of Malolos. During the sitting of the peace conference at Paris the natives were anxious that the Americans should remain as their protectors, for fear Spain would concentrate all her military force against them. Then when Spain would be deprived of all rights in the islands they expected that the Americans would retire and leave them in peaceful and undisturbed possession.

In the meantime the budding Insurrection received encouragement from the United States, and from citizens whose loyalty could not be questioned. The more conservative Americans were bitterly opposed to the purchase and annexation of the Philippines. They were opposed to any addition of insular territory, and this party by its declarations and protests against annexation gave the natives hope that a determined resistance on their part would lead to an abandonment on the part of the United States. The idea prevailed that if the natives could compel the handful of American troops to withdraw from the islands the government of the United States would never attempt to recover possession, so they plotted to overthrow the American military government before re-enforcements could be brought across the Pacific.

A plan was cunningly laid. General Pio Pilar was to get into the city with 10,000 bolo-men and other native troops variously armed, in disguise of peaceful citizens. Aguinaldo and his associates were to have command of the main force outside the American lines. Their purpose was to provoke the Americans to begin hostilities, and then, when the Americans were strung out in a thin line of battle and busily engaged with the forces in their front, Pilar was to attack them from behind and throw them into a panic which would make them easy victims. The intent to compel the Americans to appear as aggressors made it impossible to fix a definite date for the attack. The natives could not tell just how much annoyance the Americans would stand. At first the troops merely laughed at the gibes and insults, which they could not understand. When force was justified they retorted with kicks and cuffs. The difficulty the natives experienced in arousing the Americans to armed hostility made them believe that their enemies were cowards and that they would not dare oppose such an overwhelming force as the natives had massed.

General Merritt, in order to get at the intentions of the native troops, proposed a conference between commissions representing the Americans and the natives, at which the natives were to submit their plans and whatever requests they wished to lay before the American government; but when the conference met the natives refused to make any definite statements. Then it was apparent that they meant mischief and that they were unwilling to enter into a temporary understanding.

THE FIRST BATTLE

O**N** the night of Saturday, February 4, 1899, the natives had resolved to force the hand of the Americans. They drew up in formation resembling line of battle in front of the Nebraska and South Dakota regiments, and marching up to the sentries shouted insulting remarks and pushed them back by force. This was only a little more than had been attempted on several previous nights, but the movement was more extensive and the formation of the natives more menacing than usual. Finally a band of natives in charge of an officer in uniform made a rush upon Private Grayson, of Company D, First Nebraska Volunteers, on sentinel duty, who fired and brought the officer down. The squad immediately fired at Grayson at close range and then fled. Grayson was unhurt, but the object of the natives had been gained at last. American troops had opened fire upon the patriots who were demanding independence. In a few minutes a shrill clamor arose from the darkness which enveloped the native lines and then rockets began to go up, which were answered by other rockets. Signal guns were fired at various points along the American front and the Philippine rebellion was begun.

Soon the artillery joined in the melee and from the bay Admiral Dewey's warships began to shell the insurgents. The Filipinos concentrated their forces at three points, Caloocan, Gagalangin and Santa Mesa.

At 1 o'clock in the morning the insurgents opened a hot fire from the three points simultaneously. This was supplemented by the fire of two siege guns at Balik-Balik, and by advancing their skirmishers at Peco and Pardacan. The Americans replied with a heavy fire, but in the darkness they had little knowledge of its effect.

The Utah Light Artillery at last succeeded in silencing the guns of the Filipinos. The Third Artillery was pounding away at the flashes of fire, showing the insurgents' position on the extreme left. The engagement lasted over an hour. During much of the time the United States cruiser Charleston and the gunboat Concord, stationed off Malabon, hammered with the rapid-fire guns of their secondary batteries upon the insurgents' position at Caloocan. At 2:45 in the morning there was another fusillade along the entire line. When daylight came the Americans advanced. The natives outnumbered the American forces largely and fought bravely, but were everywhere repulsed and driven back with awful slaughter. The men of the Eighth Army Corps, under General Elwell S. Otis, who took charge of the American forces on his arrival in the Philippines in August, 1898, participating in the fight, numbered about 13,000. The total strength of the Filipinos under arms in the neighborhood of Manila was about 30,000, of whom 20,000 are supposed to have engaged in the battle. Heavy losses were inflicted on the enemy.

While the fighting was proceeding there was great excitement among the residents of the city, and had it not been for the splendid police system established by the Americans there would have been a general outbreak and looting. The attack by the Filipinos came so suddenly upon the American forces, although trouble had been anticipated, that soldiers then off duty, who had visited the theaters and the circus that evening, were called out and the performances stopped. Filipinos scurried everywhere, and the rattle of musketry and the booming of cannon outside the city rent the air. The residents of the outskirts of Manila flocked into the walled city with their arms full of household effects. All the carriages disappeared as if by magic, the street cars stopped, the telegraph lines were cut, and the soldiers moved hurriedly about to the stations assigned them. The stores were closed almost instantly, foreign flags were to be seen flying from many windows, and a number of white rags were hung out from the Filipino huts and houses. There were several cases of Tagals attacking American soldiers in the streets, but those who attempted it were shot and killed.

The native troops were well armed with Mauser and Remington rifles, but their shooting was ridiculously bad. General Charles A. King's brigade charged upon a numerically strong force of the enemy, and, yelling wildly, drove them helter-skelter into the Pasig River, where, in the frenzy of terror, they were drowned like rats.

The fighting during the night was necessarily somewhat desultory. The Americans were on the defensive. They simply stood their ground, returned the fire of the rebels and pressed forward whenever possible. The attack was renewed several times. At 4 o'clock in the morning, however, when daylight made it possible to engage in anything like organized warfare, the entire line of American outposts was engaged. The soldiers moved out of the city to the east and north, driving the enemy beyond the lines they formerly occupied, and capturing several villages and their defense work. These villages included San Juan del Monte, Santa Ana, San Pedro, Macati, Santa Mesa and Lorma.

In the meantime Admiral Dewey had not been idle. During the night it was impossible for him to use shells, as his fire would have been as dangerous to the Americans as to the natives, but he gave orders that as soon as it was light enough to allow the positions of the enemy to be determined with accuracy the cruiser Charleston and the captured gunboat Callao should take part in the fight. At daylight these two warships took up positions and opened fire on the enemy north of the city. Later the monitor Monadnock was ordered to cover the Filipinos to the south of Manila. The positions of the enemy were accurately located and the warships poured a heavy fire into them. The losses of the natives by this bombardment were very heavy.

To the north and south of the city the slaughter was sickening. Filipinos were literally torn into shreds by the fire from the warships. In some places the shells tore great holes in the earth and around these were scattered the dead bodies. The great number of dead that were afterward found everywhere showed that the natives were not lacking in courage, but no courage could withstand the terrible rain of death that fell upon them as the Americans approached their positions.

A NIGHT ATTACK AT MALATE REPULSED.

When the enemy retreated it was to get out of the range of the American guns as rapidly as possible.

Of the American forces in the battle the Fourteenth United States Infantry suffered the greatest losses. The regiment was quartered at Malate, under command of Major Rabe, and was assigned to the task of carrying the rebel position south of that suburb. The men fought through a country covered with a dense undergrowth, and made slow progress at first. The natives took refuge in nipa-covered huts, and until they were dislodged and driven back inflicted considerable damage on the Americans. The Fourteenth was armed with Krag-Jorgenson rifles, and these weapons proved most effective. For every life that the gallant old regiment gave it took a score in revenge.

The First Washington Volunteers and Third United States Artillery also saw severe fighting and sustained material losses. The Utah Light Artillery and the Sixth United States Artillery did effective service, and the latter helped to save the First California Regiment from being badly cut up. The guns were posted east of the city, and during the early hours of Sunday poured a deadly fire into the insurgent trenches. The men of the Utah battery were seasoned by their experience in Malate in August and conducted themselves like veterans.

During the engagement 100 insurgents took possession of Pacho church, and barricading the doors opened fire on the First California Regiment. They also fired on the ambulances that were carrying wounded Americans to the rear. The Californians sent volley after volley against the sturdy stone structure, but their fire was ineffective. The men wanted to rush in and storm the building, but Colonel Smith restrained them. Word was sent to the Sixth Artillery and the guns were ordered trained on the church. The gunners found the range very quickly, and in twenty minutes the old church was a wreck and half its occupants were dead. The First California Regiment was also attacked by Filipinos who were concealed in huts beside the road along which the Americans were advancing. To put an end to the danger Colonel Smith gave orders to burn the village.

In the district between Tondo and Malabon, to the north of the city, great slaughter was done by the gunboat Callao. This little vessel proved herself a terror. She mounted more guns in proportion to her size than any other vessel in the American navy, being full of one, two and three-pounders and machine guns. The Concord's six-inch and the Charleston's eight-inch guns likewise did great execution. General Otis's brigade had driven a large body of the enemy from their positions, and the Filipinos ran at a breakneck speed for the beach, a discouraged and panic-stricken mob. When they reached the shore they were met by a devastating fire from the warships and mowed down in great numbers. The sight was horrible.

On Sunday afternoon the Charleston joined the monitor Monadnock off Malate, which was the scene of the heaviest fighting with the Spaniards in August, and both vessels delivered their shells with telling effect. The enemy were retiring before the steady advance of the Fourteenth Infantry and furnished excellent targets for the marksmanship of the Yankee gunners.

The Filipinos now retreated, quickly followed by the Americans, as far as Caloocan, on the Dagupan Railway on the north, and on the south to Pasay, south of Malate. The burial of the dead Filipinos by our soldiers took place on Monday.

Aguinaldo had his lines strengthened, especially at Santa Mesa and San Juan del Monte, which commanded the approaches to the reservoir that supplies Manila with drinking water. It was at that point near Santa Mesa that the battle started, and it was there that the fighting was fiercest. The Americans, on defeating the enemy in that quarter, marched on towards the water-works, with the object of gaining possession of them and thus preventing the insurgents from cutting off the water supply.

By Tuesday evening the Americans were in complete control of the situation within a radius of nine miles from Manila, their lines extending to Malabon on the north and Paranaque on the south, a distance of fully twenty-five miles. The main body of the rebels was in full retreat and utterly routed.

General Hale's brigade advanced Tuesday morning and captured the water-works at Singalon. Four companies of the Nebraska regiment and a part of the Utah battery, with two field guns and two Hotchkiss guns, met the enemy on a hill half a mile out, and a sharp engagement took place, in which the Nebraskans lost one killed and three wounded. Dr. Young, formerly quartermaster-sergeant in the Third Artillery, was wounded, captured and brutally murdered, and his body when discovered was found horribly mutilated. The Filipinos were driven back, retiring in bad order and carrying with them the valves and heads of the steam chest and cylinder of the pumping machinery.

General Ovenshine's brigade advanced and took Paranaque, capturing two field guns. General MacArthur's division advanced beyond Gagalangin without loss, the enemy retreating upon Caloocan. The Americans gained control of the steam line to Malabon and 600 marines with four Maxim guns were landed from the fleet on the beach north of the city. The Third Artillery, on the main road, and Utah battery, in a cemetery, covered the advance of the troops.

Among the important points captured was a strong embrasured earthwork within sight of Caloocan. The signal corps were compelled to run their wires along the firing line during the fighting, and consequently there were frequent interruptions of communication, owing to the cutting of the wires, and signal-men were ordered to kill without any hesitancy anyone who attempted to interfere with the lines.

THE SECOND DEFEAT

THE terms of the capitulation between the United States and Spain, agreed upon on August 13, 1898, surrendered the city of Manila, the suburbs, harbor and bay to the American forces. The rest of the archipelago remained, for the present, under control of Spain. But this was merely nominal, for the insurgents were the real masters of the situation in all these places. Negotiations for the occupation of certain positions in the immediate vicinity of Manila were begun immediately after the surrender and dragged along all fall. There was some dispute as to the rights of the American troops to garrison certain places, not so much between the Spanish generals and the American commanders as between the insurgent leaders and the latter. As a matter of fact the Spaniards fully appreciated the untenability of their position and dreaded to surrender to the rebels, at whose hands they feared they would receive very little consideration, and they, therefore, secretly wished and welcomed American occupation. But the insurgents stubbornly insisted on their rights of conquest, and were unwilling to recognize the supremacy of the United States. General Otis's demand that the insurgents evacuate the Island of Panay was met with a flat refusal. At Iloilo General Rios was in possession with a large Spanish force. He was willing to yield to the wishes of General Otis and surrender the city to him if the insurgents would let him, but they would not.

General Otis replied at once, thanking the Spanish general for his generous offer, but declined to accept it without instructions from the home government, and not before the peace treaty about to be concluded at Paris established the authority of the United States beyond controversy.

In the meantime the position of General Rios became very precarious; that of the insurgents stronger with every day. The capture of the place was only a question of time, and fear of an awful fate seized the inhabitants.

On December 13, 1898, a petition for American protection was sent by a number of leading business men of Iloilo to General Otis and by him forwarded to Washington for instructions. These arrived ten days later and read as follows:

"The President directs you to send the necessary troops to Iloilo to preserve the peace and protect life and property. It is most important that there should be no conflict with the insurgents."

Upon receipt of this telegram General Otis at once notified General Rios that an American force would be sent to Iloilo. On December 24th Brigadier-General Marcus T. Miller was placed at the head of an expedition and ordered to proceed to Iloilo. Before his arrival, however, the Spanish general had given up the struggle and surrendered to the insurgents. Then followed some more parleying, exchange of notes, etc., and time passed until Friday, February 10th, when definite action was taken and the second serious conflict with the insurgents took place.

On that day General Miller was ordered to await the arrival of the St. Paul, which carried an additional force, and take the town no matter what the insurgents would say.

Upon the arrival of the transport and after a conference with other officers, General Miller, about 4 o'clock in the afternoon, sent a notice to the insurgents that they must surrender within twenty-four hours or he would land troops to occupy the town, and if they offered any opposition the town would be bombarded. They were also informed that if they burned the town he would burn Molo and Jaro, two native villages; and that if they attempted to further obstruct the entrance to the river, or add to their defenses, he would open fire at once.

On Saturday morning the Petrel signaled the Boston: "Enemy throwing up more trenches in our front." The Boston replied: "If you are sure this is so, give them a shot." She fired two 3-pounders, and soon afterward signaled: "Enemy firing on us." At the same time the enemy were seen to bring down a field gun to the beach on the Boston's side. The Boston signaled to the Petrel, and both opened fire. The Boston fired two trial shots and then dropped a 6-inch shell into a house in front of which the insurgents had stationed their gun. It was afterward learned that this house was their headquarters. Five minutes before this shell struck the house a mounted officer had galloped down and sent his horse into the compound of the house. When the Boston's shell dropped the people on board could see him, horseless, running away. As soon as the American forces opened fire the insurgents began setting fire to the town. The first house fired was an American storehouse. In a few minutes the town was on fire in five or six places, and it burned all that day and night, destroying the English, American and German consulates, several residences and warehouses, a large portion of the business section and the native and Chinese quarters. The next day, after the army had occupied the place, the custom house and a large warehouse were burned. Most of the foreign residence part was untouched.

The ships ceased firing at 10:20 A. M., and soon after the Boston sent forty-eight men and a Gatling gun ashore, while the Petrel sent thirty men.

The men from the Boston immediately took the fort, hauling down the Filipino flag, which was still flying, and hoisting the stars and stripes amid the cheers from the ships. They then immediately advanced towards the town, where they hoisted the American flag over the city.

During this time the St. Paul had moved close in to the fort, and at noon the first troops from the Tennessee regiment were landed in the ship's boats. The Arizona then moved in, and by 6 o'clock that afternoon all the troops had been landed, immediately after marching into the town, and as far as the Molo and Jaro bridges, the insurgents having retired to these villages.

It was said that the action was brought on prematurely by the navy, but the Americans had threatened that if they found the insurgents adding to their defenses they would open fire at once, and the threat had to be made good. There is no doubt that it was for the best, for it was announced that the insurgents were perfecting arrangements for burning the whole town.

The strongest rebel position in the island of Luzon at this time was Caloocan, twelve miles from Manila to the northward on the Manila-Dagupan Railroad. The railroad shops, worth a half million dollars, are located there. Aguinaldo massed his forces there with great energy, and General Otis determined to attack the town at once. General MacArthur's division was north of the Pasig River, and his left was wheeling around towards Caloocan, carrying everything before it. The city was within easy range of the guns of the warships, a wide stretch of marsh land lying between the town and Manila Bay.

It was planned to have the attack upon Caloocan opened with a bombardment by the warships. At 2:30 o'clock on Friday, February 10, 1899, the monitor Monadnock and the gunboat Concord, which had been ordered up the bay by Admiral Dewey, opened fire on the town. Their shells went true and great damage was done, alarming and intimidating the rebels.

At the same time that the warships began shelling the Sixth Artillery and the Utah Battery opened fire on the rebel intrenchments on the landward sides of the town. The country between the American position and Caloocan was covered with banana groves, bamboo hedges and paddy fields, with here and there straggling collections of nipa huts, all of which afforded excellent shelter for the native soldiers near the town who were not in the trenches. Some of these men had the reputation of being sharpshooters; but their work did not prove them experts in that line, and the damage done by them was trifling.

The artillery and the warships pounded away until 4 o'clock, when orders were given for General Harrison G. Otis's brigade, except the Pennsylvania regiment, which was held as reserve, to move upon the enemy's works. The men had been impatiently waiting for the order, and as the word was passed down the line they responded with cheers.

The Filipinos were awaiting the advance of the troops. reserving their fire with coolness, but as the Americans began to move forward the rebels started a rattling fire, which made considerable noise but did no great damage. The Americans did not return the fire, but pressed steadily forward, marching through the woods and banana groves from the left, and from the right through the paddy fields, which afforded no protection. Not a single stop was made until they reached the intrenchments, from which most of the natives hastily srcambled as the Americans drew near. The rebels tried to make their way to the shelter afforded by the town, but scores of them never reached their goal, being stopped by the American bullets. Just at this time the scurrying rebels were thrown into confusion by the discovery that they had been flanked. A company of the First Montana Infantry, under command of Major J. Franklin Bell, had volunteered to execute the flank movement, and, moving to the east, had, without being detected, arrived on the enemy's flank back in the town.

"THE KANSAS AND MONTANA BOYS CHARGED THROUGH."

The natives saw that they were trapped, and, scattering, fled like sheep, many of them dropping their weapons in their anxiety to escape. The Americans jumped the trenches, and yelling and cheering were in full pursuit. It was simply a rout, and proved that even with artificial defenses the Filipinos were no match for the Americans who were pitted against them.

There is in Caloocan a large church which for all practical purposes was really a fort. It was a substantial stone structure, strongly defended, and had been occupied by Aguinaldo and a portion of his army, he having intended to make a stand there. But when the soldiers ran into the town and drove before them the rebels who had been in the trenches the insurgents who had been in the church sallied forth and joined in the general retreat. It was found, also, that barricades had been erected at the place where the Malabon road crosses the line of the Dagupan Railway, in the center of the town. These had been torn to pieces in many places by the fire from the warships and the land batteries. As the Twentieth Kansas and First Montana Regiments entered the town from the south, some of the fleeing natives set fire to the huts, whose roofs were made of nipa grass, thinking doubtless to start a blaze that would destroy the town; but in this they were disappointed, as the Americans extinguished the fires.

The losses of the enemy were heavy, both in killed and wounded. The forces of Aguinaldo at this point were from 8,000 to 10,000 men. Most of the casualties to the Filipinos were due to shrapnel, the screaming and effectiveness of which caused terror among them. Captain Dyer's guns of the Sixth Artillery and Major Young's Utah Light Artillery kept pouring shrapnel into the enemy's line at a range of 2,200 yards, with great accuracy, almost every shot telling, and ceased fire only when the infantry approached closely to the town.

The American loss was three killed and thirty-two wounded. The Kansas and Montana boys, in their magnificent charge through a wooded ravine, suffered the principal losses. Nothing could surpass the fearlessness of their advance across an open field on the right, directly in the face of the enemy's strongest intrenchments.

After the capture of Caloocan Aguinaldo visited Polo, a few miles northwest of Caloocan, and addressed the Filipino troops there, claiming that he had won a victory, and asserting that 2,308 Americans had been killed.

THE BURNING OF MANILA

O N the night of February 22d a fiendish plot, well nigh incredible in its sweeping, uncontrolled savagery which had for its object the extermination of practically all the foreigners in Manila—men, women and children—was frustrated by the alertness of the American officials. Fire broke out in the houses of some rich Filipinos who had refused to array themselves on the side of the insurgents. A strong wind was blowing towards the Escolta, the business street of Manila, which made the work of the fire-fighters difficult. The regular fire department, manned by the natives, proved to be wholly inefficient, and their places were taken by American soldiers. The English and German volunteer engine companies did excellent work, but it was found that the hose was contantly being cut, and finally a soldier caught a Malay in the act of bending over the hose and running a long knife into it. The soldier made short work of the offender, bringing his gun down over his neck and killing him instantly.

The scene during the fire was one of great excitement in all parts of the city. Business men watched the progress of the fire toward their property with anxiety.

Platoons of soldiers, their arms stacked, stood at street corners ready to quell any uprising. At a corner, with the flames blowing toward him from the blazing block of buildings across the narrow street, an American sailor from the Olympia held the hose. Sometimes he was helped by a few soldiers, sometimes by civilians, but nobody except the sailor seemed to be able to bear the heat for any length of time. He stood his ground, determined that the fire should not cross the narrow street, and he accomplished his purpose.

Scarcely was the fire under control when a new one broke out, this time in the Tondo district, north of the city proper. It lay next to the seas, was cut off from the main part of the city by a broad street, the Calle Iris, and was occupied by natives. The tall spires and massive walls of Tondo Church, surrounded by a high wall and a stone building, used by the Americans as a police station in that district, were the only large buildings in a group of nipa huts. The incendiaries had been re-enforced in that section by about 500 native soldiers, who had in some manner crept through the lines near the sea. There was one company of the Minnesota regiment in the police station at Tondo, and General Hughes had placed another in Tondo Church to meet any emergency.

At the time the fire broke out an attack was made by the native troops on the police station. It was their intention to drive the company of Minnesota men out of their barracks and finish them off in short order. As the flames shot up to the sky, the insurgent bugles rang out long and loud, as if sounding the charge, and the insurgents tried to drive the men from the police station. They were unable to get by the guard at the gate, and then tried to scale the wall, but met with a sharp fire which prevented their climbing over. Re-enforcements soon arrived—two

THE BURNING OF MANILA.

companies of the Second Oregon and two of the Twenty-third United States Infantry. They lined out along the Calle Iris in ditches, and also at right angles to the road skirting the fire. The fire leaped and roared in mountains of flame, and to add to the general hubbub the joints in the bamboo huts burst with sharp reports like those of a rifle. Shots came toward the Calle Iris from all parts of the burning district, and the soldiers promptly returned the fire. The advancing flames drove before them a crowd of women and children carrying bundles of what they had been able to save from their homes. They moaned and chattered in fright, and piteously begged to be saved from the fiery element. Along with them came a number of men, half-naked, who probably a few minutes before had been firing into the ranks of the Americans. They were allowed to pass into the city. The fire swept fiercely with flaming tongues and hoarse roar, driven by the wind. For some time it was doubtful where it would stop, but it finally was checked at the Calle Iris.

In the booths of the Binondo Market, only 100 yards back of the Calle Iris, the fire broke out anew. The Chinamen of the district made a hard struggle to put out the flames and tore down their booths, though fired upon by the crafty insurgents who were concealed in the neighboring houses.

As the Mausers gave no flash at night, it was impossible to tell whence the shots came, and consequently they inspired double terror. Gradually the shooting ceased and the insurgents withdrew to Tondo bridge. It was truly a night of terror. A small number of Americans had stood up against a large force on the outside, and it was known that the mass of the population was opposed to the Americans. It was a crucial point in the history of the occupation of the city. Had the insurgents been able to burn the city as they expected, had they won a victory over the small American force, and got the upper hand, it would have been ten-fold more difficult for the Americans to have carried on the work of pacifying the islands. As it was, thirteen of the Americans were wounded and a large number of the incendiaries shot. Between 600 and 700 residences and business houses were burned, and the property loss probably exceeded a half million dollars. Hundreds of the natives, who had been burned out, huddled in the streets for days, making the patrol duty of the Americans much more difficult.

THE INSURGENTS DEFEATED AGAIN

O N March 7th the insurgent forces to the number of several thousand were driven from their position at San Juan del Monte with great loss. General Hale's brigade, which had been holding the water-works against the repeated attacks of the Filipinos, swept forward in the form of a V, with the open ends towards the Pasig River. This form of advance inclosed the rebel position completely and permitted a terrible concentration of fire. As soon as the lines were well under way in the massed advance the Wyoming regiment closed in, firing rapidly and effectively. Suddenly Company C sprang from the line with a cheer and dashed towards the insurgent trenches. The other companies of the Wyoming regiment rushed to the front and the entire line swept down uponthe Filipinos. Maintaining their fire for only a short time after the roaring charge, the Filipinos leaped from their earth-works and fled, closely pressed. Retreat was cut off in all directions save toward the Pasig River, and as the insurgents turned that way they were met by a pitiless shelling from a United States gunboat. The infantry lines closed in at once from the east.

In the woods the Filipinos were scattered into small bands and driven along the river front. The losses of the insurgents were very heavy, the accurate fire of the gunboat creating panic in the fleeing lines. The only casualty to the American forces was the wounding of one private.

The American forces were halted at the river for a rest. The insurgents had been utterly routed. This engagement was the result of the advance made the day before by General Hale's brigade in San Tolan and Mariquina, when the Americans met and defeated the largest body of natives yet encountered.

General Loyd Wheaton's brigade was also in action, the fighting having spread toward his flank. The Colorado, Nebraska and Wyoming regiments, with eight field pieces, the Utah regiment and two companies of the Oregon infantry were in fighting line. In the rear the Twentieth Infantry was held in reserve. Resistance was made by the natives the moment the American troops approached San Tolan, but their fire was not effective, while the marksmanship of the western regiments was superb.

A river gunboat joined in the attack and shelled the towns as in the fighting of the morning. The troops in General Wheaton's brigade were the California, Idaho and Washington regiments and the Sixth U. S. Artillery. In face of the telling fire the natives clung to their position before the towns until the shells began dropping among them. Then the American infantrymen advanced and the Filipinos fled from their earthworks. They carried some of their dead and wounded with them, but a great number were left on the field of battle. Eight Americans were severely wounded.

THE CAMPAIGN OF 1899 IN LUZON

WHILE the American troops were engaged strengthening the outer lines of defense around Manila the insurgents were concentrating to the north and south of the city, collecting ammunition and establishing supply depots, and by March a concerted effort was made by the American troops to subdue the rebellion.

The plan of the Luzon campaign in general was to operate in three directions— north, east and south—the operations in the northern part of the island to be confined to getting to the rear of the insurgent troops, making escape to the mountains impossible.

The first attempt to execute this plan was made by General Arthur MacArthur, who started with his command on the northern campaign on March 24, 1899.

General MacArthur followed the railway line to Malolos, capturing the intervening towns, which were fired by the retreating insurgents; and on the 31st he entered the insurgent capital, Malolos, finding the city burned and all records removed. Further pursuit was stopped by orders from General Otis, who believed that a combined movement which should result in the hemming in of the insurgents would be more advisable than a pursuit of the retreating enemy, and consequently he held MacArthur at Malolos until General Lawton could be sent north to aid in surrounding the insurrectionary forces.

Meanwhile General Lawton was put in command of an expedition sent south to capture Santa Cruz and Calamba, on the shores of Laguna de Bay, and locate and seize two insurgent launches.

Santa Cruz was the richest and most important city of La Laguna Province, situated on the southeastern shore of Laguna de Bay, and the insurgents were reported to be established there in full confidence. The city was captured April 10th, the insurgents retreating with heavy loss under the combined fire of the land troops and the machine guns on the American boats. Before Calamba could be taken, however, General Lawton was recalled by General Otis.

The abrupt withdrawal of General Lawton from the south emboldened the insurgents in the north, who looked upon Lawton's return as a defeat to the American forces.

As soon as General Lawton returned to Manila the second concerted move northward began with the same general plan outlined for MacArthur in March. General Lawton left Manila April 22d, the same day that MacArthur took up the advance northward from Malolos again. MacArthur this time got as far north as San Fernando, about forty-five miles north of Manila on the main railway line, which city he captured. General Lawton moved first northeast, then westward to Baliuag, one of the chief war depots of the insurgents, where he waited until General MacArthur should be enabled to secure a more advanced position and discover the whereabouts of the enemy. He was obliged to abandon the towns which he had captured farther to the east owing to the lack of men to garrison them.

General MacArthur reported that General Luna was in his immediate front with 2,500 men, and 1,000 more about five miles northeast of San Fernando, in the district lying between San Fernando and Baliuag, where General Lawton was stationed. General MacArthur thought there were about 10,000 insurgents, while his own force consisted, at the time of the investment of San Fernando, of an aggregate of 4,800 men, but by May 10th yielding only 2,640 infantry for duty on the firing line.

MacArthur's troops were thoroughly exhausted from the prolonged marches and continuous outpost duty, and he reported the fact to General Otis.

There were no fresh troops to send to San Fernando. The withdrawal of the Spanish forces in Mindanao and the Sulu archipelago, where troops must be placed, the necessity of sending others to Cebu and to increase those in Negros—all of which was imperatively demanded at this time—rendered conditions somewhat critical. The volunteer organizations had also to return to the United States without delay.

It was finally determined that MacArthur should hold San Fernando with what force he had, operating against and holding Luna as best he could; to send a detached column up the Rio Grande, and to permit Lawton to advance.

Accordingly on May 14th Lawton was ordered to proceed northward with San Isidro as his objective, and on the 17th, after sharp resistance from the insurgents, the place, strategically important, was captured.

Owing to the heavy rains it was impossible for General Lawton to form a junction with General MacArthur, and on May 19th the former was recalled. All the towns that he had captured, with the exception of Baliuag, had to be abandoned. On the return march the troops encountered great difficulties from the steady downpour and the constant vexatious demonstrations from the enemy, and while en route they were attacked at Ildefonso and Maasin, and were obliged to halt twice and drive off the enemy, which they did effectively.

The insurgents, supposing a general retreat was intended, were at once excited to great activity, and they forwarded their forces at once by rail to General MacArthur's front, concentrating near San Miguel.

On May 31st the forces in the Philippines numbered 1,201 officers and 33,026 enlisted men. Of these an aggregate of 25,809 were effective for duty. The troops sent to other islands left in Luzon 20,965. Of the whole number present in the Philippines, 16,000 were volunteers waiting to be returned to the United States, leaving 18,000 regulars owing further service.

The latter part of May it was reported that the inhabitants at Antipolo, Morong and other near towns east of Manila were suffering heavily on account of the crimes committed by General Pilar's insurgent troops, and they called for protection.

Accordingly, on June 2d, immediately after his return to Manila, General Lawton was ordered to drive off the insurgents at Antipolo and Morong. The bad roads and excessive heat, however, rendered the expedition a difficult one. The insurgents had scattered, most of them having taken the trails to the mountains, where they could not well be pursued. The town of Morong was taken without the loss of a man, and was occupied by the troops for a time, reconnoissances being made into the interior and along the shore of the Laguna.

Again on June 7th General Lawton concentrated a force of about 4,000 men to move south.

On this second southern expedition Calamba and Los Banos, two towns on the southern shore of the Laguna de Bay, were captured and held, as was also a strip of territory south of Manila.

In the meantime the insurgents in the north were again becoming active. On June 15th from 3,000 to 5,000 attacked General MacArthur's entire front and were driven back with heavy loss. After this defeat the insurgents in the north were comparatively quiet for some time.

In August the American army in the Philippines aggregated about 31,000, but only 24,000 were fit for active duty. General MacArthur, whose troops were now in better shape, had by this time extended his lines farther north to Angeles, ten miles above San Fernando, thus giving the United States control of a narrow strip of territory between Imus in the south and Angeles in the north. In this northward movement the troops' progress was impeded by frequent heavy rains, but on the 9th of August the insurgents were met and driven back towards Angeles. At 5 o'clock in the morning the attack on the rebels was opened, a battery of the First Artillery shelling Bacolor on the left. Simultaneously Colonel J. Franklin Bell's Thirty-sixth Infantry struck Bacolor from the rear and drove the rebels out. Battery M of the Third Artillery and some Iowa troops made a feint toward Maxico, while the main body of troops under General Wheaton, on the right, and General Liscum on the left, advanced, steadily pouring their fire into the insurgents and receiving heavy fire in return from the rebels, who were well protected by trenches. The rebels, however, could not withstand the determined attack of the troops and retreated, leaving their dead and wounded behind.

This engagement served to clear the country of insurgents to the rear, left and right of MacArthur's forces, who now held Calulet, six miles from San Fernando. The insurgents lost heavily in the fighting around this town, they having lost 100 killed and 350 wounded, while the losses to the Americans were five killed and thirty-one wounded.

General MacArthur's troops rested at Calulet on the night of the 10th undisturbed by the insurgents' usual night firing, for the latter had fled into the hills and out of range of the troops. Shortly after the rebels also set fire to Angeles and fled, thus leaving the place to be occupied by the American troops.

Only minor military operations were attempted in September, since, as in August, the troops were busily engaged in relieving those directed to depart from the islands, there being two volunteer regiments in Panay, Negros and Cebu, which had to be withdrawn, and also a few organizations on the outer Luzon lines which were to be replaced. This exchange was effected as rapidly as vessels could be secured to transport men and supplies. Dispositions were being constantly effected to commence the execution of a well-determined plan of operation in northern Luzon as soon as an available force would justify it, and continued caution was exercised to neutralize the enemy's aggressive movements. Since the early portion of July they had gradually become more bold because of the apparent quiet of the American army and were inclined to take the initiative wherever they might consider an opportunity offered. Their troops attacked various portions of General MacArthur's lines at the north, made various attempts to cripple the railroad between Manila and San Fernando, the continued working of which was essential for the forwarding of troops and supplies required in the contemplated northern operations and the forwarding of subsistence to the men holding that section of the country. They threatened the lines about the city of Manila, concentrating at Mariquina, San Mateo, Montalban and vicinity, in the Province of Manila and Baloocan, and to the eastward in the Province of Morong. They gathered and attacked Calamba on the Laguna de Bay, and also the strong outpost at Imus, Province of Cavite. The insurgents of the city of Manila again became somewhat confident, and under a chief, an influential Tagalog appointed to the position by Aguinaldo, actively engaged in supplying the insurgent troops with contraband of war, and in plotting for another uprising within the city's most densely populated sections.

J. FRANKLIN BELL,
Colonel, 36th U. S. Vol. Infantry.
Highest rank attained: Brigadier
General, U. S. V.

During one of the engagements of this September campaign occurred an incident of individual bravery that won for Colonel J. Franklin Bell the Medal of Honor. It is as follows:

On September 9, 1899, near the village of San Augustine, the Thirty-sixth Infantry, under command of Colonel J. Franklin Bell, left camp on that date and proceeded along the San Antonio Porac road to head off a large body of insurgents, which had attacked the troops of the Ninth Infantry, stationed at Guagua and Santa Rita, during the night. Colonel Bell, followed by Lieutenant-Colonel William R. Grove, Major Straub and two mounted orderlies, was ahead of the regiment with about twelve scouts. Just as day was dawning the advanced scouts encountered the enemy's patrol, consisting of one captain, one lieutenant and five privates, near the village of San Augustine. The scouts fired on them, and, as the insurgents started to run, gave chase. Colonel Bell, in advance of the mounted party, immediately spurred his horse to the front and seeing that the insurgents were easily running away from the scouts, pushed his horse into a gallop and charged the seven insurgents with his pistol, scattering them into the bushes on both sides of the road and compelling the surrender of the

"HE CHARGED THE INSURGENTS WITH HIS PISTOL."

captain and two privates, under a close and hot fire from the four remaining insurgents, who had concealed themselves in a bamboo thicket. As soon as Colonel Grove heard fighting at the front he ran his horse, which was the speediest in the command, to the head of the column, and, seeing Colonel Bell pursuing alone, immediately dashed to his assistance, joined him in the midst of the insurgents while they were firing from the side of the road, and assisted Colonel Bell in the capture of the rebel patrol.

By the 10th of October the process of changing armies and the approach of the dry season had reached a point where an advance towards the general occupation of the country was justified.

At that time the American lines extended from the Bay of Manila to Laguna de Bay, and included considerable parts of the Provinces of Cavite, Laguna and Morong to the south and east of Manila, substantially all of the Province of Manila and the southern parts of Bulacan and Pampanga, dividing the insurgent forces into two widely separated parts. To the south and east of our lines in Cavite and Morong were numerous bands occasionally concentrating for attack on our lines, and as frequently dispersed and driven back toward the mountains. On the 6th of October the insurgents in this region having again gathered and attacked our lines of communication, General Schwan with a column of 1,726 men commenced a movement from Bacoor, in the Province of Cavite, driving the enemy through Old Cavite, Noveleta, Santa Cruz, San Francisco de Malabon, Laban, and Perez des Merinas, punishing them severely, scattering them and destroying them as organized forces, and returning on the 13th to Bacoor.

On the north of the American lines stretched the plain of central Luzon, extending from Manila about 120 miles. This plain comprises parts of the Provinces of Manila, Pampanga, Bulacan, Tarlac, Nueva Ecija, and Pangasinan. It is, roughly speaking, bounded on the south by the Bay of Manila; on the east and west by high mountain ranges separating it from the sea-coasts, and on the north by mountains and the Gulf of Lingayen. Through the northeast and central portion flows the Rio Grande from the northern mountains southeasterly to the Bay of Manila, and near the western edge runs the only railroad on the island of Luzon in a general southeasterly direction from Dagupan, on the Bay of Lingayen, to Manila. In this territory Aguinaldo exercised a military dictatorship, and with a so-called cabinet initiated the forms of civil government, having his headquarters at Tarlac, which he called his capital, and which is situated near the center of the western boundary of the plain.

October 7th General Schwan was put in command of an expedition sent south into the Province of Cavite, whose object was to punish and if possible to destroy or break up the insurgent forces in the Province of Cavite, which had recently shown considerable activity in attacking the American line on both sides of the Tibagan River from Imus northward to Bacoor and Paranaque. This expedition of a week's duration had driven the enemy back from his intrenchments on the south line, and had penetrated as far as Dasmarinas, but owing to the necessity of employing the greater part of the troops elsewhere, and the consequent lack of sufficient force to hold the ground thus gained, it had again been relinquished to the rebels, who had been further re-enforced by portions of the defeated armies that had retreated from the northern provinces. The insurgents occupied Cavite Viejo and were practically in contact with the American lines at Imus. The troops held Paranaque, Bacoor, Big Bend and Imus, and immediately south of the city of Manila they occupied a line running through San Pedro Macati to Pasig, and thence to Taguig. Calamba and Los Banos were also held by forces as advanced posts of the general line, the control of the Laguna de Bay enabling troops at these points to be easily supplied. Beyond the lines mentioned, the theatre in which operations were to be conducted was entirely in the hands of the insurgents.

The effect of the punishment was evidenced by the quiet that had since its administration prevailed on the south line, where it had been reported not a shot was fired in fifteen days, and it was expected that the insurgents would remain quiet for some time after this expedition.

But the enemy at the south recovered their courage sooner than was anticipated, and, probably following Aguinaldo's instructions for general active demonstrations, given as soon as the northern advance was commenced, displayed unusual activity.

The constant activity of the insurgents in the vicinity of Manila, to the east in the Province of Morong, and to the south in the Province of Cavite and Batangas, had its chief inspiration in Tarlac, and was the result of the efforts of the agents of Aguinaldo, assisted by the subordinate officers of Lieutenant-General Trias, who commanded all the enemy's forces in southern Luzon. The work of recruiting and sending out men from Manila for the insurgent ranks never ceased, and supplies and munitions of war for the enemy continued to pass out, notwithstanding all efforts to stop it.

For some time no further expedition south could be organized, as every man was needed in the northward movement which was begun the early part of October. As the insurgents had moved so much farther north than was anticipated, the plan of campaign became complicated, and, though it was well planned, it could not be carried out owing to the heavy rains and the difficulty of transportation. The several divisions, however, under Generals MacArthur, Lawton, Young and Wheaton continued moving northward and drove out the insurgents wherever they met them.

By November 12th General MacArthur's troops, under Colonel Bell, had moved as far north as Tarlac, which city they entered, finding it deserted. On the next day the insurgents held an important council of war at Bayambang, Pangasinan, which was attended by General Aguinaldo and many of the Filipino military leaders, at which a resolution was adopted to the effect that the insurgent forces were incapable of further resistance in the field, and as a consequence it was decided to disband the army, the generals and the men to return to their own provinces with a view to organizing the people for general resistance by means of guerrilla warfare.

Thus the so-called Filipino Republic was destroyed. The congress had dissolved, and its president was a prisoner of General MacArthur's forces, while Aguinaldo and all of his cabinet officers were fugitives. The executive department was therefore broken up. The generals were separated, without any power of conference or concerted action, and the authority under which the insurgent army was kept in the field no longer existed. The army as an organization had disappeared.

On the 19th of November General MacArthur had entered Bayambang, the last capital of the insurgents, and ninety miles north of Manila.

In the meantime General Lawton, who had left Manila on October 15th with a force of 3,500 troops, proceeded northward, encountering the greatest difficulties on account of the heavy rains and poor roads. On the 22d of October he recaptured San Isidro, and on the 6th of November he joined General Young's column at Cabanatuan. The following day General Young began his movement to cut off all the northeastern trails to the mountains, and General Wheaton, who had reached San Fabian, connected with General MacArthur at Bayambang. On the 12th General Lawton started westward and overtook General Young six days later. By this time it was apparent that Aguinaldo had eluded General Wheaton's and General Young's columns and gotten to the north of the troops, and General Young was at once sent in pursuit, while General Lawton continued westward and joined General Wheaton at San Fabian on the 19th.

From this time on General Lawton was occupied day and night with the difficult problem of supplying and re-enforcing General Young, keeping open lines of communication over almost impassable roads in his rear and front, disposing troops to the right and left front over mountains, trails and rivers to prevent concentration of insurgents, whip and capture their scattered forces and release American and Spanish prisoners.

The campaign against the Filipino troops as an organized army now ceased and the pursuit of Aguinaldo was begun.

HEROES ON THE BATTLEFIELD

ONLY ten Medals of Honor had been awarded up to October, 1901, to soldiers and sailors for exceptional bravery during the Filipino insurrection, although many more will doubtless be awarded before the campaign in the islands is brought to a close.

Many a brave soldier and sailor wears the mark of battling with the Filipino insurgents, and many an heroic deed was performed, but only the most conspicuous have been and will be rewarded by the coveted medal.

The following nine men, besides Colonel J. Franklin Bell, whose narrative is given in the preceding pages, have thus far been awarded the Medal of Honor:

Corporal Thomas F. Prendergast and Privates Howard M. Buckley and Joseph Melvin of the Marine Corps won their medals during the battles which the Eighth Army Corps fought on the 25th, 27th and 29th of March and 4th of April, 1899, on its way from Manila to Malolos, the Filipino capital. These intrepid marines faced the Mauser bullets in exposed positions, succored the wounded under fire and encouraged their comrades by their fearlessness and almost reckless daring. Second Lieutenant George E. Stewart won his Medal in a similar manner on November 26, 1899. Sergeant Hardy Harvey of the Marine Corps was one of the most conspicuous objects on the battlefield at Benitican on February 16, 1900, where his services in aiding the wounded under heavy fire won him the unstinted praise of his superior officers.

Frequently recurring battles and skirmishes gave opportunity for the display of unusual bravery, and in a fight which occurred on March 4, 1900, Second Lieutenant George W. Wallace distinguished himself to such an unusual degree that he was rewarded with the Medal of Honor.

Gunner's Mate Andrew V. Stoltenberg, Apprentice William H. Jaeger and Seaman Andrew P. Forbeck were constantly exposed to the insurgents' fire at Samar on July 16, 1900, when that island was being pacified by General Kobbe, and were attacked by a large body of the insurgents, who with their bolos were routed and driven back with severe loss in killed and wounded, besides the several prisoners who were taken in the fight.

THE CAPTURE OF GILMORE'S PARTY

For some time there had been coming to the military headquarters at Manila rumors, vague and conflicting, but telling substantially the same story. At length, well along in March, 1899, General Otis received more definite knowledge, and it became known to the authorities beyond the shadow of all doubt that a handful of some fifty plucky Spaniards were fortified and starving in an old church at Baler, on the east coast of Luzon.

Bravery appeals to the heart of every nation on earth and stops at the frontier of no race. Admiral Dewey and General Otis, upon the receipt of this information, determined to make an effort to rescue the little band of Spaniards who for the past eight months had held out against a force of over 500 natives.

The Yorktown was assigned to this difficult task of relieving the besieged men in the heart of the enemy's country. Lieutenant-Commander James C. Gilmore had just arrived in the Philippines and he was detailed aboard the Yorktown as navigating officer.

The Yorktown steamed out of Manila Bay, and on the 11th of April came to at the entrance of Baler Bay. The alarm of the Yorktown's coming was soon made manifest in the excitement of the Filipinos, who could be seen running up and down the beach between their sentry boxes.

Under a flag of truce and with orders to communicate with the besieged Spaniards, if possible, Ensign Standley was sent ashore. Treacherous intentions were so evident, however, on the part of the Filipinos that Ensign Standley returned to the ship and reported that a scouting party was the only feasible plan under the circumstances. His plan was accepted, and he and Quartermaster Lyac were selected for the perilous reconnoissance.

It was 4 o'clock in the morning and still dark when the cutter left the ship's side to set the scouts ashore. Besides Commander Gilmore and the two scouts there was a crew of seventeen men, picked for their nerve and cool judgment. In the darkness and the profound quiet of a tropical night the two men were left upon the beach and at once plunged into the dense thicket and away on their dangerous mission.

The cutter, with muffled oars, had pulled away from the beach and was headed back to the ship, when the tropical sun shot up above the horizon, blotting out the darkness and showing to the Filipino sentries the American crew, pulling swiftly and quietly across the sun-streaked waters of the bay.

Commander Gilmore at once saw that the wily natives would guess the purpose of this night sally; that they would follow up the trail of the two American scouts, and in the dank wilderness of the tropical forest would slay them without mercy and even a chance to reach the shelter of the less unfortunate Spaniards. To avert suspicion from the two lone men he boldly changed the course of the cutter. The crew pulled up the mouth of the little river, while Gilmore stood in the bow and made a pretense of sketching the shore and sounding the waters, as if that had been the ostensible purpose of the bold excursion. The ruse worked successfully, too, at least as far as the plucky scouts were concerned. But not so with the unselfish crew of the little cutter. For many of them a horrible death was in store.

For a thousand yards they rowed up the little river. Then Gilmore thought that the trick had been played long enough and he gave the order to turn and put back to the Yorktown. They followed the left bank of the river because it was low and marshy, and there seemed no danger of attack from that quarter. Suddenly that bank rose precipitately into a bold bluff. A Filipino sentry sprang up from the creeping growth of the forest and discharged his rifle as a signal.

Then without warning a deadly volley, for the range was dreadfully short, issued from the impenetrable brush and thickets. Not a man of the insurgent band on shore was visible, and from unseen quarters volley after volley poured down upon the men struggling in the shallow water below. Almost the first volley disabled the Colt rapid-firing gun in the bow of the cutter. The first man to drop was shot through the head and his brains splattered his comrades and the boat and oars. Another fell back screaming as a ball penetrated his eye. The fingers of another were shot away cleanly as he pulled madly at his oar.

The men fell faster and faster, and the uninjured were thrown down in the bottom of the boat with the falling bodies of their comrades, but they crawled out from beneath the bleeding forms of the dead and wounded and fired back.

The men were being potted like quail in a trap and those wounded cried aloud in agony and begged their comrades in the name of God to kill them before they fell into the natives' hands for further tortures. The oars had been splintered. There were not enough men left to man them. The cutter now was filling and wabbly and, worst of all, drifting slowly to the bank from which came the hellish fire of the hidden natives.

Gilmore sat in the stern sheets at the tiller. With his disengaged hand he reached for the rifle of one of the dead men, but he found that a shot had bent the lock. The bullets cut his clothing and splashed in the hissing water about him. The thwarts and oars and seats of the cutter were splashed with the blood of his men.

Three of the crew leaped overboard and attempted to pull the cutter out into deeper water. But she was drifting slowly, inexorably, toward the bank of sand.

At last with screams of exultation there broke loose from the thicket a motley crew of savages, half nude, in shirts and breech-clouts, armed with spears, bolos and rifles. Yelling and screaming, they came down the spit of sand, brandishing their weapons and wild with savage joy.

It was now all so hopeless that Commander Gilmore at once ordered the white flag raised. The man who held it was shot in the wrist and the flag fell to the bottom of the boat, which was half fiilled with water and blood.

Then a voice, a strong voice of authority, came from the thicket. It warned the unfortunate Americans that unless they surrendered at once they would all be killed in their tracks.

Gilmore arose and threw up his arms in token of submission and there were no more shots.

About them now there gathered a wild, chattering band of half-naked natives, Tagals and Principes and other tribesmen. They stripped the Americans of their coats, hats and shoes, rifled their pockets for watches and money, and pulled rings from their fingers, but the men of the mutilated little band were cool in their extremity and attempted no mad resistance.

With hands bound behind their backs with bamboo thongs the forlorn band of survivors were lined up on the beach. There was much jabbering and gesticulating among the savage captors. Then those with guns stepped out in front of the line of prisoners. They cocked their rifles and raised them. They took aim at the breasts of the Americans. It was now but a matter of seconds and then eternity.

Then came a shout from the bank and a native officer came running toward them, yelling as he ran and waving his sword. The murderous natives dropped their guns and the Americans and Gilmore knew that for the nonce their lives were to be spared.

The native officer ordered the little band to cross over to the other bank of the river in their own blood-spattered boat. To do this they had to plug up the scores of bullet-holes and bail out the bloody water. Two mortally wounded men, who were still gasping, the Americans carried out of the boat. Under the shade of trees they put tufts of grass beneath their heads and water by their sides and left them to die alone while they wandered on into captivity. They were not allowed to bury their dead comrades, but were forced to leave them where they had fallen in the blood-covered boat.

The American captives were led by, but out of gun-shot of the old church held by the Spaniards whom they had come to rescue. They saw the Spanish flag flying from the roof and they rejoiced to know that the plucky Spaniards were still holding out against overwhelming odds.

A mile and a half they marched them through the deep jungle, the severely wounded suffering excruciating agony, and it was with great difficulty that they were dragged along on the heart-breaking march. When night came on they were put in an old bamboo church. The uninjured men were bound together with a long rope.

A day and a night they were kept in these rude quarters. Commander Gilmore was shown some respect because of his rank. His hands were not bound and his coat and shoes were returned to him.

Throughout the unspeakable horrors of that first night in captivity the wounded moaned for water and the bound men would cry to the savage guards without to bring water to their dying comrades.

THE CAPTURE OF GILMORE'S PARTY.

From Aguinaldo himself a runner came next day and ordered them to march on or drag themselves on to San Isidro, the insurgent capital. Ragged and worn out, for two days the captives were dragged through the courses of tortuous river beds, wading streams and climbing over great, jagged bowlders. When night came they had reached the mountains. It turned cold, and a dreary, chilling rain fell, adding to the sufferings of the wounded.

On that weary march through the jungle and the paths of the deep tropical forests the captives several times met with priests and friars, who, moved to pity by their desolate condition, gave them food and dressed their wounds and bleeding feet. The news that Americans had been captured spread on before them. Through every village they passed between lines of chattering, joy-mad natives, who offered them no violence, but gaped in open-mouthed curiosity at these strangers, upon whom they were looking for the first time in their wretched lives.

The governor of San Isidro was apparently favorably impressed with Commander Gilmore's appearance and address. He cross-examined him thoroughly and terminated the interview by presenting the American officer with a suit of underclothing and sending the captives off to a filthy, crowded prison. The original inmates of this place were murderers and thieves, but they met the captive Americans with kindness, even consideration.

So fearful were the Filipino captors that their prisoners might in some manner be rescued by their friends that they were kept always upon the march, dragging them about over rough and desolate mountain trails, fording streams and passing through the half-night paths of the deep tropical forests. During the time of their captivity the little band of half-naked Americans twice crossed the Island of Luzon, a distance of not less than 400 miles, and at length emerged upon the shores of the northern ocean. Some times in their endless wanderings they were met with hospitality and kindness by the natives. At other times threats were made against them, and for days at a time they knew not the moment they might all be massacred. On the other hand the Spanish prisoners, who sometimes to the number of 600 were added to their straggling column, were brutally beaten.

At Vigan the American captives had the misfortune to be placed in the power of General Tinio, a cruel, wily native, with a deep hatred for all Americans. His mind at one time was fully made up to execute them all in cold blood. Commander Gilmore, however, had made a good friend and ally in the person of the local presidente, who was prevailed upon to warn Tinio that should such a massacre of Americans be consummated, American avengers would come and burn and destroy in a thoroughly punitive manner. This admonition had the desired effect, and, further than the separation of Commander Gilmore from his men, they suffered no serious privations at Vigan. From their prison windows they could see American ships passing to and fro, far out on the bosom of the ocean, and it was maddening to the captives to know that rescue was so near and yet so impossible.

Then without warning rumors came to the little band which cheered their hearts and brought new hope to their breasts. American troops were certainly in the vicinity. This was evident in the sudden panic among the natives.

Families were hurriedly prepared for flight. The excitement grew each hour until all the natives were seized with a sudden terror. Prisoners who were suspected of being Macabebe spies were taken out and shot down without ceremony. Then on the morning of December 5th the American column routed the forces of General Tinio. The American captives were then quickly brought from their prison and hurried into the mountains. Superstitious fear of the Americans urged the captors on. They would give the Americans no time to eat or sleep. But as the little band of captives were urged on farther and farther, with the rescuers hard upon their trail, they marked their names with chalk upon the rocks and tree trunks, so that their friends might have some clue to the direction which they had taken. Into the wild mountain region they now were going. They were forced to crawl over bowlders and climb monkey-like up the cliffs by clinging to roots and the overhanging branches of trees. They were far beyond the edge of all civilization. They were in the wildernesses of unknown Luzon.

At last the extremity came. All food was gone. The men were thoroughly exhausted, starving and heart-sick. Night had come on. They had drunk their fill of water from a near-by stream, and that was all they had to satisfy their craving for the barest sustenance. The men were huddled together, wretched, without hope and ready at last to die. A Filipino approached them from the guard camp near at hand. He calmly informed them that they could take them no farther. It meant that they were to be shot where they stood and that the end had at last come for them.

Commander Gilmore did not speak for mercy. For some time the young native lieutenant stood and looked at them, pity and abhorrence in his eyes. At length he spoke again:

"I cannot do it," he said. "I will abandon you here in the mountains. Your own troops are not far away and you will be rescued."

Commander Gilmore asked him for guns that they might defend themselves; but these were denied. There was no food to give them. They had nothing, this little band of desolate Americans, but the ragged shirts on their backs. Even their knives had been taken from them by the thieving natives. They were alone, unarmed, resourceless in the heart of an impenetrable wilderness.

In a deserted hut they found a bolo and a small battle-ax. A small stream flowed past them, leaping down the mountain side. It must lead somewhere. It must have some outlet, either the eastern or northern sea.

They decided to build a raft and take this one lone chance of reaching succor and civilization. Weak and emaciated though they were, scarcely able to walk, they set to work with hope born anew in their hearts. In the vicinity they found a bamboo grove. While they were at work they saw a band of natives armed with spears and battle-axes. They came together for a last stand against fate, but fate was good to the Americans, and the natives at last drew away into the dense under growth.

Again they were at the work of construction upon the rickety bamboo rafts. The men were scattered along the beach, weak and famishing, but with light hearts they worked, for they were for the time at least free and doing something that might at last bring rescue and home.

Suddenly there was a shout from those at work along the beach.

Again the treacherous natives were upon them. They had no arms to defend themselves. The ragged men hurried to gather up stones and sticks from the shore. They would make a last stand, now that their last hope was gone. There was another yell from around the bend in the shore line. Then another. Commander Gilmore stopped and listened, and while he listened to reassure himself there came something to his mind that told him that those were not the yells of the puny Filipinos.

And still while he stood in doubt, and there came to him a mad suspicion that he tried to put down, there swung around the curve the blue shirts and the yellow khaki of the American soldiers. On they came, that little squad of plucky Americans, cheering as they raced along the pebbly beach. While still at some distance they shouted to the rescued men to lie down, thinking they were still under guard, and that they would have to fire over their heads at the Filipino captors. But they did not lie down, those pale, emaciated men. They dropped the stones that they had picked up to defend their lives and ran forward cheering, too, in weak, crackling voices, and they fell into the arms of the hardy Americans who had come for them, and cried in their weakness and sobbed their joy upon the broad breasts of their countrymen.

Then there was more cheering and hand-shaking and questions. They put Commander Gilmore and his little band of the rescued upon a huge bowlder that had toppled down from the mountain-side, and from this height Commander Gilmore saw the band of natives slinking away in the distance, for they, too, had heard those good American cheers and knew what they meant from tradition and actual experience.

On this bowlder Commander Gilmore and his little half-naked band were photographed. It was, too, the last film that Lieutenant Lipop had in his camera. One of the soldiers had a tiny American flag, and this they tied to a stick, which Commander Gilmore held aloft as an emblem of triumph at this climax to months of direst suffering.

The rescuing party was under the command of Colonel Hare, who with 150 men started out in light marching order to find Gilmore and his men. They pushed and climbed mountain ranges, swam streams, always with that little band of sufferers just ahead of them, till at last they came to their reward, that meeting on the dreary beach of Luzon's wildernees

Commander Gilmore's party was composed of the following men—Standley and Lysac, the scouts; Gilmore and his boat-crew, manned by Chief Quartermaster Walton; Sailmaker's Mate Voudoit, Cockswain Ellsworth, Gunner's Mate Nygard, Seamen Rynders, Woodbury, Brisolese and McDonald; Landsmen Dillon, Morrissey, Edwards and Anderson, and Apprentices Venville and Peterson.

During the nine months of their captivity this brave little party had traveled over 400 miles, the greater part of this distance being through the wildest and most mountainous part of the country.

Upon the arrival of the rescuing party food was given the half-starved men and preparations were at once made for the escape from the mountain fastnesses to the sea. The plan agreed upon was to build rafts and float down the river with the current. Accordingly all set to work building about forty bamboo rafts, each large enough to carry three or four men, some camp equipment and guns.

On the 18th of December all was in readiness, and the soldiers and sailors started off on their unique voyage to the sea. The narrow stream was full of large bowlders, the current swift, carrying the rafts rapidly along, thus making the trip a most hazardous undertaking. Many were the collisions with these bowlders, which were detected only when it was too late to divert the course of the rafts, and they would crash into the obstructions, throwing the little crews overboard. Scarcely a day passed but there were a number of these disasters, and then the more fortunate voyagers would again show their splendid courage by heroically rescuing the exhausted struggling men in the water. By the 25th they had lost so many of their rafts and so much of their camp equipment that Colonel Hare ordered a stop for the purpose of replacing the lost and damaged craft.

When the shore of the stream was gained the men were thoroughly exhausted, nearly half of them were without clothes, many had fever from their exposure to the water and the hot sun, and nearly all had badly swollen feet.

Those who were able were set to work cutting bamboo sticks and lashing them together, and in an incredibly short time the necessary outfit was complete, the weaker members of the party having in the meantime gathered a supply of rice.

Provisions had run down to such an extent that the fare was most meagre and the prospects of the returning party were most gloomy. The rafts drifted rapidly down stream between the precipitous bluffs which rose up from the water's edge to a height of 200 feet. Occasionally breaks were encountered in the dark canyon which revealed long beaches reaching back into an undulating country of lofty palms, cocoanut and banana trees, amidst a luxuriant undergrowth.

The few men of the party who were not overcome by exhaustion or sickness piloted the rafts down the river, but as their work required the greatest vigilance they could not enjoy the beautiful country through which they passed, and consequently the trip seemed never-ending.

Whenever a native hut was sighted some of the party went ashore to obtain provisions; but in almost every instance the men found the huts deserted. Their only recourse then was to go into the rice fields and gather what they could to carry them through until they might reach a place more abundantly supplied with food.

On they went, never knowing how far they were from civilization. Discouraged but not overcome they kept to their posts and guided the rafts with their precious burdens of sick men past the dangerous obstructions down the rapids.

Finally after eleven days' most perilous traveling the weary party rounded a curve in the river and before them lay a valley which stretched out beyond their vision. Civilization was close at hand. Disappointment was not in store for these men who had for so long a time suffered the tortures of captivity in the mountain fastnesses of an unknown country.

Before they could fully contemplate their good fortune one of the party discovered a bamboo cross upon which was floating a small white flag. Up went a shout of joy from the weary men when they were apprised of the discovery of this sign, for it meant a welcome to them or any other Americans who might see it. When a landing was made near the cross the party was met by the natives who offered them rice, tobacco, cocoanuts and sugar cane, as an offering of friendship and peace. Now that the men were assured of the friendship of the natives their feelings were given vent to in repeated and hysterical cheers.

The natives made them as comfortable as was possible under the circumstances, and that evening after they were told that the sea coast was but four days distant all turned in with the thought that at last they were safe from the vigilant and ever-spying insurgents.

On the following morning, after paying the Filipinos for their hospitality, the party again set out—this time with glad hearts—for their objective point, the sea, where they felt sure of encountering Americans.

The river widened as they progressed, but the current was still strong, causing much inconvenience and in several cases disaster to the rafts. The raft on which one of the sick men was lying crashed into a rock and threw the occupants into the water. The invalid was Private Day, and though he was rescued from a watery grave, he nevertheless succumbed to the exposure to which he had been subjected while in the water. This was the only casualty which befell the party since the start of its perilous journey on the 18th.

After a short rest at one of the villages some of the men set out in canoes in advance of the main party. They found friendly natives who gave them food and informed them that when the rest of the party arrived they would carry them in their bancas to Abulug.

Upon reaching Abulug Commander Gilmore and his party were met by an officer from the Princeton and taken aboard, where they were received by their messmates with cheer after cheer.

When the Princeton reached Vigan Colonel Hare and his men were met by General Young, who did not restrain himself in his expressions of gratitude to the noble band of rescuers, whom he said he would recommend for Medals of Honor.

THE BATTLE OF SAN JACINTO

Eᴀʀʟʏ in November, 1899, the Thirty-third Infantry, under Colonel Hare, encountered a force of the enemy between San Fabian and San Jacinto, and one of the sharpest battles of the year was fought, resulting in a complete victory for the American troops, and severe punishment, with large losses in killed, for the insurgents.

The Filipinos had concealed their presence in the vicinity of San Jacinto so well that a reconnoissance by Major Buck's battalion failed to locate their whereabouts. Through the energy of General Wheaton, who had been informed that the enemy had concentrated their forces near this place to protect and control the road from Dagupan north through San Jacinto, the Filipinos were at last located. It was necessary for the American troops to have control of this road, as it was considered probable that Aguinaldo's Tarlac army would use it on its retreat.

Thus the Thirty-third was ordered out, accompanied by a Gatling gun and a detachment of the Thirteenth Infantry, under command of Captain Howland. Five miles of the worst kind of road, cut by numerous creeks and miry ditches, had to be traversed before the enemy could be encountered. This march to action was one of the most interesting ones for all who participated. The difficulties to be overcome were endless; men and horses would sink into the miry creeks waist deep and struggle through rice fields as best they could. Not one of the numerous bridges that crossed the creeks was in a condition to be passed over by troops, not to speak of the gun. Some were hastily repaired to safeguard their passage, and in some of the more difficult places the gun had to be drawn by hand, a hundred soldiers or more pulling at the drag-rope. Nothing but the indomitable energy of the soldiers, and especially of the officers, enabled them to get the Gatling gun into action.

Finally the position held by the Filipinos was reached. This was about two miles from San Jacinto, and the fight ensued at once. The American troops had expected the enemy about a mile farther towards San Jacinto, and therefore it was somewhat of a surprise when fire was opened suddenly on the soldiers of the first battalion, which was just then crossing one of the miry rice fields. The first fire came from a number of native houses, surrounded by groves of cocoanut trees, in which sharpshooters were hidden, and also from a trench which had been thrown up across the road. The fire came at close range and was directed at the officers, for the first five men that fell wore either chevrons or shoulder-straps.

Major John A. Logan was among the first five. He saw one of his comrades fall next to him, and, passing over to where the man lay, was about to assist him, when a bullet crashed through his head.

A Filipino sharpshooter in one of the trees also shot Captain Green about the same time that Logan fell, but his wound was not serious. The troops never wavered for a moment. Crack marksmen of the regiment soon located the natives in the

DEATH OF MAJOR JOHN A. LOGAN.

trees, and but a few moments passed before the first ones came tumbling down like cocoanuts, the slayer of Logan among them. At the same time the trench in front was stormed and taken. Then the regiment deployed as skirmishers and spreading out, covering nearly two miles, rushed forward.

The Filipinos, however, were not so easily routed and put to flight this time as on previous occasions. They made a desperate stand and displayed considerable courage in holding their ground under such withering fire as was poured in on them by the American troops, who were surprised to see them keep their places even when within twenty feet of the storming column. The Filipinos lost considerably in this affair. Major Marsh's battalion alone slaughtered a whole trenchful of them, which they attacked from the flank.

The superiority of American arms and men was demonstrated again on this battlefield. The Filipinos were at last driven towards and through the town of San Jacinto, where they dispersed, and pursuit could not be taken up.

Major Marsh's battalion entered the town first and captured a large battle flag that was floating over a convent. The town had been deserted by everyone but a blind boy and an old woman, so complete was the fright of the inhabitants, who had fled to the hills. The larger part of the insurgent forces retreated towards Dagupan, and it was impossible to pursue them further, as the troops were completely exhausted. Ammunition was low and rations were carried only for two days, so they camped for the night in the town, buried the dead, among whom was found an officer in lieutenant-colonel's uniform—presumably the leader of the Filipinos in this affair—and as it was not advisable to await further supplies from San Fabian over such devastated roads the return march was begun.

CHASING AGUINALDO

Early in November, 1899, General Otis started a campaign the express purpose of which was the capture of Aguinaldo.

General S. B. M. Young was entrusted with this important though extremely difficult task, and the pursuit in which this daring and persistent general subsequently engaged became a regular man-hunt, the details of which are given by General Young, as follows:

"Aguinaldo became a fugitive and an outlaw, seeking security in escape to the mountains or by sea. My cavalry had ridden down his forces wherever found, utterly routing them in every instance, killing some, capturing and liberating many prisoners, and destroying many arms and other munitions of war.

"Our march was forced to Rosario, where we arrived sixty hours after Aguinaldo's departure. Here we found his abandoned carts, he packing his baggage over the difficult mountain trail to Tubao on carabaos. A deserter came into our lines here with the information that Aguinaldo's rear guard was in Tubao, but said that the trail was impassable for our big horses. This man willingly consented to guide us. Scattered bands of insurgents kept our outpost busy all night; we found two dead ones in the morning. The trail leading to Tubao was extremely difficult, and we passed many exhausted and abandoned native horses and carabaos in a valley extending six or seven miles southeast from Tubao to a fairly good road. Horses, cattle and carts had been in waiting for Aguinaldo at the point where the mountain trail came into this road. After preparing our camp in Tubao information was received that the enemy were moving up the coast road to join General Manuel Tinio at Aringay.

"My force was too small to allow any concentration of the enemy, and we pushed on, leaving all footsore and tired-out Macabebes with a small guard at Tubao to wait and care for weary stragglers who were being brought up by the rear guard.

"On November 19th I sent word to General Lawton that I needed additional forces, but could not wait, and asked that a battalion of light infantry, that could march rapidly without impedimenta, should follow on my trail with an officer in command who would push for all he was worth.

"At dusk we struck the enemy's intrenchments and carried them by assault. Captains Quinlan and Hall with their companies waded the river in the face of a heavy fire. Captain Chase dismounted, covering the left flank and driving back a force evidently just arriving on our side of the river from the coast road. One Macabebe soldier was wounded and died the same night. Captain Batson's left foot was shattered by a spent ball striking him on the instep, a sad and at this time a very grave misfortune, and one particularly disheartening to the Macabebes, who performed prodigious work under him.

"The enemy finding our troops crossing, fled from their up-stream works and we pushed into Aringay in rear of the trenches made to defend the coast road. The night was very dark, and we knew nothing of these trenches or the force in them until morning, after they had escaped during the night. About 8 A. M. on the 20th Lieutenant Bell and party, with sick and footsore men, arrived from Tubao, six miles distant, and I moved out immediately, leaving him and his party to guard the sick and wounded.

"Between Aringay and Booang flag communication was gained with the gunboat Samar, Ensign Mustin commanding. He was requested to open on the works at San Fernando at 2:30 P. M.

"The insurgent battalions of Union and Benguet provinces had increased Aguinaldo's strength to over 1,000 men, part of this force having followed Aguinaldo, while the remainder was with Tinio, going directly up the coast road. I overtook Chase as he neared San Fernando, and witnessed the handsomest and neatest little fight of the campaign. A trench made with bamboo revetment and ditched in front extended from the foot of the mountain across the road to the town's cemetery wall, and could be approached only through an open rice field with no cover. Captain Chase with his dismounted force, numbering thirty-seven troopers, charged up and over the works, and as the enemy's fire made it very uncomfortable around my flag we all charged, carrying the led horses up against the works.

"As Captain Chase and his men were scrambling over them, the horses were passed through an opening in rear of the west terminus of the works and in front of the southeast corner of the cemetery wall. The narrow defile, 400 yards in length, leading into the town was passed under a heavy fire from both sides, but the rush by Captain Chase and his troopers, followed by the led horses at a trot, seemed to unnerve the enemy, as none of their fire was effective; but they kept up an annoying fire on Chase's exhausted men from the hills beyond, until the Samar's guns frightened them away.

"An insurgent officer captured some days afterwards stated that the force opposed to Captain Chase at San Fernando numbered 300, 200 of this number occupying the works facing the sea, and that when Captain Chase entered the rear of the town by the road he rendered their positions untenable and they fled without offering resistance; but of this fact we were not aware until the rear of their column was on the distant hills

"Early on the morning of the 21st, leaving Captain Chase to hold San Fernando, I returned to Booang, and met Captains Parker and Swigert, who had come up the coast road.

"Captain Cunningham and his mounted scouts of Colonel Hare's regiment, who came up with Parker, were left to occupy Booang, and with Swigert's two troops I followed on Captain Wilder's trail. About six miles out we met Wilder returning with information that Aguinaldo had left two nights previously, but that he had not taken trail to Trinidad. Wilder had in the meantime sent Lieutenant Lee Hall with his company of Macabebes over the mountain trail from Naguiliang direct to San Fernando. Ordering Wilder and Swigert to return to Booang for the night, I hurried to San Fernando and arrived there at 11 P. M., Hall arriving about midnight.

"The situation was perplexing. My cavalry was crippled for want of shoes, the Macabebes were disheartened at the loss of their beloved leader, Batson, and many were sick and footsore."

On the 20th of November Aguinaldo remained at Balauang over night and passed through Bangar the following day, General Young close upon his heels and steadily gaining upon him.

General Young's forces were much depleted and worn out. Aguinaldo had been playing hide-and-seek, one day in the mountains, the next day, he or some of his generals, on the coast road. The general felt positive that Aguinaldo could be caught with fresh troops, for he had information from the best authority that Aguinaldo had a force of only 1,700 men with him, under Generals Tinio, Pilar and Concepcion, in Abra. The additional cavalry force required could have reached San Fernando in the shortest time, and the infantry could have been landed by boat at Darigayos, four miles south of that point.

On the 25th Swigert examined the country around Namaspacan, Balauang and Bangar, and Sergeant Aquilino Vasea, with two of his Macabebes on outpost duty, attacked a party of insurgents, killing one and capturing another, together with four rifles and ammunition.

The mass of the people in this section showed the strongest demonstration of friendship and welcome to the troops. They had been robbed by the insurgent commanders, and many of them feared that they would be likewise robbed of what they had left by the troops; but to assure them to the contrary, General Young sent back to the agent of the tobacco company, Don Benito Reynoldo, at San Fernando, and borrowed $2,500 on his personal security, in order that cash might be paid for all supplies needed.

It was learned here that Aguinaldo had been at Naguiliang on his way to Benguet, and that he had changed his plan of escape in deference to the demands of his new provincial re-enforcements. He then took a trail leading into Balauang, thence through Namaspacan and north on the coast road, intending to go to the province of Abra by way of Vigan.

Aguinaldo and Tinio had separated at Candon, the former going by mountain to Lepanto, the latter with a retarding force of 600 occupying and repairing trenches at Tagudin, and Pilar was left to fortify and hold the Tila Mountain Pass in his rear, near Angaqui. A captured letter showed Aguinaldo in Angaqui on the 28th, intending to go to Cervantes on the 29th of November. Tinio was going north to San Quintin to hold the Abra Canyon against a force moving up from Vigan.

DEATH OF GENERAL PILAR

O N November 30th Major March, with a sufficiently large force, was sent on
Aguinaldo's trail and encountered the force of General Pilar in the Tila Pass
soon afterward. The rebels had constructed a stone barricade across the trail at a
point where it commanded the turns of the zigzag pass for a considerable distance.
This barricade was loop-holed for infantry fire and afforded head cover for the
insurgents. Passing beyond Lingey the advance was checked by a heavy fire from
this barricade, which killed and wounded several men without having its position
revealed. Major March brought up the remainder of the command at a double
quick, losing two men during the run up. Arriving at the point he located the
insurgents' position with field glasses—their fire being entirely of Mauser rifles, with
smokeless powder—by the presence of the insurgent officer, who showed himself
freely and directed the fire.

Pushing forward, the number of men who were hit increased so rapidly that it
was evident the position could not be taken by a front attack, when the trail only
allowed the men to pass one at a time. On the left of the barricade was a gorge
several hundred feet deep, on its right a precipitous mountain which rose 1,500 feet
above the trail. Across the gorge and to the left front of the barricade was a hill,
which, while it did not permit of flank fire into the barricade, commanded the trail
in its rear; and this point was occupied by ten sharpshooters in command of Sergeant-Major McDougall, who lost one man wounded in getting to the top, and when
there rendered most effective assistance.

Lieutenant Tompkins was then ordered to ascend the slope of the mountain
under cover of a slight ridge which struck the face of the mountain about 150 feet
from the summit. From there he had a straight climb to the top, where the men
pulled themselves up by twigs and by hand. The ascent took two hours, during
which time the enemy kept up an incessant and accurate fire, which they varied by
rolling down stones on the soldiers' heads. When Tompkins's men appeared upon
the crest of the hills over their heads, he had the command of the two trenches
which were constructed in rear of the barricade, around a sharp turn in the trail,
and which were also held by the insurgents. He opened fire upon them, Major
March charging the first barricade at the same time, rushing the enemy over the
hill. Eight dead bodies were found on the trail, and the bushes which grew at the
edge of the gorge were broken and blood-stained where dead and wounded men fell
through. Among the dead bodies was that of Gregorio del Pilar, the general commanding the insurgent forces. His shoulder-straps, French field glasses, official and
private papers, and other articles which served as a means of identification, were
taken from the body.

The insurgents' report of their casualties in this fight was fifty-two; Major
March's loss was two killed and nine wounded. The major reached the summit at

4:30 P. M., and camped there for the night, finding at that point a large amount of rice, lard, etc., which had been abandoned by the insurgents and on which he subsisted his troops. In this engagement he also captured several Mausers and a large quantity of ammunition.

"At Cervantes," Major March relates, "I learned that the force at Tila Pass consisted of picked men from Aguinaldo's bodyguard, and that it was wiped out of existence. Aguinaldo, with his wife and two other women and a handful of men, were living in a convent at Cervantes, perfectly secure in his belief that Tila Pass was an impregnable position. It was the insurgents' Thermopylae. Upon learning of the death of Pilar, which news was brought in by runners across the hills at 5 P. M. of the same day, Aguinaldo hastily gathered together his effects, and with two of his women on horseback and his wife in a litter carried by Igorrotes, left the town at 10 o'clock P. M. I arrived the evening of the 3d and spent the 4th in resting the men and sifting evidence of his whereabouts. Large numbers of Spanish prisoners were abandoned in his flight, and from their tales and those of natives I located him as passing through Cayan at 2 o'clock A. M. of the 3d. I set out at 6 A. M. on the 5th for Cayan, with a picked force of 100 officers and men who were the least exhausted by their long march and the fighting. The road begins immediately to ascend and goes straight up until a height of 9,000 feet is reached.

"Upon arriving at Cayan I was met by the two staff officers of General Venancio Concepcion, Aguinaldo's chief-of-staff, with a letter proposing an interview, with the suspension of hostilities in view. I told his officers that there could be no suspension of hostilities, but that if the general and his staff wanted to come in and surrender I would guarantee them good treatment and would consent to their proposed interview at 3 P. M. He came in and surrendered and was sent to Cervantes under charge of a guard. A number of the men were now exhausted by the climb to Cayan, so I weeded out the command again and set out after Aguinaldo with eighty-six men. All this time I had been living on the country, paying or giving receipt for what I took. I now got into a country which produces very little besides yams, and then pushed on to Baguen, near Bontoc, where I found natives hostile to Aguinaldo, and learned that he had gone on through the town of Bontoc to Tuluben, evidently making for Banaueg and the road to Bayambang, three days before. He was gaining on me with fresh ponies and bearers and with his party unencumbered. I therefore rounded up the Spanish prisoners throughout the region and returned to Cervantes."

DEATH OF GENERAL LAWTON

S AN MATEO, a place which lies between a high mountain behind and a broad, shallow stream in front, with wide sand bars, has twice been the scene of battles. It is some fifteen miles to the northeast of Manila, and was occupied and abandoned by the Americans more than once.

The first engagement occurred on August 12, 1899, when an advance of three separate columns was made against the place. One, under Captain Cronin, consisted of 150 men from the Twenty-fifth (colored) Infantry. It was to move eastward from Novaliches, effecting a junction with Captain Rivers, who, with 100 men of the Fourth Cavalry, was to move from the southwest and join Cronin in or near San Mateo to intercept the retreat forced by Captain Parker of the Fourth Cavalry, who lead the attacking column. That consisted of 280 men in six companies from the Fourth Cavalry and Twenty-first and Twenty-fourth (colored) Infantry. Four of these companies were commanded by second lieutenants. Parker was to cross the river near Mariquina and follow the road leading northward upon its eastern bank. The purpose was to drive the Filipinos, known to be in the vicinity, back upon San Mateo, where they would encounter the other two columns. The general plan miscarried, but Parker's force found a busy time for some four miles. The enemy, well intrenched, were encountered near the little River Nanca. Their dispersion involved the crossing of an unusually long stretch of those abominable muddy rice fields which make military movements on the islands so arduous. The troops plunge and flounder about in muddy water from six to eighteen inches in depth. If the fire of the enemy becomes too galling it is sometimes necessary for the men to imitate the carabao, and lie down and wallow in it. A forty-minute fight took place at this point. The command was composed largely of recruits, but they showed all the pluck and dash and coolness of well-seasoned troopers. They manifested but one desire, and that was to charge forward. The first dash of the encounter was a hot one. It was made across the open and against trenches. It cost the Americans eighteen men in killed and wounded. The Filipino loss was not known. For the next four miles it was a running fight, with the Filipinos gaining at every jump. The lightly-clad native, who knows every inch of the running, rather handicaps his American pursuer at that kind of a foot-race. Parker kept them moving at a rate that sent them through the city before Cronin's arrival. Some escaped to the north. Others undoubtedly played the usual game and got away round to the right of the American line and were "Amigos" by the time they reached the rear. It is beyond question that a fair number of the Americans' opponents on the 12th were seen as industrious agriculturists at work in their fields, and all very friendly, when the troops returned a day or two later.

Cronin's march was without especial incident. Some three or four miles outside of San Mateo Captain Rivers came upon an intrenched outpost. A sharp little

DEATH OF GENERAL HENRY W. LAWTON.

engagement followed, with the usual result. The Filipinos fired a few moments and then disappeared. Their fire cost one American life and a few wounds.

Captain Parker's trip resulted in an incident worth recording. One company was under command of Captain Wilhelm, of the Twenty-first Infantry. At a certain stage of the fighting he saw four of the enemy running away at close range. He ordered his men to fire on them and bring them down. Just at the critical moment, and just in time to save them, a native woman ran out and placed herself, with extended arms, immediately behind the fugitives, in the line of the fire. There was but one thing for Wilhelm to do as an American gentleman, and he did it promptly. He ordered his men to reserve their fire and moved on, while the hurrying Filipinos got as quickly as possible out of range, sheltered from harm by American gallantry and their guardian angel.

The second engagement at this place occurred December 18th of the same year, and resulted in the death of General Henry W. Lawton, one of the bravest men in the army. The general had left Manila the night before with Troop I, Fourth United States Cavalry, under Captain Lockett, and two battalions of the Twenty-seventh and Twenty-ninth United States Infantry, under Lieutenant-Colonel Sargent, for the purpose of capturing San Mateo, where General Geronomo was known to have 300 insurgents. The night was one of the worst of the season, heavy rain having set in.

With a small escort he led the way through an almost pathless country, a distance of fifteen miles over hills and through cane-brakes and deep mud, the horses climbing the rocks and sliding down the hills. Before daybreak the command had reached the head of the valley, and San Mateo was attacked at 8 o'clock, a three hours' fight ensuing. This resulted in but few casualties on the American side, but the attack was difficult because of the natural defenses of the town.

General Lawton was walking along the firing line within 300 yards of a small sharpshooters' trench, conspicuous in the big white helmet he always wore. He was easily distinguishable because of his commanding stature.

The sharpshooters directed several close shots which clipped the grass near by. Staff officers called General Lawton's attention to his dangerous position, but he only laughed with his usual contempt for bullets.

Suddenly he exclaimed: "I am shot," and clenching his hands in a desperate effort to stand erect, fell into the arms of a staff officer.

Orderlies rushed across the field for surgeons, who dashed up immediately, but their efforts were useless, for the bullet had struck him in a vital spot. The body was taken to a clump of bushes and laid upon a stretcher, the familiar white helmet covering the face of the dead general. Almost at this moment the cheers of the American troops rushing into San Mateo were mingling with the rifle volleys. After the fight six stalwart cavalrymen forded the river to the town, carrying the litter on their shoulders, the staff preceding with the colors, and a cavalry escort following.

The troops filed bare-headed through the building where the body was laid, and many a tear fell from the eyes of men who had long followed the intrepid Lawton. The entire command was stricken with grief, as though each man had suffered a personal loss.

All except the officers were behind cover at the time the general was shot. A staff officer was wounded about the same time, and one other officer and seven men were wounded. After three hours' shooting the Filipinos were dispersed into the mountains.

THE DEATH OF COLONEL STOTSENBURG

THE death of another gallant officer, whose loss was felt alike by his men and his country, occurred some time prior to that of General Lawton, in an engagement with the insurgents near Quinqua.

The occupation of Malolos, situated on the Manila-Dagupan Railway, northwest of Manila, by the American forces, made it necessary to send out several expeditions to clean the insurgents out of neighboring villages and hamlets so as to secure the Malolos force against surprises.

Such an expedition, consisting of the First Nebraska and Fifty-first Iowa Regiments, detachments of the Fourth U. S. Cavalry and the Utah Light Battery, started towards Quinqua, northeast of Malolos, on the 23d of April, 1899.

Major Bell, with the forty cavalrymen, was in the lead, scouting towards Quinqua, when he came across a strong rebel outpost which forthwith opened a murderous fire on him, killing four of his men and wounding five. Major Bell withdrew into the next favorable position and sent for re-enforcements. Major Mufford, with a battalion of the Nebraskans, came hurrying up and attacked the Filipinos. The latter withdrew within the lines of a strong, fortified position, their rifle ditches encircling a rice field at the edge of dense woods. Here the fight came to a standstill. It was impossible for the Americans to advance farther without artillery against the heavy fire of the overwhelming numbers of the enemy.

For two hours the Nebraskans and the Fourth Cavalrymen held out in this exposed position, about 800 yards from the enemy's rifle pits.

Finally, Colonel Stotsenburg, the commander of the First Nebraska Regiment, brought up the second battalion of this regiment and the guns of the Utah Battery. He immediately ordered the attack, and, putting himself in front of his line, led his men daringly against the firing lines of the insurgents. When only about 200 yards distant from them the brave colonel was shot through the breast, and killed almost instantly. Lieutenant Sessions of the same regiment was also killed by a bullet which went through his heart.

The Nebraskans, enraged over the loss of their esteemed leader, immediately rushed the enemy, who fell back on their second line of defense. But this, too, was stormed, and soon the Americans had reached the town of Quinqua, which they occupied.

The loss of the Americans was heavy, amounting to two officers and four men killed and three officers and forty men wounded.

———

IN 1900 the American troops were scattered over the entire island of Luzon and occupied the chief cities of the other islands, including Camarines, Albay, Leyte, Samar, Mindanao, Cebu, Negros and Panay, but nevertheless many well-armed forces of Filipino insurgents operated in nearly every province of the islands. These forces, acting independently of any apparent central direction, were commanded by men who had been well known as insurgent leaders.

Early in January Captain Conchause, with three companies of the Twenty-fifth Infantry, surprised and captured a stronghold of the insurgents at Mayalang, in the Province of Pambanga. The well-selected position of the insurgents was situated on the top of a high hill where they could well protect themselves from attack, but the surprise was so complete and the attack so well planned that they were com pletely routed.

This insurgent band held as captives three soldiers of the Ninth and two of the Twelfth Infantry, but before these men could be rescued by Captain Conchause's force they were shot down and horribly mutilated. Three of the captives were found dead and the other two severely wounded when the troops came up to the abandoned Filipino position.

The fort and adjacent village were at once burned and destroyed by Captain Conchause's men, who thus avenged the death of their murdered comrades.

The tactics of the insurgents in retreating before the advancing Americans and then closing in after the troops had passed their hiding places made it difficult for all the expeditions sent out to surround or entrap them, and consequently the American forces were continually engaged in skirmishes and brushes which brought but little punishment to the insurgents. In this manner General Schwan's command was chasing a band of insurgents in January, having numerous engagements with the retreating foe whenever they would show themselves. To corner them was difficult, and when this was finally accomplished it was comical to watch the many manœuvres executed by them in order to escape.

For several days the chase was kept up in the direction of Binang, whither the insurgents were retreating. On the 5th they were located along the hill-ides near the town and fierce fighting ensued, but only for a short time, as the Filipinos realized that they were cornered and they would suddenly disappear under the rapid fire of the troops only to reappear at a different point, sometimes holding a stone wall or barricade in front of the town, but never long enough to give the Americans a good chance to capture them.

Finally, on the next day they made their last stand in the open market place of Binang, where they delivered several volleys at the advancing troops and then again suddenly disappeared. A few minutes later they began to reappear from all directions and in all streets, this time not as fighting insurgents, but as — Amigos. Their trickery, however, could not deceive General Schwan this time, and many of them were made prisoners of war.

These expeditions involved great hardships for the troops and even considerable loss of life, but they helped to teach the insurgents that the Americans meant to subdue them and do it by going after them into the very interior of their mountain faotnoaooo.

On the 12th of January the Thirty-eighth Infantry, under General Schwan, succeeded in routing the enemy at San Tomas, where they captured the town and its treasury, containing $20,000. Sixty Spanish prisoners were also released from captivity. In this engagement the Filipino losses were considerable, while the American troops lost but one man killed and one wounded.

About this time re-enforcements were sent to the Islands of Samar, Leyte and Negros, where the insurgents were showing unusual signs of activity. The inhabitants of these islands were known as the most peaceful, but when they rose in revolt they at once became the worst enemies of the American soldiers that could be found in the whole Philippine Archipelago.

At the same time the insurgents in Luzon became more troublesome, and the troops went after them with renewed vigor. On one occasion the rebels attacked a pack-mule train of twenty mules, accompanied by fifty men of the Thirtieth Infantry, in command of Lieutenant Ralston.

They were traveling along the route between San Tomas and San Pablo, in the Province of Laguna, when suddenly they were attacked by a superior force of insurgents, who first fired upon them from ambush and then dashed out upon the command, dispersing them and capturing the entire mule train. The Americans retreated in good order, taking with them their two killed and five wounded. Nine were reported missing.

The Filipino losses could not be ascertained, but as the Americans made a determined stand before retreating their losses must have been considerable. The detachment returned to San Tomas with its wounded.

Continued fighting of this character was kept up throughout the year, in which the Filipinos were almost invariably repulsed with severe losses, and, although no less than 1,000 of these engagements were fought since the outbreak of hostilities, the wily insurgents were not yet under control.

Towards the end of the year the situation in the islands was practically the same as at the beginning, with the exception that Aguinaldo was rapidly losing his power among the Filipinos, and shortly after the beginning of the year 1901 his power was completely gone, he having been captured by United States troops in command of General Fred Funston.

CAPTURE OF AGUINALDO

GENERAL Emilio Aguinaldo, the leader of the insurrection, was captured by General Frederick Funston March 23, 1901, in the following manner:

The confidential agent of Aguinaldo arrived at Pantabangan in the province of Nueva Ecija, northern Luzon, February 28th, with letters dated January 11th, 12th and 14th. These letters were from Emilio Aguinaldo ordering that General Alejandrino be supplanted in the command of the provinces of central Luzon. Aguinaldo also ordered 400 men to be sent him as soon as possible, saying that the bearer of the letters would guide these men to where Aguinaldo was.

General Funston secured the correspondence of Aguinaldo's agent and laid his plans accordingly. Some months previously he had captured the camp of the insurgent general Lacuna, incidentally obtaining Lacuna's seal, official papers and a quantity of signed correspondence. With this material two letters were constructed, ostensibly from Lacuna to Aguinaldo.

One of these contained information as to the progress of the war. The other asserted that, pursuant to orders received from Baldermero Aguinaldo, Lacuna was sending his best company to President Emilio Aguinaldo.

His plans completed and approved, General Funston came to Manila and organ ized his expedition, selecting seventy-eight Macabebes, all of whom spoke Tagalog fluently. Twenty-four had insurgent uniforms, and the others the dress of the Filipino laborers. This Macabebe company, armed with fifty Krag-Jorgensen rifles, was commanded by Captain Russel T. Hazzard, of the Eleventh United States Volunteer Cavalry. With him was his brother, Lieutenant Oliver P. Hazzard, of the same regiment. Captain Harry W. Newton, Thirty-fourth Infantry, was taken because of his familiarity with Casiguaran Bay, and Lieutenant Burton J. Mitchell, of the Fortieth, went as General Funston's aide. These were the only Americans accompanying the leader of the expedition. With the Macabebes were four ex-insurgent officers, one being a Spaniard and the other three Tagalogs, whom General Funston trusted implicitly.

General Funston and the American officers wore plain blue shirts and khaki trousers. They each carried a half blanket, but wore no insignia of rank. The Macabebes were carefully instructed to obey the orders of the four ex-insurgent officers.

On the night of March 8th the party embarked on the United States gunboat Vicksburg. It was originally intended to take cascoes from the island of Polillo and drift to the mainland, but a storm arose and three of the cascoes were lost. This plan was abandoned. At 2 A. M., March 14th, the Vicksburg put her lights out and ran in-shore 25 miles south of Casiguaran. The Americans had never garrisoned this place, and the inhabitants were strong insurgent sympathizers. Having arrived there, the ex-insurgent officers, ostensibly commanding the force, announced that they were on the way to join Aguinaldo between Pantabangan and Baler, that they had surprised an American surveying party of whom they had killed a number, capturing five. They exhibited General Funston and the other Americans as their prisoners.

The insurgent president of Casiguaran believed their story. Two of the Lacuna letters previously concocted were forwarded to Aguinaldo at Palanan, Province of Isabela. General Funston and the other Americans were kept imprisoned for three days, surreptitiously giving orders at night. On the morning of March 17th, taking a small quantity of cracked corn, the party started on a ninety-mile march to Palanan. The country is rough and uninhabited, and provisions could not be secured. The party ate small shell-fish, but were almost starved. Wading swift rivers, climbing precipitous mountains and penetrating dense jungles, they marched six days and nights, and on March 22d had reached a point eight miles from Palanan. They were now so weak that it was necessary to send to Aguinaldo's camp for food. Aguinaldo dispatched supplies and directed that the American prisoners be kindly treated but not allowed to enter the town.

On the morning of March 23d the advance was resumed. The column was met by the staff officers of Aguinaldo and a detachment of Aguinaldo's bodyguard, which was ordered to take charge of the Americans. While one of the ex-insurgent officers conversed with Aguinaldo's aide, another, a Spaniard, sent a courier to warn General Funston and the other four Americans, who, with eleven Macabebes, were about an hour behind. Having received the warning, General Funston avoided Aguinaldo's detachment and joined the column. The Tagalogs went ahead to greet Aguinaldo and the column slowly followed, finally arriving at Palanan.

Aguinaldo's household troops, fifty men in neat uniforms of blue and white, and wearing straw hats, lined up to receive the new-comers. General Funston's men crossed the river in small boats, formed on the bank and marched to the right and then in front of the insurgent "grenadiers." The Tagalogs entered the house where Aguinaldo was. Suddenly the Spanish officer, observing that Aguinaldo's aide was watching the Americans suspiciously, exclaimed: "Now, Macabebes, go for them!" The Macabebes opened fire, but their aim was rather ineffective, and only three insurgents were killed. The rebels returned the fire. On hearing the fire Aguinaldo, who evidently thought his men were merely celebrating the arrival of re-enforcements, ran to the window and shouted: "Stop that foolishness; quit wasting ammunition!"

Hilario Placido, one of the Tagalog officers, and a former insurgent major, who was wounded in the lung by the fire of the Kansas regiment at the battle of Caloocan, threw his arms around Aguinaldo, exclaiming: "You are a prisoner of the Americans!"

Colonel Simeon Villia, Aguinaldo's chief-of-staff, Major Alambra and others attacked the men who were holding Aguinaldo. Placido shot Villia in the shoulder, Alambra jumped out of a window and attempted to cross the river, and as he was not again seen it is supposed that he was drowned. Five other insurgent officers fought for a few minutes and then fled, making good their escape.

When the firing began General Funston assumed command and directed the attack on the house, personally assisting in the capture of Aguinaldo. The insurgent bodyguard fled, leaving twenty rifles. Santiago Barcelona, the insurgent treasurer, surrendered without resistance.

When captured Aguinaldo was very much excited, but he calmed down under General Funston's assurance that he would be well treated. General Funston secured all of Aguinaldo's correspondence, showing that he had kept in close touch with the sub-chiefs of the insurrection in all parts of the archipelago. It was also discovered that Aguinaldo, on January 28th, had proclaimed himself dictator. He had been living at Palanan for seven months, undisturbed, except when a detachment of the Sixteenth Infantry visited the town. On that occasion the entire population took to the mountains and remained there until the troops retired.

Aguinaldo admitted that he had come near being captured before, but he asserted that he had never been wounded, adding: "I should never have been taken except by a stratagem. I was completely deceived by Lacuna's forged signature."

He feared that he might be sent to Guam, and he was quite glad to come to Manila.

Palanan was guarded by numerous outposts and signal stations. During the fight none of the Macabebes were wounded.

The expedition rested March 24th and then marched sixteen miles the following day to Palanan Bay, where General Funston found the Vicksburg, which brought him to Manila. Commander Barry, of the Vicksburg, rendered General Funston splendid assistance.

Aguinaldo arrived at Manila a few days after his capture. He now entered the Filipino capital a prisoner of war instead of a victor and the president of an independent republic, as he had so fervently hoped. However, from the very first hour of his captivity his conduct was dignified and peaceable, his spirit of rebellion and revolt giving way to one of reconciliation and submission to an inevitable fate. On April 1st he was persuaded to take the oath of allegiance and become an American citizen.

The insurgent leader not only gracefully made his peace with the government of the United States, but on April 19th issued the following significant manifesto:

"I believe I am not in error in presuming that the unhappy fate to which my adverse fortune has led me is not a surprise to those who have been familiar with the progress of the war. The lessons taught with a full meaning, and which have recently come to my knowledge, suggest with irresistible force that a complete termination of hostilities and lasting peace are not only desirable, but absolutely essential to the welfare of the Philippine Islands.

"The Filipinos have never been dismayed at their weakness, nor have they faltered in following the path pointed out by their fortitude and courage. The time has come, however, in which they find their advance along this path to be impeded by an irresistible force, which, while it restrains them, yet enlightens their minds and opens to them another course, presenting them the cause of peace. This cause has been joyfully embraced by the majority of my fellow-countrymen, who have already united around the glorious sovereign banner and believe that under its protection the Filipino people will attain all those promised liberties which they are beginning to enjoy.

"The country has declared unmistakably in favor of peace. So be it. There has been enough blood, enough tears. and enough desolation. This wish cannot be ignored by the men still in arms if they are animated by a desire to serve our noble people, which has thus clearly manifested its will. So do I respect this will, now that it is known to me.

"After mature deliberation, I resolutely proclaim to the world that I cannot refuse to heed the voice of the people longing for peace nor the lamentations of thousands of families yearning to see their dear ones enjoying the liberty and the promised generosity of the great American nation.

"By acknowledging and accepting the sovereignty of the United States throughout the Philippine Archipelago, as I now do, and without any reservation whatsoever, I believe that I am serving thee, my beloved country. May happiness be thine.

"EMILIO AGUINALDO."

The capture or surrender of other insurgent generals of importance and prominence occurred at the same time.

On February 2, 1901, General Delgado surrendered to General Hughes, with 30 officers and 140 armed men. As a result of this surrender 41,000 inhabitants of the Province of Iloilo took the oath of allegiance. On March 15, 1901, General Trias, commander of the insurrectionary forces in southern Luzon, surrendered to Lieutenant-Colonel Frank D. Baldwin, Fourth United States Infantry, and in a manfiesto urged his followers to give up all further resistance to the American troops. Generals S. Juan and Blas Villamor, two brave Filipino fighters had surrendered early in January, 1901, and on May 1st of the same year General Manuel Tinio, who had covered Aguinaldo's retreat at the mountain passes, gave up the struggle. The surrender of Generals Alejandrino, Lacuna and Cailles, together with the capture of the entire insurgent cabinet members, plainly told of the utter collapse of the insurrection. The total surrenders of insurgents from December 1, 1900, to the last day of May, 1901, numbered 1,699 officers and 19,372 men. During the same time the casualties of the American forces were: Killed 245, wounded 490, captured 118, missing 20.

Henceforth the pacification progressed steadily, although the work did not proceed without many engagements and fights with small bands of bush-whacking insurgents.

THE MASSACRE AT BALANGIGA

THE difficulties which our troops experienced in subduing the insurrection were manifold, especially in those districts of the Islands where the insurrection had seemingly been suppressed, and "Amigos" were trying to gain the friendship of the Americans only to lure them into ambush. The shrewd and intelligent Filipinos would then form treacherous plans to surprise and destroy the so bitterly hated Americans. Woe to them if they were not always on their guard, or if the officers had ceased watching for signs and symptoms of hidden treachery.

A case where officers as well as enlisted men were cleverly lured into such a trap was experienced by Company C, Ninth United States Infantry, on Saturday, September 28, 1901, on the Island of Samar, near Balangiga, and the result of this negligence was a disaster to our troops which had no equal during the whole campaign. Not more than twenty-four of the entire company of seventy-two men escaped with their lives, the others sharing a terrible fate at the hands of the frenzied natives.

The garrison of the entire island had been too small for so large an area, being fully as large as the State of Ohio, and having but 2,500 men stationed at different places. Speedily the important towns and centers were occupied by small bodies of our men. Spain had up to this time never attempted to occupy Samar, and therefore the insurgents had believed themselves masters of the island. However, they were, as on all the other islands, conquered, and from that time on the Filipinos had carried on a guerrilla warfare. Operations against them were difficult.

The Ninth United States Infantry had seen service during the preceding summer in China, and after its return to the Philippine Islands a battalion was sent to Samar.

Previous to the arrival of the ill-fated Company C at their station colored troops had occupied the place, the inhabitants had become acquainted with the soldiers and seemed in the best of harmony with them. This, however, was a ruse, for as soon as Company C had settled down and through the seeming friendship of the natives had slackened their vigilance, the surprise was carried into effect with disastrous results.

The following details about the affair were gathered from the survivors, and it can be termed a wonder that any had a chance to escape the massacre, so well planned and executed was the surprise:

The night before the massacre the village presidente came to Captain Connell, then in command of Company C, and declared that it would take 100 more natives to do certain pioneer work which had been ordered by the command and was to be done by natives. An agreement was reached by which the work was to be started the next morning. This arrangement gave 100 or more natives a chance to come into camp with their bolos, pretending to cut underbrush with them. They chatted, laughed and carried on as if actually going to work. No sooner, however, had the last man passed the sentry than, upon a given signal, the latter was cut down, and

THE BALANGIGA MASSACRE.

with tiger-like swiftness they all dashed upon the barracks, and a fearful slaughter was begun. The soldiers were completely surprised; most of them were at the breakfast table, and their arms being on the floor above, they had no chance at all to defend themselves. The natives had divided; half of them murdered every soldier on the upper floor of the barracks, while the other half forced the mess-room, killing every one they could reach. The attack came so sudden and was carried out so fiercely that within a few minutes the dastardly work was done and a large number of horribly mutilated American soldiers were lying upon the floors.

Captain Connell apparently was awakened in his quarters by the attackers pouring in. He was alone, so he jumped from the window down where he supposed his guards were, but they had all been slaughtered. He was struck by many bolos as soon as he reached the ground. Not satisfied with killing him, the assassins hacked his body and severed the head, upon which they piled paper and sticks of wood, setting them on fire to render the face unrecognizable.

Separated from their weapons, most of the rank and file fought like heroes, with table knives, stones, clubs and such rude weapons as chance threw in their way. It was a bitter fate that befell those who closed with the Americans before they had received their death wounds.

During these trying moments many deeds of self-sacrifice were performed by our soldiers. They fought desperately, and never turned their backs upon the scene of carnage until all was lost, their comrades slaughtered and a terrible vengeance executed upon the enemy. Then they were compelled to save themselves, and, retreating slowly, fought for every foot of ground.

During the retreat a rifle in the hands of the first sergeant of the company rendered a terrible account. The sergeant killed the faithless presidente, who led the attack. With six men he also fought his way to the headquarters building to see if they could rescue or pick up some stricken comrades. Despite the mad rushes of the savages that surrounded them, they were able to secure the post colors. Then they cut their way back to the beach, where another little knot of comrades were defending their wounded companions.

After the alarm had been given re-enforcements arrived and the camp was at once recaptured. The bodies of the slain American soldiers had to be searched for all over the ground. Lieutenant Bumpus and the doctor were found upon a bridge leading up to the quarters, over a little stream. The lieutenant had a bolo cut horizontally across the forehead, almost severing the top of the head, and a deep gash down each side of the face, so that when his body was picked up the face was practically severed from the rest of his head. The doctor's body was not so badly mutilated. Some of the native dead were buried by their own crew before they fled, but Colonel De Russy was compelled to bury a very large number more after arriving on the scene.

It would be improper to dignify as battles the desultory engagements which at irregular intervals occurred after the affair at Balangiga. They were no more than skirmishes, the conflicts of wandering bands of insurgents without organization and patrolling detachments of American troops. One of the most sensational of these skirmishes in Batangas was that which Lieutenant Hennessy of the Eighth Infantry experienced. He was detailed with a scout and six trusty Filipinos to make a reconnoissance in Batangas, then the hotbed of what spirit of resistance there still remained. Lieutenant Hennessy secured information of the presence of a small company of insurgents in the immediate vicinity. By strategy, diplomacy and daring he actually captured with his little detachment of eight men (seven of them Filipinos) a body of forty-two insurgents, fifty rifles and a large supply of ammunition and rice.

At the town of Lepa, also in Batangas, a large force of insurgents attacked the American troops. Several Americans and one native ally were killed in the first volley. The natives then fled, but Troop F succeeded in heading them off and killed ten of the wily insurgents before they got back into the impenetrable jungle.

At Labo, Province of Camarines, the Twentieth Infantry was attacked by a large force of insurgents. Three Americans fell and the insurgents were beaten off with a heavy loss.

Captain F. H. Schoeffel, Co. E, Ninth Infantry, was on November 17th at a point six miles from Tarangnan, on the Island of Samar. Fifty bolo-men and insurgents, armed with rifles, broke from ambush and attempted to rush the American detachment. As soon as they encountered resistance they broke and scattered. Of the Ninth a corporal and a scout were killed and a private wounded. Sixteen of the bolo-men were found dead after the engagement, while the native riflemen escaped.

During the month of November Captain Herman Hall of the Twenty-first United States Infantry was scouting in Batangas Province, and during that period in the field he had four distinct skirmishes with the insurgents in that province. Judging from the firing of the natives on these occasions, Captain Hall estimates the number in the rebel bands from thirty to fifty; certainly no more. In no engagement did the insurgents make any effort to charge the American detachment. As a result of his reconnoissance, Captain Hall captured one insurgent officer and 50,000 pounds of rice.

On November 15th Captain Hartman and a troop of the First Cavalry came upon and attacked 400 insurgents intrenched in rifle pits at Buan, Batangas Province. The rebels were driven from their fortifications and routed and the Americans sustained little or no loss.

From an enumeration of these small engagements it is perfectly apparent that it is in Batangas Province that guerrilla warfare and desultory fighting are still continued by wandering bands of insurrectos without leadership or organization. Gen. Bell reports that they make no firm resistance; they fire a volley from ambush and then scatter before the scouts of the American troops.

Before this section is closed the records of a few brave American soldiers, who have won the coveted Medal of Honor for personal bravery during some of the important actions in the island, are given in the following lines.

It was at San Miguel, May 13th, 1899, where Filipinos numbering three hundred were vigorously repulsed and routed by the gallant action of Major William E. Birkhimer, U. S. Artillery, who with twelve men fearlessly attacked this vast superior force.

Captain William H. Sage, Twenty-third U. S. Infantry, won his Medal of Honor at Zapote River, Luzon, June 13th, 1899, by volunteering to hold an advanced position. With nine men he fought under a terrific fire from the enemy estimated one thousand strong. Taking up a rifle from a wounded man he personally killed five of the enemy and held them in check until his small squad had reached the company in safety.

The severe engagement at Bobong, Negroes, July 19th, 1899, gave Major Bernard A. Byrne, Thirteenth U. S. Infantry, an opportunity to display exceptional gallantry as a leader. The line had been broken by the insurgents and the men commenced a hasty retreat over the bridge. This the Major frustrated and without regard for his own personal safety rallied his men on the bridge, a target for Filipino sharpshooters.

An incident at the battle of Calamba, Luzon, July 26th, 1899, aroused the greatest enthusiasm among the attacking American troops. After the attack had been brought to a halt on the banks of the San Juan River, Captain Hugh A. J. McGrath, Fourth U. S. Cavalry, and Captain Matthew A. Batson of the same regiment were seen to swim the river in the face of a deathly fire. Some of their men followed and the enemy was driven from his intrenchments. The deed was so conspicuous that cheer after cheer went up from the ranks of the soldiers who witnessed the incident.

First Sergeant Charles H. Pierce, Company I, Twenty-second U. S. Infantry, and Sergeant Charles Ray of the same company won their Medals of Honor on the 19th of October, 1899, near the town of San Isidro, Luzon. A detachment of this company under the command of the Sergeant encountered strong positions of the enemy and a desperate fight ensued for the possession of the bridge. It was finally captured by our men, and with great determination held. Sergeant Pierce, although severely wounded, and Sergeant Ray. displayed exceptional gallantry in defending this bridge until relieved.

With a detachment of but four men Second Lieutenant Clarence M. Condon, U. S. Artillery, charged and routed forty entrenched insurgents, inflicting upon them heavy loss. This action occurred at Calulut, Luzon, November 5th, 1899, and for his gallantry the Lieutenant received the Medal of Honor.

Private John C. Wetherby, Company L, Fourth U. S. Infantry, the recipient of a Medal of Honor, won same on the battlefield near Imus, Luzon, on November 20th, 1899. He was carrying important orders, when a rebel bullet laid him low. However, he managed to crawl on his hands a great distance, far enough to deliver his orders and faint away.

" For most distinguished gallantry in defending, single handed and alone, his mortally wounded captain from an overwhelming force of the enemy at Mt. Amia, Cebu, on February 4th, 1900," reads the inscription on the Medal of Honor which was awarded to Private Louis Gedeon, Co. G, Nineteenth Infantry.

Corporal George M. Shelton, Company H, Twenty-third U. S. Infantry, won his Medal at La Paz, Luzon, on April 26th, 1900. It was given to him for gallantry displayed in advancing alone under heavy fire and rescuing a wounded comrade.

Exceptional gallantry was displayed by Corporal Henry F. Schroeder, Company K, Twenty-third U. S. Infantry, at Carig, September 14th, 1900. With twenty-two men he gave battle to a force of insurgents four hundred strong. No less than thirty-six of the enemy were killed and ninety wounded.

Lieutenant Allen S. Greer, Fourth U. S. Infantry, distinguished himself on July 2nd, 1901, near Majada, Luzon, by charging alone an insurgent post. With his pistol he killed one, wounded two, and captured three of the rebels, including their rifles and equipments.

THE SAMOAN IMBROGLIO

SAMOA is the collective name for a group of thirteen islands in the southern Pacific, situated between latitude 13° 30' and 14° 30' south, and between longitude 169° 14' and 172° 50' west. Its aggregate area is 1,700 square miles. The group lies almost in the direct line of communication between the American continent and Australasia, and within easy striking distance, in these days of fast cruisers, of the great streams of commerce which are perpetually passing between America and Japan, China and India. Consequently Samoa must always be regarded as a point of considerable value in the estimation of naval strategists. And of the magnitude of the commercial interests which are held to be involved in the neutrality or the proper guardianship of this group there could not be a possible doubt.

The three largest islands were Tutuila, with the excellent harbor of Pago-Pago, now in the possession of the United States, and Savaii and Upolu. Savaii takes first place as to area, being about forty miles in length and about twenty miles wide. Upolu, with the principal town, Apia, is by far the most important and valuable island of the whole group. It now belongs to the Germans.

But before this division was effected Samoa formed an object of bitter political strife of over twenty years' duration between three great nations, the United States, Germany and England. The United States claimed precedence over the other two in dealing with these islands, as Captain Meade of the United States steamer Narragansett had concluded the Pago-Pago treaty with the Chief Maumea as far back as 1872. Germany claimed that her commercial interests and possessions in Upolu surpassed all the others combined, and Great Britain showed that she was superior to the other two in the carrying trade. All three were equally concerned in the strategical position of the islands. In course of time, as the Germans preponderated in number, and also perhaps through race tendencies, it came to pass that the British and Americans usually formed one side and the Germans the other. The natives were divided accordingly. Although naturally a kindly, careless, peaceable and well-disposed race, the foreign factions succeeded often enough in inciting them to civil war and bloody strife, which caused the kanaka's latent savagery to spring forth in the commitment of all sorts of cruelties.

A certain king, Malietoa Laupepa, died in the summer of 1898, and the question of who should succeed him brought out again the slumbering antagonism in all its old intensity.

Malietoa had left a young son, Malietoa Tanu, whom the Americans and British wished to see anointed king. But there was also the old and renowned war chief and ex-king, Mataafa of Saana, who had already been appointed king by his numerous followers right after his return from an exile imposed upon him by the British, and the Germans favored him. The Chief Justice in Apia, an American, decided the legal question in favor of Malietoa Tanu. Mataafa was told by the Germans that he need not heed the justice's decision. Consequently Mataafa gathered his braves and attacked Malietoa Tanu in his camp. In the ensuing battle Tanu's forces were routed and many heads were taken. This barbaric custom of severing the heads of the dead and wounded the Samoans cannot be made to abandon, even when professing to be otherwise good Christians. They will say: "Is it not so that when David killed Goliath he cut off his head and carried it before the King?"

About this time, early in March, the United States steamer Philadelphia arrived in Apia, under Rear-Admiral Kautz, U. S. N. She was the first American warship that visited the Samoas in seven years. There were a German and two British gunboats in Apia then. The American admiral assembled a conference of the consuls and naval officers of the three powers, and thereafter issued a manifesto declaring the provisional government previously established by the consuls under pressure of the Germans to be unauthorized by the treaty commanding its members to return to their homes and threatening violence if they failed to do so; he also caused Malietoa Tanu to be appointed king. The German consul-general issued a counter proclamation to this, urging the provisional government to stand by its colors. It did. So the American admiral proceeded to carry out his threat, and, aided by the British gunboats, but not by the German, bombarded portions of the town of Apia and other places along the sea-coast, where Mataafa's followers or supporters were suspected of having taken refuge. This was on the 15th of March.

It became necessary to protect the property of Americans and English on shore against nightly raids of Mataafa's marauders, and detachments from the warships of the two nations were sent on shore.

The British gunboat Tauranga arrived and aided in the exploits of the others.

On the 1st of April an expedition consisting of 105 men of the Philadelphia and Tauranga, commanded by the British Lieutenant Freeman and the American officers Lieutenant Philip V. Lansdale and Ensign John R. Monaghan, was sent on shore toward Mulifanuu and the German plantation Vailele, east of Apia, to drive back a large force of Matafaa's followers assembled there.

Not far from the plantation the white force ran into an ambush, in which they were surrounded by 800 of Mataafa's warriors the wily kanakas concealing themselves between the palm and banana trees. Lieutenant Freeman fell dead, shot through the heart. The automatic Colt gun of the Philadelphia detachment jammed. While Lieutenant Lansdale was trying to fix it he was severely wounded in the thigh. A panic seized the men. Seeing two of their officers shot down, they retreated back to the beach. In vain did the gallant Ensign Monaghan call out to them to stand by and not leave their wounded officer to the mercy of the savages. It was a hopeless situation.

The brave young officer stepped up to his wounded comrade and made ready to defend him to the last. Lansdale was heard to call out to Monaghan to save himself. But the ensign only shook his head and then raised his revolver against the nearest of the onrushing enemy.

That was the last seen of the two men alive.

In the meantime some of the men went forward again to rescue their wounded officers, all the time imploring the main body of marines to make a stand, but the fire was too severe and they were forced to retreat.

Gunner's Mate Frederick T. Fisher, U. S. Navy, Sergeants Michael J. McNally and Bruno A. Forsterer and Private Henry L. Hulbert, of the Marine Corps, were the men who distinguished themselves in this engagement by their fearlessness in facing the ambushed enemy, and also by attempting to rescue their officers and rally the retreating men, in consequence of which they were awarded the Medal of Honor.

Towards evening French missionaries carried ominous bundles into Apia, which they had taken from the savages. In them were the heads of Lansdale, Monaghan, Freeman, two sailors, Butler and Edsal, of the Philadelphia, and one of the Tauranga.

It was a sad day's ending for the American and English settlers. The next morning the bodies were recovered.

They were laid to rest with military honors, and a simple monument now marks the spot where American and British seamen died together in the fulfillment of their duty.

This unfortunate affair stirred up public sentiment again, especially in the United States and Great Britain. The governments of the three concerned nations realized that their joint rule over the Samoas was fraught with dangerous possibilities to their mutual understanding. Naturally the representative of each of these governments would strive to gain advantages over his two colleagues, especially in the commercial field, and the much-needed harmony of action became more and more chimeric.

The three powers agreed finally to appoint a special commission, consisting of a representative of each government, they to be endowed with the necessary power to end hostilities, appoint a king and re-establish peace and order in the islands and straighten out all unsettled questions.

The three commissioners started on their voyage to Apia with all possible haste, and succeeded soon in bringing about as satisfactory a state of affairs as the extremely difficult conditions allowed.

It was plain that any arrangement based on the three-power rule could, at the best, be only temporary. This conviction probably aided in bringing about the final treaty between Germany and Great Britain in November, 1899, ratified by the United States in January, 1900, in which the difficult question was settled forever by dividing the islands. Great Britain withdrew all claims whatever, Germany, which had the largest interests involved, became owner of Upolu, Savaii and adjoining islands, and the United States of Tutuila, with the excellent Pago-Pago harbor, and surrounding islands.

Of the estimated population of 36,000 natives, about 30,000 inhabited the German possessions. The white populace was almost exclusively limited to Apia and the immediate neighborhood, numbering in all about 350 persons, of which 75 were Americans, 100 English and 175 Germans.

Both governments now in possession of the group of islands immediately reconstructed the laws and concessions in their respective domains satisfactorily, and thus it happened that the United States and Germany became near neighbors in the far-away southern seas.

So far there has been no recurrence of troubles with the natives since the days of excitement and warfare in March, April and May, 1899, and owing to the excellent management of their respective islands by both governments concerned in this group most likely never will.

The old war-chief, Mataafa, was honored by the Germans, and thereby the natives, ninety per cent of whom had been his followers, were appeased, becoming once more absolutely harmless and the most satisfied inhabitants of those beautiful islands, as which they have always been known.

THE war between China and Japan in 1894 left the interested European powers in a rather unsatisfactory state as to their relative position in the Middle Kingdom. Japan was unable to earn the full and deserved fruits of her victory, as she was turned out of Korea by the concerted action of Germany, France and Russia. Great Britain, standing isolated, could not help Japan, and Germany sought her reward for the pretended act of friendliness towards Russia by the sudden seizure of Kiao-Chau and the establishment of claims of interest over the entire Province of Shantung. Her direct pretext was the murder of two missionaries in this province. Other powers followed, or tried to follow, by similar procedure at different parts of the coast, and the hostile feeling of the "learned class" in China, which rules the country, became intense. Hatred against the foreigners had, for obvious reasons, always been strong in China. Now the secret anti-foreign societies which had also been foremost in their aversion of the "Ocean-Men," found their opportunity to strike a blow. With great activity and a secrecy only possible in China, the preparations were conducted. The coming danger was felt and soon plainly appreciated by the better-informed of European residents. But the lack of cohesion and faith in a common cause among the representatives of the different nations prevented timely concerted action, which alone could have checked the outrages that followed.

So the uprising of the most powerful organization known as the "Boxers" broke like a tidal-wave, sudden and overwhelming, over the northern Chinese lands and swept hundreds of Europeans and thousands of Chinese Christians helplessly into cruel destruction.

The several nations interested in affairs in China, who had embassies and legations in Pekin, at once united their forces and a campaign was begun against the "Boxers" and the Chinese government, which secretly supported them.

UPRISING OF THE BOXERS

THE secret society I HoChunan—that is, Fists of Righteous Harmony—known among English-speaking residents of the Celestial Empire as Boxers, is more than 100 years old. Founded in the year 1796, during the reign of the Emperor Chia Ching, the Boxers were condemned by this latter ruler through an imperial edict, which caused the order to slumber in oblivion for a full century.

Europeans in China became first alarmed about the Boxers shortly after the German seizure of Kiao Chau; it was then that the "Fists of Righteous Harmony" became widely known in north China through their intense anti-foreign agitation.

The murder of Reverend Sidney Brooks, of the Anglican Mission, on New Year's eve, 1899, was ascribed to their doings. They succeeded in distributing in almost every village throughout northern China their pamphlets asserting that their crusade was based on no human design, but on a Divine command, and would consequently be supported by Divine assistance. Their proposal was to destroy the foreigner and all his works, to restore the old habits of thought and life endeared to the people by the experience of tens of centuries.

In the fall of 1899 a great drought prevailed in all the northern Chinese land, which rendered the planting of crops useless. The Boxers, using this misfortune in their agitation, succeeded easily in rousing the feeling against the "Ocean-Men" to the highest pitch in all the rural districts; the native adherents of Christianity were denounced as aiding the foreigners.

Even the better class of well-to-do farmers joined in the anti-foreign movement and invited Boxer emissaries to their villages to preach their doctrine to the peasants. Among the powerful officials, the strongest and boldest supporter of the "Fists" was Yu Hsien, the governor of Shantung. It was said among the people that his own son was a Boxer leader, and this belief alone furnished thousands and thousands of new followers.

In December, 1899, the government removed Yu Hsien, as the violent agitation created dread in official circles against European armed intervention; but Yu Hsien was received with high honors at court, and the Empress Dowager secured immediately the appointment of him as governor of Shansi. His successor in Shantung was the shrewd Yuan Shi Kai, who soon perceived that the Boxer movement, if allowed to spread, must end in the ruin of his country, and who acted accordingly, suppressing the organization as much as was in his power. It was due to his firmness that Shantung, with a populace of nearly 40,000,000, kept quiet when the Boxers ran riot in Chihli.

Among the foreign representatives in Pekin it seems that Baron von Ketteler, a thorough master of the Chinese official language and an experienced dealer with affairs Chinese, foresaw the coming crisis. The subsequent events showed that he probably could not impress the real gravity of the situation. upon his collegues.

On the 13th of January, 1900, an imperial edict was issued urging the officials to deal leniently with the societies and to be careful not to confound the innocent with the guilty. It caused great apprehension among the foreigners and spread consternation among the native Christians in the capital.

Several foreign head missionaries of different nationalities held conferences and begged the Anglican Bishop Scott to unite all Christian missionaries in China in taking common action against the terrible danger looming up in the immediate future. But nothing was done or could be done, and the Boxers, at the door of the foreign and native Christian settlements, continued gathering adherents on all sides. They had formed alliances with all the native mutual defense guilds, and it was in these days that foreigners, walking harmlessly through the streets, were greeted in different northern cities with the ominous and fanatic yells: "Kill them! kill them!"

The foreign ministers repeatedly sent protests to the Tsung li Yamen, the Chinese foreign office, but with what results may be seen from the following Boxer placard which was posted on the walls throughout West Pekin on April 29th:

"In a certain street in Pekin some worshipers of the Iho Chuan at midnight suddenly saw a spirit descend in their midst. The spirit was silent for a long time and all the congregation fell upon their knees and prayed. Then a terrible voice was heard, saying:

"'I am none other than the great Yu Ti (God of the Unseen World), come down in person. Well knowing that ye are all of devout mind, I have just now descended to make known to you that there are times of trouble in the world, and that it is impossible to set aside the decrees of fate. Disturbances are to be dreaded from the foreign devils; everywhere they are starting missions, erecting telegraphs and building railways; they do not believe in the sacred doctrine and they speak evil of the gods. Their sins are as numberless as the hair of the head. Therefore I am wroth and my thunders have pealed forth. By night and by day have I thought of these things. Should I command my generals to come down to earth, even they would not have strength to change the course of fate. For this reason I have given forth my decree that I shall descend to earth at the head of all the saints and spirits, and that wherever the Iho Chuan are gathered together, there shall the gods be in the midst of them. I have also to make known to all the righteous in the three worlds that they must be of one mind, and all practice the cult of the Iho Chuan, that so the wrath of heaven may be appeased.

"'So soon as the practice of the Iho Chuan has been brought to perfection—wait for three times three or nine times nine, nine times nine or three times three—then shall the devils meet their doom. The will of heaven is that the telegraph wires be first cut, then the railways torn up, and then shall the foreign devils be decapitated. In that day shall the hour of their calamities come. The time for rain to fall is yet afar off, and all on account of the devils.

"'I hereby make known these commands to all you righteous folk, that ye may strive with one accord to exterminate all foreign devils, and so turn aside the wrath of Heaven. This shall be accredited unto you for well-doing; and on the day it is done the wind and rain shall be according to your desire.

"'Therefore I expressly command you to make this known in every place.'

"This I saw with my own eyes, and therefore I make bold to take my pen and write what happened. They who believe shall have merit; they who do not believe shall have guilt. The wrath of the spirit was because of the destruction of the temple of Yu Ti. He sees that the men of the Iho Chuan are devout worshipers and pray to him.

"If my tidings are false may I be destroyed by the five thunderbolts.

"Fourth moon 1st day (April 29, 1900)."

This message (the translation is the one sent by the British minister, Sir Claude Macdonald, in his dispatches) describes exactly the true meaning of the Boxer uprising.

Whatever may be the opinion about the Boxer movement during its later and last stages, it is but justice and fairness to concede to it a spirit of true Chinese patriotism. The Boxer slogan, "Death to the foreigners," which is the Chinese way of expressing the more civilized "China for Chinese," has as much justification as "America for the Americans"—the fundamental principle of the Monroe doctrine. The very fact that the Boxer movement was intensely and solely anti-foreign made it a patriotic one—from the Chinese point of view.

The question arises as to the reasonableness of this hatred of all foreign influence, this bitter feeling against the foreigner, which is without parallel among the civilized nations.

Was there a real reason for this persecution of the Caucasian? Of what grave offense were the Europeans guilty to have incurred the deadly enmity of the Chinese?

The answer to this query will at once explain the cause of the Chinese war and throw light upon the honorable and dignified course of the American government during the controversy and subsequent bloody events.

Ever since the war between Japan and China, in 1894, the European powers had looked upon the helpless empire as legitimate prey for colonial and territorial exploitation. The big powers seemed to have arrived at the conclusion that the time for the "partition of China" had come, a conclusion which they formed as if by a tacit understanding, although mutual jealousy prevented an agreement on the manner of the "partition"—the division of the spoils. The principle being recognized, the case resolved itself into a sort of land-grabbing competition. Japan, as the result of its war, had seized Port Arthur, but had been compelled to evacuate it under pressure from the united powers, who protested that the integrity of the Chinese Empire must be preserved.

Shortly afterward, however, Germany made its famous seizure; then Russia astonished the world by occupying the strategic harbor of Port Arthur under the rights of a "lease" from the imperial government at Pekin.

And then the "leasing" of Chinese territory began.

England seized Wei Hai Wei and claimed an exclusive sphere of commercial influence in the rich provinces of Kiang Su, Ngan Whei, Kiang Si, Hu Peh, Hunan and Suchuan.

France took the island of Hainan, a coaling station at Kwang Chow Wan, and claimed an exclusive sphere of influence in the provinces of Kwang Tung, Kwang Si and Yunnan.

Russia occupied Manchuria; England took another slice of property. No less than thirteen provinces, all told, were thus divided among the European powers. In exchange the benefits of modern civilization were fairly thrust upon the Mongolians, who had gotten along without it very well, and yet felt happy and contented. It was a two-fold civilization, too, industrial and spiritual, that was being introduced, for the benefit of the almond-eyed "barbarians," but it was not cordially received.

As to the benefits of modern progress the conservative Chinaman was very skeptical. In the introduction of machinery he saw only disaster and commercial calamity, owing to the over-population of the country. And as to the teachings of a new religion he was more than reserved and loath to exchange the good old faith of his forefathers for a creed which was so much in dispute among the foreigners themselves. There was the Methodist, the Presbyterian, the Roman Catholic, the Baptist, all teaching a faith of their own and decrying each other as false apostles and religious impostors. How was the Chinaman to choose? What would he gain by the exchange? Besides, these foreign missionaries were by no means as lowly and meek as one would infer from their teachings. On the contrary, relying upon the support of a powerful government which was always more than willing to punish an insult by a territorial grab, these bearers of the new religion were of a quite independent spirit, and at the slightest provocation, real or imaginary, appealed to their respective governments for protection. The missionaries became very unpopular with the masses in China, and this unpopularity was extended to every foreigner. The invasion of territory by the powers also added to the general ill-feeling, and finally developed into a hatred for everything and everybody from foreign shores.

The United States government had not taken part in the "partition of China"; it had neither "leased" nor "seized" any of the Chinese Empire's territory. The statesmen in Washington had likewise maintained a dignified and just attitude toward the court at Pekin in pressing claims for damages for insults and injuries.

It was only when it became apparent that the Chinese government itself secretly encouraged and assisted the Boxer movement, and that the lives and property of American residents were in serious danger, that the President joined in the concerted action of the European powers and participated in the war against the common enemy. Again, America was the first to withdraw its troops from the forces of the allied powers as soon as the object of the expedition, from the standpoint of the United States Government, had been accomplished.

It now becomes necessary to follow the Boxer movement in order to comprehend the events which finally led to the actual hostilities.

Nothing can better illustrate the condition in the Chinese Empire than a letter addressed by the French Bishop Favier to the French minister at Pekin, M. Pichon. This letter reads as follows:

"PEKIN, May 19, 1900.

"YOUR EXCELLENCY:

"The situation is becoming more and more menacing. In the prefecture of Pao-ting-fu more than seventy Christians have been massacred; three other neophytes have been cut to pieces. Several villages have been looted and burned, a still greater number completely deserted. Over 2,000 Christians are fugitives, without food, clothes or shelter; in Pekin alone about 400 refugees—men, women and children—have already been given shelter by us and the Sisters; in another week's time we shall probably have several thousand to look after; we shall be obliged to disband the schools, colleges, and all the hospitals, to make room for these unfortunate people.

"On the east, pillage and incendiarism are imminent; we receive more and more alarming news every hour. Pekin is surrounded on all sides; the Boxers are daily approaching the capital, being only delayed by the measures they are taking for destroying all the Christian settlements. I beg of your Excellency to be assured that I am well informed and not making assertions at random. The religious persecution is only a sham; the main object is to exterminate all the Europeans, and this object is clearly indicated and written on the standards of the Boxers. Their accomplices in Pekin are awaiting them; they are to begin with an attack on the churches and to end in an assault upon the legations. For us, indeed, here at Pe-tang, the day of attack has actually been fixed; the whole town knows it, everybody is talking about it, and the popular excitement is clearly manifest. Last night, again, forty-three poor women, with their children, flying from massacre, arrived at the Sisters' home; over 500 people accompanied them, telling them that, although they had succeeded in escaping once, they would soon all perish here with the rest.

"I will not speak of the numberless placards which are posted in the town against Europeans in general; new notices appear daily, each more clearly expressed than the last.

"People who were present at the last massacre in Tien Tsin thirty years ago are struck by the similarity of the situation of those days with that of to-day: the same placards, same threats, same notices and the same want of foresight. Then also, as to-day, the missionaries wrote and begged, foreseeing the horrible awakening.

"Under these circumstances, your Excellency, I think it is my duty to request to send us, at least to Pe-tang, forty or fifty sailors, to protect us and our property. This has been done on much less critical occasions and I trust your Excellency will consider favorably my humble application."

And the foreign diplomats at Pekin? They met and conferred and protested and exchanged civilities with the Yamen until it was too late. They believed the assurances of the Chinese officials that the Imperial Government was determined to stop all further progress of the Boxer movement, but when the ambassadors requested an explicit statement of the measures the government had taken the answer failed to come. But all of these pourparlers consumed much time and aggravated the situation. The foreign representatives were loath to believe that the Yamen was in collusion with the leaders of the Boxer movement.

MOUNTED CHINESE POLICE.

Towards the latter part of May the ambassadors sent a joint note demanding from the representatives of the Imperial Government an explicit statement of the measures that had been taken to suppress the Boxer movement. This note sounded like an ultimatum and remained unanswered. On May 27th the ministers of France and Russia telegraphed for a sufficient number of guards to protect their legations. Two days later the American and English diplomats followed suit and made similar requests. The English ambassador had been especially tardy in his appeal for help from the home office. He was the last to doubt the sincerity of the Celestial officials, the first to accept their assurances that they had no communication or sympathy with the anti-foreign movement, and it was only when the howls of the rebel mobs were heard at the walls of Pekin and the city itself was threatened that he changed his optimistic views of the situation.

On May 30th the first foreign marines were landed at Tien Tsin, but the Tsung li Yamen refused permission for their arrival at Pekin. Nevertheless the marines proceeded to march to the Chinese capital, but, a large number of troops being sent to enforce the edict of the Dowager Empress they returned to Tien Tsin. On May 31st the Tsung li Yamen yielded to the renewed pressure brought to bear by the ambassadors and on the afternoon of that day a special train brought the following international force to the metropolis of the Celestial Empire: Seven American officers and fifty men, three British officers and seventy-five men, three Italian officers and forty-seven men, two Japanese officers and twenty-three men, three French officers and seventy-two men, four Russian officers and seventy-one men, a total force of 22 officers and 338 men, who had brought with them five rapid-fire guns and a respectable quantity of ammunition.

While the arrival of these troops afforded some protection, however slight, to the European and American colony at Pekin, still their presence had a more irritating than reassuring effect on the populace. There was no use denying the fact that the foreigners were hated and that the presence of these foreign soldiers was looked upon as an armed invasion. Events then rapidly shaped themselves for the worst.

About the time the marines landed the Boxers destroyed the railroad between Shang-sin-tien and Pao-ting-fu, and kept the Belgian and Italian engineers prisoners at the former place. The escape of these men with their wives and children forms a thrilling episode of the turmoil and shows the extent to which the whole country had been torn up by the Boxers. The party consisted of some forty people, among whom were eleven women, and a few children. They managed to make their escape, thirty fleeing to Tien Tsin by the river route, the others taking an overland course. Their voyage was a succession of harrow-ing experiences and narrow escapes. They were shot at, stoned, insulted, hooted, and the clothing torn from the bodies of the wo-men, two of whom were in a delicate state of health. They were compelled to leave their boats, the mob lining up on both sides of the narrow river, shooting and pelting the roofs of the junks with stones. In their despair they had to plunge into the marshes to escape death at the hands of a howling mob of at least 4,000 Boxers who clung to their trail like a pack of hungry wolves. It came to a hand-to-hand fight, during which the women and children fought alongside of the men. With almost superhuman efforts this heroic little band beat its way through the ranks of the Chinese and continued on its way toward Tien Tsin. Here the Belgian consul had heard of their plight, and organized a relief expedition which went to the rescue of the refugees. They found the women nude, the children limped, with their clothing torn into shreds, the men were almost exhausted from fatigue and weariness, and there was not a single person in the entire group that was not

A BOXER.

injured or wounded and in dire need of medical help. Of the other party no one ever returned to Tien Tsin to tell the tale of the overland flight. The mutilated body of the wife of one of the engineers was found floating down the river and taken from the water. It told the story of the whole party.

Other murders of Europeans, mostly missionaries, were reported at Pekin from all parts of the country.

To add to the uncertainty of the situation the Dowager Empress had left Pekin and taken up her imperial residence at some other place.

Remonstrances by the ambassadors were answered with insulting impudence by the remaining officials, who declined to assume any responsibility.

On June 6th, however, Prince Ching made a frank statement to the foreign representatives. He feared that the Celestial government was not able to cope with the
Boxer movement, since it expressed the popular and universal feeling of the population. The railway from Tien Tsin to Pekin, he said, was guarded by 6,000 imperial
soldiers, but the loyalty of the troops was problematical and their efficiency in a
combat with the overwhelming number of the well-trained Boxer forces in still
greater doubt. Prince Ching regretted that he could not vouchsafe the life or property of any foreigner in Pekin, and with the Dowager Empress ill-advised, the officials
in the most important departments in league with the disturbers, he was unable to
remedy the evil, although he fully realized that by his own admission he would only
hasten foreign intervention.

The interview with Prince Ching was important from one standpoint only: it
served to impress the diplomats at Pekin that henceforth they had to rely on themselves for their own security; that they could expect no support from the Chinese
government. Urgent appeals were made to the home offices and measures were
now taken which finally led to the Chinese expedition.

ADMIRAL SEYMOUR'S EXPEDITION

VICE-ADMIRAL SIR EDWARD SEYMOUR, the commander of the English squadron in
Chinese waters, had already ordered the Phœnix and Aurora from Wei Hai Wei
to Taku, and the Humber to Shan Hai Kuan. The United States government had
already dispatched the Newark, Rear-Admiral Kempff commanding, and those of
Germany, Russia, France, Italy, Austria and Japan had likewise sent warships to
the Chinese ports.

On June 6th the senior officers of the various naval forces met in conference on
the British flagship Centurion, but definite action was not taken.

That same day the Imperial Government issued the following edict to the people:

"The western religion has existed and been disseminated throughout China for
many years, while those who disseminated it have done nothing except to exhort
the people to do good. Moreover, converts to the religion have never, under the
protection of religion, raised up disturbances; hence converts and people at large
have always remained at peace with one another, each going his own way without
let or hindrance. Of late years, however, with the constant increase of western
churches throughout the country and the consequent overwhelming numbers of
converts joining them, men of evil character have stealthily gained a footing in
their ranks, making it difficult, under the circumstances, for missionaries to distinguish the good from the bad among the converts.

"Taking advantage of this, these evil characters have accordingly, under the
guise of being Christians, harassed the common people and bullied the country-

side. Such condition of affairs cannot have been viewed with favor by the missionaries themselves. As to the Iho Chuan, this society was first prohibited during the reign of the Emperor Chia Ching (1795–1820). Owing, however, to the fact, that of late the members of this organization simply trained themselves for the purposes of self-protection and to defend their homes and villages from attack, and, moreover, because they had abstained from creating trouble, we did not issue our ban of prohibition according to precedent, but merely sent repeated instructions to the local authorities concerned to keep a proper restraint on the movements of the society. We pointed out to the said authorities that the present was not a question of whether these people were society men or not, but that the point was whether, being banded together, their object was to create trouble in the country or not. If, then, the society men should indeed rise up and break the peace, it should be the duty of the authorities to make a strict search for the law-breakers and punish them according to law. Whoever these parties may be, whether Christians or society men, the throne makes no difference in its treatment of them, for they are all children of the Empire. Moreover, in cases of litigation between Christians and the common people, our instructions have ever been that the authorities should settle them according to the rights of the matter, no favor being allowed to be shown to either party. It transpires, however, that of late years our commands have never been obeyed.

"The officials of the various prefectures, sub-prefectures, departments and districts have been proved to have neglected their duties. They have neither acted in friendly conjunction with the missionaries, sympathized with the people under them in their difficulties, nor settled litigation in the spirit of impartiality, and the consequence has been that those concerned began to hate one another, the enmity becoming deeper and deeper as occasions for ill-will multiplied. On account of this, therefore, we now find the members of the Iho Chuan Society banding themselves together as village militia and declaring war against the Christians. At the same time we find discontented spirits, in conjunction with lawless ruffians, joining in the movement for their own ends.

"Riots are the order of the day; railways are destroyed; churches burned down. Now, the railways were constructed by and are the property of the government, while churches were built by the missionaries and their converts for their own occupation.

"Do these society men and others, then, think that they will be allowed to burn property at their own sweet will? In this running riot these people are simply opposing themselves to the government. We, therefore, appointed Chao Shu-ch'iao, Grand Councilor and Governor Adjunct of Pekin, to proceed as our Imperial Commissioner to restore peace and to call upon the people and society men to disband immediately and return each man to his own vocation and daily work. Should traitors and revolutionary society men try to stir up the people to rise up and pillage and destroy the country-side, we hereby call upon the Iho Chuan people to hand over to the authorities the ringleaders for punishment according to the laws of the land. Should there be any so misguided as to persist in disobeying our commands, they shall be treated as rebels, and we hereby warn them that when the grand army arrives their fathers, mothers, wives and children will be separated from one another and scattered, their homes destroyed and they themselves slain. They also will bring upon themselves the stigma of disloyalty and of being false to their country, for it will then be too late to repent. Our heart is filled with pity when we think of the retribution that will then overwhelm our people. We, therefore, hereby declare that if, after this warning, there should still be any who refuse to obey our commands, we will immediately order the generalissimo, Jung Lu, to send Generals Tung Fu Hsiang, Sang Ch'ing and Ma Yu K'un with their commands to punish these rebels and to disperse them.

"Finally, in sending out troops the primary purpose is to protect the law-abiding people, but we now hear that those sent out by the Chihli provincial authorities have not only failed to afford such protection and restrain evil characters, but, on the contrary, have themselves been guilty of preying upon the country-side. We now hereby command Yu Lu, Viceroy of Chihli, to investigate this matter at once, and also to send trusty deputies to make secret investigations. If it be found that these military officials have indeed been guilty of encouraging their men to loot and pillage, such guilty officers are to be summarily executed. There must be no leniency or mercy shown to such offenders.

"Let this, our decree, be copied on yellow paper and posted throughout the country as a warning to the people and army, and that all may know our commands."

This edict did not have the desired effect; it pleased neither the Boxers nor the Christians. Besides, the time for imperial decrees had passed; the movement was beyond control by manifestoes.

By unanimous consent Vice-Admiral Seymour was appointed commander of the international forces stationed in China, and on June 10th decided to increase the legation guards at Pekin, permission having been obtained from the Tsung li Yamen to increase the number to 1,200 men.

Accordingly, on the evening of that day the following force, under command of Vice-Admiral Seymour, left Tien Tsin on three different trains:

One hundred Americans, 915 British, 450 Germans, 300 Russians, 158 French, 52 Japanese, 40 Italians and 25 Austrians. To make repairs to the railroad, if such were necessary, 100 coolies were taken along. The train reached Yangtsun, 30 miles from Tien Tsin, at 1 P. M. The road was in good condition and guarded by imperial troops. About four miles beyond, however, the expedition met the first obstacles and was compelled to halt, the tracks having been broken up. The troops encamped for the night and the next morning proceeded slowly towards the next station of Lofa, the roadbed having been repaired by the coolies with the material that had been carried along.

Late in the afternoon the advance guard of seventeen men, under Major Johnstone, reported that a body of Boxers had attempted to cut them off from the trains. The marines had been forced to retreat and during their flight keep up a hot running fire. The train stopped and then a force of Chinese was seen approaching, some mounted, others running barefooted, shouting, waving old swords and spears, pitchforks and clubs. They made straightway for the guns—a fanatical, frenzied crowd of some 1,500 young men and boys. When within a few yards from the guns,

"THE ENEMY WENT DOWN BEFORE THIS FIRE."

the troops poured their deadly volleys into the crowd, and the enemy went down before this fire in rows. The unfortunate fanatics again and again advanced, only to share the fate of those that were laid low in former attacks. For an hour the fusillade was kept up. After that the road was clear. There were no more Chinese to shoot at.

On June 11th the allies were re-enforced by 200 Russians and 58 French, and the day following Vice-Admiral Seymour received an additional command of 300 Russians, making the total strength of the relief expedition on the way to Pekin 2,300 men.

Lofa was reached without further incidents, and excepting constant harassings by the enemy, who could be seen on all sides of the advancing columns, no noteworthy attack took place. At this latter station, however, the progress of the expedition was interrupted, because north of this place the rails had been twisted, torn up and carried away. Henceforth the march toward the Imperial City resembled the pace of a snail, not through any fault of Vice-Admiral Seymour or his plucky troops, but because of the exigencies of the occasion, repairs being necessary every inch of the way, the hostile attitude of the population demanding the utmost caution. From June 13th to June 14th only three miles were covered by the troops.

News of the most important nature reached Vice-Admiral Seymour at this point. A large army under General Tung Fu Hsiang had left Pekin to oppose by force any attempt the allied forces might make to enter the Celestial city. At the same time, the situation at Tien Tsin and Taku began to assume a threatening aspect, and it was not long before the commander-in-chief of the relief expedition realized that the Chinese were determined to prevent his further progress and cut off his rear. Reports from Pekin also indicated that the situation there was fast approaching a critical stage.

A casual glance at Pekin will, at this juncture, be sufficient to appreciate the condition of things.

On June 11th the Japanese secretary of legation, Mr. Sugiyama, was murdered by soldiers of General Tung while on his way to the railway station. A party of legation students walking harmlessly on the streets was attacked by an infuriated mob and only escaped annihilation by defending themselves with drawn revolvers.

June 13th the summer residence of the British legation, twelve miles from Pekin, was burned; the same night the custom house and the grand stand at the race track were leveled, various mission schools and residences of Christians were forcibly entered, the contents looted and the inmates attacked. At the European graveyard the bodies were disinterred, desecrated, and the tombstones smashed. Pekin was seething with riot and disorder.

All of this was not unknown to Vice-Admiral Seymour and his brave troops of all nations. Frantic efforts to repair the railroad and proceed, even in defiance of the large body of Chinese regular soldiers, were made; repeated attempts to start the expedition were undertaken, but the difficulties increased with every foot of ground covered, and ere long the relief expedition was in need of assistance as much as the people it had intended to relieve at Pekin.

A party of Americans had an engagement with a large body of Boxers on June 13th and killed a number of them.

On the 14th the Boxers, numbering many thousands, made a foolhardy attempt to rush the trains of the allied forces, and were repulsed only when a Maxim gun was brought into play and brought death and destruction to the fanatics. A second attack, near the depot at Lanfang, met with a similar repulse.

These defeats did not discourage the Boxers. On the contrary, their wrath was increased by the sting of defeat, and what they lacked in personal experience and training they sought to accomplish by the force of overwhelming numbers. By repeating their attacks upon the foreign troops and exhausting them they expected to annihilate them.

Realizing the danger to his own men and the futility of further advance, Vice-Admiral Seymour decided to return to Tien Tsin.

And now he discovered that the railroad from Lanfang to that city had also been destroyed, even at Yangtsun, where, as has been stated, a body of soldiers had been ostensibly guarding the tracks. Thus there were as many difficulties to get back to Tien Tsin as to reach Pekin. June 15th, 16th and 17th passed, however, without severe attacks, and on the morning of the 18th the Germans succeeded in taking a number of imperial junks, loaded with railroad material. This capture was accomplished after a lively brush with the enemy. In the afternoon a battle occurred between the troops and the Boxers, re-enforced by some 5,000 imperial soldiers—the first time that governmental troops and Boxers joined forces to fight the foreign invaders.

"IT WAS NECESSARY TO MAKE SEVERAL SORTIES."

The fighting was severe. It was necessary to make several sorties to keep the Chinese in check. The latter were well armed, even the Boxers having been provided with Mauser and Mannlicher rifles, and fought with great gallantry. Had it not been that they were poor marksmen and invariably aimed too high, the result would have been disastrous to the allied forces. Late in the afternoon the battle ended; the Chinese were routed and defeated all along the line. They lost at least 500 men in killed alone.

The allies had six killed—two British, three Russians, one German—and sixty wounded—thirty British, twenty Germans and ten Russians.

June 19th and 20th the retreat toward Tien Tsin continued. The trains were abandoned and the provisions were carried along by water. The march was necessarily slow. The telegraphic communication with the coast was cut, which added to the distress of the expedition.

At the village of Pei-tsang, on June 21st, the allies met the imperial troops, who at once opened a heavy fire upon them. Vice-Admiral Seymour's men fought most determinedly and succeeded in dislodging the enemy, who intrenched themselves at the village proper.

It took four hours of hard fighting before the allies succeeded in driving the Chinese out of their trenches; then they entered the village under cover of darkness.

On June 22d an endeavor was made to open a line of communication with Tien Tsin. The allies were in possession of some forts on the left bank of the Pei-ho river, and from there a detachment of 120 marines, under Captains Boyd and Daly, started for Tien Tsin. This detachment met with such forcible opposition that it was compelled to return during the evening. The Chinese also made a violent attack upon the allies to recapture the forts, but were repulsed.

The American marines displayed great coolness and daring in this attempt to open communication with Tien Tsin, in which the exceptional bravery of the following men elicited universal commendation and gained for them the Medal of Honor:

Privates of Marines Thomas W. Kates, Alfred R. Campbell, Chas. R. Francis and Clarence F. Mathias.

Among the many wounded was the gallant American, Captain McCalla of the Newark, whose intrepid bravery had won the admiration of every officer of the troops, no matter of what nationality.

From June 24th to June 26th the troops enjoyed comparative rest. The allies held undisputed possession of the Wuku forts and arsenals and had plenty of fighting material, guns and ammunition at their disposal, and also a sufficient supply of provisions. The care of the many wounded, 228 in all, and the inability to leave the fort, either to retreat or advance, was the only embarrassment. By means of signal lights at night, rockets and similar signs of distress, and the invaluable aid of a messenger, who succeeded in breaking through the hostile lines and arriving at Tien Tsin, the foreign troops at that city were apprised of the plight of Vice-Admiral Seymour's expedition.

On the morning of June 26th Lieutenant-Colonel Shirinsky, with eight companies of infantry and marines, moved toward the Wuku forts and liberated the cooped-up allies. The joint forces then entered Tien Tsin unhampered and unopposed, to the great joy of the foreign population and the civilized world in general, which had heard nothing of the expedition for several days and had entertained serious fears for its safety.

The list of casualties of this memorable expedition is as follows: Killed — American 4, British 27, French 1, German 12, Italian 5, Japanese 2, Austrian 1, Russian 10; total 62. Wounded — American 25, British 97, French 10, German 62, Italian 3, Japanese 3, Austrian 1, Russian 27; total 228.

Thus ended the first attempt to rescue the foreigners and native Christians at Pekin.

The superior fighting qualities of the allied troops in this expedition were brought out in the various engagements with the Chinese and Boxer troops. Numerous individual acts of bravery were performed, many of them by the American sailors and marines, which won for them the admiration of not only their own officers, but also the officers and men of the foreign troops.

Among those of the Americans whose bravery was most conspicuous and who now have the distinction of wearing the Medal of Honor for their heroic deeds on Chinese soil are the following:

Chief Boatswain's Mate Joseph Clancey, Boatswain's Mates Edward Allen and William E. Holycoke; Cockswains John McClery, Jay Williams, Francis Ryan and Martin T. Torgarson; Machinist Burke Hanford, Chief Carpenter's Mate William F. Hamberger, Seamen Hans A. Hansen and George Rose, Ordinary Seaman William H. Seach, Landsmen James Smith and Joseph Killecky and Oiler Frank E. Smith of the navy, and Gunnery Sergeant Peter Stewart, Corporal Reuben J. Philips and Private Henry W. Orendorff of the marine corps.

THE CAPTURE OF THE TAKU FORTS

WHILE the relief expedition under Vice-Admiral Seymour was being driven back the Chinese government made warlike preparations which could not be ignored by the European powers. Troops were massed in the vicinity of Tien Tsin and Taku and torpedoes placed at the mouth of the Pei-ho. The commanders of the allied fleet viewed these preparations with distrust and alarm, and upon instructions from their home offices met in conference on board one of the ships to discuss the situation. It was determined to demand from the governor of Chihli and General Lo Yung Kwang, who commanded at Taku, that he surrender to the allies the strongholds on both sides of the river and withdraw his forces to the interior. They were given until June 17th, at 2 P. M., to comply.

This ultimatum was followed up by another conference on board the Russian gunboat Bobr, when the plans for a forcible capture of the forts were formulated and the preliminary orders given.

The Taku forts, five in number, on both sides of the river, were the key to the position in North China in case of war. Their occupation by the allies was therefore of great strategical importance.

The United States government, however, had held itself aloof from these negotiations. Indeed, Rear-Admiral Kempff had been instructed to refrain from participating in any action which might be construed as a declaration of war with the Chinese government, with which this country was at peace.

Consequently, although Commander Wise of the Monocacy attended the conference, he refrained from signing the ultimatum, and was, during the subsequent events which culminated in the capture of the forts, a disinterested spectator. Curiously enough, the Monocacy was one of the first boats struck by Chinese shells; the damage done was trivial.

The Chinese not only refused to accede to the terms of the ultimatum, but on June 17th opened a severe bombardment on the foreign fleet and a fight ensued which lasted fully seven hours and ended in the capture of the forts. The Chinese lost 400 men; the allies 21 killed and 57 wounded. The Germans suffered the most, but they were also credited with having held the most dangerous position during the bombardment, and their gunboat Iltis actually led the fight. The Americans took on board the Monocacy thirty-seven women and children refugees who had fled from the mission at Taku and also gave assistance to the wounded.

THE CAPTURE OF TIEN TSIN

IT now becomes necessary to revert back to the incidents which had occurred at Tien Tsin since Vice-Admiral Seymour with the relief force had left the city. In order to better comprehend the subsequent events it will be necessary to give a brief outline of the city itself, the population of which is estimated at 1,000,000.

The walled native city was of a rectangular shape. The foreign settlements and concessions were about two miles southeast of the native city, and consisted of a large French concession along the south bank of the Pei-ho River, with the British settlement southeast of it, still along the west of the river, and the extra British concessions south of the French settlement. The German settlement adjoined the British.

There was an almost continuous succession of native houses between the native city and the foreign settlement, especially on the southeast and nearer the river, while on the west there was much open ground and large patches of water, even within the famous mud wall, which in an irregular fashion surrounded the native city, all the settlements, the railway station, the north fort, and also a long stretch of the Pei-ho River.

The mud wall, about ten feet high, ten feet broad on the top and thirty at the base, was built by the Chinese to protect the city and settlements during the time of the Tai-ping rebellion. It was only a few yards from the settlements. The American consulate, almost the last house in the extra British concession, was situated only about 350 yards from the wall, where the naval guns were subsequently mounted for the defense of the settlement.

The north fort, built by Li Hung Chang, was outside the native city, on the north bank of the Pei-ho, near its junction with the Grand Canal.

Huge mounds of salt along the water, used with much success by the Chinese for the purposes of defense, were features of Tien Tsin.

AMERICANS ATTACKING TIEN TSIN.

The West Arsenal, or Joss-house Arsenal, lay west of the settlement, and due south of the native city. Between the arsenal and the city were a great number of Chinese graves and earth-mounds, of which the Chinese took advantage, digging trenches in addition for further protection; and the extensive graveyards north of the railway station, on the opposite side of the stream, were used by them in the same way.

To the south and west of the settlement were large tracts of comparatively open country, with a few Chinese houses scattered here and there, and a few low-hutted villages which afforded good shelter.

Nothing of note occurred June 11th, 12th and 13th. On June 14th 1,700 Russian soldiers arrived, originally to join Vice-Admiral Seymour's forces, but this plan was changed owing to the spirit of unrest apparent at every corner in Tien Tsin itself, and it was thought wise to keep this detachment in the city for the protection of the foreign population. On the 15th an armored train was sent out to re-enforce the British commander-in-chief, but the obstacles were so many, the hostile forces encountered on the way so strong and the attacks so fierce that the train returned to Tien Tsin in all haste, the men glad to have escaped annihilation.

That same night the Boxers succeeded in gaining the upper hand in Tien Tsin and the first attack upon the foreign settlement was made.

On June 17th, the day of the capture of the Taku forts, the Boxers, now in complete control of the native city, made an attack upon various parts of the settlement, but were repulsed. The casualties to the foreign troops were nine killed and twelve wounded. An attempt to seize the pontoon bridge leading to the station ended disastrously to the Chinese, who lost heavily during the brief but sharp engagement.

From June 18th to June 21st the Chinese attacked and harassed the settlements and kept the allies on the alert by throwing bombs and shells, posting guns and sniping across the Pei-ho River.

On June 22d several large detachments of foreign troops left Taku to relieve those besieged at Tien Tsin. They met a large force of Boxers and imperial troops and were held in check all night, losing in killed and wounded 224 men. However, early in the morning the Chinese retired and the relief force entered the settlement and relieved Tien Tsin. The Chinese troops and Boxer forces still held possession of the walled city and the fortifications and continued to shell the European concessions.

The force that by this time had been landed at Taku comprised 335 Americans, 26 Austrians, 570 British, 421 French, 1,340 Germans, 138 Italians, 602 Japanese marines and 1,050 infantry, 235 Russian marines and 3,500 troops. Japan had 2,100 more men on the way, France a battalion of infantry and a battery of artillery; Russia had already 4,000 and Germany 1,300 men on Chinese soil.

On June 22d Li Pingheng, High Commissioner of the Yangtse, and a number of high ranking officials of several Chinese provinces memorialized the throne and implored their majesties, the Emperor and the Dowager Empress, to suppress the rebellious Boxers and save the country from foreign invasion by quieting the disturbances and restoring law and order.

"The Boxers ought to be suppressed," urged the memorialists by telegraph. They are not content with having forced the country into war with the foreign powers, but they must damage foreign property. We humbly pray your majesties to immediately issue edicts ordering the severe punishment and extinction of the Boxers, to prevent the imperial troops from making further trouble, and to relieve the anxiety of those residing in the legations by informing them that there is no intention of going on with these troubles.

"We also pray that edicts be sent by wire to the ministers of China in various countries apologizing for the past troubles. * * * This will appease the anger of the foreign countries. A few days' delay may mean the breaking up of the country, and then it will be too late."

And the throne's answer to this eloquent and patriotic appeal was an "imperial edict," vague and meaningless, one calculated to have no force or weight.

In the meantime events took their warlike course at Tien Tsin.

On June 26th Lieutenant-Colonel Shirinsky and Vice-Admiral Seymour returned from Wuku arsenal, as previously described.

For the next two weeks, June 27th until July 13th, there were many skirmishes and small engagements, but no fight of real importance took place, the allies getting ready, mounting guns and preparing for the attack on the walled native city, the Chinese busying themselves by strengthening their line of fortifications.

On July 6th two battalions under Colonel H. Liscum disembarked at Taku and arrived at Tien Tsin on July 11th.

The attack on the city began early on the morning of July 13th.

The allies had at their disposal two 4-inch rapid-fire naval guns, one on the road to the arsenal, the other near the mud wall, and besides had some thirty field-pieces and eight Hotchkiss quick-firing guns. A heavy cannonade was the prelude to the ensuing fight. Under the protection of these guns a combined force of some 2,000 Japanese, 800 British, 600 French, 900 Americans, 100 Germans and 100 Austrians, all under the command of the Japanese Major-General Fukushima, advanced on the walled city from the south, while another combined force of Germans and Russians moved forward from the northeast.

The advance proceeded under the greatest difficulty imaginable: a swampy ground and lack of shelter from Chinese bullets; and the losses to the allies were heavy.

Of General Fukushima's forces the American marines were on the extreme left wing, the Japanese in the center, the British on the right and the Ninth United States Infantry on the extreme right wing. The Chinese were only too well prepared for the fray. Their modern guns, served by experienced men, dotted the walls at frequent intervals, while large bodies of regulars, all armed with the latest arms, occupied a position of vantage, being placed at the most favorable points on the wall, which, in addition, was also manned by large bodies of Boxers.

For every inch of ground the allies gained they had to fight hard and pay for with the lives of some of their brave fellows. But yield they would not, and slowly but steadily they approached the death-dealing wall, until by nightfall they were almost under its shadow.

While the conduct of the men of all nationalities was superb, that of the Americans was especially distinguished, since they bore the brunt of the fighting and were honored with the selection of holding the most difficult position, a dyke only seventy-five yards from two Chinese guns and fully exposed to the enemy's fire.

When the Americans gallantly stormed the dyke the color-bearer was shot and fell carrying the flag of the regiment with him to the ground. Colonel Liscum at once ran up to the wounded man and grabbed the flag. He waved the stars and stripes high above his head and continued the attack at the head of his wildly cheer- ing men. Presently a bullet—a muffled cry—a shout—and dead to the ground dropped the colonel. The cheering ceased. The men halted, wavered—but a single moment only. In the heat of battle there is no time to mourn even the dearest loss. Already another brave American officer, Lieutenant Charles A. Coolidge, had stepped into the breach made by the commander's fall and was leading the men with renewed vigor and pluck. And the dyke was carried. For fifteen hours the regiment main- tained a position that seemed almost a folly to hold a single instant and then retired only when commanded to do so by imperative orders.

The losses of the Americans—seventy-seven wounded and eighteen killed— express more eloquently than words can ever describe, the unflinching bravery of the American on Chinese soil.

Among the others killed of the American force was Captain Davis of the Marine Corps, and among the wounded Captains Lemly and Long and Lieutenants Butler and Leonard.

The British General Dorman, to whose brigade the gallant Ninth had been assigned, says in his official report: "I desire to express the high appreciation of the British troops of the honor done them in serving alongside of their comrades of the American army during the long and hard fighting of the 13th inst. The American troops had more than their share of the fighting."

The praise thus bestowed upon their sons on foreign shores filled the people of the United States and the government with pride, which found substantial expression at Washington by granting Medals of Honor to the men whose deeds of heroism were most conspicuous. It was not easy to differentiate between the conduct of such gallant and brave men. However, these were the fortunates who were thus dis- tinguished:

Sergeants of Marines Clarence E. Sutton, John M. Adams and Alexander M. Foley; Corporals Harry C. Adriance and Private James Cooney. These men were conspicuous on the battlefield by their almost reckless daring in the face of a heavy fire and by rescuing wounded officers and comrades from falling into the enemy's hands.

REMOVING THE WOUNDED.

Most of the wounded in this battle were conveyed down the Pei-ho in junks and flat boats, and it was a solemn procession which the many boats formed, the flag of the red cross flying from them indicating their cargo of disabled and dying humanity. The attack was resumed at dawn the next morning. The plucky little Japanese succeeded in blowing up the South Gate. The large city gates being double an effort to blow up the second gate had to be made. While this was being attempted number of Japanese scaled the big wall and the first of the allied troops were now inside the native city. With a leap they made for the second gate, and after a fierce hand-to-hand struggle overpowered the guards and forced it open. Shouts and hurrahs went up from a thousand throats as thus the long-fought-for entrance had finally been gained, and the Japanese and the American, the British and the French troops poured into the town, shooting down every Chinese who attempted to stem the tide of victory. Through the narrow streets the fight was continued, the Chinese stampeding in every direction. A large part of the town was set on fire and the frenzied Celestials hurried away, carrying on their backs their few belongings or a beloved relative they intended to save from the scene of disaster and death. The dash of the victors progressed over a route strewn with the disfigured corpses of the dead and the groaning bodies of the wounded. When darkness fell upon the gruesome scene the Americans found themselves in possession of the arsenal and the flags of all nations were flying from the battered walls of the defiant Chinese city.

The next day the city was looted by the allied troops, and the soldiers of every nationality helped themselves to the property of the conquered enemy. There was no exception, the difference being marked only by the various desires and tastes. But it must be stated that most of the property taken was either deserted by the rightful owner or in danger of being destroyed by the raging conflagrations or would have fallen into the hands of looters not of the allied forces. Indeed, the next day the looting did become general, one Chinese taking property from the other and trading it or selling it to the foreign invader.

For days after the capture of the city these Chinese looters—men, women and children—were seen digging in the ruins of burned houses and shops for valuables and fighting among themselves for the possession of every article of value found. Those who did not participate in this wholesale robbery and theft stood trembling for fear in the doorways of their homes holding in their hands small flags of truce made of paper or cloth.

They were models of meekness and displayed an air of friendliness and smiling courtesy to every allied soldier that were too ostentatious to be sincere. Tea and cold water could be had for the asking, sometimes, and more often they were tendered without even being asked for. Everybody had an inscription on his flag of truce, which read: "Poor man, please allies' officer don't kill me." "Vive la France." "A friend of England." "A friend of the great McKinley." "Hurrah Deutschland." Most of these inscriptions were addressed to the Japanese, but many were in poor English, German or French. Small, home-made, primitive-looking flags of all nations were also carried by the completely cowed Mongolians. A native without a flag or pass was at once made a prisoner or simply shot. Little mercy and no consideration were shown to anybody exhibiting defiant tendencies.

The Yamen of the viceroy was occupied by the Russians. It had been stripped of everything that was precious by the Chinese mobs, the papers and documents of great historic value, such as treaties with foreign nations, being swept in a pile by an army of coolies and thrown into the canal. The viceroy's account book was found in this lot. Among the entries was the payment of a reward of fifty taels to Major Cheng Kuo Chun for capturing two American guns June 19th, and one for the payment of 100 taels to Colonel Wan Yi T'sai for the heads of two American marines. The book also showed many and large payments to the leaders of the Boxers, which proved conclusively that the Chinese government was supporting and encouraging the anti-foreign movement.

On July 21st Vice-Admiral Seymour was able to telegraph officially that Tien Tsin and vicinity were free from Chinese forces and under complete control of the allied soldiers.

The troops, tired from long voyages, exacting marches and hard fighting, settled down for rest and recuperation during the subsequent two weeks. The commanders still kept in view an early relief of Pekin, but it was not considered wise to proceed until a sufficiently strong force had been collected to attempt a second expedition. An army of at least 25,000 men was believed to be necessary, with an equally large force to maintain the base of supplies at Tsien Tsin and along the route.

In the meantime the foreign powers kept pouring in troops at Tsien Tsin. Rear-Admiral George C. Remey, commander-in-chief of the Asiatic Station, was ordered to proceed with the cruiser Brooklyn from Manila to Taku by the United States Government, where he took charge of naval matters at the seat of war. On July

28th Major-General Adna R. Chaffee arrived at Taku as commander-in-chief of the American land forces in China, with instructions to so conduct himself in his operations as not to limit the home government as to its future course and conduct. The troops at the general's disposal were, besides those already mentioned: Fourteenth U. S. Infantry, Colonel A. S. Daggett commanding; a light battery of the Third U. S. Artillery, parts or all of the First, Second, Fifth, Eighth, Fifteenth, Twenty-fourth and Twenty-fifth U. S. Infantry, the First, Third and Ninth U. S. Cavalry, the Fifth and Seventh U. S. Artillery, also the necessary engineers and medical corps, altogether an army of 17,550 men, some 6,000 of which arrived in China before the capture of Pekin.

The other nations had likewise made ample preparations, and were sending large forces, to wit: Japan, 23,000 men; Russia, 25,000; Germany, 15,000; England, 11,000; Italy, 3,200; Austria, 2,500. These troops, however, arrived slowly and at long intervals and caused much delay. The anxiety felt in Europe and this country for the safety of the diplomats and foreign residents at Pekin expressed itself by severe criticism of the army commanders for their apparent inactivity. However, the second expedition got under way as quickly as it was possible to do so.

Nor were the commanders at Tien Tsin less apprehensive as to the fate of those imprisoned within the walls of the Chinese capital than the people in other parts of the world. Constantly arriving messages gave them an idea of the situation at Pekin and of the approaching crisis, and kept stirring them to incessant energy.

A message received at Tien Tsin July 9th stated that two legations at Pekin were still uncaptured and that the foreigners still had sufficient food and ammunition. More serious was the news from Sir Claude MacDonald, the British ambassador, which was received at Tien Tsin July 29th and read:

"We are surrounded by Chinese imperial troops who have fired upon us continuously since June 20th. Enemy are enterprising but cowardly. They have four or five cannon, used mostly for battering purposes. Our casualties are, up to date, forty-four killed and about double that number wounded. We have provisions for about two weeks, but are eating our ponies. If Chinese do not press their attack we can hold out for some days—say ten—but if they show determination it is a question of four or five, so no time should be lost if a terrible massacre is to be avoided.

"The Chinese Government, if one exists, has done nothing whatever to help us. We understand that all gates are held by the enemy, but they would not stand an attack by artillery. An easy entrance could be effected by the sluice gate of the canal, which runs past this legation through the south wall of the Tartar City."

These alarming messages caused the foreign commanders to redouble their efforts to get the second expedition under way for the relief of the besieged city of Pekin.

THE EVENTS IN PEKIN

IT was Queen Victoria's birthday, May 24th   A large party of British and other foreigners gathered at the British Legation to celebrate the festive day.   There was an elaborate banquet, and the guests sat down to enjoy the rich menu amidst pleasant speeches, patriotic toasts and general good feeling.   Following the repast was a dance in which old and young participated.   They could have heard, had they listened, the mutterings of a discontented mob penetrate to the very hall of pleasure, a noise like the rolling of distant thunder, indistinct and faint, but audible nevertheless.   It was the last celebration before the war.

Already the walls of the city were covered with rebellious, incendiary placards; already the spirit of hatred of the foreigner had made its appearance at all corners of the city.   More and more did the city begin to look like a barrel of gunpowder, to which the Boxers needed only to apply the match to cause an explosion.

It has been shown how the Boxer movement had been spreading all over the country, carrying with it death and destruction.   From Archbishop Favier's letter it was apparent that Pekin itself was in imminent peril of invasion and foreign troops were asked for and sent to Pekin for the protection of the legations.

The foreigners who succeeded in making their escape fled to Pekin and sought refuge within the various legations, which were hastily made defensible by the military.   The premises were patrolled day and night by volunteers, mostly students.

Word was received almost hourly of the progress of the Boxers.

On May 29th the electric street car line outside of the city was destroyed and the homes of many foreigners just outside the walls burned down.   The arrival of the military detachments of the foreign nations was none too soon, for the Boxers had at last entered the gates of the Imperial City.

One June 1st a general massacre of the foreigners had been planned, but the appearance of the foreign soldiers with their small cannon and the rumor that an army of several thousand more of these "foreign devils" was on the way had a salutary effect and dampened somewhat the ardor of the bloodthirsty Boxers; they graciously condescended to postpone the massacre to June 5th.   On the 2d the Chinese government informed the ambassadors that it was powerless to check the Boxer movement and advised self-protection.   On Sunday, June 3d, the last mail was received at the legations.

The British Legation offered the best chances for an effective resistance and therefore formed, as it were, the citadel of the diplomatic territorial fortress.   It was by far the largest legation, being 2,000 feet long and 600 feet broad, and surrounded by strong walls.   Its boundaries on the north were the Chinese official grounds, known as the Carriage Park, on the east a canal and on the south and west the Mongol Market, a number of Chinese houses and the Carriage Park.   Within this space there were some thirty different buildings. Here were domiciled the representatives of most foreign nations and the refugee women and children. The American, German, French and Russian legations were also fortified and saw some hard fighting during the siege. The Soo Wang Foo, grounds of a Mongol prince across the canal from the British Legation, were also made defensible and quartered 2,000 Christian Chinese and refugees. At the British Legation there were 600 foreigners and 1,000 Chinese. The military force was a little over 400 men. The Teitang, or Northern Cathedral, a Catholic house of worship outside of the legation district, was also besieged. Here were huddled together no less than 4,000 wretched, unfortunate Chinese, men, women and children, who had called down the wrath of their fellow-countrymen for no other reason than because they had embraced the Catholic faith. Nearly all of them were unarmed and utterly unfit to defend themselves, so that the sole defense rested upon the heroism of a small band of forty soldiers, sent there by the ambassadors. Archbishop Favier accomplished wonders in providing for such a large and heterogeneous crowd, keeping up their drooping spirits and conducting the defense, which was maintained until the siege was raised. It was the most remarkable feature of the whole war.

June 8th the grand-stand at the race track was destroyed and a party of Americans was attacked by Boxers and narrowly escaped death.

Wherever the face of a foreigner was seen the cry of "Sha! Sha! Sha!" (Kill! Kill! Kill!) went up, and wherever a house was found, known to have been occupied by a foreigner or a converted Chinaman, it was leveled to the ground.

Women were divested of their clothing, insulted most outrageously and tortured to death. Repeated attacks were made on the several legations and repulsed only after severe fighting.

On June 20th the most tragic incident, and one which stirred up the whole civilized world, occurred — the murder of Baron von Ketteler, the German ambassador. On the preceding day the Yamen had addressed a note to the foreign representatives calling their attention to the fact that the powers were about to take Taku by force and demanding that the ministers leave Pekin within twenty-four hours. The Yamen offered to guarantee a safe passage as far as Tien Tsin.

Upon receipt of the note the diplomats discussed the advisability of leaving, but came to the conclusion that it would be almost suicidal to risk the departure. No foreigner's life was safe in the streets of the capital, and the country between the two cities was in a still more dangerous condition. Trust the faith and loyalty of Chinese troops? None of the ministers would even consider the probability of the existence of any such virtues in a Chinese military body. However precarious was their situation, however critical, it was still considered safe in comparison with a trip to Tien Tsin.

The ministers spent all night in discussing the matter, and finally concluded by declining to leave.

The Yamen had invited them to call and give their answer, but none dared to go except Baron von Ketteler, who thereupon was authorized to convey to the Chinese officials the decision of the other ambassadors.

Shortly before 8 o'clock in the morning Baron von Ketteler and Mr. Cordes, his secretary, were on their way to the Yamen. At the Austrian outpost an Imperial Chinese guard was waiting and ready to conduct them safely to the palace. The baron, who never knew what fear was, dismissed his own guard and he and his secretary trusted their fate in the hands of the armed men of the Dowager Empress. But reliance in the honor of the Chinese soldier cost him his life. Shortly before entering the Yamen an imperial banner soldier raised his gun into the sedan chair where the German Ambassador was boxed in, a helpless victim, and shot him through the head. The treacherous deed was the signal of an apparently premeditated attack, for now other soldiers of the guard were turning the murderous steel into the chair and found a fiendish delight in the utter helplessness of their victim. Mr. Cordes, too, was attacked and dangerously wounded by a shot, but in the general uproar and melee managed to make his escape. He was able to reach the legation and confirm the news of the foul murder, rumors of which had already reached the plucky defenders. This deed, more than any other outrage, raised a cry of indignation throughout the civilized world and stirred up all the nations. In Germany, especially, feeling ran high, and the people's demand for retribution was imperative, justifying Emperor William II to at once mobilize a large force.

The murder, too, served to demonstrate the folly of leaving Pekin, as the Yamen wanted the foreign ministers to do, and they now, more than ever, were resolved to remain where they were, defend themselves as well as they could and fight it out to the bitter end.

The dismissal of Prince Ching as the head of the Yamen and his substitution by Prince Tuan destroyed the last vestige of hope that the Chinese Government would not stand by idly in case a wholesale slaughter of the foreigners was about to be perpetrated. Prince Ching was a man of broad views and strong pro-foreign tendencies. It was he who had thus far saved the foreign element. Prince Tuan, on the other hand, was an enemy of the foreigners and fanatical in his hatred of modern advance. It was well understood that his elevation was intended to mean death to the brave men and women whom the Chinese believed were at their mercy within the legation walls.

From July 20th until August 2d a heavy bombardment was kept up, being especially heavy July 30th and 31st and August 1st. The drooping spirits of the defenders were revived with new hope by the arrival of a messenger from Tien Tsin July 31st, announcing the welcome news of the speedy departure of the second relief force. From August 9th until the 14th, when the relief was effected, the Chinese soldiers and Boxers, made supreme efforts to capture the legation district, efforts which were counteracted by the heroism, almost without parallel in the history of the world, on the part of the defenders.

Nothing can better describe the condition of the besieged district than the report from General Chaffee, the American commander, who said: "Upon our entering the legations the appearance of the people and their surroundings, walls, streets, alleys, entrance, etc., showed every evidence of a confining siege. Barricades were built everywhere and of every sort of material, native brick being largely used for their construction, topped with sand-bags made from every conceivable sort of cloth; from sheets and pillow-cases to dress materials and brocaded curtains. Many of the legations were in ruins, and the English, Russian and American, though standing and occupied, were filled with holes made by bullets and shells. The children presented a pitiable sight, white and wan from lack of proper food, but the adults seemed cheerful and little the worse for their trying experience. They were living on short rations, a portion of which consisted of horse or mule meat daily. The Christian Chinese were fed upon whatever could be secured. All the surroundings indicated that the people had been closely besieged, confined to a small area without any comforts or conveniences, and barely existing from day to day in hope of succor."

"Sand-bags made from every conceivable sort of cloth," brocaded curtains"— these two expressions speak volumes for the devotion and sacrifices of the women within the legations during the siege, while the fact that the besieged were able to withstand the persistent and furious assaults, and hold out so long, is proof sufficient of the bravery and heroism of the men.

At the Pei-tang, or Northern Cathedral, when, as has been stated, Archbishop Favrier was bravely defending the lives of 4000 Chinese refuges, a similar condition of affairs existed. Owing to the location of the church in a populous section of the city the Chinese dared not use their large field pieces or any other cannon, and confined themselves to the use of small arms only.

Of the many heroic deeds performed during the siege of the legations none are worthier of praise than those which made Joseph Mitchell, a gunner's mate of the United States navy, the hero of the siege. He had captured an old Chinese cannon and worked it all alone, the only large gun the besieged had at their disposal Mitchell fought desperately during the entire siege until a few days before the relief was effected, when he was wounded and placed hors de combat. He graphically describes the affairs in the legations as follows:

"After we had reached Pekin on the 31st of May affairs grew worse for the legations daily and skirmishes were the order of the day, in some of which we had hard work to extricate our small commands from the surrounding Chinese hordes. One day, which will always be memorable to the small band that was with me, we were wedged in on three sides by the enemy, but we held two breastworks. One of these was erected at the American and the other near the German Legation, about 2,000 yards away from each other. I was stationed at the British Legation when orders were given to bring the Colt automatic gun, which I handled, over to the German Legation. I was compelled to climb the incline to the wall with my gun in the face of a murderous fire directed from both sides. To turn back, as I would have been justified in doing, never entered my mind, so I took the automatic gun about 2,000 yards over the wall to where our men were stationed. When about half way across the stretch I had to traverse, the gun which I had used with such good effect right along became jammed, and I was compelled to sit down under that heavy fire until I had it fixed, for to re-enforce our men with a broken gun was useless. Yet my efforts did not bring the necessary relief to our pressed men; the fire of the Chinese became so severe I had to leave the wall and return the same way I had come.

"At another time the only piece of artillery we had was the gun which I had constructed, and this was used all during the siege. It was known by all the besieged as "The Old International." It was about 100 years old. To mount it I took a piece of timber and lashed the gun to the station water carriage. It had no trunnions or sight, but nevertheless it was of good use. I used Chinese and German powder, Russian shell and Japanese fuses with it, and to work the old cannon I fought under the flag of every nation in the legation district and the breastworks of the enemy were leveled rapidly. Sometimes I was within six feet of the enemy, and never more than thirty feet from them.

"'The Old International' and my services were wanted everywhere, and we kept the old-timer moving from place to place just long enough to knock down newly-erected breastworks in front of the wall. This sort of work I kept up throughout the siege until I was wounded while firing. I had to work the old gun all by myself, as everybody was afraid it would burst. When wounded the enemy were only ten feet away from me."

Mitchell managed to fire the "International" successfully wherever and whenever it was used, and it was considered by all the only thing that saved the legations, and his ingenuity and heroism are known in all countries.

He seemed to know no fear. At one time during the siege the Americans, in an advanced position, sent for an Italian one-pounder. It was brought up and fired, but the fire of the Chinese was so severe that in a short time the two Italian gunners were wounded. No one but Mitchell was able to handle the gun, and he did it well until the small force was driven off the wall. Mitchell would not, however, desert the gun, and only through his energy it was prevented from falling into the hands of the enemy.

Mitchell also enjoys the distinction of having captured a Chinese flag. He had espied it in a fortification near the wall and, approaching it slyly, had made a sudden grab for the colors when he was discovered. The Chinese soldiers held on to the flag-pole. Mitchell stuck to the flag. They shouted, stabbed and shot at him, pulled at the flag-pole, but the plucky American would not let go of his prize. Presently the flag-pole broke and Mitchell ran away with the flag, which subsequently was sent to Washington as a war trophy.

"HE MANAGED TO FIRE THE 'INTERNATIONAL' SUCCESSFULLY."

From June 20th, the day on which Baron von Ketteler was murdered, until July 16th, many acts of exceptional heroism were performed in Pekin. Those which were rewarded by the Medal of Honor were performed by Sergeant E. A. Walker, Corporal John O. Dahlgren and Privates Martin Hunt and F. A. Young, of the Marine Corps, and Hospital Apprentice Robert Stanley, the latter having distinguished himself by voluntarily carrying messages under heavy fire to the commanding officers.

The following also received the Medal of Honor for distinguished conduct in erecting barricades under heavy fire from July 21st to August 17th: Privates Erwin J. Boydston, William C. Horton, Albert Moore, Herbert I. Preston, David J. Scanell and Oscar Upham, while a Medal of Honor was sent to the heirs of Private of Marines Fisher, who was killed while participating in the work of the marines just mentioned.

Besides these, Drummer John A. Murphy and Privates William I. Carr, Henry W. Davis, Louis R. Gaienne, Francis Silva and William Zion, of the Marine Corps, Chief Machinist Carl E. Peterson and Seaman Axel Westermark, of the navy, received the Medal of Honor for distinguished conduct in the presence of the enemy at Pekin.

THE SECOND RELIEF EXPEDITION

THE allied troops, consisting of about 19,000 men, among whom were the Ninth and Fourteenth U. S. Infantry, numbering 2,000 men, under General Chaffee, left Tien Tsin on the afternoon of August 4th and met a strong Chinese army intrenched at Pie-tsang the day following. An attack was commenced at once and carried out principally by the Japanese, who, after a most gallant fight, drove the enemy from their positions and into hopeless confusion and flight. The victory was followed by a quick move on Yangtsun, twelve miles from Tien Tsin, where the Chinese had made another stand. A battle raged for several hours, the Chinese behaving most gallantly and putting up a strong resistance. The losses to the allies were severe, the Russians alone losing 117 in killed and wounded. The Americans took a conspicuous part in the battle, but suffered more through an unfortunate mistake than from the bullets of the Chinese. At first the French fired into the American lines, then the English by a worse mistake sent some shells into the ranks of Co. E of the Fourteenth U. S. Infantry, under Colonel A. S. Daggett, killing eight and wounding nine of the men.

The Chinese were dislodged once more and Yangtsun fell into the hands of the allies.

The march from here to Tung-chou, at the junction of the Pekin canal and the Pei-ho, thirteen miles from Pekin, was practically unopposed by Chinese troops or Boxer bands.

The entire route from Tung-chou to Tien Tsin was guarded by detachments numbering altogether 3,000 men. The attack on Pekin was decided for August 14th, but during the night the Russians moved away and the next morning made an independent attack on the Tung-pien-men gate. They, however, failed in their attack and were thrown into confusion and saved from a worse fate by the timely arrival of the other forces of the allied troops.

The same morning Japanese and American forces advanced on the city, the former reaching the wall about 8 o'clock in the morning had to stand the brunt of the battle. Great courage was displayed by them during the day. The Chinese had evidently expected the main attack on this side, and had concentrated most of their forces there. Not before 9 o'clock in the evening was the task of blowing open and forcing the gate accomplished. Meanwhile the other forces of the allied troops had attacked from different points. The British met with little or no resistance; they having entered the city through the Shan-huo gate, which was opened for them by the Chinese themselves. They advanced towards the legations and saw that the legation guards were still holding a part of the wall. As they approached they were hailed and cheered by the besieged, and soon they reached the legation grounds closely followed by the American forces under Colonel Daggett. The reception given them as they entered through a passage in the wall, known as "the sluice," was tremendous.

The American forces, comprising the Ninth and the Fourteenth Infantry, did not fare so well as the British. They encountered greater difficulties and severe fighting. The heroism displayed by some of the men in these attacks was exceptional. Their intrepidity and dash caused the American flag to be the first planted on the Chinese wall by the allied forces.

This feat was accomplished when re-enforcements from the allied troops came to the help of the Russians, who were badly pressed, and had received severe losses. The Chinese were driven back and a small number of plucky Americans under Captain Crozier managed to scale the wall and reach the position of the Russians.

The relief of the besieged, however, did not end the fight. Russians and Japanese were still fighting at their positions, and even in the inner city volleys were delivered by the enemy into the legation grounds. This fire was stopped short by the Americans and Sikhs, who rushed the barricades and drove out the Boxers as well as the Chinese soldiers from the strongholds they had held so many weeks.

The relief of Pekin practically ended the Chinese war. Count von Waldersee, the German field-marshal, who had been selected by the powers concerned to command the allied forces, arrived on the scene shortly after, but his efforts were confined to the re-establishment of law and order within the city and Empire and avoiding outbreaks of jealousy and rivalry within the ranks of the allies themselves. The Americans, acting upon instructions from Washington, refrained from all further hostilities. As far as they were concerned the object of the expedition

THE BATTLE ON THE WALL AT PEKIN.

had been attained. Minister Conger, and with him the lives of all other Americans who had been imperiled, had been saved.

On August 28th detachments of the various troops entered the Forbidden City — the palaces of the Emperor and Dowager Empress — and penetrated to grounds upon which hitherto no "foreign devil" had ever set his foot.

The court had fled to Singan-fu, 500 miles from Pekin, and, owing to this distance, and the stubborn conduct of the Chinese court, peace negotiations consumed much time. The well known tactics of Chinese diplomacy were again employed. The negotiations were being stretched by them in the hope that the allies would fight among themselves and thus give them a chance to gain better terms than those which had been dictated.

To frustrate these plans, and also to check and disperse the renewed gatherings of large Chinese forces at several points in the province, the commander-in-chief was forced to send several expeditions in different directions. All of these expeditions, which were undertaken during a period of several months, were carried out successfully, although some of them were accompanied by heavy losses to the allied forces in the field.

Serious differences among the allies for which the Chinese had hoped actually occured, but were always amicably settled by Count von Waldersee, the commander-inc-hief.

One of the most serious differences arose when the Russians had secretly obtained a concession from the Chinese government for the occupation of Manchuria. Japan protested and actually made threats, but Waldersee's diplomacy prevented the worst, — a break which would have brought on a war among the powers.

At another time the English and the Russians got into a dispute over a stretch of railroad, for which a concession had been given to both by the Chinese government. Here again Waldersee showed his skill and tact and trouble was averted. Had it not been for this leader's wise conduct of all affairs, China would have witnessed what it had wished and hoped to bring about, a war among the allies themselves. Anticipating such a calamity, the United States Government had abstained from further actions after the siege of the legations had been raised.

After the demands of the allies, that some of the government leaders in the outrages against the "foreign devils" were to be punished by being decapitated in the presence of representatives of all powers, had been fullfilled, peace was finally concluded on the following terms:

An Imperial Prince to apologize to the German Emperor for the murder of Baron von Ketteler. Punishment of the leaders of the Boxers and three officials who were known to have been in league with them. Reparation to Japan for the murder of Secretary Sugiyama. Expiatory monuments at all cemeteries where the bodies of foreigners were desecrated.

A monument on the site of the murder of Baron von Ketteler with inscriptions in Latin, German and Chinese, expressing the regret of the Chinese Emperor for the murder. Payment of indemnity to the various nations, societies and individuals affected by the Boxer movement. Permanent legation guards at Pekin. Destruction of the Taku forts. Prohibition of import of arms and of their manufacture. Maintenance of foreign troops at all strategic points between Pekin and the sea. Change of mode of communicating with Yamen in accordance with the wishes of the powers. Reform in all trade relations and the issuing of imperial edicts for the next two years admonishing the people to treat all foreigners with becoming kindness and telling the population of the punishment meted out to the Boxers.

These conditions may seem harsh and severe, yet the Chinese government was not in a position to reject them. Besides, they were mild compared with the original demands of some of the powers. If these demands had prevailed the "partition of China" would have been an accomplished fact.

TERRORS OF THE ARCTIC

THE heroes of the battlefield are the ones most dear to and most willingly admired by the human heart. This is human nature, for their deeds being achieved in the midst of dramatic, stirring incidents and inspiring surroundings act upon the quick impulsive imagination and emotion in man. But as soon as we admit reasoning into our feeling we must concede that there have been done deeds of heroism unaccompanied by the grand scenery of the battlefield and still equalling or even surpassing anything on record in that respect as to silent courage, wonderful enduring and that grandest of all qualities in the race, the selfsacrificing grim devotion to duty unto death.

For deeds of this kind the geographic exploration of our globe, especially the search for the north pole, have offered a wide field. Most conspicious among all of these and before all nations stand out the two American arctic explorations known to the world as the Jeannette expedition of 1879-1881 and the expedition of Greely 1881-1884.

In both of these exploits participated all in all fifty-six men and officers; only fifteen of these reached the United States again; forty-one perished after untold miseries and privations. The record of their behavior under the most terrible misfortunes forms one of the proudest and most brilliant pages in the annals of American manhood and prowess.

Two lonely cairns are now standing, thousands of miles apart, one on the western foreland of the Lena Delta on the Siberian coast, the other near Cape Sabine in Smith sound, objects of passing curiosity to the roaming half wild Tunguse hunter or the spearskilled Eskimo, but silent witnesses of the heroic sacrifice of so many brave American men.

Of those who led these men the most famous are still alive: Rear-Admiral Melville, the conspicious figure in the Jeannette drama, General Greely, now Chief Signal Officer in the U. S. Army, and Vice-Admiral Schley, he of Santiago, who commanded the party that rescued Greely and his men.

Beside the American home country the whole scientific world owes gratitude and appreciation to these two expeditions. In summer 1881 the American government, through the Signal Service of the Army, established two meteorological stations, in accordance with the agreement of the International Meteorological Congress. One of these was at Point Barrow, north of Behring Strait, in charge of Lieutenant Ray, U. S. A., and the second, in charge of First Lieutenant Greely, was at Fort Conger in Lady Franklin Bay. Both of these American outposts of science were much farther north than the stations of any of the European nations, in fact, the fate of the Greely station showed that the limit of reasonable safety had been transgressed in the patriotic zeal to outdo all others.

How the valuable scientific records of this expedition were gathered in the midst of dramatic incidents of most appalling character will be desribed later on.

As to the Jeannette expedition its plan as conceived by its leader, Lieutenant-Commander G. W. DeLong, U. S. N., was an entirely novel one and had it not been for the "Noros trousers", of whom more anon, the daring Northman Nansen would probably never have undertaken his famous expedition of 1893.

In the seventh decade of the nineteenth century many geographists, including their acknowledged authority, Peterman of Gotha, believed the north pole to be surrounded by a great continent, which was supposed to stretch from somewhere north of Wrangel Land over the pole to Greenland that was considered part of it.

James Gordon Bennett, who wished to have light thrown upon this question, fitted out an expedition at his own expense and made DeLong its leader. DeLong had demonstrated to him that the Behring Strait was the proper route through which to start for the pole; this idea had never so far been entertained by any explorer of the Arctic.

After the foundering of the illfated Jeannette, when the sleigh crews worked their difficult way across the pack towards the New Siberian Islands, one of the men, seaman Louis P. Noros, left his oilskin trousers on the ice. Nine or ten years after these same oilskins, bearing the stamp of Noros' name and that of the ship, were found by Eskimoes near Goodhaab, on the eastern shore of Greenland, on the drift ice. They were taken to Kopenhagen, where the fact was published in some scientific Danish paper, and thus Nansen heard of it. The fact of this drift confirmed his conviction that there was a slow current running over the pole, and in consequence he shaped his plan, whose splendid execution brought him so much success and fame.

THE JEANNETTE EXPEDITION

Lieutenant-Commander George Washington DeLong, the leader of the James Gordon Bennett expedition for the finding of the most proper route to the north pole, had everything ready by the beginning of midsummer 1879, and on the 9th of July of the same year the Jeannette steamed out of San Francisco on her adventuresome and perilous trip. The ship had been fitted out in the most thorough and liberal way. DeLong had his own choice of officers, the men were most carefully selected, and on the commander's suggestion Congress had caused the whole crew, officers and all, to be put under the regulations and orders of the United States regular naval service.

The muster roll of the ship including officers and crew at leaving Unalaska was as follows:*)

*Lieutenant George W. DeLong, U. S. N., Commanding.**)

*Lieutenant Charles W. Chipp, U. S. N., Executive.

Master John W. Danenhower, U. S. N., Navigator.***)

Passed Assistant Engineer George W. Melville, U. S. N., Chief Engineer.****)

*Mr. Jerome J. Collins (shipped as seaman), Meteorologist.

Mr. Raymond L. Newcomb (shipped as seaman), Naturalist.

*William Dunbar (shipped as seaman), Ice Pilot.

John Cole (shipped as seaman), Boatswain.

William Nindemann (shipped as seaman), Ice Quartermaster.

*Alfred Sweetman (shipped as seaman), Carpenter,

*Walter Lee, Machinist.	*Peter E. Johnson, Seaman.
James F. Bartlett, Fireman.	*Hans Halmer Ericksen, Seaman.
*Geo. W. Boyd, Fireman.	*Heinrich H. Kaack, Seaman.
John Lauterbach, Coal Heaver.	Frank E. Munson, Seaman.
*Walter Sharwell, Coal Heaver.	*Carl A. Goertz, Seaman.
*Niels Iversen, Coal Heaver.	Herbert W. Leach, Seaman.
Louis P. Noros, Seaman.	*Edward Starr, Seaman.
*Adolph Dressler, Seaman.	*Henry D. Warren, Seaman.
Henry Wilson, Seaman.	*Albert G. Kuehne, Seaman.

Steward Charles Tong Sing. ⎫
*Cook Ah Sam.   ⎬ Chinese.
Cabin Boy Ah Sing.   ⎭

*Dog Driver and Hunter Alexey.   ⎱ Aleutes.
*Dog Driver and Hunter Aneguin. ⎰

The Jeannette had been constructed as a pleasure yacht for Arctic waters by Sir Allen Young, who owned her several years under the name Pandora. For the present trip she had been especially strengthened against ice pressure in the best and most thorough way science could suggest. She was a barkentine rigged steamer; her speed under steam alone proved to be four to six miles an hour. The arrangements for the housing of both officers and men proved comfortable and healthy.

Nothing extraordinary happened during her trip from San Francisco to the Behring Strait. In St. Michaels the two dog drivers, Alexey and Aneguin, were taken on board, and then with the supply schooner Clyde as a convoy, the voyage was continued. In Little Harbor, on the Siberian Coast, the supplies from the Clyde

---

*) Those marked by an asterisk before their names lost their lives.

**) Promoted November 1, 1879, to Lieutenant-Commander.

***) Promoted August 2, 1879, to Lieutenant.

****) Promoted March 4, 1881, to Chief-Engineer.

were transferred to the Jeannette, and on the 27th of August they parted, the Clyde sailing south, the Jeannette to the north into the unknown. After passing Behring Strait and Nordenskjold's winter quarters, near Cape Sjerdze-Kamen on the northeast coast, the Jeanette turned northward and entered the pack-ice on the 5th of September, in sight of Herald Island, bearing in a northwesterly direction. On the 6th of September the ice closed around the ship, and thus the Jeanette remained practically ice-bound until the fatal crush came, on the 12th of June, 1881.

The long interval of time between those two events showed the general monotony and dreariness so characteristic of life on an ice-bound ship in the Arctic The monotony was often rudely broken by the imminent danger of being crushed between the floes whenever the pack started moving. It seems that in this point, too, the Jeannette was less lucky than other exploring vessels, for there is hardly a polar trip of modern times on record where the vessel was so often on the very verge of annihilation as this ship in the pack off Herald Island. From the end of October there hardly passed a week in which the restless and resistless jamming of the floes did not cause the endangered crew preparing for the abandoning of the ship. It was one day in January, 1880, that the ship sprung a leak forward at the keel; the captain computed the daily amount of water entering thereby at over 4,800 gallons, which had to be pumped out by hand until a windmill pump was rigged. In the meantime the floes which imprisoned the Jeannette drifted steadily toward the north-west. In the spring of 1881 land was discovered in the southwest. When the Jeannette was only about 12 miles away from the shore, DeLong sent Melville, (Chipp, Danenhower and Newcomb were ill in bed) with Ice-Quartermaster Dunbar, Nindemann, Ericksen and Sharwell, fifteen dogs, a sleigh and a dinghy on an exploring trip on shore. This was on the 31st of May. It was a most hazardous and tiresome trip over the moving, whirling ice-fields. Melville accomplished it splendidly, though; his party reached land on the next day. He seized the island in the name of the United States, and raised the stars and stripes. It was christened Henrietta Island, after Mr. Bennett's mother, and then its position and its limits were established and surveyed. The party returned without mishap on board the ship on the morning of June 5th. Another island, further south, was discovered, its bearings were taken, and it was entered on the map as Jeannette Island.

On the morning of June 10th the movement of the ice became so violent and threatening that everyone on board believed the end of the ship to be near. In the following night the floe suddenly, with a tremendous report, split fore and aft on a line with the keel; the ship kept hanging fast to the starboard half, while the port half, on which were the dogs, the observatory, and other things, moved several hundred yards off.

When DeLong asked the ice expert, the old whaler captain Dunbar, what he thought of the situation, the man replied: "She will be either under the floe or on top of it before tomorrow night." His words came true. Careful preparations had been made for the emergency of abandoning ship ever since the first jam after the vessel was frozen in, twenty-one months ago.

During the afternoon of June the 11th the order was given by DeLong to abandon ship. This was done according to the preconceived plan, orderly and quietly, while DeLong looked on from the ship's bridge, coolly smoking his pipe. Hardly had the stores and boats been secured to the ice floe, some five hundred yards away, when the ever increasing crowding of the hummocks made the ship heel over in such a way that standing on the bridge was no longer possible. Everyone else of the crew having by this time left her, DeLong jumped from the ship upon the ice, and waving his cap and shouting, "good-bye, old ship!" he greeted her for the last time.

Towards four o'clock in the morning of the 12th of June the men were awakened from their slumber by the sudden shout of the watch, seaman Kuehne: "Hurry if you want to see the last of the Jeannette. There she goes! There she goes!" While the crew came running out and amid the rattling and battering of her timbers the ship righted and stood almost upright; the crushing floes backed slowly off and "as she sank with slowly accelerated velocity," describes Mr. Melville this last moment, "the yard-arms were stripped and broken upward, parallel to the masts, and so, like a great, gaunt skeleton clapping its hands above its head, she plunged out of sight."

So there was the crew now, cast upon the ice and left to themselves, five hundred miles from the mouth of the Lena river. Although everyone could not help realizing what a difficult and arduous task was before them, it was fortunate that none of them could read the future, that none of them had the slightest suspicion of the terrors they were to pass through, of the miseries in the midst of which so many of them were to perish.

The first few days on the ice were spent in thoroughly organizing the camp. There were five sleds, six tents and three boats, which formed the basis for the following organization:

Sled No. 1, to first cutter, DeLong.
Sleds No. 2 and No. 4, to second cutter, Chipp.
Sleds No. 3 and No. 5, to whaleboat, Melville.
Sled crews No. 1 and No. 4 to man first cutter.
Sled crew No. 2, the second cutter.
Sled crew No. 3 and No. 5, the whaleboat.

Of the six tents one was reserved as headquarters; the other five sheltered the men and were in charge of the following officers: No. 1, DeLong; No. 2, Chipp; No. 3, Melville; No. 4, Danenhower; No. 5, Dr. Ambler. From the stores and provisions saved a reserve for 60 days was packed into the sleds and was not to be touched at all as long as the rest lasted. The matter of clothing was regulated and restricted to the least possible weight; the ammunition taken amounted to twenty rounds per man. They had twenty-three dogs, and at the time of the start there were five men sick and under the care of the surgeon, namely: Chipp, Danenhower, Kuehne, Alexey and Tong Sing.

On the fifth day, the 17th, everything being ready, the expedition started south on the following evening, Saturday, June 18th, at seven o'clock. It was found more practicable and consistent with circumstances to march during the night and rest during the daytime.

The humor of the men was excellent, but the road was extremely difficult, so ragged and interspersed with hummocks, that Melville, in charge of a working gang, had to even the way before the boats could be dragged along. The hard work in the wet of the slush and over the sharp edges soon tore the footwear, and after two or three weeks the men had to resort to all kinds of tricks to keep their feet off the ice, but frequently it was all in vain. Melville says: "Many, many times, after a day's march, have I seen no less than six of my men standing with their bare feet on the ice, having worn off the very soles of their stockings. A large number marched with their toes protruding through their moccasins, some with the "uppers" full of holes out of which the water and slush spurted at every step. I have here to say that no ship's company ever endured such severe toil with so little complaint. Another crew, perhaps, may be found to do as well, but *better*—never!" Brave men! But what were all the hardships they were so cheerfully enduring in comparison to those that the near future had in store for them.

The little band had been on the march for several weeks, straining every muscle in covering some twenty-five miles as a daily average, when Captain DeLong was enabled to take an observation of the sun. Imagine his disappointment when the subsequent calculation, and after that a "Sumner" calculation for verification, revealed the discouraging fact that in spite of all their endeavors they had actually drifted twenty-five miles to the northwest. This was indeed a gloomy if not desperate state of affairs. DeLong kept his secret to himself, still the men guessed it since the result was not announced to them. The effect was plainly visible on their faces. However, a week later, when a second observation was possible, the encouraging result that they had covered some twenty-odd miles toward the southwest spread joy and new hope among the much suffering party. Slowly they continued their advance southwestward, the distance covered often amounting to not more than a mile during the twenty-four hours.

On the 12th of July land was sighted toward the southwest some twelve to fifteen miles distant, but it took more than two weeks of incessant and extraordinary toil before they finally reached this land on the evening of July 29th. It was newly discovered land, and DeLong, christening it Bennett Island, took possession of it in the name of the United States. After being compelled to have ten of the poorest of the dogs shot, and after depositing a record in a cairn, DeLong left this island with his comrades on the 6th of August. They proceeded this time in their boats, which were laden with the sleds in addition to the provisions. The crew was distributed in this manner: First cutter, DeLong, Ambler, Collins, Nindemann, Ericksen,

Kaack, Boyd, Alexey, Lee, Noros, Dressler, Goertz, Iversen; Second cutter, Chipp, Dunbar, Sweetman, Sharwell, Kuehne, Starr, Munson, Warren, Johnson, Ah Sam; Whaleboat, Melville, Danenhower, Newcomb, Cole, Bartlett, Wilson, Lauterbach, Leach, Aneguin and Tong Sing. The dinghy, which was taken in tow by the first cutter, contained the dogs, in charge of Ericksen and Lee. Later on, on the 5th of September, Munson was shifted to the whaleboat and Ah Sam to the first cutter, in order to lighten the second cutter, which acted badly in heavy weather. In the same order as they were now divided the men were soon to meet their fate, Chipp's cutter to founder on the 12th of September, with all hands on board, in a gale; DeLong and Melville to reach the land at separate places, and the former and his crew, with the only exception of Nindemann and Noros, to starve slowly and helplessly to death in the Lena Delta.

By sailing, rowing or sledging, as the occasion required, the party made their way due south, covering at an average five miles a day. On the 8th it was found necessary to lighten the first cutter's ballast by shooting two dogs; eight others had strayed away during the passage over the ice-fields, so there remained only two. On the 18th DeLong dealt out the last bit of bread. Two days later DeLong held council with Chipp and Melville, giving them directions in case the boats should become separated by the ice or the gales. It was now plain that the second cutter offered difficulties in handling, but nothing could be done to improve the seaworthiness of the boat, so they kept wearily on, through fogs and gales and ice-fields, towards the southwest, passing between Novaya Sibir and Fadeyeff Islands, then by the south shore of Kotolnoi toward Semonoffski. On the 12th of September, when about half way between the latter island and Barkin, in the Lena Delta, they were caught in a teriffic gale. By this time the boats had been lightened as much as possible, the dinghy aud the sleds having long ago been rendered into kindling wood, and only one dog remained, which DeLong meant to keep as a last resort in case provisions gave out before reaching relief. At nine o'clock in the evening of this day it was no longer possible to keep the boats together in the terrific gale and sea without seriously endangering their safety. DeLong motioned to them to take care of themselves. Melville, who was in the lead, disappeared quickly in the darkness toward the south; so did Chipp with the second cutter, who had kept about six hundred yards to the rear on the port quarter of DeLong's boat. There were in both Melville's and DeLong's boats men who declared that they had discerned the hapless cutter being swamped by a huge wave. At any rate there was nothing heard or seen after that night of either boat or crew.

DeLong kept on toward west-south-west and struck the northernmost point of the Lena Delta on the afternoon of the 17th of September, effecting a most difficult landing through a waist deep icy surf. The men were, with very few exceptions, so thoroughly exhausted that only by exerting their utmost will power they succeeded in securing the provisions and necessary stores on shore. On the morning of the 19th, after breakfast, DeLong ascertained that they had three and a half days' rations left; and they did not know where they were, except somewhere in the immense Lena Delta.

Before following further their gruesome experiences, let us turn to Melville. During the terrible night of the 12th the whaleboat hove to by means of a sea-anchor, improvised after Melville's direction by Cole and Munson; its proper position was given it by sliding the copper fire pot, the only available weight, down to the drag, and between fear and hope the thirsty, hungry, drenched and shivering crew awaited the break of morning, anxiously occupied with bailing their little craft between sets of the dreaded "three waves." But it was toward evening of the 13th ere the gale and the sea subsided sufficiently to permit a getting under way. Melville shaped his course toward the south and east, as he believed himself to be near Cape Barkin, toward which his orders directed him. The weather improved a good deal, and things would have had a brighter aspect if it had not been for the entire lack of fresh water, which caused much suffering among the utterly exhausted men. They were hardly able to swallow dry their quarter of a pound of pemmican for meals. As the condition of the weather cut off the progress toward the south, Melville took an easterly course, and found himself towards morning about twenty miles toward the east of the supposed point of Cape Barkin, consequently in Borkhoi Bay. As the weather was comparatively fine he shaped again his course to the westward, but perceiving an opening in the shore line towards the south he run into it and entered one of the mouths of the Lena estuary during the 16th of September, his men being by this time almost overcome by the agony of their thirst. Now they soon reached fresh water, which enabled them to quench their craving. Melville felt scruples. though, as to not fulfilling orders concerning Cape Barkin, and he announced at noon his intention to turn the boat about and attempt reaching the cape. The boat's bow was turned, when a timely and common sense remark of fireman Bartlett aroused suspicion in the intrepid engineer's mind as to the prudence of his maneuvre; in an inkling he made up his mind, feeling the soundness of Bartlett's view, and turned the boat again down stream. In doing so he undoubtedly saved the lives of the whaleboat's crew, as they would, without question, have shared the fate of the hapless first cutter's party, for further investigation proved Cape Barkin a barren, uninhabited place, where they all must have starved during the fast approaching arctic winter.

As it was, they continued up river, with an east wind, until toward evening they sighted an abandoned hut on the bank; they landed and established their night camp, but their stiffened, cramped and frozen limbs were so affected by the heat of the camp fire that none of the men were able to sleep, and the morning found them suffering excruciating pain, well nigh unfit to continue their journey. Yet they managed to start again; toward evening they landed and passed the night on shore at a spot which from its nature they christened "Mud Camp." In a similar manner they continued their way, always up stream, toward the south and west, when shortly after noon on the 19th they espied three natives in three boats rowing toward them. That meant "saved at last." One of Melville's men felt so enthusi-astic that he presented every one of the utterly amazed natives with a hearty kiss upon each cheek. The natives gave the men venison and fish; still Melville had his suspicions and watched them closely so as to prevent any possible attempt on their part to steal away and leave the white men in the lurch. Melville hoped the natives would easily help him to reach the nearest inhabited settlement, Belun, from where he might speedily obtain succor to ascertain the fate of the other two boat crews. But the natives refused point blank, explaining that a trip to Belun, at this time of the year meant certain death. As it was the party continued their way among the direst hardships to a place called Zeumavolioki, where they arrived totally exhausted on the evening of the 26th. They were quartered in a house and scantily provided with poor, often half decayed food by the starosta or elder. All efforts to reach Belun, said to be "sixteen days" distant proved in vain. A Russian exile named Kopaloff lived in the same house with the Americans and was a great help to them as he proved willing and more intelligent than the natives. As week after week passed without the slightest prospect of establishing communi-cation with Belun the situation became very trying, and an almost unendurable restlessness seized the leader and his men. The disgusting filth in which they lived added to their discomfort. The following scenes, described by Mr. Melville, may serve as an illustration: "Mrs. Chagra, assisted by some of her female friends, put on a large kettle of ancient but hardy geese that had long and honorably served the natives by raising numerous progeny of their kind. But they had been slaugh-tered during the summer, when in pin-feather, and hung in pairs, with their bills interlocked, across a pole, out of the reach of dogs and foxes, and as they had neither been plucked nor dressed, the juices of their poor bodies naturally gathered at their extremities, hence, ere freezing, the dead geese had generated another and more prolific family within themselves. So when such are heated for the purpose of cleaning, the natives are usually saved the trouble of opening them, for the whole after part of the fowl drops out of its own accord—anything but a pleasing sight to contemplate, particularly if the agony, or inside, be long drawn out. Still we ate of the geese, and heartily." And again: "During the nesting season the eggs are also gathered in large quantities and buried in earth until winter, their state of incubation, however far advanced, mattering but little to the accommodating taste of the native, who, in fact, makes use of all kinds of eggs, and finds no fault with the fresh ones. And though when eating them raw the presence of a young bird in the shell does not seem to perturb him, yet I have noticed that everywhere he is par-ticular, when frying his eggs, to pick out the yellow feathers from the pan. When the American sailors were supplied with such eggs there was at first some discussion in the hut as to the propriety of using the over-ripe eggs, but I finally concluded to cook them all together, and thus the identity of the poor little geese was lost in the 'scramble.'" Thus in spite of all their efforts and protests the shipwrecked sailors could do nothing but keep their patience and wait. At last, on the 10th of October, a soldier-exile by the name of Kusma Germayeff happened to arrive from Belun. Melville promised him money and the whaleboat if he would return immediately with the letters, or take one of the crew as a courier with him. In vain; only after several days was Kusma ready to depart, and did so entrusted with letters to the Russian commandant or highest official at Belun. He had promised to be back within five days.

He returned finally, but on the afternoon of the thirteenth day, the 29th of October, he having had great difficulty in passing several streams that in the meantime, through a change in the weather, had become nearly impassable. Imagine the astonishment and excitement of the Melville party when one of the three written communications Kusma brought was a crumpled and dirty scrap of paper with the following message:

> "Arctic steamer Jeannette lost on the 11th of June; landed
> on Siberia 25th September or thereabouts; want assistance to
> go for the Captain and Doctor and (9) other men.
> > "William F. C. Nindemann,
> > "Louis P. Noros,
> > > "Seamen, U. S. N.
> "Reply in haste; want food and clothing."

It was further learned from Kusma that the two men of DeLong's crew had been discovered exhausted, sick "and suffering fearfully from hunger and cold in a hut at a place called Bulchur, and that they were now on the way to Belun. Melville at once gave direction to get a fresh dog-team and everything else ready to take him to Belun. The next morning, October 30th, he started. Lieutenant Danenhower had been instructed to wait for the announced arrival of the Cossack Commandant Byeshoff, from Belun, and then to proceed with the men and him to the latter place, there to await Melville's return. The trip to Belun, in the grim Arctic winter gale, in an open dog-sleigh, with tattered clothing, was an excruciating hardship for Melville, who was yet unable to use his frozen limbs freely. On that evening they reached a place called Tamussi, where a new sleigh had to be equipped. Little did the intrepid American officer think that this very evening, some hundred and odd miles away, sealed the fate of his brave comrades with DeLong. It was on this day, a Sunday, that the heroic commander, with the last effort of ebbing life, made the last entry in his famous ice-journal.

Melville finally reached Belun, toward evening, after several days of hard traveling and many mishaps and difficulties. He proceeded at once to look up Nindemann and Noros, a whole band of natives acting willingly as his guides. The meeting can only be properly described in his own words: "They opened an outer door, but refrained from touching an inner one, which opened into the apartment where were my two comrades, Nindemann and Noros. Pausing an instant I pushed open the door, which was covered on one side with deer skin, on the other with woolen felting to keep out the cold....I remained silently standing for a brief spell to see if Noros would recognize me. He stood up, facing me, behind a rude table, not more than ten feet off, holding in one hand a loaf of black bread which he was in the act of cutting with a sheath knife when I entered. Nindemann was nowhere to be seen. A dim light straggled through an ice glazed window in the rear of Noros, and to the left, around a fire in a small alcove, a number of Yakuts were cooking their supper. At my entrance Noros glanced up from his bread but did not know me, and was about to resume operations on the loaf, when 'Halloa, Noros,' said I, 'how do you do?' at the same time advancing toward him with outstretched hand. 'My God! Mr. Melville,' he exclaimed, 'are you alive?' And then Nindemann, hearing my voice, arose from a roughly made bed, and cried out: 'We thought you were all dead, and that we were the only two left alive; we were sure the whaleboat's were all dead and the second cutter's too.'"

Melville told them that his men were safe and sound, and that he was hurrying to get relief for DeLong and his party. But as Nindemann and Noros both declared that it was useless to try to help their companions, since by this time they must all be dead, they all three broke down from grief and emotion. By and by Melville extracted from the two sailors their story.

When DeLong's party, after the landing, started on their march southward, Boyd, Ah Sam and Ericksen had great trouble to keep on their feet, which were more frostbitten than those of the others. Ericksen especially was in bad shape; the brave Dane had exposed himself unflinchingly, and, being of Herculean build, had willingly borne the brunt of the work and the hardships. On the fourth or fifth day Ericksen lay down and wanted to be left. DeLong induced him to get up again, but contemplated at that time already to send two men ahead as a relief-searching party; these were to be Dr. Ambler and Nindemann. The little band opened their last can of pemmican, (forty-five pound), and by dexterously cutting it DeLong divided it into rations for four more days. As a last resort, they had still the one dog, Snoozer, to keep immediate starvation off.

Two days later the sufferers were somewhat cheered up by a piece of good luck on the part of Alexey, the Chinook hunter; he shot two reindeer, killing both with the same bullet. They had now over one hundred pound of clear meat, and at the first deer dinner each man was allowed one and one-half pound of the fresh, delicious venison. Their daily march averaged at that time about five miles. On their way they found abandoned huts, fox traps, an old boat and other signs of the presence of man, but to all indications no human beings except themselves had been around there for a long time.

On the 27th of September, when they were again at the end of their resources for food, Nindemann and Alexey secured once more a reindeer, out of a herd of ten which they had managed to stalk successfully.

On the 1st of October Dr. Ambler amputated Ericksen's toes on both feet. On the 3d of October, no other food remaining, they had to kill the dog. DeLong allowed one-half pound of dog meat per day for each man. On the morning of the

6th of October poor, heroic Ericksen died in great agony, the first victim of the first cutter's party. His body was buried in the ice, the Captain reading the burial service.

On the seventh they ate their last half-pound of dog for breakfast. Toward evening Alexey shot a ptarmigan, (Arctic grouse a little larger than a pigeon), and they made soup of it for supper.

On the 9th of October DeLong deemed it imperative to send two of the strongest men on ahead to secure relief if possible. He selected Nindemann and Noros. They started at seven o'clock, amid the feeble cheers of their starving companions. It was a Sunday; the two men had been furnished with a copy of DeLong's chart, a rifle and some ammunition, and were instructed to make for Ku Mark Surka, which was supposed to be about twelve miles distant. As a matter of fact, Tit Ary, where DeLong thought he was himself, was nearly a hundred and twenty miles away, and the two sailors reached it after a fortnight's march, and Ku Mark Surka lay thirty-three miles beyond that.

Nindemann and Noros followed their instructions as well as they could, and by dint of marvellous exertion, coupled with miraculous good luck, they reached a hut where they were found by a native on the morning of the 22d of October, weak, sick, starving and exhausted, at the place mentioned before, Bulchur. This man fetched succor, and they were taken to Ku Mark Surka, which they reached on the twenty-fourth. All efforts of Nindemann to make the natives understand him were futile. Finally, on the twenty-seventh, Kusma Germayeff fell in with them and promised to forward to the Commandant at Belun a note which the two men composed, the identical one that Kusma delivered soon after into Melville's hands.

The latter made hurried dispositions for the transportation of the men to Verkhoyansk and Irkutsk and finally back to the United States, and then organized without delay, although still very much suffering from frostbites, a searching expedition. Following back the track of Nindemann and Moros, he searched from the 7th until the 21st of November when the task had to be abondoned on account of the wintry season and the absolute refusal of the natives to continue. But Melville, Bartlett, Nindemann, Munson, Leach, Lauterbach and Aneguin stayed in Siberia to resume the search again in the spring. The United States government sent several officers over to assist them. In the meanwhile Aneguin died at Kirinsk of the small-pox. Danenhower with the rest of the survivors reached on the 17th of December Yakutsk, from where they returned home. John Cole, the boatswain, had become insane and ended in the United States Insane Asylum.

On the 18th of February, 1882, Melville's searching party were again assembled at Belun and on the 16th of March he set out with Nindemann and Bartlett. On the 23rd of March Melville and Nindemann found the corpses. First they saw some sticks protruding from the snow at the high river bank ; they discovered one of the sticks to be a Remington rifle, they noticed a camp kettle half buried in the snow and while Melville reached out to pick it up, he stepped over something which he suddenly recognized as the arm of a man. It was the body of De Long, nearby lay Ah Sam and Dr. Ambler. Not far off lay the famous ice-journal of De Long. With the deepest emotion did the searchers open the weather-worn leaves of this priceless document. It showed that the second day after Nindemann's and Noros' leaving found the party already unable to move further. On that day they had "one spoonful of glycerine and hot water for food," with no more firewood in the vicinity. On the 18th of October Alexey died. The last page of this extraordinary monument of endurance and truest devotion to duty runs thus: "October 21st, Friday, one hundred and thirty-first day." (Since leaving the ship) "Kaack was found dead about midnight between the doctor and myself. Lee died about noon. Read prayers for sick when we found he was going. October 22nd, Saturday, one hundred and thirty-second day; too weak to carry the bodies of Lee and Kaack out on the ice. The doctor, Collins and I carried them around the corner out of sight, then my eye closed up." (De Long had suffered much from eye troubles, and, as Nindemann stated, was nearly blind, when the two sailors left on the ninth.) "October 23rd, Sunday, one hundred and thirty-third day. Everybody pretty weak. Slept or rested all day and then managed to get wood in before dark. Read part of divine service. Suffering in our feet. No footgear. October 24th, Monday, one hundred and thirty-fourth day. A hard night. October 25th, Tuesday, one hundred and thirty-fifth day. October 26th, Wednesday, one hundred and thirty-sixth day. October 27th, Thursday, one hundred and thirty-seventh day. Iversen broken down. October 28th, Friday, one hundred and thirty-eighth day. Iversen died during early morning. October 29th, Saturday, one hundred and thirty-ninth day. Dressler died during night. October 30th, Sunday, one hundred and fortieth day. Boyd and Goertz died during night. Mr. Collins dying."

This was the last entry. After searching further Melville and his companions found in a small cove in the bank the bodies of Lee, Kaack, Dressler, Iversen, Goertz, Boyd and Collins, together with the flag and the two boxes of records. Erichsen's body was found soon afterwards, and on April 6th and 7th the mortal remains of these valiant, unfortunate sons of Columbia were buried together in one grave on what is now called Monument Hill and a huge cairn with a cross erected on their last resting place. *Alexey's body was never found, and search for any signs of Chipp proved fruitless. Thus ended one of the most remarkable expeditions in all the history of Artic exploration, most remarkable indeed on account of the unprecedented endurance and unsurpassed devotion of those who took part in it.

---

*) The bodies of the dead on Monument Hill were disinterred later on and conveyed to the United States for final burial.

THE GREELY EXPEDITION

Complying with the suggestions of the Third International Polar Conference for the establishment of circumpolar stations of observation the United States agreed to organize two, one at Point Barrow, north of Behring Strait, the other at Lady Franklin Bay on Grinnell Land. The latter was established and worked by the Greely expedition, or, as it was officially called, the Lady Franklin Bay expedition, under the command of A. W. Greely, First Lieutenant 5th Cavalry, Acting Signal Officer U. S. A. The order of the General commanding the Army which assigned Mr. Greely to this new duty was issued on March 11th, 1881. On June 19th the following officers and men were detailed as Greely's command by the Chief Signal Officer, General Hazen:

Second Lieutenant Frederick F. Kislingbury, 11th U. S. Infantry.
Second Lieutenant James B. Lockwood, 23rd U. S. Infantry.
*Sergeant Edward Israel, Signal Corps, U. S. A.
Sergeant Winfield S. Jewel, Signal Corps, U. S. A.
**Sergeant George W. Rice, Signal Corps, U. S. A.
Sergeant David C. Ralston, Signal Corps, U. S. A.
Sergeant Hampton S. Gardiner, Signal Corps, U. S. A.
Sergeant Wm. H. Cross, General Service, U. S. A.
Sergeant David L. Brainard, Co. L., 2nd Cavalry, U. S. A.
Sergeant David Lynn, Co. C., 2nd Cavalry, U. S. A.
Corporal Daniel C. Starr, Co. F., 2nd Cavalry, U. S. A,
***Corporal Paul Grimm, Co. F., 11th Infantry, U. S. A.
Corporal Nicholas Salor, Co. H., 2nd Cavalry, U. S. A.
Corporal Joseph Elison, Co. E., 10th Infantry, U. S. A.
Private Charles B. Henry, Co. E., 5th Cavalry, U. S. A.
Private Morris Connell, Co. B., 3rd Cavalry, U. S. A.
Private Jacob Bender, Co. F., 7th Infantry, U. S. A.
Private Francis Long, Co. F., 9th Infantry, U. S. A.
Private William Whisler, Co. F., 9th Infantry, U. S. A.
Private Henry Biederbeck, Co. G., 17th Infantry, U. S. A.
Private Julius Frederick, Co. L., 2nd Cavalry, U. S. A.
Private James Ryan, Co. H., 2nd Cavalry, U. S. A.
Private Wm. A. Ellis, Co. C., 2nd Cavalry, U. S. A.

The plan laid out for the undertaking was in short that a chartered steamer should take the party from St. John's, New Foundland, to its place of destination;

---

*) Specially enlisted for the expedition; was a professional astronomer.
**) Specially enlisted for the expedition; was a professional photographer.
***) Private Roderick R. Schneider, 1st Artillery, U. S. A., took his place, Grimm having deserted before the start was made.

the expedition should there establish its station, the ship to return, and supply vessels to visit the permanent station in 1882 and 1883; the station should not be abandoned before the 1st of September, 1883, and efforts towards new discoveries by means of sledge parties were to be made to the northeast, the high land near Cape Joseph Henry.

On July 4th, 1881, the chartered steamer Proteus, displacement 619 tons, under the experienced ice navigator Captain Richard Pike, left St. Johns with all of the expedition on board except the surgeon, Dr. Octave Pavy, who was under contract for this expedition as Acting Assistant Surgeon and joined at Disco. Dogs and other supplies were taken on board here and at Rittenbenk. Arriving at Upernivik on the 23rd, six days were spent here in completing the last preparations. On the further way northward supply depots at Southeast Cary Island, Cape Hawks and other places were inspected and found in fairly good condition; Greely made a cache of 225 rations at Carl Ritter Bay, about 75 miles from the end of the journey. But just at entering Lady Franklin Bay the Proteus was locked in by the ice and did not reach her destination until the 12th of August. The station was established in the winterquarters of the Discovery, in Discovery harbor, and christened Fort Conger. Starr and Ryan were ordered to return with the Proteus as they showed signs of physical ailments. On the 25th the Proteus left to return home, and Greely and his companions, numbering twenty-five in all, were now left to their own resources. They were well provided with all that could serve to make life bearable in those regions. Their provisions were ample for three years, and before the ship left they had had the luck to kill musk-oxen enough to furnish besides three full months' rations of beef. Furthermore, Greely had sent back special instructions as to some essential matters for the relief parties, so, apparently, everything pointed to a successful and not very difficult future.

There was one feature, however, which might by a good many, and probably rightly, be considered a foreboding of evil. That was the early sign of an easy possibility for disharmony among the party. On the 26th of August, Lieut. Kislingbury requested to be relieved from the expedition as he did not approve of the rules; his request was granted, but before he could reach the Proteus the latter was gone. So the discontented officer had to return to Fort Conger. As he was relieved from duty he did none, nor, according to Lieut. Greely's statement, did he at any time request to be assigned to duty. It was only after Lieut. Lockwood's death in the April of 1884, that Greely deemed it proper to assign work to him. It is probably best to mention right here, that disharmony, quarrelling, theft and disobedience appeared as most painful features toward the end of the expedition. Greely himself tried to find an excuse for it in the fearful privations from which the men suffered and which rendered them irritable and unquestionably sometimes even irresponsible. Still, when the individual actions of many of Greely's men during their direst trials are compared with the behavior of other crews under similar circumstances— take for instance De Long's and Melville's men—it is plain that the selection of the members of the Lady Franklin Bay expedition must have been lacking in something The manner and actions of the surgeon especially were such as tending to undermine all discipline, and although Greely is very reticent on this point, a little reading between the lines shows how hard it must have been for him to endure these entirely unnecessary and cruel difficulties. On the other hand, the leader himself and some of the men evinced an heroism never surpassed as yet. Such men were Brainard, Long, Frederick, Lieutenant Lockwood, Elison, Biederbeck, Israel, Rice, Ralston, Connell, Gardiner, Lynn, Jewel, Ellis and the two Upernivik Eskimos, Jens Edwards and Frederick Christiansen. Besides, if bad luck and, at least in a measure, bad management had not rendered the two first relief expeditions of 1882 and 1883 unsuccessful, the latter even a dismal failure, the horrible miseries of Camp Clay during the winter and spring of 1883-'84, would never have come to pass.

At Fort Conger the party occupied most comfortable winter quarters, a well arranged, warm, dry and spacious house; as said before they were provisioned amply and exquisitely for three years and over. But Greely's orders from his superiors contained the passage that if no ship or communication had reached him by the end of summer, 1883, he should start on his march south not later than the 1st of September, 1883; that he would then find ample supply depots at Cape Sabine and Littleton Island in Smith Sound, and several other places further south.

The details of the explorers' activity during their stay at Fort Conger have no room here except the mentioning of Lockwood's, Brainard's and the Eskimo Christiansen's sledging trip along the northern coast of Greenland. They started on April the 3rd, 1882, and on May 13th they had pushed to latitude 83° 24′ north, the farthest point north so far reached by man. The place was on an island they christened Lockwood's Island. So it was by American soldiers that the British lost their record for the northernmost point which they had held undisputed for three hundred years. Lockwood's record led thirteen years until it was broken by the Norseman Nansen, who in April, 1895, reached latitude 86° 17′ north. It goes without saying that Lockwood's trip exacted much fortitude and endurance, the temperature in April, when they started, being registered at 42 degrees below zero. The lowest temperature during the whole period of the expedition was recorded in February of the same year, 62.1 degrees below zero. But such severity of climate had been anticipated and the explorers were as well and probably better protected against it than any of their predecessors. The most dangerous enemy of the Artic explorer, lack in variety of diet, was entirely eradicated; here for instance is the menu of a Tuesday at Fort Conger: Breakfast—Musk-beef hash, oatmeal, fresh bread. Dinner—Bean soup, roast musk-beef, tomatoes, fresh apples. This was the first Christmas dinner: Mock turtle soup, salmon, fricasseed guillemot (kind of a gull), spiced musk-ox tongue, crab salad, roast beef, eider ducks, tenderloin of musk-ox, potatoes, asparagus, green corn, green peas, cocoanut pie, jelly cake, plum pudding with wine sauce, several kinds of ice cream, grapes, cherries, pineapples, dates, figs, nuts, candies, coffee, chocolate; egg-nogg was served in moderate quantities, and an extra allowance of rum issued in celebration of the day.

What a contrast to Camp Clay, at Cape Sabine, when two and a half years later the rescuers found that the dead had been cut and the flesh removed to still the craving of hunger in some of the wretched survivors.

The first relief expedition sailed from St. John's on the 8th of July, 1882, in the Neptune, in charge of William M. Beebe, a former officer on the war staff of General Hazen. His orders were to convey the stores to Lady Franklin Bay, or in case this proved impossible to cache 250 rations at a place as far north as possible on the east coast of Grinnell Land, if possible in sight of Cape Hawks, and the same amount on Littleton Island in Smith Sound, the rest of the stores, amounting at least to 2,000 rations, to be brought back to St. John's. The reason of this last order, if ever there was any, has never been accounted for. Beebe, trying to fulfil his orders, attempted four times to reach Cape Hawks but never came nearer to it than ten miles. Finally he made up his mind to cache 250 rations, a whaleboat and some wood at Cape Sabine. Then, during the first days of September, he renewed his efforts twice to penetrate northward, but in vain. At last he stored 250 rations at Littleton Island and returned with the rest of his stores to St. John's; 2,000 rations which "would have kept better in the ice upon the rocks of Cape Sabine," as Commander Schley sarcastically remarks in his description of the different relief trips. For any mistake or misjudgment in this first attempt for relief the responsibility rests not with Beebe, who obviously did his full duty, but with those who shaped orders for him.

The second expedition, of 1883, was intended to leave St. John's by June 15th so as to improve as much as possible the probability of its reaching Discovery Bay. In February 1883, First Lieutenant Ernest A. Garlington of the 7th Cavalry, who had been stationed at Dacota for six consecutive years, was assigned to command it. The Proteus, which had taken Greely north, was chartered for this purpose, and the United States Steamer Yantic, Commander Frank Wildes, was to act as a tender as far as Littleton Island. Garlington had been fully impressed by his superiors and was probably equally fully aware himself of the momentous importance of his task and that the "to be or not to be" of the Fort Conger party depended almost wholly upon his action. It is impossible to go here into the details of this unfortunate relief trip; there are to many technical questions involved which raised a storm of dispute among the professionals, and they were of such a nature that no agreement could be reached; all that might be said is that the fault of failure should rather be found with the method than with individuals. The Proteus reached Smith Sound alone, lingered before Cape Sabine without adding new provisions to the two caches there, got beset soon after, on the 23rd of July, not far from Cape Albert in Kane Sea, and was crushed by the nip and sent to the bottom on the evening of the same day. Garlington saved some of the stores on board, and a clever young naval officer, Lieut. Colwell, U. S. N., who happened to be a volunteer passenger on board the hapless Proteus, took some five hundred rations on shore in a whaleboat and made a depot a few miles northwest of Cape Sabine, known afterwards as the "wreck-camp cache." Then both the relief party and the Proteus crew turned south in their boats and, after missing the Yantic a considerable number of times at different places in Smith Sound, met her at her arrival in Upernivik on the 2nd of September. Any further effort was useless then as the season was too far advanced, and the expedition corps returned to St. John's on the naval vessel. "It is my painful duty to report the total failure of the expedition." Thus began the first despatch of Garlington to the Chief Signal Officer at Washington, dated St. John's, September 13th, 1883.

So after the three ships Neptune, Proteus and Yantic had, during 1882 and 1883, taken not less than 50,000 rations up to or beyond Littleton Island, they had only cached about a thousand in the vicinity; the rest was brought back to the States or lost with the Proteus!

What was to be done now! By this date, the one of Garlington's first despatch, Greely and his men were without doubt two weeks under way from Fort Conger, on their perilous fall march toward Cape Sabine, trusting for their subsistence to the promised supply depots along the coast. The whole nation was incensed and deeply concerned. However, careful deliberation decided that the season was to far advanced to send out another expedition this same year; according to all human experience and calculation such an undertaking must come to grief. The only thing to do, therefore, was the careful preparing of a third expedition which must start for the north next spring at the earliest time possible. It must be stated here that Greely himself and some other men of experience in the Arctic took a different view. According to Greely's opinion the party could have been saved by another expedition during the same fall of 1883.

As is was, the task was this time entrusted to the navy, and the Navy-Departement secured by purchase from British firms the two steam whalers Thetis and Bear before the beginning of spring 1884. The British naval vessel Alert, one of the ships of Nares' expedition in 1875, was presented to the United States by the English government. This vessel was intended as an auxiliary ship. The officers appointed in command of these ships were Commander W. S. Schley, the Thetis and in charge of the expedition; Lieutenant H. H. Emory, Jr., the Bear; and Commander G. W. Coffin the Alert. The Bear left first, steaming out from New York Harbor on the 24th of April, 1884, one week later the Thetis followed. The Bear arrived at St. Johns on the 2nd of May, and on the 13th at Godhavn. The Thetis reached St. Johns on the 9th of May where she found the coaling steamer Loch Garry which was chartered to take 500 tons of Cardiff coal to Littleton Island for the use of the expedition. Both vessels left on the 12th and reached Godhavn on the 22nd of May. On the 29th the Thetis and Bear met at Upernivik. The Alert, which left New York on the 10th of May, reached Upernivik on June 13th, the Loch Garry waiting for her. The Thetis and Bear had already left for the north on the 28th of May, their next object being Melville Bay. The expedition did not know, of course, whether Greely had really started south from Fort Conger towards the end of summer or whether he had concluded to pass through his third winter there. The relief squadron was therefore prepared to look for him along the west coast of Smith Sound from Cape Sabine northward, and, if not successful in finding him, to attempt with all means to push through to Discovery Bay. Under great difficulties and dangers, and managed with commendable skill, these two ships worked their way toward Smith Sound during the first weeks of June having as companions several Dundee whalers who were perfectly willing to neglect their professional work to make an effort in finding Greely first so as to gain the reward of $25,000 which the United States government had offered on the 16th of April to any party bringing in Greely and such men as might be with him or furnishing reliable news about him. The Thetis and Bear managed to outstrip the whalers, though, and touched Carey Islands and Littleton Island on Saturday, the 21st of June. Finding no trace of Greely they started for Cape Sabine at 3 o'clock p. m. on Sunday, June 22nd, with a heavy gale blowing over the stretch of 23 miles which constituted the strait.

Let us now turn to Greely and his comrades. He had made up his mind during the summer that the march toward the south would have to be attempted since there was no sign of any relief vessel. August 8th was set for the day of departure which was carefully prepared. Bad weather on that day frustrated the plan, but they left on the afternoon of the next day for Cape Baird, on the southern shore of Lady Franklin Bay, twelve miles distant. As the situation was, there were the following small depots distributed along this coast: Between Fort Conger and the first depot station, Carl Ritter Bay, Greely had himself established an intermediate small depot at Cape Baird, as the distance to the Bay was 75 miles. At the latter place there were cached 225 rations or nine days' supply by the Proteus on her way up to Lady Franklin Bay. Sixty-two miles further down, at Lake Collinson, was the Nares depot, of 250 rations. The next one, of eight or ten days' supply, established by Nares, was at Cape Hawks, on the west shore of Kane Sea. Finally at Cape Sabine, 53 miles further, there were in several small caches about a thousand rations in all which were estimated representing about forty days' supply. At Littleton Island, 23 miles across the Sound, there were some more depots, but they are of no interest in connection with Greely as his party was not able to reach that spot.

So at the time when Greely left his base at Fort Conger, between that place and the last, the fatal Camp Clay, north of Cape Sabine, there were only provisions for perhaps seventy-five days' subsistence altogether. And it was now August, and more than three hundred days were to pass before relief reached the remnants of the unfortunate little band in June 1884. If only Greely could have anticipated this. But he had no choice; there were his orders and he must obey them.

On the perilous march southward the party progressed mainly by boat, their steam launch towing the other boats until she had to be abandoned in the ice on September 10th. After extraordinary dangers and trials the brave men effected a landing near Cape Sabine towards evening on the 29th of September. They had covered about 500 miles on their retreat from Conger, 400 of which were made in the boats, in fifty-one days. Greely felt greatly relieved when he had finally gathered his little band around him on *terra firma*, all safe and sound, for now there was a fair prospect of finding game in sufficient number to ward off privation from hunger should relief fail. The party established a camp of ice and stone huts not far from where they landed, and Greely sent Sergeant Rice and some others further up along the coast-line to reconnoiter the caches. Rice returned on October 9th with the record of the Colwell cache and of the foundering of the Proteus. From the word ing Lieutenant Greely **gained** the impression that "everything within power of man" would be done to rescue them and he decided therefore to proceed north of Sabine and await help in the vicinity of the Colwell caches. The state of the ice and the tides in the sound rendered the passage of twenty-three miles across to Littleton Island entirely impossible.

Greely declared afterwards that could he have known that no help would be sent him that year he would certainly have turned his back to Cape Sabine and star-vation, to face a possible death on the perilous voyage southward along shore. In the caches near Cape Sabine, Rice found about 1,300 rations, and in Payer Harbour the whaleboat which had before been abandoned by the party.

The camp of the party having been shifted to its new location, a stone and ice hut was built, the whaleboat put on the walls of the house as ridge-pole, and this im-provised roof covered with canvas. Greely says of this building: "The scarcity of rocks prevented our building higher walls. Sitting in our bags the heads of the tall men touched the roof; under the whaleboat was the only place in which a man could get on his knees and hold himself erect." This, then, was Camp Clay, situated north around the promontory of Colwell cache cove, and on this dreary spot the fast approaching winter evolved the drama which left of this healthy, strong and intre-pid band of twenty-five only six to return alive to their home and country to tell the tale.

On the 1st of November the reduction of rations commenced. Greely had detailed Long and the two Eskimos as hunters of the party who were frequently joined by Lieutenant Kislingbury. Greely's hope was that they might kill some walrus, two of which would have furnished provisions sufficient for subsistence till April. But fate would not have it. The hunters shot occassionally a seal, or some dovekies (sea birds), and once a bear. Sergeant Brainard caught shrimps regularly, but sometimes the catch amounted to only a few pounds. Later on, when every-thing gave out, they ate lichens which they gathered from under the snow on the rocks.

In November, when the wintry blasts began to chill the poor, helpless sufferers in their miserable hut in the dreary Arctic night, and the fearful pangs of hunger were first felt in all their agonizing cruelty, they realized for the first time the horrors that were yet to meet. On December 22nd, Brainard, the most cheerful and energetic man of the whole party, Greely himself excepted, wrote in his diary: "Mouldy bread and two cans of soup make a dinner for twelve. At Fort Conger ten cans of soup were needed to begin dinner. But even the dire calamity which now confronts us is insufficient to repress the great flow of good nature in our party generally." It was during this month that the first signs of collapse were noticed among some of the men. On the 14th of January it became obvious that Sergeant Cross was very badly off; he acted as if demented, and showed signs of physical weakness. Ralston, Lynn, and Jewel had fallen into a state of apathy from which they could only be aroused with great difficulty. Lieutenant Lockwood, the hero of the farthest north, began to be suffering from a deep mental depression.

On the 18th of January, Cross died, the first man in the expedition to pay with his life for the awful sufferings his body had been forced to endure. They sewed him up in canvas and buried him on the summit of a nearby hill, Greely reading the service of the Episcopal church at the burial. Such ceremonies at the occasion of death were soon to cease, for the latter became too common and the mourners too weak and indifferent. The sick were now Lieutenant Lockwood, Jewel, Ellis and Elison. The latter had his limbs frozen two months previous in an exploring expedition and finally lost his hands and feet so that his comrades were compelled to feed him. He never complained in spite of his terrible extremity, but suffered in silence and was still alive and mentally entirely well when the rescuers reached them five months later.

At that unspeakably dreary mid-winter time early in 1884 the main hope of the explorers and their grand theme of conversation was the belief that Garlington was at Littleton Island with abundant provisions and only waiting for the first chance to relieve them.

On the 2nd of February Rice and the Eskimo Jens started on an attempt to cross Smith Sound to Littleton Island. Rice was held in high esteem by Greely on account of his cheerfulness, his readiness to do whatever might be required of him, and his excellent judgment. The two men took six days rations and one of Lieutenant Kislingbury's guns and departed early in the forenoon. Four days later they were back in camp and reported open water off Brevoort Island as far as they could see. Greely wanted the Sound frozen over and told his men that he trusted this state would arrive with the beginning of March. During this month it was noticed that Private Henry was stealing provisions. Greely gave orders to watch him carefully. Frederick, who had many times distinguished himself by deeds of extraordinary endurance and unselfishness, was promoted to Sergeant, the same as Long, the indefatigable hunter of the party. During the end of March the apathetic spirits of some of the party became revived and more hopeful than at the beginning since Long and Rice had been fairly lucky in the last week in catching shrimps and killing dovekies. But depression set in again on April 5th when the faithful Eskimo Christiansen, who had suffered by attacks of delirium the previous day, died during the forenoon. On the next day, April 6th, Lynn became unconscious early in the afternoon and died six hours later. On that same day at midnight two of the bravest men of the party, Rice and Frederick, set out to the accomplishment of a task, which cost one of them his life and showed the splendid mettle, the grand unselfish-ness of the two heroes who had volunteered for it against even the wish and advice of the commander himself. They went to attempt to find one hundred pound of English beef which had been abandoned near Baird Inlet in November 1883, such abandonment having become necessary at that time to save the life of frostbitten Sergeant Elison. The two men had this dangerous expedition in mind since March but Greely objected foreseeing the fatal result. However, since the men persisted in declaring their ability and strength to do it, Greely, realizing the desperate straits to which the whole party was now reduced, gave finally, although reluctantly, his con-sent. So at midnight a hearty godspeed and a feeble cheer sent the courageous pair on their hazardous trip.

On the 8th of April, in the afternoon, Lieutenant Lockwood expired; utter exhaustion and mental depression evidently combined to hasten his end. On one of the following days the party was much startled and shocked by the return of Fred-erick alone who announced the death of Rice. According to his story they reached the old camp at Eskimo Point on April 9th, left their equipment there except the sled and proceeded to the cache where the beef was left, six miles away. They found this place in the afternoon but the meat had disappeared. They had to turn back to Eskimo Camp to rest; on the way Rice collapsed. Frederick did everything he could for him, cooked some food and gave him rum with ammonia; he even stripped his coat which he wrapped around the feet of the already dying man. Sitting on the sled in his shirt-sleeves he held Rice's head in his arms until death came, towards eight o'clock in the evening. Frederick buried him and then he drudged his way in an intense snowstorm to where the sleeping bag was left. Resting there a little while, he continued on his march, and by superhuman efforts he succeeded in reach-ing Camp Clay. There it was found that this man, as loyal as he was fearless, had brought back Rice's ration which he never touched in spite of his fearful exhaustion and his craving for more food.

On the 12th of April Jewel died from weakness through lack of food. It was on this very day that Sergeant Brainard discovered the form of a bear among the rocks and hummocks. Long and Jens succeeded in killing it. "This game seemed to in-sure our future," wrote Greely in his journal on this day of joy.

In spite of such rare moments of luck the horrible daily sufferings caused signs of rapid collapse to become frequent in the party. On the 14th of April Lieutenant Kislingbury broke down, and Gardiner, Israel, Salor, Connell, Whisler and Biederbeck showed a distressing weakness, the usual forerunner of worse symptoms and the end. On the 25th happened a very disagreeable incident: Private Henry, taking advantage of the commanders temporary illness, obtained some extra alcohol and became help-lessly drunk on it. Henry was a powerful man, weighing over two hundred pounds, and the fact that he could have handled any two of the exhausted other men ren-dered him bold and reckless in his depredations on food and drink until the measure was filled and fate met him in the shape of a Remington bullet fired by order of the commander.

A few days later, untiring and faithful little Jens Edwards, the skilled Eskimo hunter, lost his life while out hunting in his kayak between the floes. Long, who watched him from the shore, noticed that the man was in trouble, but could not help him as before many seconds the forepart of the kayak rose high out of the water and Jens disappeared below the waves to be seen no more.

It was during these terrible weeks of suffering and disaster that a quarrelsome, mutinous disposition began to spread among the weaker men. Leaving alone Dr. Pavy who had all along been extremely troublesome on account of his utter lack of discipline and reliability in statements it came to pass that two or three of the weakest in character and vital energy talked back to Greely or did not mind orders. The commander, who was suffering intensely from temperary heart trouble and different other serious ailments brought on through exposure, felt necessarily extremely grieved and irritated at such painful occurrences but refrained from serious measures for several reasons, the strongest being that mental excitement was a welcome antidote against the dangerous and increasing apathy and a stimulant to the fast failing energy of the men.

On May 19th Ellis died, on the 23rd Ralston. Ralston, Israel, who was also in a hopeless condition, and Greely occupied the same sleeping bag. Ralston was seized with the death-struggle while all three men were in the bag. Israel struggled out of the bag after his comrade's death, but Greely felt so weak and benumbed that he stayed in the bag for four hours until the chill of the dead body drove him out. On that same day a tent was erected with great difficulty and occupied by those who were ill. The stronger ones remained in the dilapidated hut whose interior by this time was in a fearful condition. The next day Whisler passed away, and Sergeant Israel followed on the 26th. Israel was a graduate of the University of Michigan at Ann Arbor, Mich., a professional astronomer and a highly cultivated young man whom his zeal for science induced to enlist for this expedition which cost him his life. Lieutenant Kislingbury was the next to go; death claimed him on the 1st of June. There were thirteen men left now, every one of them being seriously affected by the protracted lack of nourishment and the cruel exposure. Salor and also Dr. Pavy died between June 3rd and 6th. On this latter day occurred Henry's execution. As he was caught again and again stealing, Greely issued an order on that day to Brainard, Long and Frederick, that the man must be shot. The order was promptly executed, Greely does not say by whom of the three. Bender died on the same day, Gardiner on the 12th and Schneider on the evening of the 17th. The next days were spent by the few surviving men in dumb agony and suffering which no pen can describe. On the 21st Connell became unconscious and was seemingly dying. A fierce gale blew down one end of the tent, but the men were too weak to put it up again. On the evening of the 22nd, Greely, turning feebly towards Brainard and Long, remarked that he just heard the whistle of a steamer. The two men started out to investigate. Brainard returned soon with the sad report that nothing was to be seen. Long went further to set up the distress flag which had blown down.

But Greely had not been mistaken; the whistle was that of the Thetis which was recalling her searching parties from Colwell's cache, around the promontory towards the southeast. Soon after the steam-cutter of the "Bear," in command of Lieutenant Colwell, U. S. N., rounded the cape which separated the cove of Colwell's cache from Camp Clay. On the top of a little ridge, a small distance from above the ice-foot, was plainly outlined the figure of a man. The coxswain in the cutter waiving an American boat flag, the man on the hill—it was Long—responded by waiving the distress flag of Camp Clay. Lieutenant Colwell had soon reached him and was shocked by his ghastly, emaciated appearance. A few moments later Greely was aroused from his lethargy by hearing his name called by strange voices. But he could not move. When Lieutenant Colwell came up he saw before him, on his hands and knees, a dark man clad in tatters, with wild staring eyes. When Colwell stepped up the man raised himself a little and put on a pair of eye-glasses. "Who are you?" asked Colwell. The man stared but gave no answer. "Who are you?" again from Colwell. One of the men said: "That's the Major—Major Greely." Now Greely spoke the following words: "Yes—seven of us left—here we are—dying like men—did what I came to do—beat the best record." Then he fell back in a faint.

But the agony was over at last. The seven men, Greely, Brainard, Long, Biederbeck, Frederick, Elison and Connell, were taken on board the two vessels, where everything was made as comfortable as possible for the poor sufferers. They reached home in safety with the exception of Elison who died in Godhavn, July 8th, from the effects of his injuries and an amputation.

The bodies of the other nineteen dead were also taken home; that of the Eskimo Christiansen was buried at Godhavn. The eighteen Americans, including Elison, were brought to the United States where they were buried with military honors.

Thus closed a chapter of Arctic exploit which is and will always remain one of the most stirring and dramatic in that great history of extraordinary adventures.

BATTLES AND ENGAGEMENTS

ILLUSTRATIONS

TITLES

MEDAL OF HONOR-MEN MENTIONED

MEDAL OF HONOR WINNERS

The following two pages are devoted to the names and ranks of men who won their Medal of Honor during the several wars and expeditions against the Indians, in Naval Combats during the great Civil War and during the Spanish-American War. Their names have not been mentioned on previous pages. The grounds of award differ in the individual cases, but they all properly come under the general head of "For distinguished gallantry in action outside the line of duty."

INDIAN WARS

ACHESAY,
  Sergt., Indian Scouts.
ALBEE, GEORGE E.
  Lieut. 24th U. S. Inf.
BAILEY, JAMES E.
  Sergt., Co. E, 5th U. S. Cav.
BRADBURY, LANFORD
  1st Sergt., Co. L, 8th U. S. Cav.
BARNES, WILLIAM C.
  1st Class Priv. Signal Corps,
  U. S. A.
BARRETT, RICHARD
  1st Sergt., Co. A, 1st U. S. Cav
BEAUFORD, CLAY
  1st Sergt., Co. B, 5th U. S. Cav
BERTRAM, HEINRICH
  Corp., Co. B, 8th U. S. Cav.
BESSEY, CHARLES A.
  Corp., Co. A, 3d U. S. Cav.
BISHOP, DANIEL
  Sergt., Co. A, 5th U. S. Cav.
BLAIR, JAMES
  1st Sergt., Co. I, 1st U. S. Cav.
BOYNE, THOMAS
  Sergt., Co. C, 9th U. S. Cav.
BRATLING, FRANK
  Corp., Co. C, 8th U. S. Cav.
BROGAN, JAMES
  Sergt., Co. G, 6th U. S. Cav.
BROPHY, JAMES
  Priv., Co. B, 8th U. S. Cav.
BROWN, BENJAMIN
  Sergt., Co. C, 24th U. S. Inf.
BURKE, PATRICK J.
  Farrier, Co. B, 8th U. S. Cav.
BUTLER, EDMOND
  Capt., 14th U. S. Inf.
CANFIELD, HETH
  Priv., Co. C, 2d U. S. Cav.
CARR JOHN
  Priv., Co. G, 8th U. S. Cav.
CHIQUITO
  Indian Scout.
CO-RUX-TE-CHOD-ISH (MAD
  BEAR)
  Sergt., Pawnee Scouts, U. S. A.
CRIST, JOHN
  Sergt., Co L, 8th U. S. Cav.

DANIELS, JAMES T.
  Sergt., Co. L, 4th U. S. Cav.
DAY, MATTHIAS W.
  1st Lieut. and R. Q. M., 9th
  U. S. Cav.
DAY, WILLIAM L.
  1st Sergt., Co. E, 5th U. S. Cav.
DEARY, GEORGE
  Sergt., Co. L, 5th U. S. Cav.
DENNY, JOHN,
  Sergt., Troop B, 9th U. S. Cav.
DICKENS, CHARLES H.
  Corp., Co. G, 8th U. S Cav.
DONAHUE, JOHN L.
  Priv., Co. G, 8th U. S. Cav.
ELSATSOOSU
  Corp., Indian Scouts.
ELWOOD, EDWIN L.
  Priv., Co. G, 8th U. S. Cav.
FERRARI, GEORGE,
  Corp., Co. D, 8th U. S. Cav.
FOLEY, JOHN H.
  Sergt., Co. B, 3d U. S. Cav.
GARLAND, HARRY
  Corp., Co. L, 2d U. S. Cav.
GARLINGTON, ERNEST A.
  1st Lieut., 7th U. S. Cav.
GATES, GEORGE
  Bugler, Co. F, 8th U. S. Cav.
GEORGIAN, JOHN
  Sergt., Batt. U. S. Eng.
GOODMAN, DAVID
  Priv., Co. L, 8th U. S. Cav.
GREAVES, CLINTON
  Corp., Co. C, 9th U. S. Cav.
GRESHAM, JOHN C
  1st Lieut., 7th U. S. Cav.
GUNTHER, JACOB
  Corp., Co. E, 8th U. S. Cav.
HAMILTON, FRANK
  Priv., Co. E, 8th U. S. Cav.
HARDING, MOSHER A.
  Blacksmith, Co. G, 8th U. S.
  Cav.
HARRIS, CHARLES D.
  Sergt., Co. D, 8th U. S. Cav.
HAUPT, PAUL
  Corp., Co. L, 8th U. S. Cav.

HEYL, CHARLES H.
  2d Lieut. 23d U. S. Inf.
HILL, FRANK E.
  Sergt., Co. E, 5th U. S. Cav.
HILL, JAMES M.
  1st Sergt., Co. A, 5th U. S. Cav.
HINEMANN, LEHMANN
  Sergt., Co. L, 1st U. S. Cav.
HOOVER, SAMUEL,
  Bugler, Co. A. 1st U. S. Cav.
HUBBARD, THOMAS
  Priv., Co. C, 2d U. S. Cav.
HUFF, JAMES W.
  Priv., Co. L, 1st U. S. Cav.
HYDE, HENRY J.
  Sergt., Co. M, 1st U. S. Cav.
JARVIS, FREDERICK,
  1st Lieut., Co. F, 54th Ohi Inf.
JIM
  Sergt., Indian Scouts.
KEENAN, BARTHOLOMEW,
  Trumpeter, Co. G, 1st U. S.
  Cav.
KELSAY
  Indian Scout.
KOSOHA
  Indian Scout.
KELLEY, CHARLES
  Priv., Co. G, 1st U. S. Cav.
KILMARTIN JOHN
  Priv., Co. F, 3d U. S. Cav.
KIRK, JOHN
  1st Sergt., Co. L, 6th U. S
  Cav.
LENIHAN, JAMES
  Priv., Co. K, 5th U. S. Cav.
LEONARD, PATRICK
  Corp., Co. A, 23d U. S. Inf.
LEWIS, WILLIAM B.
  Sergt., Co. B, 3d U. S. Cav.
LYTLE, LEONIDAS S.
  Sergt., Co. C, 8th U. S. Cav.
LYTTON, JEPTHA L.
  Corp., Co. A, 23d U. S. Inf.
MACHOL
  Priv., Indian Scouts.
MAHERS, HERBERT
  Priv., Co. F, 8th U. S. Cav.

MARTIN, PATRICK
  Sergt., Co. G, 5th U. S. Cav.
MATTHEWS, DAVID A.
  Corp., Co. E, 8th U. S. Sav.
MAYS, ISAIAH
  Corp., Co. B, 24th U. S. Inf.
McBRYAR, WILLIAM
  Sergt., Co. K, 10th U. S. Cav.
McDONALD, FRANKLIN M.
  Priv., Co. G, 11th U., S. Inf.
McDONALD, JAMES
  Corp., Co. B, 8th U. S. Cav.
McNALLY, JAMES
  1st Sergt., Co. E, 8th U. S. Cav.
MEAHER, NICHOLAS
  Corp., Co. G, 1st U. S. Cav.
MILLER, DANIEL H.
  Priv., Co. F, 3d U. S. Cav.
MOQUIN, GEORGE
  Corp., Co. F, 5th U. S. Cav
MORRIARTY, JOHN
  Sergt., Co. E, 8th U. S. Cav.
MORRIS, JAMES L.
  1st Sergt., Co. C, 8th U. S. Cav.
MURPHY, PHILIP
  Corp., Co. F, 8th U. S. Cav.
MYERS, FRED
  Sergt., Co. K, 6th U. S. Cav.
NANNASADDIE
  Indian Scout.
NANTAJE.
  Indian Scout.
OLIVER, FRANCIS
  1st Sergt., Co. G, 1st U. S. Cav.
ORR, MOSES
  Priv., Co. A. 1st U. S. Cav.
OSBORNE, WILLIAM
  Sergt., Co. M, 1st U. S. Cav.
PENGALLY, Edward
  Priv., Co. G. 8th U. S. Cav.
POWERS, THOMAS
  Corp., Co. G, 1st U. S. Cav.

RACRICK, JOHN
  Priv., Co. L, 8th U. S. Cav.
REED, JAMES C.
  Priv., Co. A, 8th U. S. Cav.
RICHMAN, SAMUEL
  Priv., Co. E, 8th U. S. Cav.
ROGAN PATRICK
  Sergt., Co. A, 7th U. S. Inf.
ROWALT, JOHN F.
  Priv., Co. L, 8th U. S. Cav.
ROWDY
  Sergt., Co. A, Indian Scouts.
RUSSELL, JAMES,
  Priv., Co. G., 1st U. S. Cav.
SALE, ALBERT
  Priv., Co. F, 8th U. S. Cav.
SCHNITZER, JOHN
  Wagoner, Troop G, 4th U. S.
  Cav.
SCHROETER, CHARLES
  Priv., Co. G, 8th U. S. Cav.
SCOTT, ROBERT B.
  Priv., Co. G, 8th U. S. Cav.
SEWARD, GRIFFIN
  Wagoner, Co. G, 8th U. S. Cav.
SHELDIN, JOHN
  Blacksmith, Co. C, 8th U. S.
  Cav.
SPENCE ORIZOBA
  Priv., Co. G., 8th U. S. Cav.
SPRINGER GEO.
  Priv., Co. G, 1st U. S. Cav.
SMITH, ANDREW I.
  Sergt., Co. G, 8th U. S. Cav.
SMITH, OTTO
  Priv., Co. K, 8th U. S. Cav.
SMITH, ROBERT
  Priv., Co. M, 3d U. S. Inf.
SMITH, THEODORE F.
  Private., Co. G, 1st U. S. Cav.
STANCE, EMANUEL
  Sergt., Co. F, 9th U. S. Cav.

STANLEY, EBEN
  Priv., Co. A, 5th U. S. Cav.
STANLEY, EDWARD
  Corp., Co. F, 8th U. S. Cav.
STAUFFER, RUDOLPH
  1st Sergt., Co. K, 5th U. S.
STEINER, CHRISTIAN
  Saddler, Co. G, 8th U. S. Cav.
STICKOFFER, JULIUS H.
  Saddler, Co. L, 8th U. S. Cav.
STRAYER, WILLIAM H.
  Priv., Co. B, 3d U. S. Cav.
SUMNER, JAMES
  Priv., Co. G, 1st U. S. Cav.
TAYLOR, WILLIAM N.
  Corp., Co. K, 8th U. S. Cav.
THOMPSON, JOHN
  Sergt., Co. G, 1st U. S. Cav.
TRACY, JOHN
  Priv., Co. G, 8th U. S. Cav.
TURPIN, JAMES H.
  1st Sergt., Co. L, 5th U. S.
  Cav.
VOKES, LEROY H.
  1st Sergt., Co. B, 3d U. S. Cav.
VON MEDEM, RUDOLPH
  Sergt., Co. A, 5th U. S. Cav.
WALKER, JOHN
  Priv., Co. D, 8th U. S. Cav.
WARD, CHARLES H.
  Priv. Co. G, 1st U. S. Cav.
WATSON, JOSEPH
  Priv., Co. F, 8th U. S. Cav.
WEISS, ENOCH R.
  Priv., Co. G, 1st U. S. Cav.
WHITCOME, JOSEPH
  Priv., Co. B, 8th U. S. Cav.
WILSON, MILDEN H.
  Sergt., Co. I, 7th U. S. Inf.
WOODALL, ZACHARIAH
  Sergt., Co. I, 6th U. S. Cav.
YOUNT, JOHN P.
  Priv., Co. F., 3d U. S. Cav.

WAR OF THE REBELLION — NAVY

ANDERSON, AARON
  Landsman, U. S. S. Wyan-
  dank.
ANDERSON, ROBERT
  Quartermaster, U. S. S. Cru-
  sader.
ANGLING, JOHN
  Boy U. S. S. Pontoosuc.
ASTEN, CHARLES
  Qarter-gunner, U. S. S. Sig-
  nal.
AVERY, JAMES
  Seaman, U. S. S. Metacomet.
BARRETT, EDWARD
  Second-class Fireman, U. S.
  S. Alaska.
BARTON, THOMAS C.
  Seaman, U. S. S. Hunchback.
BETHAM, ASA
  Cockswain, U. S. S. Pontoosuc.
BIBBER, CHARLES J.
  Gunner's Mate, U. S. S. Aga-
  wam.
BLAIR, ROBERT M.
  Boatswain's Mate, U. S. S.
  Pontoosuc.
BRADLEY, CHARLES
  Boatswain's Mate, U. S. S.
  Louisville.
BREEN, JOHN
  Boatswain's Mate, U. S. S.
  Commodore Perry.
BROWN, JAMES
  Quartermaster, U. S. S. Alba-
BYRNES, JAMES
  Boatswain's Mate, U. S. S.
  Louisville.
CLIFFORD, ROBERT T.
  Master-at-Arms, U. S. S. Mon-
  ticello.
CONNOR, WILLIAM C.
  Boatswain's Mate, U. S. S.
  Howquah.
GILE, FRANK S.
  Landsman, U. S. S. Lehigh.
CONLAN, DENNIS
  Seaman, U. S. S. Agawam.

COTTON, PETER
  Cockswain, U. S. S. Baron De
  Kalb.
DITZENBACK, JOHN
  Quartermaster, U. S. Monitor
  Neosho.
DORMAN, JOHN
  Seaman U. S. S. Carondelet.
ERICKSON, JOHN P.
  Capt. of Forecastle, U. S. S.
  Pontoosuc.
FERRELL, JOHN H.
  Pilot, U. S. Monitor Neosho.
FRANKS, WILLIAM J.
  Belonging to U. S. S. Mar-
  mora.
GARVIN, WILLIAM
  Capt. of Forecastle, U. S. S.
  Agawam.
HAMILTON, THOMAS W.
  Quartermaster U. S. S. Cincin-
  nati.
HARDING, THOMAS
  Capt. of Forecastle, U. S. S.
  Dacotah.
HARRINGTON, DANIEL
  Landsman, U. S. S. Pocahön-
  tas.
HARRINGTON, DAVID
  First-class Fireman, U. S. S.
  Talapoosa.
HATHAWAY, EDWARD W.
  Seaman, U. S. S. Sciota.
HAWKINS, CHARLES
  Seaman, U. S. S. Agawam.
HILL, JOHN
  Chief Quarter Gunner, U. S.
  S. Kansas.
HINNEGAN, WILLIAM
  Fireman, U. S. S. Agawam.
HORTON, JAMES
  Gunner's Mate, U. S. S. Mon-
  tauk.
HORTON, JAMES
  Capt. of Top, U. S. S. Consti-
  tution.

HUSKEY, MICHAEL
  Fireman, U. S. S. Carondelet.
IRVING, THOMAS
  Cockswain, U. S. S. Lehigh.
JACKSON, JOHN
  Seaman, U. S. S. C. P. Will-
  iams.
JOHNSON, JOHN
  Seaman, U. S. S. Kansas.
JOURDAN, ROBERT
  Cockswain, U. S. S. Minne-
  sota.
KANE, THOMAS
  Capt. of Hold, U. S. S. Ne-
  reus.
LAFFEY, BARTLETT
  Belonging to U. S. S. Petrel.
LAKIN, DANIEL
  Seaman, U. S. S. Commodore
  Perry.
LANN, JOHN S.
  Landsman, U. S. S. Magnolia.
LAVERTY, JOHN
  Fireman, U. S. S. Alaska.
LELAND, GEORGE W.
  Gunner's Mate, U. S. S. Le-
  high.
LEON PIERRE
  Capt. of Forecastle, U. S. S.
  Baron De Kalb.
MACK, JOHN
  Seaman, U. S. S. Hendrick
  Hudson.
MAGEE JOHN W.
  Fireman, U. S. S. Tallapoosa.
MARTIN, WILLIAM
  Boatswain's Mate, U. S. S.
  Benton.
MATTHEWS, JOSEPH
  Captain of Top, U. S. S. Con-
  stitution.
McDONALD, JOHN
  Boatswain's Mate, U. S. S.
  Baron De Kalb.
McWILLIAMS, GEORGE W.
  Landsman, U. S. S. Pontoosuc

MERTON, JAMES F.
Landsman, U. S. S. Colorado.
MONTGOMERY, ROBERT
Capt. of Afterguard, U. S. S.
Agawam.
MOORE, WILLIAM
Boatswain's Mate, U. S. S.
Benton.
MORTON, CHARLES W.
Boatswain's Mate, U. S. S.
Benton.
MULLEN, PATRICK
Boatswain's Mate, U. S. S.
Wyandank.
NEIL, JOHN
Quarter Gunner, U. S. S. Aga-
wam.
NIBBE, JOHN H.
Quartermaster, U. S. S. Pe-
trel.
NUGENT, CHRISTOPHER
Sergt. of Marines, U. S. S.
Fort Henry.
O'BRIEN OLIVER
Cockswain U. S. S. Canandai-
gua
Ohmsen, August
Master-at-arms, U. S. S. Tal-
lapoosa.
ORTEGA, JOHN
Seaman, U. S. S. Saratoga.
PETERSON, ALFRED
Seaman, U. S. S. Commodore
Perry.
PYNE, GEORGE
Seaman, U. S. S. Magnolia.
PURVIS, HUGH
Private Marine, U. S. S. Al-
aska.
REGAN, PATRICK
Seaman, U. S. S. Rensacola.

RICE, CHARLES
Coal Heaver, U. S. S. Aga-
wam.
RINGOLD, EDWARD
Cockswain, U. S. S. Wabash.
ROBERTS, JAMES
Seaman, U. S. S. Agawam.
ROBINSON, ALEXANDER
Boatswain's Mate, U. S. S.
Howquah.
ROBINSON, CHARLES
Boatswain's Mate, U. S. S.
Baron De Kalb.
ROBINSON, JOHN
Capt. of Hold, U. S. S. Yucca.
ROUNTRY, JOHN
Fireman, U. S. S. Montauk.
SCHUTT, GEORGE
Cockswain, U. S. S. Hendrick
Hudson.
SMITH, EDWIN
Seaman, U. S. S. Whitehead.
SMITH, JAMES
Seaman, U. S. S. Kansas.
SMITH, OLOFF
Cockswain, U. S. S. Rich-
mond.
SMITH, THOMAS
Seaman, U. S. S. Magnolia.
STODDARD, JAMES
Belonging to U. S. S. Mar-
mora.
SULLIVAN, JOHN
Seaman, U. S. S. Monticello.
SULLIVAN, TIMOTHY
Cockswain, U. S. S. Louisville.
TALBOTT, WILLIAM
Capt. of Forecastle, U. S. S.
Louisville.
TAYLOR, JOHN
Seaman, Picket-boat, N. Y.
Navy Yard.

THIELBERG, HENRY
Seaman, U. S. S. Minnesota.
THOMPSON, WILLIAM
Signal Quartermaster, U. S. S.
Mohican.
VERNEY, JAMES W.
Chief Quartermaster, U. S. S.
Pontoosuc.
WARREN, DAVID
Cockswain, U. S. S. Monti-
cello.
WEEKS, CHARLES
Capt. of Foretop, U. S. S.
Susquehanna.
WILLIAMS, ANTONIO
Seaman, U. S. S. Huron.
WILLIAMS, ANTHONY
Sailmaker's Mate, U. S. S.
Pontoosuc.
WILLIAMS, HENRY
Carpenter's Mate, U. S. S.
Constitution.
WILLIAMS, JOHN
Boatswain's Mate, U. S. S.
Mohican.
WILLIAMS, ROBERT
Signal Quartermaster, U. S.
S. Benton.
WILLIAMS, WILLIAM
Landsman, U. S. S. Lehigh.
WILCOX, FRANKLIN L.
Seaman, U. S. S. Minnesota.
WOOD, ROBERT B.
Cockswain, U. S. S. Minne-
sota.
WOODS, SAMUEL
Seaman, U. S. S. Minnesota.
WOOD, JOHN
Boatswain's Mate, U. S. S.
Pittsburg.
WRIGHT, WILLIAM
Yeoman, U. S. S. Monticello.
YOUNG, HORATIO N.
Seaman, U. S. S. Lehigh.

SPANISH-AMERICAN WAR

BAKER, EDWARD L., JR.
2d Lieut., U. S. Philippine
Scouts.
BROOKIN, OSCAR
Priv., Co. C., 17th U. S. Inf.
CANTRELL, CHAS. P.
Priv., Co. F., 10th U. S. Inf.

CUMMINS, ANDREW J.
Sergt., Co. F., 10th U. S. Inf.
FOURNIA, FRANK O.
Corp., Co. H, 7th U. S. Inf.
KELLER, WILLIAM
Priv., Co. F, 10th U. S. Inf.
LEE, FITZ
Corp. Troop M., 10th U. S. Cav.

RESSLER, NORMAN W.
Sergt., Co. D, 7th U. S. Inf.
SHEPHERD, WARREN J.
Corp., Co. D, 7th U. S. Inf.
WANTON, GEORGE H.
Priv, Troop M, 10th U. S. Cav.